THE
PATRIARCH

The Rise and Fall of the Bingham Dynasty

Susan E. Tifft
Alex S. Jones

SUMMIT BOOKS

New York London Toronto Sydney Tokyo Singapore

Summit Books
Simon & Schuster Building
Rockefeller Center
1230 Avenue of the Americas
New York, New York 10020

SUMMIT BOOKS and colophon are trademarks
of Simon & Schuster Inc.

Designed by Levavi & Levavi/Nina D'Amario
Manufactured in the United States of America

10   9   8   7   6   5   4   3   2   1

Library of Congress Cataloging in Publication Data
Tifft, Susan E.
    The patriarch: the rise and fall of the Bingham dynasty/
Susan E. Tifft, Alex S. Jones.
        p.   cm.
    Includes bibliographical references (p.   ) and index.
    1. Bingham family.   2. Bingham, Barry, 1906–1988—Family.
3. Publishers and publishing—Kentucky—Biography.
4. Educators—North Carolina—Biography.   5. Kentucky—Genealogy.
6. North Carolina—Genealogy.   I. Jones, Alex S.   II. Title.
CT274.B52T54   1991
929'.2'0973—dc20   90-21435
                                                        CIP

ISBN 0-671-63167-5

Photos 1, 2, 4, 6, 7, 11, 14, 15, courtesy of Mary and Barry Bingham Sr.
3, used with permission of Jane Peabody Durham
5, used with permission of the Henry M. Flagler Museum Collection
8, 10, 18, 21, 25, used with permission of AP/Wide World Photos
9, 12, 13, 16, 17, 19, 20, 22, 23, 26, 27, 28, 31, 32, 33, 34, 35, courtesy of *The Courier-Journal*
24, used with permission of Charles E. Bascom
29, 30, used with permission of Eleanor Bingham Miller
36, used with permission of Nick Mills/Photographer, Louisville, Kentucky
37, used with permission of Charles H. Traub, New York

Acknowledgments

A great many individuals helped to nurture this book. We will never be able to express adequately our thanks to all of them.

Our first debt of gratitude goes to Arthur Gelb, former managing editor of *The New York Times*, now head of the New York Times Company Foundation, who is responsible for suggesting that we work together as a team. Arthur and Barbara Gelb co-authored *O'Neill*, the definitive biography of Eugene O'Neill. Throughout our project, they provided affection, encouragement, and the heartening certainty that a loving marriage can survive the rigors of a literary partnership.

Arthur also had the wisdom to steer us to our agent, Kathy Robbins. There cannot be a more capable adviser and advocate, or a more treasured friend. We were equally blessed to work with James Silberman, editor-in-chief of Summit Books, whose skill and insight vastly improved the final product, and whose confidence in the project never flagged. We are indebted as well to Dominick Anfuso, a senior editor at Summit, who provided cheer and good suggestions in equal doses.

We could not have completed a book of this length and detail without the generosity of our employers, *Time* magazine and *The New York Times*, both of which granted us several months of leave to work on the manuscript. We are particularly obliged to the Gannett Center for Media Studies at

Columbia University and its executive director, Everette Dennis. Susan's fellowship at the Center in 1987 offered her time for reflection and reporting during the critical first stages of our inquiry.

Laurel Shackelford, a talented *Courier-Journal* editorial writer who helped us with research in Louisville, was dogged in her quest for material on the newspapers and the family, never complaining as we made request after request for information. Her expert detective work shines through on many pages of *The Patriarch*. We are also thankful to John Gallagher, who aided us with research in New York City and Boston, and to Elena Siddall, who combed through libraries and archives in Richmond.

Our insight into the Bingham family's early life in America has many fathers. Chief among them is Harry McKown, a reference associate in the North Carolina Collection at the University of North Carolina at Chapel Hill, who tirelessly answered our queries and pointed us to valuable sources. William S. Powell, professor emeritus of history at UNC; William S. Price Jr., director of the North Carolina Division of Archives and History; and Richard Nelson Current, university distinguished professor of history, emeritus, at the University of North Carolina at Greensboro, were also generous with their time and knowledge.

We are deeply grateful to James J. Holmberg, curator of manuscripts at the Filson Club in Louisville, and to Joan Runkel, curator of the Henry Morrison Flagler Museum in Palm Beach, for their able assistance. Our thanks are due as well to Nicholas J. Fiumara, M.D., adjunct clinical professor of dermatology, Boston University School of Medicine; clinical professor of dermatology, Tufts University School of Medicine; and lecturer in dermatology, Harvard Medical School, whose knowledge of medical practices in the early part of this century was immensely useful to us as we tried to reconstruct the final days of Mary Lily Kenan Flagler Bingham.

Amanda George and Sharon Worthy-Bulla swiftly, cheerfully, and accurately transcribed many of our tape-recorded interviews, saving both our time and our sanity.

Finally, we want to thank our families and friends—and each other—for the love and forbearance that made this book possible.

Susan E. Tifft
Alex S. Jones

New York City, 1990

For our parents

Contents

PARADISE

And some have said that Eve in Paradise
Stood often by the gates, and pressed her face
Close to the bars, and warmed them with her sighs.
And Adam sometimes turned from Eve's embrace
To dream of earlier nights, and Lilith's eyes.

Some say Eden was a lonely place.

Barry Bingham Sr.
Age twenty

BINGHAM GENEALOGICAL TREE

Rev. William Bingham, 1754-1826
Migrated from County Down, Northern Ireland,
to North Carolina 1789

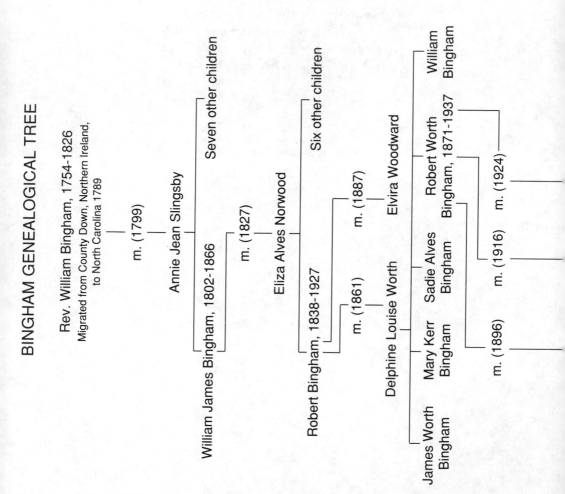

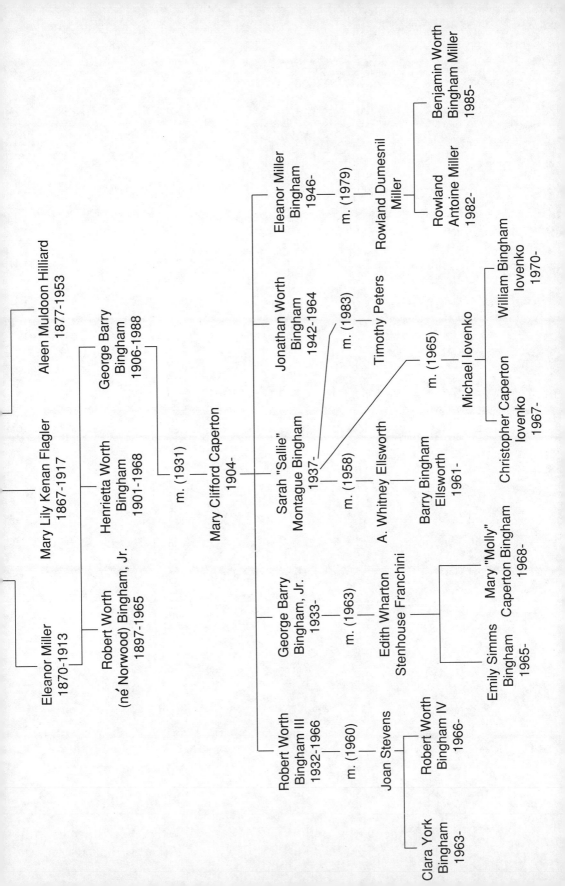

Eleanor Miller
1870-1913

Mary Lily Kenan Flagler
1867-1917

Aleen Muldoon Hilliard
1877-1953

Robert Worth
(né Norwood) Bingham, Jr.
1897-1965

Henrietta Worth
Bingham
1901-1968

George Barry
Bingham
1906-1988

m. (1931)

Mary Clifford Caperton
1904-

Robert Worth
Bingham III
1932-1966

m. (1960)

Joan Stevens

Clara York
Bingham
1963-

Robert Worth
Bingham IV
1966-

George Barry
Bingham, Jr.
1933-

m. (1963)

Edith Wharton
Stenhouse Franchini

Emily Simms
Bingham
1965-

Mary "Molly"
Caperton Bingham
1968-

Sarah "Sallie"
Montague Bingham
1937-

m. (1958)

A. Whitney Ellsworth

Barry Bingham
Ellsworth
1961-

m. (1965)

Michael Iovenko

Christopher Caperton
Iovenko
1967-

William Bingham
Iovenko
1970-

Jonathan Worth
Bingham
1942-1964

m. (1983)

Timothy Peters

Eleanor Miller
Bingham
1946-

m. (1979)

Rowland Dumesnil
Miller

Rowland
Antoine Miller
1982-

Benjamin Worth
Bingham Miller
1985-

PROLOGUE

For such a sad day, Barry Bingham Sr. seemed incongruously cheerful. As he stood in the doorway of his office at the family newspapers, the flesh was puffy around his eyes, but he looked younger than his seventy-nine years, very handsome, and unexpectedly merry. "Oh, come in, come in," he said in his own unusual accent, a mixture of the patrician South, stiffened by Harvard, and finished with a touch of England and a trace of Kentucky. It was a cello voice, warm and formal, and he frequently donated its services to recording books for the blind.

On the previous day, Thursday, January 9, 1986, Barry Sr. had announced that he would exercise his power as controlling owner and sell the family companies: *The Courier-Journal* and *The Louisville Times*, WHAS-TV, WHAS AM/FM radio, and Standard Gravure, a printing subsidiary. The businesses would be put up for auction.

To the Binghams—even those who had pressed hardest for a sale—the family holdings, especially the celebrated newspapers, were far more than income-producing assets. They were the psychic bricks and mortar of their lives, the passport under which they traveled the world beyond Kentucky, and the reason why the Binghams were not simply rich people but were The Binghams of Louisville. By declaring an end to the Binghams' nearly seventy-year reign as Kentucky's most powerful media dynasty, Barry Sr. was, in a profound way, declaring the end of the family as well.

Typically, the announcement had been made not in person but on paper. Barry Sr.'s statement, posted around noon on a company bulletin board, characterized the decision as an "unwelcome duty." But, he said, "times change," and he cited the burden of increased costs and the problem of inheritance taxes. At the insistence of one of his granddaughters, who argued that he would appear ludicrous otherwise, he reluctantly included a reference to "divergent interests" among family members. The memo concluded by expressing his confidence in the skill and dedication of his sole surviving son and namesake, Barry Bingham Jr., who had managed all of the companies for the past fifteen years.

Located next to Barry Sr.'s statement was one by Barry Jr., denouncing the decision as "a betrayal" and tendering his resignation. His memo said the decision to sell was "irrational and ill-advised." In a stormy meeting between father and son before the announcements were posted, Barry Sr. had angrily accused Barry Jr. of effectively declaring that his father was senile.

In his memo, Barry Jr. said he would never have devoted his life to the family businesses had he known that his parents would ultimately sacrifice his show of duty and dedication to the "interests and priorities" of his sisters, Sallie and Eleanor. Earlier, face-to-face with Barry Sr., he had been less controlled and thundered that his father was rewarding their "stunning greed."

News of the sale had reduced scores of staff members to tears, prompted anxiety throughout Kentucky about the fate of the papers, and splashed the unhappy family's private torment across front pages throughout the nation. Barry Sr. had also forfeited forever the chance to pass on the papers and related companies to another generation of Binghams and had wounded his only living son so grievously that the younger man was radiant with pain.

Yet Barry Sr., the patriarch, was now receiving members of the press like a genial host whose only concern was to put at ease some new acquaintances who had arrived for the weekend. For the occasion, he wore an elegant dark blue suit from Barneys, the expensive New York clothier. He had a closet full of even finer suits from Anderson & Sheppard, Ltd., the Savile Row tailor, but he rarely wore them in Louisville. He saved his custom-made clothing for more sophisticated cities like New York, Washington, London, and Paris; the Barneys label was good enough for local consumption.

Barry Sr. pointed out mementoes scattered around the office in an effort to divert attention from the thin, forbidding figure of Barry Jr. a few feet away. Despite his obvious distaste at being in the same room with the man who had sold the companies out from under him, Barry Jr. had agreed to pose for a picture with his father as a journalistic courtesy to *Time* magazine. The son stood frozen and furious as his father conducted his chatty tour and the *Time* photographer tinkered with his lights and cameras.

"That was my grandfather's battle flag from the Civil War," Barry Sr. said, fixing his gaze on a tattered remnant of the Confederate Stars and Bars that had once been carried by the 44th North Carolina Regiment and now hung on his wall. "It belonged to Robert Bingham, who was a captain in the infantry and was captured in a skirmish on the way to Gettysburg," he said. "The regiment was almost wiped out in Pickett's Charge, you know. If he had not been captured, he probably would have been killed."

With this he paused, as though momentarily contemplating just how this particular brush with fate should be wedged into the larger family mosaic. Barry Sr. was fascinated with the concept of destiny and with the eerie patterns and unlikely turns of fortune, good and bad, that riddled the family's history.

Then he pointed to a black-and-white photograph. "That was the Japanese surrender ceremony on the deck of the *Missouri* in 1945, which shows just the view I saw from where I was standing. I was on Admiral Nimitz's staff. And that," he said, indicating a small square of paper mounted on the wall, "is the Pulitzer Prize for public service we won in 1967. That's the top Pulitzer, you know."

The wallpaper in the office was the color of shellacked pine, creating a sepia tone that evoked the 1940s; the faint, musty smell was reminiscent of old letters. The room had been carved out of unused space in the late 1960s, and in 1971, after turning the company reins over to his son, Barry Sr. had moved to this isolated chamber from the more spacious office that Barry Jr. now occupied on the same floor.

A bust of Franklin Delano Roosevelt stood on a ledge behind the couch, along with a framed cartoon of Barry Sr. with a huge bouquet of spring flowers in his arms. On the wall behind the plain wooden desk were three large photographs. Each showed a young man dressed for hunting and holding a rifle. "That's Worth," said Barry Sr., pointing to the picture on the left. The athletic, glamorous-looking man stared back at the visitors with a confident, cocky smile. Worth, the oldest son, had been the Binghams' golden boy, the heir apparent tapped to run the family newspapers until his bizarre accidental death in 1966.

"And that is Jonathan," said Barry Sr., nodding toward the right-hand photo. His youngest son, the fourth of his five children and the one with a whimsical "Irish plainness," had been the first to die, also in a freak accident.

"And, of course, Barry Jr.," he said, indicating the middle picture, positioned a few inches higher than the other two. It showed an easygoing, robust young man in his twenties who was barely recognizable as the one standing mute and clinch-jawed nearby.

On the desk itself were two small photographs of Mary Bingham, the woman of searing intellect who had been Barry Sr.'s wife for over fifty years. The pictures, which appeared to have been taken in the 1930s, were by far the most elegant in the office. In one, Mary relaxed in a chaise longue with a cigarette; in the other, she sat in a grand salon with sunlight pouring through the window, dressed in a chic evening gown.

Mary had been a golden-haired beauty in those days and, even now, she retained a piercing charisma. Through exercise and spartan meals of consommé, she maintained a slim figure. But it was Barry Sr., with his head of silver hair, luminescent eyes, and gleaming white teeth that he had had capped at sixty-five, who had grown ever more handsome with age.

Pictures of the other people in Barry Sr.'s life were on a chest against one wall. The top was cluttered with photographs of his nine grandchildren and special friends like Percy Haly, the shadowy backroom politician who had been Barry Sr.'s political mentor in the 1930s. It was here that he placed Sallie, the older daughter, who the previous day had cheered the news that the papers would pass from Bingham hands, viewing it as a triumph for all women in male-dominated families. Next to Sallie was a photo of Eleanor, the youngest child and the object of much of Barry Jr.'s wrath for what he considered to be her underhanded role in the decision to sell.

Just outside the door was a picture of the Judge, Robert Worth Bingham, the father Barry Sr. revered like an icon. Not surprisingly, Barry Sr. displayed no photo of his wealthy stepmother, Mary Lily Kenan Flagler Bingham, whose mysterious death had made the Binghams rich, enabling them to buy *The Courier-Journal* and *Times*, but whose memory still haunted the family like a vengeful ghost.

Barry Sr.'s sunny tour was interrupted when the *Time* photographer asked father and son to stand together. Barry Sr. flashed an accommodating smile as he gingerly moved closer to his son, looking everywhere but at the glowering countenance next to him. As the two men stood side by side, Barry Jr. was asked whether he had decided to honor his father's request to remain at the helm of the companies until the sale process was complete.

The focus of attention shifted to Barry Jr. He hesitated, his waxed regimental mustache twitching slightly. Finally, in a flat, stony voice, he said, "I have not yet decided what my role will be."

As he listened to his son, Barry Sr. stared into a blank middle distance, his head slightly bowed. And for a brief moment, thinking himself unobserved, his composure failed and the mask fell. His face sagged and seemed to lose its rosy color, his lips pursed in a grimace, and his pale blue eyes brimmed with grief, regret, and protective tenderness for the fifty-two-year-old son he often referred to as Young Barry, the child closest to his heart. He looked suddenly wizened and in despair. It was as though, in gazing back across the years, he saw clearly the tortured, complex journey that had led the family to this moment, and judged that it could not be otherwise.

And then, abruptly, his eyes snapped back into focus. He practically skipped across the room to a stuffed mallard mounted on the wall, and reached for it. "That's about the only duck I ever shot," he told the photographer, clearly gratified to find yet another distraction. "Be sure to get the bird."

In the ensuing days, Barry Sr. gave a series of candid interviews that shocked people who had known him for decades. The impenetrable affability, which he had long used to keep out interlopers, had been somehow breached by the announcement of the sale. Over and over again he tried to explain himself, in part, perhaps, to demonstrate that he was not senile and in part to justify his decision to scuttle the ownership of his beloved company.

Even his closest associates marveled at his momentary transparency. "We all seem to have some inhibitions about each other," Barry Sr. told a *New York Times* reporter. "It's very hard to express to each other the way we feel sometimes. It might have been much better if we'd been a more Latin-type family with a lot of outbursts, tears, screams, and reconciliations. But that has not been the way any of us operates." At the end of the interview, surprised at his own willingness to share his personal thoughts, he wryly thanked the journalist for "being my father confessor."

He did not reveal everything about his decision to sell, of course. In fact, he kept hidden, even from Barry Jr., the key incident that, after a titanic struggle to avoid a sale, finally tipped the balance. That Barry Sr. should remain silent about such a sensitive piece of the puzzle was thoroughly in character. The enigmatic man at the center of the Bingham family had been guarding secrets for a lifetime.

BEGINNINGS

On a cold Saturday afternoon in December 1937, Joseph P. Kennedy, the forty-nine-year-old multimillionaire, movie magnate, and father of a future president, strode down a quiet corridor in Johns Hopkins Hospital on a mission he did not relish. For a hypochondriac like Kennedy, courtesy calls on the sick and dying were highly disagreeable. Still, this was an obligation he could not ignore. He removed his hat, exposing a thinning crop of Irish red hair, and entered a room in the hospital's V.I.P. section.

The man he had come to see, Robert Worth Bingham, looked ghastly. The owner and publisher of Louisville's *Courier-Journal* and *Times* and, for the past four years, Franklin D. Roosevelt's ambassador to Great Britain, had just one week to live before cancer, as yet undiagnosed, would claim him. Bingham smiled a greeting through the pain. He had insisted that no opiates cloud his mind when Joe Kennedy came. He wanted to appear as strong and confident as possible, knowing that his visitor would give the president a full report on his condition. Struggling to resurrect the old authority in his voice, he told Joe that he definitely intended to seek an unofficial role in the Roosevelt administration once he recovered. Perhaps, he said, as a personal adviser to the president.

Bingham's youngest son, Barry, stood by the older man's bed as he had almost continuously since Thanksgiving, when his father had returned to

the United States for treatment of a malady the press speculated was malaria.
At thirty-one, Barry wore the kind of sophisticated clothes the stylish Kennedy could appreciate. But his smooth face and cheery, deferential manner
made him seem younger than his age, and less mature. There was something
childlike in the way he embraced his father's fable about recovery, thus
avoiding the unpleasant and obvious reality.

Despite his physical agony, the older Bingham's political instincts remained sharp. He had expected Kennedy's visit after the events of the past
week. Three days earlier, on Wednesday, December 8, Bingham had dictated a letter of resignation to President Roosevelt, saying that his health
made him unable to do "my necessary duty to you and to the country."

The news came as no surprise to the White House. Bingham had long
been infirm, and for over a year Roosevelt had been searching for a graceful
way to replace him. Indeed, in late November, even before the ambassador
had decided to resign, the president had quietly offered the diplomatic plum
to Joe Kennedy, chairman of the U.S. Maritime Commission, who had
been frustrated in his attempts to win a cabinet post and, with characteristic
cheek, had set his sights on the Court of St. James's. Announcing Kennedy's
new assignment would be delicate, however, and Roosevelt had made it
clear he wanted to wait a while. He did not wish to create the macabre
impression that he was rushing Bingham to his grave.

But the matter was soon taken out of the president's hands. On December
9, the day after the ailing man had resigned his post, the news of Kennedy's
appointment burst onto the front page of *The New York Times*—a result of
Kennedy's overeagerness and his long-standing alliance with Arthur Krock,
the paper's Washington bureau chief.

Krock had his own reasons for publishing the story. Decades earlier,
while Krock was working at the Louisville newspapers, Bingham had
double-crossed him—or so he thought. Now he was only too glad to get
even. Publicly embarrassed, Roosevelt hotly accused Krock of trying to
hasten Bingham's death, and dispatched Kennedy to the former ambassador's bedside to make amends.

Bingham was determined that the moment not belong entirely to Kennedy. Propped up on pillows, the frail sixty-six-year-old ambassador listened as Kennedy apologetically explained that the leak had been
inadvertent, an accident. Bingham waved the incident aside as if it were of
no importance, and steered the conversation back to what he intended to
do for Roosevelt once he was himself again.

Bingham and Kennedy understood each other perfectly. In 1931, they
had been members of "Roosevelt Before Chicago," a group of wealthy Democrats whose money and muscle had helped launch F.D.R.'s first presidential
bid. Bingham was rewarded with the ambassadorship; Kennedy got the

Securities and Exchange Commission. In 1936, Kennedy had visited Bingham at the American embassy in London, marveling at the opulent furnishings and the palatial scale of the building, a gift to the American people from J. P. Morgan.

Joe Kennedy knew that, in some respects, he was a Yankee version of this self-created Southern patrician, a man who had gone from near-poverty in Reconstruction North Carolina to incredible wealth and the most prestigious post in the diplomatic service. But unlike Bingham, who had successfully obscured his Irish ancestry, Kennedy would never quite escape the taint of the Irish stereotype: a poor, hard-drinking, uneducated immigrant.

The Binghams were Protestants from Northern Ireland, the stronghold of the hard-working Scotch-Irish—so-called because they had emigrated to Ireland from Scotland. Robert Worth Bingham's father had taken great pride in being Scotch-Irish, but his ambitious son had realized at an early age that an English pedigree was socially preferable. Over many years, Bingham spent thousands of dollars on genealogists in an effort to establish that his great-great-great-great-great-grandfather was the third son of Sir George Bingham, an English nobleman who had emigrated to Ireland around 1600 from Bingham's Melcombe, an estate in Dorset.

Unfortunately, there was no proof that Sir George even had a third son. But that had not stopped Bingham from declaring himself Anglo-Irish and naming his Louisville mansion Melcombe Bingham in honor of his "ancestral home." In Kentucky, his baronial airs were well known. An English butler looked after his Louisville estate, and Bingham ate in the continental style, with his fork in his left hand.

Like Kennedy, Bingham had traveled far from his roots, making and remaking himself until his character was an alloy of fact and fiction. Over the next fifty years, the Binghams and the Kennedys would continue the alchemy, one clan becoming the royal family of Kentucky, the other of the entire nation. Both would suffer the loss of two sons and would try vainly to keep the family's hopes and ambitions alive in the sole surviving son.

But all that was in the future on that December day in 1937. After a few pleasantries, Kennedy found to his relief that he would not have to endure one of Bingham's doomsday lectures on Hitler; the old man simply was not up to it. Kennedy looked intently into Bingham's death-bright eyes, searching for the tough political infighter he had once known. All he saw was fatigue and a slight glimmer of contempt. Kennedy knew that Bingham thought him a bit common and unschooled in foreign affairs. No matter. His duty done, Kennedy shook hands with Barry and disappeared down the hospital's hallway.

For a moment, Barry was left alone with his feverish father. He knew that he would inherit everything when Bingham died: *The Courier-Journal* and

Times, the radio station, WHAS, and Melcombe. But he took little pleasure in the prospect of running the empire without the older man's often ill-advised but always certain direction.

Death and birth. Endings and beginnings. It was Bingham tradition that the best man in each generation be given dominion over what had been built, along with the responsibility to rework and improve it before passing it on again. That is what he would do when his father died, Barry thought: take his good name and the newspapers, burnish them both, make them stronger, more renowned, then pass them on.

The dream would prove to be admirable but false. Dependent, like the South itself, on artifice, half-truth, and denial, the Bingham family would ultimately dissolve from within, eaten away by the corrosive power of its own invention. "This family is very complex and not everything is as it appears," said a Bingham in-law decades later. "You have to wrestle with a lot of myths if you want to understand this family."

Fittingly, the Bingham saga in America began with an engaging tale of good fortune, bad luck, and fate.

As family lore had it, William Bingham, an unmarried, thirty-five-year-old Presbyterian minister, left County Down, Northern Ireland, and arrived in 1789 with a contract to teach the sons of Scotch-Irish immigrants in Wilmington, North Carolina. But, not realizing that his new country might have two towns with the same name, he booked passage to Wilmington, Delaware. When he disembarked, he discovered that he would have to travel the intervening four hundred miles on foot if he was to make good on his teaching commitment.

While trudging from Delaware to North Carolina, William spied something round and sparkling in the road. He speared the mysterious object with his walking stick and discovered that, miraculously, he had found a diamond ring in the wilderness. After making inquiries at the next village and finding no claimant, he sold the ring and rode horseback the rest of the way to his destination, only to discover that his position had been given to someone else when he had not arrived as expected. By 1793, he had recovered sufficiently to establish his own boys' academy, which came to be called the Bingham School. In 1799, he married the daughter of a well-connected Tory.

Generations later, Robert Worth Bingham would insist to his son, Barry, that this unlikely sequence of events was true. The story of the diamond ring was perhaps the first great Bingham myth, told and retold to prove that from the moment the Binghams arrived in America, they were a special family.

The more enduring myth of Robert Worth Bingham's childhood, however, was of the lost glory of the Old South. Born on November 8, 1871, at Oaks, the family farm, near Hillsboro, North Carolina, "Rob" was too young to experience life before the Civil War. He grew up surrounded by the bitterness of Reconstruction, keenly aware of the South's poverty, humiliation, powerlessness, and frustration.

But he also grew up hearing his father, Robert Bingham, a former Confederate captain, speak glowingly of the region's antebellum world, a world described as one of comfort, chivalry, and civilized behavior, with loving slaves and considerable wealth. The truth was somewhat less grand. The Binghams ran a respected but rustic boys' school and lived the life of the lower gentry, which was more hardscrabble than Arcadian.

At first, the war had little effect on the Binghams. Robert spent the first few months after North Carolina's secession courting seventeen-year-old Delphine Louise Worth, the pious daughter of a North Carolina physician who had made his fortune in copper- and gold-mining. In December 1861, they were married.

The cause of Southern independence soon proved irresistible. Robert mustered a company of men from the small villages around Oaks and left his frail older brother, William, to oversee the Bingham School. The 129 recruits joined the Confederate Army as Company G of the 44th North Carolina Regiment, with Robert as their captain. Church bells pealed, guns fired salutes, and townspeople paraded and shouted for joy as the new soldiers marched off to do battle with the North.

Robert's experiences as a Confederate officer only reinforced the family's conviction that it had been singled out by fate, for he was saved from death not once but twice by coincidences of timing.

The first moment came in mid-June 1863, when Company G was diverted from its march northward with Robert E. Lee's army to help guard the critical railroad bridge over the South Anna River outside Richmond. The balance of Lee's forces tramped on to Gettysburg, the decisive battle of the Civil War, where 28,000 Rebels were slaughtered, including most of Robert's regiment.

The second came when Robert and sixteen other Confederate officers were captured while defending the South Anna bridge from Yankee assault. At Fort Norfolk, Virginia, their first place of internment, the men found themselves in one of the war's most bizarre conundrums. In 1831, not long after Nat Turner's Rebellion, the Georgia legislature had passed a law condemning to the gallows any Northerner who entered the state to "tamper with the Negroes." Just ten days before the battle at the South Anna bridge, Confederate troops had captured seventeen Union officers in Georgia and promptly announced their intention to hang them under the old state law.

Outraged, the North vowed to retaliate by stringing up Captain Bingham and his compatriots. Fortunately for Robert—and future generations of Binghams—Gen. William H. "Rooney" Lee, Robert E. Lee's oldest son, was also incarcerated at Fort Norfolk. Rather than see General Lee's boy "hanged like a dog," Georgia reluctantly backed down and agreed not to execute the Union officers. Robert Bingham's life was once again spared.

Instead, Bingham and his companions were transferred, first to the "pestilineal cells" of Fort Delaware, a crude configuration of sheds on an island in the Delaware River, and then to the notorious prisoner-of-war camp on Johnson's Island in Lake Erie, two and a half miles from Sandusky, Ohio.

In the journal that he kept on scraps of paper throughout his ordeal, Robert recorded the shames and slights of prison life. He was particularly offended when a group of well-dressed Northern women—"the she Yankee brute," as he dubbed them—peered through opera glasses at Rebel prisoners while they bathed naked in the Delaware River.

But the worst period of his imprisonment was the winter he spent on Johnson's Island. Robert's bunk was near the door, making him particularly vulnerable to exposure. On New Year's Day, 1864, several of his fellow-prisoners froze to death as a biting wind blew in off Lake Erie and rattled the thin walls. "I never felt such weather," he wrote. "The windows have ice a half an inch thick on them." To supplement his meager rations, Robert trapped mice for food.

After ten months in captivity, he was finally set free in a prisoner exchange at Point Lookout, a sandy, barren spit of land at the mouth of the Potomac River. Following a brief visit home to see his wife, he reentered the fray. Between then and the South's surrender a year later he took part in ten pitched battles during the siege of Richmond and Petersburg.

On Palm Sunday, 1865, Robert Bingham, "ragged, hungry and barefoot," crouched in an apple orchard near Appomattox Courthouse while General Lee, resplendent in his full-dress uniform, surrendered to a mud-spattered Ulysses S. Grant. Three days later, when the Confederates marched up to stack their weapons and relinquish their flags, Robert worried that the Yankees would erupt in humiliating whoops of victory. "I just thought I couldn't stand it if they cheered," he recalled later.

When the moment of final surrender came, however, there were no signs of disrespect. Instead, the 44th marched down a sunken road between banks of blue-clad soldiers standing smartly at carry-arms, the salute of honor. Bingham's men were crying like children and he was weeping with the rest. But to his relief, there were no shouts from the enemy ranks. The Union troops stood in a silence so complete that Robert was compelled to look up. When he did, he saw tears streaming down their cheeks as well.

Although Robert revered Robert E. Lee, he also blessed the memory of

Ulysses S. Grant, because he and his men had been so compassionate in conquest.

Robert could now go home, but a changed world awaited him. He had left North Carolina an inexperienced and immature second son. Now he returned as something of a hero, toughened in battle and sobered by his deprivations. The war had also been hard on his wife, Dell. She had lost two of her three brothers and, though pregnant with her second child, she was in poor health. Her firstborn, a round-cheeked boy named Jimmy, had died two months before his second birthday while Robert was trapped in trench warfare at Petersburg. Dell had been en route to the battlefield when she learned that the baby had succumbed to a fever.

The sliver of prosperity the Binghams had enjoyed before the war was now gone and, like many of their neighbors, they were destitute. To finance the war, the Confederate government had extracted levies in kind, demanding the family's chickens, vegetables, and meat for the battlefront. The Binghams' slaves had been set free by the Emancipation Proclamation with no compensation for the loss. Confederate currency had become so worthless that it was contemptuously referred to as "rags" and "shrunken cabbage," but Robert's brother, William, had patriotically insisted on accepting it as payment for tuition, giving the family no hope of accumulating hard currency.

During the war, the Binghams had added a military dimension to their academy, renaming it the Bingham Military School. In late 1864, to be closer to supply lines, the family had moved operations from rural Oaks to a flat, wooded parcel of land outside nearby Mebaneville, now Mebane, where a railroad depot, post office, and several small stores made life more manageable. When Robert arrived home several months later, he found his family living not in the tidy white farmhouse at Oaks but in temporary log barracks caulked with mud. He immediately sank into a brooding despondency.

The crop at Oaks failed that summer and the whole region was overcast with the gloom of a conquered territory. In September, only nine students showed up for classes. Elderly, ill, and unable to accommodate himself to the ruin around him, Robert's father died soon after Christmas. Only when it became clear that the old man was near the end did Robert finally rouse himself and, in accordance with his father's wishes, rejoin the school as a Latin and English teacher.

Into this angry and impoverished world, Robert Worth Bingham, "Rob," was born in 1871, Robert and Dell's fourth child. From his earliest days, the family's struggle for money and prestige—an obsession that swept the humiliated South—was as pervasive and insistent as the aggressive Confederate pride that sprang up after Appomattox.

The Bingham Military School that Rob knew as a child had a distinctly Confederate cast. The cadets wore gray uniforms and drilled in tight formation with huge .59-caliber smoothbores. Rob's father and his uncle William were active promoters of the regional romance and beamed discernibly when cadets delivered commencement addresses with titles such as "Southern Chivalry" and "Adieu to the Confederacy."

Mingled with the South's reverence for its past was the fury of the old order struggling to reassert itself. "We who were born here will never get along with the Negroes," raged Dell's uncle, Jonathan Worth, who was elected governor of North Carolina just months after the South's defeat. "The fools and demagogues of the North insist they must be our equals. This will not be tolerated."

The Binghams and other members of the Southern gentry soon made that abundantly clear. While he was still a toddler, Rob watched, terrified, as a huge form, draped in white, approached the house. He huddled behind his mother's skirts until the ghostly figure removed its tall, pointed hood and Rob saw, to his great relief, that the apparition was his father, dressed in his Ku Klux Klan robes.

Few areas experienced as much Klan violence as Alamance County, where the Bingham Military School was located. The year before Rob's birth, a mob of white-hooded horsemen dragged the county's most prominent black citizen from his bed and lynched him from a tree in his own front yard. There was no proof that the Binghams took part in that execution, or any other, but afterward his uncle William was arrested, along with eighty-two other Alamance citizens thought to be involved in Klan activity.

Coupled with the Binghams' determination to recapture the power of their class and race was a constant anxiety about money. Uncle William's death in 1873 at the age of thirty-eight only heightened their sense of distress. Robert immediately assumed the title his brother had taken as head of a military academy—"Colonel Bingham"—and became the school's fourth headmaster.

With borrowed funds and the new colonel's natural talent for self-promotion, the business improved rapidly. By the 1880s, the Bingham Military School was able to attract the sons of the best families in the region. Log huts gave way to neat wooden barracks with corn shuck mattresses, trim parade fields, and the first gymnasium at a boys' prep school in the South.

As he got older and his responsibilities multiplied, Col. Robert Bingham became a terrifying disciplinarian. Cadets who were late for class or had untidy rooms were summoned to his office and taught a lesson by "Dr.

Black" or "Dr. Brown," the names Bingham gave the leather straps he used to administer punishment.

At the same time, the Colonel showered fatherly devotion on Rob. He clearly favored his oldest son and could often be seen riding about the grounds on horseback with the little boy balanced uncertainly in front of him in the saddle.

Colonel Bingham was not the only adoring presence. Rob's mother, his black nurse, and his two older sisters, Mary and Sadie, treated him with the deference due the family heir, and he became used to getting his way, especially with women. Weaned on the boiled ham, butter beans, biscuits, and apple pie that the school cooks prepared, the brown-haired boy shot up handsome and straight, with his father's easy athleticism and Dell's good manners, charm, and quiet intensity.

As he matured into adolescence, attending classes at his father's school, Rob came to understand more fully the precariousness of his family's situation. The proximity of Dell's relatives, the well-heeled Worths, only magnified the Binghams' sense of being under financial siege. For most of Rob's childhood, he watched his father scheme and plot in an effort to boost the Bingham fortune—with only intermittent success.

But the most crushing burden of Rob's early life was the death of his mother. In 1886, after six months as an invalid, Dell finally succumbed to a vague malady that had dogged her since the death of her firstborn. Years later, when he was an old man, Robert Worth Bingham would describe his mother as "Melanie to the last emotion," a reference to the kind, pure-hearted character in *Gone With the Wind*.

Dell's death took away the one person who could temper Colonel Bingham's bitterness about the South's defeat and the family's worries about money. The sudden loss catapulted him into a depression rivaling the one after Appomattox. When the "nervous prostration" became prolonged, his doctors ordered him on a sea voyage, hoping that the fresh air and change of pace would prove steadying. But Colonel Bingham never fully recovered. The soft, loving side of him flickered out, and all that remained was the moody dictator his cadets knew so well. Lonely and desperate to find a new mother for his children, Robert hastily remarried less than a year after Dell's death.

His new bride was Elvira Woodward, a stiff South Carolina school-teacher. Vy, as she was known, had none of Dell's nurturing sweetness, and the Bingham children, who now ranged in age from nineteen-year-old Mary to eleven-year-old Will, Rob's younger brother, treated her like a cipher in their Mebaneville home.

Rob loathed Vy and resented his father's mounting imperiousness. At the Bingham Military School, he had dismissed his classmates' snickers about the Colonel's grandiose behavior as typical schoolboy mockery. Now he appraised his father with a freshly critical eye. To sixteen-year-old Rob, the Colonel did not seem shrewd, or even very smart. And the Bingham Military School? A dead end if a young man's goal was to rise and live in luxury like the Worths.

Rob was determined to escape. In 1888, he took his first step, following Bingham tradition by enrolling at the University of North Carolina, entering as a sophomore.

———

At the university, Bob, as he now preferred to be called, had more plans than resources, but he compensated for that lack with a winning air of self-assurance. His years among the Bingham cadets had made him a man's man; his mother had imbued him with a gentleman's bearing and manner. The combination made him prized company among both men and women.

He consciously sought out friendships with young men from families whose names and economic circumstances were somewhat better than his own. Within weeks, he had forged close alliances with Shepard Bryan, the son of a North Carolina judge, and William Watkins Davies, a philosophy major and writer who would later become his law partner in Louisville.

Dell had drilled her son in scripture and religious piety. But at UNC, Bob became something of a libertine, leading dances and playing football at a time when dancing was banned on campus as "promotive of various evils" and football was associated with rowdies. With "Shep" Bryan, "Dave" Davies, and Wray Martin, another classmate, Bob helped organize the Order of the Gimghouls, a secret fraternity with ideals based on chivalry and knighthood.

Bob's dawning political ambitions found an outlet in the Dialectic Literary Society, a debating club, and in various university offices. Aware that merit was no guarantee of victory, he was not above rigging elections. When Bob ran for chief ball manager—a position that gave him the privilege of leading school dances in ermine regalia—he got Dave Davies to entice an anti-Bingham freshman named Mumpsey away on a buggy ride, leaving his proxy with Dave. Bob was subsequently elected by one vote—Mumpsey's.

He also discovered that personal charm could be a source of great power. Irene Langhorne, who twirled with Bob till sunrise at the last ball of the season, likened him to "a prince out of a romance," and it was clear that his male companions felt similarly enchanted. Bob was "a social success always," said one classmate. "He was at home anywhere, and I have seen him many times entertain a party of twenty or thirty after a dance and have the full attention of all."

His academic performance was less noteworthy. He excelled in Latin,

Greek, and English, core subjects at the Bingham Military School. But his father's parochial curriculum had ill-prepared him for the chemistry and German courses he now needed to pursue a career in medicine, the profession he secretly planned to enter in the hope that it would bring him prosperity and acclaim, as it had Grandfather Worth.

Bob's plans quickly unraveled. He barely passed physics. Then, after the first semester of his junior year, he contracted malaria and was forced to drop out. He never received a degree.

In those days, however, the lack of a diploma was no bar to entering medical school, and in the fall of 1890, Bob did just that, enrolling at the University of Virginia. His choice of a medical career infuriated his father, who had expected him to honor the Bingham teaching tradition. But Colonel Bingham took solace in the knowledge that his youngest son, Will, then a freshman at UNC, would soon be available to help him in the enterprise. Even so, he refused to subsidize Bob's medical education. To pay his tuition bills, Bob had to borrow money against stock in the Worth family business that he had inherited at his mother's death.

These quarrels with his father did not prevent Bob from having a glorious time in Charlottesville, where he was elected to Phi Beta Kappa, named captain of the school's first football team, and celebrated as a great lady's man. One of his most ardent male admirers was Hugh Young, a muscular Texan who, like Bob, was the son of a Confederate officer. Both men prided themselves on their "quick, decisive manner," and Bob saw in Hugh's knowledge of opera and art a delicious wider world that he yearned to experience.

While Bob was savoring the heady atmosphere of Charlottesville, the Bingham Military School suffered repeated disasters. In December 1890, two fires, one allegedly set by a "crazy incendiary" angry at the Colonel's harsh ways, demolished most of the classrooms and the gymnasium. A third unexplained fire two months later finally convinced Colonel Bingham to uproot his school and seek a new location.

After visiting twenty-five potential sites, he finally settled on Asheville, a mountain town of ten thousand near North Carolina's western border. There, on a bluff outside the city overlooking the French Broad River, Robert Bingham set about erecting a model academy, complete with swimming pool, showers, and fireproof cottages. The Colonel's removal to "Bingham Heights," as he immodestly named the plateau, was the boldest and most financially risky venture of his career. But he thought he could see the future clearly that summer of 1891, later writing to a friend that he felt confident he was laying the foundation for yet another generation of Bingham schoolmasters.

How naive that must have seemed to him in retrospect. In July 1891, Colonel Bingham's youngest child, Will, suddenly died, the victim of a ruptured appendix. For several years, Bob had justified his abandonment of the family business by arguing that Will was always available to take over. But his brother's death put an end to that possibility. Reluctantly, Bob gave up his medical studies and went to Asheville.

For the next four years, he taught Latin, smoldering in resentment of his autocratic father and chafing at the schoolmaster's life that seemed to his newly refined sensibilities like a rough suit of homespun cloth. The only bright spot was a brief romance with Mary Lily Kenan, a beguiling young woman from a socially prominent and well-to-do North Carolina family whom Bob met in 1894 at Hugh Young's graduation from the University of Virginia.

The Kenans and the Binghams were old acquaintances. Colonel Bingham had attended UNC with Thomas S. Kenan, Mary Lily's uncle, and the two had endured the same Yankee prison together. Bob's sister Sadie had been Mary Lily's contemporary at Peace Institute, a women's finishing school in Raleigh.

Bob quickly became smitten with the vivacious, dark-haired beauty, and the couple had what Mary Lily later called "an affair," a word that, at the time, meant a flirtatious dalliance rather than a sexual tryst. It did not last long. Mary Lily wanted a grander life than a Latin teacher could provide, and they soon drifted apart.

Colonel Bingham's ripening idiosyncracies only intensified the blow of the breakup. Now white-haired and magisterial, the Colonel had become a living caricature of the Old South. He wore his gray officer's cape winter and summer, and on the cadets' day off, rode into town in an old victoria driven by an elderly black in a silk top hat.

So ridiculous was the sight of the bristling Colonel that Asheville native Thomas Wolfe later lampooned him in his novel *The Hills Beyond* as the self-deceiving Theodore Joyner, a man who spoke of the Lost Cause in a "solemn whisper." Wolfe was only slightly less biting when describing Bob, reborn in the book as "Silk" Joyner, Theodore's son. Silk "sensed the right thing before anyone else even suspected its existence," Wolfe wrote. "And 'the right thing' with Silk . . . was, simply, the advantageous thing." The characterization would prove to be remarkably accurate.

———

In February 1895, Samuel Adams Miller, a manufacturer and waterworks executive from Louisville, committed suicide at the Asheville train station. Miller, fifty-six, had been in town for three months, recuperating from what doctors vaguely diagnosed as "melancholia and insomnia." He had been driven to the station to meet his daughter Eleanor and was sitting quietly in the car when suddenly he bolted out of the vehicle, ran to the platform, and threw himself beneath the wheels of the approaching train.

A few months later, Bob Bingham, restless from the confining routine of school, descended from Bingham Heights and rode into town, looking for companionship. It was summer, and he sought out the cool, broad porch of the Battery Park Hotel, an elegant hostelry with a bowling alley, marble rotunda, and a commanding view of the mountains.

Gazing down the length of the porch, he spied a petite brunette sitting in a rocking chair and, using intermediaries, he wangled an introduction. Her name was Eleanor Miller, Sam Miller's youngest daughter, and she had come to Asheville with her family to escape Louisville's blistering heat. He remembered her name from that winter's tragedy, and knew from newspaper accounts that her father's estate was worth at least a million dollars.

To Bob's delight, Eleanor, known as "Babes," was not the typical wealthy heiress. She was vivacious and whimsically funny. Although Bob had never been known to tell a joke, he liked being around people who made him laugh; it moderated his natural intensity. When Babes teased him about being too serious and self-important, he was oddly entranced, not angry or deflated. For her part, Eleanor felt stirrings of attraction for this confident and handsome young man who seemed to have ambitions far beyond his family business.

At twenty-four, Eleanor was old enough to be considered a spinster, and it is unclear whether it was she or Bob who pushed the idea of marriage. Bob was well aware, though, that he was marrying above his station. "I am safely conscious of the great thing I am asking of you," he wrote Eleanor's mother in a letter requesting consent to their engagement. But if he were given half a chance, he said, he knew he could convince Mrs. Miller that Eleanor would not be making a mistake to wed "a man who lives as I do." By Christmas, 1895, the couple's plans were set: He would leave Asheville, marry Eleanor, and study law in Louisville.

Colonel Bingham instantly saw how his own enterprise might benefit from Bob's marriage to a wealthy woman. But that was poor compensation for the loss of his sole remaining heir. When Bob had come back to Asheville in 1891, the Colonel had assumed that he would be his successor as head of the Bingham Military School. Now the Colonel's hopes for perpetuating the family business were permanently shattered. Although his two daughters had married instructors, and one, S. R. McKee, would eventually run the academy in its waning years, the old man knew that without his son, the school was unlikely to survive.

In May 1896, the Binghams boarded the train in Asheville en route to the wedding in Louisville. For Bob, the trip marked the beginning of a whole new life, and in the compartment, his sisters laughed and bantered with the nervous young bridegroom. But Colonel Bingham just stared out the window as the train pulled away and the buildings of the Bingham Military School became smaller and smaller, finally disappearing altogether as the tracks curved northward.

BEAUTIFUL
BOB BINGHAM

The trip to Kentucky took the better part of a day and ended at Louisville's Union Station, an elaborate stone structure whose name annoyed the town's many Confederate sympathizers. As the Binghams emerged from the cavernous depot onto Broadway, they came face-to-face with one of the nation's most bustling metropolises, a city that had a population of nearly 200,000—or so boosters claimed.

Louisville chauvinists liked to brag about the town's up-to-date electric streetlights and trolleys. Window screens were a new invention and immensely popular. One circular featured a huge black fly with a message emblazoned on its wings: "No more to wade in butter and beans, I am kept outside by Dow's wire screens." But underneath its futuristic sheen, Louisville was little changed from the eighteenth century. Though Henry Ford was only a month away from driving his horseless carriage through Detroit, the powerful odor of manure would hover over the streets of Louisville for several more decades.

Just two weeks earlier, Louisville had played host to the Kentucky Derby, the horse race that, since its founding in 1875, had drawn national attention to the city. The lush Kentucky spring had already brought forth tulips, forsythia, tender chartreuse shoots of grass, and a bounty of white magnolias.

In a convoy of carriages, the groom and his party set out from Union Station for the Galt House, the city's most elegant hotel, located several blocks from the swirling brown waters of the Ohio River. The high-ceilinged rooms were too expensive for North Carolina schoolteachers, but Bob Bingham considered the cost a necessary extravagance. He was determined not to be patronized by the well-to-do Millers, and had already taken pains to ensure that he made the right impression.

Days before, in a story about his engagement, *The Courier-Journal* had obligingly regurgitated the biographical information he had sent, noting that Bob was "prominently connected in North Carolina," the grandson of Dr. John Milton Worth, who was the "proprietor of five cotton mills" and "perhaps the richest man in the state." The suggestion of wealth and position was gratifying, if misleading: It was true that his grandfather was prosperous, but Bob Bingham was virtually penniless. Still, he hoped that the newspaper notice would reassure Louisville's monied upper crust that he was a fit match for the daughter of one of the city's leading families. Gaining the confidence of Eleanor Miller's mother, Henrietta, however, would be a different matter altogether.

Mrs. Miller viewed her prospective son-in-law with ill-concealed suspicion. She did not like the fact that he was ten months younger than her daughter and of undistinguished professional background. The haste of their romance also bothered her, and she morosely speculated that he was a gold digger. Soon after proposing, Bob had jettisoned his Presbyterian heritage and joined the Episcopal Church, the Millers' denomination, demonstrating an unattractive eagerness, she felt, for upward mobility and social acceptance.

Her fears were rooted in her own experience, for Mrs. Miller was herself a wealthy man's daughter who had married an ambitious but socially inferior suitor. Her father, Dennis Long, had made a fortune manufacturing boat engines and pumps for waterworks. Sam Miller, on the other hand, was the lowly manager of a flour mill when he proposed to Henrietta Long, a position he soon abandoned to go work for his new father-in-law. Financial success and a partnership in Dennis Long & Company followed, along with stakes in other ventures.

A slender man with thinning hair and a full mustache, Sam Miller had been blessed with a genial and sweet temperament. He worked hard—frequently to the point of nervous exhaustion—but he also had a dreamy, faraway quality and often lost himself in music and literature. Early in the marriage, he built a handsome red-brick Victorian home with a fish-scale shingle mansard roof on Louisville's fashionable Fourth Street and furnished it with paintings, statuary, and books on Napoleon, his personal hero.

Despite their money, the Longs and the Millers had never penetrated the innermost circle of Louisville's social elite. Neither Dennis Long nor Sam Miller were members of the Pendennis Club, an organization, established in 1882, that included the most substantial business and professional men of the city and state. Wounded by the exclusion, Miller organized the rival Kenton Club, which was less expensive and had "a more social turn." He was sitting as its first president in 1895 when he abruptly ended his life.

Mrs. Miller had been disgraced by her husband's public breakdown and "sensational suicide," as one Louisville newspaper called it. Within the family, his death was described as a regrettable accident and rarely mentioned. "I never heard my grandmother talk about that," said Barry Sr. "It was just not discussed."

Determined not to let the gossipy matrons of Louisville get the better of her, Mrs. Miller staged a dazzling Wednesday evening wedding for her daughter at Calvary Church, the Gothic-spired Episcopal cathedral favored by Louisville's best families. There were eight bridesmaids, all swathed in Paris muslin, and a program of harp, organ, and violin music. Eleanor's sister sang a solo and the bride, outfitted in a lace-trimmed dress of ivory brocade satin, walked down the aisle on the arm of her brother, carrying a bright bouquet of sweetpeas. White magnolias—hundreds of them—garlanded the stairs and surrounded the mirrors and chandeliers of the Miller home, the site of the reception. Only the mother-of-the-bride looked incongruously dour and cheerless as Kurkamp's Orchestra struck up the first dance. Although the traditional one-year mourning period for her husband had expired months ago, Mrs. Miller wore black.

The newlyweds honeymooned in Chicago, then went to the University of North Carolina at Chapel Hill, where Bob took a summer course in law to prepare himself for the rigors of legal studies at the University of Louisville. That fall, Bob and Eleanor returned to Louisville and moved into an upstairs apartment in Mrs. Miller's four-story house. The arrangement was one of necessity, not desire. As a student and later as a struggling young lawyer, Bob had no money for a home of his own. By 1897, he had earned his law degree, passed the bar exam, and launched a new career.

Louisville at the time was a glittering, raffish bazaar with a veneer of Victorian stuffiness where a small group of men schemed and plotted for political power, forged shifting alliances, and, in the city's half-dozen newspapers, lambasted their enemies with exuberant broadsides. It was no place for the timid or the weak. For Bob Bingham, steeled by the experience of Reconstruction and consumed with a single-minded desire to get ahead, it looked like fertile hunting ground.

Prosperity, earned off the traffic that glided up and down the river or clattered along the rails, had been as much an accident of geography as effort, making Louisville smug and a bit pompous. Easy profits and easy virtue went hand in hand. Whiskey was available in ice-cream parlors, and the row of brothels near the riverfront had become a celebrated lure for tourists and travelers.

At the same time, the city burghers had raised rules of etiquette to the status of religion. Bob soon found that there were strictly observed standards for everything from clothing to the proper form for dinner invitations. The Louisville Social Directory decreed that men must "never wear a watch guard with full dress, never wear diamonds, never wear patent leather shoes with knickerbockers, and never do as you please in matters pertaining to dress."

The rules governing politics were almost as explicit, the product of Louisville's peculiar history. The city's name itself was a political back-scratch. It was christened Louisville in 1779 to encourage King Louis XVI of France to continue his support of the American Revolution. During the Civil War, when the Ohio River and the L&N—the Louisville & Nashville Railroad—made the town a hub of wartime commerce, enterprising Louisvillians traded shamelessly with both sides, shipping coffee, bacon, and other goods to Yankees and Rebels alike.

Though slavery was legal in Kentucky, many citizens opposed secession. At first, the state adopted a policy of neutrality, but ultimately it sided with the Union—a fitting straddle, perhaps, for the birthplace of both Abraham Lincoln and Jefferson Davis. In Louisville, it was not uncommon to see recruits destined for the Union Army marching up one side of the street while Rebel recruits stepped smartly down the other.

After the war, ex-Confederates poured into Louisville to start fresh in one of the few Southern cities that had escaped ruin and military rule. But was Louisville really Southern? Characteristically, the town tried to have it both ways. In circulars aimed at prospective customers from the South, city promoters stressed that Louisville was on the *south* bank of the Ohio, unlike Cincinnati, its arch rival upriver. But Ohio and Indiana customers were told that Louisville was a "live Western town"—although the West had long since moved on. The truth was that Louisville was a hybrid, a place where Southern gentility co-existed with Midwestern commercial intensity. Leading citizens sipped bourbon toddies on the back porches of their stately homes only after a day of mercantile hustle.

The combination made Louisville politics a heady mixture of business, sport, and social diversion. Like the rest of the South, Kentucky had gone solidly Democratic after the war to counter the threat of newly enfranchised blacks. In Louisville, the kingpin of the Democratic machine was John H. Whallen, a saloonkeeper of Irish origins who had endeared himself to the city's many immigrants and working stiffs by charging just a nickel for a schooner of beer. The L&N, *The Courier-Journal* and *Times*, and other Louisville power brokers had no particular love for Whallen, but at election time they had little choice but to play his game if they wanted their candidates in office.

Robert Worth Bingham observed the city's dealmakers with fascination and envy. Like Silk Joyner, his opportunistic prototype in *The Hills Beyond*, Bob had an intuitive political sense. In his heart he knew he was destined for a life far grander than that of a colorless attorney, drawing up lawsuits and contracts and eating dinner every night at his mother-in-law's table. With a nose for power and a hunger for some of his own, he set his sights on public office. His fifteen-year swim in the murky waters of Louisville's municipal politics would shape his adult character as much as the aftermath of the Civil War had his youth, earning him contempt as well as renown and creating in him a moral certainty that would make him seem almost priggish in old age.

His political beginnings were quite modest. After several years with the firm of Pryor, O'Neal & Pryor, Bob persuaded Dave Davies, his old friend from UNC, to leave Atlanta and join him in a new partnership, Bingham & Davies. The firm did a respectable trade, fed in large part by business from the Miller and Long family enterprises as well as regional and national clients such as Aetna Insurance and the National Biscuit Company.

Bob was sensitive to suggestions that he was using his wife's money and social prominence to rise above his station, and he lashed out fiercely at anyone he felt had besmirched his reputation. When he heard that an acquaintance of Davies's had snidely commented that Bob Bingham was "doing the great club and society act in Louisville," he confronted the man and hotly accused him of labeling him as "nothing more . . . than an ordinary drunkard." The statement was an extreme exaggeration of the original gossip, but the frightened man promptly denied all and wrote Davies a conciliatory letter saying that he knew Bob was "a gentleman at all times" and had "a most excellent standing with everybody in Louisville."

Regardless of what was actually said, Bob's "club and society act" clearly impressed the social gatekeepers of Louisville, for in 1899, just three years after his marriage to Eleanor, he was invited to join the prestigious Pendennis Club. In 1902, to boost his position still further, he put up the funds to establish a Bingham prize in debate at UNC, though he was not a graduate and barely thirty years old.

He took an expensive cure at the sulphur springs of Carlsbad, a health resort in Czechoslovakia, for the high blood pressure, headaches, and chronic eczema that plagued him. He had no trouble paying for membership in the Juniper Hunt Club, a 25,000-acre spread for quail shoots on Florida's Lake George, where black-tie dinners accompanied by live organ music were staged in elaborate tents. And after he saw the name "Bingham" in Burke's Peerage, he thought nothing of hiring a lawyer in Belfast to track down his family's Irish and English roots.

The gestures bespoke wealth, but it was the Millers' money, not Bob's, that made his foreign trips and costly club memberships possible. As a lawyer, he was only marginally successful, and most of his clients continued to come to him through Miller family connections. Money was a constant headache. It took him four years to pay off a $300 debt to an Asheville law firm that he had incurred before his marriage to Eleanor, for instance, and he never bought life insurance over $10,000, renewing the policy each year on a twelve-month term basis—the cheapest form possible. He continued to live in Mrs. Miller's Fourth Street house and listened in resentful silence as she lectured him about finance, a topic on which she fancied herself to be an expert. Although he had been professionally established for several years, he had yet to repay a $2,500 loan his grandfather Worth had made him to help defray his law school expenses.

As it turned out, he would never have to. When his grandfather died in April 1900, he left Bob no stock or money but he did forgive the debt. Bob was furious. He had expected the rich relation he had bragged about in Louisville to divide his estate equally among his surviving children and grandchildren. But he discovered that in the last two years of his life the old man had changed his will, essentially disinheriting Bob, leaving a pittance to Bob's sisters, Mary and Sadie, and, instead, favoring their aunt, Addie Worth McAlister, who had cared for him in his final illness.

Spurred on by his outraged father at Bingham Heights, Bob filed suit, charging that the McAlisters had taken advantage of the dying man's "enfeebled intellect" and coerced him into rewriting the will. Vowing that he would "not stop until the McAllisters [sic] have disgorged the last dollar which they have wrongfully and fraudulently taken from my sisters and myself," Bob pursued his aunt and cousins for years, taking the case to the North Carolina supreme court when the lower court went against him.

It is likely that his grandfather, who was cranky and headstrong, had arranged his affairs precisely as he wanted. Shortly before his death, Dr. Worth told a relative, "Bob seems to care more for his old Grandaddy's money than the Granddady [sic] himself and if he don't mind, he won't get anything." But where self-interest was concerned, Bob could be blind and a bit dishonest, wrapping his desire for wealth, power, and position in a gauzy cloak of high-minded principle. "The most contemptible thing in the world to me is a man or woman who has not strength enough to stand up for what they [sic] thought was right," he told Sadie's husband, R. T. Grinnan, during the fight over the Worth will. In the end, the McAlisters agreed to buy out the Binghams' stock in the Worth companies. But after court costs were subtracted, the amount was so small, and divided so many ways, that Bob and each of his sisters got only $3,500.

Bob Bingham's moralizing soon found an outlet in Louisville politics. Although he was repulsed by Whallen's tactics and sympathetic with the gathering reform elements inside the Democratic party, he kept his eye on the main chance. He correctly surmised that he could do little in Louisville politics without the blessing of the machine, and he tried at every opportunity to be of service.

In 1903, Bob's toil in the Democratic vineyards paid off and he was appointed to fill the unexpired term of the county attorney, who had moved on to another post. In the general election of 1905, he easily secured a full term in his own right, running on the machine slate and bitterly denouncing the Republicans.

The municipal election of November 1905 was perhaps the filthiest and most violent in Louisville's history. Fed up with Whallen's bossism, Reform Democrats and Republicans united under the Fusionist banner and offered J. T. O'Neal, a partner in Bingham's first law firm, as their mayoral candidate. On election day, the city braced for trouble. Police were out in force by 5:00 A.M., liquor was unavailable all day, and guns and truncheons were forbidden near polling places.

The precautions did not stop the Democratic machine from stuffing ballot-boxes and physically threatening the opposition. To no one's surprise, everyone on the Democratic slate was elected, including County Attorney Bob Bingham. The Fusionists cried foul and immediately challenged the results. The process wound slowly through the legal system and was not resolved until 1907.

Bob's first instinct, as usual, was pragmatic. He feared Whallen's thugs and did not want to antagonize the powerful men who had nourished his fledgling political career. Personally, he was disturbed by the machine's contemptible performance—but not enough, apparently, to denounce it or to resign what he later admitted was a stolen office.

In April 1907, the matter was decided for him. To the surprise of the entire state, the Kentucky Court of Appeals declared the 1905 election invalid and promptly removed all the Democrats elected eighteen months earlier, including the mayor, sheriff, city council, and the county attorney, Bob Bingham. The governor, J. C. W. Beckham, was put in the ticklish position of having to appoint replacements for these offices until new elections could be held. On the one hand, he had to satisfy the reform-minded Fusionists or risk riots in the streets. On the other, he was a Democrat and did not want to antagonize Whallen.

Helm Bruce, a Fusionist leader, helped resolve the dilemma. There was at least one member of the past administration, he said, who might be acceptable to both sides as interim mayor: Bob Bingham. Beckham carefully considered the pros and cons. True, Bingham's silence in the aftermath of the 1905 fracas had convinced many machine leaders that he was still a party loyalist despite his known sympathy for reform. At the same time, as county attorney he had made a determined, if unsuccessful, effort to enforce a state law requiring saloons to close on Sunday, a move that had won him the admiration of Protestant ministers, prohibitionists, and other Progressive elements.

In late June 1907, Governor Beckham appointed Bingham mayor, reminding him that he had only four months to serve until the next election in November. As Beckham had hoped, both the Fusionists and many Whallen followers were pleased. But Henry Watterson, the pro-Whallen, anti-Prohibition editor of *The Courier-Journal*, was decidedly unenthused, noting grumpily that the new mayor was "not a very orthodox Democrat."

He was right. Convinced that Whallen's hold on power had been permanently weakened by the 1905 election scandal, Bingham daringly vowed to be a reform mayor. His first order of business was to reward his prohibitionist supporters by enforcing the widely flouted Sunday Closing Law. He took the oath of office on a Saturday and the following day—for the first time in memory—the city's saloons did not open. "Louisville Dryer Than Ever Before in History" proclaimed the stunned *Courier-Journal*.

That was just the beginning. Within a month, Bingham had flushed out the corrupt police department with the help of his law partner, Dave Davies, whom he appointed chairman of the Board of Public Safety. Bingham fired the police chief, reduced most officers in rank, and gave fifty patrolmen their walking papers for allegedly participating in election fraud.

Such tactics made Bob a hated enemy of the political machine that had once embraced him. One day, a Whallen strongman appeared in City Hall, pulled out a pistol, and informed Mayor Bingham that he was going to kill him—but not until he had told the traitor what he thought of him. Before the man could get two words out of his mouth, Bingham wrestled him to the floor and grabbed his gun. Minutes later, the dazed would-be assassin found himself sitting on the street.

The incident seemed more fitting to the Wild West than to self-consciously genteel Louisville, but it was not unusual. When Bingham exposed the fact that his predecessor, Paul Barth, had taken a city-owned saddle horse with him when he was forced to leave office, *The Louisville Times* pounded the mayor unmercifully. Fed up with the abuse, Bob threatened to kill the *Times*'s managing editor. The statement may have been more than bluster: Bob Bingham always carried a gun. "If you crossed him, God help you," said another *Times* editor decades later.

The Barth affair turned out to be Bingham's undoing. The reformist press, led by Louisville's *Evening Post*, trumpeted the scandal day after day. Finally, Barth wrote the city a personal check for $750 to cover the cost of the horse. A few days later he committed suicide, opening a floodgate of charges from *The Courier-Journal*, *The Louisville Times*, and others that the mayor and his overzealous henchmen had driven Barth to his death.

Bob's budding political career was mortally wounded by Barth's demise. When voters went to the polls in November 1907, Bingham's name was not on the ballot. Instead, the Whallen machine, gleefully back in the driver's seat, nominated one of its own for mayor.

For a while, Bob returned to his law practice and made a respectable living out of representing some of the city's largest companies, including B. F. Avery and Sons, a plow manufacturing firm in which the Long family had an interest. But he could not resist politics, and in 1909 he announced himself a candidate for the Democratic mayoral nomination. Predictably, the party rebuffed him.

Meanwhile, Bingham's preoccupation with Louisville politics had taken its toll on Dave Davies and, soon after Bob's second attempt to become mayor, the firm of Bingham & Davies dissolved, although there was no apparent diminution in the friendship. Bob became part of McChord, Bingham & Page; Dave practiced alone. The breakup came just as Bob Bingham's political career was on a downward arc. In 1910, realizing that his chances with the Whallen machine were nil and that Reform Democrats were powerless, Bob agreed to run for a seat on the Court of Appeals as a Republican.

The move made him look like a man who would do anything to win public office. *The Louisville Times* savagely assailed Bingham's politics as "changeable . . . as the colors were in Joseph's coat." Few were surprised, including Bob, when he lost to the Jefferson County circuit judge Shackleford Miller, the candidate of the Democratic machine.

But Bob's willingness to switch party labels soon helped him. After Judge Miller took up his new position, the Republican governor appointed Bingham to fill Miller's spot on the Circuit Court bench. In January 1911, Bob Bingham, former aide-de-camp of the Democratic machine, former reform mayor, and former Court of Appeals candidate on the Republican ticket, became "Judge Bingham," a title that, as so often happens in the South, clung to him for the rest of his life. The honorific was a bit misleading, however: Bingham sat on the bench for only ten months.

Stung by his earlier defeats, Bob declined to run for the post in a special election later that fall and never stood for office again. In 1913 and 1917, friends tried to persuade him to make a bid for mayor, but he refused. In both elections, the Democrats kept control of City Hall and the machine continued to dominate local politics.

After abandoning his dream of a political career, Bob had more time to devote to his family, which had swelled and changed in the years since he had begun his odyssey. A son, Robert Norwood Bingham, had been born less than a year after he and Eleanor were married. Four years later, in 1901, Henrietta Worth Bingham arrived, named in honor of Bob's formidable mother-in-law.

The new additions made Mrs. Miller's large turreted Victorian cramped and crowded. The house had plenty of bedroom space, but there was only one bathroom, located on the second floor at the top of a carpeted stairway. And Mrs. Miller and the Binghams were not the only ones living there. Eleanor's brother Dennis had never left home. Even after he wed a rather unattractive young woman named Lucy, he saw no reason to change his circumstances and remained happily in the cluttered household, shooting pool with his friends in the shadowy upstairs attic.

In 1905, just months before the notorious elections, Eleanor became pregnant for the third and final time. On February 10, 1906, she delivered a son, George Barry Bingham, in the spare bedroom of the Fourth Street house. The Judge named the new arrival for John George Barry Bingham, Fifth Baron Clanmorris, the head of the Anglo-Irish family to which he was desperately trying to establish kinship. The connection was extremely tenuous, though, and when Barry was old enough to ask where his name had come from, Judge Bingham hemmed and hawed, vaguely alluding to noble relations. At one point, he suggested that Barry was named for the Baron's son, also a "Barry Bingham," who had been a decorated hero at the Battle of Jutland, but the notion was preposterous. The Battle of Jutland, a World War I naval engagement, occurred in 1916, ten years after Barry was born. As a consequence, Barry grew up never really knowing which ancestor he was named for—or indeed if they were his ancestors at all.

The new grandchild convinced Mrs. Miller that Bob and Eleanor needed a home of their own. She provided $50,000 for construction costs, taking care to place the deed to the house and the land, a grassy tract east of town overlooking Cherokee Park, in Eleanor's name. The furnishings were Bob's responsibility, and he went heavily into debt buying sofas, tables, and linens for his new residence, which perched above a large rock and the ruins of an old mill.

The three Bingham children, of course, knew nothing of such difficulties, and remembered the Cherokee Park home, their summer residence, and the Millers' Fourth Street house, where they spent the winters, as the country and city versions of heaven. For Robert, Henrietta, and Barry, life was a smooth, predictable idyll, with rhythms as sure as the seasons that dictated their residences, and warmth as near and welcoming as the large, extended family to which they belonged.

Because he was afflicted with a lung ailment and often confined to bed, little Barry spent more time at Grandmother Miller's than did his siblings. On summer afternoons, he took naps on a sun-warmed blanket in her small backyard, drifting off to sleep as the hens clucked and scratched in the wired-off chicken pen and George, Mrs. Miller's coachman-turned-chauffeur and handyman, hovered quietly in the background. Inside, the sounds of the city—the cries of the vendors, the click of horses' hooves on cobblestone—floated up to Barry in his second-floor sickroom as he lay still under the covers. Even at night, when the taps and shouts became fainter through the heavily curtained window, he took comfort in the urban hum; it made him feel less alone.

Barry's illness was diagnosed as a tubercular condition and bed rest deemed the only cure. His sickliness set him apart from Robert and Henrietta, who, like their father, were vigorous athletes. Barry cheered when his sister and brother won tennis tournaments in nearby Central Park, and watched enviously as they glided down snow-covered hills on sleds in winter. Isolated and indulged, he was well aware that he was different. For his fifth birthday, he requested that only the servants be invited to his party—George and his wife, Sarah, who cooked for the Millers, and Lizzie Baker, the black nurse who looked after him. He neither knew nor cared for children his own age.

Instead, Barry's days were spent in the company of adults, soaking up what he later described as the "slight feminine air of mystery" that permeated the Fourth Street house. He often roamed through its rooms, daydreaming and playing solitary games. From the downstairs parlor, with its horsehair sofa and grand piano, he would walk to the dark library, heated and dimly lit by a coal fire in winter. Then up to the second-floor landing, where an old black telephone with "South 295" printed on the base loomed high above him, just out of reach.

More fascinating was the speaking tube that served as an intercom for Grandmother Miller, who would whistle through it to the kitchen when she wanted Sarah to put on some black bean soup for lunch. But best of all was the circular tower at one end of the house, reached only by a winding iron stairway. From this perch, Barry spent hours surveying the streets and yards below and, in the distance, the businesses and shops of Louisville, pretending all the while that he was a king in a castle. It was in this tiny room that the Binghams and the Millers gathered in 1910 to watch Halley's comet streak across the night sky.

On summer evenings, Barry was allowed to stay up late while aunts and uncles assembled on Grandmother Miller's front porch, rocking in wicker chairs, sipping strong, sweet, iced tea, and playing euchre, a popular card game. Barry rarely saw his father, who was too consumed with his law practice and political plots to pay much attention to his wife and children. Even when he stayed at the Cherokee Park house, Barry glimpsed his father only early in the morning as he strode out the door, leaving behind a trail of tobacco smoke and the slight, agreeable smell of lemon-scented shaving lotion.

Sometimes on weekends Bob Bingham would take his family out for a drive in his Model 21 Rambler. If the tour took them downtown, he would stop at Solger's at Fourth and Broadway and allow Robert, Henrietta, and Barry to scoop bags of penny candy from the rows of glass jars inside. When he was feeling particularly flush, he would stop at Jennie Benedict's, Louisville's finest confectionery, and buy each child an ice-cream sundae crowned with a cherry.

Bob's frequent absences and natural aloofness made him a demigod to his children. They all longed desperately for his attention and approval, but it was Barry who knew he was least likely to get it. His physical frailty and emotional sensitivity simply made him too eccentric and effeminate for his self-consciously masculine father.

As a result, Barry idealized his father far more than the others. In Bob Bingham's chiseled face, Barry saw not a humorless lawyer, obsessed with getting ahead, but a classical hero, "a gentleman of the old school, brought up in the atmosphere of chivalry that survived in the South." The image was reinforced, no doubt, by Bob's role as King Menelaus in an outdoor production of *The Trojan Women* when Barry was about six. Decades later, Barry could recall in detail the magnificent sight of his father stepping onto the makeshift stage in a suit of armor and a Roman-style helmet topped by a mane of dyed horsehair.

However admiring he was of his father, the golden center of Barry's life was his mother, Eleanor, who was as warm, cheerful, and loving as Bob Bingham was serious and distant. Like her three children, Eleanor often felt lonely and a bit neglected by Bob. To compensate, she heaped affection on Barry, whose illness kept him at home more than his siblings. Often, when she sat sewing in the sunny front parlor of the Cherokee Park house, she would burst spontaneously into song, inviting Barry to join her in duets. "She taught me how to sing something called 'To You Beautiful Lady, I Raise My Eyes,' " he said. "I remember her with the happiest feelings."

On the Fourth of July, 1912, Barry sat in his mother's arms in a chair on the lawn outside the Cherokee Park house. The evening was warm, the sky cloudless. As dusk fell, red, green, and gold fireworks blossomed and thundered in the open bowl of the park below. When the crackles and whistles finally came to an end, Barry's eyes followed the parade of fire balloons—

colored lanterns with lighted candles inside—as they processed in regal splendor across the valley, carried on a current of soft night breezes. Nestled in his mother's lap, with his father nearby and the magical lights ascending, Barry experienced what he would come to remember as the last truly secure moment of his childhood.

The following spring, Eleanor took the train to Asheville to visit her son Robert, who had followed family tradition and enrolled in the Bingham Military School, now run by the Colonel and his two sons-in-law. Eleanor loved going to "The City of the Sky," especially since it gave her a chance to see Bob's sister Sadie, who was her dearest friend as well as her relation by marriage. So close were the two women that years earlier, in her will, Eleanor had designated Sadie to be her executor and the guardian of her children should she and Bob both die.

As the train carried Eleanor back to Louisville, however, she began to be filled with a sense of doom and fear. Suddenly she had a premonition that something terrible was about to occur. She became so agitated that the next day she caught a train back to Asheville. "If anything should happen to me or to Bob," she told Sadie, repeating what was in the will, "I want you to be the one to take care of my children, especially my youngest son."

Eleanor's intuition was chillingly accurate. Several weeks later, on April 27, 1913, she agreed to go on a Sunday drive to her mother's country house, where the family planned a relaxed afternoon of dinner and conversation. Her brother, Dennis, was behind the steering wheel. Mrs. Miller and twelve-year-old Henrietta sat in the front seat; Eleanor, Barry, and Frank Callahan, a young cousin from Chicago, tucked themselves in back. Lucy, Dennis's wife, stayed behind, as did Bob Bingham, who had to catch a train to Cincinnati for a court appearance the next day. After the laughing party roared off into the fragrant Kentucky spring, Bob set out alone for Union Station.

Half an hour later, shortly before 2:00 P.M., Dennis approached O'Bannon's Crossing, a deadly intersection where the road crossed two parallel sets of tracks: those of the interurban streetcar line, and those of the L&N Railroad. Before venturing across, Dennis stopped the car to wipe his glasses. A shed and the O'Bannon grocery obstructed his view to the right and the rumble of the automobile engine muffled the sound of an interurban streetcar that was at that very moment barreling down the tracks from town. Dennis let out the clutch and the car lurched forward. Eleanor and the others screamed for him to stop. The interurban's horn blared. But it was too late.

The interurban struck the automobile's rear right fender, hurling the car against a telephone pole so fiercely that the pole snapped in two. Frank Callahan flew out of the car and onto the grass, but was not seriously hurt;

the others were thrown to the floor. Eleanor, clutching seven-year-old Barry in her lap, hunched forward to protect him. When the interurban plowed into the automobile's rear, she pitched sharply to the front, then, in whiplash fashion, was thrown backward against the lightly upholstered steel frame of the seat.

Barry had been asleep until moments before the accident. Although the day was sunny and clear, he would always recall it as rainy. "I can remember being [woken] up by the terrible noise and then seeing this dreadful light, the headlight of the [interurban] approaching us, and the rain falling through it and then there was a crash," he said. The impact knocked him unconscious. When Barry came to, he was lying in a strange room. His sister, Henrietta, was pacing back and forth, crying hysterically.

Barry never saw his mother again. Her skull was fractured at the base of the brain. Along with the others injured in the accident, she was taken by the interurban to Louisville, where ambulances whisked them to Norton Infirmary. In a twist of black irony, the L&N train ferrying Bob Bingham to Ohio passed the horrible scene at O'Bannon's Crossing only minutes after Eleanor had been taken away. Bob saw the crushed car and the broken telephone pole, never realizing that the victims of the dreadful accident were members of his own family.

That evening, Dennis, who suffered only a scalp wound, reached Bob at the Sinton Hotel in Cincinnati. Bob rushed back to Louisville, arriving by 9:30 P.M., and went directly to the hospital. He was at his wife's bedside when she died six hours later.

Sixteen-year-old Robert did not get back in time to say goodbye to his mother. He and Sadie had set out from Asheville the moment they had heard about the accident, stopping in Knoxville to change trains. While awaiting their connection in a Knoxville hotel, Sadie received a telegram saying that Eleanor had died. She swooned and tumbled down the hotel staircase, to the horror of her already-traumatized nephew.

Barry did not attend his mother's funeral, which was held at the Cherokee Park house. Instead, he was confined to bed at Grandmother Miller's. "The shades were lowered and I couldn't understand what in the world was happening," he said. "I had never seen the shades pulled down in the daytime like that." Eleanor was only forty-three, a month away from celebrating her seventeenth wedding anniversary. Bob had never expected his energetic wife to die so young and had no grave in which to bury her. Instead, she was interred in the Miller-Long plot at Cave Hill Cemetery.

In the ensuing weeks, Bob Bingham seemed to bear his sorrow with admirable stoicism. He went to work as usual, seeing clients and carrying on with his affairs. He was determined not to collapse into a despairing depression as his father had done at the death of his first wife, Dell. But, like Colonel Bingham, Bob had depended heavily on his spouse. Eleanor had shored him up, kept his home cheerful and light, and opened her family's purse to support his ambitions. He had been able to trust her. In his rather selfish and inattentive way, he had loved her terribly, and her absence left him shocked with longing and loneliness.

Sadie, too, had watched Colonel Bingham nearly go mad at the death of Dell. Now she began to fear for Bob. For unknown to everyone but her, he had adopted a poignant ritual. A few weeks before the accident, Bob and Eleanor had gone to a spring ball where a motion picture—then a novelty —had been made of the dancers as they waltzed around the floor. Eleanor loved to dance, and she had twirled delightedly, laughing and mugging for the camera like a girl half her age.

During the long afternoons in the weeks after her death, Bob went to a movie house near his office and bribed the owner to open early. Then, at Bob's instruction, the projectionist ran the homemade movie over and over. For those few, brief moments, Eleanor was alive again, waltzing and smiling and laughing at the camera. Bob sat alone in the silence of the darkened theater, looking up at the screen as his sunny, raven-haired wife twirled and twirled and twirled and twirled.

THE MAD WOMAN
IN THE ATTIC

"It's a grave mistake," Sadie told him when Bob wanted to withdraw his oldest son, Robert, from the Bingham Military School and bring him back to Louisville. Robert had always been lazy and inclined to coast on his good looks, but in the disciplined atmosphere Colonel Bingham maintained at the school, he had shown real promise. His grades were excellent and at the end of his junior year he had been chosen to be the leader of the student corps of cadets, which was both an honor and a responsibility. Sadie, who had observed her nephew closely, knew that he was psychologically fragile, a condition made worse by the loss of his mother. "Staying at Bingham could be the making of him," she told her brother.

But Bob was lonely and ignored Sadie's counsel. That fall, instead of riding the train back to Asheville, Robert entered Louisville Male High School, the most prestigious secondary education facility in the city. Several months later, in an effort to please his father, he legally changed his name from Robert Norwood Bingham to Robert Worth Bingham Jr. Bob was immensely flattered. He had high hopes for this boy, now his true namesake, and he began entertaining ambitious visions of Robert's future.

It soon became clear, however, that Robert would never live up to his father's expectations. Though Bob Bingham had brought his son back to Louisville to serve as his companion, he was too obsessed with his own grief and his grueling schedule at Kohn, Bingham, Sloss & Spindle, his third and final law firm, to pay much attention to him. The elderly cousin he had hired to look after his children provided adequate housekeeping services but little in the way of warmth or guidance. Left to his own devices and angry at his father's virtual abandonment, Robert rapidly began to deteriorate.

Outwardly, he showed no distress over his mother's death. A few months after her funeral, he tapped his feet impatiently at a Louisville ball, prevented from dancing by the obligatory year of mourning. Frustrated, he leaped onto the band platform and took over the drums, banging them loudly and grinning.

Soon Robert's life began to revolve around boozy parties that frequently put him in such a glazed condition that he did not know where he was. All too often, Bob Bingham would return home from a business trip to find that Robert had not been sighted for days. Embarrassed and angry, he would search Louisville's bars and brothels until he located his son, sleeping off the effects of his latest tear in a seedy hotel. But he did little to discipline the boy.

Robert was the most handsome of the Bingham clan. Dark-haired and athletic, he was, as Barry often said later, the *beau idéal* of young manhood, and he always made a stunning first impression. The promise of his exterior, however, was inevitably betrayed by the confused, unhappy personality within.

At Louisville Male, as elsewhere, Robert was initially thought to be a leader, a gorgeous combination of breeding, physical grace, and self-confidence. But as the months wore on, his drinking and depravity revealed him as he truly was: uncertain, fearful, and totally incapable of discipline. His grades, in the 90s at the Bingham Military School, plummeted. In June 1914, he graduated from Louisville Male without distinction. In a poignant coda to his misery and self-indulgence, the editor of the yearbook inscribed under Robert's senior picture: "He came to us for knowledge all athirst / But his books he has forsaken, / So our faith in him is shaken, / And oh, we hoped so much for him at first."

That seemed to sum up his father's feelings as well. Bob Bingham, with one eye on the next rung of the social ladder, had hoped that his oldest son would one day go to Harvard, thus opening the door to the wider world of Northern society that still remained out of reach, even to a former circuit court judge and mayor of Louisville. Eleanor's death had severed his direct link to the Miller fortune; forging ties with Harvard would provide a definite boost in prestige. But Robert failed the Harvard entrance exams and in the fall of 1915 entered the University of Virginia, his father's alma mater, where, according to Barry, he "had a good time and was a real Virginia playboy."

In his business and political dealings, Judge Bingham tended to invest those he favored with more virtue than they deserved, then unceremoniously cast them out when they disappointed or displeased him. He treated his children in much the same way.

When Robert failed to live up to his father's expectations, the Judge continued to supply him with money, but in almost every other respect wrote him off. Instead, he refocused his hopes on Henrietta, whom he petted and spoiled extravagantly. To please her father, Henrietta pursued sports with a fervor more befitting an adolescent boy than a refined Southern belle. Horseback riding, golf, tennis—she did them all and did them well. When she entered Louisville Collegiate, the city's most elite girls' school, in 1915, she was instantly elected captain of the basketball team. The Judge basked in her accomplishments and Henrietta became, for a time at least, the center of his emotional life. "He was in love with her," said John Houseman, the actor, who came to know Henrietta several years later. "It was a real Southern father/daughter thing."

That left little room for seven-year-old Barry. He tried desperately to push his mother's death out of his mind, but his body refused to cooperate. For months, he could not walk normally, though there was no evidence of spinal injury. Even after he managed to get out of bed, he navigated the house on tiptoe as though fearful of arousing and driving away his one remaining parent. For a time, he woke up screaming at night, haunted by the memory of the interurban's blinding light.

The shock of the crash caused Barry's allergies to flare, and the little boy wheezed and sneezed pathetically. Because of his multiple ailments—or perhaps just to get him out from under foot—the Judge dispatched him to Asheville, then a well-known center for the treatment of tuberculosis and other lung diseases. There, atop his aunt Sadie's house, Barry lived in a specially built room with tremendous windows on all four sides. As part of the cure, fresh air was let in winter and summer, giving him a life-long taste for frigid living quarters.

With the move to Asheville, Barry began several years of a bedouinlike existence, shuttling between the mountains of North Carolina and the sad house in Louisville. His mysterious illness had long set him apart from his father and siblings, but it had never before caused him to be exiled. Now Barry felt rejection, along with a dim sense that he was being punished for his mother's death. After all, she had given up her life sheltering him in her arms. The knowledge made him frantic to recapture the love and security he had once known, and unusually fearful of loss and emotional pain.

Propelled by guilt and loneliness, Barry became a supplicant for his father's affection—indeed, for affection in general.

Colonel Bingham, still consumed with the business of the school, was a remote figure, treating his grandson to striped peppermints from his desk drawer but rarely showing any warmth. Mary, Barry's other aunt, had inherited the Colonel's austere bearing and no-nonsense attitude. What Barry needed was a substitute mother, and Sadie, who had never had any children of her own, was only too happy to oblige. Petite and dark, like Eleanor, Sadie was a kind-hearted, accessible woman who laughed easily and took pleasure in everyday things. The rustling of autumn leaves, a perfect rose in a summer garden, a steaming cup of tea—these were the delights on which she dwelled amid the dull regimen of Bingham Heights.

Her talent for focusing on distracting, cheerful details no doubt had its roots in her marriage, which, though long-lived, was entirely platonic. When the marriage was still unconsummated several months after the vows had been spoken, Sadie approached her sister. "Isn't something supposed to happen?" she asked timidly. Mary questioned her closely and discovered to her horror that her sister, a virgin on her wedding day, was a virgin still. And so she remained for the rest of her life, too fearful even to ask her impotent or possibly homosexual husband, R. T. Grinnan, what was wrong.

Sadie's pent-up sexual energies were redirected into an intense maternal concern for her battered nephew. Sensing Barry's distress, she schooled him in her sunny approach to life and he became her apt and eager pupil. Concentrating on small pleasures and looking for the positive in the bleakest situation became Barry's escape route from emotional pain, first of his mother's absence and later of his own sons' deaths and the explosive fight over the family newspaper company. "I really tried to model myself on [Sadie]," said Barry. "The glass is always half full for me, not half empty."

With Sadie as mother, mentor, and confidante, Barry's time in Asheville was in many ways blissfully happy. He grew strong on the "fried everything" and hot biscuits that the black cooks dished up. Because of his lung problems, he was given a reprieve from school and instead became lost in the city's motion picture houses, where he watched cliff-hanging serials such as "The Perils of Pauline" and "The Diamond from the Skies." He and Sadie shared the same birthday—February 10—and every year they would gather (along with a former slave named Booze Basin, who claimed it was his birthday, too) for a celebration. "My aunt Sadie used to say, 'You know, I think if I were dead and you walked in the room, I'd rise up and begin to laugh,' " said Barry. "We laughed at things so much together."

Barry's tastes and proclivities, already more feminine than that of most young boys, grew increasingly so under Sadie's care. He liked stamp-collecting and other indoor pursuits, and was far less given to rough-housing than were the Asheville townies or the brawny Bingham cadets. While other boys battled for supremacy on the football fields of Bingham Heights, Barry rejoiced in a life largely free of competition. Asheville's ease only made Louisville, with its haunting fears and expectations, all the more stark and frightening.

When he was well enough, he would travel home for two- and three-month stretches, taking the Carolina Special from Asheville to Louisville, with an intermediate stop in Knoxville, where he would descend with the other passengers and rush into the dingy station room for a hasty meal of sandwiches, fried chicken, and fruit pies. The child who greeted Judge Bingham on these visits appeared younger than his years and delicately pretty. But the sad, self-contained way he carried himself gave him the air of someone much older. Vulnerable and desperate to avoid another sudden wound, Barry carefully refrained from placing emotional demands on his father. "I may have given him a kiss, but he didn't make a big thing out of it. He treated me really more as an adult," he said.

Despite the outward reserve, Barry was a terribly angry little boy and had a violent temper. He was furious at the turn his life had taken and enraged that his father would cast him out so unfeelingly. He could not bear to be teased. Once, when his brother and sister were tormenting him, he snatched a red hot poker out of the fire and, waving it in the air, set out after them. Another time, provoked by the taunts of a young playmate, Barry grabbed the boy's crotch, squeezed hard, and held on tight until Lizzie, his black nurse, tore the screaming pair apart.

As he got stronger and his visits to Louisville became longer, Barry began taking classes at the Richmond School, a private institution that had just opened in a turreted stone building on Third Street. It was the first formal education he had had in years, although his lack of classroom training hardly seemed to matter. Motivated by a craving for escape, Barry read voraciously, taking special delight in *The Wizard of Oz* and a junior encyclopedia a relative gave him for his birthday.

The rowdy boys at the Richmond School had little appreciation of such tastes. They liked sports, something Barry openly shunned, taking comfort instead in his superior intellect. Luckily, he found a confederate, Archie Robertson, who lived next door to the school. When classes were over for the day, the two would adjourn to Archie's gas-lit house, where they ground out their own student newspaper on a little hand press. "My life at that age was certainly blighted by my utter inability to do anything that required a minimum of physical coordination," Barry later wrote. "But at least I was able to fall back on the undisputed fact that Archie Robertson and I were much the brightest children in the class and that Archie was even more grotesquely inept than I was on the grubby playing fields of the Richmond School."

Being the class prodigy might have been a more isolating experience had it not been for one special teacher, Nannie Lee Frayser, who was also the assistant principal. She revered good writing and was a born storyteller. Fairy tales, stories from her childhood: Nannie Lee was a schoolmarmish Scheherazade, seducing her charges into a love of language. Barry floated on the cadence of the prose.

With his affection for words and solitary pursuits, it was only a matter of time before Barry drifted into writing himself. At the age of nine, he joined the Aloha Club, a children's literary organization that produced a four-page supplement for the Louisville *Courier-Journal* every Sunday. The section was run by the paper's music and theater critic, Anna Hopper, a beloved figure known to the children as "Aunt Ruth." Along with Sadie and Nannie Lee, "Aunt Ruth" became a strong, motherly presence in Barry's life.

At the club's weekly meetings, held at *The Courier-Journal*, Barry discovered that writing won him praise and commanded attention, things he rarely got from his father. As more and more of his work got published, Barry's reclusiveness began to fade, replaced by a kind of absurd humor. He once promised to bring a pet to the meeting, only to collapse in laughter at his companions' discomfiture when he opened the box and out scuttled a cockroach. "Isn't Barry the essence of glorified prose writing?" Aunt Ruth wrote in one Aloha Club supplement. "Gentle reader, he isn't as angelic as his cherubic countenance would lead one to imagine."

Alohans published under what Aunt Ruth grandly called "noms de plume," many of which derived from popular fiction of the time. "Rebecca of Sunnybrook Farm" appeared alongside "Phronsie Pepper," "Monsieur Beaucaire," and just plain "Bill of Louisville." After flipping through a favorite book on flowers, Barry decided on the prissy name of "Bluet." When Aunt Ruth gently pointed out that it did not sound like a boy's "nom," Barry obligingly stuck the word "Master" in front.

During the long stretches between Aloha Club meetings, Master Bluet was alone a great deal. "Won't somebody take pity on me and write to me?" he asked plaintively in a letter published one summer Sunday. "I'm just crazy to correspond with some of the members." During those interminable evenings, Barry would sit for hours, composing the saccharine, sentimental poetry so characteristic of childhood. Much of it was hauntingly wistful, written to a vague female figure whose caring ways closely resembled Eleanor's. "The rainbow is beautiful, / 'Tis certainly true," Barry wrote two years after her death. "But I must confess freely, / I'd rather see you."

Despite the loneliness and inner turmoil, Barry would later tell friends that his childhood had been innocent and carefree. The real world did not impinge, he said, until the German sinking of the British liner *Lusitania* in May 1915. But that event, so critical to the eventual entry of the United States into World War I, provided less of an introduction to the world's cruel possibilities than did the reappearance of his father's old college love, Mary Lily Kenan, who was destined to change the Bingham family and its fortunes forever.

———————

Before air-conditioning provided relief, anyone with wealth or sense tried to escape the leaden summer heat of Louisville. Thus it was only natural that Judge Bingham and his three children retreated to the cool breezes of Asheville in mid-August of 1915. To be sure, Bingham had other reasons for going. His sister Sadie had been widowed only eight months before, and he knew that his presence would be a temporary comfort to her. As important to a man of Bingham's ambition, Asheville had become a powerful magnet for the upper crust. In 1890, George Vanderbilt, grandson of industrialist Cornelius Vanderbilt, had turned the city into a Southern version of Newport by choosing it as the site of Biltmore, his 250-room Louis XV country estate. Now the monied and the merely curious flocked to the city's proliferating hotels and spas to take in the "healing breath of the pine." Mindful of his plunge in social and financial status since his string of political defeats and the death of Eleanor, Judge Bingham approached Asheville with a mixture of envy and dread.

There was another unsettled soul in Asheville that summer; Mary Lily Kenan Flagler had been driven to North Carolina from New York a month earlier, accompanied by her invalid mother, her two sisters, and her nineteen-year-old niece, Louise Wise. The women and their servants had taken up residence in the Grove Park Inn, a massive resort of brown mountain stone so popular that, the summer before, the managers had had to turn away eight hundred guests. From this comfortable headquarters, the ladies spent their days reading, going to dinner parties, visiting friends, and taking in the splendor of the Smoky Mountains, which greeted them each morning with a hazy crown of mist.

Like Bob Bingham, Mary Lily had been widowed for more than two years. Her husband, multimillionaire Henry Flagler, had been John D. Rockefeller's partner in Standard Oil and the prime mover behind the development of Florida. When he died in May 1913, less than a month after Eleanor, he left Mary Lily an estate valued at between $80 million and $100 million. The sum made her the wealthiest woman in the United States, and perhaps the world. But it failed to repair the emotional emptiness she had often felt during her husband's last years.

As he had gotten older, Flagler, more than thirty-five years Mary Lily's senior, had grown deaf and halting and increasingly eccentric, leaving his wife to host their opulent entertainments by herself. Now, at forty-eight, she had a vast sum of money and delighted in spending it. But she was also suspicious of prospective suitors. Just over five feet tall, plump and dark-haired, Mary Lily was well past the age when looks alone could attract a mate. Still, drawn by her incredible wealth, men fawned over her shamelessly. The transparent sycophancy left her feeling flattered but unfulfilled. Would a man ever love her again for anything other than her money?

There was more than a hint of irony in the question, for Mary Lily Kenan had clearly been dazzled by Flagler's fortune when the two first met in 1891. To be sure, her own family was well off, though its upper-middle-class prosperity was no match for the gilded excesses of a leading industrialist like Flagler. Still, the Kenans could rightfully hold their heads high. Mary Lily's great-great-grandfather, James Kenan, fought in the American Revolution, helped obtain statehood for North Carolina, and served as the first state senator from Duplin County. Her grandfather had been a congressman in the Rebel government of Jefferson Davis.

Mary Lily's childhood was spent in a modest white-frame house on Nun Street in Wilmington, where her father, a taciturn Scotch-Presbyterian, worked as a wholesale merchant. In the worst days of Reconstruction, her mother sewed most of her children's clothing, aided by a black seamstress. But by the time Mary Lily was old enough to "come out," the family had regained much of its economic footing.

At eighteen, Mary Lily went to Raleigh, the state capital, to take classes at Peace Institute, a respected finishing school. But as was the custom, women's studies were far from rigorous and she spent much of her time at the home of her uncle, Col. Thomas S. Kenan, a former state attorney general who, the year after her arrival, was elected clerk of the state supreme court.

Mary Lily had a clear, sweet singing voice and was in great demand on the party circuit. She also had her share of beaus, including at least one serious marriage proposal. But for unknown reasons Mary Lily turned the young man down, and by the age of twenty-three was back in Wilmington with her parents, unattached and at loose ends.

Her love of parties and gaiety drew her to the Pembroke-Joneses, a Wilmington couple who had moved to New York and shuttled between a luxurious town house on East 61st Street and the playgrounds of the rich at

Newport and along the Florida coast. To relieve Mary Lily's boredom during the gray North Carolina winter, the Pembroke-Joneses invited her to stay with them at their estate, Airlie-on-the-Sound, in St. Augustine in the early weeks of 1891. There, Mary Lily reveled in the lavish balls, grand gowns, and delicious society gossip. She marveled that elegant hotels like the Ponce de Leon and the neighboring Alcazar, opened just three years earlier, could rise from what was once marshy wasteland.

She met the creator of this improbable oasis one day while lunching with the Pembroke-Joneses aboard the *Narada*, a friend's yacht. Henry Flagler and his wife, Alice, were among the guests and Mary Lily could not help but notice that everyone paid inordinate attention to the tall, white-whiskered man who faintly resembled her own father. Then sixty-one, Flagler had made the development of Florida his second career, using the millions he had earned from Standard Oil. In Florida, he was regarded as a benevolent patriarch, endowing hospitals, building roads, and lining everyone's pockets as he turned the state into a vacation home for the well-to-do.

But he had not always been so beloved. Flagler had had few scruples during the early days of the oil industry. In her landmark history of Standard Oil, muckraker Ida Tarbell described Flagler as "quick to see an advantage and quick to take it," as ruthless in his creation of the company's stranglehold on the nation's oil supply as he was cavalier in his personal life.

Indeed, when his first wife died of a bronchial ailment in 1881, Flagler had shown no outward signs of grief and two years later married Ida Alice Shourds, an aspiring actress eighteen years his junior. Shifting his gaze to the business possibilities of Florida, he built Kirkside, a fifteen-room home in St. Augustine, as a winter residence. The couple was residing at this seaside estate when Flagler was introduced to Mary Lily Kenan.

Over the next several years, Henry and Alice saw much of Mary Lily in St. Augustine and Newport. But soon, for no apparent reason, Alice began to deteriorate mentally. She held seances, consulted Ouija boards, and wrote a check in the amount of one million roses instead of dollars. By 1896, she was too far gone to remain at home, and Flagler confined her to a New York sanitarium, where she lived until her death.

As Alice grew more unstable, Flagler looked elsewhere for comfort and found himself increasingly drawn to the soothing Southern ways of Mary Lily. He loved her singing and would often ask her to perform such antebellum ballads as "I Want You My Honey" and "Little Alabama Coon." Soon, Mary Lily and her friend Eliza Ashley, Flagler's niece, began to accompany the aging tycoon on business trips to New York, St. Augustine, and Palm Beach.

For a social moth like Mary Lily, the life of indulgence and splendor that

Flagler made possible was irresistible. With Eliza along to give the appearance of propriety, Flagler and Mary Lily were soon frequently seen in public, dining in the finest restaurants, wearing the most up-to-date fashions, and flirting discreetly at the toniest parties. The couple grew closer and bolder even while Flagler maintained a mistress, Helen M. Long, in a house at 27 East 57th Street in New York.

For a woman of breeding and station, traveling with a married man, even one chaperoned by his niece, was a clear violation of proper behavior. But Mary Lily was willful and spoiled, with a broad streak of wildness. She did not seem to care that she was getting a reputation, even among Flagler's sophisticated set, as a woman of loose morals. It was not until the New York scandal sheets began gossiping about the liaison—the trips together, the glittering gifts—that the Kenans moved to protect the family name. An entourage of relatives, including Mary Lily's father, arrived on Flagler's doorstep and told him point-blank: "You've tainted her. Now no other man will go near her."

Flagler was used to silencing his critics with cash. To compensate Mary Lily for her diminished marriage prospects, he signed over $1.5 million of Standard Oil stock to her and gave her younger brother, Will, a talented, ambitious engineer, the lucrative job of designing the power plant for his latest venture, the Breakers Hotel in Palm Beach. By 1903, to no one's surprise, Will was the consulting and construction engineer for all the Flagler hotels.

By then, however, Flagler had long since decided to make an honest woman of Pudgy, as he affectionately called Mary Lily. On August 24, 1901, just ten days after his divorce from Alice, the couple exchanged vows at Liberty Hall, the home of Mary Lily's grandfather in Kenansville, North Carolina. The groom arrived in his private railway car, "The Rambler," a $70,000 oak-paneled, copper-roofed mansion on wheels, which he parked on a siding in nearby Magnolia. He even brought his own orchestra for the reception. And when the moment came, Mary Lily, draped in satin and white chiffon, looked serenely proud despite the years of innuendo. Her niece Louise, then only five, was her sole attendant. Mary Lily was thirty-four; Flagler was seventy-one.

Within weeks, Flagler had engaged Carrère and Hastings, the firm that later designed the New York Public Library, to build a palace of white marble for his new bride. By the spring of 1902, Whitehall, a $2.5 million Spanish-inspired extravaganza, stood gleaming on the shores of Lake Worth in Palm Beach. Flagler filled it with $1.5 million worth of furnishings, including rare Aubusson tapestries, Arabian laces, Louis XV furniture, paintings by Gainsborough and other famous artists, and the largest pipe organ ever installed in a private home. To roost in the palms and orange trees on the grounds, he bought colorful parrots, clipping their wings so they couldn't fly away. Whitehall quickly became America's Taj Mahal, "more wonderful than any palace in Europe."

The grand scale of her new home made Mary Lily the center of Palm Beach society. Caruso sang in the music room. Victor Herbert played the organ. John Jacob Astor and Woodrow Wilson, then president of Princeton University, were frequent visitors. As Flagler grew older and more feeble, he groused to friends that he would have preferred to live in a "little shack." But Mary Lily became ever more enamored of the dizzying whirl, hosting elaborate dinners and theme parties with her cousin, Owen Kenan, Flagler's personal physician, when the aged millionaire seemed uninterested or indisposed.

The endless festivities and her husband's growing isolation made strong drink increasingly attractive. Mary Lily's cocktail of choice was fruit juice mixed with grain alcohol, a concoction that masked the taste as well as the appearance of liquor while carrying twice the kick of bourbon. Women, even those in Mary Lily's world-weary circle, were not supposed to imbibe. As a practical matter, however, many turned to alcohol-laden nostrums such as Lydia Pinkham's Vegetable Compound (40 proof) and Boker's Stomach Bitters (84 proof) to relieve menstrual cramps, "nerves," and other "female" ailments. Some even sought comfort in the laudanum bottle, although many over-the-counter cough syrups and tonics also contained cocaine and opium.

Mary Lily may have been in one of her alcohol-induced fogs when Flagler tumbled and fell in a downstairs bathroom at Whitehall in March 1913. No one heard him cry out, and it was several hours before he was found, sprawled on the floor. He lived for only two more months and near the end was out of his mind. When he finally died on the morning of May 20, all the businesses in Palm Beach closed for the day.

Flagler's death left Mary Lily wealthy beyond belief. But it also left her in the hands of her domineering brother, Will, who by then was an executor of Flagler's estate and, within five months of the funeral, a director of the Flagler enterprises. Flagler once joked that his brother-in-law had been "born at the age of fifteen," and there is little doubt that Will, the youngest in the Kenan clan and the only boy, had appealed to the businessman in the shrewd tycoon.

Mary Lily was content to leave the day-to-day decisions concerning her vast holdings to Will and two other Flagler officials, who, under her husband's will, had been appointed as trustees to oversee the estate for at least five years after his death. All the same, she wished that he and the rest of the family would pay more attention to her. Overnight, she had gone from party frocks to widow's weeds, and instead of offering sympathy and companionship, Will and her happily married sisters, Sarah and Jessie, seemed to look upon her as the Kenans' cash cow. They issued stern warnings against remarriage, saying that any prospective mate was likely to be an opportunist hungry for her inheritance and, by implication, theirs.

So it was hardly surprising that the family took careful note of the unattached men who came to call on Mary Lily in Asheville during the summer of 1915. From the moment of her arrival, she was in great demand among the town's elite. Dinners at Fernihearst, a local mansion; dances and card parties at The Manor, a hotel and spa. Mary Lily reveled in the spotlight and did her share of entertaining, even throwing a large private party for friends at the Grove Park Inn.

Among those who sought her out during those first weeks in Asheville were the Binghams. Mary Lily was delighted to spend an afternoon visiting Sadie, her old schoolmate from Peace Institute, and Colonel Bingham, her uncle's college contemporary and wartime comrade. When Bob arrived some days later, his father suggested that he, too, renew his friendship with the woman who had entranced him in Charlottesville almost twenty years before.

Reluctant to be accused of fortune hunting, and perhaps embarrassed by his diminished circumstances, Bob put the meeting off as long as he could. When he finally did go to pay his respects, he brought his oldest son along. Cupid's only conquest that day may have been young Robert and Louise, Mary Lily's niece, who subsequently went to Asheville's Japanese Ball together and motored to a mountain inn for lunch.

By the end of the summer season, it was widely gossiped in Asheville that Mary Lily was soon to be remarried. But the rumored bridegroom was not Bob Bingham. Her new beau was Westray Battle, a well-connected widower and former navy physician who compensated for his mangled left hand (the result of an injury at sea) with a jovial manner and an elegant waxed mustache. By the time Mary Lily left for her apartment at the Plaza Hotel in New York in early October, the expectation was that the two would soon be wed.

What derailed the prospective alliance is not known. Perhaps it was Battle's age: at sixty-one he may have been an uncomfortable reminder of Flagler's geriatric frailties. Or maybe it was his ill-timed trip to England that fall that left her lonely and open to other suitors. Whatever the cause, Bob did not hesitate to move into the vacuum. He began making frequent business trips to New York, always staying a few extra days to spend time with Mary Lily.

The rekindling of a college romance appealed to the young girl still inside

Mary Lily. The fact that he had admired her long before she became a wealthy widow made her feel secure. By the following summer, word began to circulate that she and Bob Bingham were on the verge of becoming engaged. Only one wrinkle remained: how to arrange Mary Lily's financial affairs so that the Kenans would not oppose the match.

Despite their past family associations, the Kenans considered Bob, who had three children and considerable debt, an unsuitable mate, and they were not shy about showing it. Bob had not felt such suspicion and disdain since Eleanor's mother, Mrs. Miller, had first fixed her patronizing gaze on him twenty years earlier. It was galling, and he was humiliated and angry. To prove his prospective in-laws wrong, he ceremoniously declared that he wanted no part of her fortune.

In mid-August 1916, Judge Bingham visited Mary Lily at the Greenbriar Hotel in West Virginia to hammer out the details. By September, Mary Lily had a long and detailed will, signed and witnessed in West Virginia, that gave most of her estate to her family and named her brother, Will, as an executor. Bingham was not mentioned in the document, and he gave his word that he would formally renounce any claim to her estate as soon as they were married.

With that assurance, the Kenans reluctantly blessed the union, and in early November, the New York papers announced the news of "Mrs. Flagler's Romance." Outside Louisville, Bingham was just a small-town politician and hardly her social equal, but Mary Lily seemed genuinely excited. "One of my friends said to me, 'Why, this is not a very brilliant match, is it?' " she told *The New York Herald.* " 'Yes it is,' I replied to her. 'It is of the heart and what can be more brilliant than that?' "

On her wedding day, Mary Lily appeared "young, radiant and full of life" as she walked down a makeshift aisle in the flower- and plant-filled music room of the Pembroke-Joneses' posh East Side town house. Her dress, an afternoon gown of gray velvet and tulle, was appropriately subdued for a second-time bride. Only her jewelry, a $122,000 string of graduated pearls, betrayed the extent of her fabulous wealth. Louise, again her sole attendant, was not so subtle; she wore a flashy dress of ankle-length white broadcloth trimmed in white fox fur, set off smartly by a satin and fur hat.

Hugh Young was Bob's best man. But of the fifteen guests, Sadie was his only relation, dabbing her eyes at the first strains of *Lohengrin.* Neither his father nor his sister Mary made the trip, and the three Bingham children were clearly not welcome. The Judge was worried that the delicate understanding he had forged with the Kenans would disintegrate if they were exposed to Robert's drinking, Henrietta's tomboyish swagger, and Barry's violent outbursts, so he had conveniently gotten rid of them. Robert was in his freshman year at the University of Virginia; Henrietta had been hastily dispatched to Stuart Hall, a girls' school in Staunton, Virginia; and Barry had once again been banished to Asheville. "I didn't know anything about my father's plans to marry," Barry said. "It didn't mean anything to me."

The Wilmington, North Carolina, papers wrote excitedly of the newlyweds' trip to Canada and the Pacific coast, but in fact there was no honeymoon. Instead, Judge Bingham and his bride came back to Louisville aboard Mary Lily's private railcar for a series of parties in their honor. The Ballards, the Whittys, the Todds—the Binghams' hosts came straight out of the Louisville social register, indicating that, through his marriage to the nation's wealthiest woman, Bob Bingham had finally arrived in Louisville society. Why, even irascible Henry Watterson, who only eight years earlier had denounced Bingham as "not a very orthodox Democrat," now invited him to lunch at the Pendennis Club.

The couple took up residence in a suite at the Seelbach Hotel while Mary Lily looked for a house to rent. At first, Mary Lily seemed deliriously happy, writing to her family that she "wouldn't trade places with any woman in the world." But the romance, built largely on Bob's desire for wealth and position and Mary Lily's memories of a handsome college beau, quickly began to unravel. Bob was away a great deal on business, and Louisville was hardly Palm Beach or New York. Mary Lily soon grew restless and bored.

Money was also an issue. Within three months of their marriage, Mary Lily had spent $50,000 paying off Bingham's real estate and stock debts and signed over $696,000 in securities so that he could have an income—about $50,000 a year—independent of her. Bob had full use of her three automobiles, including a sleek Packard, and was the cheerful beneficiary of her frequent and generous gift-giving. Even Sadie received a string of pearls from her girlhood friend.

But Mary Lily's wealth was also her chief source of power. Bob was well aware of the financial gulf between them, and it upset the traditional roles of husband and wife to which he was accustomed. He was embarrassed to be on a petticoat payroll, even as he loved the flattering attention it brought him. When the University of North Carolina invited him to deliver the 1917 commencement address, he was delighted. But he knew the honor was not due solely to his oratorical gifts; the university also hoped that Mary Lily would bankroll a new building. Bob's guilt, anger, and wounded pride only added tension to a relationship that had started in youth but had not yet reestablished itself on an adult footing. "I think my father thought of Mary Lily as he had known her as a girl rather than as she later became—

the doyenne of Palm Beach," said Barry. "She was really an entirely different person by this time in her life."

Mary Lily's growing disenchantment deepened during the Christmas holidays of 1916, when Robert, Henrietta, and Barry returned to Louisville from their respective outposts. Not having children of her own had been one of Mary Lily's great frustrations, and she spent days shopping for presents to give her new family. By mid-December, when Robert's girlfriend, Sophie Albert, and her cousin came to call, the brightly colored packages were piled high in a bedroom at the Seelbach. Sophie was not impressed with the display. She knew that the Bingham children were deeply suspicious of their new stepmother and would almost certainly view the presents as an attempt to make up for their banishment from Louisville. "They don't want any of those things," Sophie told her cousin when they had left the hotel. "They just want to come home." Henrietta soon made that clear. The moment she saw the presents, she threw them on the floor unopened and stalked out of the room.

To her credit, Mary Lily made every effort to develop a warm relationship with her volatile and spoiled stepdaughter. Just before New Year's, she took over an entire floor of the Seelbach for a party in Henrietta's honor. The room where the dancing took place was decorated like a Louis XV garden, and couples waltzed under baskets of red and pink roses and showers of colored confetti. There were expensive favors for everyone. The next day, *The Courier-Journal* gushed that the scene had been like "a fairyland."

But Mary Lily, despite her vaunted love of children, had had virtually no experience with them. She had little understanding of the jealousy a fifteen-year-old girl might feel toward her mother's replacement, a jealousy made all the more intense by Judge Bingham's treatment of Henrietta as his hostess and confidante in the years following Eleanor's death. "The Judge really ruined her life," said John Houseman, Henrietta's onetime beau. "He gave her a notion of tremendous power and then remarried."

Disillusioned by the children's rejection, Mary Lily became withdrawn and depressed. No longer were her letters home glowing paeans to marital bliss. "She complained of how she'd done everything for [the Bingham children] and they had shown no gratitude," said Thomas Kenan III, Mary Lily's distant cousin and the Kenans' unofficial historian.

Alone in a new city, with few intimates and her dreams of a warm family circle shattered, Mary Lily turned to her old friend—liquor. She began to take long naps during the day and to disappear from social engagements on the excuse of colds or headaches. Soon, Bob, who rarely took more than a bourbon toddy before dinner, could not ignore the slurred speech and somnolent manner. On the advice of his physician friend, Hugh Young, he explored the possibility of moving to Washington, D.C., to work for Herbert Hoover, then Food Conservation Commissioner, in the hope that Mary Lily might agree to be treated for alcoholism at nearby Johns Hopkins. But nothing ever came of the idea.

Perhaps thinking that a return to old routines would do her good, Judge Bingham agreed to accompany Mary Lily to New York during the early weeks of 1917 and to Whitehall for the high season at Palm Beach, officially kicked off each year by a Washington's Birthday Ball. He implored Robert and Henrietta to join them in Florida, but they would have none of it. It was a bald power play—"your new wife or us"—and ultimately the Bingham children won. "My father found Whitehall oppressive and the society shallow and ostentatious," Barry recalled. In fact, Bob was as fond of extravagance as Mary Lily; his decision to leave was probably motivated more by her alcoholic binges or his discomfort at being treated like a small-town gigolo by Palm Beach socialites than by guilt about his children. Whatever the reason, in April he abandoned Mary Lily to her parrots and palmettos and returned to Louisville and Asheville to be with his family.

Despite its troubles, the marriage appeared pacific to outsiders, even ideal. Soon after Mary Lily came back from Florida, the couple moved out of the Seelbach and into Lincliffe, a three-story, stucco-and-stone Georgian Revival mansion overlooking the Ohio River several miles east of town. Built by hardware magnate William R. Belknap, Lincliffe featured an oak-paneled library and billiard room, green-and-white marble mantels, a walled formal garden, and two servants' cottages. For weeks, attendants unpacked and arranged Mary Lily's many belongings, which included a mahogany-and-gilt Louis XV bedroom set, a leather sofa, a statue of Napoleon, Dresden plates, forty-eight place settings of sterling silver, thirty dozen napkins, four Royal Bokara rugs, and twelve sets of linen sheets embroidered with her name.

As soon as the last crates and barrels were emptied, Mary Lily set about planning an elaborate housewarming party. By then it was early June, and she decided that the event could safely be held outdoors. When the Binghams' four hundred guests arrived around eight in the evening, they could hardly believe their eyes. Lincliffe's winding driveway and manicured grounds were softly lit with electric lights hidden inside red paper lanterns. More than forty waiters served the seven-course dinner, held on the front lawn of the estate under a massive canopy of fresh rambler roses.

After the meal, guests moved from one activity to another. A live orchestra played dance numbers outside; card tables and games were set up in the spacious public rooms; and in the sun parlor, a string quartet performed classical selections. To cap the evening, Mary Lily showed a silent film, *Diplomacy*, at midnight in the sunken garden. It was, wrote *The Louisville Herald*, "one of the most brilliant entertainments ever given." Thrilled with the praise, Mary Lily gave the caterer, Jennie Benedict, a platinum and diamond pin and added the price of an automobile to the bill.

Within days, fashionable Louisville began its seasonal pilgrimage to cooler climes. But Mary Lily, who normally spent the summer in the mountains or at Satan's Toe, her forty-room Long Island retreat, stayed behind. Unknown to most of Louisville, the heiress, who had just turned fifty, had been experiencing chest pains, heart palpitations, and general lethargy. Since Christmas, 1916, she had been seeing Dr. Michael Leo Ravitch, a bespectacled Russian immigrant and local dermatologist.

The Judge, who suffered from eczema, shingles, and other nervous skin disorders, had been a patient of Ravitch's for over ten years. So had his sisters, Sadie and Mary, who went to him for more general complaints. Bingham knew him to be an able physician, despite Louisville's deep prejudice against Jews and the medical profession's sneering contempt for "beauty doctors."

The Kenans would later say that Ravitch had a bad reputation around town, and perhaps he did, for dermatologists in the early part of the century treated not only acne and sunburn but venereal disease, then considered partly an affliction of the skin because of its unsightly lesions. Many of the medical journal articles Ravitch wrote were on syphilis and gonorrhea, and a large part of his practice was made up of patients with social diseases.

Whether Mary Lily was one of these is not definitively known. But there is a strong case for believing that she suffered from cardiovascular syphilis and, what is more, knew that she had the ailment when she married Bob Bingham. Almost certainly she got the infection from Flagler, her only other known lover, who kept one mistress and perhaps others. His second wife's insanity reinforces the suspicion since, before the discovery of penicillin, as many as half of all institutionalized mental patients were presumed to be syphilitics. So does Flagler's $1.5 million pay-off to Mary Lily during their courtship, a sum so staggering for the time that it suggests a wrong far more permanent and damaging than diminished marriage prospects.

Bingham, on the other hand, was an unlikely transmitter. The incubation period for cardiovascular syphilis is ten years or more, and it is highly unlikely, given their family ties and the strict mores of the small-town South, that Bingham and Mary Lily had intimate relations during their brief romance in 1894. He had also fathered three children who were free of such syphilitic symptoms as mental retardation and meningitis. Most compelling, though, were the four Wassermann tests performed on Bingham toward the end of his life, tests that could have detected past bouts of venereal disease as well as live infections. All four were negative.*

Bob was no doubt horrified when Mary Lily revealed such an embarrassing secret to him after their wedding. He was an unusually fastidious sort, so skittish that he could not listen to Sadie talk about where milk came from without squirming. And because of his tendency to see people as all good or all bad, he was cruelly unforgiving. A wife who had fallen off a pedestal would find it nearly impossible to redeem herself. When Mary Lily turned to drink for solace, Bob's revulsion multiplied.

Ironically, alcohol only exacerbated her condition, lowering the heart's resistance to the disease. Her husband's rejection made Mary Lily's situation even more pitiable, for once the syphilitic infection enters the heart, the prognosis is almost always death. According to one account, Mary Lily suffered heart trouble as early as 1903; according to another, not until the fall of 1916, just before her wedding in New York. Either way, when the symptoms recurred in Louisville, she was forced to ask Bob for the names of suitable local physicians. There were clearly more experienced doctors in New York and Boston, but Bingham suggested Ravitch, knowing that he was close by, capable, and, most important, discreet.

Compared with many venereal disease doctors of the day, Ravitch was medically conservative. Other physicians had already embraced Salvarsan, or "606," an arsenic compound that had been available in the United States since about 1911 and was widely touted as a miracle cure for syphilis. But in his papers and articles, Ravitch urged caution about the drug, saying that "disastrous results have been encountered by some experimenters." Instead, he relied on mercury rubs and injections—old-fashioned remedies that had been in use since the nineteenth century.

This approach was reflected in Mary Lily's regimen, which Ravitch outlined in detail in an article entitled "Chronic Syphilitic Aortitis," published in the Kentucky Medical Journal in April 1917, several months after he began seeing her. While not naming Mary Lily as the patient, the article describes a routine that is very similar to the treatment her relative, Thomas Kenan III, says she received. The prescription included plenty of bed rest, a nourishing diet, intermittent exercise, freedom from worry to lower blood pressure, and injections of mercury and water two to four times a week, supplemented by a "syphilitic cocktail" of mercury bichloride, potassium iodide, and syrup

* He did not catch the disease from Mary Lily after the two were wed because transmission requires an active lesion and her affliction was well beyond that stage by 1916. See Robert Berkow, M.D., ed., The Merck Manual of Diagnosis and Therapy (Rahway, N.J.: Merck Sharp & Dohme Research Laboratories, 1982), p. 1617.

of sarsaparilla. Even if a patient followed the regimen to the letter, "a complete cure is a difficult thing to achieve," wrote Ravitch.*

Most of Louisville was unaware of Mary Lily's grim prospects. Observant society ladies probably thought her frequent trips to the Atherton Building, where Ravitch and many other doctors had their offices, were for routine medical matters. Judge Bingham, however, remained cold and detached. After the housewarming party, he made it a point to be out of town more than ever, leaving Mary Lily in the company of Hannah Bolles, a girlhood friend from Wilmington who had been a guest at Lincliffe since late May.

It was during one of these absences, when Bingham was away in Asheville, that Mary Lily hit upon an idea that she thought might get her back into her husband's good graces. Less than a month after their wedding, Bingham had kept his promise and signed a document formally renouncing any share in her estate. Had he not signed this postnuptial document, his verbal pledge to make no claim on her riches, given at the Greenbriar in September of 1916, would have meant nothing. Legally, Bingham, once married, would have been entitled to half of Mary Lily's fortune. Perhaps because he had so honorably followed through on his prewedding vow— and perhaps, too, because she knew she was gravely ill—Mary Lily decided to leave Bingham a $5 million inheritance, hoping that her generosity would, for a time at least, soften his feelings toward her.

In two afternoon drives with Dave Davies, Bingham's former law partner, Mary Lily broached the idea of a codicil to her will. She had known Davies since their youth in North Carolina and trusted him completely; she was sure she could count on him to keep a confidence. That was especially important to Mary Lily, who feared that her relatives, if they found out, would bully her into revoking any unilateral change in her will. She knew how difficult they could be. In 1913, when her first husband, Henry Flagler, had been ill, the Kenan family had intentionally delayed notifying his estranged son until the old man was in a coma, making it impossible for Flagler to have a change of heart on his deathbed and increase the small amount he had left his son in his will.

Mary Lily's fear of her family's reaction was clear in two early drafts of the codicil. In one version she made a point of declaring that she had a right to dispose of her property as she pleased. A second version required that the codicil be kept secret from the Kenans until her death. But later

---

* A further indication that Mary Lily was treated with mercury is that she required $430 worth of dental work during the last three months of her life, a huge sum for the day. See *Final Settlement in Re: Estate of Mary Lily Kenan Flagler Bingham*, Jefferson County Inventory and Settlement Book 152, December 22, 1927. According to Dr. Nicholas J. Fiumara, adjunct clinical professor of dermatology, Boston University School of Medicine, clinical professor of dermatology, Tufts University School of Medicine, and lecturer in dermatology, Harvard Medical School, one side effect of mercury was that it caused the gums to become sore and the teeth to loosen.

she felt uneasy about the imperative tone of the drafts and asked Davies to strike any reference to her family.

When Mary Lily finally executed her codicil, she went about it in the same impulsive, willful manner that characterized the rest of her life. On Tuesday, June 19, 1917, at about 1:00 P.M., after taking a mercury shot at Ravitch's office, Mary Lily dispatched her chauffeur to pick up Davies. Thinking he was being summoned for yet another drive or perhaps for lunch, Davies did not bring the drafts of the codicil with him. But when he arrived, sweeping past Mary Lily's maid in the waiting room and entering Ravitch's office, he found that legal business was precisely what she had in mind. So he agreeably scribbled the one-sentence codicil from memory on Ravitch's letterhead and witnessed it along with the physician. The unorthodox procedure took just forty-five minutes.

The Kenans would later wonder why such an important document had been written and executed in a doctor's office. Davies's explanation was that Mary Lily pointedly refused to visit him at his place of business because "she was a woman . . . of great wealth and . . . in the public eye . . . and preferred to let this matter remain in secrecy." For the same reason, she never filed the codicil with the existing will, which was in the possession of her executors and trustees. She told Davies that she did not want "her brother William and . . . her family to have knowledge of everything she did with her own property." Instead, she presented the codicil to Bob Bingham sometime in late June and presumably he put it in his safe-deposit box. Whether it improved her relationship with her husband is not known.

Over the next several weeks, Mary Lily's condition worsened. In early July, Judge Bingham purchased three lots at Cave Hill Cemetery with enough room for sixty-six bodies. In the largest of the three, he reburied Eleanor, his first wife.

Whether innocent or calculated, the timing of these actions would later look suspicious. For on July 12, even as the Cave Hill gravediggers lowered Eleanor into her new resting place, Mary Lily suffered a "severe attack" in her bedroom at Lincliffe. Ravitch and his partner and son-in-law, clinical pathologist Sol A. Steinberg, were immediately summoned; from then until her death, they virtually lived at the Bingham estate. At some point, Walter Boggess, a general practitioner and former professor of medicine and chest diseases at the University of Louisville, also moved in, along with two nurses. Realizing the gravity of the situation, Judge Bingham wrote at once to Mary Lily's minister, George M. Ward, at his summer house in Massachusetts. But he made no attempt to locate the top medical practitioners in the country and rush them to Louisville, something a woman of Mary Lily's means could easily have afforded.

How Mary Lily was medically treated during her final days is not known.

Thomas Kenan III, Mary Lily's distant cousin, said that, while at Lincliffe, Ravitch overdosed her on morphine, woke her up in the middle of the night for alcohol and water injections, subjected her to hot baths, and forced her to take twice-daily walks. He also said there were four nurses, not two, and that several were fired when they protested the massive doses of drugs.

Some aspects of Kenan's story make no sense. Alcohol and water injections would have irritated the skin but have no therapeutic purpose. The shots were also unlikely to have been morphine: Kenan said they made Mary Lily cranky and restless, and morphine induces sleep. It is more probable that the injections were the same mercury and water shots Mary Lily had been receiving for months. Morphine may have been used at other times, however, to dull pain and stimulate the heart. As for the baths and daily walks, they were standard fare for syphilitics of the era.

It is impossible to know whether these ministrations, so primitive-sounding to modern ears, hastened Mary Lily's death or offered her comfort in what was an inevitable final illness. Either way, on the evening of July 26 she slipped into unconsciousness, was given oxygen, and within seventeen hours died. The official cause of death: "edema [sic] of the brain," exacerbated by "myocarditis," an inflammation of the heart muscle and a symptom of cardiovascular syphilis. Perhaps to avoid gossip about her condition, Ravitch, the only venereal disease specialist on the medical team, did not sign the death certificate, leaving that to Boggess and Steinberg.

During her last hours, Judge Bingham, Dave Davies, Mary Lily's brother Will, her sister Jessie, and her friend Hannah Bolles stood vigil at the bedside. Conspicuous by her absence was Louise, the favorite niece who had been with Mary Lily at so many other critical junctures in her life. The young woman knew nothing of her aunt's demise until she and her husband of two months, Lawrence Lewis, read the newspapers the next morning.

In the first few days following Mary Lily's death, Judge Bingham and the Kenans were allies in grief. After a brief service at Lincliffe, the mourners loaded the casket onto a private railroad car and rode to the funeral in Wilmington. There, despite Bingham's spacious new Cave Hill lots, Mary Lily was buried in Oakdale Cemetery. Letters of sympathy poured in. "I love to think that you made her so happy these last few months," wrote one woman to the Judge. "I have lost one of my dearest friends."

Exactly one week after her death, Will Kenan and the other executor, W. A. Blount, filed Mary Lily's will for probate in West Palm Beach. The action shocked Kentucky, which had assumed that the papers would be filed in Louisville and had anticipated collecting some $8 million in inheritance taxes. For the Kenan family and the Flagler companies, the location made perfect sense: most of Mary Lily's property was in Florida and the state had no inheritance tax. But where wealth is concerned, what seems like common sense to one party may look like self-interest to another. Eventually, nineteen states made claims on Mary Lily's estate.

The news of her legacy—estimated at about $100 million—made banner headlines across the country. Louise got all the real estate, including Whitehall and Kirkside; the pearls, valued at more than $295,000; and a lump sum of $5 million when she turned forty. The remaining $181,000 worth of jewelry, including an emerald pendant trimmed with diamonds and a platinum mesh bag studded with tiny rubies and diamonds, went to her two sisters. All the Kenan siblings shared equally in the Standard Oil stock and her brother, Will, even got special treatment—$50,000 a year for twenty-one years for the trouble of serving as an executor. But despite her generosity, Mary Lily clearly expected postmortem fights. How else to explain the existence of a "no squabble" clause in the will, which stipulated that any beneficiary who tried to contest the will and frustrate her final wishes would promptly be cut off?

The Kenans soon had a chance to test the strength of that provision. In late August, Judge Bingham strode into the Jefferson County Courthouse in Louisville and filed his $5 million codicil for probate. The unexpected document caused a sensation among the Kenans, who had already begun to hear disturbing rumors of foul play in Mary Lily's death. According to Thomas Kenan III, the family received letters from half a dozen Louisville citizens, including a "prominent doctor" and a "prominent minister," suggesting that Mary Lily had been sealed off from visitors at Lincliffe and possibly murdered. "Everybody thought Bingham married her for her money," said John Herchenroeder, a former Courier-Journal editor who was a teenager in Louisville at the time.

But personal politics probably also played a part. The "prominent doctor" was almost certainly Dr. Jacob Flexner, whose younger brother, Abraham, had held a grudge against Bingham for years. Jacob had treated Henrietta for diphtheria as a child, and in 1904 served alongside Bingham at the Louisville Medical College, where the Judge taught a course in medical jurisprudence. But the following year, Abraham and the Judge fell out over the management of Abraham Flexner's private school, a facility in which the Judge's son, Robert, was a student. As a result, relations with the Flexner family became permanently soured.

The barrage of letters and the appearance of the $5 million codicil may explain why Louise and her husband, who had come to Lincliffe to pack Mary Lily's things, abruptly left town without a word to the Judge. Their destination: the Greenbriar Hotel in White Sulphur Springs, where the rest of the Kenan clan had hastily convened to consider a contest to the codicil. The Judge may yet get his $5 million, wrote The Louisville Evening Post in late August, but "the outlook . . . is distinctly for a bitter fight."

A lot of tough talk would eventually ensue, but the "bitter fight" never materialized, at least not in court. On September 4, Bingham's counsel, Alex P. Humphrey, and the Kenans' lawyer, Helm Bruce, met in a packed Jefferson County Courthouse to determine whether the June 19 codicil was valid and should be admitted to probate. As a partner in the most prestigious law firm in Louisville, Bruce was in many ways a logical choice for the Kenans. But he had also been politically close to Bingham in the past, backing him as a candidate for interim mayor in 1907 and doing legal work for Bingham's former mother-in-law. Whether the Kenans were aware of Bruce's ties to Bingham is not known. His withering cross-examination of Dave Davies certainly did not suggest that he was pulling his punches. "Judging from the testimony, there is not all harmony in the air," the presiding judge, Samuel W. Greene, said wearily after Bruce had completed his questioning.

Under Kentucky law, only one witness was required to attest to Mary Lily's signature and soundness of mind. Since Davies and Ravitch had both seen her sign the document, either could have fulfilled the function. Still, it must have looked odd when Davies told the court that Ravitch, the only witness with firsthand knowledge of Mary Lily's medical condition, was on vacation in Maine and would not appear. Was his absence calculated to avoid divulging the details of her embarrassing illness? Or was it because he had been part of a conspiracy to secure the codicil and then commit murder, all at Bingham's direction? And why didn't Judge Greene interrupt the proceeding and subpoena Ravitch? The answers are lost to history. Bingham, too, was nowhere to be found that day, though he was not legally required to be there. Several days earlier he had left for Atlantic City, then a popular health resort, presumably to get away from the screaming headlines and vicious gossip.

That left Davies to describe the events leading up to the creation of the codicil and the bizarre signing ceremony at the Atherton Building. Why was Mary Lily seeing Ravitch, asked Bruce. "That is a medical matter I wouldn't know very much about," answered Davies. Did she appear to be drugged? "She had nothing in her manner that would indicate any such thing." Did you ever hear her speak of receiving hypodermic injections? "I did not."

Undaunted, Bruce plunged on. Were you aware that the younger Binghams' lack of appreciation had caused Mary Lily "very great pain," and that "she told Judge Bingham that his children could not come into her house?" At this, Alex Humphrey leaped up to object. "If the gentleman wants to contest this codicil I demand that he shall say on whose part he is contesting it here." Objection sustained, said Judge Greene. After a few more barbed questions, the codicil was duly admitted to probate without a hint of legal action by the Kenans.

On an ad hoc basis, however, the family did conduct its own investigation into the alleged murder conspiracy. Leading the charge was Graham Kenan, Mary Lily's cousin and brother-in-law. "He could never rest until he put [Mary Lily's death] right," explained Thomas Kenan III. Justice was probably not his only concern. Graham, a Wilmington lawyer, had been left nothing in Mary Lily's will, although he certainly stood to benefit indirectly from the vast inheritance she had bequeathed his wife, Sarah, Mary Lily's sister. Of all the members of the family, Graham had the least to lose under the "no squabble" clause. After all, how could he be cut out of a legacy he never had? Following several closed-door meetings, Graham was deputized to go after Bob Bingham.

With Graham as their front, the Kenans secured the services of the William J. Burns Detective Agency and pursued their suspicion of murder. Burns, the founder of the firm, had had a checkered career, barely escaping prison for jury-tampering and kidnapping. But since cracking the bombing of *The Los Angeles Times* building in 1910, he had enjoyed a reputation as "the only detective of genius" in the United States. The Kenans had hired the best in the private eye business, if not the most honest. One of his agents' first acts was to break into Ravitch's office and steal the narcotics records on Mary Lily.

But that was hardly the family's most gruesome tactic. In late September, just as Bingham was returning from Atlantic City, rumors raced through Louisville and New York that the Kenans had ordered a secret exhumation and autopsy of Mary Lily's body. The Judge immediately dispatched his college friend Shepard Bryan to Wilmington to see if the ghoulish reports were true. But Bryan was too late. Days earlier, at the Kenans' request, three prominent physicians had arrived in Wilmington, registered at a local hotel under assumed names, and, after midnight, driven out to Oakdale Cemetery. There a group of "badly scared Negroes" dug up the grave and opened the coffin. Whether due to fright or the odor of the decomposing body, one of the doctors became ill while the others busily set to work excising the heart, kidneys, and several other vital organs. "I'll never forget it," said Robert's girlfriend, Sophie. "I picked up a newspaper and saw the headline that Mary Lily had been dug up by her relatives. I almost fainted, it was so horrible."

The remains, locked in a metal box, traveled to New York with the physicians, and were subsequently cut, stained, and examined at Bellevue Hospital. Hugh Young later secured oral confirmation from two of the pathologists—friends of his from Johns Hopkins—that suspicious substances were not present in the body. But the Kenans would not allow the autopsy to be released, nor would they permit the doctors to say independently what they had found.*

For the next month, however, papers across the country repeated the Kenans' assurances that the autopsy report would soon be forthcoming, and that a codicil contest was imminent. There were even fresh rumors, attributed to Louise, that Dr. Ravitch had received $50,000 and a Packard car for taking care of Mary Lily. Behind the reports, no doubt, was the fact that Judge Bingham had traded one of Mary Lily's Packard roadsters in for a new four-passenger model only three weeks after her death. The transaction cost $1,000—a hefty sum in those days—but there is no evidence that he gave the car to Ravitch. If Mary Lily had promised her doctor an automobile, it would certainly be in keeping with past behavior: She had given Jennie Benedict virtually the same gift in June for catering the party at Lincliffe. As for the $50,000 figure, Louise may have simply confused it with the amount Mary Lily gave Bingham early in their marriage to pay off his debts.

The Louisville papers, so divided on politics, quickly united behind the wronged hometown boy. "Somewhere there is a Mephistopheles, or a gang of them, watching over this great fortune to see that none of it escapes the Kenan clutches," wrote *The Louisville Evening Post* after Mary Lily's grisly exhumation. With no incriminating autopsy report or proof of coercion or murder, though, the sensational stories gradually began to fade away. In the spring of 1918, the Kenans finally folded their tents and grudgingly agreed to honor the codicil. "Mary Lily's brother just said, 'Give Bingham his money and good riddance,' " said Thomas Kenan III. Accordingly, on July 27, 1918, exactly one year to the day of Mary Lily's death, the Judge got his $5 million, all of it free of federal inheritance tax.

The payment was in no way a vindication of Bingham, who continued to be dogged for the rest of his life by rumors that he had murdered his wife. Nor did the remaining millions assure the Kenan family of happiness. Louise, thrice-married, died bitter and disillusioned at forty, having sold Mary Lily's beloved marble palace, Whitehall, to hotel developers and Satan's Toe to D. W. Griffith, the silent screen mogul. Graham, the family member who so vigorously pursued Bingham, died in 1920 as a result of the Spanish influenza epidemic, which took the lives of half a million Americans. Even her brother and two sisters, so generously remembered in her will, lost control of their most valuable asset, the Florida East Coast Railway, on the eve of the Depression.

For the Binghams, the ignoble roots of their great wealth would become,

---

* The autopsy and detective reports have never been released. Thomas Kenan III was given the opportunity to reproduce these documents verbatim in this book. He refused.

as John Houseman put it, "the mad woman in the attic," a painful, embarrassing topic rarely discussed. Even succeeding generations of Kenans would pass down the tale that the family had been hexed. According to Thomas Kenan III, in the autumn of 1917, when talk of Mary Lily's murder had reached fever pitch, her Haitian maid—the same woman who had waited patiently outside Ravitch's office on the day the codicil was signed—took revenge by placing a voodoo curse on the Binghams.

EDEN WAS A LONELY PLACE

In the wake of Mary Lily's death, Barry got his fondest wish: His father, hungry for companionship, called him home from Asheville. In the fall of 1917, the eleven-year-old boy returned to Louisville to disquieting stares and whispers, overjoyed that Judge Bingham wanted him back but terrified of risking exile yet again. Amid packing crates and sheet-shrouded furniture, he and his father lived at Lincliffe while Mary Lily's things were inventoried, appraised, and shipped to her family. As soon as the task was done, they moved into temporary quarters in an apartment on Cherokee Road and awaited payment of the $5 million legacy.

In December, Henrietta, still at boarding school in Virginia, came home for Christmas and never went back, reinstated, as she was, as the mistress of the household. Robert continued to drink his way through the University of Virginia and tried to escape his father's reproving gaze as much as possible.

Mary Lily's death, much like Sam Miller's suicide two decades earlier, was rarely mentioned within the family. Judge Bingham was disinclined to discuss it with his children and they, wisely, never asked. "I realized, even when I was very young, that this was a painful subject which he really didn't want to talk about very much," said Barry. "So I only heard bits and pieces from him over a period of years. . . . It was obviously a thing that continued to make him intensely unhappy." Feeding his distress, no doubt, was the withering disdain of Louisville's aristocracy, a group to which the millionaire-to-be now felt he had a right to belong.

But the Judge's altered fortunes made little impression on the city's oldest families—the Speeds, the Belknaps, the Chenoweths, and the Dumesnils. To them, Bingham was an unpedigreed pariah and nouveau riche social climber. Some were even inclined to believe the rumors of foul play. "Why, he was as crooked as a hound's hind leg," said one elderly doyenne of Old Louisville. "He simply was not received."

To escape such messages, Barry retreated to his familiar world of poetry, private pleasures, and self-invention. World War I, which the United States had entered in April 1917, provided a merciful distraction. Barry chronicled the Allies' progress on a map of the western front, moving colored pins from place to place as the newspapers reported battles. At the Richmond School, he helped raise Victory Gardens and even knit a scarf to warm the shivering soldiers in France.

Such deeds, though, did not prevent him from being assigned the part of the enemy in a school pageant of nations. "I was obliged to goose-step across the lawn as the Kaiser's Germany," he recalled ruefully. He often felt isolated and neglected at home. At one Aloha Club meeting, Barry arrived in grimy knickers and tattered knee-high hose. "I marveled that with his wealth, he had such a hole in his stockings," recalled Wilson Wyatt, a fellow-Alohan.

The Judge had little time or inclination to fuss over a small boy's clothing. He was too busy pondering what he would do with his $5 million bequest, an amount that promised abruptly to make the Binghams one of the nation's richest families. He relished his good fortune, but he was well aware that it had come at a terrible price: a stain on his reputation. Worse still, as his friend Hugh Young sailed for Europe with General Pershing and his former law partner Dave Davies landed in France with the Red Cross, Bingham remained behind, disqualified from overseas duty by poor eyesight. He applied for the Officers Reserve Corps, but was turned down because, at forty-five, he was over the age limit.

The two rejections weighed on him heavily. Military service was not only consistent with his growing conviction that the United States must be involved in world affairs, it might also force his detractors to admit that he was a man of courage and honor after all. It was in this state of brooding reflection that Arthur Krock, an editor of *The Courier-Journal* and *Louisville Times*, found Bingham at the Pendennis Club in the spring of 1918. Krock, one of the club's few Jewish members, was engrossed in Somerset Maugham's *Of Human Bondage* in the oak-paneled library when Bingham walked in and stood disconsolately at the window.

Krock asked him what was wrong and Bingham told him about being turned down by the military. "Abstention in wartime is completely alien to the tradition of my family," he said. "And I don't know of anything useful to my country in its need that is available to me." Krock seized the opportunity. "Wouldn't you be performing a great public service as the owner and publisher of *The Courier-Journal* and *Times?*" Bingham gaped in astonishment. "Are they for sale, and could I buy them?"

The Judge was well aware that the Haldeman family, which had owned the papers for more than seventy years, was falling apart. Indeed, months earlier, while Mary Lily was still alive, he had represented the winning faction in a dispute over who should control the papers. Selling, however, was a different matter altogether and he was shocked to hear the news.

Perhaps he did not realize how strained relations had become. Since the death of Walter N. Haldeman, the head of the family, in 1902, *The Courier-Journal* and *Louisville Times* had been run by an uneasy quartet: Haldeman's three children—Will, Bruce, and Isabel—and *The Courier-Journal's* fiery editor, "Marse"* Henry Watterson. Isabel proved to be a passive partner, but the others were extremely stubborn and cantankerous.

At the start of World War I, Bruce fell out with Watterson over the editor's harsh anti-German editorials, which frequently included the battle cry: "To Hell with the Hapsburg and Hohenzollern!" Bruce complained that the vitriol was offensive to Louisville's many German advertisers and subscribers; business was suffering. Watterson made it abundantly clear that he did not care.

The breach became permanent early in 1917 when Bruce refused to publish one of Watterson's anti-German broadsides. In a series of private meetings, Marse Henry, Will, and Isabel decided to dilute his power. They created an executive committee to make decisions, a move that caused Bruce to file suit, saying that the action violated an earlier agreement, signed by his siblings, making him president for life. Bob Bingham was retained as counsel to represent Marse Henry and Will.

On July 27, 1917—the day Mary Lily died—Bruce lost in the Kentucky Court of Appeals and, bitter and angry, withdrew from active management. But without his business savvy, the papers faltered. As worrisome, Marse Henry and Will Haldeman were both over seventy, and neither had suitable heirs. The prospect of a total sale became more inviting with each passing day.

The executive committee finally instructed Krock, then editorial manager of the two papers, to locate a new owner "worthy of the paper's heritage"—

---

* "Marse," slave dialect for "master," was an honorific that followed Watterson for most of his adult life.

meaning a Democrat. Watterson, who was openly talking of retirement, favored William Randolph Hearst, who had ready cash but an unsavory reputation for jingoism. On the other hand, Krock's choice, Ohio governor James M. Cox, was a Yankee, a matter of great importance to Will, Watterson, and Bennett Young, Isabel's lawyer, who were Confederate veterans. With no consensus on a new owner, and the Haldemans and Watterson clamoring for action, Krock was in a quandary when he encountered Judge Bingham in the Pendennis Club that fine spring day in 1918.

In theory, it was an ideal match. Bob Bingham was locally known, a Democrat, with Confederate credentials and deep pockets. From Bingham's point of view, the papers were a sound business investment and, far more important, a means of acquiring political power without the kowtowing and compromise that went with elective office. Henry Watterson had given *The Courier-Journal* a regional and national reputation while the *Times*'s intense local focus made it a potent force among Louisville Democrats. To exchange mere money for the influence and prestige the combined properties represented was, to Judge Bingham, the bargain of a lifetime.

By the summer of 1918, a deal had been struck and on August 6, just ten days after receiving his legacy, Bingham took control of the "Old Lady on the Corner." The price came to a little more than $1 million for the combined shares of Will, Isabel, and Henry Watterson, plus $418,300 for the percentage controlled by Bruce, who refused to sell for another year. The total—roughly $1.5 million—amounted to less than a third of Bingham's new fortune.

Watterson and Will Haldeman announced the transaction on the front page of *The Courier-Journal*, praising Bingham and asserting, somewhat defensively, that they felt "no need to apologize for our disposition of the property." As if to prove them right, Bingham vowed to use the papers' power "justly and wisely . . . to further the progress of our city, our state, our nation."

———————

Judge Bingham, a man once hounded by creditors, could not resist showing off his new wealth. Within a week of buying the papers, he treated Barry and Henrietta to a spending spree in New York. Ensconced at the Plaza Hotel, the trio sampled room service, took in a Booth Tarkington play and two Broadway musicals, visited Grant's Tomb, traveled the length of Fifth Avenue by bus, and kept a sharp lookout for child star Mary Pickford, whose suite was just one floor below theirs.

On the same trip, they visited Swampscott, a summer resort north of Boston, where Barry got his first glimpse of the ocean and had the exquisite pleasure of meeting silent screen idol Anita Stewart, who was making a film on the beach. "She petted me and patted my head, all those things," said Barry. "It was the great adventure of my childhood."

When he returned to Louisville, Judge Bingham began looking for a grand home to reflect his new status. In March 1919, he bought Bushy Park, a twenty-room Georgian mansion high on a ridge overlooking the Ohio River that had once belonged to Louisville flour magnate Charles Ballard.

With the acquisition of the stately brick house, Judge Bingham began a process of personal reinvention every bit as powerful as the South's own myth of its glorious past and gilded future. He rechristened the property Melcombe Bingham, after the Dorset estate of his supposed English ancestors, and began entertaining as the owner and publisher of important newspapers.

Gradually, Judge Bingham transformed Melcombe, with its broad lawns, circular driveway, glass double doors, and gleaming white columns, into an English manor house so wildly out of place in Kentucky that it might have been imagined by Evelyn Waugh or P. G. Wodehouse. He imported a British valet named James, took to having afternoon tea at the newspapers, and spoke with an accent many Louisvillians mistook for Oxford English. Cartoons in the rival paper, *The Herald-Post*, depicted him as "Lord Bing," complete with top hat and cane. *Courier-Journal* and *Times* reporters were known derisively as "the British press."

He indulged his passion for hunting on a grand scale, acquiring several prize dogs and an electric treadmill to keep them in shape. "He was like Lord Chesterfield," said an old family friend. "An English lord who was the epitome of graciousness." It seemed somehow fitting that the first name in Melcombe's guest book should be Lloyd George, Britain's World War I prime minister, who visited the estate in 1923.

Maintaining such a household had its drawbacks, of course. Compton, the Judge's English butler, had trouble understanding the Kentucky twang that confronted him on the phone, and he winced visibly while announcing female guests with pet Southern names like Sissy and Honey. He was also quite lonely, and at night the melancholy sound of Compton's flute wafted over the estate as he serenaded his little dog in their cramped attic quarters.

To outsiders, a British butler seemed pretentious and put on, but the Judge was impervious to criticism. He had been scrambling and scratching all his life to escape the humiliation and poverty of Reconstruction. Now that he had actually done it, he felt a certain smug self-confidence. Outsiders might view him as a man who had merely married wealth, but he saw himself as a man who had worked hard for what he owned and had every right to be as ostentatious as he pleased. "He liked style and elegance," said Barry's wife, Mary Bingham. "In his fastidious way, I think he thought that English servants were somewhat cleaner than black servants."

The Judge's baronial tastes were also reflected in his furnishings. He favored antique tapestries and dark burgundy rugs in the wide entrance hall, and gold-plated flatware and mahogany appointments in the dining room. The library eventually contained over a thousand books, including 337 volumes on Joan of Arc. Collecting works on the French martyr had been a passionate interest since his early days in politics, and Bingham bristled when visitors suggested that he saw something of himself in the valiant saint. "I'm afraid he didn't like to be kidded about that kind of thing," said Mary.

Up the broad maroon-carpeted staircase was the second-floor hall, decorated with cloisonné vases, gilded mirrors, and large oil paintings. The Judge's bedroom, which overlooked the river, was aggressively masculine, with framed hunting scenes on the wall and a stuffed quail looking permanently quizzical in a glass case. In the adjoining study, he kept old guns and rifles and hundreds more books, many of them popular novels that he felt self-conscious about displaying in the formal library downstairs.

It took several years for Melcombe to ripen into the caricature it ultimately became. In the meantime, to make up for his earlier negligence, the Judge indulged his offsprings' every whim, watching with helpless bemusement as they turned his elegant new mansion into a combination speakeasy and playhouse. "He was so good to his children," said Robert's girlfriend Sophie, "he let us wreck the place."

The ringleader of these bacchanals was inevitably Robert, who had long since given up trying to please his father and now seemed actively engaged in punishing him for his obvious disapproval. After three years of debauchery at the University of Virginia, he departed without a degree. He attempted to salvage some self-respect by enlisting in the Naval Aviation Service, but the war ended in November 1918, just as he was completing his training. He then enrolled in Tulane University in New Orleans and spent three months sleeping off the effects of nights in the French Quarter before his father discovered that he had not attended a single class and brought him back home.

By the time Robert was twenty-one, drinking had gone beyond its original purpose—to defy his father—and had degenerated into chronic, pathetic alcoholism. He hid liquor in the water compartments of toilets and once drank a whole bottle of perfume for the alcohol. It made him violently ill, but when he recovered, his first impulse was to search for more and he ended up downing an entire bottle of Cointreau. Unable to control his son, Judge Bingham acted as though there was nothing out of the ordinary in Robert's behavior. "He'd just laugh it off," said Sophie. "He laughed off practically everything they did."

And the Bingham children did a lot. At Robert's instigation, ragtime bands from New Orleans played all night in Melcombe's music room while throngs of casual friends and strangers staggered about under the influence of bootleg whiskey. The next morning the Judge would find chicken legs and remnants of Tomato Surprise inside the grand piano. Once, as a Thanksgiving prank, Robert turned live turkeys loose in the upstairs hall, where they flapped wildly from room to room before the wide eyes of the frightened servants. On another occasion, he drove a car through the front door and left it parked at the foot of Melcombe's broad double staircase.

But his most venomous assault came on Judge Bingham's birthday. Barry, to get attention and please his father, had, soon after his mother's death, started writing plays in honor of the Judge's birthday. Every November 8, he and Henrietta mounted a performance before the Judge and an appreciative audience of servants. The plays were typical childish melodramas, although the accompanying songs, which Barry also wrote, sometimes contained slightly ribald lyrics. "Soaking, soaking, I'm just soaking my parts," went one. "Soaking, soaking, where each odor starts."

Robert felt nothing but contempt for these celebrations, which he saw as a fawning attempt by his brother to win their father's approval, and he flatly refused to participate. But one year, in an act of revenge, he did deign to appear. He entered the room stark naked with a crown of ivy on his head. In his hands was a large, wrapped package. To the astonishment of all, he marched up to his father and presented him with the gift: a box of manure.

Barry was not completely aloof from the clamorous mayhem of Melcombe either. He had his own tribe, which included Henrietta, their cousin Martha McKee, and Sophie Albert, who, though almost twenty, spent more time reading and playing with the Judge's youngest child than with his older siblings. Like Barry, Sophie had lost her mother at a young age. She felt a sympathetic attraction to the blond-haired little boy, more so even than to Robert, who had once asked her to marry him.

Cut off from most adult influences, Barry and Sophie invented a secret language, which they dubbed "Melcombian," after the estate. There were no grammatical rules. Words simply sprouted full grown when they sounded right. A social climber became a "soladda"—a compression of "social" and "ladder." Barry's bossy grandmother, Mrs. Miller, became "Larco Grumps." There was even a word in the Melcombian dictionary for "Pew, I smell your dirty armpits."

Parcheesi tournaments, another favorite pastime, took on the air of medieval masques, with players donning elaborate costumes for the "finals." During one such ceremony, Sophie startled the Judge by dressing up as a local girl who had recently been murdered. She threw a nightgown over her clothes, smeared it with red paint, and surprised him in the upstairs hall. "He almost screamed," she recalled.

Judge Bingham was equally forbearing when, at Barry's request, Curtis, Melcombe's handyman, built a wooden slide on one side of the mansion's double stairway. Soon after it was in place, the Judge looked up from a dinner party to see an apparition in a tuxedo flash across his field of vision. The blurred figure was a cousin and contemporary of Robert's, who had used the slide to speed himself to a debutante party. "Isn't that my dinner jacket?" the Judge calmly asked his companions before looking back down at his plate.

For Barry, the lawless Melcombe existence came to an end in the winter of 1920 when his father decided he should return to Asheville and attend the Bingham Military School. Nothing could have been more distasteful to a boy with Barry's sensibilities than an all-male military environment. The school did not even have private bathrooms; all the cadets sat on rows of open holes in a large latrine.

But Barry had begun to learn how to get what he wanted from his father, and, with the Judge's help, he managed to avoid the most loathed aspects of cadet life. He lived with his aunt Sadie, not in the barracks, and was exempted from mandatory athletics and drills. Though he was grateful for the reprieve, the special treatment marked him as a mama's boy and he made no friends. His flowery poetry, published in the yearbook, *From Reveille to Taps*, only branded him further as an object of ridicule. Although he never complained to his father, he yearned to be back in Louisville.

He got his wish after only one semester, when Sadie quietly told Judge Bingham of Barry's unhappiness. But what lay ahead was arguably no better. Having watched Robert's failed attempt to enter Harvard, the Judge now pinned all his hopes on Barry, who was more conscientious and academically gifted than either Robert or Henrietta. And this time there would be no mistake: He would find a school with a reputation for preparing boys for admission to the elite university.

He consulted Barry's uncle, a Chicago stockbroker, who reported back that the best place was Middlesex School in Concord, Massachusetts. Judge Bingham immediately contacted the headmaster, Frederick Winsor. "I am very eager to secure a place in your School next Autumn for my son, Barry," he said. "I have concluded that he should go to Harvard and that your School is the best preparatory school for him in the country."

There was, however, no vacancy in the fall of 1921. The only opening was in several weeks, in the middle of the spring term. Though not ideal, Judge Bingham jumped at the chance. He was determined that one of his sons would go to Harvard; if that meant starting Middlesex at the end of a semester, so be it. "Shall not let this opportunity pass," he cabled Winsor from Bocagrande, his winter fishing retreat in Florida.

Barry, however, was filled with dread. So far, he had managed to huddle behind one forgiving female after another—first his mother, then Sadie, then his teacher Nannie Lee Frayser, then Aunt Ruth, and, later on, his older playmate Sophie. Now, on the "wind-swept plains of North Concord," as he chillingly referred to the place, he would find no such allies. "Barry is a young boy of a very unusual type," one of his Middlesex references advised Winsor. "He has always had everything he wanted, which is not in itself unusual, but in addition he is not of a gregarious nature. He is curiously self-sufficient. . . . Also he is not athletic, or I should say, has never tried to be [and] he has a particular bent for poetry. . . . All these facts taken together make me feel that he is just the type of boy that needs Middlesex."

On the cold April day he was to enroll, Barry and his father had a gloomy lunch at the Copley Plaza Hotel in Boston, then drove twenty miles to Concord where Middlesex's gray buildings stood like sentries on 250 acres of icy, treeless tundra. While registering with Miss Chase, the headmaster's secretary, Barry got an inkling of just how out of place he would soon feel as the school's only Southerner. "Oh, you're the little boy from Kentucky, aren't you?" she said brightly. "You know, we have another little boy here from South America."

In 1921, Middlesex was just beginning its third decade of operation. Founded in 1901 as a nondenominational feeder school for Harvard, it was religious—chapel every morning and church on Sunday—but in the intellectual tradition of Emerson, Thoreau, Hawthorne, and other local eminences. Headmaster Winsor, known to the boys as The Boss, was a short, balding man with a rolling gait, a bushy mustache, and penetrating eyes that, according to one contemporary, "sought out . . . minor transgressions like blue searchlights."

The Middlesex regimen reflected Winsor's personal brand of New England Puritanism: cold morning showers, rigorous bed checks, no smoking, no photos of parents in dorm rooms, a clean white shirt every day, and exercise rain or shine. Unused to such discipline, Barry felt persecuted and confused. To make matters worse, his mid-term status left him without a roommate, magnifying his solitude. He comforted himself by gorging on slabs of devil's food cake at Concord's Red Bridge Tea Room.

Though Barry nursed a lifelong hostility toward Middlesex, the school matured him in a way that the disorder of Melcombe never could. His combustible temper, so apparent in the years following Eleanor's death, gradually disappeared. Tantrums simply had no effect on the hard-boiled teachers at Middlesex. What replaced these outbursts was a glowing ember of hurt and pain. "I realized life was not going to be easy and it wasn't going to do me much good to get angry about it," he said. "So I began to retreat into wounded feelings, which is a much less healthy way to face these things."

For Barry, those first weeks at Middlesex were like boot camp. He flunked algebra, necessitating a summer tutor, and stumbled over the trip wires of prep school life like a raw recruit on night patrol. Each day at lunch, he listened with foreboding as his name was called out for breaking the rules. Being late for breakfast, having to use the toilet during class—these infractions and others like it were punishable by "rounds," laps of the school's quarter-mile elliptical driveway. By the end of Barry's first quarter at Middlesex, he had incurred no less than twenty-seven rounds—about one for every two days he was there.

By the following fall, he had managed to whittle his rounds in half. But he had another problem that added immeasurably to his misery: a perception, delicately addressed by his English teacher in a letter to Judge Bingham, that he was homosexual.

[Barry] is naturally appreciative of what is beautiful and true in life and literature. Either because of this trait being more apparent in him than it is in most boys, or because of something that I do not know of, a few of the fellows are inclined to think him "soft." As far as I can judge, Barry is not himself, as yet, conscious of this feeling on their part. There are two contingencies I feel sure you will be as concerned as I am to guard against: one, that he shall be thought of and treated as effeminate by the other boys; the other, that this reproach of theirs shall drive him to killing out the love of the beautiful and the expression of that passion for beauty.

Aghast at the inference, the Judge immediately requested that Barry be exempted from Middlesex regulations and allowed to come home for Thanksgiving. Headmaster Winsor cabled his permission, but added tersely, "This is highly irregular and I wish it could be avoided." Once behind the protective walls of Melcombe, Barry suddenly became too sick to return. Like the allergies that had erupted after his mother's death, his illness was probably psychosomatic. His teacher's protestations to the contrary, Barry could hardly be unaware that his classmates thought him weak and dandified. Just the prospect of going back to their taunts and jeers may have brought on physical symptoms.

But his sickness also had a premeditated quality. Barry was a boy beset with conflicting desires. On the one hand, he wanted desperately to please his father. On the other, he wanted just as desperately to avoid the unpleasant aspects of life, an ever-lengthening list that included math, athletics, criticism of any sort, and, of course, the dour rigor of Middlesex. Falling ill accomplished both ends: It elicited sympathy from Judge Bingham and gave Barry a legitimate reprieve from boarding school. Though only fifteen, Barry had learned how to manipulate people for his own ends while still retaining their love—a technique that would serve him well throughout his life.

As usual, Judge Bingham offered no resistance. He seemed quite content to play along with the ruse as long as Middlesex agreed to hold Barry's place. "His condition is not alarming in any way," he wrote Winsor. "[He has lost weight but] he has no temperature, no cough and cannot be said to be tubercular in any way." But, he added, the doctors think it best to be on the safe side and keep Barry at home.

For the rest of the academic year, Barry stayed cozily at Melcombe, working occasionally with a tutor. As spring gave way to summer, he spent long, lazy days submerged in the family's new swimming pool. In July, armed with take-home exams and a summer reading list, he sailed off to Europe with his family, seemingly quite fit.

What appeared effeminate at Middlesex seemed boyishly suave and charming in the Binghams' world overseas. There, Barry appeared remarkably self-confident. While in London that summer, he became smitten with Fred and Adele Astaire, then performing a new dance called the Charleston in the hit musical *Stop Flirting*. Determined to meet them, he sent a note to the theater saying he represented *The Courier-Journal* and wanted to interview them. On the appointed night, he showed up at the Astaires' dressing room in a rented top hat and tails, handed Adele a white orchid, and proceeded to pepper them with questions. They penetrated his disguise in an instant, for he had forgotten to bring a notebook or a pen. But they never let on.

His mysterious infirmity apparently cured, Barry returned to Middlesex in the fall of 1922. The intervening months had matured him and he used his strengths—charm, a facility with language, and an offbeat sense of humor—to keep his tormentors at bay. After sitting through Headmaster Winsor's mandatory lecture on the dangers of self-abuse, he sent the other boys into howls of laughter with his new name for the practice: "self-amuse."

A young Catholic English teacher took an interest in his writing and sparked a brief religious phase. But by the end of his junior year, Barry had had enough of Middlesex. Despite his failure in math—which his housemaster, "Bugs" Raymond, attributed entirely to his lack of discipline—he had done well enough in English, history, French, and Latin to be ranked fifth in a class of nineteen. Unlike Robert, he had handily passed the college entrance exam, and all he needed was a second modern language to make a run at Harvard. The university might have waived the requirement if the headmaster of Middlesex had recommended it. But Winsor adamantly refused. He was damned if this pampered pup would once again flout the rules.

Barry, as usual, got his way. He spent his senior year at Melcombe being tutored in German and never graduated from Middlesex. His antipathy toward the school remained strong. As a gesture of conciliation, Middlesex finally granted him a diploma in 1981, but he returned the favor by giving only small, occasional donations.

For Barry, that long, last year before college was deliciously sweet. With his father's indulgent backing, he and his sister, Henrietta, opened the Wilderness Bookstore in downtown Louisville. The shop had some decent books, and even a few first editions, but it was more of a lark than a business. The younger Binghams did not hesitate to close up early and passersby got used to seeing a sign—"Gone to the Races"—dangling in the window.

———————

By then, Henrietta was twenty-two and something of a celebrity in Louisville. She ran with the exotic Bloomsbury crowd in London and had a daring penchant for cigarettes and fashionable flapper dresses. In superficial ways, she had changed a great deal since the death of Mary Lily. Secure again as her father's hostess, she no longer flew into schoolgirl rages when other women hovered around him at parties. The Judge, for his part, doted more slavishly than ever on his daughter, inflating her capabilities to match his hopes. "My father had the highest expectations for Henrietta," said Barry. "He thought she was brilliant."

When Judge Bingham sent Henrietta off to Smith College in 1921, he told her he was sure she would get her degree and then go on for a Ph.D. In fact, Henrietta had little interest in intellectual pursuits and rarely read a newspaper or a book. It took her months to wade through *Anna Karenina*, and she later told friends it was an experiment she did not care to repeat. Barry overheard the Judge's exhortations and thought how little his father seemed to understand Henrietta as she really was. Like her brother Robert, she ended up with no degree of any kind.

Instead, at Smith she met English professor Mina Kirstein, a tall, intense Bostonian five years her senior. The two women were rare economic equals; Mina's father, Louis, was a partner in Filene's Department Store. But whereas the Binghams were political, the Kirsteins were artistic, intellectual, and avant-garde. At Smith and Columbia University, where she earned her M.A., Mina was whispered to be bisexual and a radical feminist. During her long lifetime, she would edit and translate an anthology of Proust's letters, work with Orson Welles and John Houseman in the Mercury Theatre of the Air, and be awarded the French Legion of Honor; her brother, Lincoln, would co-found the New York City Ballet.

All this was in the future, of course, when Mina and Henrietta met in the fall of 1921. Like her siblings, Henrietta was drawn to strong, maternal figures. Mina, in turn, was taken with Henrietta's freshness and her "gentle, encompassing warmth." Handsome rather than pretty, the Louisville ingenue also seemed perpetually troubled, which only added to her mysterious charm.

So it seemed quite appropriate when Mina, overflowing with motherly concern, petitioned Judge Bingham to underwrite a year of analysis for Henrietta with Dr. Ernest Jones, Sigmund Freud's disciple and biographer-to-be, in London. Such treatments were much in vogue among the moneyed set at the time and Mina assured the Judge they would do Henrietta good. Besides, she said, she was going to England herself for a sabbatical and would look after Henrietta personally. Unable, as usual, to say no to one of his children, Judge Bingham gave the adventure his blessing and Henrietta dropped out of Smith, never to return.

In England, the Bingham and Kirstein wealth made possible a very comfortable life-style. For their weekday use in London, the women leased Grove House, off the Fulham Road. On the weekends they journeyed to Hurstpierpoint, their country retreat in Sussex, so that Henrietta could indulge her taste for fox-hunting. "The Kentucky heiress," as she was known, was soon a familiar sight among the titled and the well heeled, careening through cobblestoned hamlets in her Bentley and popping up at the best parties in luxurious silks and furs.

Had it not been for Mina's literary connections, Henrietta might have contentedly remained in this conventional social circle. But the "Bloomsberries," as Mina called the artists and writers of the Bloomsbury set, were natural companions for the brainy Smith professor, and soon she and Henrietta were regulars at the group's bohemian gatherings.

In the world of Virginia Woolf and Lytton Strachey, Henrietta was an inexplicable smash hit. She had little sense of humor or artistic ability, and she was too self-involved to be a particularly good listener. Still, she had a certain seductive charisma. With her lightly accented speech, magnificent wealth, and refined manners, Henrietta personified a glamorous stereotype of the South. The family newspapers, though little known in England, only heightened the mystique. Giddy on her fourth martini, Henrietta would sometimes boast that one day she would return to Louisville and take over the Bingham empire.

Her legs were unfashionably muscular from years of riding, but she had no trouble attracting suitors of both sexes. David Garnett rhapsodically described her face as "the perfect oval of a Buddha" and dedicated one of his books to her. At a winter party at Grove House, Henrietta perched atop the piano in a purple velvet dress, playing soulful melodies on the saxophone and singing gospel songs. Many of the guests, men and women alike, fell in love with her that night, including John Houseman.

One of her most passionate lovers was Dora Carrington, the Bloomsbury circle's blond bisexual artist. After seeing Henrietta at a party, Carrington excitedly wrote a friend that she had met a woman with "the face of a Giotto Madonna. She sang exquisite songs with a mandolin, Southern-state revivalist nigger songs. She made such wonderful cocktails that I became completely drunk and almost made love to her in public. To my great joy, Garnett told me the other day she continually asks after me and wanted me to go and see her."

The affair progressed off and on for more than a year, with dramatic reunions and brutal leave-takings. Once, during a secret rendezvous in a Knightsbridge flat, Carrington and Henrietta ate biscuits and garlic sausage and drank tea with lemon without saying a word. "I hardly ever speak to her," wrote Carrington. "We are the most silent of friends!"

Despite such becalmed moments, Henrietta's homosexuality had a frenzied obsessiveness about it that led some to believe that she yearned to recapture her mother's love, or purposely kept men at bay so that her father could remain the one, true romance in her life. Either way, the excitement of unconventional affairs filled Henrietta's need for turmoil. "She really enjoyed that," said one woman who knew her well. "She was always in some relationship that was tremendously full of drama."

For all of Henrietta's torrid flings, however, she was not really available for love or marriage. The only important relationship in her life was with her father. And with the Oedipal tugs came complexities and contradictions. The Judge adored and indulged her, dominated and controlled her. She, in turn, alternated between childlike dependence, brazen manipulation, and outright efforts to escape the pull of his power.

She was in one of her manipulative moods in the spring of 1923 when she came back to America and refused to reenter Smith, instead running the Wilderness Bookstore in Louisville with Barry. Her time at home was brief, and the following summer she sailed again for England. The pattern was thus set: flights from Louisville and triumphal returns, followed by more flights and more returns.

The long absences inflicted deep wounds on her father. John Houseman later said he came to believe that the reason Judge Bingham married for a third and last time was because he realized, finally, that Henrietta could not be counted on to remain by his side.

The Judge had married Eleanor for love and Mary Lily for money, but he married Aleen Muldoon Hilliard, the matronly widow of a Louisville stockbroker, for peace and quiet. Beautifully dressed and brimming with the social graces of the Old South, Aleen was more ornamental than intellectual, more conventional than spontaneous, all of which seemed mercifully reassuring to the Judge after the chaos of Melcombe. "She behaved like a correct wife," said a family member. "It never would have occurred to her not to do what was expected of her." In Louisville, the match was viewed as a logical merger of two people drawn together by a need for companionship.

Taking a chapter from the Kenans' book, Bob Bingham asked Aleen to renounce her right to her half of his estate in exchange for $1 million. That done, they were married in August of 1924. Perhaps to avoid the Louisville gossips, they took their vows in St. Margaret's Church in London before a small assemblage of family and friends.

Once back in Kentucky, they settled into a low-key "lord and lady" relationship that included separate friends and separate bedrooms. The latter was perfectly acceptable to Judge Bingham, who was extremely fussy about the way his bed was turned down. Only Lizzie Baker, Barry's black nurse, was able to do it precisely as he liked; a wife between the sheets would have disrupted the routine.

The marriage had little discernible effect on Robert and Barry, who called Aleen by her first name rather than "mother." But for Henrietta, the wedding was a watershed. When not pub-crawling in London or visiting speakeasies in Harlem, she flounced self-importantly through Melcombe's wide halls, treating Aleen like a dim-witted houseguest. In the hope that it would help shake off the father-fixation that had tormented her for so long, she decided to lose her virginity. In John Houseman, then a struggling grain broker in Kansas City, she found a willing, unthreatening accomplice.

Houseman had been besotted with Henrietta since meeting her at Grove House in 1922. So when she suggested, five years later, that they unburden themselves of their virginity during a vacation in London, he was both delighted and terrified. With businesslike efficiency, Henrietta took full charge of the mutual deflowering. On the appointed day, she picked up Houseman in her black roadster, took him to Ernest Jones's office, where she was still in psychoanalysis, and told the doctor of their mission. After a few cautionary words to Houseman about Henrietta's Oedipal yearnings, the psychoanalyst blessed the venture and the couple roared off to a chic seaside hotel in Brighton.

The evening, which Houseman remembers "with a mixture of embarrassment and pleasure," began with a sumptuous dinner and ended in a hotel room with bright red curtains. "Henrietta thought it would fix things," Houseman said of her determination to bed him. "She thought I was going to save her from her problems. But I was very mother-fixated myself. She picked the wrong man." After they returned to the States on the *Aquitania*, there was vague talk of marriage, but it went nowhere. They soon broke up and Houseman went back to Kansas City.

As for Barry, his father's remarriage came on the eve of his freshman year at Harvard. While moving into Gore Hall that crisp fall day in 1924, he had contradictory emotions: fear that his unorthodox schooling had left him unprepared, relief at finally fulfilling his father's expectations, and dizzy, heady joy at the prospect of real freedom.

His life up till then had been anarchical, not free. He had always been branded the alien, the odd-ball, the limp-wristed sissy who wrote poetry, had too-perfect manners and no interest in athletics. And then there was his father, doting and compliant on the one hand, but full of insistent demands on the other. Barry longed to escape to a place where he could relax and just be himself. With cunning accuracy, he realized that Harvard might be such a haven, an institution that was tolerant of eccentricity and at the same time so awe-inspiring that it would be Judge Bingham—not Barry—who would feel out of place. "The overwhelming experience of Harvard to me was a sense of liberation," said Barry. "For me it was the right place at the right time." Indeed it was, for waiting for him behind the stone facade of neighboring Radcliffe was a strong, complex woman with a peculiarly similar history of her own: Mary Clifford Caperton of Richmond.

BABY'S AWAKE NOW

Late at night, as they huddled in bed, Mary Caperton and her sisters could hear their mother and father fighting. The pattern was always the same. First came their distraught father, Clifford Caperton, despairing over the latest sheaf of bills. Then came their mother, Helena, shrilly lambasting her husband for being an inadequate provider. Next the little girls heard their mother weeping, her sobs echoing off the walls of the modest brick house on West Avenue that was, she continually reminded them, a decided step down from the Linden Row town house where she had grown up. Finally, the tears became muffled as the couple found solace in sex, their only area of mutual satisfaction.

The old families in Richmond were well aware that Clifford Caperton could ill-afford his wife's refined tastes on the salary he received as a representative of an advertising agency. And they knew that her membership in the Colonial Dames of Virginia, while an envied badge of distinction, did nothing to feed and clothe the Capertons' son and six daughters.

But to Helena Lefroy Caperton, a well-born Richmond belle, pedigree and position were all important. The Civil War and financial panics of the late nineteenth century had made genteel poverty commonplace in families such as theirs. Though necessities might be scarce, one could still take pride in being a member of a First Family of Virginia. Most Southern patricians looked down on Yankee aristocrats, but Virginia's gentry patronized even their Southern brethren. And Richmond's elite considered themselves preeminent in Virginia—la crème de la crème de la crème, as it were. Helena Caperton, a descendant of Peter Montague, a Virginia planter with blood ties to both the Tudor and Stuart royalty, felt she had good reason to be a snob. Regardless of the cost, she was determined that neither she nor her little girls would lose their place in Richmond's society.

Appearances had to be maintained, lace-trimmed petticoats bought, young ladies' educations provided for, and debut parties arranged. Helena set her jaw and spent what she had to. Then, inevitably, the arguments would ensue, again and again, over and over, until Clifford Caperton came to be viewed even by his own children as a hen-pecked bumbler. "We all just felt terribly sorry for him," said Mary, the Capertons' fifth child and fourth daughter. "I hate to say that, but he was a failure."

Clifford Caperton was not without a distinguished background of his own. In West Virginia, the Capertons were a leading family; his uncle had been a U.S. senator. But it was his mother's people, the Stiles, who had offered Clifford his best chance for a bright future. While Clifford was still a teenager, his uncle, Maj. Robert Stiles, invited him to come live in Richmond with him, study law, and eventually join his firm. The move was a social as well as a professional coup, for Major Stiles lived in one of the grand brick town houses on Linden Row, Richmond's most fashionable street, so named because of the beautiful linden trees that grew in one of the gardens.

Clifford had no inkling, of course, that the woman he would eventually marry lived at the opposite end of Linden Row. There, in a town house identical to his uncle's, dwelled John Henry Montague, "one of the famous wits of Virginia," president of the Merchants and Planters Savings Bank and the Virginia Paper Company. Sharing his household was his widowed daughter, Sallie Montague Lefroy, and her only child, the vivacious and willful Helena.

Mary Caperton grew up on tales of family glory, graceful wealth, and loving and lasting marriages, tales passed down like fine heirlooms from her grandmother Sallie, known to her grandchildren as "Artown" (pronounced Artone), to her mother, Helena, and then on to her and her five sisters. From the tenderest age, the six blond Capertons were told that they were "Montague girls," a term synonymous with women of seductive beauty and belle-like charm.

The phrase also suggested a certain joie de vivre that could, if coaxed, skirt the rim of scandalous behavior. It seemed only fitting, Richmond's grand dames knowingly clucked years later, that Alice Montague, a Balti-more cousin, became the mother of Wallis Warfield Simpson, the Duchess of Windsor—perhaps the ultimate "Montague girl."

The family's sense of wealth and social position also derived from the Montague connection. As a child, before the Civil War left Richmond in ashes, Artown had made summer pilgrimages to Cherry Grove, the ancestral family plantation, where, she later wrote, "swarms of darkie children greeted our annual arrival with peals of joy."

After the South's surrender, the Montagues remained solvent, though not as well-heeled as before. In an effort to restore some of the city's prewar gaiety, Artown's father and several other Richmond leaders organized the Richmond German, a debutante party named after a popular Prussian dance of the era. Receiving an invitation to The German was inviolate proof that a young lady was well-born, and the ball soon became a way for the old families of antebellum days to demonstrate their superiority to the new people who poured into Richmond as the city rebuilt itself.

Forty years later, Mary and her sisters were raised with the expectation that they, too, would make their debut at The German and then enjoy a year of fun and abandon before pursuing marriage—preferably a match as romantic and full of wealth and happiness as their grandmother Artown's.

Even as they listened to their parents squabble over bills, Mary and her five sisters clung to the sentimental ideal of marriage that Artown described. As she told the tale, she had been swept away by a dashing blond foreigner, Jeffrey Arthur Lefroy, who had taken her on a honeymoon trip to Carriglass Manor, his family's estate in southern Ireland. There she had mingled with his titled relations before making a triumphal return to Richmond with eighteen trunks of wedding gifts. It was better than a fairy tale. To a group of girls in hand-me-down clothes, Artown's silky narrative made marriage sound like life's surest road to contentment and plenty.

But the story had a vein of tragedy as well as romance. During a second trip to Ireland, Artown's husband became ill with tuberculosis. Though he alternated between periods of remission and relapse, he finally died in 1884, after only seven years of marriage. Artown was devastated. With nowhere else to go, she returned to Richmond with her only child, five-year-old Helena, and moved back into her father's Linden Row home. Though just thirty-four, she wore black for years.

Helena soon became the petted, spoiled focus of the Linden Row house-hold. When Buffalo Bill brought his Wild West Show to Richmond, Grand-father Montague invited him home for dinner. To return the hospitality, Buffalo Bill asked the little girl to sit next to him the next night when he drove the Deadwood Stage around the arena, pursued by a band of wild

"Indians." The real object of Colonel Cody's attention, however, was Artown, who had no interest in a second marriage. As a token of his esteem, he gave the lovely young widow a silver-handled riding crop inscribed "with enduring admiration from Buffalo Bill."

Each night, Grandfather Montague sat next to Helena at dinner, drilling her on new words and their Latin origins. She quickly picked up the game, and as a small girl astonished strangers by interrupting their conversations to inquire, "What is the root of that word?" Artown took her on annual trips to Ireland, where she was the adored only child of the late adored son. By the time she was eighteen and ready to make her debut, Helena was pampered, strong-minded, and very beautiful—traits she considered the natural birthright of every "Montague girl."

When Clifford Caperton moved in with his uncle down the block in the mid-1890s, Helena set her cap for him. All her life she had heard stories of her mother's connubial bliss. She was well grounded in the myth that all husbands were stalwart, all wives devoted. Her mother and Grandfather Montague had neglected to mention anything that might sully this shimmering image of married life, such as incompatibility, alcoholism, or worries over money.

Clifford Caperton was anxious to marry Helena, but he wanted to wait until he could establish himself in his uncle's law office. As an attorney, he at least had a hope of keeping his bride in the life-style she had always known. Helena, however, insisted that the wedding be now. The couple was duly wed and Helena became pregnant almost immediately. Clifford, the once-aspiring lawyer, took a job with the telegraph company.

The Caperton marriage was sexually tempestuous and unusually fruitful. By the time Mary Caperton was born on Christmas Eve, 1904, Helena, twenty-six, already had a son, Arthur, and three other daughters—Rose, Helena, and Sarah. Two more girls, Harriette and Melinda, would follow Mary. As each baby arrived, Artown would wring her hands and wonder aloud, "But who will provide the drawers and the petticoats?"

The Richmond Mary Caperton knew as a child had a flourishing red-light district, yet was so puritanical that an advertisement for Bull Durham Tobacco had portions of the bull's anatomy painted out by order of the mayor. Water troughs stood downtown well into the twentieth century, families never locked their doors, and children played freely in the network of alleys where carriages, horses, and buggies were kept.

A proper household required at least a maid and a cook, which the Capertons managed even during their most desperate periods. Children had nurses and ladies spent their days gardening or doing volunteer work. Unless an invitation specified informal attire, it was understood that gentlemen were to appear in black tie and ladies in evening gowns.

For the six little Caperton girls, city life in Richmond before World War I had a sweetness and an innocence now almost unimaginable. In summers, before bed, their nurse Louise would dress her charges in their thin cotton nightgowns and herd them out to the streetcar tracks that ran in front of the house. There, the barefoot girls and their black guardian would wave down the driver, then clamber aboard the open summer car and race to the front where they would sit side-by-side on the cane seats, giggling and squirming and delighting in the cool breeze as the streetcar made its circuit in the twilight, disembarking at their stop when it came around again.

Though it had been half a century since Appomattox, the Lost Cause was still a live topic of conversation. On Sunday afternoons, Great-Grandfather Montague would arrive home from church with a retinue of old Confederate veterans. They would gather around the Montague table, telling and retelling tales of battlefield bravery to a less-than-appreciative audience of small, blond Caperton girls. "The dead hand of the Civil War was heavy on everything," said Mary. "I remember being terribly tired and bored." Still, Mary's parents puffed with pride when she was chosen to model for a panel of the city's famous Battle Abbey mural depicting scenes from the Civil War.

The Capertons first lived on North Harrison Street, about nine blocks from Linden Row. On winter mornings, the house was icy cold. Nurse Louise would arrive before dawn and quietly ascend the stairs to the third floor where the six Caperton girls slept. "She'd build a fire in the nursery and warm the long flannel drawers on the fender," said Mary. "Then she'd get us up and we would stand in a row, buttoning the one in front of us in a file." Then came a forced march to the frigid bathroom down the hall. The only heat came from fireplaces, except for a Lectrobe stove in the dining room, which created an island of warmth that Mary often claimed as her own. "It had a curved front and glass doors you could open and this great red glare came through," she said. "Very warm."

The only bounty the Capertons knew was an abundance of mouths to feed. Shocked at first by the novel experience of financial deprivation, Helena Caperton soon became obsessed with money and applied her considerable will to the fine art of making-do. She cleverly chose godmothers who could afford expensive coats for her girls, for instance, then passed the garments down to the next child in line. As Helena saw it, her principal duty was to make sure that her girls married well, which in her book meant wedding a man who was either rich or had prospects of becoming so. She took on the challenge with unembarrassed calculation.

If the Caperton girls could not be heiresses, she told herself, then they would attract wealthy mates with their looks and breeding. Helena's campaign was so successful that the society pages of *The Richmond Times-Dispatch* routinely referred to Mary and her siblings as "the six beautiful Caperton sisters."

Mary respected her mother's uncommon energy, and was in awe of her ability to find humor in the family's bleak financial situation. But she was disgusted that her mother would waste her time and intelligence on schemes to get party frocks and bows when the family was genuinely hard up. Once, in a moment that seemed emblematic of Helena Caperton's misplaced priorities, Mary went to the icebox to get food for a guest and found nothing inside but a half-dozen orchid corsages.

If Mary thought her mother shallow, Helena Caperton considered her fourth daughter a dismal failure as a "Montague girl." The other Capertons prized their looks, adored the social whirl, and disdained intellect as a handicap to marriage. But Mary loved books and the life of the mind. From earliest childhood, she knew she was different. "My sisters were fair and had wonderful pale gold hair, great big blue eyes and they all danced," she said. "I didn't even have a date until I went to college. I was considered a blue-stocking." The term, always used pejoratively, referred to women considered to be prim, brainy wallflowers.

Coloring every aspect of life was the constant anxiety about money. "Looking back on my childhood, I know that, even at 12, I was . . . confused and uncertain," Mary later wrote. "I was rather deeply upset and depressed even as a pre-adolescent child by the rather grim financial difficulties we were always facing at home, and by the consequent tension and misery that marked the definitely tempestuous relationship between Father and Mother."

Not knowing what else to do about Mary's scholarly bent, Helena Caperton decreed that she should take violin lessons. Mary had no interest in the instrument, and less talent, but her mother cajoled her English godmother into underwriting lessons. For years, Mary trudged to the home of Madame Hattenberg, who, she later concluded, was "a drug fiend," and took the lessons that regularly reduced her to tears.

Mary's real passion was the classics, a curiosity ignited by Artown, who endlessly corrected her grandchildren's grammar and word usage. "You love your mother; you do not love shad roe," Artown would observe with pious insistence. If the word in question had a Latin root, its meaning was traced and it was lucidly and quite positively explained. To misuse a word was to abuse a word, the older woman told Mary, which was both vulgar and unkind to the nobility of the English language.

By the time Mary was fourteen, she had all but dropped out of school.

Since her mother had decided that she was going to be a violinist, there seemed little need for formal education beyond the casually attended classes she took in English and history at Miss Virginia Randolph Ellett's School for Girls, known as Miss Jennie's, the institution-of-choice for young ladies from good Richmond families.

But Mary had caught the attention of Louise Burleigh, a young Radcliffe graduate who directed Richmond's community theater. The two had become friends while touring Virginia auditoriums and courthouse squares one summer with a production of *Gammer Gurton's Needle*, an early English farce in which Mary had played Dame Chat. After years of observing the Caperton family, Louise was well aware that Mary felt out of place.

Louise soon determined that Mary should go to Radcliffe. To the grand dames of Richmond, the idea seemed positively heretical. If local girls went north to college, which was rarely, they almost always went to Bryn Mawr, a school that offered the cachet of an Eastern education without the onus of being excessively Yankee. The cost of a Seven Sisters education was also far beyond the Capertons' means, and Mary's preparation had been so haphazard that she was unlikely to be admitted anyway. She would have to study intensely for the next several years to qualify, Louise knew, a feat that seemed impossible in the mayhem of the Caperton household.

Radcliffe sounded like paradise to a Richmond blue-stocking, and Mary appealed to her mother for support. To her surprise, she cooperated, concocting a plan whereby Mary would return to Miss Jennie's as a full-time student, leave the confusion of the Caperton household, and live with Louise on Plum Street a few blocks away.

Helena Caperton had no objection to a daughter moving out. She was too preoccupied with her own budding career as a writer, which brought in a little money as well as an opportunity to brag about her artistic abilities. When her childhood playmate, Nancy Langhorne, was elected to the British Parliament as Lady Astor in 1919, Helena sent a sketch of the family, "The Virginia Viscountess," to the *Ladies' Home Journal*. She also enclosed a snapshot of the new MP as a child, sitting in a goat cart. To her delight, a check came back. From that moment on, Helena Caperton fancied herself a literary genius and lived for the acceptance slips that seemed to compensate for the other frustrations of her life.

Not surprisingly, she tended to exaggerate the role her writing played in keeping the family solvent. She told a Richmond newspaper that whenever one of the little girls needed a new dress, she would "hold a baby on one knee and bang a typewriter on the other." But she did not even start writing for pay until her youngest child was a teenager, and she never earned more than pin money. Mary bristled at her mother's bombast. The family did have a financial savior, she said, but it was Artown, whose inheritance was gradually reduced to nothing by Helena Caperton's spendthrift ways.

———

For three years, Mary and Louise Burleigh amicably shared a house, though the arrangement had its problems. Louise was madly in love with a concert pianist who had studied with the Russian composer Liatoshinsky, and Mary was often in a fury with him because he was extremely cavalier with Louise's reputation. He would come to dinner, and then, because he was an insomniac, force Louise to sit up all night reading *Beowulf* and Shakespeare aloud. He was also a violent racist and would gladly have been a member of the Ku Klux Klan had the group not been considered so common by then. "Older people in Richmond would corner me and say, 'What goes on? He's seen coming out of her house at five in the morning.' . . . And I would say, 'Well, there's nothing in that because I'm right there and I know.' "

To her relief, Mary saw little of her family during those years. Most of her energy went into the furious struggle to prepare for the entrance examinations for Radcliffe. She enjoyed the discipline, and the learning itself was a pleasure as palpable to her as romance or athletics were to other adolescents.

Miss Jennie Ellett's School, the precursor of present-day St. Catherine's, reflected the headmistress's rather parochial theories of education. Mary learned all the Plantagenet kings and endless passages of Shakespeare, for instance, but had only the vaguest notion where Colorado was located. Her passion for the classics intensified after coming under the influence of Miss Edmonia Lancaster, and as examinations neared, Mary went "voluntarily and with good will" to her house every Saturday morning to do Latin composition.

The hard work paid off. The faculty of Miss Jennie's and the members of her graduating class elected Mary "June Queen," the school's highest award, which went each year to the student "whose attainment, honor and influence best represents the class."

At seventeen, Mary declared to "a more or less inattentive family" that she intended to compete for a Distant Work Scholarship to underwrite her Radcliffe education. Despite her eccentric daughter's previously announced intention to go to college, Helena Caperton seemed genuinely stunned. She had somehow never thought Mary was serious about the proposition. Higher education was not expected or desired in a Montague girl; several of Mary's sisters did not even finish high school.

Helena found it especially hard to believe that Mary cared nothing for the one year of gaiety allowed her sisters before marriage or a job. She considered a year of play a good investment in man-hunting; higher education, however, would only make her daughter less attractive to a prospective groom. Just as disturbing, Mary's decision meant that the money the family had planned to use for her debut would now have to be spent on college, making her the only Caperton girl not to "come out" at the Richmond German. Mary did not care; she considered a debut ridiculous under the circumstances, and her mother "thought this was part of my being such a blue-stocking so she forgave me."

After four examinations, Mary won the scholarship, which provided $400 a year, enough to cover tuition. Summer jobs and the small sum provided by her parents would pay for room and board, books, clothes, and other living expenses.

In September 1924, Mary climbed aboard a train with Louise Burleigh and set out for Radcliffe. Once in Boston, the pair motored along the Charles River, where the trees were just beginning to take on their vivid autumn color, and then crossed into Cambridge. They went through Harvard Square, glimpsing the spacious green of Harvard Yard behind the brick gates, and up Massachusetts Avenue to Radcliffe, which had its own separate campus and was a fifteen-minute walk from Harvard. Louise accompanied Mary into Briggs Hall to make sure the single room she had been assigned was clean and neat. She helped Mary unpack, and then, with a quick hug, was gone, leaving Mary to wallow in fear and homesickness.

———————

Mary found that she was one of only two girls in her class from the South. She considered her schoolmates, who were mostly from New England and New York, rather stiff. They, in turn, thought her curious and strange, and mistook her shyness for timidity. Because of her Virginia accent, Mary also had the novel experience of being considered frivolous—the exact opposite of her problem in Richmond. The other girls, she said, assumed "that I was a light-minded, Southern belle-type, which I was far from being."

Such annoyances, however, were trivial compared with the joy Mary discovered as a Radcliffe freshman. In later years she would say that the Radcliffe experience was her first exposure to greatness. " 'Harvard is a nursery for independent and lonely thought,' " she said, quoting William James and adding parenthetically that women had a special need for such places because the pressures for "conformity, orthodoxy and narrow conservatism beat more fiercely [for them] than they do for men."

She was rapturous at having nothing to do all day but learn from some of the nation's most famous scholars. To her, it was an extraordinary luxury. "I get so impatient with young people now who complain about Harvard and how they hate the lectures," she said later. "I just thought it was the most wonderful thing in the world."

When Mary went home for Christmas her freshman year—the time when most Richmond belles made their debuts—she brought bottles of fruit flies with her. She was cross-breeding them, she told her horrified mother, to get red eyes and gray bodies, and gray eyes and red bodies. To Helena Caperton, Mary showed every sign of incipient spinsterdom, a fate she regarded as the ultimate misfortune. Indeed, Radcliffe's image was one of dowdy women with high intellects and little charm who would eventually become schoolmistresses. To trade a Richmond debut for revolting experiments in fruit fly husbandry only confirmed Helena Caperton's worst fears.

Mary lived up to her mother's nightmare. At Radcliffe she lugged a black leather binder from class to class, taking notes in a small, compulsively neat hand. She reassembled and summarized her lecture notes, then painstakingly made more notes while reading the assigned books. "I used a pen with a thin nib," she said, "and carried about, with an insufferably pedantic air, a bottle of soot black ink."

In large part, her view of life was permanently influenced by Irving Babbitt, a remote and terrifying man who preached a rigorous, unforgiving brand of humanism. "He was an overpowering intellect," Mary said. "He would come in with his green bag, pull out twelve or fifteen books that he wanted to quote from and just deliver his lecture. He never made any contact with anybody. He was like some god who descended to the desk and sat there to instruct you in the way you should cope."

Babbitt taught French literary criticism, but the course was really just a vehicle for the transmission of his stern system of values. He detested Rousseau, who believed that man, untouched by civilization, was naturally good, and he found the whole Romantic movement and its notion of noble savages pernicious. He was a rationalist who abhorred impulse and loved discipline, both intellectual and emotional.

But he also placed a high value on intuition, which he felt could spring from a hidden spiritual source. He idolized Pascal, who said, "The heart has its reasons, of which reason is ignorant." In a Babbittian world, sex would be kept in its place; the object of life would be to constrain the natural mind. "He was not a joyous thinker," Mary recalled, noting that his conclusions were perfectly compatible with Richmond's Victorian rules of behavior.

Mary's own views were as severe as Babbitt's. She knew that it was her talent for discipline, her ability to sublimate her "natural" self in pursuit of a higher goal, that had helped her escape her chaotic family and the confining world of Richmond. But she was more understanding of human foibles than

Babbitt. "He was too savage about impulse, though I really think that the natural mind is instinctively evil," she said years later. "If you watch small children, they're naturally quite aggressive, selfish, egocentric. This is the way they are. This is human nature in the raw. If you observe people, you know that there really is such a thing as original sin. Any other view of human nature is quite sentimental. But I haven't got such a terribly gloomy view. A self-disciplined human being can be a noble, wonderful piece of work. . . . Also, every now and then, I'm taken off of my views. You seem to see quite simple people who are just good. It doesn't happen very often, but sometimes you do."

Though her philosophy was puritanical, Mary had a definite taste for the amenities of dormitory life. Irish maids in aprons and caps brought tea to the girls on rainy Cambridge afternoons. On Sundays, they would deliver a breakfast tray of popovers and fishballs for fifty cents—a treat Mary longed for but could rarely afford. The sight of such luxury inflamed Mary's mind so thoroughly that years later she had breakfast in bed virtually every morning.

She joined the Radcliffe Idler, a theatrical club, and the Choral Society. She had little social life, however, because Harvard men barely acknowledged the unfashionable blue-stockings of Radcliffe. There were few opportunities to meet Harvard students anyway, since most classes were sex-segregated. The only person who ever approached the status of beau was a Harvard boy whose father was a jeweler in Richmond. Although he and Mary came from the same town, the two had never met until they went to Cambridge; he was Jewish, and the Capertons simply did not receive Jews. When he came to call on Mary the summer before her sophomore year, Helena Caperton and Artown gave him a frosty welcome and the relationship petered out.

Unlike most of her Radcliffe classmates, Mary was not set on a career as an elementary or high school teacher. She really had no idea what she would do after college. By the spring of her sophomore year she was twenty-one and drifting toward a life as a classics scholar, perhaps a professor, specializing in ancient Greek. Then, suddenly, everything changed.

———

About a mile away from Mary's mean existence, Barry Bingham was living the life of a Jazz Age college boy, lubricated by liquor and plenty of money. His hair slicked down and parted in the middle, his clothes elegantly tailored and his galoshes fashionably unbuckled, he roared around Cambridge in a Stutz Bearcat, the embodiment of twenties chic. On lost weekends in New York, he rushed to Club Montmartre to gaze calflike at Julie Johnson, an adagio dancer who performed with her husband, George Murphy. After spending all night in a speakeasy, Barry would join friends for breakfast at Childs on Columbus Circle and watch the sun rise orange and red over Central Park. The group would then roll blearily back to Harvard, making vulgar puns and singing such hits of the day as "When My Baby Smiles at Me." In his dormitory on Harvard Yard, the biddies, as the school's maids were called, shook their heads disapprovingly as they tidied up his disheveled room.

Between bouts of drinking, Barry was almost as taken with the feast of learning as Mary was. He gravitated to Harvard's grand and idiosyncratic literary classicists. One professor, Willard Conelly, dressed for his composition course as though he were living in the eighteenth century. His Shakespeare teacher, Professor Kittredge, charged madly about the lecture platform, taking all the parts of the play. Kittredge was especially renowned for the demonic way his white beard waggled when he incanted, "Double, double, toil and trouble, fire burn and cauldron bubble" from *Macbeth*. Barry's Bible teacher made the Old Testament "resound as the most stirring literature in the English language" and another, who taught a course on the Romantic poets, provided "a lifetime joy, planting seeds of lyrical verse to blossom in memory on many a wakeful night."

It was a time to entertain radical ideas that had yet to seep into Louisville's consciousness. In the cloister of his Harvard existence, Barry seemed unperturbed when, for the first time in his life, a black student sat down next to him in a poetry composition class.

Race may not have been the barrier at Harvard that it was in Kentucky, but there was plenty of social stratification nonetheless. Wealth was important, and Barry was clearly among Harvard's rich boys. But it did not ensure acceptance and Barry never received an invitation to join one of Harvard's "final clubs," then the standard for social success. "I didn't aspire to it," he said obliquely. "I had other things I was interested in and I was enjoying my life tremendously."

The explanation is not persuasive. In later life, Barry was an almost compulsive joiner. But it is logical that he would not have been considered "final club" material. Regional snobbery was as pronounced at Harvard as it had been at Middlesex. Southerners were rare, and even sixty years after the Civil War, many people viewed them as both backward and traitorous. Barry also bore the taint of the Mary Lily scandal, which had been widely reported in Northern newspapers just seven years earlier. For an insecure boy who craved acceptance, exclusion from Harvard's inner circle must have been a scorching humiliation, though, characteristically, Barry took pains not to show it.

He made campus dramatics his principal extracurricular activity and became so hungry for moments in the spotlight that he would take almost any role. He sang "Muddy Water" in blackface as part of a modern-dress production of *The Taming of the Shrew*. That led to an even more preposterous bit of casting as a turtlenecked football hero in *Brown of Harvard*.

On weekends there were debutante parties at the Somerset Hotel in Boston and drunken gatherings in Brattle Hall after Dramatic Club performances. The chief intoxicant was homemade gin, "a Prohibition concoction with raw alcohol for kick, glycerine for smoothness, and juniper drops for flavor"; to buy it, Barry sometimes sold his lecture notes to less studious classmates.

Though he did well academically and thought of himself as a hard-drinking jazz baby, Barry was emotionally immature. His writing, published in *The Harvard Advocate*, the campus literary magazine, was overwrought and hilariously revealing. In a short story called "White Carnation," a poor shopgirl named Molly meets a courteous, blond boy named John, who is "different" and clearly of a higher social and economic class. "John" bears a striking resemblance to Barry, of course, and the story mingles some of the Freudian sexual candor then in vogue with a sense of innate superiority that had been drummed into him since childhood; ". . . her love for John became more and more a sort of worship," went the overheated prose, "the worship of a more humble human for a young god too beautiful to dwell on earth."

Though they did not yet know each other, Barry and Mary were remarkably similar. Both were intellectuals, more comfortable with ideas and books than people, and afflicted with a sense of being different that caused them to lurch between uncertainty and arrogance. They were socially handicapped by their Southern background; both had escaped to college from dysfunctional families and chaotic, even traumatic, households, and were profoundly adrift, searching for a safe harbor.

There were also striking differences. Mary was a poor girl in a school that catered to the rich, totally lacking in experience with the opposite sex and unsure of her physical attractiveness and social skills. Yet in other ways she was uncommonly sophisticated. She had been alone, uncoddled, and independent since she had left her family and moved in with Louise Burleigh. Underneath the Tidewater accent and pale blond curls, Mary had a granite-like confidence that was founded on the twin pillars of her intelligence and her capacity for hard work.

Barry, on the other hand, seemed the very picture of self-assurance, but it was mostly a sham. He was wealthy and good-looking, with handsome clothes and savoir faire. While he knew he had brains, he was frightened that his spotty education would be found out at Harvard. His high-living background and trips abroad had given him a patina of worldly wisdom, but in fact he was almost as inexperienced as Mary, and considerably less self-aware.

She had struggled head-on with the obstacles in her life; he had maneuvered around his, avoiding pain rather than confronting it. He came across as a beautiful, smiling boy, a prince from Kentucky, full of joy and enthusiasm. Like some people who are gifted mimics or musicians, Barry had a natural talent for focusing on the positive. But his apparent good cheer was more dark and impenetrable than it seemed, luring people closer even as it made real intimacy impossible.

In the spring of their sophomore year, Barry Bingham and Mary Caperton finally crossed paths at a try-out for the Radcliffe Idler production of *A School for Princesses*. Mary came to the audition in Pittman Hall with her close friend Rhodita Edwards. Barry was among the many men who had pursued red-haired Rhodita, who was an upperclassman, but she had concluded that he was much too young for her.

Mary was in a crowd near the door when she looked up from her script and saw Barry standing by the fireplace. "That really is a lovely looking man," she thought. Rhodita introduced them and, for Mary, something stiff and unyielding suddenly gave way inside her. They both got parts in the play and Mary was astonished to find herself, for the first time in her life, unreservedly smitten. "I was at a loss from that moment. I fell madly in love with him then," she said.

—————

Ruby Newman caught a glimpse of the stunning young couple as they made their way to one of the small tables that encircled the dance floor at the Ritz Roof. Ruby, the orchestra conductor at the Roof, had not become the rage of Boston just because his baton could produce a snappy fox-trot. He was equally adept at coaxing crumpled ten-dollar bills out of the Harvard undergraduates who frequented the place. He knew what would entice this particular college boy with the slicked-back blond hair and elegant manners to drift casually by the bandstand later with a word of thanks and a generous tip.

Ruby murmured to the band and they shuffled their music. Then, at a wave of Ruby's arms, came the sensuous rhythms of "Bang on the Big Drum, Baby's Awake Now." As Ruby well knew after months of watching Mary Caperton and Barry Bingham dance together, this suggestive tune about a young girl's awakening to romance was "their song."

With Barry as her willing tutor, Mary pursued fun—pure fun—for the first time in her life. Often on weekends, they would travel to the Boston suburbs to visit their friend Harriet Owen, a self-proclaimed lesbian who loved watching her husband ply Harvard and Radcliffe undergraduates with drink. It all seemed very daring and sophisticated, this adult sense of thumbing one's nose at Prohibition. If the liquor gave out, the group would wobble out en masse to dig up more from the cache Harriet kept buried in the garden.

Until Barry, Mary had never really danced, much less drunk herself into a stupor. Now she was terrified that she had neither the looks nor the charm to hold him. And there was some competition. Her older sister Helena, who had parlayed her beauty into marriage to a rich Louisville stockbroker, told Mary that she should desist because Barry was the property of a friend of hers in Louisville. Mary curtly told her sister that she had no intention of retreating.

Mary did keep Barry as far away from her grasping mother as possible, however. In letters home, she never mentioned him. "I didn't want her to get into it," she said. She knew that Barry was just the kind of match her mother and grandmother had rhapsodized about, a man with nineteenth-century English-Southern sensibilities and lots and lots of money. The prospect of a son-in-law as rich and well connected as Barry would have sent her mother into a frenzy of plotting and scheming that Mary knew Barry would find vulgar, comic, and ultimately so repugnant that a lifetime connection with the Caperton family would be unthinkable.

In later years, Mary and Barry described their romance as a deep friendship that ripened into love. But it was more complex and bumpier than that. The essence of their rapport was an ability to fill each other's empty places: his orphan-boy's need for a strong, disciplined, adoring female; her yearning for a man who appreciated her intellect, was male without being frighteningly masculine, and made her feel financially secure.

From Barry's perspective, Mary was pedestal-perfect—a well-born Southern woman who, as he later put it, was "a combination of blond beauty and classically trained brains." Her inexperience made him feel grown-up and masterful, and she had a droll, dark humor that, like his, delighted in the absurd. They groaned in unison when a Harvard wit transformed the popular song, "Where's My Sweetie Hidin'?" into "Where's My Sweetie, Haydn?" and they raced around Boston together in the Stutz Bearcat, howling conspiratorially at any folly or foolishness they happened to find.

They were boon companions and best friends. "I do wish I could always be with you when anything ridiculous happens to me," Barry later wrote her. "I think just how you would laugh, and how we would nudge each other, and I can hardly stand not having you right there at the very moment."

By contemporary standards, theirs was a chaste romance. Radcliffe required girls to sign out on dates and be in by 10:00 P.M. Often, after a meal at the Splendid in Harvard Square, Barry and Mary would linger on the porch of her dormitory until the house mistress, Miss Field, tapped on the window to give warning and then cracked the door to say, "Ten o'clock, Mary dear." "We both were absolutely liberated and perfectly delighted with everything," Mary recalled. "[Barry] was so attractive and so handsome and so gay and charming—so buoyant and full of life and spirit and just perfectly adorable."

Mary seldom saw Barry's lonely, melancholy side—a side he consciously kept hidden from her. By the time he arrived at Harvard, he was proficient at Aunt Sadie's method of dealing with unpleasantness. He methodically focused on life's happy details: the way sunlight struck a leaf, the rhythms of Shakespeare, the ridiculous lyrics of a college drinking song. But beneath his frantic joie de vivre, Barry had convinced himself he was destined to die young, certainly before the age of thirty.

As a child, he had overheard doctors tell his parents that his lung ailment made a long life unlikely. His mother's early death and his own survival of the fatal accident had given him a sense that he was living on borrowed time anyway. He also believed it was possible to sense impending disaster; certainly, as Sadie had told him many times, his mother had quite correctly felt her own end looming. Barry was sure he had been given a portent of what was to come and, secretly, he resigned himself to an early demise.

The one person who knew of Barry's premonition was Francis Parks, his closest friend at Harvard. One night, after guzzling bootleg whiskey at a party, Barry and Francis talked for hours about how they expected their lives to unfold. "I want to live to be ninety years old," Francis said. "I have so many things I want to do." Barry confided his own ambitions: He wanted to have a child and to write and publish one book; then he expected to die. He was not particularly upset about it; thirty seemed far away.

Although he and Mary talked about almost everything, he never told her of his apprehension. He did not want to inflict the notion on her, he said, though no doubt she would have considered it a vital piece of information. To Barry, the prospect of a finite future made an elegant, if morbid, framework for his headlong pursuit of pleasure. Telling Mary would only lead to troublesome questions and dampen everyone's fun.

Besides, Mary had plenty of reasons already for fearing that her relationship with Barry would not end in marriage. Even as Barry complimented her on her perfect complexion and slim figure, the vast difference in their worlds was never far from her mind. They saw a great deal of each other, but Barry also traveled in elevated circles to which she had no access. Because of his wealth and his father's Boston connections, he was often invited to local debutante parties. Mary, needless to say, was not, and many nights she watched him toddle off in tuxedo or tails to a grand ball without her.

In the summers, to earn money, Mary ran a tearoom near Concord, New Hampshire, owned by her friends, the Pens. Mildred Pen, who lived in Cambridge and was an associate of Louise Burleigh, more or less adopted Mary, giving her clothes and the chance to make a few dollars baby-sitting. Mary ran the restaurant with typically uncompromising élan. "I had one menu," she said. "I gave them open-face tomato and mayonnaise sandwiches and devil's food cake, and if they didn't like that, they had to leave."

Mary was perfectly content to spend her summers in New England, especially since it allowed Barry to visit her freely, out of range of her family. But to Barry, New Hampshire was just one stop on a holiday circuit that usually included London, Paris, Geneva, and other gathering places of the idle rich. As Mary dryly observed, Barry would come to see her "just for a few days when he was not abroad or in California or somewhere."

―――――――

As graduation neared, it became clear to Mary that Barry was not going to marry her. She had arrived at Radcliffe with no ambition other than to enjoy learning. But after meeting Barry, she had pinned all her hopes on becoming Mrs. Barry Bingham. She was disappointed, wounded, and a little bewildered by his reticence to wed. Still, she had her pride and wisely never brought up the subject. Since marriage was clearly not at the top of Barry's agenda, the practical question for Mary became, "Now what?"

Ever since the Stutz Bearcat beckoned, Mary's studies had suffered. Even so, she graduated cum laude and her classics thesis was so impressive that she became the first woman to win a Charles Norton Fellowship for a year's study in Greece. Despite these honors, the Capertons did not come to watch her get her diploma. They claimed they did not have the money, even though a few months earlier they had contributed handsomely to a cousin's coming-out party at Richmond's swank Jefferson Hotel. Mary was relieved rather than angered; the Capertons did not belong in the world of Harvard and Radcliffe.

Barry, on the other hand, declared that he intended to stick with his before-thirty agenda and write a novel. Judge Bingham was displeased but forbearing, taking heart from the Harvard yearbook where, under his name, Barry had listed "journalism" as his future profession.

That spring, as Barry marched purposefully to commencement exercises, he, like virtually everyone else in the Harvard class of '28, saw a rosy future. The stock market crash was still over a year away and fortunes were being made overnight. "It looked as though the good times would never end," he said. "Some of my friends quite literally went out of college saying that before they were thirty years old they would be millionaires. They were going to go into the stock market and make a killing."

Despite his playboy antics, Barry managed to graduate magna cum laude, mainly by filling up his schedule with English and other subjects at which he excelled without much effort. Judge Bingham spared no expense marking this benchmark in the family's ascendancy. He glided into Boston on his yacht, the *Eala*, and invited Mary and the Pens to a luncheon onboard. There, for the first time, Robert Worth Bingham came face-to-face with Mary Caperton, a self-made woman every bit his equal in tough-minded determination.

To Mary's annoyance, Barry seemed eager to create the impression that she was just one woman among many he liked. She was hurt when he did not present her to his father as "his girl" and then ignored her at several of the graduation week festivities. When Barry and his sister, Henrietta, loaded their friends on the boat and sailed down to New London for the races, Mary was not Barry's date. Instead, she went with one of the secondary beaus she kept in reserve for the times Barry went to his Boston debutante parties.

The young man "got awfully importunate and I really was put to it to get away from him," she said. "He kept trying to get into my robes." Mary was obliged to take refuge on the yacht, where her standing with Barry was unclear. As the crowd cruised back to Cambridge, Henrietta, Francis Parks, Barry, and the others were in high spirits. But Mary surveyed the future and saw only one thing to be happy about: that Barry had promised to join her while she traveled to Greece to take up her fellowship. Perhaps during the summer their relationship would quicken, she thought. But then she shook her head. She was too brutally honest with herself to sincerely believe that was going to happen.

In later life, many of Mary's acquaintances found it hard to imagine that she had ever been giddy or flirtatious. She was usually so serious or wickedly witty. It was only with Sarah, her favorite sister, that Mary could be girlish herself. Sarah was twenty-four, one year older than Mary, and had been engaged to a North Carolina man who had died of a ruptured appendix just days before they were to be married. The death sent Sarah into a deep depression, and somehow Helena Caperton scraped together the funds to send her off on a European holiday with Mary en route to her fellowship in Greece.

In Paris that summer, Bricktop, the famous black jazz singer, was all the rage. Barry had come to know her on his many trips to Harlem nightclubs, and Mary was impressed that, night after night, Bricktop made a point of stopping at their table. "She was crazy about Barry," Mary said.

Sarah, though, was still mourning the death of her betrothed and felt too melancholy for club-hopping. When Mary would return bleary-eyed at dawn, her sister would crawl out of bed and into her arms, where she would weep for hours. When Mary finally set off for Greece, Sarah went back to the States. The last thing Mary saw as the train pulled away from the Paris station was her sister running up and down the platform, waving her arms and crying madly.

Mary spent those first hot nights in Athens trussed up in the anti-bedbug costume that she had brought at her mother's insistence. Each evening before bed, she would step into an enormous bag of pink flannel, then cinch it around her neck with a drawstring. At the top was a second bag of mosquito netting that went over her head.

Barry was not plagued by such inconveniences. In the clean mountain air of St. Moritz, Switzerland, he eagerly took up the routine of a writer's life. "I was holed up in a room, writing all day," he said. "Everything just kept pouring out and I wrote and wrote and wrote." He soon hit a block, though, and thinking that familiar surroundings might help, he came back to Asheville and lived in the same upstairs room in Aunt Sadie's house that he had inhabited as a child.

The Bingham Military School was all but abandoned by the time Barry returned. Colonel Bingham had died two years earlier, while Barry was at Harvard, and the school had never reopened. When a group of former students offered to buy the name and keep the school in operation, Judge Bingham had refused. But Aunt Sadie, Aunt Mary, and their families continued to live in the abandoned barracks and, as time went on, Bingham Heights came to resemble a windswept ghost town.

Barry's book, which he called *Battle in the Dark*, after a Walt Whitman quotation, was told from the point of view of a nine-year-old boy—precisely Barry's age when he lived in Asheville following his mother's death—and was loosely based on a girl who had worked for his aunt Mary. In the novel, a poor, illegitimate mountain girl has a baby out of wedlock. Deserted by the baby's father, she marries an older man who loves her but whom she does not love. Finally, she takes the baby and flees the unhappy marriage. "What happened to her after that was left hanging," said Barry.

The themes of shame and desertion, defiant pride and flight, certainly rang chords in Barry's life. In fact, he felt so strongly about the way the book ended that, when a British publisher agreed to bring it out but only if the faithless lover and heroine were reunited, Barry refused. No happy ending, he said. He tried unsuccessfully to interest American publishers in the work. Finally, the book, which Barry came to call his "turgid novel," was put in a drawer, where it remained.

Mary returned from her year in Greece in the summer of 1929 and, that fall, joined Little, Brown, the Boston publisher, working in the publicity department. She shared an apartment on Beacon Hill and spent her days writing blurbs for book jackets and persuading newspapers to publish reviews. "I was quite good at that, rather astonishingly," she said.

As a single woman, Mary's life-style was so modest that she barely noticed the stock market crash that October. Neither did Barry, but for different reasons: Judge Bingham had never invested heavily in stocks. He had paid cash for his businesses, had little debt, and a steady stream of profit from his newspapers. Compared with many, he was unscathed by the sudden collapse in prices.

Shortly after the crash, Judge Bingham took Barry to his Georgia hunting preserve, Pineland Plantations. Amid the yelps of golden retrievers, the conversation turned to Barry's future. The Judge had gone along with the novel-writing project; he had been patient. Now it was well over a year since Barry had graduated from Harvard. It was time for him to decide what he wanted to do.

Barry later maintained that his father did not pressure him into joining the family business. But he felt an enormous weight of expectation. He knew that if he did not take up his role as heir, it was highly probable that the Judge would eventually sell out. In many ways, Barry welcomed the prospect of working at the Bingham newspapers and WHAS, the radio station his father had started eight years earlier. True, it meant relinquishing some freedom and independence. But it also meant the chance to live a useful and interesting life, a comfortable and powerful life, and, most important, it ensured that Barry would continue to bask in his father's approval. "I [just] thought this is probably what I was going to do," he said, "not out of a sense of duty to my father necessarily—although that was a part of it, I guess."

Working for the Bingham enterprises, of course, meant living in Louisville, something his brother and sister had violently rejected. But Barry was more compliant and eager to please than either Robert or Henrietta. "I'm not a natural-born rebel as both of them were," he said, "and I enjoyed my life there." The deal was made. Barry would start after the Christmas holidays.

———

Barry began his career in January 1930 at WHAS radio, not at *The Courier-Journal* or *Louisville Times*. The choice had as much to do with station manager Credo Harris, the Judge's trusted friend, as it did with the medium itself. Bingham knew that his son was green and immature, and he felt confident that Credo would keep a sympathetic eye on Barry while he learned the ropes.

Barry settled into comfortable quarters in an Italian-style villa about a hundred yards from Judge Bingham's Melcombe mansion. The house had originally belonged to the daughter of a Louisville judge, and his father had bought it, along with the surrounding acreage, shortly after World War I. Because of its comparatively small size, the place came to be called the Little House, while Melcombe was known as the Big House. To make life more comfortable, the Judge assigned one of his English valets to wait on Barry in his new surroundings.

As the months passed, Barry wrote regularly to Mary, offering her hilarious accounts of life in the radio business but little in the way of passion. For one program, he was obliged to speak in a Negro dialect with a white woman "who brushes her hair with a toothbrush and is fat, hysterical [and] over-sexed. . . . She claims to have introduced Edgar Guest to the world."

In his off hours, he entertained guests in a manner reminiscent of his jazz-baby days at Harvard. When a cousin visited him at the Little House, "we went out on the town nearly every night, and grew so devoted to a road-house called Snyder's that we could hardly bear to miss an evening," he wrote. "One night we went tearing out there and . . . ate an enormous frog-leg dinner and talked as bad as we were able about everybody, and finally left after insulting all the other customers by howling at the way they danced."

His long-standing fear of rejection and pain kept Barry from showing any real emotion. Only occasionally did the mask fall and his need for Mary show through. When he left for a European vacation with the Judge and Aleen, Mary came to New York to see him off. "I miss you so intensely at night that I feel bitterly alone, almost as though I were lying in a grave," Barry wrote her from his stateroom on the *Mauretania*.

That fall, Judge Bingham moved Barry from WHAS to *The Louisville Times*, where he was assigned to the police beat. The press room at police court provided Barry with even more absurd material. He loved clambering into the paddy wagon for whorehouse raids and got so that he could remain unmoved when he saw "floaters"—dead bodies—dragged out of the Ohio River. To dispel the notion that he was just the boss's son, Barry sneaked swigs of moonshine with the horse race writers and after work piled reporters into his father's fancy car for trips to Tiger Jim's, a black nightclub. There, night after night, Barry and his companions would throw back drinks and listen to "Old Rocking Chair's Got Me."

———

Mary was growing angry and increasingly impatient. Despite occasional visits and a constant stream of letters, her college romance with Barry seemed to be wilting. "Barry would come see me in Boston but it was very unsatisfactory," she said. "I felt that our relationship was diminishing in a rather sad way. I began to be discouraged whether he would ever come to the point of proposing. I wasn't self-assured enough to feel that I really meant that much to him." She was bored at Little, Brown and watched with a mixture of envy and annoyance as Barry indulged in parties and the thrill of ambulance-chasing—all without her.

With characteristic firmness, she decided to take action. On October 29, 1930, exactly one year after the stock market crash, Mary wrote Barry and told him that she was quitting her job and going to stay with a friend in Paris. "I don't know how long I shall be abroad," she said. "My plans are very indefinite. I wish I could see you. I feel very far away from you and it makes me feel sad and strange. . . . I love you, Barry darling."

Barry admitted that her letter gave him the "most numbing sense of loneliness," but there was no marriage proposal, no plea for her to stay in the States. In November, Mary left for Paris, ostensibly to study French. Despite Barry's relative indifference, she wrote him in her typically frank and passionate way. "I feel that you are naturally and necessarily so engrossed in what you are doing that nothing else matters very much just now," she told him. "But I do hope you won't forget me . . . whether I am in Paris or anywhere in the world doesn't really matter because my inmost thoughts and my deepest feelings are always bound up in you, and do love me, darling, because I feel that I am really yours, and that I can't help it, but I hope that you feel something like this too."

The relationship could have gone on like that for years, or just evaporated, had it not been for the premature death of Barry's college friend Francis Parks. After learning that Francis had been killed in an automobile accident, Barry changed, almost overnight, from the feckless, callow youth he had been only a year earlier. He vividly recalled the night Francis had told him he wanted to live to be ninety. Now Francis was dead in the prime of his youth. Eerily, his fate was precisely the one Barry had expected for himself.

Barry felt he had been given a reprieve, a pardon. He had a new obligation to live life purposefully, to abandon his faith in premonitions in favor of a belief in the kind of cosmic arithmetic that would now spare him simply because Francis had died. Snuffing out two young lives would be too much. Fate and luck were not predictable anyway, he decided, and the thought freed him.

Besides, for all his talk of dying young, the finality of Francis's death scared him. "It was the first death of anybody of my generation," he said. "That feeling of mortality—it's frightfully difficult. I took it pretty hard." He felt profoundly lonely. Suddenly, having a partner and ally with whom to face life's uncertainties shot to the top of his list of priorities.

His letters to Mary became more sober, more worried, and more tender.

"I realize that I've been a troublesome lover, my dearest Mary, a very unsatisfactory one, and it may be that you have spoiled me with your unspeakably lovely sympathy and understanding," he said. "I have been such a damn fool on many occasions. I have had such growing pains and such flashes of a funny kind of wildness at times in these years. . . . I am looking entirely toward the future, and, God willing, we have hardly reached the beginning of a great love."

Delighted with Barry's sudden transformation, Mary was glad when, early in 1931, she took ill and had to come back to the States. Barry excitedly cabled back that he would meet her ship in New York. The small French steamer rocked horribly during the crossing, and Mary spent most of the voyage in a nauseous haze. But she forgot her troubles when the ship docked in the early afternoon and she saw Barry, handsome and fair, waiting for her with "his arms absolutely full of daffodils."

The couple raced out in the March mist for the Gypsy Bar, a speakeasy near the present-day "21" Club on 52nd Street. Over bootleg gin, Barry finally proposed and Mary instantly said yes. When they blurted out the news to the bartender, he opened a bottle of champagne and delivered a long, sentimental speech on love. They picked out a diamond at Tiffany & Co. that very day. "Despite all that has been written and said throughout the course of time, I consider that being in love is the most underestimated thing in the world," Barry wrote several days after the engagement was officially announced in Richmond and Louisville.

Helena Caperton yearned to stage the kind of dignified wedding for which the best families in Richmond were famous. But despite the absence of Barry's perpetually inebriated brother, Robert, the June 9, 1931, nuptials of Barry Bingham and Mary Caperton were neither quiet nor refined.

Guests of the groom and guests of the bride challenged each other to cockfights. Barry's best man, a Louisville boy and former Yalie named Bobby Carrier, drank so heavily that he fell down and cut his face. When he arrived at the altar, his head was wrapped in bandages. The night before, he had crashed a party Henrietta was hosting for the bride and thrown his shoe into the chiffon-draped masses, hitting one of Mary's friends in the bosom. Mary was just happy that her sister Helena managed to stay sober. Earlier that spring, at another family wedding, Helena had decided to bleach her hair, and when it had turned out green she had drowned her anguish in drink. The wedding party had arrived at the church to find her seated on the curb, drunk and sobbing.

Despite their social pretensions, the Capertons were unprepared for the Bingham way of doing things. On the day of the wedding, Barry ordered his valet to dress in white tie and tails and go to the Caperton house with a bottle of champagne. Because of his attire, Helena Caperton assumed he was a member of the wedding party and invited him in as a guest.

The wedding was far more opulent than the perpetually strapped Capertons could afford, but luckily Mary's patron, Mildred Pen, came through with a large check for the reception at Richmond's fancy Commonwealth Club. Helena Caperton's contribution was to slip a "Lily Maid"—a diaphragm—into her daughter's honeymoon luggage. "Dear, I'm putting this little . . . Well, you'll find it useful," she said awkwardly. Such was Mary's sex education.

The newlyweds spent their wedding night at an inn near Charlottesville, Virginia, and then traveled to Nantucket, a place they would one day come to avoid. On June 30, they set sail on the *Carinthia* for a cruise of Scandinavia and Europe. "Except at night in bed our life was not very different from that time we were together in Paris two summers before," said Mary. "It was so wonderful to be together." New brides often find it hard to adjust to having their mates close by all the time. Not Mary. She had waited for this moment for almost five years. "I was delighted to have my privacy invaded," she said with satisfaction.

THE FAMILY JEWELS

Barry and Mary came back to Louisville in October 1931 and set up housekeeping in the Little House. Barry wanted to resume his duties on the police beat, but his father thought it unseemly for his newly married son to be out every night chasing thieves and prostitutes. Reluctantly, Barry moved over to *The Louisville Times* copy desk and shortly thereafter became a general assignment reporter.

In 1931, newspapers in the United States were on the brink of change. The Depression had already sent many dailies into insolvency or persuaded strapped owners to sell out to thriving chains like Hearst. Overall, the number of papers in the country was shrinking. Of the seven dailies that had flourished in Louisville at the turn of the century, only three remained —*The Courier-Journal* and *The Louisville Times*, both owned by the Binghams, and *The Herald-Post*, bought by John P. Gallagher at a bankruptcy sale the same month Barry and Mary returned from their honeymoon.

The fiery, one-sided, personal style of nineteenth-century journalism was dying out; Horace Greeley, Charles A. Dana, and other singular voices were gone. With fewer papers, the ones that remained had to cover the news more objectively. At the same time, publishers found merchants disinclined to buy advertising—a source of revenue that now rivaled subscriptions—if their news columns offended large groups of potential customers.

The result was that newspapers were becoming blander, if arguably more responsible, institutions that were businesses as much as thundering editorial forums.

Judge Bingham personified this trend. Not long after he purchased the papers, a rival publication characterized him as typical of rich men who buy newspapers "to satisfy and to subserve an ambition. . . . The newcomers are convinced that money will buy anything." There was more than a smattering of truth in the statement, as Barry well knew. He was twelve when Judge Bingham took control of the Louisville papers, old enough to observe how his father used them to reward his allies, punish his enemies, and advance his pet political causes. As Barry grew older, he would nod in knowing agreement when family friends said that ownership of The Courier-Journal and Louisville Times was "better than a perpetual Senatorship."

The first power play Barry saw close up was with Henry Watterson, the legendary Courier-Journal editor who had agreed to stay on under Bingham ownership in exchange for the title "editor emeritus." Judge Bingham knew almost nothing about running newspapers, but he was smart enough to realize that Marse Henry, then seventy-eight, was The Courier-Journal's greatest asset. In April 1918, just months before the sale to Bingham, the old man had even won the prestigious Pulitzer Prize for his editorials.

Indeed, the irascible Watterson quite literally was The Courier-Journal. He had been instrumental in bringing about the birth of the paper, a merger of Walter Haldeman's Morning Courier and George Prentice's Daily Journal, on November 8, 1868. The date was three years to the day before Robert Worth Bingham was born, a coincidence not lost on Barry, who made much of the fact that his father and The Courier-Journal shared the same birthday. "It can lead one to believe that he and the paper were destined to come together," he said.

Soon after buying the papers, however, Judge Bingham and the crusty Watterson crossed swords over women's suffrage, an issue that by 1919 had generated enough support to be proposed as an amendment to the U.S. Constitution. Bingham's brand of Progressivism made him a staunch advocate; Watterson was unalterably opposed.

To Judge Bingham's distress, his new editor emeritus used his column in The Courier-Journal to lash out at the "feminine freaks" and "horsey girls" who marched down Pennsylvania Avenue for the vote. Bingham retaliated by publishing a long, unsigned editorial just three weeks after buying the papers that artfully reversed The Courier-Journal's earlier stance against suffrage. Men may find it hard to see "their goddesses in the role of ward-heelers or stump-speakers," said the article, but that "is a sentimental ground for opposition." From here on out, The Courier-Journal "is going to dance the 'Votes for Women' one-step . . . until the band plays 'Home Sweet Home.' "

The final break between Bingham and Marse Henry came not over suffrage, however, but the League of Nations. Though Watterson supported America's entry into World War I as an unavoidable necessity, at heart he was an isolationist. Bingham, on the other hand, was an ardent internationalist and a fawning admirer of President Woodrow Wilson.

In the winter of 1919, when the president hurried home from the peace conference in Paris to stump for the League, the Judge made every effort to help him. "Day after day we printed the truth about the League," he told Barry. "Day after day we printed the actual Covenant." Bingham also let his son in on a political trick. Knowing that country newspapers often had space to fill, he sent them preset type and graphics that could be popped into the paper with no extra labor. The material, which reflected Bingham's views, was usually published without alteration.

Even as Bingham-inspired editorials pleaded for ratification, Watterson's column denounced the League as "a fad" and a "petty conceit." Though the Judge did not try to muzzle Marse Henry, it was clear that *The Courier-Journal's* two-faced, for-and-against editorial policy could not go on indefinitely.

On April 2, 1919, Watterson offered his letter of resignation, which Bingham accepted with ill-concealed relief. With the old editor's departure, the paper became less personality-driven and noticeably more tame. "Watterson loved the Irish, the South, the Negro, the valiant, the oppressed, and the unequal," wrote one Louisvillian at the time. "Today *The Courier-Journal* has no loves."

That was perhaps an exaggeration, for the paper did reflect Judge Bingham's definite, often progressive, and sometimes self-serving views. But it was also true that the Judge, who took the title of company president, thought of himself more as a proprietor than a publisher. Except for those in top management, he had little day-to-day involvement with the staff at Fourth and Green, and the new blood he introduced to the papers' upper echelons arguably had even less journalism experience than he did.

It was these personnel shifts that led to Judge Bingham's second showdown, this time with Arthur Krock, the talented veteran who had recruited Bingham as a buyer. Before the sale, the Judge had led Krock to believe that he could keep his position as editorial director of both papers. But on the day he took over from the Haldemans, Bingham announced that his friend Wallace T. Hughes, a Chicago attorney for the Rock Island Railroad, would become vice-president of the company, supervising the publications' editorial and business functions.

To make up for the loss of his position, Bingham sent Krock to France to cover the Versailles Peace Treaty negotiations in the winter of 1919. It was a plum assignment and Krock won the French Legion of Honor for his syndicated dispatches, but when he returned to Louisville, he found that, in his absence, Bingham had diluted his responsibilities still further. No longer would Krock have anything to do with the prestigious *Courier-Journal*. Instead, he was made editor of *The Louisville Times* and given a seat on the new executive committee, which was, he acidly noted later, "that in name only." Krock considered the maneuver "unfair and unsavory" and remained with the Bingham papers only four more years. He eventually moved on to *The New York World* and later to *The New York Times*, where he won four Pulitzer Prizes.

While Bingham evicted journalistic giants like Watterson and Krock, he replaced them with men of more mercantile and narrowly political instincts, men whose value derived mainly from their personal loyalty to him. He put Gen. Percy Haly, head of the so-called Beckham wing of the state Democratic party, on his payroll as an adviser. He also placed his new general manager, Emanuel "Mannie" Levi, a young attorney who had worked with him in his law firm, on the board of directors of a local bank in which Bingham was a top stockholder.

Under Judge Bingham and his hirelings, the papers thrived on a steady diet of accident stories and syndicated features. "*The Courier-Journal* at that time was a sad little paper," said Molly Clowes, who then worked for a rival daily. "It was a most colorless thing, with the weirdest prejudices and curious columns." Stories such as "Child Weavers of Persia" appeared alongside "Afghanistan: Land of Deceptive Courtesy," "Ancient Blue Laws of Connecticut," and a joke column called "Grins and Groans."

Despite its idiosyncrasies, Bingham's *Courier-Journal* also took some courageous and unpopular positions. The paper had little sympathy for the xenophobic hysteria that gripped the country in the years following World War I, for instance. While Henry Ford's *Dearborn Independent* alleged that the Jews were plotting world domination, Bingham denounced any form of anti-Semitism. When the Ku Klux Klan burned a cross half a block from the mayor's home in Louisville, he lashed out at the organization, to which his own father had once belonged, as "un-American and un-patriotic."

The Courier-Journal also managed to score some reporting coups, one of which led to its second Pulitzer Prize. The winning reporter, twenty-one-year-old William Burke "Skeets" Miller, wriggled 125 feet down into a Kentucky cave to interview a dying man trapped under a seven-ton boulder. *The New York Times* gave the story eight full columns. Years later, Robert Penn Warren wrote a book about the incident.

Even while wallowing in misery at Middlesex, Barry had been aware that owning *The Courier-Journal* and *Louisville Times* gave his father automatic power and prestige as well as a vehicle for bringing about political change. He had seen firsthand how a newspaper owner could harness his personal wealth to the vast reach of a communications empire and catapult himself, and a cause, into the national spotlight. In Judge Bingham's case, that cause was tobacco cooperatives.

In 1921, Bingham had contributed $1 million of his own money toward the financing of a tobacco cooperative in Kentucky. His aims were partly altruistic: By pooling their product and sharing storage and marketing costs, tobacco growers for the first time had some protection against bad crops and plummeting prices. But the idea also made good business sense, because tobacco was a mainstay of the Kentucky economy.

To help put these new groups on solid legal footing, the Judge's associate, Aaron Sapiro, drafted legislation that became the model for cooperative marketing laws in at least thirty-eight states. Kentucky's bill, passed in 1922, came to be known as the Bingham Act. "I think it gave him more satisfaction than just about anything else he did," said Barry of the Judge's role in the cooperative movement.

The statement sounds odd considering Bingham's later distinctions in public life, but Barry knew how wounded his father had been by the gossip that accompanied his marriage to Mary Lily and the purchase of the newspapers that her death made possible. The success of the tobacco cooperatives, at least, was a free-standing achievement, something Bingham had done entirely on his own. "Like all human beings, I like to be liked," the Judge later wrote to a friend. "But above all . . . I must be respected."

The Judge's work with tobacco co-ops also introduced him to such financiers as Bernard Baruch, who wanted to consolidate farming to make it attractive to big business, and gave him valuable political contacts throughout the state. By 1924, he was under mounting pressure from Kentucky Democrats to run for governor. To their surprise, Bingham refused, saying he thought it improper for a newspaper owner to aspire to elected office. Barry applauded the decision and pointed to it frequently as proof that his father was unusually high-minded.

As with so many other aspects of his life, though, Judge Bingham had made a principle out of pragmatic necessity. According to at least one account, he yearned to be governor, but his powerful enemy, Louisville banker James B. Brown, would not have it. Perhaps more important was the likelihood that becoming a candidate would have allowed his enemies to dredge up the Mary Lily scandal and hamstring his papers politically.

Being a kingmaker, however, carried no such risks, and Judge Bingham enthusiastically embraced the role. Along with his salaried counselor, General Haly, he schemed, pulled strings, and made or broke candidates for state and municipal office, often using the news pages and editorial columns of *The Courier-Journal* and *Times* to shape and win races.

By most measures, he used his power for good, fighting the entrenched bipartisan combine that ran the state. If he satisfied himself that the ends were honorable, Bingham did not quibble about the means. For years he supplemented the salary of the state's well-regarded chief highway engineer because, under Kentucky's constitution, the man could only make $5,000 and was about to leave. The supplement effectively put a government official on the payroll of the state's most powerful publisher, but Bingham saw no impropriety, since the public benefited by keeping the engineer.

Although the Judge was a Democrat, he did not limit his papers' endorsements to Democrats any more than he had limited his own candidacy to a single party during his earlier attempts to win municipal office. Indeed, many of the Republicans he backed, like William B. Harrison, who served as mayor and later ran for governor with *The Courier-Journal*'s support, were forward-thinking politicians and good managers.

That mattered little in the state's charged partisan atmosphere. When *The Courier-Journal* editorialized against giving soldiers a one-time bonus from the U.S. Treasury for serving in World War I, a Democratic congressman from Kentucky railed against Bingham on the floor of the U.S. House of Representatives, calling him a "North Carolina mountain carpetbagger" and a "political hermaphrodite" with a "decided leaning toward the Republican Party."

Until Barry and Mary came back to Louisville in 1931, the Judge viewed such assaults less as a burden than a badge of honor. He scorned the corruption of Kentucky's Democratic party even while he maintained strong ties to the party's national organization. But that year, as Barry observed close up, his father's sour relations with state Democrats got in the way of his national political plans.

With a gubernatorial election scheduled in November 1931 and a presidential election in November 1932, the political winds in Kentucky were blowing at gale force. Herbert Hoover, a Republican, was unpopular with many Americans because he opposed federal aid for people thrown out of work by the Depression. For the first time in a decade, the Democrats felt they had a chance to recapture the White House. The governor's race in Kentucky was considered a stalking horse for the national election, and the state Democratic party was determined to win it.

Judge Bingham, however, supported the Republican nominee for governor, a move he knew was politically risky. "If the Democrats win here the group in power will want to 'punish' me," he wrote Col. Edward House, a former aide to President Wilson, a few days before the election. "If they lose they will blame their loss on me, and be very bitter. They will still control the State [Democratic] Committee and would seek revenge by fighting anybody in whom they thought I was interested."

When the Democrats swept Kentucky that fall, Bingham's backing suddenly became the kiss of death for any national Democratic hopeful, putting the Judge in a terrible bind. How could he publicly support New York governor Franklin Delano Roosevelt in his campaign for the presidential nomination, then just gearing up, without damaging the politician's chances in Kentucky?

At that point, Bingham's relationship with Roosevelt was only slight. The two had met briefly when Roosevelt was assistant secretary of the navy during Wilson's second term, but he knew intuitively that F.D.R. was an optimist and could help pull the country out of the trough of the Depression. As important, he felt certain that, like Robert E. Lee, Roosevelt was "a gentleman."

Soon after the gubernatorial election, Bingham sent General Haly to New York to confer with Colonel House about how best "to secure the Kentucky delegation" for Roosevelt. Almost as an afterthought, he included a $1,000 contribution "for pre-campaign expenses," admonishing House to funnel the gift to Roosevelt through Kentucky senator Alben Barkley so that his enemies in the state Democratic hierarchy would not know he was backing F.D.R. and, therefore, use Bingham's support to attack the aspiring candidate.

The amount of money Bingham eventually gave Roosevelt for his first presidential campaign has never been accurately determined; figures range from $5,000 to $50,000. Whatever the sum, it was sufficient for the Judge to be considered a member of what came to be known as the "pre-convention committee" or "Roosevelt Before Chicago," a group of about seventeen wealthy supporters, including Henry Morgenthau, Jesse Straus, and Joseph P. Kennedy. "That same year, everyone on the paper got a 10 percent pay cut because of the Depression," said John Herchenroeder, a *Courier-Journal* reporter at the time. "That didn't set too well."

Judge Bingham did not shed his cloak of secrecy until after the Democratic National Convention nominated Roosevelt in July 1932. But then he went all out. It was the first presidential campaign that Barry had seen up close, and he felt mounting excitement as *The Courier-Journal* published editorial after editorial for the Roosevelt-Garner ticket.

The general election campaign that fall was fevered and emotional. In Kentucky, many people considered Roosevelt a Socialist and the Judge did everything in his power to counteract such opinions. Working out of a temporary office in the Park Lane Hotel in New York, he formed a publishers' group to support Roosevelt and, on one occasion, wrote a scathing letter to the Associated Press, castigating the wire service for slanted reporting about the Democratic nominee.

In late October 1932, Bingham checked into Johns Hopkins Hospital to have an ulcer removed from his buttock, damage caused by excessive radiation administered years earlier as part of a treatment for neuroeczema. Days later, with the wound still fresh, he hurried back to Louisville to host Franklin and Eleanor when they arrived for a last-minute campaign stop. To his delight, the Roosevelts agreed to use his open car to transport them back to Union Station. As the vehicle made its way through the city streets, small clumps of well-wishers waved and cheered, and Bingham, physically uncomfortable though he was, swelled with pleasure.

Well before the election—indeed, well before Roosevelt was even a candidate—Bingham's name had been on a list of possible cabinet appointments in a Democratic administration. But as late as two weeks before Roosevelt's victory, Bingham told his old friend Shepard "Shep" Bryan that he had no desire for any kind of presidential post. "There are plenty of people who could hold up any cabinet jobs as well or better than I could, and who would probably want it, which I do not," he wrote Shep, then a judge in Atlanta. "I greatly prefer to stay on the outside."

Such protestations were, at best, a distortion. The Judge had set his sights on a position in the Roosevelt administration—secretary of state—and as soon as Roosevelt won, he prevailed upon Colonel House, his longtime friend and mentor, to promote him for the post with the new president-elect.

Bingham's friendship with "House the Mouse," as the short Texan was derisively known, had deep roots. Described by one historian as President Wilson's "alter ego," House had served as chief delegate to the Versailles Peace Treaty negotiations and had been a strong advocate of the League of Nations, a stand that made Judge Bingham a natural admirer and ally.

For years, Barry had watched his father cultivate House with lavish flattery and praise. Judge Bingham cheerfully reprinted his windy articles in *The Courier-Journal* and sent him letters brimming with obsequious compliments. "There is no doubt in my mind that you are the most potent individual force in the world today for peace, goodwill, understanding, for the actual preservation of civilization itself," he wrote House in 1925. And, seven years later: "I have never known you to be wrong about anything."

With such devotion as a foundation, Colonel House was only too glad to lobby for his friend with the new administration. On the strength of his recommendation, the Judge was one of the first people called to Warm Springs to confer with the president-elect in December 1932. But when Roosevelt finally announced his new secretary of state the following month, it was not Bingham but Cordell Hull, a U.S. senator from Tennessee. The Judge was disappointed, but he admired Hull and had privately hoped to see him selected for vice-president instead of John Nance Garner. Because of their mutual respect, and their bond as fellow-Southerners, Hull strongly urged Roosevelt to nominate Bingham as ambassador to Great Britain, which he did within days of the March 4 inauguration.

The appointment of a wealthy backer to a choice overseas post was hardly unusual. Jesse Straus, president of Macy's department store, got France; Josephus Daniels, owner of the Raleigh, North Carolina, *News & Observer*, was given Mexico. What was different about Bingham's selection, though, was that his political enemies publicly objected to it.

Abraham Flexner, whose brother, Jacob, had floated rumors of foul play in the weeks following Mary Lily's death, recycled the gossip now. After peddling the story to Bernard Baruch without success, he visited Secretary Hull, who promptly ejected him from his office. But Andrew Jackson May, a Democratic congressman from eastern Kentucky who was part of the state's corrupt bipartisan combine and no friend of Bingham's, gladly took up the cudgel on the floor of the U.S. House. A scant week after the nomination, he regaled his colleagues with a half-hour speech entitled "From the Police Court to the Court of St. James's." Mary Lily died under "mysterious and suspicious circumstances," he said, giving "Robert Worthless Bingham" the "filthy lucre" to buy *The Courier-Journal*, which he then turned into the "political harlot of the Republican Party" and the "Judas of the Democratic Party."

The resurrection of murder rumors was not the only reason the Senate Foreign Relations Committee decided to hold over Bingham's confirmation. To many, he was simply too pro-British—in his mannerisms, his loyalties, and his policies. For years, Bingham's papers had favored forgiveness of Britain's World War I debts, or, in the absence of that, a deal that would give the country the "longest time and the lowest rate [of] interest to which we can get Congress to agree."

The proposition made good economic sense. If the United States forced Britain to repay the funds in full, it would cripple one of the nation's best customers for wheat, cotton, tobacco, and retail goods. But many Depression-ravaged citizens felt differently. They saw leniency as unpatriotic and were not shy about expressing to Roosevelt their distrust of Bingham. "England has had about as much to say about running this country as the real Americans," one Chicagoan complained in a letter to the White House. "It should be possible to find some other qualified man."

Such protests did not hold up Bingham's ambassadorship for long. After he gave written assurances that he would faithfully represent the U.S. government on the debt question regardless of his own opinions, the Senate Foreign Relations Committee unanimously confirmed him on March 22, just two weeks after his nomination.

The move to England in May 1933 was in many ways Judge Bingham's triumphal final act of self-invention, but he was not really well enough to enjoy the experience. Although he gamely tried to ignore it, Bingham had been in failing health for years.

The allergies and skin disorders that had sent him to foreign spas and dermatologists as a young man were only the most visible manifestations of his grinding inner tension. As he had gotten older, Bingham had become plagued by migraine headaches, and often disappeared into his darkened bedroom for hours until the pain subsided. He had difficulty sleeping and his digestion was, at best, unpredictable.

During Bingham's four-and-a-half-year tenure as envoy to Great Britain, poor health crippled the possibility of any real accomplishment. Except for a spirited show of loyalty to Cordell Hull during the World Economic Conference in the summer of 1933, his record was marked by illness, frustration, error, long absences, and homesickness.

The British, however, seemed pleased with Bingham, a man they correctly sensed was sympathetic to their customs and national goals. The Judge in turn felt grateful that the British did not question his English antecedents or his qualifications as an aristocrat. Over the course of his ambassadorship, he received honorary degrees from Oxford, Cambridge, and the University of London—so many, in fact, that his critics accused him of being willing to travel any distance to add another to his tally.

Back in the United States, detractors complained that he was too much of an Anglophile and internationalist to protect American interests. In one speech before the Edinburgh Philosophical Institution, for instance, Bingham suggested that Britain and the United States stabilize their currencies by tying the dollar and the pound together. Furious, Hull cabled Bingham that the American people, still waiting for domestic prices to settle, were not ready for such a move.

Such stumbles did not endear the ambassador to the White House, where he was continually in bad odor for his long and frequent absences from the embassy. As a publisher and political kingmaker in Kentucky, Bingham had fashioned a life of freedom and ease. Now, well into his sixties, he was expected to account for every moment of his time. Under State Department rules, he was limited to two months' leave a year, but his shooting vacations in Scotland, lengthy homestays in the United States, and several incapacitations due to ill health ate up far more than that. From 1933 to 1936, he took a total of 337 days of leave—almost a third of his time on the job.

In letters to Barry and several close friends, Bingham revealed his growing disillusionment with the duties of an ambassador. He was especially distressed at the social tedium of the job, which included presenting Americans at court, hosting teas and dinners, and receiving an endless parade of visitors.

These functions also added to his financial burdens. In the wake of the 1929 stock market crash, Congress had been understandably reluctant to appropriate liberal living and entertainment allowances for U.S. ambassadors, most of whom were wealthy men anyway. By 1936, an ambassadorial allowance was only $4,500 a year. Any costs above that—even for official dinners, trips on embassy business, and diplomatic gifts—came out of an envoy's own pocket.

For the first time since Mary Lily's millions had made him a man of means, Bingham began to worry about money. He was often overdrawn on his account. When the embassy building needed repair, Bingham fretted that he would have to move out and rent a large house in London at his own expense.

Not every aspect of life in London was grim, though. On mornings when he was feeling up to it, Bingham would leave the palatial embassy at 9 Prince's Gate and go for walks in nearby Hyde Park. Early each fall, he traveled to Guthrie Castle, halfway between Edinburgh and Aberdeen, for several weeks of bird-hunting. He rarely spoke of the Irish part of his heritage. Instead, he spent hours writing to distant English relations in an attempt to nail down the precise nature of his British pedigree, and paid several visits to Bingham's Melcombe, the twelfth-century estate in Dorset for which his own Kentucky mansion was named.

One newspaper account described Bingham's time in London as "somewhat of a family reunion," and in many ways it was. With the exception of Barry, every member of the Judge's immediate family lived in England during his tenure. But it was hardly a cozy arrangement.

Robert, like Henrietta before him, had turned into an expatriate. In 1922, the Judge had helped form Standard Gravure, a company that began by printing circus posters and ended up producing rotogravure sections for *The Courier-Journal* and many other papers. Bingham's unfounded hope was that his oldest son would eventually run Standard. Robert went down to the office a few times but, as with so many other aspects of his life, the effort was halfhearted and he did not stick with it.

Soon thereafter, on a transatlantic voyage, he met a Scottish woman named Phyllis Clark. Barry, who shared a cabin with Robert on the ship, was dumbfounded when his older brother became smitten with Phyllis, who was "large, hearty, and not very attractive." They were married in 1927. The whole family went to Edinburgh for the wedding, including Barry, who served as his brother's best man. Barry endured most of the traditional hour-and-a-half Scottish Presbyterian ceremony in erect and solemn silence, but when the minister got to the part in which he declared that the couple was marrying in order to avoid "the sin of fornication," it was all Barry could do to choke back the laughter.

For a while, the couple settled east of Louisville on a small farm purchased by the Judge. But Robert never did much work on the place, preferring instead to live off the trust fund his mother and maternal grandmother had left him, and the $1,000-a-month allowance his father still willingly provided. His drinking problem became, if anything, more pronounced, and he smoked several packs of cigarettes a day. Phyllis was well aware of Robert's failings and overflowed with missionary zeal, at least at first. "She was going to reform him the way so many people think they're going to," said Barry. "Later on she was very abusive to my father because she said he had not really told her the extent of my brother's problems."

Boredom soon overwhelmed them both. In 1928, after less than a year in Louisville, the couple moved back to England and set up housekeeping in a little cottage in Buckinghamshire, near Chequers, the country estate of Britain's prime ministers. With the Judge's help, Robert bought stock in Carter Merchants, Ltd., an import-export business in London, and once again tried to launch a career.

When his father was appointed ambassador to the Court of St. James's five years later, Robert was furious. Bound to the Judge by money as much as affection, he had spent most of his life in open rebellion, alternately tormenting his father and avoiding his reproach. Now he would once again be in the older man's shadow, cast in the role of the child. He wanted desperately to stay out of the embassy whirl.

But there was little he could do to avoid it and soon, to his surprise, he became mildly enamored of the diplomatic high life. He and Phyllis danced at balls at Buckingham Palace and attended fancy dinners at the embassy; when F.D.R.'s mother, Mrs. James Roosevelt, arrived in England for a visit, Robert went with his father to Southampton to meet the ship.

His personal relationship with the Judge, however, remained predominantly financial. Robert continued to use his father as a blank check, often shamelessly. A summer cruise, additional stock in Carter Merchants, even an operation for Phyllis—no purchase was too large or too small, it seemed, not to require parental assistance. When Judge Bingham offered to buy his son a new car, Robert instantly angled for the deluxe model with leather upholstery.

As compliant as the Judge was about such matters, he was rigid when it came to the appearance of propriety, especially if the behavior in question had the potential to damage him personally. It did not bother him when Phyllis began spending most of her time in Scotland, leaving Robert to catch the train to Edinburgh every weekend. But when one of her male acquaintances moved into the spare bedroom with his girlfriend, Bingham put his foot down. He demanded that Robert tell the young man that he and his female companion had twenty-four hours to leave. "It might come out publicly that [Phyllis's friend] was keeping this woman in Robert's house," the Judge told Barry. "And I have my own interest to look after, as well as his."

Henrietta had less trouble pleasing her father, even though she conducted a rather obvious affair with tennis star Helen Hull Jacobs during much of her time at the embassy. At thirty-two, she too had yet to burst free from her father's magnetic pull, and was both attracted and torn by the prospect of following him to England. The Judge would not accept the post without her, she told friends, a statement they dismissed as typical Henrietta-like hyperbole. But for her the pressure seemed real. "She knew that if she went —it was sort of a premonition—that it would in a way be the end of her life," said John Houseman, who lunched with her in New York the day before she sailed. "I always felt strongly that she dreaded it, but I think the temptation to be the ambassador's wife—he was married but she was the one who was the top girl—[was too great]." In what may have been a last-ditch effort to save herself from her father, Henrietta asked Houseman to marry her. He refused.

Despite her misgivings, England proved to be a liberating place for Henrietta. She effortlessly recaptured her earlier niche in London society, hosting parties for the "Bloomsberries" at the embassy and skimming the glittering outer edge of the Prince of Wales's circle. She took a cottage at Long Crendon in Buckinghamshire, and motored there in her Bentley for the country's smartest weekend hunts. With the embassy as her stage set, she evolved into an even more mysterious and glamorous figure than she had been before, sometimes wearing a fedora and carrying a walking stick in a style suggestive of Marlene Dietrich.

Henrietta was indeed the "top girl" at Prince's Gate, outshining Aleen in every way—in the stylishness of her wardrobe, the sophistication of her manners, and, most important, in the certain knowledge of the special place she held in her father's heart. "The Judge was absolutely wax in her hand," said Mary. "You'd see her manipulating him. It was very painful to watch." Like an attentive beau, Bingham showered her with expensive clothes and jewelry; anything Henrietta wanted she was to have.

The rivalry between daughter and stepmother was obvious to anyone who cared to notice. It was Henrietta who planned the embassy's meals, from everyday breakfasts to opulent dinners. It was she who stood next to her father in newspaper photograph after newspaper photograph. Aleen, constitutionally unsuited to social warfare, signaled her surrender early on, and the Judge, characteristically, had neither the energy nor the will to defend his wife.

Aleen's position as second consort unavoidably took its toll, however.

One night, after an evening at the theater, she came back to the embassy to discover Henrietta in the midst of a dinner party with Noel Coward, Beatrice Lillie, and David Garnett. "You know I've no right to be here at all," Aleen said in a flustered voice. "Well, now that you've found your way," Coward responded with deadpan sarcasm, "I do hope we shall often see you here again." Garnett thought the playwright rather cruel—mainly because the essence of his comment was true. "The lady was a nonentity in her own house," he later wrote. "[She] would be overlooked and would rejoice that she was."

Perhaps because of her unthreatening subordination, Aleen became, much like house servants of earlier periods, the repository for Henrietta's most intimate secrets, including the fact of her lesbianism. Indeed, it was Aleen who invited Henrietta's lover, Helen Hull Jacobs, to stay at the embassy whenever she was in London.

Helen and Henrietta had met during the summer of 1934 at a reception for the Wightman Cup Team. By then, Helen, seven years Henrietta's junior, had already won the U.S. Women's Singles three years in a row as well as two U.S. Doubles championships. She would go on, in 1936, to win Wimbledon. Unlike Henrietta, who prided herself on her special brand of Southern charm, Helen was an unfettered tomboy. She once shimmied up the mast of an ocean liner in an evening dress and was matter-of-fact about her lack of interest in men. "Miss Jacobs isn't keen about the boys and says 'Maybe I'll never get married,' " *The New York World-Telegram* coyly observed.

Despite her public flamboyance, Helen was conservative at heart and, like most athletes, intensely self-disciplined. She rarely drank, enjoyed walking, bicycling, horseback riding, and other active pastimes off the court, and went to bed early. Her habits were a dramatic counterpoint to Henrietta's unstructured life-style, and as the relationship deepened, Henrietta found a stability and an inner peace she had never known. "I don't believe I've ever seen Henrietta so settled and happy," Barry wrote his father in the fall of 1935, when the two women were vacationing in Louisville. "She has been leading a wonderfully healthy life, playing tennis and riding every day and doing very little drinking."

Unlike so many of Henrietta's blazing affairs, the relationship with Helen was strong and slow burning. "Our friendship was a very placid one," Helen recalled. "We never fought over anything, nor did we have reason to." After a while, the pair settled into a comfortable routine. Each year, Helen stayed in London at the embassy through Wimbledon, then returned to the United States, where she had writing commitments and, for a time, designed sports clothes for Harrods and Izod. While she was in England, she would go with her border terrier, Scrap, out to Henrietta's cottage in Long Crendon for extended stays. On weekends, the Judge and Aleen would join them for small dinner parties and receptions.

Encouraged by her lover, Henrietta for the first time gave serious thought to establishing a permanent home in Louisville. Her dream had always been to own a horse farm and, on one of her stateside visits with Helen, she found just the location: a rolling rise of land outside Louisville, above Goshen, with a view that Barry considered "more magnificent than anything I had ever imagined existed on the Ohio." Judge Bingham sold some of his securities to purchase the place, and Henrietta christened it Harmony Landing.

Happy though he was at his daughter's changed demeanor, the Judge felt uneasy at the thought of remaining in England without her. His earlier disillusionment with his post had matured into an intense desire to go home that grew as his health worsened.

The Judge's homesickness was matched only by Roosevelt's mounting eagerness to replace him. In the spring of 1936, during one of Bingham's trips to Washington, Harold Ickes, F.D.R.'s secretary of the interior, dropped by the ambassador's suite at the Carleton Hotel for a glass of Kentucky bourbon. After the routine niceties, Bingham told Ickes that he wanted to return to the States "on account of the health of his wife."

It was a ruse, not a reason. Aleen had had an operation the previous summer, but the Judge had barely noticed it, leaving her to recover on her own while he sailed for a vacation in the United States. That night, Ickes made note of the conversation in his diary, adding that a candidate rumored to replace Bingham was Henry Morgenthau, then secretary of the treasury.

That fall, less than two weeks after F.D.R. won a second term, Bingham's political counselor, General Haly, went to New York for a confidential chat with Colonel House, who had recently talked with the president. House told Haly that Roosevelt had casually mentioned that Wisconsin Democrat Joe Davies, a multimillionaire and longtime friend of the First Family, was interested in the Court of St. James's. Reading between the lines, House asked Haly to deliver a message to Judge Bingham: send in your formal resignation, as all diplomats are expected to do after an election, but accompany it with a personal note asking for another year "to wind up the things you have been . . . doing in London."

When Barry got wind of the plan, he injected himself into the situation with uncharacteristic firmness. The shame of the Mary Lily incident had made him acutely aware of appearances. He knew that reputations could be made or broken overnight solely on the basis of how something looked. And how his father looked to others mattered a great, great deal to him.

He counseled the Judge to reject House's one-year solution as "weak and untenable." He feared that such a short extension would invite his father's critics to cavil that he had hung on only to attend the coronation of King Edward VIII, then scheduled for May 1937 despite scandalous talk of his intention to marry the American divorcée Wallis Warfield Simpson. Either come home immediately, said Barry, or remain indefinitely. "I hate the thought that the President would think you were only interested in staying there until after the big show was over," he wrote. "I can't stand the thought of your coming back . . . in anything except the strongest and most dignified way."

The letter had the desired effect. In labored tones, the Judge explained to Colonel House that he really did want to remain in London after all. To Barry, he sent a reassuring message: "It was a grand letter you wrote me, and I agree with you in every syllable of it. It is a Godsend to me that you do write me so frankly and so wisely." Maybe this fair-haired boy has the spine and political horse sense to be a good newspaper publisher yet, he told himself. The Judge could hardly know it, but it would be only a matter of months before Barry would be forced to find out.

COMING OF AGE

Despite his father's obsession with politics, Barry grew up with almost no interest in public affairs. So did Mary. In 1928, she had supported Al Smith, the Democratic presidential candidate, mostly because he was criticized for being Catholic and the irrationality of religious prejudice enraged her. But she had virtually no knowledge of Al Smith's views or Democratic party principles. Throughout the 1920s, her convictions, like Barry's, consisted of little more than a vague sympathy for outcasts and the needy.

The 1929 stock market crash changed all that. Although the Depression barely affected the Binghams, they could not help but be touched by the pervasiveness of soup lines, apple sellers, and the unemployed. For Barry and Mary, as for many other young, well-educated Americans, the beggar-liness of the era galvanized their belief in New Deal liberalism, a belief that would remain unshaken even decades later.

It took a personal brush with the poor, however, to turn them from sympathizers into zealots. The incident occurred late one October night in 1932, when Barry and Mary were in New York City visiting Judge Bingham, who was there raising money for F.D.R. After a champagne dinner and dancing at the Stork Club, they climbed into a taxi and headed for the 26th

Street pier, where the Judge had docked his yacht, the *Eala*. En route, the taxi stopped at a red light and a man in a beautifully cut but shabby suit approached the car. He stood on the running board, peered in and said in polite, well-spoken English, "I am hungry. Will you give me some money?"

Startled, Barry dug into his pockets and offered the man some change. "I'm afraid we were terribly frivolous," said Mary. "It just shocked us deeply to see this." Until that moment, she and Barry had dismissed the victims of the Depression as "other people." It had never occurred to them that highly educated professionals had also been destroyed by plant closings, bank failures, and other upheavals beyond their control.

Gen. Percy Haly was also a factor in the younger Binghams' political awakening. In the years before Judge Bingham became ambassador, Haly would often join Barry, Mary, and the Judge at the Big House for a breakfast of eggs and grits, along with spirited talk of local, state, and national affairs.

Mary took to such discussions as naturally as her husband—perhaps more so. Left to his own devices, Barry would have been content to be just a "charming, lovely, sweet, obviously bright person," as one Louisville friend put it. Few people felt that he was as serious or as fully formed as Mary, and even in later life Barry did not dispute the analysis. "I'm much more like a fast-running stream running over rocks with a lot of sunshine on it," he explained. "Mary is much more the kind of person [to have] deep pools in that stream."

From the moment she arrived in Louisville and moved into the Little House, Barry's carousing friends sized Mary up as a prim, disapproving schoolmarm. Bobby Carrier, the man who had aroused her ire by throwing a shoe at her bridesmaids, was one such person. When they were first married, he was a constant visitor at the Little House. Mary viewed him as ill-mannered and "not a good influence" on Barry. He was, she felt, a malignant Falstaff figure who appealed to the libertine in her young Prince Hal.

One day, after playing tennis, Mary went to her shower only to find Bobby already in it, sudsing up. He had no qualms whatsoever about commandeering their private bathroom. "That was the last straw," said Mary. "I told Barry that I really couldn't put up with it anymore. To me, he was unattractive, uncongenial and in our hair every minute." Barry did not fight it. Bobby Carrier—his best friend in Louisville—was effectively banished from the Binghams' social circle.

Mary also clashed with the city's female establishment. Her aristocratic Virginia accent and blue-stocking temperament gave her the appearance of being stiff and proud. She, in turn, found Louisville less refined than Richmond and rather dull. She was quite comfortable discussing family histories and the exploits of long-dead aunts and fourth cousins—a conversational mode she knew all too well from her upbringing. But local gossip bored her and she despised the Louisville custom of serving enormous Sunday dinners preceded by sweet Manhattan cocktails "that absolutely slugged you."

Mary's standing was not enhanced by her almost total lack of housekeeping skills. Soon after settling into the Little House, she invited the Judge and Aleen for an elegant meal, which she planned to cap with a bourbon-laced frozen mousse. When the moment arrived for dessert, she rang the small bell by her place to signal the next course, but no servants appeared. Minutes went by in pregnant silence with nothing but loud whispers coming from the kitchen. Finally, James Henry, the black waiter, appeared with his long arms sticking out of his white cotton jacket. He placed a little note in front of Mary that read: "Cream very soft and roony." Mary had put so much bourbon in the mousse that it had refused to freeze. The concoction eventually appeared and was hailed as a dessert soup.

The absurdity of the situation appealed greatly to Mary, who delighted in Judge Bingham's finicky alarm when the viscous confection was placed before him, Aleen's thinly veiled pleasure that something had gone awry, Barry's anxiety that his father was going to insult his new bride or vice versa, all topped by John Henry's perplexed and despairing note, laboriously printed on a tiny piece of paper. It was a wonderfully ridiculous scene. Unfortunately for Mary, she found many of the conventions—and people—in Louisville equally absurd, and showed it.

One of her few kindred spirits was Caroline Cox, an older woman who seemed to have more substance than the rest. She and Mary had met through the Thursday Club, a group of Louisville matrons, including Aleen, who gathered for luncheon once a month. When she felt she knew Caroline well enough, Mary ventured to ask what she knew was a heretical question. "What do married women do all day?" she said. "I get up and I do the ordering and do what has to be done in the house and then I have nothing more to do." "Well, my dear child," the older woman responded. "You have your garden, you're going to have children, and then there's always reading." But, Mary responded piteously, "there's so much empty space."

———————

Caroline was right about one thing: Mary was going to have children. The first baby arrived on Saturday, May 7, 1932—the day Burgoo King won the Kentucky Derby—and the couple named him Robert Worth Bingham III. That morning, Mary had been sitting quietly with Aunt Sadie on the lush green lawn in front of the Little House when she felt the baby coming. Barry, sick in bed with scarlet fever, could not play the role of nervous father in the hospital waiting room, so James Henry drove Mary into town, looking wild-eyed at the wheel.

Worth had arrived almost exactly ten months after their wedding. Barry and Mary were lax about family planning and their children came, as she delicately put it, "as the circumstances arose." "I was instructed by Aleen not to have a child too early," Mary said with a sigh, "but I slipped up. Things got beyond me." By the New Year, she was pregnant again.

On September 23, 1933, Mary had another boy. Barry wanted to name him Hugh Erskine—Hugh in honor of Dr. Hugh Young, Judge Bingham's great friend, and Erskine for an ancestor of Mary's. But Mary adamantly refused to consider any name but George Barry Bingham Jr. The baby had arrived in the wee hours, and Barry drove back to the Little House at dawn. "It was a particularly brilliant, crisp, cool, blue morning and the sun came up as I drove out the River Road, feeling sleepy and terribly happy and relieved," he said. "The condition of the weather seemed to me at the time an augury of the kind of disposition he might have."

By then, Franklin Roosevelt had been in office for half a year and the Judge had been in London for four months. The 1932 election had been a watershed for Barry. It was the first presidential campaign in which he had had a personal stake, mainly because of his father, and his nascent enthusiasm for the New Deal was fully aroused. Shortly after the inauguration, at the Judge's insistence, he worked as a reporter in the Washington bureau of *The Courier-Journal*, watching in fascination as Roosevelt's "Hundred Days" took shape and his father went through his troubled confirmation hearings.

Barry came back to Louisville several months before Barry Jr. was born, but he was on fire with Potomac fever and wanted desperately to return to Washington. Six weeks after the birth, he pressed Mary to leave both babies and accompany him to the capital.

The request was willful, self-centered, and perfectly in keeping with the upper-class English model of parenthood Barry had been raised to emulate. But he also had good reason to think Mary would accede. During Barry's first stint, she had felt few qualms about abandoning ten-month-old Worth to an old Irish nurse and taking up residence in Washington's Shoreham Hotel in order to be with her husband. Now that there were two infants to look after, however, she was "a good deal torn."

But Mary loved the larger world that Washington represented and loathed the prospect of her dashing young husband running around wifeless in the capital. After some discussion, she assented. "The fact that she had two small children at home might have deterred another person," Barry said. "But she was perfectly willing to turn them over to responsible people and come up there and be part of the life I was plunging into."

It was an exciting time to be in Washington. There was an intoxicating sense that the world was being remade and Barry felt fortunate just to be an observer. F.D.R. cultivated journalists from pro-Roosevelt publications, and twenty-six-year-old Barry Bingham soon found that he was one of a handful of White House correspondents invited to the Oval Office on a regular basis for informal group discussions. One day, Barry summoned the courage to ask about a bill pending in Congress. "Well, Barry, I think I can tell you . . . " Roosevelt began as Barry flushed with the thrill of being recognized. "There was an intimacy about it that was indescribable," he recalled later. "It was just the most delightful way to get baptized in big-time political reporting."

Barry became hooked on politics and spent hour after hour talking and thinking about it. But for Mary, confined to her suite at the Shoreham Hotel and worried about the children, time hung heavy. "We did a tremendous lot of going out to cocktail parties and dinners and things," she said. "I remember hem-stitching handkerchiefs for Barry during the day."

After seven months in Washington, the young Binghams decided to experience the world of international diplomacy that the Judge's new position made possible. In the spring of 1934, they gathered nurse and babies, packed their bags, and sailed for England on the *Majestic*.

While in London, Mary's distant cousin, Wallis Warfield Simpson, already notorious as the mistress of the Prince of Wales, invited them over for cocktails. Inside her Bryanston Square flat, Barry and Mary found the Prince holding court with what they considered to be the tackiest people imaginable. "The Prince had an unerring instinct for the most frivolous and indeed trashy Americans he could find," said Barry. "He plainly felt more at home with them than with his own countrymen." Barry was startled when Mrs. Simpson handed him a sugar cube and asked him to bite it in two. He obliged. She then dropped half of it into an Old-Fashioned and handed the glass to the Prince.

———————

In 1933, before sailing to England to take up his ambassadorship, Judge Bingham had promoted Barry from Washington correspondent to associate publisher. Barry knew his father wanted him to take over the newspapers someday, but he was also aware that the Judge thought him too inexperienced to be in charge after just three years' work, and so had intentionally left his role undefined. What his father envisioned was a long period of grooming, with Emanuel "Mannie" Levi, his general manager and right-hand man, instructing Barry on the premises—an idea that both teacher and pupil found highly repugnant.

Barry considered Mannie obsequious in the extreme, a trait that pleased the Judge, who mistook his aide's fawning sycophancy for loyalty. "Mannie was a real Uriah Heep," said Barry, referring to the forelock-tugging character in *David Copperfield*. Mary had a harsher assessment. "He was quite terrifying, like some Fagin or something," she said. "Really evil."

However, neither Barry nor Mary could argue with his success as a newspaper promoter. Under Mannie, the daily *Courier-Journal* had doubled its circulation to over 50,000 in the first five years of Bingham ownership, and by 1931 had doubled that again to 100,000. But the feat was due more to promotional gimmicks and Mannie's willingness to strong-arm advertisers than a concern for editorial excellence. "The story in the newsroom was that Mannie didn't even know where the city desk was located," said John Herchenroeder, who worked under Levi in the 1920s and 1930s.

While Barry had been growing up, attending Middlesex and then Harvard, Mannie had been Judge Bingham's chief lieutenant and surrogate son, managing the business with great independence and basking in his mentor's complete confidence. He was almost exactly Robert's age and had stepped into the role that naturally would have gone to Robert had alcohol and a lack of ambition not made the proposition out of the question. When Barry arrived on the scene as the presumed heir in 1930, Judge Bingham expected Mannie to take on the role of benevolent older brother, eagerly tutoring the boss's other boy in the family business.

Unsurprisingly, Mannie instead viewed Barry as his arch rival, a spoiled, undisciplined rich kid who, like his two siblings, had no stomach or aptitude for work. The prospect of sharing power with him while the Judge was in England was annoying at best, and made him uneasy. What if Barry tried to assert himself and jettison the apprenticeship role to which his father had assigned him?

Mannie took comfort, however, in the notion that if he waited long enough, Barry would tire of the routine at *The Courier-Journal*, move back to Switzerland with his new wife, and resume life as an aspiring novelist— subsidized, of course, by generous checks from the Judge. "It was his solid conviction that I would stay a while and then say to my father, 'You know, I really don't believe I want to do this after all,' and just drift away as my brother had done before me," said Barry. "He felt certain that he was going to inherit the mantle and . . . become publisher of the paper a short time after my father left."

Barry had no intention of letting that happen. He knew that Mannie had greatly underestimated him, and his father. Almost from the moment Judge Bingham left, Barry looked for an opportunity to mount a coup d'état. And when the moment came, he orchestrated it with considerable finesse and understanding of his father's foibles. It was exactly the sort of power play the Judge would have admired had he realized what was happening. Ironically, Mannie himself provided the opening.

In October 1934, a few months after Barry had returned for good from Washington, Mannie wrote Judge Bingham about a proposal to secretly buy *The Herald-Post*, Louisville's struggling Republican daily and the only rival newspaper in town. The idea was tantalizing. In one masterstroke, Judge Bingham could turn an obnoxious competitor into an ally and create for himself a position of unprecedented political influence in Louisville and Kentucky. Through *The Courier-Journal* and *Times*, he already wielded great power in Democratic circles. With the behind-the-scenes acquisition of *The Herald-Post*, he would have a clear, if hidden, hand in shaping the Republican agenda as well.

But the main attraction of the plan was money. Throughout the 1920s, *The Courier-Journal* had been locked in a fierce and expensive circulation war with *The Herald-Post*, offering pogo sticks, "Flossie Flirt" dolls ("with real hair just like Mamma's"), automobiles, and even a $10,000 model home as rewards for large subscription sales. The intense competition had eroded profits. With monopoly ownership, it would no longer be necessary to woo subscribers with such tricks. What is more, if the Judge owned all the papers in Louisville, he could raise advertising and subscription rates at will without worrying about a rival undercutting his prices. And with both the Democratic and Republican papers in Louisville locked up, large newspaper chains such as Hearst would find it financially infeasible to launch a competing publication.

Barry was unaware that Mannie was promoting this scheme. Two years earlier, Judge Bingham had entertained a similar plot to buy *The Herald-Post* and Barry had thrown cold water on it, declaring himself "stumped" at how the owner's identity could ever be concealed. To Barry's relief, however, that deal had fallen through and he had never given the notion a second thought. This time, knowing Barry's feelings on the matter, Mannie purposely kept the younger Bingham in the dark. Barry did not learn of the project until Judge Bingham was on the verge of signing documents to acquire *The Herald-Post*.

It was one of the pivotal moments of Barry's life. He knew that if the secret arrangement ever came to light, his father would be exposed as unprincipled and politically two-faced: a high-level appointee in a Democratic administration running a Republican newspaper. He would also look dishonest, financially greedy, and power hungry. The thought of such stinging criticisms triggered all the feelings of humiliation and disgrace that Barry had tried hard to bury ever since Mary Lily's death seventeen years earlier.

So, for the first and only time in his life, the normally acquiescent son defied his father. He was prepared to quit, he told the Judge, if the deal for *The Herald-Post* went through. "Unalterably opposed to entire plan," he said in a terse cable to the U.S. embassy in Britain. "Regard it utterly impossible in view of your official position. Feel so strongly would be unable to continue present work under those conditions." The missive had the intended effect. As soon as he received it, Judge Bingham placed a transatlantic telephone call to Barry and capitulated completely. "Greatly relieved," Barry cabled back. "Urge you tell Mannie as your own decision."

That same day, Barry sat down and composed a five-page handwritten letter to his father explaining in detail his objections to the *Herald-Post* plan. But first he soothed the Judge's smarting ego, using the techniques of flattery and false modesty he had learned from the wily politician himself. "I am pleased and proud that you accepted my opinion as being of value," he wrote. The sentiment was counterfeit and Barry knew it. His father was rarely afflicted with self-doubt. Indeed, Judge Bingham felt uncommon certainty about everything, from how his bed should be turned down to which candidate was worthy of political support. Barry was keenly aware that he had not changed the older man's mind; his father simply wanted to prevent his son from quitting.

Covering his tracks after getting his way was to become a pattern for Barry, who did not hesitate to wield power but preferred to cultivate the image of a charming compromiser. In fact, within the month, he would tell his father with a straight face that "I am completely undecided about the whole matter [of *The Herald-Post*], and I won't be able to make up my mind at all until I have talked it all over with you." Such solicitousness was calculated to make the Judge feel that he had not been whipped in a fight, but rather had come to a meeting of the minds with his son. Privately, Barry was not undecided at all; he was merely being politic.

Barry took extraordinary pains to make his case. "You have built up two splendid papers in Kentucky in the past fifteen years, through your energy and ability, and particularly through your complete integrity," he wrote the Judge. "If it should ever become public knowledge that you had operated a Republican paper, under a concealed form of ownership . . . I believe it would be absolutely fatal to the welfare of these newspapers. . . . Even if we run into the stiffest kind of competition . . . I would not be willing to buy immunity at the price of your taking a serious risk to your reputation."

Barry knew it was important that his father consider him reasonable and open-minded, because he wanted his criticisms of Mannie to be taken seriously. Mannie is "growing increasingly autocratic and dictatorial," Barry wrote the Judge. He "handles advertisers so roughly that he stirs up a constant ferment of resentment, and he has most of the employees here in fear of his harsh manner. Since you went away . . . his natural ambitions have expanded into a lust for power that is disturbing." Barry labored to

assure his father that he was "on the pleasantest personal terms with Mannie." But, he said archly, he did regard his state of mind as "not quite
normal."

Barry's chief complaint was that there was "not one policy of the New
Deal" that Mannie "does not condemn and decry," an especially embarrassing circumstance in light of the Judge's official position in the Roosevelt
administration. If Bingham were to buy *The Herald-Post* and put Mannie in
charge, Barry predicted, "it would be temperamentally impossible for him
to avoid using such an opportunity to crack at various Roosevelt policies."
What is more, he said, as a Republican newspaper, *The Herald-Post* would be
obligated to attack Neville Miller, Louisville's Democratic mayor, "whom
you practically put in office yourself."

By return post, Judge Bingham reassured Barry that he had "called off the
Herald-Post matter in any form, as I should defer to any strong opinion of
yours," although, he added, "I am not sure you are altogether right in this
instance."

The *Herald-Post* imbroglio taught Barry something positive about his own
ambition and power, and something negative about the Judge. Unavoidably, it darkened the rosy portrait he had always painted of his father,
although for public consumption he continued to describe him as a near-
saintlike figure who refused on moral grounds to build a newspaper monopoly in Louisville. "I'm sorry that he didn't see [the impropriety of the *Herald-
Post* deal] right away," Barry admitted many years later. "It's so strange. This
seems to give a distorted picture of my father, who has always seemed to
me a man of the highest principles."

———————

Successfully scuttling the acquisition of *The Herald-Post* gave Barry the confidence he needed to root out Mannie Levi once and for all, along with his
aide-de-camp, Howard Stodghill, the circulation director. The first opportunity to talk to his father about the matter, however, did not arise until
Christmastime, 1934, when the Judge and Aleen sailed back to the United
States on the *Empress of Britain*.

By then, Judge Bingham was already somewhat disgruntled with Mannie.
It was becoming increasingly clear that his son and his general manager
were on a collision course. What is more, only a month earlier, Mannie had
tactlessly insinuated that former governor J. C. W. Beckham, the Judge's
longtime friend and political ally, was unfit to run for office because he was
"a decrepit old man." The phrase had stuck in Bingham's craw. In a letter to
Barry, he huffily observed that Mannie's views demonstrated his "tendency
to prejudice and violence in some respects." Besides, he added, "Beckham is
almost exactly my age."

Mannie tried his best to make up for the gaffe. On Christmas Eve, when the Judge and Aleen arrived at Louisville's Seventh Street station, he arranged for the *Courier-Journal* drum corps to meet them and a fleet of motorcycle policemen to escort them to the Court House Square, where live Christmas turkeys were ceremoniously presented to the papers' newsboys. That night in his official diary, the Judge recorded that he was "much moved."

It was not until several days later that Barry got a chance to discuss how intolerable life was at the newspapers under Levi and Stodghill. The setting was Pineland Plantations, the Judge's 1,200-acre hunting preserve near Albany, Georgia.

Barry had wanted to ask his father to fire Mannie and Howard during their Pineland pilgrimage the previous year, but the Judge's old friend, Hugh Young, had urged patience. "Don't rock the boat," he had told Barry. "You're very young. You're inexperienced. And these men are old associates of your father's. Just try to get along." Barry had dutifully followed Hugh's advice until the *Herald-Post* flare-up. Now, in early January 1935, he felt the time was right to tell his father what was on his mind: He wanted a free hand at the papers and Levi and Stodghill out.

He got ample opportunity to make his arguments during the dawn-to-dusk shoots that were part of the Pineland routine. Early each morning, the Judge and his party left the wooden lodge and drove in a station wagon to that day's hunting spot, where fresh horses awaited them. Judge Bingham was the only man who did not ride. Instead, he took out after game in an open-backed, horse-drawn contraption that resembled a Roman chariot. The effect was imperial and slightly ridiculous, but Bingham had little choice. The skin on his buttocks had been painfully tender ever since he had had the ulcer removed from the area a month before Roosevelt's election.

The discomfort did not diminish his enjoyment of the sport. When the dogs spotted a covey of quail, came to point, and flushed the birds, he was always the first to make a hit. Indeed, his marksmanship was so expert that by the end of the quail season, he insisted on shooting only male birds. After a morning in the cool, sunny air, the men would regroup for a lunch of freshly killed quail grilled over an open fire. Though Barry had no taste for hunting, he marched out to the fields day after day to please his father. Mary did not shoot at all.

After cocktails and dinner, Barry, Mary, the Judge, and Aleen played bridge by lanternlight. It was then that Barry and Mary hammered home Mannie's many inadequacies: He was vehemently against the child labor amendment, a New Deal reform, because it might interfere with the use of newsboys, they said; he blacklisted locals who were "too liberal," keeping them and their activities out of the news columns; and he complained loudly and often about the Democratic mayor, giving aid and comfort to the Republicans. Judge Bingham listened patiently to the laundry list of sins but remained unconvinced. Mannie "has good qualities which are hard to see through his ugly exterior," he told Mary. "I want to keep him on so long as he is useful and can be endured."

It was not until February 3, 1935, that Bingham saw for himself how difficult Mannie could be. On that day, he and Barry met in Atlanta with Levi and Stodghill, at the latter's insistence. The agitated pair said they had just learned that a Republican banker friendly to Walter Girdler, proprietor of *The Herald-Post* since 1933, had managed to persuade five of Louisville's largest retailers to switch $50,000 in advertising from the Bingham papers to *The Herald-Post*. What is more, they said, the advertisers had pledged to boycott the *CJ & T* if the Bingham papers complained about the pact.

To bring the merchants to heel, Levi and Stodghill proposed refusing to renew their advertising contracts. The Judge was appalled at the stupidity of the suggestion. He knew such a move would invite retaliation from every Republican businessman in town. He and Barry instantly quashed the idea and instead called a meeting of all parties in the Judge's Louisville office that so mollified the advertisers that they backed down.

By the time Judge Bingham returned to England in March 1935, Barry had secured his father's permission to look around for a potential addition to management ranks. Convinced that something radical had to be done, Barry began contacting newspaper organizations and friends in the press, asking them who they thought might be right for Mannie's job. As the weeks went by, one name kept popping up: Mark Foster Ethridge, an outspoken New Dealer ten years Barry's senior who had started out as city editor on the Macon, Georgia, *Telegraph*. Ethridge had moved to the Associated Press and *The Washington Post* before taking charge at *The Richmond Times-Dispatch* in 1934 as publisher and general manager. Mary's sister Sarah, who made frequent trips to Richmond to see the Capertons, confirmed that Ethridge had performed miracles at the paper. Would Barry and Mary like to meet him, she asked? The Binghams eagerly said yes.

Early in the summer of 1935, Sarah gave a small dinner party to bring Barry and Mary Bingham together with Mark and Willie Snow Ethridge. The two men were stylistic opposites. Slim and dapper in his tailor-made suit, Barry spoke in the lilting, erudite phrases that instantly telegraphed "Harvard." Mark had never finished college. He was smallish and egg-shaped, with chipmunk cheeks and shaggy eyebrows. The blue eyes, however, were alert and friendly, and he moved around the room with decisive energy.

Mark had grown up with eight brothers and sisters in Meridian, Mississippi, a town near the Alabama border. Both parents were voracious readers and young Mark got plenty of encouragement to discuss ideas. Something his father, a lawyer, once said stuck with him: "Nothing that embarrasses anybody is ever funny." Mark always said that was why he felt constitutionally incapable of enjoying jokes at the expense of Negroes.

At forty, he was infinitely more experienced and confident in his views than Barry. He took the unusual position, for instance, that it was not his job as general manager to sell advertising. The object of a newspaper was news, he said, and profits were a by-product, like sparks shooting off a grinding wheel. He wanted to produce the most aggressive, thought-provoking newspaper possible. If that were done and done well, he believed, money would inevitably follow.

Barry was taken with Mark's philosophy, as well as his sincere Southern liberalism. He especially liked the fact that he had spent more than twenty years in the newspaper business. "He was the kind of person I knew could teach me more about journalism," Barry said.

As important, he sensed intuitively that Mark's expert management skills would free him from the day-to-day obligations of actually running the papers. Soon after Barry had started at the Bingham companies in 1930, he had confided to Mary that "the worst feature [of work] is the lack of time for the amenities of life, reading, writing letters and all that." Five years in Louisville had only reinforced that view. With Mark at the helm, he knew he could produce a great newspaper and still have time to pursue his many pleasures and interests. Barry was certain he had found Mannie's replacement.

For his part, Mark was pleased at Barry's New Deal convictions and impressed with the younger man's "great intelligence and . . . vision." He indicated that he would seriously consider an offer if one were made. The trouble was, with Mannie still in place, Barry had no job to give.

Luckily, Mannie helped accelerate his own ouster. Two months later, in August 1935, when the Judge arrived for a six-week stay at Virginia Beach with Barry, Mary, and the boys, Mannie greeted him with a renewed plea to buy The Herald-Post. The Judge refused, writing disingenuously in his official diary that it was "disappointing that he should even suggest such a proposition." The encounter prompted Mannie to pen a series of angry letters complaining that the Judge had lost confidence in him and no longer consulted him on important matters. The Judge snapped back that he had repeatedly demanded financial reports from Mannie that had never been produced. After six months of deteriorating relations, Mannie made one final, desperate gambit.

In February 1936, when Judge Bingham was in the States yet again for his annual hunting holiday, Mannie sent an urgent telegram saying he had to see him. There, in the Pineland lodge, Mannie said that he knew the Judge wanted Barry to succeed him as publisher at the papers. Given that, he said, he had no choice but to resign. Judge Bingham made no move to convince him otherwise. Instead, he wished Mannie well in his future endeavors, adding as an aside that he assumed he would not trade on his privileged position at the company by going to work for *The Herald-Post*. Rising up to his full height, Mannie allowed that he had, indeed, been approached by *The Herald-Post* and was seriously considering the offer.

The ploy was Mannie's trump card but Judge Bingham did not blink. He knew that Mannie hoped the prospect of his defecting to the rival news-paper would scare him into displacing Barry and maybe even compel him to sell Mannie stock in *The Courier-Journal*, something he had steadfastly refused to do. A few days later, his schemes exhausted, Mannie haughtily informed the Judge that he had decided to accept an offer to become publisher of *The Chicago Herald & Examiner*, a Hearst newspaper.

Barry was ecstatic. As soon as he learned of Mannie's resignation, he arranged for his father to meet Mark Ethridge. The Judge was as taken with him as Barry had been. "The more I talked to him, the more eager I became to have him come to the *CJ*," Judge Bingham wrote, "and when he left I felt that he was inclined to do so." Back in Richmond, Mark discussed the offer with his superiors and marveled at how different Barry and Judge Bingham seemed from "the sorry little newspaper" they were producing.

Judge Bingham's favorable impression was reinforced by President Roo-sevelt. Roosevelt had known Mark since 1925 when the two had met over dinner in Warm Springs, Georgia, where F.D.R. swam to relieve the effects of polio. Mark was working at the nearby *Macon Telegraph* at the time, and the paper's publisher and Roosevelt were old friends. Over the ensuing years, Mark had stayed in touch with the rapidly rising Democrat, who appreciated the panegyrics Mark penned to the New Deal in *The Washington Post* during the early 1930s. When Judge Bingham asked F.D.R. his opinion of Mark Ethridge, the president's response was instantaneous: "You couldn't do better."

By then, however, Mark had gotten a counteroffer, and was uncertain about coming to Louisville. He met again with the Judge in Washington and told him that the principal owner of *The Richmond Times-Dispatch* had agreed to sell him a 10 percent stake in the newspaper if he stayed. "I want to be a newspaper proprietor someday," Mark explained, "and this seems like a way to build the necessary capital."

The Judge told Mark that he could not offer him any stock in *The Courier-Journal* and *Times*; his plan was to pass all of it to Barry at his death "so as to put him in the same position that I had been in conducting the newspapers." Instead, he offered Mark a $24,000 salary, handsome by the standards of the day, and an unwritten promise to help him purchase his own newspaper later on. As long as Mark remained in Louisville for "a reasonable period" of time—at least five years—and taught young Barry the ropes, he said, he would lend him $150,000 "on very easy terms" for the acquisition of a paper. The proposition struck Mark as fair and he agreed to start work as general manager of *The Courier-Journal* and *The Louisville Times* in late April 1936.

On the same day that the Judge and Barry offered Mark a job, they interviewed a slender, thirty-four-year-old banker named Lisle Baker for the position of company secretary. General Haly had spotted Lisle in Frankfort, Kentucky, and recommended him to Barry as a person who could bring economic and financial sophistication to the Louisville newspapers, something the Judge, Barry, and Mark definitely lacked.

Lisle was a native Kentuckian, born in Monticello, a small courthouse town near the Tennessee line. He graduated from Centre College in Danville, Kentucky, and attended Columbia University before starting a banking career in the state capital at Frankfort. There, General Haly, a client, quickly detected in the taciturn young man a rare combination: banking acumen and politically progressive views. By the time Barry asked him to come to Louisville for a talk, Lisle held the position of cashier, director, and trust officer of the State National Bank. He knew nothing about journalism, but he liked the sound of what Barry said he hoped to create: a great, liberal, Southern newspaper. On April 1, 1936, just three weeks before Mark's arrival, Lisle began functioning as secretary of the Bingham company.

With Mark and Lisle in place, life at *The Courier-Journal* and *Times* was transformed. The books had been left in a shambles and Lisle in his methodical way set about imposing order. By the fall of 1936, he had prepared a precise analysis of the company's financial status. The neatly typed sheets and ledgers were revolutionary to the Judge, who had never really known how much his business was generating or costing. So confidence-inspiring was Lisle's approach that Barry quickly asked him to become the family's private financial counselor, a position of total trust.

Mark's first concern was newsroom morale, which had suffered greatly under Mannie's rages and dictums. The word went out: Blacklists are a thing of the past; the general manager's door is always open. Mark's special gift was his ability to forge personal relationships, from the top of the staff to the bottom, and he took pains to cultivate reporters. He liked working with people directly and ignored the accepted protocol of going through editors, who did not seem to mind because he treated them, too, with respect and warmth.

The new breezes blowing through the newsroom extended to advertisers as well. One of Mark's first acts was to hold a reconciliation banquet for over seven hundred local and regional businessmen. While the guests rustled in their seats in the ballroom of the Brown Hotel, the Judge, home once again from London, rose to introduce Barry and then sat back down. As he listened to his son talk, he had "such a large lump in my throat I was afraid I wasn't going to be able to introduce the next speaker."

The growing tenderness between father and son was apparent in their letters, which now began with "dearest" and ended with "devotedly." The Judge was proud of his dutiful, adoring son. Barry, in turn, basked in his father's confidence and approval. Both men seemed delighted to be getting, finally, the emotional sustenance for which each had yearned.

As if it had been preordained, in late October, just six months after Mark's arrival, the struggling *Herald-Post*, the paper Judge Bingham had once called a "putrid excrescence," finally shut its doors for good. The Bingham organization benefited by picking up "Popeye," "Blondie," and popular syndicated columnists such as Walter Lippmann and Walter Winchell. There was "an audible cheer all over town," Barry told his father wryly, "when we restored that God-awful Popeye to his frantic audience."

To Barry, life at that moment seemed splendid indeed. He had his own managers in place, men he could trust. The despised Levi was gone and Stodghill had just recently left for a job in Philadelphia. And now, with the death of *The Herald-Post*, his papers had unfettered power in a market that only promised to grow in prosperity and influence. To make everything perfect, the Judge was talking with increasing frequency of returning from England once and for all so that he could hunt, play with his grandchildren, and act the part of elder statesman while his son ran the family business.

Barry's sense of calm equilibrium was soon shattered by the Louisville Flood, a catastrophe that put the Bingham-Ethridge-Baker team to its first real test. The rain began on Christmas Day, 1936. On New Year's Day, 1937, the forecast was for more rain. On January 6, it rained a full inch in Louisville, and the next week brought such torrents up and down the Ohio Valley that "the rain-soaked earth yielded water from the lightest footfall like a squeezed sponge." By January 13, the Ohio River was up three feet; a week later it had surged eighteen feet, and before the month was out it crested at forty-one feet above its normal level. Louisville had no flood control reservoirs and no levees. There was nothing to keep the swollen river in bounds. The deluge was Louisville's greatest recorded natural disaster.

In mid-January the sewers became backed up with river water, and soon the whole downtown and much of the low-lying residential area looked like a surreal Venice. *Life* magazine dispatched Margaret Bourke-White to shoot pictures of the catastrophe. Drinking water became scarce. Over 200,000 people had to evacuate their homes and some two hundred died, mostly from pneumonia. The mayor, Neville Miller, declared martial law and, in an attempt to bolster the city's soggy spirits, handed out buttons that said "I Dare You to Catch Me Not Smiling."

Mark worked the newspapers like a general under assault. Reporters congregated on the dry upper floors of the *CJ & T* building, composing their stories by kerosene lamp and sleeping on cots. Publication of *The Louisville Times* had to be suspended, but Mark arranged for *The Courier-Journal* to be printed in neighboring towns and then delivered to Louisville via a network of passable roads. Crowds gathered to await the newspaper trucks, which dropped twine-tied bundles at designated spots. At the flood's peak, *The Courier-Journal* consisted of just four pages, one of them blank, but the paper never missed a day.

Barry had the critical job of running WHAS. Radio was the only source of information for most of the stricken Ohio Valley, and it was used for disaster relief as well as for news. Hour after hour Barry stayed at the microphone, intermittently yelling "Send a boat! Send a boat!" when he had information about the precise location of flood victims.

During the day, Mark and Lisle caught a few hours' sleep at the Seelbach Hotel; at night, the women on the staff took the beds. Barry, however, drove each evening over dry back roads to the Little House, where Mary was in the final stage of her third pregnancy. On Friday, January 22, she shook Barry awake and told him she had to get to the hospital immediately. Before Barry could get dressed, Loubelle Retter, the gardener, appeared at their bedroom door. "Mr. Barry," he said, "the back road done wash out."

By then, Mary's water had broken. While she dressed, Barry and Loubelle threw wooden planks across the hole where the road had collapsed. Then the couple tumbled into the car and Barry, with Mary beside him clutching his arm, drove in a great rush across the planks. Even in this most desperate of situations, Mary's Montague breeding shone through and she sat primly on the seat, teeth clenched, in a stylish dress and hat. As each lurch of the car rattled her swollen body, however, she became more and more uncomfortable. "We'd go down a street and then you'd see the water and we couldn't get through," she said. "I finally said, 'Do you think I could take my hat off?' And Barry said, 'Of course, darling.'"

They abandoned their original plans to go to a hospital in downtown Louisville, and instead headed for Baptist Hospital, which was on a little rise at the east end of town. When the car pulled up, the head nurse whisked Mary onto a stretcher and clapped a cone of chloroform over her nose. But the entourage never made it to the delivery room. Sarah Montague Bingham was born in the hospital elevator. Barry and Mary called her Sallie.

Barry was so thrilled to have a baby girl that he took the unusual and expensive step of telephoning his father in London. After giving birth, Mary lay in her room and began to regain consciousness. As she struggled up out of the fog, she heard an eerie, disembodied voice that seemed to come from the sky. It was an airplane with a loudspeaker on its wing. The pilot was slowly circling the neighborhood warning residents to take typhoid shots.

Three days later, Judge Bingham called Secretary of State Cordell Hull and asked permission to come back to his flood-stricken home. Mary was still in the hospital when he arrived and although he was thin and clearly in poor health, the Judge insisted on parading up and down the hall with his tiny granddaughter in his arms.

He found Louisville to be less devastated than he had feared. The flood, in fact, had engendered a kind of defiant pride and community spirit. When the worst of the emergency was over, Mark composed a full page ad with an upbeat headline—"The Sun Shines Bright On My Old Kentucky Home" —and ran it in *The New York Times*, *The Herald-Tribune*, and *The Wall Street Journal*. The ploy was meant to bring national advertisers back to *The Courier-Journal*, and it worked.

From Judge Bingham's perspective, the flood's greatest tragedy was the loss of his old friend Percy Haly. The aging politico kept an office on the third floor of City Hall and during the disaster chased up and down the stairs constantly. On one of these trips he suffered a heart attack. In mid-February, after several days in the hospital, he died.

Judge Bingham helped make arrangements for the funeral, which was to be held in Frankfort. And then, awash with the conflicting emotions stirred by his granddaughter's birth, Haly's death, and the natural cataclysm, he sat down and wrote a long, rambling letter to Margaret Mitchell, author of the new best-seller, *Gone With the Wind*.

The letter was sentimental and overwrought, but in many ways it was the Judge's benediction, the final cry of a man who, as his own end approached, found himself haunted by the Old South that ultimately defined him despite the personal metamorphosis he had struggled all his life to achieve. "I do not thank you for *Gone With the Wind*," he wrote, "I bless you." He told Mitchell of his father's suffering in the Civil War, of the poverty and humiliation of Reconstruction, and of his mother, who had seemed so much like Melanie. "They were saints, both of them, my mother and Melanie. They were great ladies, as my grandmothers were, and they both glowed with an inner fire, a spiritual fervor, which illuminated them and all around them."

He concluded the letter in high emotion. "To a voiceless people, you have become the voice. In behalf of a people not only tortured and robbed, but cynically and cruelly maligned, you have told the truth. . . . You have done a service . . . most of all for us of your own South, for us who would be worthy of our tradition of calm, unflinching courage, of dignity in the face of any tragedy, of honor to the end, of chivalry and who, striving to live up to our heritage, would have it pass in its entirety to those who come after us."

The following day, the Judge decided he was too worn out to go to Haly's funeral and instead left immediately for Pineland Plantations. Barry and Mary did not go to the service either. When they learned of Haly's death, they were in Florida vacationing with their two boys and the newborn Sallie while electricity was restored to the Little House. Barry felt great guilt at not returning for the funeral. In his father's absence, he had grown extremely close to General Haly, and the old pol had treated him like a protégé. For the rest of his life, a small, framed photograph of Haly hung in a place of honor on his office wall. It had been taken by Margaret Bourke-White during the flood, just days before his death.

———————

Early in the summer of 1937, Barry and Mary went to England to visit the Judge and found that his earlier eagerness to leave the embassy had become an urgent determination to return home. The cost of the post was oppressive, he said, and he yearned to play the role of doting grandfather.

The birth of his grandchildren had brought out a protective streak in the Judge. When a wealthy woman was kidnapped less than a mile from Melcombe, he dashed off a hysterical letter to Barry ordering him to hire bodyguards and a "trustworthy" chauffeur ("preferably a white man"), and to carry a "short barreled revolver, of the type which I always carry when I am at home." Except for the gun, Barry dutifully followed his father's instructions.

The Judge had stayed on for the coronation, not of Edward VIII, who abdicated to marry Mrs. Simpson, but of King George VI. For the occasion, he had even donned the requisite silk knee breeches that one of his predecessors, Charles G. Dawes, had refused to wear because they made him look "like some damned jack-ass." But now he wanted to return to Louisville and enjoy his final years with his family. He told Barry that he had written Colonel House about the matter, informing him that he hoped he could retire—"with full honor and dignity . . . of course"—the following December.

That fall, he took a short vacation with Barry and Mary at the Greenbriar in White Sulphur Springs, the mountain resort where Mary Lily had composed her will more than twenty years earlier. There he took steps to make legal his plans for succession at the newspapers.

In public, the Judge made a show of being fit, but in private he had grown increasingly hypochondriacal. His appetite had fallen off and he had more and more trouble sleeping. Several doctors had examined him, including his friend Hugh Young, but they could find nothing wrong. "I hope you'll discourage him from taking his temperature all the time," Hugh wrote Mary before the meeting at the Greenbriar. "It's very bad for him to be so obsessed by his health."

On the hotel's broad white porch, a group of Louisville lawyers, including Barry's childhood friend, Wilson Wyatt, presented the lengthy will and trust documents that they had been working on for months. An earlier will had divided Bingham's estate into thirds, leaving Robert, Henrietta, and Barry equal amounts of stock and property. The new document made Barry the sole inheritor of all the stock in the family businesses, reaffirming the Judge's belief that a newspaper should be controlled by a single proprietor. It also left Barry the Big House, the Little House, and all the grassy acres at the Bingham compound.

Barry did not lobby for the consolidation of power, though he knew his father wanted to reward his steadfastness and felt that Robert and Henrietta had proven themselves incapable of running the business. "I can't say it was a surprise," he said, "but I certainly did not anticipate that he was going to do this to such a clear-cut extent."

Under the terms of the will, Robert and Henrietta were left no stock in the Bingham companies. Instead, until their deaths, they were to receive $15,000 a year each in income, generated by equal blocks of preferred *Louisville Times* stock that Barry would actually own. Henrietta also got free title to Pineland Plantations and Harmony Landing, her horse farm outside Louisville. Robert, who had borrowed heavily from his father during his lifetime, simply had his debts forgiven.

The most brilliant and complicated part of the will was a scheme to reduce the size of Judge Bingham's estate for tax purposes while creating a flow of income to pay the premium on a $500,000 life insurance policy he had taken out on himself, with Barry as the chief beneficiary. The instrument came to be known as Trust #9. It left a substantial block of stock in the family companies, in trust, to Barry and Mary's born and unborn children. While Barry and Mary were alive, dividends from the stock went to them, with the understanding that the money would be used to pay for the insurance policy.

The Judge signed his will on September 30, 1937, and three weeks later sailed back to England. In less than a month, however, he felt too ill to go on and cabled Secretary of State Hull that he intended to enter Johns Hopkins Hospital immediately for tests. "I've had a hard time," he told Hull by telephone on November 17. "If I can get a rest—a little rest—I feel I will be all right."

Despite his age, sixty-six, and the chronic nature of his illness, the Judge acted as though the trip were just another routine visit to the States. He brought several new guns and fishing rods with him and, when Barry came to Baltimore for a visit in early December, he spoke with keen anticipation of the house party he hoped to have at Pineland Plantations after Christmas. "He told the doctors that Georgia was the only medicine he really needed," Barry recalled.

Still, the Judge knew he had neither the energy nor the inclination to go on with his official duties. On December 8, he sent his resignation to President Roosevelt, paving the way for Joseph P. Kennedy to become his successor. Several days later, after exploratory surgery, Bingham slipped into unconsciousness. Hugh Young, who had been bedridden himself with pneumonia for several weeks, made it to Johns Hopkins just in time to witness his friend's final hours. "As I bent over him, saying 'Bob, this is Hugh,' a faint smile crossed his face and he gurgled some reply," he said, "but I fear he did not recognize me."

Soon, Robert Worth Bingham was dead, the victim of Hodgkin's disease, a slow and insidious form of cancer diagnosed after an autopsy. Although the Judge had been in pain only toward the end, the postmortem showed that every vital organ was almost eaten away. At his bedside were his beloved sister Sadie, Barry and Henrietta, and Aleen and her son by her first marriage, Byron Hilliard.

Only Robert was absent. When Barry had finally realized that the Judge was seriously ill, he called him in England and suggested that he come home at once. But Robert was reluctant. "Must I really?" he asked plaintively. "It's going to be very difficult for me." Barry was at first aghast, then grateful to be spared Robert's alcoholic binges. "Well, maybe you'd better not," he told him.

The New York Times put the news of Ambassador Bingham's death on the front page. President Roosevelt provided his special railway car, the "Maryland," to transport the body from Baltimore to Louisville, where it was met by Kentucky governor A. B. "Happy" Chandler and taken immediately to Calvary Church. There, where young Bob Bingham and Eleanor Miller had exchanged wedding vows in 1896, the casket lay in state as staffers from *The Courier-Journal* and *The Louisville Times* filed respectfully past.

The Judge's oldest friends—Dave Davies, Shepard Bryan, and Hugh Young—joined Marvin McIntyre, F.D.R.'s secretary, and Ronald Lindsay, the British ambassador to the United States, at the funeral, which began with the comforting cadences of the Twenty-third Psalm. During the service WHAS radio went off the air for three minutes as a gesture of respect. The flag at the capitol in Frankfort flew at half-mast.

Though he had never been in uniform, the State Department arranged for Judge Bingham to be buried with military honors. Eight army sergeants from nearby Fort Knox carried the casket from the church to the hearse. When the car arrived at Cave Hill Cemetery, 160 soldiers and 6 officers stood at attention on either side of the road, then presented arms as the coffin was borne past. Finally, Robert Worth Bingham was laid to rest next to his first wife, Eleanor, whose gravestone, at his direction years earlier, had been inscribed with the words, "Loveliest and Most Beloved."

For days, tributes poured into Louisville from cabinet members, Kentucky politicians, and the thousands of everyday citizens who read Bingham's two newspapers or listened to his radio station. On December 23, some seven hundred British notables, including Foreign Minister Anthony Eden, attended a memorial service for Bingham in Westminster Abbey. Robert and his wife, Phyllis, made a special point of going.

Except for that single gesture, however, Robert reacted to his father's death much as he had to his mother's: with seeming indifference. Henrietta, on the other hand, was inconsolable for months. Helen Hull Jacobs said it was the only time she had ever seen her cool, detached lover in a highly emotional state. Though nearly thirty-seven, Henrietta was still a daddy's girl, dependent on her father for financial and emotional security. After his death, she gradually slid into a life of alcoholism and idleness.

Mary appeared strong and stoic, but the Judge's death had no less impact on her. Clifford Caperton had been so weak and ineffectual that she had come to view the Judge, with his firmness, money, and charm, as a kind of idealized substitute father. "I was devastated," she said. "I felt that my whole world was so shaken. I could not imagine what life would be like without him."

Of them all, Barry was the most disconsolate and adrift. "I not only felt green with grief from losing this devoted parent," he said, "but I felt that my anchor in my business life was being removed. I had always counted so much on Father's advice and sympathy."

Two days after Christmas, the Judge's will was filed for probate. His estate was valued at $4,625,000 and Barry was admitted as executor. Although the document essentially disenfranchised Robert and Henrietta, they expressed no objection—at least not at the time. Because the will was signed just three months before the Judge's demise, they could have contested it on the grounds that it was written "in contemplation of death," but they never considered a legal wrangle. "Neither my brother nor my sister had the smallest interest in running these operations and didn't want to live in Louisville above all things," said Barry. Years later, however, Robert's resentment would grow so inflamed that he could not bring himself to speak to his younger brother or even to be in the same room with him.

A VERY
SATISFACTORY LIFE

Sitting in the office that had once belonged to his father, the new president and publisher of the Bingham media companies contemplated his future. He was fearful, bereft, and a bit overwhelmed. He was also, at thirty-one, a man of breathtaking wealth and power. *The Courier-Journal* and *The Louisville Times* were now Barry Bingham's newspapers, free and clear, but he was unsure precisely what that meant. For years, he and his father had spoken of their shared ambition to produce the finest newspaper outside of New York. The Judge's will had even included some high-minded language characterizing the papers as "a public trust." Now it was up to Barry to make all that a reality.

His first move was to write President Roosevelt a note of thanks for the honors he had accorded the Judge in death. "[My father] has bequeathed me no heritage so important . . . as the devotion to the cause of true and enlightened liberalism, which you exemplify in the world today," Barry wrote four days after the funeral. "If there should ever be any service that the papers or I personally could perform for you, I am at your command." The president responded by issuing a vaguely worded invitation to "run up to Washington" for a talk sometime, adding that when he had read Barry's letter, he had had "a feeling that Bob, himself, might have helped you pen it." Like it or not, Barry was still very much in his father's shadow.

In those first years after Judge Bingham's death, Barry struggled, tentatively at first, then with increasing confidence, to assert his power as the
heir to the Bingham companies. It was not easy. Since Mark's arrival in
1936, Barry had served without complaint as a sort of sorcerer's apprentice
to his new general manager. Though technically his superior, Barry almost
always deferred to Mark's judgment and looked up to him—and Lisle,
too, to a lesser extent—as a mentor and older brother. Over time, the three
men had become a close-knit triumvirate, with Mark focusing on advertising and news, Lisle on contracts and finance, and Barry on the editorial
page.

But Mark's dominance was apparent. Soon after Judge Bingham's death,
former Kentucky congressman John Young Brown found out that F.D.R.
was on the verge of contacting Barry about an important political matter in
Louisville, and took pains to reroute the White House to Mark. "My information," Brown said, "is that the one that really controls the situation . . .
is the President's friend Mark Ethridge . . . [not] Barry Bingham."

Barry's paper, too, was really Mark's in those early days. During the first
four years of his tenure, Mark introduced some eighty changes, including
easier-to-read type, new makeup, the practice of continuing page-one
stories to the back page of the section, and a weekly news summary called
"The Passing Show." He boosted salaries, installed Jimmy Pope, a feisty
fellow-Georgian, as managing editor of *The Courier-Journal*, and dramatically
increased the space for news.

His most ambitious start-up project was a locally edited Sunday magazine, produced by *The Courier-Journal* and printed in color on Standard Gravure's rotogravure presses. Soon other papers around the country followed
suit with their own Sunday supplements and Standard Gravure, the perpetual weak sister of the Bingham operation, was deluged with hefty printing
contracts. "[The Sunday magazine] not only did a lot for the paper, it did a
lot for Standard Gravure," Lisle recalled. "It was a double-barreled type of
decision."

The news columns often reflected Mark's P. T. Barnum-like flair for promotion. To attract readers, he found out when every little town had its
Mule Day or Tobacco Festival and then "covered the hell" out of the event.
To help establish Louisville as a shopping mecca, he brought high school
seniors from the surrounding countryside into town every spring for a tour.

With the help of the Works Projects Administration, Mark also got a six-
week opera going in the summer and, in the fall, brought big names like
Rudy Vallee and fan dancer Sally Rand to Louisville in an effort to attract
customers to the heavily advertised downtown clothing sales. These moves,
Mark said with a satisfied smile, were "all for the betterment of Louisville,
and incidentally, for the financial betterment of the advertising department."

If Barry's professional standing remained uncertain, his home life was very "satisfactory," a word that in the private language of Barry and Mary reverberated with meaning. Because of their wealth and social position, they were able to fashion a world in which love, work, and play came together in perfect harmony. Most days began the same way. They arose a little before eight and had a leisurely breakfast on trays in their bedroom. Barry arranged to have two copies of *The Courier-Journal* delivered to the house and they read them in comfortable silence while Mary ate her egg in bed and Barry took his on the chaise longue.

The newspapers anchored their lives, giving them a sense of purpose as well as money, power, and prestige. As she sipped her coffee, Mary turned the crisp, wide pages, reading carefully and critically. Often she broke the morning hush to comment on a statewide political race or a bill before Congress. This quiet hour in the morning became the best time for the two of them to talk about the papers' policies. Should we endorse him? What should a *Courier-Journal* editorial say on this? How should we cover that?

Barry usually left for the office about nine, dressed in the fine suits and diamond stickpins of a stockbroker. Like his father, Barry took great pleasure in clothes. He bought his shirts at Turnbull & Asser, the London shirtmaker, and had his shoes custom-made at Maxwell's. He instructed the servants to keep his summer clothes and winter clothes in separate closets. He hated to be rushed about sartorial decisions and carefully laid out the next day's suit, shirt, and tie each night before he went to bed, delighting in the supple feel of the fine cloth.

On Sundays, the schedule ran a little later and breakfast was particularly sumptuous: brains and eggs, sweetbreads and bacon, or some other delicacy. But always, there was a schedule. Barry and Mary agreed that the regularity of hours had an aesthetic appeal all its own, rather like orderly rooms and clean fingernails.

In the early years of their marriage there was plenty of time for intimate dinners and amateur theatricals, activities that almost disappeared from their lives later on. Barry and Mary were still jazz babies in many respects, and loved to make pilgrimages to Manhattan. "In that day it was fun to go to New York, go to the theater, see friends," said Mary. "We knew quite a lot of people in that sort of crowd."

"That crowd" included Harold Guinzburg, publisher of Viking Press, and his wife, Alice, whom they had met at a party in London and instantly recognized as kindred spirits. Mary considered Jews superior in every way and often shocked Louisville hostesses by saying that she yearned to be Jewish. She was particularly mesmerized by Alice's face, which she considered the embodiment of aristocratic Hebraic beauty, "as if she were David's daughter or something."

The Binghams' New York circle also included Alexander Woollcott, the Algonquin Roundtable wit whose waspish nature made him the model for the demanding houseguest in *The Man Who Came to Dinner*. He owned a seven-acre island in the middle of a Vermont lake, and during weekend house parties there he took Mary as his croquet partner. Together they would stumble over a course that was "nothing but roots and hills."

Woollcott returned the visits with maddening frequency. "[That] was really very onerous, because when he came to stay, he required your undivided attention," said Mary. "Children must be done away with. Every minute he wanted you to sit and talk to him and he never wanted to walk anywhere. . . . One morning early I heard a terrible cry from the guest room and rushed to see [what was the matter]. He had sat on a frail Italian chair—he was very fat—and had broken it into pieces. And instead of being apologetic, he said, 'I'm going to sue you!' . . . He felt we were a Southern curiosity."

The Binghams' privileged lives were complemented by the daily demands of their growing brood. For Barry, the children were another source of delight, another blessing among so many. He loved reading aloud to them at bedtime, and even grew sentimental about toilet training as he stood patiently over Worth and Barry Jr. in the bathroom, running water to inspire their efforts.

To Mary, childbearing and child-rearing were the duties of a good wife, and she set out to be one with the same determination she had applied to classical Greek at Radcliffe. In her view, the primary purpose of a parent was to instruct, correct, discipline, and guide. That kind of love, she felt, was infinitely more demanding and difficult to maintain than the unconditional affection conventional mothers offered.

Like most women of the era, Mary accepted children as a responsibility that was principally hers, but she did not feel a natural affinity with them. "One's children do not seem to me to be as much a part of one's own inner and personal life as one seems to move on the periphery of theirs," she once wrote Barry. "Their very dependence upon you and the whole condition of being a parent makes one into an adjunct, or a secondary kind of creature. . . . I hope I am a conscientious and reasonably adequate mother, but I can't believe I have a real talent for being one." In her mind, the duties of parenting were subordinate to what she often referred to as her "real life"— the time she spent alone with Barry.

In the twilight of their lives, Barry and Mary would wonder whether their children's natures were more the product of heredity or environment. Yes, being reared Binghams, with all the opportunities and freedom that meant, could not have helped but shape each child, they said. But that was really secondary to genetics. Barry and Mary firmly believed that their offspring were essentially the people they were going to be from the moment they arrived on earth.

Like the ancients, hungry for reassurance, Barry searched for omens on days of great importance. It had seemed a good sign that Worth was "made," as Barry and Mary liked to describe it, at the Napoleon Hotel in Paris while they were on their honeymoon. For him to be born on the day of the Kentucky Derby also suggested luck.

Barry Jr. was conceived over the 1932 Christmas holidays in the cool air of Pineland Plantations, another pleasant memory. "We had had one of those tremendous dinners with all kinds of quail and *lots* of wine," recalled Mary. "Barry and I went out for a walk to get rid of the fumes from dinner. . . . And that was when that happened."

Sallie was started on or about the first day that her godfather, Mark Ethridge, went to work at *The Courier-Journal*, a day that Barry eventually came to look upon as one of the luckiest in his life. But she was born during the flood of 1937, the worst natural disaster in Louisville's history, timing that he came to view as darkly portentous.

Given Worth's stormy disposition, it is a wonder the Binghams had any children after him. In his early years, Worth was moody, petulant, and difficult. "He had terrible fits and tantrums and throwing himself on the floor," said Mary. "A very strong temper."

In keeping with the common wisdom on child-rearing, Mary decreed that children should be fed and "aired" at fixed times, and she sometimes woke Worth up to push a bottle into his mouth. But he revolted against schedules. Being put in a playpen for his obligatory airing absolutely enraged him, and he shook the bars violently, screaming for release. After one particularly frenzied protest, Mary freed him from the pen and he bashed his head against the marble floor until blood ran from his nose.

Barry Jr., sixteen months younger than Worth, was more acquiescent. He thrived on Mary's stringent rules, and his equable nature triggered in his father a surge of recognition. "I always felt it very strongly with him," said Barry. "I'm not saying I was more fond of him than I was of any of the other children. I was fond of all of them in different ways, but I just felt from the very early stages of his life a kind of natural bond between him and me. . . . I guess he was a little bit more dependent on me, perhaps, than the other children." On the family's weekly trips to Calvary Church, that dependence was obvious. Worth always walked with Mary; Barry Jr. fell in beside his father. "There was just that feeling of a kind of natural sympathy which is beyond analysis," Barry said.

When the boys were very little, picking up marbles with their toes each night to prevent fallen arches, the Binghams thought that the dark-haired, brooding Worth would be a lifelong introvert and inept at games, while the bubbling, golden Barry Jr. was sure to be the family's social lion and star athlete. Worth did not even look like a Bingham, they pointed out, while "Baba" had the white, Jean Harlow-like hair they had had when they were children. "Worth was a more interesting child," said Mary, "and Barry was a more lovable one."

But by the time they were of school age, it was clear that Worth would be the dominant personality in every respect. He matured into the all-American boy, a gregarious, elegant athlete who fearlessly struck out in new directions. Barry Jr. adored his older brother and, in return, Worth became his fierce protector. Once, when a little boy pushed Baba aside and snatched one of his toys, Worth pummeled him to the ground. Even at this young age, the filial relationship became set: Worth was the leader, Barry Jr. his happy, passive acolyte.

Worth's virile brand of leadership was alien to his parents, who had both been solitary and cerebral children. They considered him "conventional"— the same dull word they often used to put down Aleen. Barry Jr., however, was "unusual," an adjective of high praise.

As important, Barry Jr. shared his parents' delight in the ridiculous and had a facility for off-beat observations. "He was very amusing as a child," Mary said. "He saw things . . . as we did, more than Worth." The Binghams found it charming when Baba, then three, spurned a flaming plum pudding one Thanksgiving because, he said, it might "set his insides on fire."

At eight, he composed a rhyme for his father that went, in part, "Way down South in the land of cotton, / Take of [sic] your shoes and your feet smell rotten . . ." The family had not seen such verse since Barry had rhapsodized about soaking his privates in the tub during one of the Judge's birthday theatricals. It was such lighthearted moments as these that caused Barry to think of his second son as a "merry little boy."

Barry Jr.'s native cheer flagged soon after he started classes at the nearby Ballard School. Ballard was technically part of the county school system, but it was also heavily subsidized by wealthy Louisvillians who wanted their children to get a state-of-the-art education. Attracted by sizable salary supplements, instructors from Columbia Teachers College and other incubators of excellence flocked to Ballard, where the approach was unstructured and progressive. Ballard did not teach reading using the traditional phonics method, for instance, in which sounds are associated with letters and then words are sounded out. The progressive model then in vogue was "look-say," a system in which each word was learned as a whole.

Mary would later speak bitterly of Ballard's newfangled ways, insisting that the school's reliance on the look-say method was responsible for Barry Jr.'s severe reading problems. Whether that was the cause or some form of dyslexia, it was clear soon after Barry Jr. arrived at Ballard, where Worth had enrolled a year earlier, that he was not learning to read. Humiliated by his halting attempts to keep up with the other children, he quickly changed from the happy-go-lucky boy his parents had known to the oafish class clown. As his misery compounded, he comforted himself with food, growing chubby, pale, and withdrawn.

Since Barry Jr. gave no evidence of a physical handicap, his teachers simply thought him lazy and urged him to work harder. Barry and Mary even speculated that he might be slow, a curse in a family that prized books and intellectual pursuits. Barry Jr.'s effort to read became his earliest and longest battle, one that colored his adult life as much as it tormented his childhood. Barry and Mary briefly considered sending him to a psychiatrist, but concluded that since his problem was not mental or emotional, the sessions would do no good. Barry was particularly empathetic because of his own experience as a childhood outcast. "I feel so deeply identified with the dear creature that it baffles me to be unable to fathom this strange difficulty under which he labors," he wrote Mary.

Worth was four and a half when Sallie was born, Barry Jr. almost three and a half. They soon dubbed her "Miss Priss" because she was so finicky. Sallie's age and gender kept her outside her brothers' long-established confederacy and she came to look on them as royalty might look on barbarians. They were not entirely uninteresting to her, but they were definitely inferior.

Even as a tow-headed toddler, Sallie was curiously introspective and self-sufficient. Her dreams were frighteningly vivid and she often woke up howling. The nightmares were so dramatic and recurred with such regularity that Mary came to suspect that they were consciously staged events, though she could never be sure.

During her waking hours, Sallie inhabited a private world fashioned by her rich imagination. In her daydreams, she was not the spindly and nervous little girl who passively suffered the ill-natured teasing of her older brothers. In her mind, she was a beautiful heroine, the romantic center of titanic struggles and maelstroms of emotion.

While Mark improved *The Courier-Journal* and *Times*'s news coverage and bottom line, Barry led them into controversy, a stance made possible, in part, by his wealth. "I really did not feel courageous," he said. "But I did feel that I was protected from economic deprivation as a result of the positions I took." To give other opinions an outlet, he inaugurated a policy of running every letter-to-the-editor that was not libelous, and started an opposite editorial (op-ed) page, which carried a wide range of thought.

Barry's liberal beliefs and activities were frequently out of sync with Louisville's conservative mainstream. One Easter Sunday readers were stunned to see a full-page ad for the National Committee for Planned Parenthood in *The Courier-Journal*. "The first key to strong national health—BIRTH CONTROL," the ad said. "Think what that means! A race that is vigorous, healthy, happy and self-reliant—the real hope of Democracy." On one side of the page was a list of sponsors for the ad and at the very top was the name of the newspaper's publisher, Barry Bingham.

The city's large Catholic population considered the ad a "deliberate assault on our cherished principles" and threatened a boycott of the paper. Hundreds canceled their subscriptions. A grand jury was convened to find out whether the ad amounted to "an invitation to abortion," then illegal.

But Barry did not back down. Instead, he offered readers who had canceled their papers a refund on the unused portion of their subscriptions and explained *The Courier-Journal*'s position in a strongly worded editorial. "Those objecting to the paper's conduct seem to think a newspaper should not have an opinion which a number of readers do not like," it said. "This would mean that a newspaper would have no opinion at all." Such stands made the heir to Judge Bingham's media empire a figure of controversy and scorn, but not of hatred. "They thought I was a naive New Deal fool who took his positions without fully realizing their implications," Barry said.

The hate was soon to come. Barry lit the fuse himself in 1940 when he selected Herbert Agar to be editor of *The Courier-Journal*, a title that, at the Louisville papers, meant supervision of the editorial page, not the news columns. Agar was a brilliant writer and spellbinding orator who had won the Pulitzer Prize for history in 1934. But he was also committed to "agrarianism," a redistribute-the-wealth idea that many conservatives considered communistic.

Although Barry was in awe of Mark Ethridge's journalistic talents, he was by temperament more in tune with the scholarly Agar, who had been a friend of Henrietta's and had written speeches for the Judge in London. His hope was that Agar would bring national recognition to *The Courier-Journal*, as Henry Watterson had done decades earlier.

Agar's views were, if anything, more at odds with Louisville than Barry's. Until Hitler's invasion of Poland in September 1939, Agar was a passionate pacifist. By the time he arrived in Louisville in January 1940, however, he was "the most outspoken and the most vile of all interventionists in the world," as Mary admiringly put it.

The Binghams had adopted the Judge's protective feelings toward England and were pretty much "vile interventionists" themselves. By late 1939 and early 1940, Barry and Mary had become obsessed with the notion that the United States must act decisively before Germany invaded Britain.

So it was no surprise that, soon after Agar's arrival, *The Courier-Journal* became one of a small handful of papers demanding that America go to war. "All of us were breathing fire to save England and freedom," recalled Jimmy Pope, then the *CJ's* managing editor. The position amounted to an incitement to riot in militantly isolationist Louisville. The city's large German population was particularly offended by Agar's saber-rattling editorials, which they felt contained wide veins of anti-German bias reminiscent of Watterson's "To Hell With the Hapsburg and Hohenzollern."

Years later, well after the Binghams had been vilified for their stand on school integration and busing and *The Courier-Journal* building had been attacked by brick-wielding mobs, Barry and Mary would say that the period just before World War II was the worst of their lives. "We were really persecuted then," said Mary.

At dinners and cocktail parties, people would buttonhole them, shake their fists, and say, "Your sons are too young to go to war, but you want to send *our* boys overseas to fight another country's battles." As the papers' interventionist editorials became more frequent and shrill, even Louisville's best hostesses were not above calling the Binghams "Anglomaniacs" over the trout almondine. The atmosphere became so poisoned that Barry and Mary stopped going to the River Valley Club, the city's most elite country club.

Except for the showdown with Mannie Levi, Barry had avoided confrontation all of his life. Eventually, he might have toned down the paper's strident editorials rather than face continued animosity from his dinner partners. But the woman he had married would not let him. Mary had spent her whole life defying convention. She was far less concerned about her discomfort, and his, than about principle.

With Mary egging him on, Barry took stronger, more uncompromising stands than was his natural inclination. It was a role Mary would play throughout their long marriage. "I think I have a nastier disposition than Barry," she said. "I'm inclined to strike back and he isn't so much. Barry would rather come to some accommodation—not giving up his principles, but, if possible, reasoning with people—while I'm inclined to be very ugly and say nasty things."

Mary's style was never to march into her husband's office and say, "Let's do this!" Instead, the two discussed things, often over long walks through the dun-colored pastures and thickly wooded acres surrounding the Little House. "There's nothing like a good long walk to air all kinds of views," she said. "And as we talked, we would just come to an agreement that a stand had to be taken."

WARTIME

By early 1941, *The Courier-Journal*'s war cry had escalated from a hearty call to arms in support of America's British kinsmen to grim warnings that a German victory would mean the end of Western civilization itself. Most of Louisville still viewed Europe as too far away to be of much concern. Isolationist sentiment was so pronounced that even the city's Jews did not publicly support the Binghams. Though Barry and Mary no longer went to dinner parties, close friends informed them that the papers' warmongering continued to be a staple of conversation. "If Barry feels so damn strongly about it, he should join up himself," some guest would inevitably declare after his second martini. The remark was usually met with knowing nods. Fat chance, they seemed to say. After all, Judge Bingham had been an ardent internationalist, too, and he had not served in either the Spanish-American War or World War I.

At thirty-five, Barry was eligible for the recently established draft, though few in Louisville thought a man of his wealth and position would ever be called. The suggestion that he was a hypocrite or even a coward disturbed him terribly, and he and Mary had endless discussions about what was to be done. He had already concluded that he must enlist, but he knew that his wife felt excruciatingly ambivalent and frightened.

On the one hand, Mary recognized that unless Barry demonstrated that he had the courage of his convictions, it would be impossible for him to hold his head up in Louisville. On the other, her husband was absolutely essential to her happiness. The thought of him going off to war made her breathless with panic and fear. She hated it, but finally, after months of agonized debate, she told him, "Barry, you really must enlist. It's terribly important to show that you believe in your own principles." In the spring of 1941, Barry volunteered for the navy.

The induction was handled in classic Bingham style. Barry called Secretary of the Navy Frank Knox, the owner of *The Chicago Daily News* and an old friend of Judge Bingham's. Within weeks, he was appointed a lieutenant in the naval reserves and ordered to report to the training station at Great Lakes outside Chicago.

He felt little anxiety about leaving his newspapers, radio station, and printing company in the hands of Mark, Lisle, and Herbert Agar. His relationship with Mark, especially, had seasoned into a satisfying partnership. To make sure there was no question about who was in charge while he was gone, he even transferred his title of publisher to Mark, a decision that would later give him sleepless nights.

In late May 1941, Barry and Mary drove in silence to the Tenth Street station where he was to catch the train for Great Lakes. Although the country had not yet entered the war, they both felt that years were apt to pass before their sweet, regular life at the Little House would resume. Mary watched the train depart and went home alone, deeply depressed.

Barry was in a somewhat different mood. The next four and a half years would be his first chance to perform solo, without the tight net of his father, Mark, or Mary to catch him. Although more than three years had passed since Judge Bingham's death, Barry left for the military still an immature young man, burdened with the peculiar kind of self-doubt that only the sheltered sons of the rich know. He felt excited, just as his grandfather Robert Bingham had eighty years earlier when he marched off to battle the Yankees amid cheers and church bells. Like his grandfather, Barry yearned to discover who he was and what he was made of. Like his grandfather, he felt sure that war would provide an opportunity to find out.

―――――――

The early days of Barry's military career were hardly auspicious. At Great Lakes he was not even taught how to salute. "I was never sure I made the correct gesture," he said. "I was so afraid I'd get my thumb near my nose." Because of his journalism background, he was assigned to public relations, and spent his first months in the navy mailing out sailors' photos to their hometown papers.

By the fall of 1941, he had wangled a more glamorous assignment in

Washington working for the newly formed Office of Facts and Figures. Archibald MacLeish, then librarian of Congress, headed the thinly veiled propaganda mill, and he and Barry quickly became friends. When *Time* magazine profiled the O.F.F., it noted that Washington columnist Joseph Alsop was an employee, along with "rich, personable Lieut. Barry Bingham."

Since it looked as if he might be in Washington indefinitely, Barry brought Mary, the three children, and several servants up from Kentucky and bundled them into a three-story town house at 2812 N Street in Georgetown. There, for a few months, life seemed to regain its balance. Barry's hours were regular and he was even under orders to wear civilian clothes. "They didn't want it to appear that Washington was becoming an armed camp when we were still not in the war," he explained.

There was plenty of time for reading and talking with Mary and for walking on the towpath that wound through Georgetown. The boys were happy at St. Albans School, a private academy on the grounds of the National Cathedral, and Sallie spent contented afternoons in the town house's small backyard garden.

On weekends, the Binghams shared a country cabin near the C&O Canal with Adlai Stevenson and his family. Barry and Adlai had first come to know each other through William Allen White's Committee to Aid the Allies, a group pushing for U.S. intervention in the war. But it was in Washington, while Adlai and Barry were working for the navy, that the acquaintance blossomed into friendship.

On Saturday, December 6, Barry and Mary traveled to Richmond to watch Melinda, Mary's younger sister, take her wedding vows. It was a typical boozy Caperton blowout, and the next day the family struggled to recuperate with scrambled eggs and milk punches at Richmond's elegant Commonwealth Club. In the middle of the meal, Rush, the club's black headwaiter, walked up to the table and motioned for silence. "Ladies and gentlemen," he said solemnly, "I must inform you that the Japanese have attacked the American fleet at Pearl Harbor."

The group quickly clustered around the club's radios and listened as newscasters speculated that a Japanese invasion was imminent. Back in Louisville, Wilson Wyatt, the city's recently elected mayor, was advised by the War Department to put guards on the four Ohio River bridges in case of sabotage. On December 8, the United States declared war on Japan. Three days later it declared war on Germany and Italy.

Suddenly, Washington was a sea of uniforms. Barry reported back to the Navy Department, but was quickly transferred to the Office of Civilian Defense under Fiorello La Guardia. Because of his familiarity with England, Barry was dispatched to London to see what Americans could learn from Britain's already well-established civil defense systems. La Guardia was convinced that New York and Washington would soon be under siege. Mary packed up the children and moved back to Louisville.

Barry's three-month assignment, which began in January 1942, took him deep into London's air-raid shelters and through the wreckage of Coventry, but his experience was that of a privileged observer. He enjoyed elegant accommodations at the Connaught Hotel, took long walks in Hyde Park, and reveled in the luxuriousness of Dytchley, a friend's country estate outside Oxford. He went often to the theater and took late supper at the Savoy Grill, once sitting at a table next to "the unspeakable" Clare Boothe Luce. As he would throughout the war, Barry used his wealth to avoid the meanness of military life.

But, inevitably, there were unpleasant situations that neither money nor influence could improve. When Barry came back to the United States in April, he had to spend seven long days in Lisbon waiting for a connection. He finally managed to get a plane out, but it landed in forty-two places over five days before touching down in New York. To pass the time, he played Russian Bank, a popular card game, with Alexander Korda, the movie producer, who sat in an adjoining seat.

At one of the refueling stops—a primitive port in Brazil—Barry deplaned and walked into the airport's public rest room. He approached the toilet, began to unzip his fly, and then stopped cold. Ahead of him, like just another fellow in the men's room, was a strange, furry creature. It was an anteater taking a drink, its long, slender tongue plunging noisily into the bowl. The situation was absurd—just the kind of moment Barry loved sharing with his wife. "I gave it a good kick in the slats," he told her when he returned, "and went about my business."

Barry returned to Washington but, with characteristic luck, managed to be in Louisville on June 1, the day his fourth child and third son was born. He had been assigned to make a speech in the area and could stay for only a few hours.

The baby had been conceived the previous August during a Cape Cod holiday with Henrietta, who had drunk herself into such a stupor that she had to be institutionalized. Barry's fortuitous arrival for the birth made up for the unfortunate circumstances of the child's beginnings. "It seemed such a wonderful omen to me that he was there," said Mary.

They named the baby Jonathan Worth after a great-great-uncle of Barry's who had been a Reconstruction-era governor of North Carolina. Barry's more direct ancestor was his great-grandfather, Dr. John Milton Worth, Jonathan's brother, an estimable but less celebrated figure. Barry knew little about him, however. Judge Bingham had never forgiven Dr. Worth for slighting him in his will and had rarely mentioned him to his children. Besides, linking the Binghams to a governor seemed more prestigious and fit in neatly with the Judge's ongoing efforts to burnish the family name, a campaign Barry now embraced as his own. Had Barry bothered to check, he would have discovered that Governor Worth was a virulent racist who had closed down North Carolina's public school system rather than permit freed slaves to learn how to read.

Despite the demanding presence of a newborn, Mary was determined to spend every moment she could with her husband. After a brief family vacation, Mary and the entire Bingham ménage, including several servants and a laundress, moved back to the N Street house in Washington.

Almost immediately, Barry got word that he would have to leave again for London at summer's end, this time for an indefinite stay. The knowledge that they would soon be parted made the final days at the Georgetown house precious and bittersweet. "You were looking so particularly lovely in the pink chiffon part of the evening pajamas you used to wear sometimes," Barry wrote Mary later as he recalled their last weeks in Washington, "and we went walking through the hot, quiet streets of Georgetown to try to talk away our unhappiness." All before had been prelude; now the war began in earnest for them both.

The night Barry returned to London was "the most beautiful, clear, moonlit night I've ever seen in my life." Londoners called the bright glow a "bomber's moon," and Barry soon learned why. A friend drove him around the city and he viewed the devastation wreaked by the blitz. As they passed St. Paul's Cathedral, Barry marveled that the building stood majestically intact, as if by divine intervention, while all around it lay rubble and ruin.

Barry worked out of Naval Headquarters under Adm. Harold R. Stark, Commander of U.S. Naval Forces in Europe. His job: press relations. With Weldon James, a U.S. Marine lieutenant, rabid New Dealer, and former correspondent for *Collier's*, he established comfortable living quarters in a chintz-curtained flat in Grosvenor Square and set about enjoying the electric atmosphere of wartime London. Barry's workdays were long and tiring, but he consciously maintained the refined manners and bonhomie that had served him so well in peacetime.

In fact, to reporters like Ernest Hemingway and Richard Strout, Barry seemed at first to be little more than a slick, rich, party boy dandily attired in tailor-made uniforms—an image they soon discovered was deceptive. "When you'd get to doing business with him you'd find that he was enormously efficient," said Bill Walton, who covered the war for *Time* and *Life*. "If you wanted something out of the navy and you wanted it fast, you'd go to Barry. He was one of the brightest guys in London."

Not every hour was filled with work. The city's theaters were amazingly vibrant and Barry took full advantage of them. At the opening of *Peer Gynt* at the Old Vic, he was thrilled to find himself seated between the actor Rex Harrison and the economist John Maynard Keynes. Afterward, he dined at the Savoy Grill with Michael Redgrave and watched with great interest as Noel Coward, Henrietta's old acquaintance, drifted among the tables. Barry also haunted the Windmill Theatre, a place where old-style vaudeville mingled with burlesque and the orchestra simply played louder during bombing raids. At the climax of each show, several women stood in stiff, statuelike poses, wearing "nothing but a distant and decorous smile." English law permitted nudes to appear on stage, but only if they were motionless.

The official social scene revolved around seated dinner parties, spartan affairs sponsored by older, established women who often received government support for their efforts. The point was to bring American diplomats and officers together with their British equivalents. One of London's most renowned hostesses was Lady Sibyl Colefax and her entertainments were known as "Sibyl's Ordinaries."

The fare was simple but drink was plentiful, thanks mainly to Americans who earned their keep by bringing large quantities of claret, purchased at the officers' club or on the black market. Beautiful women were also in bounteous supply, especially to Americans, who were much in demand as lovers. When Angier Biddle Duke took up with the Duchess of Westminster, London gossips took to calling them "The Duke and Duchess of Westminster."

Barry played along with the game. "Isn't she a beauty? What are the chances with her?" he would say sotto voce to other male guests as they stood together at Lady Sibyl's parties. After the war, Lady Nancy Astor, Helena Caperton's old friend, tried to reassure Mary of her husband's fidelity. "The Mayfair harpies were after Barry the whole time," she said. "But he was conspicuously faithful to you."

Bill Walton, however, was skeptical. "I think it very unlikely that he was away that long and celibate," he said. "I didn't know anyone who was." But, he admitted, "I don't remember him with any specific woman." Years later, even Worth, Barry's oldest son, would speculate that his father had had an affair early in the war.

Barry certainly had opportunities for flings, but it is unlikely he indulged. His fear of confrontation and abandonment, deeply rooted in his childhood, was simply too great and he had never been a risk taker in emotional matters. Also, unlike most Americans in Britain, Barry was not anonymous; his father's ambassadorship and his own highly visible presence in London social circles before the war made that impossible. An affair—even the whisper of one—was sure to be relayed back to Mary sooner or later by one of their mutual acquaintances, and Barry could not bear the thought of her wrath or, especially, her rejection.

That did not, however, keep him from being intensely proud of his sex appeal. Barry liked the feeling that he was admired and desired as long as there was no chance of actual entanglement. While flirtation and suggestive jokes came easily to him, it was Mary who was more comfortable talking frankly and longingly about sex. Her letters were passionate and frequently included allusions to how much she missed "midnight feasts," their elegant code words for lovemaking.

In a birthday letter, she wrote, "The greatest joy in life for me is giving something to you (from your breakfast tea, to those high moments of our whole togetherness, lovely and shared, yielding and yielded, in all the senses and all the mind and heart)." And when Barry took the flat in Grosvenor Square, she daydreamed about somehow coming over to join him. "It sounds so attractive," she wrote, "and I am delighted to hear about the big bed. Do you think, darling, there is any chance at all that it might come in handy in the Spring?"

———————

While Barry lived the wartime equivalent of the London high life, Mary struggled to adjust to a lonely existence as a single parent. When she and the children left the N Street town house in August 1942, they did not return to the comfortable familiarity of the Little House. Instead, they moved to the wide halls and musty smells of the Big House, which Aleen had vacated to take up her duties in New York as president of Bundles for Britain. With gas rationed and automobile trips circumscribed, Mary suddenly found herself marooned on a huge estate with five servants and four small children.

Robert's old room, with its water-stained wallpaper and pea green paint, went to Worth and Barry Jr., who made much of the fact that it was a strictly male domain. Jonathan slept in Judge Bingham's former room and Sallie took over Aleen's chambers, which were connected to the Judge's by a bath.

The boys returned to the Ballard School, and Sallie, now old enough for kindergarten, eagerly joined them. On her first day, she "marched off . . . in a starched dress and pigtails so tight that her cheekbones nearly protruded through the skin," Mary wrote. "She is mad about going, but wishes they would teach her to read because, as she says, she already knows how to play." Sallie's determination to read surprised and delighted Mary, and she told Barry that "she may turn out to be a more efficient scholar than either of the boys."

Barry was fearful that his children's privileged lives would cause them to throw their weight around at the Ballard School, which enrolled several students from "the Point," a quasi-shantytown by the river's edge. In Louisville, Barry took great pains not to draw attention to his money. He recalled with acute embarrassment how Judge Bingham's pretensions had been laughed at and ridiculed. As a result, his own children grew up feeling both superior and somehow ashamed. Later, Sallie would say that going to Ballard with boys and girls "who sold worms for a living" made her feel guilty, not proud, and prompted an uncomfortable sense that she did not deserve her wealth.

Left at home with Mary and the servants, Jonathan played most days in the duck yard. From the start, the Binghams' third son touched something tender in Mary. She felt more maternal toward him than she did toward the other children. "He nearly jumps out of his skin with pleasure when I go back to his room to get him in the morning," she told Barry, "and he has a wonderfully endearing way of clasping his arms around your neck and burrowing his face down on your shoulder."

As the wartime months slowly passed, Mary came to feel twinges of guilt about the special warmth she felt for this blond child with the plain Irish features. "I know that I have probably lavished a good deal more of my famished affections upon him than I was ever tempted to lavish upon the other children when they were his age," she wrote. "I do not think it is my besotted eye, but I think he looks more like you than any of the others did at his age. And he has a quality of gaiety and sympathy that enchants me because it makes me think of you."

Mary was determined not to let life in the Big House take on the grimy air of a large nursery, and to that end she imposed incongruously formal rituals on her brood of children and servants. At supper, the older boys changed into clean shirts and both Sallie and Mary arrived in dresses. Lounging on the table was forbidden, as was baiting Sallie—one of the boys' favorite sports. Each Bingham was expected to do his or her part to achieve an adult level of conversation. Mary's only concession was to have dinner at six o'clock, an hour that she regarded as barbarous. "It all sounds offensively like the early empire builders in the wilderness," she told Barry.

Worth struggled hard to fill the breach left by his father. During Sallie's sixth birthday party, he suddenly rose from the table, hoisted his silver mint julep cup of milk above the cake and blazing candles, and made a toast. "To Sallie! May she have many and happy birthdays." The others were similarly delighted by grown-up charades. On Sundays, they often joined Mary for what they called, with studied nonchalance, "a drink before lunch." Around a fire in the music room, Mary took sherry as her three companions demurely sipped tomato juice.

Sunday was also the day to instruct the children in their religious heritage. Mary had been reared an Episcopalian, but as an adult she did not feel particularly compelled to pray. She was never able to make a spiritual connection that way. But she loved the beautiful, familiar language of the Episcopal liturgy from *The Book of Common Prayer*, which to her ear was like the English poetry she so adored.

Both Barry and Mary were embarrassed by overt expressions of faith. Once, during a meeting of Louisville's Women's Action Committee, Mary was asked to lead a moment of silent prayer, a practice she considered "unendurably tacky." She did so politely but had no idea how to bring the "moment" to a close. "The only thing to do was to rustle papers and push my chair back, which did finally bring all the women out of their trances," she said.

Barry ascribed their discomfort to the "easy, cheap cynicism of the twenties," an attitude he did not want to inflict on his children. They were free to make their own spiritual judgments, he said, but only after getting the sort of literate Christian grounding both he and Mary considered as essential for an educated person as a knowledge of Shakespeare.

Mary attacked the project with characteristic thoroughness. The weekly trip to Calvary Church in downtown Louisville, fueled by precious gas stamps, became one of the Binghams' few wartime outings. Each Sunday, Mary rolled Sallie's thin blond hair into long corkscrew curls, then dressed her in her church uniform: black velvet in winter, pastel cotton in summer. Next came the white gloves and black patent leather shoes that made Sallie squirm in shame because she thought her feet looked too big. Done, Sallie sat in the car and waited for her mother to herd her brothers, reluctantly attired in gray flannel suits, out the front door.

Sallie found a special comfort in church. The responses and the prayers that never changed reassured her. She loved listening to the murmur of the congregation as it rose from the pews to sing a hymn or recite a reading. But even at the age of six, she felt that the stern condemnations of sin in the Sunday sermons were meant just for her.

During the service, she drew angels on a pad of paper, neatly printing "Angel Sallie" under each one. Then she peeled angel after angel off the pad and watched them flutter to the floor because, she said, "I knew in my heart they were not worthy." When she sent several of the drawings to her father overseas, he told Mary that the angels did indeed look "as though they had a good deal of demon blood" in them.

Back at the Big House, Mary conducted her own version of Sunday school. The object was to teach the great stories and parables of the Old and New Testaments and her approach was briskly frank. Despite their tender age, she made it as clear as she possibly could "that adultery and fornication mean just that."

In the Bingham household, Bible study was as much a competitive sport as an exercise in religion, and the three pupils responded accordingly. With his discerning ear, Barry Jr. easily picked up the colorful phrases and rhythmic cadences of the stories. He could repeat verbatim that the seven poor ears of corn had been "blasted by the east wind" and that Jacob "gathered his feet up in his bed" before he died. But Mary found him "mulish" when it came to memorizing less exotic passages. "I'm afraid he has . . . absolutely no idea of how to study anything," she wrote her husband. "I was trying to make him remember the straight lines from Abraham to Joseph (no progeny of handmaidens included) and it took Barry all morning to master this. I think he is fairly lazy."

Worth did not have Barry Jr.'s ear for language, but he made up for it with dogged determination. Soon after his father left for the navy, Worth became very devout, and Mary dismissively characterized his insistence on daily Bible-reading as evidence of a predictable "pre-adolescent religious phase."

Although she was the youngest, Sallie could quote Jacob's responses to the voice of God word for word. In an effort to appear adult, she even embraced some of the more subtle and snobbish attitudes of the household. When Mary told her that Rachel, Jacob's wife, had named her son Dan, Sallie interrupted in a dismayed voice. "But, Mother, isn't that a rather common name?"

Despite the nearly four years difference in their ages, Sallie rocketed ahead of Barry Jr. in reading. While he was still unable to make sense of the neatly typed letters his father sent home, Sallie breezed through a stack of Sarah Crew stories and "Danny Deever," a poem by Rudyard Kipling.

Worth knew that reading aloud was a special torment for Barry Jr., and though he never allowed others to pick on his brother, he was quite capable of humiliating him himself. Once, in a burst of meanness, he set up a reading contest between Sallie and Barry Jr. By the time Mary came upon the sorry scene, Barry Jr. was practically in tears. "Barry was in the midst of an extremely stumbling and inept rendition of a paragraph from a book Sallie was reading," she told her husband. "Sallie had, of course, read off every bit with great ease and expression. . . . I've never seen the poor darling look so flushed and miserable, or read worse."

It became clear soon enough that Sallie was indeed a peculiar and remarkable child. On one April afternoon shortly after her sixth birthday, Sallie went to her mother and said she wanted to dictate a poem she had made up. In increasing perplexity and some anxiety, Mary took down the words. "It has an eerie and rather frightening William Blake quality," she wrote Barry, and an "ambiguous and threatening quality of God."

The poem did, in fact, have a musical, chantlike rhythm:

"God will, God will not
Bless the lamb that He has mocked . . .
God will, God will not
Curse any of the world that He has got."

When Barry received the poem several weeks later, he was awestruck. "Do you think it is possible that we are nurturing an Emily Dickinson? . . . I keep coming back to that strange turn of phrase, particularly the use of the 'lamb that He has mocked.' Why mocked? And yet somehow it is lyrical and poetic, like the tiger burning bright," he said, referring to Blake's famous poem.

From London, he sent Sallie a red leather book with blank pages so that she could record her future works. For Sallie the book became a kind of permanent reproach. She spent hours copying and recopying poems, trying to make her handwriting perfect so that she would feel comfortable showing the pages to her father when he came home. Barry felt no less guilt about his talented little girl. She was growing up without him. He pledged to make it up to her after the war.

———————

Despite Mary's strong hand in their lives, it was the household servants who made the wheels turn at the Big House. The stuffy white English staff of Judge Bingham's day had given way to a corps of black men and women whose participation in the household went far beyond ordinary domestic chores. They were like a second tier of family to the children, and genuinely loved and prized by Barry and Mary, who spoke of them affectionately as "our dear nigs."

The cook, Cordie Stokes, called the children "honey" and specialized in Southern fare, but with a bit of direction, she could prepare anything. The children especially loved her rendition of "floating island," a mountain of meringue drifting on a sea of sweet custard. Ollie Madison, the wiry downstairs maid, was wonderful with silver and waited at table, something her husband, Curtis, was loath to do.

Curtis was an accomplished cabinetmaker and had once made such a perfect copy of an eighteenth-century French chest, that Judge Bingham had set him up in business. He could not handle the pressure, however, and soon returned to the Big House as a chauffeur and handyman. He tended the furnace, waxed floors, and even installed tiny electric lights in Sallie's dollhouse. He and Ollie were devout Catholics, which the Binghams considered a most peculiar choice for black people.

Loubelle Retter, the gardener, and his ever-changing staff of two, maintained the vast grounds. Lizzie Baker, Barry's old nurse, was long past great physical exertion, but she counted linens to make sure none were missing, helped Cordie cut up vegetables, and, as the most senior servant, reigned in the kitchen as a sort of dowager queen. Life at the Big House was the entire world to these longtime retainers, who lived together in remarkable harmony on the spacious third floor, where Compton the butler had once trilled flute serenades to his dog.

The chatter and laughter around the kitchen table, where the servants took their meals, was irresistible to the Bingham children, who frequently ate at the clean, scrubbed table, surrounded by the rich smells of bubbling pots. The servants felt comfortable enough to joke with their charges, but they treaded lightly and were carefully deferential.

In turn, Worth, Barry Jr., and Sallie were expected to treat the household help with courtesy and respect. When Barry Jr. shot Curtis with a slingshot, raising a great knot on his head, the handyman, in an uncharacteristic fit of anger, broke the weapon in two. That night the atmosphere in the kitchen was surly and silent until Barry Jr., at Mary's insistence, offered a tearful apology to his victim.

Lucy Cummings, the only white servant, rarely ate with the rest of the help. The short, plump Kentucky woman had come to the Bingham household several months before Sallie was born and stayed on as a nursemaid and governess. Nursie, as the family called her, was raised poor. She never married and bore a wide burgundy scar on her face, the result of having fallen into a fire as a child. She had a rare talent for taking care of young children, combining an air of strict authority with a loving and sensitive nature.

From her box of "pretties"—spools, pins, and knickknacks of all kinds— she created a variety of magical games. For birthday parties and other special occasions, she concocted a mesmerizing centerpiece by mixing water, red ink, citric acid, and mothballs in a big glass bowl. The chemical reaction made the mothballs bob up and down furiously and appear to chase each other around.

Mary thought it almost eerie the way Nursie could tell two days ahead of time that a child was going to be sick. She would spy her gathering nose drops and other medicines in the nursery and then she knew that the Big House was in for a spell of infection. Somehow, Nursie's deprived life had not made her bitter. Instead, it had given her an intuitive empathy, which she applied liberally to her young charges.

Mary's tough-love theory of child-rearing stood in stark contrast to Nursie's unconditional compassion, and often left her in great disfavor with what she primly termed "the kitchen." When Worth was eleven, he flagrantly disobeyed his mother by going into downtown Louisville without permission and then compounded the crime by missing the 5:30 P.M. bus home. When he called for a ride, Mary coldly informed him that gas was scarce and he would either have to wait for the 7:30 P.M. bus or walk the five miles back to the Big House through the sheets of spring rain.

That night at dinner, Sallie and Barry Jr. glowed with virtue when the front door opened and "a creature of . . . forlornity and pathos appeared outside the comfortable candle-lighted aura of the dining room table." Though Worth had taken a raincoat and hat that morning, he had left them at school and was shedding cascades of water from his blue jeans onto the red and blue oriental rug. With as much nonchalance as she could summon, Mary told him to take a bath and then come down and have the plate of food that had been kept hot for him.

Even before Worth's dramatic entrance, Mary's unyielding attitude had aroused the kitchen. Cordie had conspicuously shuttled to the front door at regular intervals to gaze down the road, and Lizzie had turned down the beds "with her lip pouted out like a Ubangi." Throughout supper, the three black women whispered a disapproving chant. "That poor little boy! . . . . Walking out here from town!" Even Curtis's back at the sink showed indignation.

All this prompted Mary to march into the pantry and tell one and all that Worth had been very disobedient and naughty, that they were not to sympathize with him, and that it was all for his own good. But she knew that her talk would have little effect. When Worth finally changed into dry clothes and came downstairs, he was treated to all manner of pats, hugs, and exquisite tidbits from the kitchen.

Later that night, to Mary's surprise, he was neither rebellious nor surly when she went to hear his prayers. He said he had gone into town to buy a friend a canteen. "I pointed out the inadequate nature of this excuse for a serious breach of discipline," Mary wrote her husband, "and was altogether as repulsive and righteous as it is the duty of parents to be under such circumstances."

The next morning Mary found Worth to be the "model of sweetness and amiability," confirming her faith in discipline and her scorn for women who saw their "normally aggressive, normally egocentric children as so many potential little Oedipuses and Electras." It was her responsibility, she felt, to apply the "wholesome hand of authority" to their "wicked little bottoms."

———

Mary's life during World War II was further complicated by what she called her "poor relations"—her mother and her many sisters—and the continuing problems of Henrietta and Robert.

Helena Caperton often boasted that she had brought her daughters up to marry gentlemen, but the truth was starkly different. Most of the Caperton girls married abusive alcoholics or became alcoholics themselves. Mary was the only one who had money and a stable marriage, making her the natural benefactor of her financially strapped mother, siblings, nieces, and nephews.

When the children of Mary's divorced sister Rose were on the verge of being put in foster homes because their father refused to pay child support, Mary agreed to underwrite the entire family. After Clifford Caperton's death in 1939, she bought her childhood home in Richmond so that her mother would have a secure place to live. "I wore Sallie Bingham's clothes," said Melinda Page Hamilton, a Caperton cousin. "I couldn't wait for the boxes to come. We had no pride when it came to beautiful things."

Of course, it was actually Barry's money, not Mary's, that provided the allowance checks and "beautiful things" that were sent off to Richmond each month. Some of Mary's relations felt shame and resentment about taking handouts from the Binghams, who, as they often reminded themselves with considerable satisfaction, had been "nothing" in antebellum North Carolina compared to the Montagues of Virginia. Under the circumstances, Mary had no patience for such ancestral snobbery. "If you were not the most generous and magnanimous human being that ever lived, the whole business would bore and irritate you to distraction," she wrote Barry after confessing that she had overextended herself to aid her sisters and now needed more funds deposited in her bank account.

Mary repaid Barry's beneficence by trying to keep Henrietta and Robert sober. After Judge Bingham's death, Henrietta was haunted by black, despairing moods that frequently led to ugly drunken scenes. The notorious Cape Cod incident marked the nadir of her affliction and, for several months afterward, she seemed to pull herself together. She even took to working for the Victory Garden campaign and organizing outings for Worth and Barry Jr. at Harmony Landing. On a car trip to Colorado with John Houseman and the composer Virgil Thomson, she chastely limited herself to beer.

But soon after her return, Henrietta careened into a long alcoholic spree. In an effort to help, Mary spent several days at Harmony Landing hiding bottles and delivering lectures on sobriety. The unsolicited attention only brought out Henrietta's abiding resentment of her picture-perfect sister-in-law. "I'm afraid I rouse all the rebellious and nihilistic feelings in her to an even greater pitch," Mary told Barry after describing the "Wuthering Heights atmosphere" at the farm and Henrietta's screaming rage at finding the wine closet padlocked.

The cycle of depression and debauchery became so pronounced that Barry and Mary considered committing her to a sanitorium in Lexington.

They urged her to try electric shock treatments, therapy that had helped Helena, Mary's older sister, control her abuse of the bottle. But Henrietta firmly refused.

The large number of drunks on both sides of the family made Barry and Mary fearful that, one day, they, too, would succumb. After Barry read *The Lost Weekend*, a novel that chronicled the disintegrating life of an alcoholic, he became so worried that "the family failing" might infect him that he gave up drinking altogether for several weeks.

Mary's favorite sister, Sarah, was a closet alcoholic, nipping secretly, then gradually moving into vehement unreasonableness and stupefaction, followed by intense depression and pathetic alibis to justify her drunkenness. Her husband had made the martinis too strong, she would say, or she had not had enough to eat. Mary felt that Sarah's inability to admit her addiction was a legacy of Prohibition. "All of us who grew up then are inclined to feel that to refuse a drink or to admit publicly that we can't drink is some sign of moral decrepitude," she said.

Sarah's weakness eventually became so pronounced that Mary and Barry decided they had been wrong to name her as the children's guardian in the event they both died. Quietly, without telling her, they took the letter designating Sarah out of their strongbox, destroyed it, and replaced it with a new one naming Edie Callahan, a family friend.

Early in the war, Barry's brother, Robert, sued his wife, Phyllis, for divorce, alleging "extreme cruelty." She had taken a lover and then brazenly brought him into their Buckinghamshire house to live with them. "Robert was most humiliated by that," said Barry. After the breakup, he moved back to the States and tried with only fitful success to abstain from alcohol.

Robert's personality had grown less acid with age, but his indecisiveness remained unchanged and he became even more pitiable, burned-out, and dependent. The once-chiseled face was now marred by teeth pitted and blackened from years of cigarettes and neglect. Plagued by his father's eczema and skin disorders, he broke out frequently in boils.

Robert visited Louisville often—mostly to see Henrietta—and was lunching on roast beef at the Big House one Sunday when Worth asked him what he did for a living. Henrietta and Mary put down their forks and waited in rapt attention for his answer. Robert muttered something so quietly that Worth asked him to repeat it. He cleared his throat and tried again. "In peacetime," he said, "I worked for a commercial bank involved with South Africa."

Worth then asked what he did now that the war was on. "I help the British," Robert said, glancing at his luncheon companions with the expression of a cornered rabbit. The excruciating awkwardness of the moment caused everyone at the table to lower their eyes. But it left Worth unsatisfied in what Mary described as his "deep desire to place us all in highly creditable and conventional pigeonholes."

Less than two years after his divorce, Robert remarried. His new bride was Felice Desmit, a Belgian stenographer who had done some work for him. Mary and Barry had little information about her before the wedding. All the Binghams knew was that "some woman" was living with Robert at the Roosevelt Hotel in New York. No one even knew her first name. Robert just referred to her as "Desmit," "that wretched girl," or "my typewriter," a British and somewhat pejorative term for "secretary."

The news of their marriage was so staggering that Aunt Sadie phoned Barry in London to say that Robert had actually wed "Ophelia," as Sadie dazedly called her. Felice was thin, knobby, and unattractive—what Barry termed "a very earnest bourgeoisie"—and the family immediately suspected her of avarice. Mary tartly described her as someone who should be in the cage of a French restaurant counting sous. "She has a sharp, shrewd eye for the main chance," she wrote Barry. "I would not be surprised if she has definite plans about Robert's future and the papers. I hope she will not plant a canker in his mind about his situation, but I fear very much that she will."

Her fears proved to be unfounded. The marriage was eccentric, but Felice seemed genuinely to care for Robert. She forced him to give up alcohol and sedatives, which he and Henrietta acquired regularly and in quantity through their psychiatrists. The marriage, however, was totally platonic. Robert's physical and psychological afflictions had left him completely impotent. His relationship with Felice was one of patient and nurse, charge and custodian. The couple soon rented a two-room apartment on East 68th Street in a town house that had once belonged to Averell Harriman, and Felice hovered protectively over her new husband while he smoked cigarettes and gulped cup after cup of coffee—up to fifty a day—to distract himself from stronger drink.

———————

Soon after Mary had returned from Washington and moved into the Big House, she had become a vice-president and director of *The Courier-Journal* and *Times* company and WHAS radio. At Barry's suggestion, she also sat on the papers' editorial board. "Mary knows my views on things better than anyone else," Barry told Mark. "You should consult her if there is a question." Mark agreed to the arrangement mostly to please his boss, but he soon discovered that Mary more than carried her weight.

In fact, Mark later said she was the best editorial writer *The Courier-Journal* ever had. Mary was sharply self-critical. "I find it hard not to fall into a scolding and omniscient vein in writing editorials," she told Barry. "This effort of mine on [the] rubber [shortage] is rather typical of my weaknesses, being somewhat pretentious and high flown."

Only once during the war did Mary and Mark fall out over what position the paper should take. They argued about the matter for some time but could not find common ground. Finally, in exasperation, Mark said, "Mary, let's call up Barry in London and ask him what he thinks." Mary looked at Mark in horror. "No, that isn't necessary," she said firmly. "Barry left you in charge of the papers and if you don't exercise that authority I won't have any respect for you."

Mary's rancorous style became something of a private joke. Once she wrote an editorial about Col. Robert McCormick, publisher of *The Chicago Tribune*, a paper that had long criticized the liberal policies of *The Courier-Journal*. "He's a God-damned son-of-a-bitch, the nephew of a syphilitic bastard," Mary typed into her copy. When Mark read the piece he gasped and fumbled for his blue pencil. "She knew, of course, that it couldn't be printed," he said later. "She just had to get her loathing out of her system."

Even shorn of libelous expletives, Mary's blast at the *Tribune* retained sufficient strength to be noticed by Turner Catledge, future managing editor of *The New York Times*, and Marshall Field, owner of *The Chicago Sun-Times*, who asked for copies. Soon she was catapulted onto the local lecture circuit and, with hands trembling and voice cracking, she appeared before meetings of the Kiwanis and Rotary clubs. Barry was delighted. "I have always wanted the *Courier* to have that touch of dynamic liberalism, expressed literately and with distinction," he told her. "It is wonderful that you should be doing it, my darling."

The war changed the complexion of the newsroom as well as the editorial board. With so many men away or working in defense plants, the papers were forced to hire more female reporters. The numbers were never large— two or three on each publication—but to older male editors, the shift seemed radical. "[*The Louisville Times*'s editor] said the other day that if he had to take on many more women, he was going to have to start wearing skirts to feel at home," Mark joked to Barry.

Mark had his own blind spots about women. He once denied a female editor a raise because he thought it would make her husband, a lower-paid reporter, feel bad. But he could also be an unusually encouraging boss. When several female reporters wanted to leave the paper to get college degrees, he helped them fit their work schedules around courses at the University of Louisville. With Barry's blessing, he even arranged for the papers to pay the tuition.

It was Mark's personal touch that both men and women remember. Every afternoon around 4:00 P.M., he would stroll through the newsroom, stopping casually at various desks to ask reporters what they were working on. One day he encountered Mary Phyllis Riedley, a new general assignment reporter, staring into space. She could not find a lead for her story. "Well, what happened?" asked Mark. "Tell me about it." The novice dutifully recited the details. When she had finished, Mark said, "Now, sit down and retell it to that typewriter. All writing is, is talking to a typewriter."

Working at *The Courier-Journal* was Mary's only real pleasure during those trying war years. She still took breakfast on a tray, but now three days a week she caught the country bus, a real "Toonerville number" that she enjoyed for the "cheerful neighborhood air" it exuded as it went "swooping and swerving down the River Road." After changing to a city bus at the edge of town, she made her way to the paper in the old post office building at Third and Liberty.* Although the Binghams lived just a few miles outside Louisville, the trip took over an hour each way.

The deadlines and deliberations at the office diverted Mary's attention from the plodding domesticity of the Big House, the burdens of errant family members, and the emotional emptiness of her life without Barry. The evenings passed more quickly when she had homework from the office— books, magazines, and newspapers to read; editorials to go over and correct. She hated to admit it, but the children did not really provide company or consolation.

Indeed, her professional life was so satisfying that she felt guilty about not liking motherhood more. "I'm afraid I am a very unnatural mama," she wrote Barry, "as I really regret the prospect of long days minding the swimming pool instead of days delving into *The Congressional Record* and following minutely the curious convolutions of American politics."

Barry gently admonished her to stay home more with the children and cut back on her work hours. Instead, she took over *The Courier-Journal's* book page and began publishing reviews of children's books. "I believe I can manage this fairly easily," she assured him. "An hour's work a day will be ample for the job."

Mary's position at the newspapers sparked pointed remarks from other war widows who thought it abominable that she was spending time at her husband's business instead of ladling out coffee at the Tenth Street station canteen. Eventually, Mary managed to ignore the carping and concluded that the other women simply did not feel as she did. How could they possibly understand what she was going through?

It was true that the good matrons of Louisville could hardly have guessed

---

* Green Street was renamed Liberty Street soon after World War I, thus changing the papers' address but not their location.

that this cool, intellectual mother of four was almost out of her mind with yearning for her husband. It was only when she wrote to Barry that she allowed herself to confess just how barren her life had become, despite the children and the job. "I cannot hide the fact from myself that all of this is quite unreal, and a kind of false, bustling activity while my real and important life, my life with you, is suffering a dreadful amputation," she told him.

Mary's letters showed clearly the torture she felt at their separation. Barry's correspondence, though fond and loving, did not betray the same helpless, compulsive need. His chatty notes from London seemed calculated to keep Mary slightly at bay, as if he were fearful that the intensity of her emotion, if unleashed, might smother and engulf him.

Years later, Worth would say that his father loved humanity, but no one in particular. Mary, on the other hand, had little affection for humanity, but she loved one person, Barry, with a total, white-hot, consuming passion. "The quite bald and simple truth is that you are my whole life," she told him, "and now that you have gone away, even the darling children can do little to alleviate the desolation."

Mary repeatedly tried to find ways to join Barry in London, though it would have meant leaving the children with Nursie and the other servants for weeks or even months. Her first idea—conducting a study on the English system of day care—fell victim to the peculiarly middle-class notion that women should not work. "I thought I would scream," Mary wrote Barry in frustration when the project was rejected.

Then she attempted to persuade Radcliffe to sponsor a study of how the war was affecting the liberal arts at English universities. When that faltered, she tried to interest Macmillan in a book and even went so far as to seek a visa. At the State Department, she ran up against "a perfect ogress" of a bureaucrat who said, "Mrs. Bingham, haven't you got young children?" Mary replied that she had four. "Well then, I'm not going to give you a visa."

When Barry's boss, Admiral Stark, heard that Mary was trying to pull strings to get to London, he quashed the effort once and for all. Though Stark was sympathetic with her plight, he thought morale would plummet if some wives were allowed to visit their husbands and others were not. He called Barry into his office and told him, "If your wife comes to London, I'm going to ship you out to the Pacific at once." To show that he meant business, he even forbade his own wife to visit him during his tour of duty. Mary's scheming abruptly came to an end.

Perhaps to compensate, Admiral Stark arranged for Barry to return to the States for the Christmas holidays in 1943. Mary got a message, in code, that he was to arrive and frantically traveled by train to New York City. There she waited day after day at the St. Regis Hotel, venturing out only briefly for tea and then rushing back to see if there were any messages. Early one morning, to her convulsive joy, Barry appeared at the door of her room and they had three delicious days together.

The night before he was to return, Mary sobbed all during the musical *Oklahoma*, then the rage of Broadway. The next day, she watched morosely from the terminal as his plane disappeared down the runway. "Those times were really so fraught with delight and terror," she said.

All through the spring of 1944—"the most beautiful spring I've ever seen, one of those that the poets write about," Barry recalled—there was a feeling of anticipation and tension in the air. Everyone in England knew that the Allies were planning to invade France, but few knew exactly where or when.

Barry's job was to look after the war correspondents scheduled to go over with the troops. Among his charges was Ernest Hemingway, who had muscled his wife, *Collier's* reporter Martha Gellhorn, out of the press pool and taken her place. When she learned what her husband had done, she stormed into Barry's office. "That son-of-a-bitch has ruined everything in my life," she screamed, "and now he's going to steal the best story I ever had."

In May, about two weeks before the invasion, Barry mounted Operation Mock Turtle, a trial run for reporters. He rounded up several dozen correspondents in the Savoy Bar and called the rest to his office. Trying hard not to show their excitement and fear, the men gathered their typewriters and duffel bags and clambered into two buses that took them to the west coast of England. Once they arrived, they were informed that the trip was phony, that it was just a way to get them in practice for the real thing.

Most of the reporters were bitterly disappointed, but Barry had arranged a consolation prize to suit his own tastes. For three days, the men bedded down in a lovely country house belonging to Daphne du Maurier, drank fine liquor from the well-stocked bar, and enjoyed the thick Cornish cream. "Someone told me afterward that this was one of the dream weekends of his life," said Barry.

On May 31, Barry once again summoned his reporters. He ushered them into a long, narrow room and ostentatiously locked the door. "Gentlemen, this is it!" he said. Hemingway, exotically decked out in a deer-stalking outfit, stared back at Barry from underneath a broad expanse of white bandage. Earlier that week, during a blackout, he and an inebriated companion had driven a car into a water tank, propelling Hemingway into the windshield. The wound required fifty-six stitches and as a result "his entire head was bound up so that he looked like an oriental potentate."

Barry escorted his charges to Portsmouth, where they were transferred to battleships. He then hastened back to London and impatiently awaited the moment when "the curtain really rose"—June 6, 1944—D-Day. Barry's assignment was to expedite the flow of newspaper, magazine, and wire copy from reporters in the field to their publications. It was an important job, but being far away from the fighting made him feel left out and a bit cowardly. "It had to be done this way," he wrote Mary, "but I was missing the chance to see some excitement and action which would have made my whole service in the Navy more tolerable."

The day of the invasion, Barry awoke very early and heard the sound of plane after plane flying toward the English Channel "like a locust swarm." Then the work began in earnest. Volumes of dispatches poured into Barry's office. He and his staff rushed the copy to censors and then pounded the men mercilessly to let the news go through. The moment the copy was cleared, it was transmitted back to the States by radio.

About ten days after the invasion, Barry finally managed to see the war up close, when he finagled a spot on the cruiser *Tuscaloosa*. From the bridge, he watched as the ship bombarded the port of Cherbourg. The big guns boomed for several hours; it was the first time he had ever been under fire. Once the city fell, Barry was put ashore in a landing craft so that he could set up facilities for American correspondents.

For a week, he and three or four other officers lived a kind of Big House-in-exile existence in a bombed-out cottage. There was a workable stove on which Barry prepared several gourmet meals by mixing C-rations with scallions and shallots from the nearby garden. Since there was no safe drinking water, the men brushed their teeth with cognac. While rooting around in the yard, he found a small, abandoned teddy bear. The following Christmas, he sent it to Jonathan.

In November, the navy awarded Barry the Bronze Star for his work during the Normandy invasion. Admiral Stark commended him specifically for being such a "cheerful and diplomatic liaison" with the Royal Navy, the U.S. Army, and the British Ministry of Information, reinforcing Barry's natural tendency to value his personal charm and his skills as a compromiser. These qualities were, in fact, extremely important in wartime Britain, where many citizens deeply resented the Americans for entering the war late and then bossing the other participants around. "There was a feeling that Americans were overpaid, over-sexed and over here," said John Templeton-Cotill, then a young British officer. "But Barry was the kind of American everyone liked."

While pinning the medal on Barry's uniform, Admiral Stark told him that the citation expressed the sentiments of the whole command, and also of the authorities in Washington, who were still talking about the good job he had done. It was the first time Barry had been recognized for a professional achievement that was purely his own, and the power of the moment surprised him. "I was more heavily assailed by a combination of embarrassment and pleasure," he wrote Mary, "than I have been since the day of our wedding, when I struggled through such mists of emotion to keep a clear view of you coming down the aisle at the beginning of the service."

That Christmas, Barry gave Mary a portrait of himself he had had commissioned in London. "It is the very most lovely present you could have devised," she told him when she learned he had begun the sittings. But when the painting arrived and was unveiled Christmas morning, she had a quite different reaction. She recognized the face of her husband—the bright, pale blue eyes, blond hair, and aquiline nose. At the same time she had "a pretty sharp feeling of anguish" because the face seemed so grave and sad. Somehow, some way, the artist had seen "that lonely character" that Barry kept carefully hidden from everyone, even Mary, and had captured it on canvas.

With typical candor, Mary told Barry she did not like the painting. "It does not shine out with your peculiar and lovely and delight-giving quality. . . . It is [this quality] you have, above all others, of making everything more intense and meaningful and joyous. There is nothing of that in this portrait."

———

With Barry overseas, the task of finding proper Eastern boarding schools for the boys fell to Mary. She was increasingly suspicious of the progressive peculiarities of the Ballard School, especially where Barry Jr. was concerned, and felt that being separated from the Big House ménage and having the influence of male teachers would do both boys good.

Like Judge Bingham years earlier, Mary and Barry were determined that their sons would go to Harvard. Other schools, even those in the Ivy League, were just not acceptable. When one prep school proudly told Mary that most of its seniors had listed Princeton or Yale as their first choices, she refused to consider the place. "I am bigoted enough to feel that it would be a minor tragedy if the boys should decide to go to either one of these institutions instead of to Harvard," she told Barry.

Underlying the Binghams' desire to send their sons away was a desperate hope that Barry Jr. could finally overcome his reading handicap and rebuild the self-esteem he had lost during his school years in Louisville. "The choice [of boarding school] must be made on the basis of the best place for [Barry Jr.]," Barry told Mary. "Worth will do well anywhere." After consulting several teachers and education experts, Mary wrote off to a half dozen institutions for catalogues and appointments.

One adviser who was aware of Barry Jr.'s difficulties told Mary to look into the Emma Pendleton Bradly Home. Mary did not know until the information arrived, however, that the place was an endowed hospital for children with serious behavioral disorders. Barry Jr. saw the literature and, as Mary put it, his "horror-loving imagination lingered over the dreadful description." Later that night, she overheard him telling Nursie that one of the proposed schools was "a hospital for jittery children."

After visiting the Fay School outside Boston and Eaglebrook in Deerfield, Massachusetts, the Binghams decided to send the boys to Eaglebrook, mostly because it had a good remedial program for Barry Jr. Mary was also impressed by Eaglebrook's crisp assurances that it made every effort to discourage homosexuality. "All the masters are married, and the older boys are constantly watched for signs of undue attachments," she told Barry.

Nursie spent most of the summer of 1944 sewing name tapes on the boys' clothing, counting and sorting underwear and T-shirts, and generally trying to avoid thinking about the ragged hole that would soon be left in the fabric of the Big House. Even Mary came to dread her sons' leave-taking. "I am already beginning to think of those fall afternoons with the starlings in the beech trees and the sun slanting across the lawn, and no little boys making the afternoon hideous with their shrill differences about the football score," she said.

Preparations for the boys' departure were interrupted in July when Mary accompanied Mark Ethridge and his wife, Willie Snow, to the Democratic Convention in Chicago. The Louisville papers had long been firm supporters of Roosevelt's vice-president, Henry Wallace. Several years earlier, Mary had entertained him in Louisville; he had even played tennis on the Big House courts. But F.D.R. was worried that Wallace's advocacy of Soviet-American friendship and his support of Negro rights would hurt him with party conservatives and Southern Democrats, and was inclined to throw him off the ticket. Mary and Mark were aghast. Such an action, they felt, would call into question the very principles of the New Deal. They vowed to do what they could to shore up support.

At the convention, they took out a $1,000 ad in *The Chicago Tribune* to publicize a poll showing that voters favored Wallace by a wide margin. When the Wallace people asked if they could hand out ten thousand copies of a pro-Wallace editorial that had appeared in *The Courier-Journal*, Mark said yes while Mary fretted about what the request implied. The piece must have been quite "low and . . . narrowly partisan," she said, to even be considered for such a purpose.

Their efforts were in vain. After seconding F.D.R.'s nomination, Wallace went down in flames and a Midwest moderate—Sen. Harry S. Truman of Missouri—was nominated, all with the behind-the-scenes complicity of Roosevelt. "Congratulations on your magnificent fight," the president told the bereft Wallace in a telegram the next morning. Mary and Mark were furious. "The President seems convicted of having perpetrated one of the most brutal double-crosses that expediency has devised," Mary told Barry.

Back in Louisville, Mary composed a wounded letter to Eleanor Roosevelt, who had been a guest several times at the Big House. She begged for an explanation that would restore her faith in F.D.R. and counter the charge that he had conspired with urban political bosses and Southern reactionaries to stop Wallace. Mrs. Roosevelt wrote back that she, too, "deeply" regretted the vice-president's defeat. But in a veiled admission that her husband was congenitally two-faced, she told Mary that she did not "understand why you should have been surprised."

In his own letter to the president, Mark was more direct. "I think you have made the greatest moral and political mistake of your career in the way in which you brought about the nomination of Senator Truman," he said. "As a newspaper publisher, I shall go on supporting you, but I am much less happy about it than I have been and I think you ought to know it."

Mary's and Mark's letters were upsetting to Roosevelt. *The Courier-Journal* was one of the few Southern papers the president could count on for constant, spirited support, and he wanted to do whatever was necessary to mollify its outraged publisher and the wife of its owner. In late August, at Roosevelt's invitation, Mary and Mark met with the president in the Oval Office. As they settled into chairs around his desk, F.D.R. looked over his glasses. "I didn't get you up here to hold a postmortem—that is, unless you want one," he said.

An uncomfortable silence ensued, which Mark finally broke by telling Roosevelt that he felt the war had put him at the mercy of the "service brass hats." Mary could barely speak. She got all "mazy" and melted in the presence of "that man." "I am a stern and disciplining parent, but it would be as hard for me to maintain a feeling of righteous indignation against one of the children as against [F.D.R.]," she wrote Barry. "I suppose this is the greatest hazard of giving women the vote. They are inclined to practice politics on the sea-anemone level—that is, the level of involuntary and passionate attractions and repulsions." As she was being ushered out, F.D.R. praised Barry and said he hoped he could come home soon. All Mary could manage was "a huge dry grin."

In London, Barry hungered for every scrap of information about the presidential audience and cabled Mary for news. Her detailed account, which he received several days later, prompted him to launch into a rare, unfavorable critique of his father that could as easily have been about himself. "The conduct and attitude of [F.D.R.] reminds me so strongly of Papa on the defensive that I can get the precise feel of the reception he gave you," Barry said. "The effort to divert the conversation into extraneous but acceptable channels, the marvelous front that is erected against criticism, the artful avoidance of issues while seeming so candidly to accept the policy of a free and open discussion—all these seem to me the marks of an honorable and righteous soul caught in a trap of embarrassment and guilt. I really deplore his whole conduct of the interview most deeply . . . [but] I must say I feel a little more sympathy with this sort of dishonest behavior because of the strong comparison it makes in my mind with similar situations I can remember through the years at home."

———————

In September 1944, Mary took Worth and Barry Jr. to New York City for a few days of fun before the commencement of their boarding school lives. After lunch at the Automat, a Broadway show, and a night of dancing at the St. Regis Roof, Mary walked them to Grand Central Station, where a master from Eaglebrook was waiting to accompany them on their trip to Massachusetts. "There was a sudden swish through the gates and with time only for hasty kisses the little boys were swept away," Mary told Barry sadly, in a phrase that somehow summed up the end of childhood.

Worth, lean and athletic, enthusiastically embraced the independence that boarding school represented. Barry Jr., a pudgy misfit, was far more tentative. "He does love his home comforts and his freedom from study and toil at the Ballard School," Mary wrote. Barry Jr.'s ambivalence was magnified further by his failure to pass fifth grade the previous spring in Louisville and by an embarrassing testicular condition that required him to take pituitary shots. "I cannot say that there has been any change in his tiny parts so far," Mary told Barry a month after the treatments began, "but he has lost four pounds."

Because of his sorry record at Ballard, Barry Jr. was put in the fourth grade at Eaglebrook, something he found hard to comprehend. "I by some mastake [sic] have ben [sic] put in the 4th grade but I will get it straten [sic] out," he wrote Nursie. Mary considered his note "such whistling in the dark that I can hardly bear it." Due to lack of a summer tutor, his reading and spelling had slipped even more than usual; Eaglebrook tests judged his reading ability to be at only a third-grade level, though he was eleven years old.

Despite such setbacks, Barry Jr. steadily improved during his first year at Eaglebrook. He lost weight and took up stamp-collecting. The headmaster and his wife told Mary that he was good company, and they often asked him to sit at their table at dinner—a position of high honor.

But he clearly missed the comfortable security of home and his longing for his father became acute. At the Big House, he had worn his father's undershirts, refusing even to give them up to be washed. The cool cotton had made him feel closer, somehow, to his adored and absent parent. Now, in his dreary cubicle at Eaglebrook, he hung his father's portrait alongside a print of St. George and the dragon that Barry Sr. had owned as a child. When Mary came for a mid-semester visit, Barry Jr. rushed to meet her with "waves of color rolling up into his already high-colored cheeks, and large tears standing in his eyes."

Worth, on the other hand, seemed headed for what his father ruefully called a "model boarding school career." He made the football team, skied, skated, and boxed intramurally, played cornet, and eagerly embraced an adolescent affection for nicknames, calling his two English roommates "Smit" and "Swaddle" and not minding at all when they hailed him back as "Worthless." After a stirring speech on the evils of the poll tax, he made the finals in Eaglebrook's public speaking contest, choosing "the tariff" as his topic. "I think Worth is, as we have always thought he would be, a pushover for the old school-tie spirit," Mary told Barry.

Worth's one-of-the-boys conventionality was such a striking contrast to his father's own eccentricities at Middlesex that the older man found himself oddly detached from his firstborn. "I feel quite capable of judging his good qualities from what might almost be called an impersonal standpoint, devoted as I am to him," he wrote Mary. "It may be because for some reason I have never particularly identified the child with myself."

Back at the Big House, Sallie luxuriated in her brothers' absence. Because she was a girl, the third in line, and "perfectly adequate," as Mary put it, she had never gotten as much attention as Worth and Barry Jr. Mary sometimes took lovely naked swims with Sallie in the Big House pool, but she rarely mentioned her daughter in letters to Barry while going on for page after page about her sons. Little girls, Mary felt, were "naturally prissy in the extreme" and "full of easy, rather dull conversation." Boys, in contrast, had "more broadly based" discussions and "their exchanges [are] more humorous than the little girls'." It was hardly surprising that, when grown-ups asked seven-year-old Sallie whether she missed her brothers, she "frankly and brutally" answered no.

Like her own mother, Mary valued beauty in girls, but unlike Helena Caperton, she also valued brains. She was delighted when Sallie read all of Aesop's fables by herself and started in on the Oz series. Sallie's "prideful and insensate appetite" for books reminded Mary of herself, even though she was well aware that a highly developed mind could doom a woman to spinsterhood. "I believe that blue-stockingness in otherwise normal and comely women is easier to curb than light mindedness," she told Barry, "and I think Sallie is probably going to be quite pretty enough to be able to afford some intellectual life."

Without the ceaseless competition and striving to keep up with Worth and Barry Jr., Sallie became noticeably less nervous. Her table manners improved and she even practiced piano without being bludgeoned into it.

In the kitchen, she worked quietly with Cordie learning how to fry bacon and make biscuits, and at dancing class, she became a favorite of the little boys, if only because she tirelessly carried most of the conversational burden. "I had hardly realized what a predominant part of my time and interest was devoted to the boys, and how much she played an also-ran part until they went away," Mary told Barry as she marveled at the change.

But Sallie was still a natural recluse. She only invited her Ballard classmates over to play after her father wrote her a letter suggesting she enlarge her circle of acquaintances. The doting attention of Nursie, "the nigs," and her mother seemed to nourish Sallie's starved ego far more than the equivocal companionship of children her own age. "I think that the thing that must be avoided in her case is the development of the princess fixation—an idea that Lizzie, Ollie, and Cordie assiduously build up, and one which she is only too willing to entertain about herself," Mary wrote Barry.

Perhaps because of the extra attention, Sallie's relationship with her brothers gradually improved. On a vacation trip home, Worth taught her to play Ping-Pong. By mistake, he gave Sallie a stinging blow under the eye with his paddle and Mary was "pleased at her fine efforts to control her perfectly legitimate tears and [Worth's] solicitude and apologies." Barry Jr., too, gave evidence of a more tender attitude toward his sister. Once Mary found herself interrupted by phone calls just as she was trying to fix Sallie's hair and leave for a luncheon appointment. Noticing his mother's distress, Barry Jr. said, "Here, let me do that." As Mary rushed to the phone, he carefully unplatted Sallie's braids and brushed out her pale blond hair "with long loving strokes."

———

As 1944 drew to a close, the war in Europe was entering its final phase and Barry knew he could probably arrange an assignment in the States. At one point he was even offered a job commanding a battle-damaged ship up and down the Mississippi, stopping in small ports to boost the war effort. But he would have none of it. Although his service had been longer than most, he had worked at a desk job; he had not dodged bullets. "It would have been nonsense for me to ease myself into any such arrangement," Barry later said of the safe berth he had passed up.

He missed Louisville and his life with Mary, but not enough to abandon the thrill and obligation of war just yet. He had enjoyed his glamorous life in London immensely, and the taste of success and recognition he had gotten from his work on the D-Day invasion was still fresh. Besides, Mary's consuming need for him had had years to gather power, and it frightened him. Her letters spoke of feeling "banished, as poor Romeo used that word in an anguished moan in Father Lawrence's cell," while Barry continued to keep his notes light and airy, full of amiable chat about the latest gossip, his work in London, the children, and the newspapers.

Although he knew Mary was frantic to have him home, he decided to keep his independence a bit longer. He told her he was going to take an assignment in the Pacific. Mary was shocked, hurt, and full of fear. Many people thought the war might rage on in the Pacific for five years or more. But she gamely tried to play the role of dutiful wife. "However this decision came about . . . I know that if you . . . made it, it is the right thing," she said when she first heard the news.

After getting a few tantalizing days alone with Barry on a short home leave early in 1945, however, she found herself slipping, by her own admission, "into a really suicidal frame of mind." She and Barry had been apart for more than four years. She had run her children's lives and the complicated affairs of the Big House all by herself. She did not understand why Barry would pass up a chance, any chance, to accomplish the only important thing in life, as far as she was concerned—their togetherness.

In February, she insisted on taking the train with him from Louisville to San Francisco, where he was to join the Pacific Fleet. After two blissful days in a hotel suite, they were parted once again. "I believe of all our goodbyes this one was the worst," she told Barry several weeks later, "and I am doing very badly at getting over it."

Barry flew to Guam, the site of his new assignment, via Pearl Harbor, where he roomed with Roger Straus, who would later help start the publishing firm of Farrar, Straus & Giroux. It was to be his last pleasant moment for some time. On Guam, he found his job as head of public relations for Adm. Chester Nimitz frustrating and of little consequence. Nimitz loathed publicity and wanted nothing to do with Barry. So night after night he sat in his room, a cell-like affair with a cement floor and a lone lightbulb, flipping through books or listening to the radio.

Mary wrote letters full of "passionate regret" that he had accepted an assignment so unworthy of their "anguish and heartbreak." Without London's theaters and restaurants to distract him, Barry had long hours to think. He, too, began to wonder what he was doing and where his life was headed.

As early as 1943, he had told Mary of his desire to become editor of *The Courier-Journal* when the war ended. Herbert Agar had vacated the position in August 1942 for a commission in the navy, and Mark had begun lobbying to take over the job, which involved running the editorial page, before Agar's chair was even cool. But Barry wanted to retain the option of taking the title himself. "I want the maximum amount of freedom," he told Mary at the time. "Mark's assumption of the job [now] . . . would tend to make the situation more rigid."

Barry knew he was on the horns of a dilemma. He had taken the titles of publisher and corporate president mainly because he owned the newspapers and his father had had them. But he had no real interest in the actual work a publisher does: overseeing company finances and the day-to-day operations of the papers. Indeed, Barry's business skills were so minimal that he had never even learned how to read a balance sheet.

He had wanted to be editor of *The Courier-Journal* from the moment his father had taken up residence in the U.S. embassy in Britain in 1933, but the Judge had discouraged him. The job was too restrictive, his father told him, and would prevent him from pursuing the balanced, Epicurean life that was his God-given due as a gentleman. "It would mean a grind for you every day in the year," he had written Barry at the time, "and would not give you time for the other things you ought to do in a public way and for your own pleasure and health."

Until he left for the navy, Barry had enjoyed the best of both worlds. He had had the title of publisher while Mark, the general manager, had really done the work, leaving him free to dip in and out of the paper as he chose, writing an editorial here, pushing a liberal position there. He had had maximum power, prestige, and freedom.

Now the situation was different. Mark had been publisher during the war. If Barry came home, stripped him of the title, and demoted him back to general manager, Mark was likely to leave—and that would be a disaster for the papers. Mark had helped make *The Courier-Journal* and *Times* nationally recognized, a fact of which Barry was very much aware. He also realized that Mark was the key to his personal freedom. As long as Mark ran the papers, Barry could serve on boards, take trips, and leave for long stretches without worry.

Moreover, unlike his father, Barry really did want the day-to-day routine of the editorial page, that ivory tower from which he could write, think, and satisfy his yearning to do productive work. But what about giving up the title of publisher, the highest position on the masthead? To the world, that would suggest that he was firmly and forever Mark's subordinate. During his prewar apprenticeship, he had not minded so much. Now that he was almost forty and had four years of military service behind him, the thought rankled.

In the summer of 1945, as Barry mused about these matters, *PM*, a New York tabloid, published an admiring two-part series on *The Courier-Journal* and *Times* that gave fresh urgency to his concerns. In the first article, Mark was cast as the liberal savior of two reactionary Southern papers while Barry was depicted as the prosperous absentee heir. "It made me quail to read of us as 'bright and wealthy young people,' " he wrote Mary. "The use of the term 'wealthy' makes shivers go up and down my spine. . . . It is curious what a stinking tacky refinement that is for the word 'rich,' which has a kind of vulgar gusto about it."

The second installment, which again hailed Mark's stewardship, aroused competitive feelings in Barry. "I can truthfully say that I have never had a qualm of jealousy in connection with Mark, and yet I can only explain my feelings about the *PM* story in that manner," he wrote. "Whatever it is, I intend to root it out immediately, for I do not propose to let my relations with Mark be marred by any such specter in the future."

Another man might have boiled over with resentment and envy. Barry, typically, looked inward. The war had matured him and given him a new sense of self-confidence. Whatever pangs of jealousy he felt toward Mark were now redirected toward the construction of a master plan for his life.

Barry knew he wanted the satisfaction of daily work as well as the Epicurean existence his father had written of more than a decade earlier. While Barry sat in his cryptlike room on Guam, brooding about the future, he began to see a solution that would satisfy both needs. Unlike most men, he had the wealth to craft whatever life he wanted for himself. He could work or play as much or as little as he chose.

It was Barry's singular strength that he consciously decided to pursue work, pleasure, and commitment to others in equal doses, and then followed that plan with rigor and discipline. "I am seriously contemplating the possibility of taking the title of editor of the *CJ* and devoting my time almost exclusively to the day-to-day editorial work," he wrote Mary. "[But] I don't want to spend the next 20 years simply hurrying back and forth to the office, with no pattern for making my time contribute toward the goal of social usefulness which I know is the only thing which would bring satisfaction to either of us in the long run. . . . We have been given a really great opportunity for usefulness, not only because of the papers, but because of our own personal happiness and the richness of our lives together. It is necessary for our future happiness, I am convinced, for us to find ways to make these great blessings contribute more materially to the happiness and well-being of other people."

On April 12, 1945, President Roosevelt died of a cerebral hemorrhage. Less than a month later, on Worth's thirteenth birthday, Germany surrendered. Barry celebrated the victory with a can of beer on Iwo Jima, which had been recently secured by U.S. Marines. The night was humid and the mood indifferent. "I couldn't find anyone who felt keenly interested in events that far away," he said. "They were glad about the news in Europe, but not jubilant. This was the Pacific: another world, another war." Barry scrounged a second can of beer and drank it alone in the dark, listening as "Sentimental Journey" wafted through the thick air from a nearby radio, making him think of home.

He still had one more grand moment to come. On August 15, nine days after the atomic bomb was dropped on Hiroshima, Japan surrendered. Three weeks later, Barry found himself handling American press relations for the surrender ceremony on the deck of the *Missouri*. Admiral Nimitz, his boss, had wanted the formalities held below decks so that he could display his magnificent crest of white hair for the cameras. Nimitz's rival, Gen. Douglas MacArthur, however, wanted to be immortalized wearing the beat-up officer's hat that was his trademark and, not incidentally, covered his balding head. He insisted that the ceremony be outdoors, where military protocol required hats—and he won.

Barry secured a spot for himself at the rail directly above the table where the surrender document was to be signed. Just as the ceremony began, a great wave of planes came roaring overhead, and for a split second Barry thought the Japanese air force had arrived to get its final revenge. He looked upward and to his great relief was able to make out the U.S. insignia on a fuselage. Later, when Nimitz stepped up to sign the surrender document, Barry snapped a picture—a photograph that was to become yet another addition to his office wall.

Several days later, he was back on Guam, impatiently waiting for a plane or a ship out. Barry had enough points to leave the navy, but he knew it could be weeks or even months before he would get a transport. "It was such an anticlimax after Tokyo Bay," he said of that uncertain period. "I wondered how long I was going to be sitting on that island out there." Listening to the radio, with its news of America and up-to-date music, he felt suddenly lonely for Mary and the life he had left behind five years earlier. He had changed a great deal since then, he knew. What he could not fully comprehend as yet was how much home, and its inhabitants, had changed in his absence.

———————

Mary was at a garden party near the Ohio River on the August day Japan announced its surrender. Her host's servants, listening to the radio in their upstairs quarters, heard the news first and came running out, breathless, to announce it. Soon the airwaves were filled with "The Star-Spangled Banner" and other patriotic songs. "Practically every one of us cried except Mary," recalled Jacques Albert, the husband of Barry's childhood friend Sophie. "She just sat [still] because she was so overwhelmed by the idea that this meant Barry could come home. The one who had more of a right for full collapse, you know, was just taking it all in."

From his room on Guam, Barry wrote Mary suggesting that, when he finally returned, they take a vacation down South so that he could stop in Asheville and see Sadie. He fantasized about a family vacation with his wife, his favorite aunt, and all the children. "Wherever we go, the thought of being with you all through the day and through the night, of waking up in the morning and turning to take you in my arms, is the promise of such joy that nothing in my life has ever compared with it," he told her.

After the years of solitary nights and domestic drudgery, however, Mary was unwilling to share her husband with anyone. In October 1945, Barry got a chance to escort some American prisoners of war back to San Francisco. Mary was at the airport when the plane landed and rushed up to embrace him. She accompanied him to Great Lakes, where his service was terminated, and then insisted they go off alone, just the two of them—no Sadie, no children. Barry consented.

At a country inn in the Berkshires, Mary and Barry walked and talked in the crisp fall air, crunching leaves under their feet and reviewing everything that had happened to them during their long separation. Sallie and Jonathan stayed in Louisville with relatives and did not see their father until the trip was over. Worth and Barry Jr. did not see him until they came home from Eaglebrook at Christmastime. But Mary, more famished than ever for her husband's companionship and touch, finally had her "real life" back. "I couldn't detect any change," she said of Barry, with complete happiness and a hint of relief. "He seemed as lovely and as adorable as ever."

RETURN TO NORMALCY

From the moment Barry arrived back in Louisville, the city's cattier gossips eagerly looked forward to a battle at *The Courier-Journal* and *Times*. "Do you think Mark Ethridge will give the papers back to Barry?" they asked each other, arching their eyebrows knowingly over the cocktail glasses.

They were soon disappointed. No power struggle ensued. Barry simply put in place the plan he had agonized over during those lonely nights on Guam. He knew that Mark was the key both to the papers' continued success and his own personal happiness. He also knew that Mark was well within his rights to leave since Judge Bingham had died before making good on his promise to help him buy his own newspaper. And Barry was almost sure that Mark *would* go, in fact, if he tried to take back the title of publisher.

Before the war, Barry had played the part of the pupil while Mark had taken the role of his older, wiser mentor. Barry had been insecure about his abilities and all too often it had showed. But military service had seasoned the thirty-eight-year-old newspaper heir in much the same way that apprenticing at a non-Bingham property might have in less turbulent times. "I had a lot of responsibility in the Navy," he said. "I think it did something for my self-confidence."

So, even though Mary felt it was a grave error, Barry let Mark retain his wartime rank of publisher. "Titles don't really mean anything much to me," he explained. "It's a question of what you're doing and how you're getting on." To the uninitiated, of course, Mark appeared to have triumphed over his younger boss. His name, with the title "publisher" after it, appeared on the first line of *The Courier-Journal*'s masthead, where the newspaper's chain of command was displayed every day. To the right of Mark, on the same line, was Barry's name, with the title "president." Below that, Barry's name was listed again, as editor of the editorial page.

Failing to reclaim the publishership surprised many people in Louisville and, as Mary had feared, it cost Barry some prestige. But to close observers it was clear that he had surrendered his papers in name only. After visiting Louisville in February 1946, a *Time* reporter cabled his editor: "Now there is no doubt who is boss. Mark Ethridge even appeared somewhat subdued. . . . I did not sense any friction between President Bingham and Publisher Ethridge, but I did get the very distinct impression that Bingham is going to run the show."

By stooping to conquer, Barry ensured that his most critical employee did not leave for another newspaper. In return, Mark made it possible for Barry to realize his father's vision of a balanced life and to spend time away from Louisville in pursuit of an ever-widening array of political, philanthropic, and social interests.

The Bingham-Baker-Ethridge troika had gelled in the late 1930s, but with Barry in an understudy role. Now it became more a trio of equals. Many staffers remember the postwar period as a Golden Age. "It was nirvana when those three men ran the place," said John Richards, who started as a teenage tour guide at the paper in 1948 and eventually worked his way up to senior vice-president of all the Bingham companies. "And I mean they ran it! It was manageable. They made decisions in the men's room."

In the sphere he claimed as his own—the editorial page—Barry was conscientious and, for his time and region, quite progressive. But his whole soul was not caught up in the paper the way Mark's was. Concentrating on the Bingham business to the exclusion of political, charitable, and other activities was not consistent with the goal of "social usefulness" Barry had set for himself in the Pacific. "I really built my life in those days around the five-day-a-week editorial conference," he said. "And then the rest of the day was whatever else I needed."

He arrived for work each morning a little after 9:00 A.M. having already digested several newspapers, including that day's *Courier-Journal*, a French daily, and one or two English newspapers. At 10:30 A.M. he convened a meeting of *The Courier-Journal* and *Times* editorial-page staffs to decide the day's topics and positions. He rarely went out to lunch, preferring instead to spend the noon hour reading in his office, catching up on correspondence or writing editorials and speeches.

He usually stayed to look over *The Courier-Journal* editorial page before it went to the composing room at 2:30 P.M. After that he was free to attend meetings of the Louisville orchestra board, the Little Theater board, and other civic, educational, and cultural organizations. By 6:30 P.M. he was back at the Big House, ready to read aloud to the children before they went to bed. The day was busy, productive, and mercifully predictable and Barry, so buffeted and bruised by the multiple upheavals of his childhood, took comfort in the routine.

Mary, too, emerged from the war with more self-confidence. She had always been outspoken, but her work at *The Courier-Journal* reinforced the trait and gave her a new sense of assurance about her professional abilities. No longer was she the dutiful wife hem-stitching handkerchiefs in a hotel room while her husband raced off to press conferences in the Oval Office. She had conferred with President Roosevelt herself!

In a bow to the conventional view that women should give up their wartime jobs when the men returned, Mary left her seat on the editorial board. She did not want to be her husband's employee in the normal sense. Instead, she continued to shepherd the book page and influence the papers from an office strategically located next door to his. Indeed, Mary was such a towering force at *The Courier-Journal* and *Times* that the same *Time* correspondent who had taken note of Barry and Mark's relationship suggested that the magazine do a press story on the "doll-like blond" who was running the book section. "Nobody, not even in the newspaper business, has heard much about her, but she is one of the real powers in the operation of the *CJ*," he cabled, adding that Mary "looks like a Park Avenue socialite babe but . . . has a tough, keen mind behind her beautiful blond facade. She gazes at those who talk to her with wide open blue eyes, which seem innocent of any guile, but one generally discovers one's brains have been thoroughly picked."

While Barry ran the editorial board and Mary ran the book page, Mark ran practically everything else, or so it seemed. He sat in on the editorial conferences, kept a keen eye on the newsroom, and in many ways was the papers' public persona in Louisville and the rest of the country.

With the title of publisher and the hands-on presence of an editor, it was Mark, not Barry, who was often seen as the moving force behind the *CJ & T.* The perception was so strong that the F.B.I., in a confidential background memo on the papers, once described Barry as the owner but Mark as "the real boss of the entire syndicate." "Mark Ethridge made the paper what it was during the thirties and forties," said Molly Clowes, who joined *The*

Courier-Journal when her former employer, the *Herald-Post*, folded in 1936. "Barry was away so much of that time. But then Barry seemed to be almost jealous that people would feel that Mark had more influence on the paper than he did. That's not a nice way to put it. It wasn't jealousy in a petty sense. It was a feeling of 'Well, I own the paper and I did as much as he did.' "

Mark was key to the papers' success, but it was Barry's elevated vision of what the papers could be and his willingness to forgo large profits that made the excellence of the *CJ & T* possible. Years later, some staffers would cynically suggest that Barry just wanted to be able to *say* he owned great newspapers; it gave him entree and a place at the table in the grand intellectual and political circles in which he liked to travel.

The view had an element of truth. Certainly Barry liked bragging about excellence more than bragging about profits, which is what most newspaper owners talk about on the golf course. But he also sincerely believed that his newspapers should lead public opinion, not just reflect it. And he had the honesty to realize that he had neither the background nor the will to bring about such a vision on his own, that he needed a Mark Ethridge and a Lisle Baker, or people like them.

The result was an unusual power-sharing arrangement in which Barry remained aloof from the day-to-day operation of the business but was ultimately responsible for its direction. "He had a presence," said Maury Buchart, who started in ad sales in 1956 and later became general manager. "You knew he owned the papers. But at that time I didn't realize he wasn't doing the day-to-day running of them. I only found that out later."

Nowhere was Barry's detached style more apparent than on the financial side of the papers. For a newsman, Mark was good with numbers; he was hardheaded and he understood the need for controls. Barry, plagued by poor math grades at Middlesex and Harvard and sheltered by his wealth, never grasped the subtleties of business. Company employees balanced his personal checkbook. Legend had it that he traveled like a monarch, taking only enough cash to tip the bellboys.

Lisle Baker, whose duties spanned everything from setting ad rates to settling strikes, was the Binghams' chief financial officer, but even he treated the companies like a mom-and-pop store. He felt that annual budgets had little meaning in the newspaper industry; instead, he asked department heads to forecast their costs on a month-to-month basis. Profits were calculated by subtracting the annual sum of these expenditures from the companies' yearly revenues. The entire financial report was copied by hand onto a single sheet of paper—no duplicates—and discussed at the one and only board meeting the companies held each year.

The cornerstone of Lisle's financial management was an almost pathological aversion to debt. As a Depression-era banker he had watched businesses crumble because they had borrowed unwisely, and he was determined to insulate the Binghams from risk. Had Barry been more financially sophisticated, he would have overruled Lisle on the grounds that borrowing money is often sensible. But the Bingham reverence for journalistic quality carried with it a corollary notion that to be financially savvy was somehow "common." The result was an ignorance about business that often left the empire vulnerable to naive blunders. A prime example involved the decision, in 1948, to build a new headquarters for *The Courier-Journal* and *Times* at Sixth and Broadway, its present location.

During the war, it had become apparent to Mark and Lisle that the old structure at Third and Liberty was woefully inadequate. There was no room for a library, and WHAS radio and Standard Gravure were crammed into a warehouse next door. After getting Barry's approval by mail, they quietly acquired the necessary land from the fifteen to twenty small residential and business owners then on the site, using a bank officer as a front to keep the price low. By the end of the war, a New York architectural firm had been hired and ground was ready to be broken.

Just one problem remained: debt. Constructing the new building was going to require the Binghams to take on a sizable mortgage for the first time in their lives, and the idea sent shivers down Barry's spine. He had almost no knowledge of what it was like to owe money. His largest assets —the Big House, the Little House, and the companies—had been given to him at his father's death, with inheritance taxes covered by the estate. The Judge himself had paid cash for the papers in 1918.

To avoid going into debt, Barry, Lisle, and Mark decided that the companies should raise the money to build the new building by selling off WHAS radio, along with a construction permit for a television station, to Crosley Broadcasting Corporation. Barry felt little remorse. He did not care much for electronic media anyway; it was the newspapers that mattered.

But like Judge Bingham, who had so often wrapped acts of necessity in a cloak of high-minded principle, he wanted to ennoble the decision to sell. For public consumption, he glossed over the real reasons, saying that television, then in its infancy, would inevitably alter the nature of radio and he wanted to concentrate his resources on *The Courier-Journal* and *Times*, the family's primary enterprise. A year later, when the F.C.C. refused to let the deal go through, Barry added another layer to the myth by asserting that the government had told him the station's public service record was just too good to risk losing to new owners.

The real reason, however, was that WHAS's signal overlapped with that of WLW, Crosley's Cincinnati station, giving Crosley a larger presence in one market than the F.C.C. allowed. There were other suitors for WHAS, including Bob Hope, but ultimately Barry decided to keep the station and take on the debt instead. As it turned out, the F.C.C. performed a great service for the Binghams: over the years, WHAS radio and its companion television station, which went on the air in 1950, generated millions of dollars in profits. But the episode did little to change Barry's fear of debt or to spark an interest in the intricacies of corporate finance.

Almost exactly nine months after Barry came back from the navy, the family's fifth and final child was born. The couple named her Eleanor Miller Bingham after Barry's late mother. Although she was unplanned, "the fruit of a joyful reunion," Mary and Barry often said she was a wonderful argument for having offspring late in life.

Gregarious, tow-headed, and the family's only southpaw (which Barry took to be a sign of a highly creative mind), Eleanor grew up in a household that was busier and less rigidly child-centered than her older siblings had known. Freed from the unnatural domesticity that the war had imposed, Mary spent more and more of her time at *The Courier-Journal*, as well as at board meetings of Radcliffe College, the Urban League, the National Conference of Christians and Jews, Americans for Democratic Action, and a host of other political and charitable organizations that frequently took her away from the Big House.

Barry's and Mary's whirlwind schedules left little time to fret over Eleanor, whom the tongue-clucking matrons of Louisville took to calling "the poor little rich girl." "For the younger child in a big family, by the time they get around to you they're exhausted—all they care is that you should have the basic skills—walk, talk, and feed yourself," Eleanor said later. As a result, Eleanor matured into a curiously self-sufficient child. On the surface, she appeared warm and easy, but underneath, Eleanor was contained and unsentimental like her father, who rarely attached himself too strongly to any one person for fear of a painful rejection or separation.

She giggled appreciatively when houseguest Marietta Tree, wife of British MP Ronald Tree, crossed her eyes to make her laugh, and she took no offense when Sallie took to calling her by the made-up name of "Undine the False Other." Mary was astonished one night when Eleanor, then only three, mounted Melcombe's grand staircase and announced that she was putting herself to bed. "She was always a most agreeable and affectionate child and lots of fun," said Mary. "Somehow or other we were more lighthearted around her than the others. I don't remember worrying about her very much. She may have been rather neglected, come to think of it."

Mary and Barry were as attentive as their hectic lives allowed, but all of the Bingham children felt shut out by their parents after the war. Barry's four-year absence had made Mary ravenous for his attention and time, and the marriage, always close, drew tighter. To the outside world, and certainly to their five children, Barry and Mary came to represent a closed corporation, a watertight unit that, as one friend put it, was not just wedded but welded. "It's one of those partnerships where you almost can't tell where one person ends and the other begins," said Sallie years later.

Though most of their friends viewed the marriage as ideal, some did not. "It looks beautiful on the outside," said one longtime acquaintance. "But it's too obsessive. Just being close to your wife is not everything. If you've got children, they've got rights, too, emotional rights."

Much like his own father and grandfather, Barry seemed wary of forging intimate bonds with his children. He loved reading aloud to them and putting them to bed when they were little. But as they got older he kept a certain distance, never maintaining a conversation with any one of them for very long. "He's like that," said one family member. "You get so close and then the screen comes down and he backs off."

Barry treated his offspring much like he did other people he considered to be close friends. He drew them to him with charm and effusive graciousness, but he took care never to unlock the final door, never to reveal himself totally. His goal was to strike a delicate balance, giving just enough to get the warmth he needed but not so much that he would feel vulnerable. That way, he could preserve his independence, and theirs. "I felt that there was always going to be a relationship between us," he said of his children, "but that it was not a thing that should be binding. That is always the question: how close can a bond be without being binding."

Like her husband, Mary had been an unusually self-sufficient child and she valued that quality in her sons and daughters. In one wartime letter she worried that Jonathan, who sobbed each time she left for *The Courier-Journal*, was much more of "a mother's boy" than either Worth or Barry Jr. had been at his age. "Do you remember how we used to notice their great self-reliance, and lack of sentimentality when we went away?" she asked Barry. "That attitude is certainly a far healthier and more attractive one than is my poor darling Jonathan's."

The younger Binghams wanted desperately to crack the barrier that separated them from their parents. Out of frustration and a need for intimacy, they turned hopefully to each other, with the two smallest, Eleanor and Jonathan, becoming natural allies and the two oldest, Worth and Barry Jr., already connected by the common experiences of school, summer camp, and boyhood adventures. The two pairs formed separate generations, almost separate families, within the Bingham clan, leaving Sallie, the lonely, artistic outsider, to wobble uncertainly in the middle.

Despite these divisions, the Big House seemed relatively tranquil during the early postwar years. Worth's removal, first to Eaglebrook and then, in the fall of 1946, to Phillips Exeter, contributed greatly to the lack of tension in the household, if only because Sallie was free of her most feared and hated enemy, the person who convinced her, as she later put it, that "boys are evil." "He was a bully," she said. "He scared the living daylights out of me. . . . It's not [that the teasing was] so extreme. It's just that it was so hard to get at Worth. There was no way you could pay him back because Worth didn't care what you said or did to him. If there had been a way to get back at him, maybe it wouldn't seem so awful."

Of all the Bingham children, Sallie was the most thin-skinned and the most haunted, full of fears and fantasies that neither her parents nor her siblings could understand. She cried when her brothers made fun of her braces, her straggly blond hair, and her "Indiana accent." Later, Mary would wonder whether she should have done more to put a stop to Worth's mean-spirited put-downs and Barry Jr.'s willing complicity in the torture. But she did not consider their shenanigans abnormal or out of bounds. "Nursie would not have allowed [the boys] to be too outrageous," she said, "and I don't remember any incidences of their physically manhandling her." Sallie, she reasoned, would eventually develop some emotional armor and hold her own. "She was just an oversensitive sort of child who couldn't take what most children do take," she said. "I expect she was, in a way, an unhappy child."

With Worth away, however, Sallie had few reasons to be miserable. She continued to shine at Ballard, where, in accordance with the school's progressive philosophy, she was not required to study math or other subjects she did not like. As a consequence, she grew up much like her father, unable or unwilling to keep a checkbook or understand the financial machinery of everyday life. "[Even now] we are hard-pressed to know our multiplication tables," said Mary Clowes Taylor, Sallie's classmate at Ballard and a niece of CJ & T editorial writer Molly Clowes.

Sallie's main preoccupation was reading and writing; she was rarely without a book in her lap. One day after school she came into the morning room of the Big House to find Mary poring over books to be donated to a hospital sale. She picked up *The Pied Piper of Hamelin*, crouched on a packing box, and became so engrossed that she read the whole thing before taking off her hat and coat.

Occasionally, Sallie would invite classmates over for dinner or a weekend slumber party, but she had few close friends. After school let out in mid-afternoon, she was inclined to disappear behind the thick, protective walls of the Big House, where she could talk with Nursie or retreat to her room with a pad of writing paper or a book.

Her distrust of the outside world made her unusually dependent on the swirling life of the Bingham household for emotional sustenance. She studied the family the way a painter would a flower, observing it, magnifying it, exalting it. Her parents, the servants, and her brothers and sister would later serve as a source of material for her fiction. "I'm the born outsider," she said. "The one looking on, the observer. I was very quiet and silent growing up and certainly didn't do any rebelling that was very open. But what I was doing all the time was absorbing it all with the greatest fascination, because it was fascinating."

Years later, Sallie would see herself as the debunker of family fictions. But as a child, she, more than anyone, fed on the notion that the Binghams were divinely blessed, perhaps because by doing so her shyness and awkwardness did not matter. As a member of a clan that she later would describe as "mythic," she felt automatically entitled to respect and recognition in a world that she viewed as dangerous and uncertain. "It was very special. Even then there was no family like it," she said. "I never met anybody that I thought was comparable. My parents were such outstanding liberals and were constantly under attack. . . . They were much better-looking than anybody else. They led a more glamorous life. They didn't seem to have to waste a lot of time with the petty boring details that other people wasted so much time on. They were more interested in ideas."

It was this richness, Sallie said, that made a writer out of her, although her relationship with her father, which grew especially close after the war, probably had as much or more to do with it. Jonathan and Eleanor were still too little to be good company for him. Sallie, with her literary bent and solitary nature that reminded him so much of his own, soon became Barry's chief source of pleasure and pride.

Each evening after supper and before bed, father and daughter would sink into armchairs in front of a fire (in winter) or recline on the chaise longues scattered around the side terrace (in summer), and in his mellifluous voice Barry would read aloud from Twain and Dickens while the little girl listened intently. Sometimes, Sallie would give him her poems to critique. Over time, the bond grew tighter.

The experience reinforced Sallie's already swollen sense of superiority and fed her perception of herself as different from other children. "Oh, I think she had an idea from the very beginning that she was an original genius," said Mary, who believed that human egos, Sallie's especially, needed to be kept firmly in check by "Christian humility [and] classical proportionateness."

Barry's admiration was less conditional, and he encouraged his daughter's talent with every means at his disposal. In the summer of her eleventh year, he arranged for the Binghams' outdoor amphitheater, which was sometimes used for productions of the Louisville Ballet, to serve as the backdrop for

Sallie's own curious version of Hamlet. Taking on the dual role of director and actress, Sallie slashed the Shakespearean classic to one hour and reduced the lines of all the parts except her own—Ophelia. "It was the only Hamlet known to man in which Ophelia was really the main character," said Mary.

Three years later, Barry bankrolled another of Sallie's productions, a one-act fairy tale opera set to the music of Schubert and performed by students from the University of Louisville. "Sallie's later attitude [of being unloved as a child] is so odd because her parents were so encouraging and just every little spark of talent was fanned and brought along," said Molly Clowes.

Barry's flattering attention, born in part of his own frustrated ambitions as a novelist, made for a strong, almost Oedipal bond between father and daughter and cemented a relationship that, by definition, excluded Mary. "I didn't enter into that confederacy," she said. Indeed, Sallie looked down on her mother, as she did almost everyone else in the family. She was convinced that she and her father were the resident intellectuals. Her mother was really not in their league.

Not that she did not regard Mary as capable, but her abilities, Sallie felt, were more those of a domestic overseer. She saw her mother as the effortless, gossamer-gowned manager of dinner parties, the sunbonneted gardener, planting bulbs and arranging flowers, and the stern parent fussing over grades and after-school piano lessons. "She ran the enormously complicated machinery of that family, but I always thought that she missed something," said Sallie. "I'm sure she would revile me if I said that."

Along with the condescension came anger. To Sallie, Mary was the nagging disciplinarian who was forever correcting her manners or telling her to keep her heels down when she went horseback riding. Once, when Sallie was seven or eight, she exclaimed that Popo, the family's black standard poodle, had "dainty" feet. Feeling that the child had misused the word, Mary flew into a rage. "Dainty feet!" she exclaimed. "Why that's the most absurd remark I've ever heard."

Sallie bitterly resented such cutting appraisals. "Mother has a tongue that could take your skin off," she said. But Mary's tongue was also the only tongue in the household. Barry, ever eager to be associated with pleasure, shrank from the tears and silences such outbursts caused. It was Mary who monitored the children's school performance and worried over their posture and hounded them to write thank-you notes. It was she who corresponded with boarding school headmasters about illnesses and missed exams. "I've never heard Barry criticize the children to their faces, even when a father would normally reproach a child for its behavior," said Jacques Albert. "I've never heard him say a word. The brunt always fell on Mary."

Her parents' close marriage, her own fierce intimacy with her father, and her fear of her mother's scalding criticism made Sallie a jealous rival for

Barry's time and affection. She idealized him far more than she did the family as a whole. He was her mentor, protector, and, later, perhaps even her fantasy lover. No one, not even her three husbands, would ever compare with him. "He was the star," she said. "Everybody in the family knew that and everybody in Louisville knew that. . . . He was just one of those people that everybody adores." Long after the Oedipal stirrings of childhood normally fade, Sallie continued to feel possessive of her father. "Yeah. That's really unpleasant, but I think maybe that is it," she confessed years later. "Of course, [daughters feeling competitive with their mothers for their fathers' love] happens a lot in families."

———

Sallie's view of her father was inflated even more by his appointment, in the spring of 1949, as head of the Marshall Plan in France. For Barry Sr., as he was now called to distinguish him from his adolescent son and namesake, the post was a heady substitute for the kind of experience his father had had, at a much later age, as ambassador to Great Britain. Through his newspapers and his involvement in Americans for Democratic Action, Barry Sr. had campaigned vigorously for the sweeping economic scheme to rebuild Europe. Now, from his perch in Paris, he was to dole out U.S. aid to restore French ports, harbors, and railroads destroyed during the war and to build gleaming new dams for electrical power. The assignment was even more "satisfactory," as he and Mary would say, because he would have the opportunity to work with such top U.S. foreign policymakers as Averell Harriman and Dean Acheson.

The press of diplomatic business and the glitter of their social life in Paris took Barry Sr. and Mary even farther away from the daily schedules of Worth, Barry Jr., Sallie, Jonathan, and Eleanor—all of whom moved to France for the one-year posting. But Barry Sr. persuaded himself that any scars that resulted from his inaccessibility would eventually fade, replaced by glowing memories of the family's life abroad. "I was so busy [in Paris] . . . that I didn't get very much time to spend with the children," he said. "But the experience is something I think they will remember [warmly] all their lives."

By the time of Barry Sr.'s appointment, Worth, then barely seventeen, was in a fragile and precarious state. Like his siblings, he desperately wanted his parents' approval. At the same time, he resented their disdain for his all-American virtues. Out of defiance, he refused to apply himself academically at Exeter. His best subject was Bible study—a result of Mary's relentless Sunday readings—and he made a respectable B-plus in that. But in his other courses, Worth limped along with C's and D's. He failed algebra and geometry altogether.

Worth's status as a well-rounded boy had never commanded much respect from his parents. They assumed he would excel at sports, perform more than adequately, if not brilliantly, in his studies, and probably be president of his class. But they felt he was totally lacking in many of the traits they prized most. On an application form, Mary spelled out his failings with savage honesty. Worth, she said, was "very untidy, unpunctual [and] a bad procrastinator" with only a "vestigial" interest in the arts and an "average" sense of humor. In other words, he was both undisciplined and dull—two black marks in the Bingham household.

At Exeter, Worth seemed determined to punish his parents for their brutal evaluation of his talents. He became laconic, rebellious, and antisocial. One master at Exeter wrote Barry Sr. and Mary that their son was "uncooperative, unfriendly and very inattentive." Even so, the Binghams were unaware of the depth of Worth's difficulties until, six months before the family was to depart for Paris, Exeter abruptly expelled him for drinking. A friend in Louisville had sent him bottles of gin through the mail, and on the night before Christmas vacation began, he had consumed nearly a pint of it and passed out on the frozen lawn of the Unitarian Church. Several classmates found him, dragged him into the vestry, and pinned a note to his coat telling him they would be back early the next morning to rescue him. Unfortunately, the church pastor discovered Worth before the boys could return. One quick call to the headmaster's office and Worth was out.

Exeter sent an airmail special delivery letter to Mary and Barry Sr. announcing the news, but it failed to arrive before Worth's train got back to Louisville, so he was forced to tell them himself. Most parents would have been stunned and stone-silent, or red-faced with anger. Mary just took Worth's hand and squeezed it. "We've really let you down," she said. The comment left Worth bewildered and a bit frustrated. The one positive aspect of this disaster was that it demonstrated to his parents that he needed help and attention just as much as Barry Jr. or Sallie did. Now Barry Sr. and Mary were telling him that he was not responsible for his actions—they were. He felt even more invisible and unappreciated than he had before.

Barry Sr. seemed more concerned about appearances than the expulsion itself. He knew that Worth and his friends got drunk occasionally as a sort of adolescent rite. But he had hoped that his son would be smart enough to realize that a gentleman can indulge a weakness, any weakness, as long as the rules appear to have been obeyed. It was the conspicuousness of the infraction that troubled Barry Sr. more than the infraction itself. "We were pretty well aware of his drinking," he said. "But it never occurred to me that he would be so indiscreet, poor boy, as to let himself get caught."

Thanks to the efforts of Thurston Chase, his old headmaster at Eagle-brook, Worth quickly managed to get into Lawrenceville, an all-male boarding school just outside Princeton, New Jersey. "He is a boy who may be reacting somewhat to a sense of inferiority," Chase told Lawrenceville in a letter pleading Worth's case. "His mother and father are both so very successful, so very charming, and altogether respected that Worth may feel he just can't live up to their standard of perfection."

It was an affliction that plagued all the Bingham children. Barry Sr. and Mary had grown up in chaotic, dysfunctional families and had not only survived but triumphed in every respect—in their stunning good looks, their academic achievements, their professional accomplishments, even in the romantic closeness of their marriage. The Bingham children could not help but feel that it was their responsibility, their duty even, to equal their parents in every category and, if possible, to surpass them—a daunting proposition.

In Worth's case the pressure was compounded by a sense of being disapproved of by his father, who, after the Exeter expulsion, compared him more and more to his wasted Uncle Robert. For years, Barry Sr. had been too preoccupied with Barry Jr.'s weight problems and reading difficulties to pay much attention to Worth. He wrote infrequent letters to his oldest son and showed only a pro forma interest in his athletic victories. He felt that Worth did not need him the way the others did. "Worth was strong and outgoing, so his father didn't spend much time with him," explained one Bingham in-law. "He was always helping Barry Jr. Worth, he thought, was capable of taking care of himself."

Getting kicked out of Exeter was a bright, burning flare, a clear sign that Worth felt neglected and needed more time with his parents. But neither Barry Sr. nor Mary felt comfortable having a heart-to-heart talk with their son. Instead, they arranged for him to have weekly sessions with Lawrenceville's school psychologist, Ben Balser. Several months into the semester, Mary traveled to Princeton for a consultation. Dr. Balser shocked her with his analysis of what was troubling Worth. "He's in love with you," he said. At first, Mary looked stunned, then she laughed. "Well, if he is, he'll certainly be quickly disillusioned because I'm in love with his father and I make no secret of the fact!"

Worth's adolescent confusion complicated the Binghams' move to Paris in the summer of 1949. Initially, Mary felt that he should finish out his senior year at Lawrenceville, where he had found some understanding teachers and congenial classmates. Indeed, he had made such an effort to improve his grades that he was in the honors group in English. But his housemaster wrote the Binghams that Worth was still "restless," "purposeless," and disturbingly adrift compared with other boys, "although his sophisticated attitude gives the impression of real maturity."

The evaluation spurred Mary to pull him out of the school and bring him to France with the family. "I am a little concerned at leaving him so far away, even in your good hands," she wrote Lawrenceville's headmaster. "Dr. Balser believes and I do too, that a closer identification with the family and particularly his father, is very important for Worth at this time."

Barry Sr. managed to get Worth on the waiting list at Le Rosey, a fashionable Swiss boarding school noted for the number of princes and counts among its clientele. The plan was for Worth and Barry Jr. to spend the summer at a lycée in Lausanne perfecting their French while Barry Sr. worked in Paris and the rest of the family, including three-year-old Eleanor, seven-year-old Jonathan, and twelve-year-old Sallie, soaked up the thatched-roofed charm of Cabourg on the Normandy coast.

The lycée in Lausanne was strict and claustrophobic. No drinking was allowed and Barry Jr., just fifteen and fresh out of Eaglebrook, ended up rooming with a Turk who spoke only halting French and English. Driven by an adolescent desire for absolute answers to life's confounding riddles, Worth found himself drawn to the Oxford Group, also known as Moral Rearmament, an anti-Communist, quasi-Christian organization that was all the rage in Europe at the time. Movement disciples, who gathered at the organization's mountaintop headquarters high above the town of Caux-sur-Montreaux, preached a gospel of honesty, purity, unselfishness, and love that appealed to Worth's troubled spirit. He dragged Barry Jr. along to several meetings, where participants were encouraged to confess their transgressions. At one, a man from Detroit stood up and talked about the number of virgins he had deflowered. That did it. The Movement was "too weird" for Barry Jr. and he wanted nothing more to do with it.

But Worth was entranced; here at last were clear, definite guidelines to live by. Toward the end of the summer he announced to his parents that he had no intention of going on to Harvard as they had hoped. After he graduated from high school in the spring of 1950, he said, he would travel the world with Moral Rearmament, putting on morality plays. He persuaded Mary and Barry Sr. to come to Caux to see the organization for themselves. To their acute embarrassment, they found Worth so suffused with piety that "he confessed to us all sorts of things we never did want to hear about at all."

Barry Sr. compared Worth's newfound ardor with his own brief brush with Catholicism at Middlesex. For all of Worth's seeming devoutness, however, he was still easily recruited to sin. Toward the end of the summer he met a dissolute young Englishman whose family had sent him to Caux to shape up—something he clearly had no intention of doing. "Listen," the boy said to Worth. "There's a bar halfway down the mountain. Why don't we go and have a few drinks?" Worth put up no protest. Several hours later, after one too many whiskeys, the two hit upon the idea of leaving Moral

Rearmament and going to Paris. They walked out of the bar and stole the first car they saw.

Before they had even crossed the French border, though, Worth sobered up enough to realize that he had made a terrible mistake. With considerable effort, he convinced his partner to turn the car around, head back to Caux, and park the vehicle exactly where they had found it. As they sped up the winding road leading to the bar, they saw in the rearview mirror the headlights of a police car in hot pursuit. They stepped on the gas, raced up to the top of the mountain, leapt out, and ran into the woods, tiptoeing into their rooms at Moral Rearmament headquarters shortly before dawn.

At breakfast the next morning, the gendarmes were waiting; they had found a Moral Rearmament pamphlet with Worth's name on it in the front seat of the stolen car. Worth called his father from the local jail and Barry Sr. arrived on the overnight train from Paris to bail out his son, paying the police handsomely to forget the whole affair.

Still, even the Senior Binghams had to admit that, in general, Worth seemed to have gained some depth as a result of his experience at Moral Rearmament. "It was very hard to swallow this revolutionary idea of Moral Rearmament's about following God's guidance," Worth wrote Lawrenceville's headmaster later that fall. "But I saw that this was the chance for me to be part of a cure for the world rather than its disease. . . . The last two months have been vastly more pleasant and satisfying than my old completely selfish existence." He even said, disingenuously, that he had given up drinking.

Worth's infatuation with Moral Rearmament faded soon after he enrolled, not at Le Rosey, which the Binghams decided was too snobby and exclusive, but at Lycée Jaccard, a spartan, family-run school on Lake Geneva. The lack of heat, hot water, extracurricular activities, and English-language textbooks soon left Mary wondering gloomily whether they had made the right decision in not sending Worth back to Lawrenceville. Her fears were not allayed when the headmaster at Lycée Jaccard appeared in Paris that winter and declared that he would not recommend Worth for Harvard because he was convinced he had written foul words on the bathroom walls, something Worth admitted he was quite capable of but, in this case, had not done.

The scene reminded Barry Sr. of his own difficulties years earlier when Middlesex had refused to recommend him for college. But because of the family's Harvard connections and Worth's workmanlike scores on the college entrance exam, M. Jaccard's explosion was not the end of the world. Worth left Lycée Jaccard and joined the rest of the family in Paris, where he signed up for courses at the Sorbonne but rarely went. By late spring, he heard from Harvard: He had gotten in.

Barry Sr., who had been named a Harvard Overseer after the war, was not altogether surprised. In the fall of 1949, he had written personally to the university's admissions director asking for "advice" about Worth's prospects. Several weeks later, Lawrenceville's headmaster had put in a good word with Harvard and had written Mary that he was "confident" that the combination of his recommendation and Barry Sr.'s past association with the school would do the trick.

The postwar housing shortage in Paris was acute. It was not until several weeks before Christmas, 1949, that the family finally located a house at 17 Rue Alfred-Dehodencq near the Bois de Boulogne. Until then, they had made do in quarters at the Hôtel James & D'Albany, a suite of rooms made all the more claustrophobic by the presence of a high-strung French governess.

Mary had insisted on bringing Nursie to France, mostly because she felt it was important for Jonathan and Eleanor to have continuity of care. But she thought better of it almost immediately. Nursie, who had rarely been out of Kentucky, despised the French, made no effort to understand the language, and found the food highly suspicious. "I finally realized that as long as Nursie was around the children would never have anything to do with French culture," said Mary. So she got a red-haired French nanny ("a distant cousin of Charles de Gaulle and she never let you forget it") and permitted Nursie to return to Kentucky to take care of her ailing mother. The Frenchwoman's arrogance, however, soon became unbearable. When Mary finally hired a replacement, Madame reacted to the news by locking herself in her room and staging a screaming, crockery-throwing fit.

Unlike Worth, Barry Jr. lived at home during the family's year abroad and attended the American School, where classes were taught in English. "With his reading problem, we felt he would just not survive if he had to deal with French," said Mary. He loved wandering up the Champs-Élysées to the American commissary and accompanying his mother to Christian Dior and Pierre Balmain, where Mary and the wives of the other diplomats bought their clothes. He admired the cool sensuality of the Foujita nude his parents acquired at the city's Independent Salon and hung on a wall in the Rue Alfred-Dehodencq house. After seeing a production of *Tristan and Isolde* at the Paris Opera, he was hooked on opera for life. "That was when the needle really went in," he said.

But he was shocked at the behavior of his American School classmates, many of them military brats who spent most of their time gulping bottles of cognac. In disgust, he joined the Société Nautique de Beaux Hommes, a French rowing organization. The sessions were physically and culturally painful. The instructor rode a bicycle along a path beside the river and shouted orders in French, straining Barry Jr.'s already tenuous grasp of the language with technical terms like "square up the blade." "I didn't even know what I was supposed to do," he recalled. "I just kept trying to watch everybody else." Worse still, at 190 pounds, he was so heavy he "practically sank the boat."

Embarrassment and the knowledge that his parents were going to enroll him in a new boarding school—Brooks, in North Andover, Massachusetts —when the Marshall Plan year came to an end, finally drove Barry Jr. to embark on a serious diet. As a little boy, he had blushed crimson when his mother dragged him to the chubby sections of Louisville's men's stores. Now he summoned the will to refuse even the rich French desserts that reminded him of the butter-and-cream-laden cuisine of the Big House. Mary and Barry Sr. were delighted, relieved, and a bit puzzled. A year in France seemed an odd time to lose weight, they thought. Why was he doing it now? "It wasn't a question of his having a girl," said Mary. "I think he just came to realize what a handicap it was. He never was grotesque. He was just plump and he had very fair, curly hair. It just made him look sort of like a simpleton, I think, to be so fat."

Sallie had the opposite problem, which put her through her own peculiar kind of hell. At twelve, she had already shot up to her full height of five feet ten inches, and the rapid growth made her thin and pale as an eggshell. To build up her strength, Mary insisted that she come home from the French convent school she attended for a hot lunch and nap in the afternoon.

The regimen did little to fill Sallie out or to allay her fears that she was a "giantess" who would never be attractive to boys. Sallie's deteriorating self-image only redoubled her fear of life outside the family circle. She had to gather her courage anew each day just to take the bus back and forth to school. One time Barry Jr. spied her with a ticket in her hand standing in line and helplessly allowing dozens of Frenchmen to elbow her aside to get on the bus. "She was a very, very uncertain child and very timid," said Mary.

Home was still the sphere in which Sallie felt most secure, so it was natural for her to become the guardian of domestic traditions. That year in Paris, despite unfamiliar surroundings, she insisted that the family put on its annual Christmas Eve play. The event had started several years earlier as an adaptation of the boyhood theatricals Barry Sr. had staged for the Judge, but the date had been changed to Christmas Eve because that was Mary's birthday. In the early days, *A Christmas Carol* was a favorite selection, with Barry Sr., dressed in a flowing academic gown, taking the part of Scrooge and one of the older boys ominously rattling chains in the Big House basement to suggest Marley's ghost.

Later plays became less traditional, with larger audiences that often included such distinguished family friends as Adlai Stevenson. During one such production, Sallie, by then a fully-bloomed adolescent, poured herself into a long satin gown she had found in the attic. During a crucial scene, the dress burst and Sallie spent the rest of the evening trying to hide her décolletage from the peering eyes of the audience.

In Paris, Sallie chose *Rumpelstiltskin* as the family drama—mainly because Jonathan seemed perfect as the magical dwarf—and several *Life* photographers came to capture it. The ermine-trimmed costumes were far more elaborate than the makeshift arrangements of the Big House and the formal Parisian salon in which the production took place gave the show a regal and removed air. For a moment, the Binghams, costumed as royalty, appeared to be just that.

Such warm family gatherings were, however, infrequent. Most evenings, Barry Sr. and Mary were away at dinner parties, the theater, or diplomatic gatherings. Their absence made Sallie and Barry Jr. more dependent on each other's company than had ever been the case in Kentucky. Each night they ate supper together and studied side by side in the grand Rue Alfred-Dehodencq house, but filial affection somehow never took root. "They never had a relationship," said Mary. "I don't think anything ever developed between them."

Meanwhile, Sallie's loathing of Worth took on a dark sexual cast. Just before sailing for home in the summer of 1950, Barry Sr., Mary, and the three older children went to London for a brief vacation. One evening when Barry Sr. and Mary were out and Sallie was already in bed, Worth and Barry Jr. came back to the hotel trailing American friends from boarding school. Worth, as usual, was drunk, and he and one of his pals burst into Sallie's room whooping and hollering and, according to Sallie, poking and pinching her through her thin nightgown. Terrified, Sallie battled her way to the bathroom, locked the door, and spent the night huddled in the tub. "The Lord preserve me," she wrote in her diary the next day. Years later when she would recount the story to her female friends, Sallie would always say she was sure Worth had been about to rape her.

During the Marshall Plan year, *The Courier-Journal* continued to prosper under Mark Ethridge's firm hand. Circulation rose from 336,000 to 375,000 and the paper was rapidly making a name for itself with its in-depth coverage of foreign news and culture, and editorial crusades for Negro rights and fair treatment for labor. By 1952, a group of several hundred newspaper publishers around the country ranked *The Courier-Journal* fourth in a list of the nation's Top Ten papers, behind *The New York Times*, *The St. Louis Post-*

Dispatch, and *The Christian Science Monitor.* "Why leisurely Louisville should be blessed with one of the best daily newspapers in the U.S., and why *The Courier-Journal's* earnings rank among the nation's top ten," said *Fortune* magazine, "are questions that defy the short answer."

There was no such praise for the afternoon *Louisville Times,* which remained so gossipy and parochial that it was known in some circles as "Barry Bingham's Five-Penny Dreadful." When the *Times's* longtime managing editor neared retirement, Mark saw a chance to raise the paper's sights. In late 1951 he recruited forty-three-year-old Norman Isaacs, the acerbic editor of the recently defunct *St. Louis Star Times,* to do the job.

Born in Manchester, England, and raised in Canada, Norman felt at home with the Binghams' British affectations. In St. Louis and in Indianapolis, where he had started out as a sports reporter, he had built a distinguished record of involvement in civic works that satisfied the family's strong desire for community-minded editors. He was also keenly interested in fairness and journalistic ethics.

Norman's main strength was that he had a take-no-prisoners style that both Barry Sr. and Mark knew was necessary if the dead wood at the *Times* was to be cleared out. He quickly set about refurbishing the afternoon paper, building a stable of talented writers that included Peter Milius and Richard Harwood. By 1956, the *Times* had won its first Pulitzer Prize, the Bingham papers' third. But success came at a price. Many staffers were offended by Norman's purple language, his gruff manner, and his habitual yelling and screaming in the newsroom. His Jewish origins and suspiciously foreign background were additional minuses in Louisville, where the most prestigious country club, even today, effectively bars Jews.

But perhaps the most persistent complaint about Norman was that he shamelessly played up to the Binghams, taking Mary out for long lunches and insisting that Barry Sr.'s pet causes receive front-page coverage. Later, when he became executive editor of the papers, with responsibility for both *The Courier-Journal* and *Times,* members of the editorial board complained that he tried to bully them into taking positions that agreed with his own. "He was a Machiavellian character," said former *Courier-Journal* editorial writer John Ed Pearce. "A lot of people in town couldn't understand why Barry hired him or kept him."

Whether they could understand it or not, Norman was critical to the strength of the Bingham media empire in the 1950s and 1960s. The *Courier* had already been ascendent for some time. WHAS radio and TV were growing and prospering; Standard Gravure was snapping up more lucrative printing contracts with each passing year. The renewal of *The Louisville Times* under Norman Isaacs's able stewardship finally gave sinew and tone to the Binghams' weakest link.

Norman became a sort of adjunct member of the Bingham-Baker-Ethridge troika, allowing the Bingham empire, like America itself, to enter the decade of the fifties with a sureness of purpose, confident of its values, vision, and abilities. But like the country, too, there were invisible cracks beginning to form just below the surface that, left unattended, would one day contribute to the disassembling of the empire.

Mark and Willie Snow Ethridge's relationship with Barry Sr. and Mary was one such hairline fissure. In contrast to the Binghams' patrician formality, the Ethridges were open, gregarious, loud, and down-to-earth. They loved parties, encouraged clutter in their century-old white house, and cheerfully set another place if a visitor dropped by unexpectedly around dinner time. When the Kentucky Press Association convened in Louisville, Mark would drink till dawn with the good old boy publishers of small-town papers; for the Senior Binghams, appearing at such gatherings was a distasteful duty.

The Ethridges' spontaneity appealed to the jazz baby in Barry Sr., but they were a bit rough-hewn for Mary. "Mr. Bingham and the Ethridges seemed to have great rapport," said Mary Phyllis Riedley. "I don't think Mary Bingham felt the same way about them. . . . I think they were a little too, well, common maybe."

Willie Snow thought nothing of grabbing the first man she saw at a party and dancing his legs off, for instance, something that struck Mary as unladylike. Willie just figured it was the only way she would ever get to kick up her heels, since Mark hated to dance and preferred to hold court while clutching a glass of Scotch. At one of the Ethridges' annual Derby parties, Willie boldly stepped out with Ray Bolger, the actor who fifteen years earlier had danced his way to fame as the Scarecrow in *The Wizard of Oz*. To thank the Ethridges for their hospitality, Bolger performed an impromptu soft shoe in their living room to "Once in Love with Amy."

Willie was equally well known for her homespun literary efforts. While raising four children, she managed to write fifteen breezy autobiographical books in which she referred to Mark as "the roommate." Publicly, the Binghams applauded Willie's writing, but in private they could be savage. "I have only read a little of [*This Little Pig Stayed Home*]," Mary once wrote to Barry Sr. "In spite of Mark's warmer-than-ever-before reception of it, I find this effort, too, pretty excruciatingly embarrassing."

Lisle Baker and his wife, Mary Elizabeth, were less aggressively social than either the Binghams or the Ethridges. By temperament Lisle was a Southern gentleman, restrained and polite no matter what the provocation. With his crisp white shirts and bright bow ties, he provided a sartorial counterpoint to Barry Sr.'s Savile Row elegance and Mark's shaggy dishevelment. He was hardly one to boast or give offense.

Mary Elizabeth, however, struck Barry Sr. and Mary as overly impressed with her Wellesley degree. "I really can't imagine, when I look at her, why men ever countenanced the higher education of women," Mary told Barry Sr. "I think [Mary Elizabeth] would be very skilled at making a good jelly, if she had never been allowed to go to Wellesley. But to hear her talk about [world] affairs is plain torture."

Barry Sr.'s natural remoteness increased the just-below-the-surface tension at the Bingham companies during the 1950s. He and Mark and Lisle had adjacent offices, and during the work day visited each other frequently. But to other staff members, he was a vague figure and an object of considerable awe, a man they referred to respectfully as "Mr. Bingham"—never "Barry." Unlike Mark, who believed that everyone, from the lowliest delivery boy to the papers' top editors, should feel free to come talk to him, Barry Sr. kept his office door tightly shut. Except for those on the editorial board, he was virtually invisible to his employees. On the rare occasions that he communicated with them, it was usually in the form of a handwritten note expressing praise for a story or a photograph. He let others dole out criticism.

Barry Sr.'s need to avoid unpleasantness made it almost impossible for him to discipline or fire anyone. Norman Isaacs readily admitted that one of the reasons he came to have the power he did was because Barry Sr. was unwilling to get into a fight with him. "Barry has one weakness," said Norman. "Just one: He is terribly uncomfortable with confrontations."

While clearing out the underbrush at The Louisville Times, for example, Norman decided he had to get rid of a political reporter Barry Sr. had known since grade school. On Mark's advice, Norman went to see Barry first. "When do you have to do it?" Barry Sr. asked, a hint of fear rising in his voice. "Right away," said Norman. Barry flipped over a calendar he kept on his desk. "Can you wait five days? I have a meeting in San Francisco," he said. Norman nodded. "He never questioned my judgment or my need to take strong action," Norman said later. Barry's only concern was, "I gotta get out of here somehow."

Barry Sr.'s detached style meant that he rarely knew how much money his employees made. "I don't think he ever understood that we were starving," said John Ed Pearce, who earned an annual salary of about $9,000 in the mid-1950s after ten years at the paper. When people were clearly in trouble, though, Barry Sr. was delighted to come to the rescue. When the sports editor's wife got a fishhook in her eye, he chartered a plane to rush her to a special clinic. When the Sunday editor had a stroke, he sent him to Jamaica for a vacation, all expenses paid.

Barry Sr. had a well-earned reputation for taking flowers to the sick, paying his respects at funerals, and dispensing comfort and funds in large doses to his faithful minions. It was a standing joke among *CJ & T* reporters and editors that they worked on a plantation. "I would call it enlightened despotism," said Jean Howerton Coady, a former reporter. "You knew they would take care of you but they didn't pay you a hell of a lot."

The Binghams took particular pains to please the first families of Louisville by finding jobs at the paper for their daughters, sons, nieces, and nephews. For years, Adele Brandeis, daughter of U.S. Supreme Court Justice Louis Brandeis, did what was politely called "research" for the editorial writers. "She was one of those genteel people that the Binghams sort of gave jobs to, like the debutantes," said Mary Phyllis Riedley. "No one took her all that seriously."*

Barry Sr. considered the editorial page his personal domain and ran it much like he ran the rest of his life. He claimed that he invited robust debate, but in fact he dictated precisely the policies he wanted while conducting the daily editorial conference in a way that allowed him to avoid personal clashes. Each morning he arrived with a set list of topics to be discussed. He always asked the editorial writers and cartoonists if they had other items to add, but, sensing his discomfort, they rarely did.

Mark's approach was less structured. When he ran the conference in Barry's absence, he had no set agenda and began meetings by asking writers what they felt was important in that day's news. Inevitably, each person's special cause surfaced and squabbles ensued. "Mark's conferences were better than Barry's because he made you work," said Molly Clowes. "You had to think of things. Barry didn't like arguing and he didn't like controversy about subjects."

Although Barry Sr. wanted the staff to like him, even love him, there were inevitable pockets of discord. One concerned his involvement in Democratic politics and state and community affairs. Barry Sr. encouraged his reporters and editorial writers to observe public life firsthand, especially at the local level. He felt they had an obligation to get out of the office and learn what was happening in Louisville. But it was clear that, in his own case at least, friendships with politicians and civic officials came first and the newspapers second.

The intertwined relationships often caused difficulties. "We'd ask him, 'What did you discuss at this meeting or that meeting?' " said Molly Clowes.

---

* The debutantes and their sponsors presented the papers with a special kind of problem. In those days, most of the society section was actually written by the grand dames of Louisville and no news was more important than the coming out parties of the city's well-born young ladies. Refined though these matrons were, however, they could not always be trusted to protect the papers' moral tone. In one celebrated incident, executive editor Jimmy Pope came flying out of his office just before the paper was to be printed, waving a proof of the women's page in his hand. "How did this happen?" he screamed. The reason for his alarm became clear when the women's page editor read the headline her society madam had, in all innocence, submitted: "Debutantes Rest Between Big Balls."

"And he would say, 'Oh, that's something they probably wouldn't want me to talk about.' Mark was involved in about as many outside activities as Barry was but he talked about them. In fact, he got himself in great arguments with people because he talked about them."

Like the Judge, Barry Sr. rejected elected office as inappropriate for a newspaper owner, but he saw no conflict in working as a *consigliere* behind the scenes to bring about the election of others. In 1952, when his friend Adlai Stevenson made his first run for the presidency, Barry Sr. was a close adviser. After Stevenson lost to Eisenhower, Barry Sr. joined him and several other of the candidate's friends for a "fact-finding" trip around the world.

In Stevenson's 1956 bid, Barry Sr. assumed an even more active role, co-chairing the candidate's national volunteer organization. Like many newspaper owners at the time, Barry Sr. did not consider his political involvement a conflict of interest. "It didn't seem strange or peculiar," he said. "If a publisher joined a political campaign in the 1980s, there would be a lot of talk about it. There really wasn't at that time."

Before World War II, intervention had been the main issue on which the normally acquiescent Barry Sr. had stood firm. In the 1950s, the issue was racial integration of the public schools, a change that Louisville was better prepared to accept than most Southern cities. The community's public transit system had been desegregated as early as 1871. By the early 1950s, Louisville's public libraries, public golf courses, and most of its hospitals were open to both races.

Still, the actual process of integrating the city's 45,000 students, over a quarter of whom were black, was a delicate and difficult chore. On May 17, 1954, when the Supreme Court's decision in *Brown* v. *Board of Education* came down, putting an end to the doctrine of "separate but equal," the five-person Louisville Board of Education was in the midst of a debate about buying milk coolers. As news of the decision was read, members fell silent. Board president William Embry then cleared his throat and told the group that they must begin planning for desegregation immediately, even if the Court allowed them five years to do so.

The result: Louisville's newly integrated schools opened peacefully on Monday, September 10, 1956, a little over two years after *Brown*. Only five protesters showed up. No one paid much attention to them and they did not return the next day. Less than two hundred miles away, in the towns of Clay and Sturgis, Kentucky, the reaction to school integration was so violent that the governor had to call out the state militia. *The New York Herald Tribune* and several other top papers took to describing Louisville's triumph as the "quiet heard 'round the world."

The strategy was simple. Louisville had decided to integrate all grade levels at once, redistrict the system without regard to race, and, as a sort of safety valve, to permit black and white parents alike to transfer their children out of the schools assigned to them. The role of *The Courier-Journal* and *Times* was critical. Within days of *Brown* v. *Board of Education*, the papers began crusading for peaceful enforcement of the law, highlighting on their news pages every instance of successful, nonviolent integration in the country and gently editorializing against prejudice.

The approach seems low-key by current standards. "We tried to make our position pretty firm, but not too insistent, not too shrill," said Barry Sr. Even so, the papers' stand earned Sallie, Jonathan, and Eleanor taunts at the all-white, private academies they attended, and brought a deluge of hate-mongering late night phone calls to the Big House.

As a matter of principle, Barry Sr. always had his name and number listed in the telephone book. It was easy for angry readers to call the newspaper owner at any hour—and they did. "Lots of times you could hear a jukebox in the background and it was obviously a call from a bar," he said. "In about 90 percent of the cases it would end with something like, 'You're nothing but a nigger lover.'" The insults never seemed to faze Barry Sr., who managed to sink back into a sound sleep after even the most bitter attack. But Mary would often lie awake until dawn. In order to get a good night's rest, she finally took to answering the phone herself. "Hello, I'm the housekeeper," she would say. "I'm afraid I can't disturb Mr. Bingham right now." The subterfuge left most tormentors nonplussed.

Barry Sr. enthusiastically embraced school integration, but Mary was far less ardent, mostly because she felt that mixing students of different capabilities would bring the most gifted ones down. "I want blacks to be educated and to have equal opportunity and all the rest of it," she said. "On the other hand, we cannot sacrifice the bright children to a social requirement."

Mary's attitude toward race had been apparent during the war, when she had forbidden Worth from inviting the son of the Binghams' black gardener to join him in the family swimming pool. "It amazes me that any child brought up in this part of the world would not have taken in through his pores a sense of the mores which forbid inviting nigs to swim in the pool," she told Barry Sr. at the time.

Less than ten years later, however, the mores of Louisville had changed dramatically. Within a year of *Brown*, racially segregated ticket lines at the bus station were eliminated, the public parks were open to both blacks and whites, and, in 1956, even the public swimming pools were integrated. The city fathers' strategy was to coax compliance rather than to demand it. Barry Sr., whose talent as a liaison had won him honors in World War II, was on the mayor's committee to help smooth the path for integrated facilities, and in that role he made dozens of personal visits to theaters and restaurants to try to persuade owners to open their doors to blacks.

The first place he succeeded was a popular seafood restaurant called Leo's Hideaway, where the proprietor initially integrated the dining room by inviting two black ministers to dinner. When several of the white patrons objected to their presence, Leo took them aside and said, "But you don't realize. These men are rectors." "Ohhhh," came the understanding reply. "They're rectors, are they? Well, maybe it's all right to let them eat here." As the white customers sat back down, however, one of the black men pulled out a racing form. "I wish that had not happened," Barry Sr. said. "Nonetheless, the rectors integrated that restaurant." By 1961, more than 185 eating establishments had dropped their racial barriers. Only one theater and one hotel remained closed to blacks.

For all their chest-beating for integration in the 1950s, however, the Bingham newspapers did not have a black reporter on staff until 1961, when Norman Isaacs hired Charlayne Hunter as an intern on *The Louisville Times*.* The twenty-year-old woman was already well-acquainted with controversy. Earlier that year she had been one of the first two blacks to attend the University of Georgia, sparking riots and demonstrations. Her arrival was not universally hailed at the Louisville papers either. When executive editor Jimmy Pope heard that Hunter was coming, he put up such a fuss that Mark was forced to fire him.

Pope had been instrumental in the maintenance of another policy that seemed inconsistent with the Binghams' generally liberal stand on race. Although blacks had always been pictured on the news pages, they were barred from the women's pages and the society sections. Louisville's white-gloved matrons would cancel their subscriptions, went the reasoning, if their daughters' wedding pictures appeared next to those of black women. "Nobody questioned the policy," said Jean Howerton Coady. "We just accepted the double standard."

In one particularly painful incident, the papers sent a photographer to Fort Knox to take pictures of a Girl Scout camping trip. During the outing, a deer suddenly wandered out of the woods, walked up to the troop's only black member, and permitted the little girl to pet it. The *CJ* photographer snapped away while the other Scouts looked on admiringly. When the picture appeared in the newspaper, the deer and the white children were clearly visible. But Jimmy Pope had cropped the black girl out. All that could be seen was a small dark hand on the animal's neck. When the little girl's father wrote in to ask how he should explain the incident to his

---

* Under her married name, Charlayne Hunter-Gault, she went on to co-anchor "The MacNeil/Lehrer NewsHour."

daughter, Mary Phyllis Riedley, then on *The Courier-Journal*'s women's page, answered him with brutal honesty. "I told him that Jimmy Pope was a bigot," she said. It was not until 1963 that blacks were pictured on the society pages.

AN AMERICAN IDYLL

During the 1950s, Sallie, Jonathan, and Eleanor got used to seeing a constant stream of famous visitors trooping through the broad downstairs hall of the Big House. One spring, the Duke and Duchess of Windsor came for the Derby and ate red snapper and Trigg County country ham in the Binghams' dining room. When the British photographer Cecil Beaton arrived for a visit, he became fascinated with Lizzie Baker, Barry Sr.'s old black nurse, and insisted on taking pictures of her with her head wrapped in colorful cotton like Aunt Jemima. Even the stiffest dinner guests melted after a round of charades in the Binghams' cozy study, with Barry Sr. relishing the challenge of acting out a word before a crackling fire. "It was an idyllic life, an idyllic American life," said Marietta Tree, a frequent visitor during those years.

The Kentucky Derby, held on the first Saturday in May, was a natural showcase for Mary and Barry Sr.'s expanding circle of rich, powerful, and lettered friends. Lured by one of the country's preeminent social and sporting events, people who would not dream of going to Louisville at other times of the year fell over themselves in the scramble for invitations, arriving by the carful with handsome leather luggage.

On that weekend, Sallie, Jonathan, and Eleanor were banished to the second-floor sleeping porch in order to make room for their parents' guests.

There they huddled happily under thin blankets, feasting on leftover Derby pie, a gooey chocolate and nut confection, and telling ghost stories to the accompaniment of a mournful night owl. "Certainly no out-of-town guest looked as wearily on the milky May dawn as the child who had spent the night on a sleeping porch," Sallie wrote years later.

For the Binghams' adult guests, the Derby routine was a test of physical endurance. Like Mardi Gras in New Orleans, the annual two-minute horse race was Louisville's excuse to let loose, get drunk, and show off. "The day before the Derby you arrive and have a skimpy lunch," recalled Marietta Tree. "Then you go to a cocktail party and dinner party that night. Then the next day, again a light lunch and you dash to the Derby. Afterward you go to someone's beautiful house, white fence around it, green lawn going on for miles, and the mint juleps begin. You treat it like an ordinary cocktail party, but you know about two people there. You don't leave until 11:30 P.M. and when you get home you are so tired you just think you are going to die. Then Barry and Mary call and say, well, dinner is at 12:30 A.M. at the River Valley Club. And you are dying to go to bed, but you change into black tie and an evening dress and have dinner. And then you stay up until three or four and by this time all the Louisvillians are drunk. Barry and Mary adore this; they stay till the last second. Then the next day, more dead than alive, you get up, have a huge lunch and sit under the pink dogwoods. Then you finally crawl on the plane. We went twice and [my husband] said, 'Why did we do it? I don't understand, we must be fools.'"

Barry Sr. and Mary were more oversubscribed in their public lives during the 1950s than they had been in all the years prior to World War II. Barry Sr. spent weeks out of town each year serving on the boards of the Rockefeller Foundation, the Asia Foundation, the American Society of Newspaper Editors, and the advisory board for Pulitzer Prizes.

Mary, too, was consumed with worthy projects. Appalled by Kentucky's high illiteracy rate, she spearheaded a campaign to get "bookmobiles"—libraries on wheels—into every county in the state. She begged and pleaded with all sorts of groups, from a truck drivers' local to the United Daughters of the Confederacy, to donate money and books for traveling libraries. She testified on Capitol Hill for rural library funds and even persuaded Kentucky movie theaters to put on special matinees, asking two books as the price of admission. The hard work did not go unnoticed. Eventually, Mary received an honorary degree from the University of Louisville and a special citation from President Eisenhower.

But the surfeit of activity meant that Jonathan and Eleanor, who were still quite young, had even less contact with their parents than Worth, Barry Jr., and Sallie had had when they were little. "I don't think there was a lack of love," said Catherine Luckett, a friend of Jonathan's. "But there was a lack of time to give them a great deal of attention. I don't remember the Binghams lighting much. I have an image of them going out the door." Mary's sister Helena routinely checked in on the Big House when Barry Sr. and Mary were out of town. Once she arrived to find Jonathan frantically bandaging a friend who had bumped her head on a piece of furniture during a game of hide-and-seek. The mishap had driven the little girl's tooth right through her lip.

With his delicate build, pale good looks, and quick smile, Jonathan was more like his father physically than either Worth or Barry Jr. His droll sense of humor appealed to adults as well as children and he possessed a vivid imagination. Within the family he was called "Toad" because his nature seemed so like the frenetic adventurer in *The Wind in the Willows*. "He could make up rhyming operettas with the silliest nonsense and then suddenly one would find oneself going right along with him and making up nonsense just like that, that's how contagious it was," said his friend Tani Cutchins Vartan.

Barry Sr.'s long absence during the war had made Jonathan unusually comfortable with women, who were attracted to his sensitivity, warmth, and vulnerability. "I think maybe he had a bit of my Barry's insight," said Mary. "He was enormously sympathetic to people." Jonathan's place in the family, though, was uncertain. "He sometimes felt that the two older boys were the heroes and he sort of came after," Mary said. The sense of being second-rate gave Jonathan a wan and somewhat sad cast despite his surface nonchalance. "I think of him as slightly the neglected boy," said Catherine Luckett.

But being the youngest son also had its rewards. Less was expected. Unlike Worth and Barry Jr., who were burdened with perpetuating the family dynasty, Jonathan had the freedom to be independent, to go his own way. Once, during a school math test, he completed the first problem correctly, then refused to do the others. "Jonathan, didn't you know the answer?" the teacher asked. "Of course I did," he replied impatiently. "But the other problems were identical. You work them out the same way. So why go through all that? I already showed you I could do it."

Jonathan had a wide mischievous streak. When he was three, he sneaked out of his room at nap time, scooped Sallie's goldfish out of their bowl, and took the doomed and wriggling creatures to bed with him. As he got older, he focused his devilish tendencies on incendiary devices. He was fascinated with Barry Jr.'s elephant gun and used to take it out on a knoll near the house and blast noisily in the direction of the river. He shot rabbits through the screens in his bedroom window and plotted to "blow up Mam'selle," the French-born replacement for Nursie, who left the Binghams in the early 1950s.

Like his older siblings, Jonathan went to the Ballard School for his early education. Every weekday, Curtis, the Binghams' chauffeur and handyman, drove Jonathan and several other neighborhood children to the bus stop in a black Cadillac. Mary dressed her son in English schoolboy style—gray flannel pants and a blue blazer—but Jonathan worried that the outfit made him look stuck up. Like Sallie, he felt vaguely ashamed of his family's wealth. So each day he stripped down in the car, changed into a pair of blue jeans that he carried in his satchel, and then stuffed the blazer and pants under the bench at the bus stop. On the way home, he reversed the process.

Other parents began helping with the car pool in 1952, when Jonathan and a few local boys enrolled in Louisville Country Day, an all-male academy. One day both driver and passengers were in ugly moods and conducted the early morning trip in silence except for the occasional whoosh of a passing car. All of a sudden, ten-year-old Jonathan broke the stillness. "Oh, fuck!" he said, then slumped back into a moody torpor. "That's Jonathan," said his friend David Morton. "He was just a bright, quirky, funny kid."

In his three years at Country Day, Jonathan did barely respectable work. By the time he left in eighth grade, he stood twentieth in a class of twenty-five. His best marks were in English and biology, his lowest in Latin. "He is an avid reader," Country Day headmaster Harry Ludwig recorded in a letter of reference. "He literally 'eats up' books on science, etc. However, when it comes to studying fundamentals, be it arithmetic, grammar, Latin forms, etc., Jonathan just can't be bothered." He was equally lackadaisical about athletics, especially team sports—a serious liability for a boy in the rah-rah fifties.

His grand obsession was science. He set up a chemistry lab in the Big House basement and was forever manufacturing foul-smelling potions. Once, to study the effects of insomnia, he deprived himself of sleep for days. When the Binghams had trouble with their telephones, they asked the phone company to investigate, only to discover that Jonathan had rigged up his own secret system for calling his friends. "He had all these colonies of mice down in the basement, for what reason or purpose we didn't know or care very much," said Barry Jr. "Jonathan was a satellite in his own orbit."

Barry Jr., nearly grown and away at school, viewed Jonathan and Eleanor through a blurry lens. "They were so remote," he said. Sallie was too engulfed in her writing to offer much companionship either. Eleanor was constantly told to be quiet when she came home from elementary school because Sallie was upstairs working. "She was redeeming the family by being a creative writer," Eleanor said. "None of this shoddy journalism stuff. This was real writing."

Because of the physical and emotional absence of other family members, Eleanor and Jonathan were thrown together more than most brothers and sisters. Jonathan and his friend David Morton would sometimes hitch up one of the Binghams' horses to a small buggy they kept in the barn and parade around the fields and lawns with Eleanor and Ina Brown, David's cousin, sitting serenely in the back. "That was a great moment for the little girls," said Mary.

For the most part, though, Jonathan viewed Eleanor as a noisome little sister, more of a nuisance than a suitable companion. "She was a fat, dirty-faced kid," said David. "Jonathan teased her mercilessly, because after all, poor Eleanor, she was the last in line." For years after his death, Eleanor promoted the myth that she and her brother had been soulmates, but the truth was more pedestrian. For Eleanor, left to her own devices much of the time, Jonathan was just the most constant face in the household, and he felt the same bond of familiarity with her.

Like Jonathan, Eleanor had none of the hysterical drive to achieve that bedeviled the older trio of Bingham children. By the time she was old enough to go to school, Mary and Barry Sr. had become thoroughly disenchanted with Ballard's progressive tenets and sent her instead to Louisville Collegiate School, where her Aunt Henrietta had won spelling bees and played basketball decades earlier.

Collegiate accepted girls from kindergarten through high school, dressed them in shapeless blue and white uniforms, and consciously kept classes small, usually no more than fifteen to a grade. Like Miss Jennie Ellett's School in Richmond, Collegiate promised well-born girls a classical education and, eventually, a place at one of the country's elite universities. Sallie, the family's best student, had already been excelling at Collegiate for several years when Eleanor, chubby and uncertain, arrived for kindergarten in 1951. Her grades were mediocre and she soon became, by her own admission, the class clown, staging pranks to amuse the other girls.

On the surface, Eleanor seemed the most independent of the Bingham clan. When the family had sailed for home after the Marshall Plan year, she had climbed purposefully up the gangplank without glancing back at the French woman who had taken care of her for months. "Eleanor didn't give a damn about leaving Mademoiselle," laughed Mary. "There was no emotional moment there at all. She was always self-contained and very adequate." At twelve, Eleanor ended a story in the Collegiate yearbook with a blunt, Aesop-like moral about self-sufficiency. "If you want something done well," she wrote, "do it yourself."

But there was a defensive quality about her sturdy insouciance. Born too late to benefit much from the plodding constancy of Nursie, she grew up under the supervision of several different nannies. "I sense that she has great pain," said one friend. "She would develop attachments and then have to break up." Eleanor soon found comfort in food, and became, like Barry Jr., "a great eater," which only exaggerated her broad features.

Driven by a deep need for affection, she also turned outward, making friends easily, laughing louder and more heartily than anyone at life's absurdities. But there was often an angry edge to her antics. Deep down, she was furious that she got so little of her parents' time and attention. One day the servants phoned Mary at the office and told her that Eleanor had commandeered the Big House tractor and was zooming around the property, grinding up the grass and bumping into trees. "I feel sorry for Eleanor," said a *CJ* staffer who knew her. "I just feel she got the rawest deal."

When Eleanor was ten, Jonathan was packed off to boarding school. Mary felt that her youngest son was not applying himself at Country Day, and she worried that his laxness would only grow worse if he stayed in Louisville. "In the suburban life of young people it is almost impossible to make them follow a proper regimen for studying," she said. "The weekend seems to be entirely given over to pleasure of all kinds, rolling around in automobiles and everything else. It's really much easier just to send them to a boarding school where they have study hours and have to do things they're supposed to do."

So, in ninth grade, Jonathan entered Brooks School. Barry Sr. and Mary chose the small, all-male New England academy for many of the same reasons they had sent Barry Jr. there several years earlier: It was less competitive than Exeter and it specialized in problem cases. The Binghams were particularly impressed with the headmaster, Frank Ashburn, who personally greeted his charges by name after chapel each evening, and with Barry Jr.'s kindly English tutor, Fessenden Wilder.

Like Barry Jr., Jonathan became manager of the hockey team, rowed, worked on the yearbook, and suffered under nicknames like "Bing" and "Bing-bones." By his senior year, he managed to become a prefect, a sort of dormitory policeman, despite a brief brush with disciplinary action himself for smoking. But Mary's hopes notwithstanding, his grades remained low. He got C's and D's in English. Even in science, his strongest suit, he never made better than a B.

Jonathan's main talent seemed to be an ability to make friends, friends of all stripes and backgrounds, from New England brahmin Ellery Sedgwick III, second cousin of actress Edie Sedgwick, the Andy Warhol camp follower, to Joe Hammer, a self-described "goody-goody" who went on to be an investment banker, to Bob Turner, a staff member of *The Shield*, the school paper, who later became a reporter for *The Boston Globe*.

His best pal was Charlie Bascom, a dark-haired classmate from St. Louis who roomed with him in a converted farmhouse at the farthest end of the campus. The Southerner and the Midwesterner could not help feeling different in a school dominated by "those horrible people from Long Island," as Charlie put it. They were also drawn to each other by a common love of electrical gadgetry and a deep distrust of authority. "Jonathan didn't toe the line," recalled Joe Hammer. "He was wild, flamboyant, excessive in some ways. He and Charlie were the mad scientists."

Charlie first became aware of Jonathan when he was invited to visit the "house" that Jonathan had managed to build inside a nearby woodpile. "It was all very secret," said Charlie. "You could walk right by it and never know because it looked just like a woodpile. We used to meet there and do nothing." The two boys constructed a bicycle built for two, joined the ham radio club, went on expeditions to Radio Shack in Boston, and sneaked out on weekends for booze. Their most elaborate project involved wiring their dormitory room so that the light would go out when a prefect opened the door—an ingenious way to get around the 10:00 P.M. "lights out" rule. "It was super," said Charlie. "Our finest hour."

But even Charlie knew little of Jonathan's life as a member of Kentucky's royal family. Concerned about being thought too wealthy or well connected, Jonathan kept no family pictures on his bureau. He never mentioned the Big House, the fluttering servants, or the famous visitors who regularly flowed through the Binghams' lives. "When Bob [Turner] and Joe [Hammer] and I visited him in the summer in Louisville, we saw all this stuff firsthand and it was amazing," said Charlie.

Especially enviable was the casual freedom that Jonathan seemed to enjoy as his birthright. During these visits, Jonathan and his friends would go to parties that lasted till 2:00 A.M., adjourn for "The Breakfast," an after-party party consisting mostly of beer, hard liquor, and rock-and-roll bands, then careen home and collapse in a heap on the upstairs sleeping porch. After one of these marathons, Jonathan and his friends pulled up at the Big House about 7:00 A.M. just as Barry Sr. was leaving for work. The older man did not break stride. "Well, gentlemen, did you have fun?" he asked cheerily as he went on his way. Said Joe Hammer: "At our homes, most of us would have been grounded."

It was during these interludes that Jonathan's boarding school friends came to know a brilliant, mercurial Louisville boy named Peter Ardery, who would eventually go to Harvard with several of them. Peter, a classmate of Jonathan's from Louisville Country Day, came from a blue-blooded but unmonied Kentucky family. While the wealthier Louisville boys went away to Groton, Exeter, and St. Paul, Peter, much to his shame, remained at home. Once, when several of Jonathan's Brooks buddies dropped by for a visit, Peter apologized repeatedly for the modest size of his house. "He was somewhat of a Gatsby figure," said Joe Hammer. "He was always on the outside looking in."

Jonathan was spellbound by Peter, who aced exams without seeming to study and shared his mania for Chuck Berry records and high-speed cars. There was an unpredictable, rebel-without-a-cause quality about him that appealed to Jonathan, even as Peter yearned for the money, position, and cosseted security of life inside the Big House. "Peter was extraordinarily wild," said Charlie. "We didn't all like him, but we were fascinated." Over time, Peter became the performer, Jonathan his adoring audience.

Peter often drank himself to the point of unconsciousness, while Jonathan held his liquor so well that friends suspected him of watering his bourbon. The results were often mindless pranks at Peter's expense. Early one morning after hours of partying, Peter passed out on the Binghams' kitchen floor. Jonathan fetched Curtis's chauffeur's hat, put it on Peter's head, and watched as Charlie Bascom grabbed a fire extinguisher from the wall and sprayed the comatose figure with foam.

———————

As fascinated as Jonathan was by Peter Ardery, the true magnetic figure in his life was Worth. For years he had heard outrageous tales about his older brother. Like the time Worth had thrown a beach party using an old toilet as a punch bowl, ladling out refreshments in a grand mockery of Louisville debutante balls. Or, on another occasion, when he had smirked at the cherry on top of the fruit cocktail and announced to the room that he had had "every cherry in town."

Just before Worth left for Harvard in the fall of 1950, Barry Sr. gave him two pieces of advice: Don't make your drinking friends your best friends and don't join a club. Worth did both. He became a member of the Delphic Club, known as "the Gas," and spent hours at its Linden Street headquarters sipping Scotch and playing poker. He signed up for naval ROTC; went out for the swim team; played house squash, soccer, and tennis; and joined the ski club. The lectures, tutorials, and college dramatics that had entranced his parents more than two decades earlier held little allure, although Worth did manage to apply himself in Prof. Walter Jackson Bate's legendary course on Samuel Johnson. He also made a fetish of taking Fine Arts 13, a grueling survey course, and badgered his friends into doing the same on the grounds that no educated man should be ignorant about art. But these spurts of academic rigor were not the rule. "He really was not intellectually minded and he did very little work," said Barry Sr. "He just barely got through."

Worth's ambivalence about women was apparent at Harvard. Through his mother, he had come to know the withering power a strong, intelligent female could have over a man. Out of fear as much as choice, he had few female friends, preferring instead the safe, uncomplicated camaraderie of men. His relationships with women were often aggressively sexual and predatory. In Cambridge, Worth rounded up unattractive girls who wanted to meet Harvard men and brought them back to his room for "horror shows" —parties in which the main entertainment was mocking and ridiculing the women. Once, at a Boston party, he unzipped his fly to display a wristwatch coiled around his penis. He acquired hard-core porno films—then illegal— and charged admission to screenings. Intellectuals were "wonks," women were "crunts." "He had a very dirty mind," said one family member. "I mean, really foul."

Worth and a classmate once enticed two unsuspecting Radcliffe women to a nudist colony outside Boston, stripped to the buff to play volleyball, and then invited the horrified (and fully clothed) girls to join them. When Boston Psychiatric Hospital put out the word that it would pay volunteers to experiment with mind-altering drugs, Worth persuaded several friends to sign up with him. After taking an early version of LSD, he sat and moaned for two hours.

Watching his son's performance from afar, Barry Sr. fretted that Worth was becoming too reliant on the good looks and charm that had doomed Robert and Henrietta. "Things were so easy for him," he said. "He just thought he could get away with most anything. And he did." To help straighten Worth out, he arranged for him to work summers at *The Louisville Times* under a stern taskmaster: Norman Isaacs.

For Worth, Norman became a mentor, teacher, and disciplinarian, roles that Barry Sr. had neither the time nor the skill or inclination to play. "I was his second Papa," Norman said. But before he could begin the molding process, Norman had to settle Worth down a bit. On his first day of work Worth showed up wearing tennis shoes, dirty gray dungarees, and an old shirt. Norman told him he looked like a bum. "You get your ass home, get in some decent clothes, and get back here within the hour," he barked. In forty minutes, Worth was back at the paper, breathless but appropriately attired in a jacket and tie. Norman was still not satisfied. "You couldn't have gotten out there and back in forty minutes," he said. "If you get pinched for speeding on the River Road, I'm going to put the story right on page one."

That was the beginning of a rule that applied to all the Bingham children as they became adolescents. "We hoped they wouldn't disgrace us," said Mary. "But we told them that the newspaper was absolutely obligated to expose any of their misadventures."

The papers paid far more attention to their triumphs than their transgressions, however. The Bingham children were considered celebrities whose lives were inherently newsworthy. Late one summer, Joe Creason, *The Courier-Journal*'s self-anointed folklorist, wrote a story about an expedition he had taken with Worth and Barry Jr. to Murphy's Pond, a large snake-infested pool in western Kentucky. The piece ended with seventeen-year-old Barry Jr. shooting a cottonmouth so expertly that he splintered its spine.

Such moments of recognition were especially sweet for Barry Jr. Still handicapped by his reading disability, he continued to struggle in school, but succeeded nonetheless in following Worth to Harvard. Exactly how he got in is a mystery. His SATs were poor. He took the tests twice, never scoring higher than low 500s and high 400s on the verbal part, and even dipping down into the 300s in math.

Harvard's acceptance letter dumbfounded Barry Sr. and Mary, who had resigned themselves to the idea that Barry Jr. would end up at a less competitive place like Trinity. "He's got the most amazing will," said Mary. "He was absolutely determined to get into Harvard. If he hadn't, I think it would have been a terrible defeat for him. We were overjoyed when he made it."

Mary was probably right when she speculated that Harvard had made allowances for the son of a Harvard Overseer and a Radcliffe trustee. Barry Jr. himself attributed his acceptance to the special attention he got at Brooks. "I for one will never forget that you all made it possible for me to go to Harvard—and to stay in once I got there," he wrote his Brooks housemaster, Fessenden Wilder, years later. Even after graduating from Harvard with a degree in history, he continued to tell friends that every educational institution he had ever attended had considered him "a calculated risk."

Barry Jr. joined Worth at Harvard in 1952, but compared with his older brother's free and easy existence, his college days were rigid and grimly circumscribed. Worth used to worry that Barry Jr. had no friends. He tried to get him into the Gas, but Barry Jr. was so nervous during the "punching season," when prospects were looked over, that for one of the few times in his life he got drunk and ripped a phone out of the wall, poisoning his chances for a bid. Instead, he joined the less prestigious Iroquois Club, made the naval ROTC rifle team, and played French horn in the university marching band.

His primary passion was crew. When classes broke for spring vacation, Barry Jr. stayed on campus, rowing up and down the Charles River each morning and afternoon until his hands looked like raw roast beef. He went to enormous lengths to keep his weight down. "I never ate lunch for four years," he said. "If you want to make crew and you have my metabolism, that's the only way to do it." His parents saluted his determination, but they took little interest in rowing, which Mary considered "a masochist's idea of fun." When Harvard won the Eastern Sprints, Barry Jr. sent an excited telegram home. "My parents didn't even know what in the hell it was," he recalled with some bitterness. "They didn't even know it was a boat race."

Because of his reading problem, Barry Jr. was naturally drawn to nonprint forms of communication. One day at Harvard he dropped by the commons room in between classes and became mesmerized by the Army-McCarthy hearings then being broadcast on television. He completely forgot about his next class and sat staring at the black-and-white screen. "I said to myself, 'If that little black box has the power I see in it, I want to get into that line of work.'" The magnetism of the "little black box" would eventually lure him back to Louisville to run the family's broadcasting stations, just as Worth would be pulled inexorably to the newspapers.

When Barry Jr. reached his twenty-first birthday without smoking, his father rewarded him with an African safari. Barry Jr. became thoroughly enchanted with the continent and sent back canister after canister of film to the *CJ* Sunday magazine. In Tanzania, he met a European who wanted to sell his tea plantation on the slopes of Mt. Kilimanjaro; for a while Barry Jr. fantasized about buying it.

A year later, Barry Jr. told a *CJ* reporter that his life plan was to graduate from Harvard, complete his commission in the Marine Corps, and then return to Africa as a photographer. "Africa was it," said Mary Clowes Taylor, who dated him briefly. "He was totally absorbed in his dream. But who knows what was on his mind? He was still young and foolish, as we all were."

The prospect of living out of a jeep invigorated him. The outdoor life made him feel securely masculine and self-confident, and gave him a sense of unfettered freedom that he rarely experienced at home. At such moments, he seemed once again to be the merry little boy his parents had known.

The years of harsh dieting and rowing had hardened his body and chiseled his face, accentuating his handsome blond features. After graduating from Harvard in 1956, he went to Quantico, Virginia, for his Marine Corps training and spent many weekends with Melinda Page Hamilton and his other Virginia cousins. To them, he was "gorgeous and divine," a witty, humorous young man who treated them to movies, photography lessons, and late-night horseback rides. "He was an absolutely charming, delightful boy," said Marietta Tree, who hosted him at Heron Bay, her Barbados estate, when he was in his early twenties. "I can't believe that Barry today is the same boy that I knew then and loved so. He's so stiff now. He's so bursting with anger."

Unlike her brothers, Sallie did not want to go away to boarding school. Instead, she continued to attend classes at Collegiate, running home in the afternoons to draft poems in her room on clean white lined bond paper. On the surface, she seemed conventional, even docile. At a gathering of Young Churchmen at St. Francis in the Fields, where the subject that day was the generation gap, she defended her parents—and those of her friends—as being "not so unreasonable." She got good grades and showed no signs of the sullen rebelliousness that had afflicted Worth during his teenage years. "She was the perfect child," said Eleanor. "She never really put a foot wrong her entire adolescence."

But inside, Sallie was filled with resentment, especially toward her stiff and seemingly perfect mother. One short story written in high school describes a mother so cold and self-absorbed that she gingerly kisses her children on the ears to prevent smearing her lipstick. "Sallie always had a very ambivalent attitude toward her mother," said Barry Sr. "I never felt that this was a solid thing. I felt it was just a phase that she was passing through. . . . But I'm afraid she's never really recovered."

Sallie's emerging sexuality only made matters worse. Like most teenage girls, she was both terrified and obsessed by the prospect of physical intimacy. One Saturday afternoon, Sallie and several of her friends pulled up to a stoplight in downtown Louisville and heckled the necking couple in the next car so mercilessly that the man drew a gun on them. True to the Binghams' tell-all standards, the incident turned up in the Sunday paper.

Worth's attitude toward his sister compounded her anger and confusion. She flushed hot with shame when he whispered nasty things under her door during an ocean crossing on the *Queen Mary*. On other occasions he did not hesitate to call her a slut, as if to say, "This is the kind of treatment you can expect from men if you become sexually active." He did not want Sallie to behave like some of the girls he took out. She was furious one night when he rammed his car into the back of her date's Cadillac because they had lingered too long in the elliptical driveway outside the Big House.

In the spring of 1954, Sallie donned a long white dress and, along with other Collegiate seniors, walked down an aisle strewn with red rose petals to receive her diploma. To Sallie, her blond hair cut short and softly curled, life at that moment must have seemed as much on the brink of happy change as any bride's. In the school yearbook, her classmates voted her "most individualistic" and listed "Don't Fence Me In" as her theme song. The line under her class picture hinted at her isolation: "I would beat a hidden way through the quiet heather spray to a sunny solitude." Weeks earlier, she had won a national award for one of her short stories. Now the future lay before her, pristine and uncharted. The possibility of remaking herself dangled deliciously in the future, just out of reach.

Sallie had effortlessly gotten into Radcliffe, following the by now well-established Bingham tradition of going to Cambridge for school. That summer, as if to signal her eagerness for a new life, she challenged the double standard Worth and her parents so fiercely defended by losing her virginity to a college dropout. Suspecting the worst, Mary and Barry Sr. summoned her to their bedroom, where Mary screamed that Sallie was ruining her reputation and acting like "a bitch in heat."

Sallie entered college in the fall of 1954. Worth had graduated the previous spring and was living at a safe distance in Norfolk, Virginia, where he had followed up his ROTC training with active duty in the navy. Barry Jr., just back from Africa, had begun his junior year at Harvard. Consumed with crew and his scholastic struggles, he saw little of his younger sister.

Sallie's four years at Radcliffe would be the high point of her life. Like her mother decades earlier, she arrived a shy, sheltered girl, one of only a handful of Southerners, branded by her accent and silent ways. But by the time she graduated—like her father, magna cum laude—in 1958, she would be the toast of the campus, a promising young writer with a three-book contract from Houghton Mifflin and a marriage proposal from a Harvard man who shared her patrician background and literary ambitions. For Sallie, life would never again be quite as sweet or as full. "She was extravagantly admired in college," said Mary. "I've always been convinced that very early success is hard to take. It's like being the head of the football team, I think. Life is never as good afterward."

In comparison with the prim constraints of Kentucky, Cambridge seemed alluringly exotic. Most of the Radcliffe girls had gone to Eastern boarding schools and were already well versed in makeup, foul language, and the independence of dormitory life. Louisville Collegiate School had not even permitted co-ed dances. "We led sheltered lives in the most sheltered homes in the most sheltered environment," said Sallie's Collegiate classmate Mary Clowes Taylor. "[We were] just a rarified, isolated, introverted group of girls."

The freedom at Radcliffe was intoxicating and a bit burdensome. For the first time in her life Sallie was confronted with a host of worthy competitors. When her freshman creative writing professor asked how many students in the room had had their work published, almost every girl held up her hand.

Sallie spent most of that first year in a lonely, locked battle to succeed. She hated the cold weather, the ammonia and linoleum smell of the corridors in her brick dormitory, and the puffy French toast the dining halls served on Sunday evenings. She was so painfully shy that she went to her single room in the dark rather than ask for a lightbulb. She peddled to class on a black bicycle, studied on the third floor of the Radcliffe library under buzzing fluorescent lights, and felt a gnawing sense of guilt when she took time off to buy a wide-skirted dress and rhinestone earrings. "What a shame! What a shame to waste an education," she lamented. "I paid for that Saturday with two days in the library."

Years earlier at the Big House, Sallie had discovered the black leather binder her mother had owned at Radcliffe, with the lecture notes copied in that impossibly erect and tiny hand. Now the memory of it haunted her. She worried that she was no match for her or for the other college girls. "They all seemed more iron-willed than me," she said.

But Sallie's period of uncertainty was brief. The summer after her freshman year she made her growing self-confidence plain by refusing to "come out," an act of rebellion that Mary and Barry Sr. found annoying and foolish. They were embarrassed, of course, that Sallie had so conspicuously rejected Louisville's customs. But they had also hoped that the parties and tea dances might make Sallie less of a hermit in her hometown. It mattered little to Mary that she herself had refused to "come out" in Richmond years earlier. That was different, she argued. The Capertons could barely afford food and rent, much less orchids and orchestras; for the Binghams, a debut was a comfortable expense. Sallie would hear none of it. After days of tearful arguing, she left for Europe.

Nonetheless, the Binghams did their duty and hosted an elaborate debutante party for three of Sallie's friends, complete with dancing on the Big House porch. To Mary Clowes Taylor, one of the honorees, the evening was memorable for its moment of surreal violence. "A typically weird Bingham twist," she said, referring to the family's reputation in Louisville for being "different." As was usual during outdoor parties, the family's standard poodles roamed freely among the revelers. Suddenly, on the shadowy lawn just beyond the dancing, one of the dogs turned on the other and broke its neck right in front of the stunned and horrified guests. In a grotesque tableau, the orchestra played on while the waiters dragged the dead animal away.

━━━━━

In her sophomore year, Sallie became a familiar author in *The Harvard Advocate*, the campus literary magazine that had once published her father's work. She was one of only two women in a writing class taught by the poet Archibald MacLeish, Barry Sr.'s wartime superior at the Office of Facts and Figures, and by the end of her junior year, she had won the coveted Dana Reed Prize, an award given each year for the best undergraduate writing in a Harvard publication. She was the first woman ever to do so.

Her prize-winning story, "Winter Term," was a disturbing portrait of female dependency and male ambivalence. In it, a college boy named Hal tries desperately to break away from his girlfriend, Eleanor, who, lacking confidence in her other attributes, attempts to bind herself to him through sex. Hal "wondered how much of her desire was passion and how much grasping; girls used sex to get a hold on you, he knew."

The frank language of "Winter Term," coupled with the unapologetic sex scenes, caused a minor scandal. A Radcliffe dean, worried about damage to alumni giving, asked Sallie to delete all references to Cambridge before the piece was reprinted the following year in *Mademoiselle*. Sallie's godfather, Mark Ethridge, wrote a tongue-in-cheek note professing concern for her "spiritual and moral welfare." Word circulated in Louisville that the Binghams had bought up every copy of the magazine to prevent people from reading it.

The truth, however, was that Barry Sr. had bought multiple copies so that he could send them to friends. He and Mary were genuinely proud of Sallie's artistic achievement. "I didn't feel shocked," he said. "I think a creative writer has a right to put those things down on paper." As for Mary, she considered "Winter Term" first rate, "one of her few stories that attacks a universal theme."

Like most of Sallie's writing, "Winter Term" was highly autobiographical and the sexual fumbling she described almost certainly happened to her. Although she was still inherently shy, much of the insecurity about her physical appearance had melted away by the end of her freshman year. Her height was now an asset and she thought of herself not as the gangly "giantess" who had once waited timidly at a Paris bus stop, but as a willowy blond sylph. "Sallie had a great sense of herself," recalled a woman a class ahead of her at Radcliffe. "I always thought she had something of a horse face, but she thought of herself as beautiful." Her growing stature as a campus literary figure fed her hungry ego, making her appear self-assured. For the moment at least, the unworthy "Angel Sallie," the frightened child within, was successfully buried. "At that point I think she was a pretty arrogant young woman," said Barry Sr.

Sallie had a number of affairs in college. The most celebrated was with Jonathan Kozol, who went on to write *Death at an Early Age* and *Illiterate America*. In 1958, he fictionalized their romance in a novel called *The Fume of Poppies*. Kozol described "Wendy," believed by everyone to be Sallie, as a woman who is "all sex and wants to be." Radcliffe classmates confirm that Sallie made it clear she loved going to bed with men. Arthur Kopit, a Harvard contemporary, even cast her as a stripper in his campus play, *On the Runway of Life You Never Know What's Coming Off Next*.

Despite the vaunted feminism of her later years, she had few close female friends. "I like distances," she wrote at the time. "I am glad that the girl next door does not know whom I go out with, and I do not miss talking to her about Fine Arts 13. . . . It is easier for me to study in a room full of strangers, and I like to walk down a street without seeing anyone I know. This, to me, is freedom."

In her senior year, Sallie became involved with A. Whitney Ellsworth, the editor of *The Harvard Advocate* who would later go on to co-found *The New York Review of Books*. She became intrigued when her carefully typed *Advocate* offerings came back with thoughtful notes attached, signed A. W. E. "I don't know who that is," she used to joke, "but I certainly am in awe of that person."

Whitney appreciated and encouraged her artistic talent in a way no man had done since her father. But the resemblance to Barry Sr. went far beyond a mutual interest in writing. Like the elder Bingham, Whitney had the air of an English dandy and an almost foppish interest in clothes. While other students showed up at crew races in sweatshirts and pants, Whitney came in a shirt and tie, blazer, and gloves. "In those days I was so naive, I thought he was gay," laughed a female contemporary.

The attire seemed natural to the scion of a wealthy New York and Connecticut family known for its interest in art, literature, and philanthropy. Despite small flashes of rebellion, Sallie's most deep-seated desire was to re-create her parents' life, and snaring Whitney was the fulfillment of that fantasy. Already, Sallie had outshone her mother at Radcliffe, achieving a better academic record and wider renown. Now she had captivated a man who seemed practically identical to her father in looks, dress, literary tastes, and wealth, but who came from a background even more established and distinguished than that of the Binghams. Why, the Ellsworths lived at One Sutton Place, arguably the best address in New York City! Whitney's father had attended Eton and shot wildlife in India with Kermit Roosevelt!

In June 1958, Barry Sr. delivered the Radcliffe commencement address, warning the young women that they had been born in the wrong generation if they wanted sheltered, secure lives. A month later, Sallie and Whitney announced their engagement. The previous summer, Sallie had almost decided in favor of Ned Bonnie, a steeplechase horseman from Louisville, but that would have meant coming home, assuming conventional responsibilities, and stepping out of the limelight. Flushed with her college triumphs, Sallie set her sights on a grander future. The buzz in Harvard Square was that she was marrying Whitney to manage her writing career.

The resemblance to their own relationship was not lost on the Senior Binghams. "It seemed almost a repetition of what Mary and I ourselves had gone through," said Barry Sr. "We'd been in the same class in college and it turned out to be a long and happy marriage. I must say I was optimistic that it was going to be the same thing. . . . Sallie and Whitney just looked like a couple of blond gods as they went around together."

Worth and Barry Jr., however, felt patronized by Sallie and her Harvard beau. When the couple announced their plans, Worth sent a congratulatory telegram to "Shitney" Ellsworth. Then, when the inevitable protest ensued, he insisted that Western Union had garbled the message. "They did not have two minutes of time for each other," said Barry Jr. "Worth thought Whitney was a pompous ass."

The summer before the wedding, Sallie worked as a guest editor at *Mademoiselle*, the same honor the magazine had bestowed on the doomed writer Sylvia Plath a few years earlier. Then she left with her family on a tour of Europe. The trip was the last vacation the whole Bingham clan would ever take together, and it had a grand, fin de siècle aura about it. After an ocean voyage on the *Mauretania*, the family traveled to London, Brussels, Venice, and the Dalmatian coast, ending up in Dubrovnik, the Yugoslavian seaside resort. While in one of the antique shops along the River Liffey in Dublin, Barry Sr. and Mary purchased Sallie's wedding present: a set of eighteenth-century flat silver.

In Vienna, Worth and Barry Jr. broke away, flying to Brazaville to begin a six-month safari that would take them to the Belgian Congo, Kenya, Tanganyika, Nyasaland, and Mozambique. Barry Jr., fresh out of the Marine Corps, was still bursting with romantic hopes of living in Africa. Worth went along, so family legend has it, to prevent his brother from "going native."

The safari had a magical quality. A hotel manager in the Congo arranged pygmy dances for them. In Uganda, they climbed an active volcano and stood shivering at the crater's edge while a thousand feet below a lake of booming, thundering lava sent molten rock flying into the air. In October, two months before their journey's end, Worth and Barry Jr. drew straws to decide which one of them would make the long trek to Louisville for Sallie's wedding. Worth lost and went through five changes of planes getting home, returning to Africa less than ten days later.

Despite Sallie's earlier shows of defiance, she insisted on a state wedding in the grand Bingham manner, and Barry Sr. and Mary were only too happy to oblige. "I think she enjoyed what Aunt Sadie used to call the 'prominence' of it," chuckled Mary. Indeed, the wedding was in many ways Sallie's announcement that she had finally won the competition with her mother, a battle that had begun in childhood with jealously guarded evenings in her father's lap, progressed through the fears and awkwardness of adolescence, and finally ended triumphantly in a brilliant career at Radcliffe and marriage to a man whom even casual acquaintances could see was a younger version of her father.

Two flower girls and four bridesmaids in wheat-colored taffeta, carrying dark pink geraniums, preceded the bride to the altar at St. Francis in the Fields. Sallie, resplendent in candlelight satin and pearls, wore the same

Limerick point lace veil that her mother, her grandmother Caperton, and her great-grandmother Lefroy had worn on their wedding days. In her hands she clutched creamy white calla lilies. For the reception, the Big House was blanketed with flowers. An orchestra played waltzes as Sallie and Whitney tried gamely to repeat the steps they had learned especially for the occasion.

Whitney, however, was unimpressed with the Binghams' efforts to put on a proper society wedding. While opening the presents, he made disparaging remarks about the taste of some of the family's less wealthy acquaintances. "He intimated that none of our Kentucky friends had given them anything worth having," said Mary. "I thought it was particularly unattractive and an ill-bred sort of thing for him to do."

From then on, the Binghams had the sense that Whitney felt he was slumming during his visits to Louisville. "He was a funny young man, a terrible snob. He thought Kentucky was sort of a barbarian place," Mary said. To be sure, Worth's vicious prank during the wedding only reinforced that opinion. As part of his "going away" outfit, Whitney had bought some fine yellow Italian leather gloves. While decorating the car with "Just Married" signs and streamers, Worth made sure to coat the steering wheel with black axle grease. Whitney's gloves were ruined.

Yet even that did not mar the perfection of the moment. The marriage between the star of Radcliffe and her well-born Harvard editor seemed to be a divinely blessed union, yet another installment in the Binghams' fated lives. Sallie seemed headed for a dazzling career. Her promise as a fiction writer appeared limitless. She had a book contract with an established publisher and a marriage that evoked enviable comparisons with that of her parents. She was rich, well educated, more beautiful than ever in her life, and now she was clearly outside her parents' sway. What could possibly go wrong?

THE HEIR RETURNS

On a hot August evening in 1957, Joan Stevens was nibbling peanuts and nursing a drink with a date in the cocktail lounge of the Chatham Bars Inn when Worth Bingham ambled in. He was beautiful—tall and athletic, his vivid blue eyes set off by a deep tan and dimples, and his clean, dark hair brushed back. But it was his "male essence" that struck Joan like a thunderbolt. "I was absolutely bowled over," she said. "He was so handsome and elegant, so in control yet so wild, so rakish."

The cocktail lounge of the Chatham Bars was a popular hangout for Worth, who had accompanied his family to a succession of rented vacation homes on Cape Cod every August since childhood. Each summer, the Chatham Bars filled up with prosperous families who returned year after year to spend a few weeks at the Cape. Joan's parents could not afford their annual month-long stay at the rambling white frame hotel, so her grandmother always discreetly paid the bill.

On the Chatham Bars's broad veranda overlooking the Atlantic, men in crisp blazers and madras trousers accompanied sunburned ladies in cotton dresses on predinner strolls. The clientele welcomed the dress code (tie required at dinner) and enjoyed the safety of being among one's own kind: white, Protestant, and sufficiently distinguished, either financially or genealogically, to be considered upper middle class, but not upper class. To the patrons of the Chatham Bars, "upper class" carried un-American and faintly decadent connotations of elitism. "Upper middle class" somehow suggested superiority based on merit.

Joan was already well aware of Worth's notorious reputation. In 1955, while she was attending classes at Harvard Summer School, a "fast" woman down the hall had scandalized her by declaring that she was sleeping with Worth Bingham, an "older man" who had graduated the year before. The woman had even bragged that she and Worth had nude dinner parties together! Among Joan and her sheltered clique, it was understood that Worth Bingham almost never took out nice girls. "He didn't waste his time on them," she said.

Worth had been stationed in Boston with the navy then, but he still spent hours at his Harvard club. He rarely came with a date, though, because he did not consider the girls he usually preferred suitable for public display. So Worth was alone when Joan, who was seeing another "Gas" man that summer, met him for the first time.

Now, two years later, Worth was on vacation from *The Minneapolis Tribune*, his first journalistic foray outside summer jobs at *The Courier-Journal* and *Times*. When he walked into the lounge of the Chatham Bars and spied Joan, he invited himself to sit at her table, completely indifferent to the obvious annoyance of her date. The next day, Worth called Joan up and asked her out. Thrilled and somewhat fearful, Joan began her plunge into the world of the Binghams, a world that seemed infinitely more glamorous and exotic than her own.

For one thing, the Binghams were Democrats, which in Joan's experience was simply impossible for nice people, especially nice *rich* people, to be. In her family of golf-playing Republicans, Franklin Delano Roosevelt was still referred to as Satan. The Binghams had also graduated from Harvard, a place that seemed intellectually more dangerous than Yale, where many of Joan's beaux had gone. And unlike others of comparable wealth, the Binghams were members of the mysterious and slightly unsavory upper class.

Dating Worth, Joan soon found, was confusing, delicious fun. On the one hand, he treated her like one of the guys. He wanted her to be easy and companionable, not prissy and demanding. He expected her to laugh at dirty jokes, hold her liquor, and, on the high-speed car rides he favored, to scream with pleasure not fear. But at night, he wanted her to be very much a woman. Those late summer evenings they would nestle together on the beach beneath Worth's camel's hair coat and he would demand that she "come across." Joan, a virgin, was inexperienced at sex and refused to go beyond heavy petting. "I almost didn't know what was going on," she said. "There was lots of necking and it was pretty exciting. It was *very* exciting."

Joan had graduated from Connecticut College the previous June. Around

Labor Day, she left to attend the School of the Museum of Fine Arts in Boston. Worth returned to *The Minneapolis Tribune*, where he had only recently saved himself from being fired.

Barry Sr. deeply regretted that he had never worked anywhere but the Louisville papers and was determined that Worth not repeat his mistake. *The Minneapolis Tribune* enjoyed an excellent reputation and the owners, the Cowles family, were patrician liberals like the Binghams. Still, Barry Sr. had been uneasy about speaking to John Cowles Sr., the publisher, about a job for Worth, and left the task of actually setting up the apprenticeship to Norman.

Barry Sr. was quite comfortable soliciting special treatment for the children of friends. He wrote recommendations by the score. But when it came to seeking favors for his own sons and daughters, he was overcome with embarrassment. There was something humiliating about asking a peer to give his child a wage-paying position. He had always felt faint contempt when friends called him on behalf of youngsters whose records were spotty, and he knew that with the exception of Sallie, who had distinguished herself as a model student, his children looked decidedly second-tier on paper. The thought of their being viewed as unqualified made him squirm with distress. And he might be refused, a thought that only redoubled the potential for misery. His solution, whenever possible, was to pass the task of actually asking for the job to others, mainly Mark and Norman, who had their own high-level contacts.

Worth was hurt by his father's clear reluctance to help him, mistaking Barry Sr.'s desire to avoid pain for a lack of interest in his son's welfare. But the arrangement was just fine with Norman. With Barry Sr. in his fifties and Mark in his early sixties, he had grand visions of a Worth Bingham–Norman Isaacs axis. Norman made one quick call to Minnesota and Worth was duly hired.

In Minneapolis, Worth made a bad first impression. "This young man turned out to be the stereotype of the spoiled brat," Robert T. Smith, the paper's city editor, told a *Time* reporter several years later. "His writing was abominable, he was inaccurate, lazy, and fully aware of what he considered to be his God-given position in the newspaper world. He wasn't worth a good goddamn." When confronted with an error in his copy, Worth would laugh, correct the mistake, and toss it back at the city desk with no word of apology. He routinely arrived late—often with a hangover—and sat in the newsroom working crossword puzzles or ogling *Playboy* because he could not be trusted with anything but the most inconsequential story. After two months, Smith got fed up and Norman received a call: Worth was just days away from being dismissed.

The following Sunday, Norman sat down at his typewriter and composed a fatherly six-page letter. "For Pete's sake, listen to what I say," it started. "One of the first things you have to get through your noggin is that *every* guy in every newspaper office is being watched all the time. . . . Put your feet up on the desk and there's a little mental note in somebody's head." Norman went on to point out that Worth's newspaper career was about to abort before it had begun. He reminded him of how bad it would look if he came home a failure. He laid out the situation in stark detail and took pains not to scold. "I think you do [want to be a newspaperman]," he said in conclusion. "Then, for God's sake, get in there and show 'em!"

Ten days later, Worth wrote to thank Norman for the "swell" letter he had written. "I feel that everyone else is more worried about my job than I am," he said somewhat defensively. But he had taken Norman's advice to heart. "It would be silly for me to say that everything has changed and that I am now the star reporter of the *Tribune* staff. However, a complete over-hauling of my approach and a lot more care in my work have brought results. . . . Perhaps it is foolhardy of me, but I have never had any doubt that I can out-write, out-dig, and out-think just about anybody here. I am also capable of doing the sloppiest, laziest, most unimaginative job around, and will do it consistently unless someone throws the fear of God into me." Somehow Norman's letter had done just that. "Once Worth got that thing, he just stopped, changed gears, and became Worth Bingham the newspaperman," Norman marveled later.

Worth pleaded with his Minneapolis editors for a second chance and was told he could stay on a probationary basis. It was a turning point in his professional life. Even Smith, his chief critic, later admitted that Worth turned into a top-notch reporter almost overnight. Of the dozen *Tribune* correspondents dispatched to Wisconsin to cover a ghoulish murder case, for instance, Worth was the only one who managed to locate the suspect's girlfriend. "He sweet-talked her right into speaking with him," said Norman. "He could charm the birds out of trees when he wanted to." When a berserk gunman was wounded by police and taken to the hospital, Worth was the reporter who got his deathbed confession. He bluffed his way into the hospital elevator, and then into the treatment room, where he took down a minute-by-minute account of the dying man's last words.

Worth resigned from the *Tribune* in the summer of 1958 so that he and Barry Jr. could go on their safari. He did not reconnect with Joan until that fall, more than a year after their torrid August together on Cape Cod, when he returned briefly to Louisville for Sallie and Whitney's wedding. Between the champagne toasts and the tossing of the rice, he called Joan in Boston and invited her to go skiing with him when he got back from Africa for good that winter. The invitation was a high compliment. Worth prided himself on his athletic prowess and Joan was almost as skilled as he was on the slopes. It was a bond deeper than sex, as far as he was concerned.

Joan said she would think about it and hung up. She very much wanted to go, but there was a small complication. By then, she was engaged to another man and the wedding was set for Thanksgiving, just six weeks away. The invitations had already been addressed and stamped.

Worth's call made her reconsider her decision. True, Joan's fiancé was the kind of man she had been groomed to marry. He had gone to Yale, then to Harvard Business School, and was now in an advertising firm where he had the Coco Puffs account. On dates, he and Joan would go to supermarkets and check out how many boxes of the sugary brown cereal faced the aisle. "Do I really want to spend my life worrying about whether this product is going to sell?" she asked herself.

No. She would rather spend her time with someone less predictable. Like Worth. She promptly broke the engagement and decided she would go skiing with the Bingham heir when he came back from Africa. Her mother went into total collapse. But then, giving up the chance to snag a Harvard M.B.A. was the sort of thing Joan's mother simply could not understand.

———

Joan's parents came from Portsmouth, Ohio, a little town on the Ohio River about midway between Louisville and Cincinnati. The real force in the family was Joan's paternal grandmother, Clara York Stevens, known as Ta-ta, who ruled through a domineering personality and the money that had come down to her from her father's trolley car company.

Ta-ta was a widow and terribly plain, but she had great dignity and style. Twice a year she checked into the St. Regis Hotel in New York City and bought a full season's worth of clothes at Henri Bendel. She read *The Wall Street Journal*, managed her own money, played a shrewd game of bridge, and would not dream of going through a summer without putting white linen slipcovers on all the furniture. Politically, Ta-ta was a hard-shell Ohio Republican. It was her view that Dwight Eisenhower was a closet Democrat.

Joan's father had been a Portsmouth rich boy, and her mother the pretty daughter of a dentist bankrupted by the Depression. Although they grew up together, their romance did not flourish until they saw each other in Massachusetts, where her mother attended Wellesley and her father M.I.T.

Against Ta-ta's wishes, Joan's father dropped out of Harvard Business School to get married and work in a Steubenville, Ohio, steel mill as an electrolytic engineer. Two daughters, Joan and Emily, arrived in rapid succession. When Joan was six, the family settled in Leetsdale, northwest of Pittsburgh. But Joan's mother ("a born social climber," said Joan) soon insisted that they move down the road to Sewickley, a Pittsburgh suburb with snob appeal similar to that of Lake Forest, Illinois, or Grosse Pointe, Michigan.

The Stevens family may have had an impressive address but they could afford only a thin slice of the grand Sewickley life-style. Ta-ta filled in the gaps. She kept her son on an allowance, made it possible for Joan and her sister to attend Sewickley Academy, a private school, and took Joan on a tour of Europe when she was fourteen. For "finishing," she sent her to Miss Porter's School in Farmington, Connecticut.

Joan was in her senior year at Miss Porter's when her father, only forty, had a stroke. Over the next seven years, he slowly lost touch with reality until, unable even to recognize his own children, he had to be institutionalized. The gradual deterioration was heartbreaking. "Once he got on the train and went to Steubenville and holed up in the hotel he and my mother had lived in when they first got married," Joan said. "I had to go down and get him. He had locked himself in the room. He was living in the past, and those were pleasant memories."

Her father's condition was hideously embarrassing to a teenage girl. Joan was humiliated when dates came to her house and had to make conversation with her father while she finished dressing. Summer visits to the Chatham Bars were worse. "He'd drool at the table," she recalled with a shudder.

To protect her father, and the family pride, the Stevenses huddled together in a tight defensive unit. As a result, Joan had felt unusually sheltered and unworldly when she entered Connecticut College in the fall of 1953. She was desperate to escape her family's dull, respectable cocoon, where money was the chief concern and status a close second. From her perspective, the Bingham clan represented an exotic alternative to her pedestrian world, and Worth, especially, was as fascinating and frightening as a bird of prey.

In December 1958, when he returned from Africa, Worth called Joan up and canceled their planned ski trip. He was about to move to San Francisco to work for *The Call-Bulletin*, another job Norman had engineered, he said, and he had to go out there right away. Ever since breaking off her engagement, Joan had been casting about for something to do. By coincidence, she had arranged to transfer from Boston to the San Francisco School of Fine Arts. "Why, I'm going to San Francisco, too!" she told Worth incredulously.

From that moment on, Worth and Joan were inseparable. They flew down ski slopes, hiked through Yosemite National Park, listened to Allen Ginsberg and Jack Kerouac read aloud in smoke-filled coffeehouses, and stared dreamily at each other as Mel Torme crooned ballads at the Hungry I.

Despite his marginal talent, Worth even took a painting course at the School of Fine Arts. When Joan declared the results abominable, he decided to prove her wrong by selling his canvases on Stinson Beach, the glistening expanse of sand and rock just north of San Francisco. While Joan splashed in the ocean, Worth paid passersby ten dollars each to take the paintings off his hands. When she emerged, flushed and dripping from the Pacific, all the artwork was gone. "Oh, my God, maybe I'm missing something in these paintings!" she thought. "Maybe there's something sort of fresh and primitive that I hadn't seen before." Only later did he confess that he had duped her.

The tale was emblematic of their relationship. Joan made Worth feel safe. With her, he could experiment—with art, with emotional vulnerability— without worrying whether he would slip in her esteem or lose the upper hand. Joan was bright and funny but not threateningly intellectual or acidly witty like his family. She was also easygoing, game for anything, and shared his ribald sense of humor. At the same time, she was "a lady." She knew which fork went with which course—a sign of overall good breeding—and was overtly sexual only behind closed doors. She never questioned his dominant position in the relationship, but her knowledge of art gave her an area of expertise that won his respect.

Worth loved playing Pygmalion to Joan's Galatea, especially in the area of fine food and wine—Bingham sacraments. Joan had grown up on roasts and mashed potatoes and was so ignorant of food that she could not tell the difference between a head of cabbage and a head of lettuce and had no idea what "sauté" meant. Worth took pains to instruct her, delighting in the novel experience of being considered refined. "He changed my life," Joan said. "He opened up the world."

In return, Joan was unconditionally affectionate, with no extravagant ambitions for herself or for him. In this supportive atmosphere, Worth was able for the first time to reveal his doubts and weaknesses. As the moment neared for him to return to Louisville and assume the role of heir to the Bingham newspaper empire, he let Joan see just how terrified he sometimes was. "Worth would get drunk and cry for fear that he might not be up to it," Joan said. "It" was a murky soup of family expectations having to do with everything from how one dressed and spoke to who one's friends were. Compared with Sallie's soaring literary success and Barry Jr.'s knowledge of opera and photography, Worth felt lumbering and clumsy. He knew his father still viewed him contemptuously as a well-rounded man, a phrase that meant he was mediocre overall but, unlike the problem-plagued Barry Jr., undeserving of help.

Worth felt closest to his mother, who, during his stay in San Francisco wrote him long, didactic letters with lots of instructions and admonitions—letters that, to him, demonstrated her love. His fundamental feeling was that he had somehow been born into the wrong family, that it was *he*, not Sallie, who was the true outsider. As she got to know Worth better, Joan was shocked to discover that beneath the stunning poise were deep pools of doubt. "He walked through life with natural self-confidence," she said. "He felt comfortable in his own skin. But he also used to get in brooding moods. That's when the insecurity would come out."

Worth proposed to Joan in the summer of 1959, while she was in Sewickley for a brief vacation. She had been gone only a few days, but Worth missed her so much that he impetuously caught a plane to Pennsylvania and took her out to dinner at the Tin Man, a chic restaurant overlooking Pittsburgh. Afterward, they drove back to Joan's house and woke her startled mother to tell her the news.

That Christmas, Worth brought Joan to Louisville. She had met Barry Sr. and Mary briefly in San Francisco and had come away from the encounter marveling at Barry Sr.'s easy charm and Mary's beige chiffon dress and matching satin shoes. But she had never seen the Binghams in their natural habitat.

It was a jolt. "I barely slept the whole time, I was so nervous," she said. "Adlai Stevenson was staying there, too. I had never met anybody who was anybody and I was very self-conscious. Everything that they talked about was absolutely riveting and fascinating. There was lots of politics. Sex was discussed at the dining room table, something that was really shocking. They would talk about people's affairs." She was sure the family assumed she was sleeping with Worth.

Each morning, a beaker of fresh orange juice and a thermos of hot coffee arrived in Joan's room on a tray set with crisp linen and delicate china. Underneath the heavy silver dome lay creamed chicken livers on toast or tiny, thin corncakes with melted butter and a pot of jam with candied lemon rind—never mundane fare like eggs and bacon. At dinner, there were finger bowls at every place. Whitney Ellsworth, who was also a guest that Christmas, was particularly kind to Joan, as though he sensed that they were both alien creatures. But Sallie was haughty and distant. "She was just very full of disdain for this poor ordinary girl," said Joan.

Each evening, Sallie swept down the broad double staircase in fantastic couture clothes, passing dramatic arrangements of fresh flowers on her way toward the dining room. Mary followed in one of her flowing tea gowns. Barry Sr. appeared at the table in a crimson smoking jacket and velvet shoes. "That's the way one dressed for dinner in Louisville. You can imagine how this threw me," said Joan.

Over Christmas, the family gathered in front of the fireplace in the music room for a photograph that seemed to capture the Binghams at the height of their elegance, achievement, and togetherness. Only the way family members looked at each other betrayed the pain and the subterranean alliances that would one day contribute to the family's collapse. The four Bingham men stood in suits and ties, with Barry Sr. smiling down at Mary, seated below the blazing sconces, as if in the thrall of a private joke. Worth gazed protectively at Joan, dressed in a schoolgirl sweater, skirt, and penny loafers, as she sat gingerly on the couch next to Whitney and Sallie. Eleanor, overweight and dressed in a jumper, huddled behind Mary and looked at Jonathan. Barry Jr., blond, martially erect and very handsome, looked at no one.

———

Joan decided that the wedding would take place on February 14, 1960— Valentine's Day—in San Francisco. She wanted to avoid the embarrassment of her mentally incapacitated father, who she knew was too sick to leave Sewickley, and she also had no desire to expose the Binghams to the town's country-club Republicans. Under Worth's tutelage, she had become a passionate convert to liberalism, and felt zealous distaste for the parochial attitudes of the people with whom she had grown up.

The wedding came off with elegant ease. The Stevens family imported their own pastor for the occasion and the Binghams hosted a rehearsal dinner at Trader Vic's. When Joan walked down the aisle in a short white dress with satin appliqués, she clutched white tulips and lilies of the valley in one hand and the arm of her sister's husband in the other. Barry Jr., as the best man, stood proudly on Worth's left.

After a sumptuous luncheon at the Fairmont Hotel and a large evening reception at Ondine's, a trendy waterfront restaurant across the bay in Sausalito, Worth, twenty-seven, and Joan, twenty-four, set out for a two-month skiing trip and honeymoon in Switzerland. That spring, when the newlyweds returned to the United States, they flew to San Francisco, piled their belongings into Worth's beat-up station wagon, and drove to Louisville. They moved into a cottage in Skylight, a small rural community some distance from town, and Worth began work as assistant managing editor of *The Louisville Times*.

Left alone most of the day, Joan frantically tried to learn how to cook. She arose each morning before 6:00 A.M. to make Worth a breakfast comparable to the gourmet affairs he was used to at the Big House, and then worked feverishly to put an edible meal on the table by the time he came home. "The first two and a half years of my [married] life I spent doing nothing but cooking," she said.

The first time Barry Sr. and Mary came to dinner, Joan fussed for three days in preparation. She made shrimp curry, served it on her wedding china, tiptoed through the inevitable conversational minefield at the table, then collapsed in exhaustion. The next day, Worth got up early to wash the dirty dishes before heading off to work. "I am sure that I was not what they had in mind at all," Joan said of her in-laws. "I think they wanted somebody who had gone to Radcliffe and was more intellectual. But they came to give me much more credit than I deserve for shaping Worth up. He really shaped himself up."

Although his new title sounded grand, Worth did everything from repairing presses to editing copy at *The Louisville Times*. At Norman's insistence, he started in circulation, knocking on doors to sell subscriptions and riding around in the *CJ & T*'s red and black trucks delivering papers before it was light. He even spent several weeks in the mailroom and the composing room, where he learned how to make up a page. "His father wouldn't know how to make up the front page," said Joan. "Norman mapped out everything he did."

After several months on the *Times*, Norman switched Worth to *The Courier-Journal*, where the paper's statewide coverage gave him license to roam Kentucky, a place he still knew little about. On one trip to the gloomy coalfields and remote hollows of eastern Kentucky, Joan tagged along. They drove back into the mountains following twisting, unpaved roads beside creeks polluted from mine runoff. Along the streams, interspersed with mountain laurel, were soggy mattresses and old ice boxes—the detritus of poverty. When the car finally lurched onto the silent Main Street of an isolated hamlet, Joan was stunned to see a *Courier-Journal* vending box on the corner, just like the ones in downtown Louisville. "It just seemed so high brow for these places [to have such a paper]," she said, "but rather wonderful."

That summer, in Los Angeles, John F. Kennedy, the son of the man who had succeeded Worth's grandfather at the Court of St. James's, was nominated as the Democrats' presidential candidate. For the third and final time in his life, Adlai Stevenson tried to capture the nomination. Barry Sr. pleaded with his old friend not to do it, but Adlai was adamant and Barry Sr. reluctantly went along. Only after Stevenson conceded defeat did *The Courier-Journal* come out for Kennedy.

In the fall of 1960, Worth was dispatched to cover the presidential campaign and found himself on Richard M. Nixon's whistle-stop train one week and the Kennedy bus the next. It was then that he became addicted to politics. As a child, he had accompanied his father and Barry Jr. to state and national political conventions, and he could hardly have escaped the political talk around the Bingham dinner table. But until 1960, he had never personally felt the rush of excitement that a political campaign engenders. Now, with some pride, he told friends that he never bothered to read the international section of the paper anymore. Domestic political news was the only thing that was important. "He loved, loved, loved, loved politics," said Joan. "He was just consumed."

While his son played the impartial newsman, Barry Sr. acted as a behind-the-scenes Democratic partisan. He had a private lunch with Kennedy when he passed through Kentucky, and occasionally talked strategy with him. That November, when Kennedy won by a slim margin, it came as no surprise that Barry Sr. was a prime candidate for an ambassadorial post.

Several countries were discussed, the most likely being Italy, but Barry Sr. was not asked to take the one he really wanted: Britain. That went to David K. E. Bruce, the man whom Barry Sr. had succeeded as head of the Marshall Plan in France just twelve years earlier. "The President liked Barry a lot and would have loved to have used him," said Kennedy intimate Bill Walton, who had known Barry Sr. in wartime London. "But [Great Britain wasn't offered] because his father had been there and they thought he ought to go someplace on his own."

With Camelot in full bloom, Worth was assigned to The Courier-Journal's bureau in Washington covering Congress. The move reminded Barry Sr. of his brief stint in the capital at the beginning of the New Deal, and he found it immensely satisfying that his oldest son was following so neatly in his footsteps.

There was a difference, however. In the early 1930s, Franklin D. Roosevelt had been old enough to be a father-figure for Barry Sr. This dashing forty-three-year-old president, on the other hand, was roughly of Worth's generation, a new generation, poised to sweep away a stale and musty past, making it far easier for Worth and his new wife to identify directly with Jack and Jackie. It was not lost on Joan, for instance, that both she and Jackie were tall, slim, and dark-haired, and graduates of Miss Porter's. Soon, she, along with millions of other American women, began sporting the slightly teased chin-length pageboy Jackie preferred.

Worth, too, felt that his life and Jack Kennedy's were unusually similar. Besides their connections to the Court of St. James's, both were athletic and occasionally wore back braces to ease the pain of past injuries. Both were Harvard men. Both had charisma, a taste for vulgarity, and a predatory swagger around women. Both were the anointed heirs in intensely political, wealthy families that, incongruously, also prided themselves on being liberal Democrats.

Soon after Worth and Joan arrived in Washington and settled into a Georgetown town house, Barry Sr. and Mary threw a small luncheon in their honor at the F Street club. The Senior Binghams' connections entitled Worth and Joan to occasional invitations from family friends such as Philip and Katharine Graham, owners of *The Washington Post*, and journalist Clayton Fritchey and his wife. There were also trips to the White House for lunches with Pierre Salinger, the president's press secretary, and various ceremonial functions, including a reception Jackie hosted for several hundred Miss Porter's alumni.

Most of the time, though, Worth and Joan enjoyed the company of like-minded people their own age. They became particularly close to Ward Just, then a *Newsweek* correspondent, and Herb Schmertz, a congenial New Frontiersman who would later become the top spokesman for Mobil Oil.

In 1962, Worth and Ward teamed up to write two articles for *The Reporter*, a liberal magazine of opinion. One, called "The President and the Press," described in detail how J.F.K. punished reporters who displeased him. The other, "All the Bright Young Men," profiled several Kennedy appointees in their early thirties. Barry Sr. was suitably impressed, and for the first time seemed to take Worth seriously as a journalist.

But Worth's greatest coup was yet to come. In July 1962, *The Courier-Journal* and *Times* ran "Our Costly Congress," a six-part series on how U.S. senators and congressmen spent money on themselves in the form of the franking privilege, office gyms, and padded staff salaries. The series won the National Headliner award and was published in condensed form by *Reader's Digest*.

To Barry Sr., "Our Costly Congress" represented Worth's high-water mark in Washington. It was time for his son to return to Louisville, he felt, just as he himself had done in 1933 when his father left for England. There were lots of reasons to call Worth back: Joan was pregnant with her first child; after the Bay of Pigs, the bloom of Camelot had dulled somewhat anyway; and the congressional term was ending.

So in November 1962, as the bright colors of fall faded into the gray tones of winter, Worth and Joan relinquished their glamorous Georgetown life for what Worth had long known was his destiny: serving at the helm of the Bingham family business. Like his father before him, Prince Hal was going home. And Barry Jr. was not far behind.

———

While Worth was in San Francisco soaking up newspaper experience and courting Joan, Barry Jr. was in New York City sitting out a year-long training program at CBS television. His passion for Africa had not subsided, but he had finally yielded to professional realities. Instead of buying his beloved tea plantation, he had opted to investigate television—the "little black box" that had first fascinated him in college.

He soon discovered that the CBS experience was utterly useless. Every week, he and two other trainees were rotated into different departments, making it nearly impossible to learn anything well. Because they were expected to write reports on what they had seen, the regular employees treated them like spies and never gave them substantive work. Even so, the program was much in demand, and, to get Barry Jr. in, Mark Ethridge had had to remind CBS that the Binghams owned a valuable affiliate, WHAS.

Only months after Barry Jr. arrived, however, Mark had a policy disagreement with CBS and switched WHAS's affiliation to ABC. Furious, the network lost its ardor for Barry Jr. When his year's training was up, the only job he was offered was recruiting new affiliates—a dig he assumed was deliberate. He wanted news or public affairs and so declined.

Barry Sr. came to the rescue, quietly contacting the president of NBC News, an old friend and social acquaintance. Barry Jr. was duly hired as a television researcher at $75 a week. This time, the fit clicked. In a medium not based on the written word, Barry Jr.'s reading difficulties did not matter, and his rigorous work habits and taste for detail proved to be valuable assets. "He was full of enthusiasm and gay-hearted," Mary said of that brief interlude in New York. "He was doing what he loved to do."

Soon, Barry Jr. was invited to join Lou Hazam, one of NBC's premier documentary producers, in Washington. Like Norman Isaacs, Hazam had a reputation for strong opinions and acerbic asides. He quickly became for Barry Jr. what Norman already was for Worth: a mentor and father-figure, someone who did not consider Barry Jr. a "calculated risk," but solicited his ideas and encouraged his professional growth.

When Barry Jr. suggested that NBC do a documentary on the Nile, Hazam enthusiastically bought the idea. For eight weeks, Barry Jr. did research on the historic sites and villages the crew should shoot as it made its way from the Nile's origin in Burundi to the Mediterranean. Shortly before they were to depart for Africa, Hazam casually dropped by Barry Jr.'s cubicle. "How about coming along?" he said. "You've got to be kidding!" Barry Jr. exclaimed in astonishment and pleasure.

The eighteen-week shoot was a hair-raising experience. Burundi was in the midst of a revolution, and villages were engulfed in flames and gunfire. The trip, said Barry Jr., was "like shooting heroin into an addict. I'll live a long time before I have another experience like that." Several months later, Hazam asked him to take part in a second documentary, this time on William Shakespeare.

The long hours and foreign travel left little time for romance. While his son was still in New York, Barry Sr. had mailed him a pair of theater tickets and encouraged him to take out Candida Mabon, a girl Barry Jr. had met more than a decade earlier during a vacation at a Wyoming dude ranch. The Seniors were convinced Barry Jr. had been in love with her since then but was simply too timid to pursue a relationship. Barry Sr. would never have considered such blatant meddling with Worth, but he felt, as he had since Barry Jr.'s early childhood, that his second son "needed" him. The matchmaking turned out to be in vain. Barry Jr. reported back that the evening had been wonderful, but Candida was already engaged.

Although he was slim, blond, and as muscular as a Greek god, Barry Jr. had little luck with women. His reading disability and long years of being overweight had made him painfully shy and a bit naive. In 1961, soon after he moved to Washington, Joan arranged for him to take an Austrian girl to the Kennedy inauguration. Barry Jr. came away from the encounter entranced and invited her on a skiing trip to Lake Tahoe, where he paid for everything from boots to lessons. As soon as the woman returned to Washington, however, she moved in with her lover. Barry Jr. was humiliated.

Soon thereafter, Barry Jr. met Edith Wharton Stenhouse Franchini, a graceful blond divorcée who lived in Washington with her two small sons. To Edie, Barry Jr. seemed handsome, wealthy, well educated, and amusing —"a real cut-up," she said. She also saw in him a way out of her dreary life as a single parent. He, in turn, saw her as a damsel in distress, someone he could rescue, like a powerful white knight. After so many years of being in distress himself, it was a role he ached to play.

———————

Edie was a sixth-generation Washingtonian, the daughter of a prominent architect. She had graduated from Holton Arms School, a prestigious private girls' academy, been presented at the Washington Debutante Ball, and gone to Smith College. In her junior year, she studied abroad in Florence, Italy, and met Massimo Franchini. Though he had no title, Massimo later came to be known in *The Courier-Journal* newsroom as "the no-account Count."

And with good reason. Massimo was the son of a wealthy family from a small town outside Florence who, like so many other idle young Italian men, spent his days hanging around the local university whistling at pretty girls and drinking espresso. "He was a *vitellone*," explained Diana Fetter de Villafranca, a classmate of Edie's. "In Florence, that means a kind of ne'er do well." Before long, Massimo met Edie, attracted by her striking good looks, and they quickly became involved. At night, he would sneak into her bedroom, wearing tennis shoes to muffle the sound of his footsteps.

Edie was as sheltered and uninitiated as her refined background suggested. She soon became pregnant, returned to the United States, and dropped out of school. Years later, she would gloss over the crisis, saying that she had left Smith "for romance." Though Massimo eventually came to the States, married her, and lived in Boston, the "romance" was short-lived.

Twenty months after the birth of their first child, Philip, a second son, Charles, arrived. The responsibilities of parenthood were too much for Massimo. After a year or two, he returned to Italy and washed his hands permanently of Edie and the little boys. When the divorce came through, Edie moved back to Washington, where she worked as a clerk-typist at the American Institute of Architects and struggled to raise her children, dependent for much of her support on her parents.

Edie was classically beautiful. There was a serene quality about her, tempered by an insightful intelligence that was at once pragmatic and kind. Despite her unhappy experience, or perhaps because of it, she had remarkable self-confidence. The combination of strength and need, sinew and softness, was powerfully attractive to Barry Jr. Throughout 1962, he spent as much time with Edie as his work schedule would allow, attending the opera—something they both adored—walking in Washington's many parks, and listening to classical music.

Barry Jr.'s world at that moment seemed nearly perfect. "The River Nile" aired in October and "Shakespeare: Soul of an Age" was broadcast on the last day of November. He and Edie seemed headed toward a permanent relationship. Then, like a thunderclap, he received a phone call from his father: It was time to come back to Louisville and join the family business.

Later, father and son would remember this incident quite differently. "I didn't press him," Barry Sr. said. "It was, I thought, a pretty clear mutual understanding that he was ready to come back to Louisville and wanted to work in radio and TV." But Barry Jr. recalled that his father had told him "in no uncertain terms" to come home.

Barry Jr. did not want to go. "I was courting Edie and I wanted to do it in Washington rather than Louisville," he said. "Besides, I really loved my work." When he told Lou Hazam of his dilemma, Hazam offered to promote him from field producer to director, with a hefty increase in pay. The offer sent Barry Jr. into a tailspin of ambivalence. Now he had a genuine alternative to life in Louisville, but he knew in his heart he was not free to take it.

For one thing, Barry Sr. had told his son that he was deeply concerned about WHAS radio and TV. The president was a borderline alcoholic and the stations were slipping in quality. WAVE, WHAS's chief competitor, was pounding the Bingham broadcasting outlets in the ratings. The message,

Barry Jr. felt, was, "You've done your duty somewhere else. Now it's time to come do your duty at home." The assumption was that he would return —whether he liked it or not.

Reluctantly, Barry Jr. turned down Hazam, resigned from NBC, and packed his bags for Louisville. "I thought I had a responsibility to my family to give it a try," he said. After her own experiences with single motherhood, Edie well understood the concept of putting the needs of others ahead of one's own and did not try to talk him out of it. Like Barry Sr., she just assumed that this aspect of Barry Jr.'s life was nonnegotiable.

Worth and Barry arrived home from Washington within several weeks of each other in the fall of 1962. "I think my father realized that if he let either of us keep on doing what we were enjoying so much for too many years, well, eventually, he would get neither of us," Barry Jr. said. The prodigal sons returned to Louisville for good, Worth to be assistant to the publisher at the newspapers and Barry Jr. to be assistant to the president of WHAS, Inc., which included the television and radio stations, with the vice-presidency of Standard Gravure thrown in for good measure.

Worth and Joan abandoned their home in Skylight and moved into the Little House, which Worth as the firstborn son had always known would be his. Barry Jr. moved back into the Big House with his parents, taking up quarters in the second-floor room he and Worth had shared as children. Within months, he asked Edie to marry him and move to Louisville. The wedding was set for late November 1963. Barry Sr. was delighted. Everything was working out according to plan.

———————

In one respect, however, it was a melancholy time at *The Courier-Journal* and *Times*. Mark Ethridge, who had been so instrumental in bringing the papers to national prominence, was in the process of being gently but firmly pushed out. One reason had to do with his age: He was approaching retirement and Barry Sr. wanted to pave the way for Worth's ascension. The other was that Mark had become an embarrassment. Over the years, his drinking had increased so alarmingly that even he began admitting to close friends that he was probably an alcoholic.

Mark had always had a prodigious capacity for strong potables. He loved to sing at parties and toward the end of the evening would invariably gather guests around a piano for a chorus of "The Battle Hymn of the Republic." Even at staff baseball games, Mark turned up with a glass of whiskey in his hand. Yet, remarkably, he never seemed incapacitated. "You'd think you had him in a weak spot, so you'd say something brave," recalled former Bingham executive John Richards. "He'd tell you about it the next day even though you thought he couldn't stand up. Amazing guy. He was always out there at 8:00 A.M. drinking an ice cold Coca-Cola at the machine and you knew he felt awful."

Mark took several shots at lunchtime and still put in a full afternoon of work. As he got older, though, he began to return later and later from the midday meal, his gait uncertain and his speech slurred, mortifying the reporters and editors who still idolized him. After work he adjourned to Teek's World Famous New York Bar, a favorite *Courier-Journal* haunt, and drank for hours with pressmen and compositors. "Mark had the strongest head of almost any man I've ever known," said Barry Sr. "But it began to catch up with him. He was beginning to be seen as an old office drunk almost."

One afternoon, after a particularly boozy lunch, Mark began weaving in his car and was promptly pulled over by a Louisville policeman. The cop blanched when he saw that the driver was the publisher of *The Courier-Journal* and *Times*, and tried to make a graceful exit. But Mark demanded that he be arrested like any other citizen and insisted that the news be reported on the front page. In a journalist less given to alcoholic excess, the gesture might have made a point about newspaper ethics. In Mark's case, it was sad and a bit pathetic.

Mark's increased drinking was rooted partly in depression over changes in his role at the newspapers, changes flowing from decisions Barry Sr. had made about the future of the family companies. In 1960, the three Bingham enterprises, which had until then been under one corporate roof, were separated into The Courier-Journal and Louisville Times Company Inc., WHAS Inc., and Standard Gravure Inc. Each had its own voting and non-voting stock. Barry Sr.'s tax advisers had told him that, with three kinds of stock, he could more easily accomplish his two fundamental goals: He could pass voting control to the Bingham children who ran the companies while also providing dividends through nonvoting stock to the Bingham children not involved in the day-to-day operations.

In mid-1961, with Worth waiting in the wings and Mark recently turned sixty-five, Barry Sr. had taken back the title of publisher, adding it to his other titles of editor and president. Although he insisted that the move represented "no break" in the Bingham-Baker-Ethridge power structure, Mark felt shunted aside. As compensation, Barry Sr. had made him chairman of the board of the three Bingham companies, but Mark knew he was being told to be less and less involved in the day-to-day running of the papers. He was on his way out.

The multiple changes piqued the curiosity of the F.B.I., which had monitored Mark's behavior ever since he had written editorials critical of the bureau and its head, J. Edgar Hoover, during the McCarthy era. In 1962,

F.B.I. headquarters asked a local agent to get in touch with *CJ* city editor John Herchenroeder, the agency's principal contact at the newspapers. Later, in a memo to his superiors, the agent reported that Mark had been unhappy for some time. He had wanted to buy stock in the company, but Barry Sr. had refused. Mark had then invested money in some weekly newspapers. They had not done well and he had subsequently sold them. "Since Mr. Ethridge's efforts to secure an interest in the *CJ & T* were rebuffed," the agent concluded, "his own aggressively militant interest and enthusiasm in the two Louisville newspapers has somewhat diminished."

When Worth came back to Louisville for good in the fall of 1962, Barry Sr. asked Mark to stay on another year to help train his son and Mark agreed. Despite their mutual love of parties and newsroom banter, however, Worth and his father's top aide never became intimate friends. Soon after Worth's return, Norman Isaacs took him aside and warned him not to follow Mark's example too closely. He was especially worried that Mark would make Worth his permanent drinking partner at Teek's, undermining Worth's authority and encouraging his already proven weakness for liquor. "It's all right to stop in for a beer," Norman advised Worth. "But it would be smart if you only had one and got the hell out of there. You don't want to be like Mark."

Worth's coolness only redoubled Mark's sense of being shoved out. As the moment of his retirement and final leave-taking neared, he felt increasingly angry about his treatment, especially about his financial settlement. His unhappiness was apparent to everyone but Barry Sr., who described Mark's severance package as "very substantial." Years later, when the subject resurfaced, Barry Sr. would say with astonishment and no small amount of hurt that Mark had never complained about the terms of his departure. Mark's wife, Willie Snow, however, was not so circumspect. "She beat my ear at a dinner party one night," said John Richards. "She was really, really bitter." Willie found Mark's retirement package—reportedly a pension and a modest onetime bonus—appalling. She thought Mark had been treated shabbily, especially since men of lesser stature at *The Washington Post* had become millionaires overnight when the company had gone public and the stock they had been allowed to buy had dramatically increased in value.

After years of loyal service, she had expected the Binghams to make it possible for Mark to retire a rich man. Barry Sr., however, felt that he owed Mark only comfort and security. Like most men and women of wealth, he lived in ignorance of the day-to-day financial worries of ordinary people. As with staff salaries, he simply did not know that he could or should do more. "I think it's the Bingham mentality," said one former *CJ & T* executive. "That kind of thing simply doesn't occur to them." Mark's heavy drinking only increased the strain. It embarrassed Barry Sr. and disappointed Mary, who considered alcoholism less a disease than a failure of will.

For public consumption, however, Barry Sr. and Mark continued to treat each other with gentlemanly regard. Several days before he left, Barry Sr. sponsored a stag luncheon for three hundred at the Pendennis Club where the mayor presented Mark with the city's first Distinguished Citizen Award. The staffs of the two newspapers threw a party in his honor, and even the International Mailers Union offered a special tribute. Norman, who a year earlier had been named executive editor, with jurisdiction over both papers, wrote a farewell column describing Mark as "the world's greatest living, working newspaperman." But it was Barry Sr. who, despite his past jealousy of Mark's professional visibility and his current discomfort with his drinking, paid him the highest and most sincere compliment: "He made it possible for *The Courier-Journal* and *Times* to be what my father and I had always wanted them to be."

Finally, on September 15, 1963, Mark left the newsroom for the last time, slipping out quietly after pinning a note on the bulletin board. "I will always be proud of these papers—the best combination dailies in the United States," it began.

The message went on for a paragraph or two. But it was the ending that, years later, after Jonathan and Worth had died, the papers had been sold, and the family lay in ruins, would seem so prescient, even eerie. For almost thirty years, this round, rumpled man had been like a guardian angel hovering protectively over the Bingham family and its newspapers. From the moment he arrived in 1936 until this cool autumn day in 1963, everything had gone exquisitely, almost inexplicably right. The papers had become synonymous with courage and quality even as Barry Sr., Mary, and their five children had glided from one triumph to another. The family had indeed been "special" and "mythic," as Sallie so often said.

Now, his duty done, Mark scribbled the fragment of an old drinking song. "Sometime when your voices are well lubricated," he wrote, "I hope you will take one more and sing for me:

> Adieu, kind friends, adieu.
> I can no longer stay with you;
> I will hang my harp on a weeping willow tree
> And may the world go well with thee."

The world did not go well with Mark Ethridge. Though he lived almost twenty years more, he came back to Louisville infrequently. After two years as editor of *Newsday* on Long Island, he taught journalism at the University of North Carolina at Chapel Hill until a stroke made that impossible. He died in 1981.

As for the Binghams, soon after their guardian angel hung his harp on the willow tree, their luck changed, too. "I feel sort of like a fellow who's been basking in the sun," Don Towles, a staff member, wrote Mark shortly after the legendary newspaperman had left. "And then the sun moves to the other side of the world."

DEATH OF A DREAM

Almost exactly two months after Mark's exit, President Kennedy was assassinated in Dallas. Although the Binghams, like the rest of the world, were shocked and shaken, Barry Jr. went ahead with his plans and married Edith Wharton Stenhouse Franchini eight days later in a chapel on the grounds of Washington's National Cathedral. Worth served as his best man, Jonathan as an usher. Returning to Louisville, the newlyweds and the two Franchini boys moved into a white frame house on River Hill Road, not far from Barry Sr. and Mary.

The modest dimensions of their new home suited Edie, who made it clear from the outset that she had no intention of running a Bingham-style household. Joan, Worth's wife, was in awe of Edie's indifference to the Bingham mystique. "Edie would have us all over and she'd serve this crap!" Joan recalled with astonishment. "And I just said, 'God, I really admire this girl for spooning this up,' because I was so cowed by the fabulous food that came out of the Big House."

Barry Jr. tried hard to be a good stepfather to Philip and Charles, then eight and seven. He read stacks of books on parenting and took them on weekend hikes and bicycle trips. But they were troubled children. At Chatham the summer before he and Edie were married, Philip had thrown a violent temper tantrum during an afternoon game of croquet. As the others watched aghast, he fell to the ground screaming, swinging his mallet in wide arcs. Barry Jr. turned to Edie. "This isn't going to be easy," he said.

And it wasn't. The boys' biological father had nothing to do with them and, soon after marrying Edie, Barry Jr. decided to adopt them. The Binghams' lawyers sent letter after letter to Massimo Franchini asking for his permission, but they got no response. Finally, one of the attorneys reached him by phone in Italy and Massimo gave his sons away without apparent qualm.

Despite these problems, Barry Jr. found marriage and fatherhood fulfilling even as he brooded about the flatness of his professional life. In 1964, two years after leaving NBC, he gloomily told a friend that he was the only person he knew who had graduated from college in 1956 and was still in a training program. "I'm not saying I was about to kick over the traces and leave town," he said later, "but if you had asked me what my satisfaction quotient was, I would have said under 70 percent."

At first, Barry Jr. displayed a kind of jaunty pep about his job with the family companies, an attitude old Bingham hands regarded as transparent bravado, much the way Mary had years earlier viewed Barry Jr.'s assurances to Nursie that his being held back a grade was a "mastake" and he would get it "straten" out. He seemed determined to convince people that he was a capable executive with national experience who was going to transform WHAS radio and television into stations of network quality. However, he quickly discovered that broadcasting in Louisville was ill-suited to such grand ambitions. WHAS-TV was only the second-ranked station in the nation's fortieth market. It had neither the money nor the staff to make the kind of serious documentaries he had helped create at NBC.

After some quick calculations, Barry Jr. decided that WHAS could afford to produce just one first-class documentary a year. He made himself producer and plowed $60,000 into a sixty-minute program about Shakertown, a Kentucky village that had once been home to the celibate religious sect. The following year he produced a program about the effects of stripmining. The shows received little critical acclaim, "nor did they deserve more than they got," Barry Jr. admitted later.

Since the prospects for quality television programming seemed poor, Barry Jr. focused his attention on radio and decided to start a classical music station. One of the things he had enjoyed most about living in New York and Washington was the abundance of such stations. If he could not bring decent broadcasting to Louisville one way, he reasoned, he would do it another. It was the Binghams' opinion that, since they were obliged to live in Louisville, they had a right, even a duty, to make the city a place they wanted to be. While undemocratic and patronizing, this missionary view was largely responsible for transforming a scruffy, midsized industrial town into an improbable oasis of theater, art, dance, and music.

In the 1960s, FM was very much a stepchild of AM. The Binghams had once run an FM station, but had not been able to make it pay. In the early 1950s, they gave up the license, which was for a powerful 100,000-watt station. When Barry Jr. found that no one had claimed it, he applied for it. At the time, Louisville already had two classical music outlets run by non-commercial owners, but they were not up to Barry Jr.'s standards. He commissioned a survey to find out whether adding a commercial classical station to the mix made any sense. When the results told him the enterprise was practically guaranteed to fail, he brushed them aside and plunged ahead anyway.

Lisle Baker thought the idea was hare-brained and financially irresponsible. He had already had a taste of Barry Jr.'s profligate spending in connection with a new building for WHAS-TV, and he did not like it. Soon after Barry Jr. returned to Louisville, the Binghams had decided to move WHAS television and radio out of the fifth, sixth, and seventh floors of the newspaper building and into a home of their own down the block. Deputized to come up with plans for the new headquarters, Barry Jr. had toured the country looking at outlets of comparable size, then ordered up a building with the finest and most up-to-date equipment.

Lisle had warned Barry Sr. that the place would be too big, unnecessarily sophisticated, and wildly expensive. But Barry Sr. did not care. The building was a payoff to Barry Jr. for coming back to Louisville, he told Lisle, and he wanted to keep his son happy. The new broadcasting station ended up costing $6.3 million. "They built the Taj Mahal," snickered a former Bingham executive. "There were just certain things Barry Jr. wanted in there and it had to be good, it had to be first class."

The plan to start a classical music station revived memories of the WHAS building affair and sent Lisle into a fevered campaign to stop it. As a practical matter, Barry Sr. agreed with his conservative financial adviser, but once again he would deny nothing to his son. "You know this is not the right thing to do," Lisle warned. "I understand that," Barry Sr. replied. "But this is what we're going to do because I think Barry has to have a chance."

Several days after WHAS-FM went on the air, Barry Jr. exulted in a letter to a former teacher that he had brought a "cultural revolution" to Louisville. The fact that the station made no financial sense seemed not to bother him. "Some people may doubt that we made a good business decision," he wrote, "but certainly no one can attack us in the name of aesthetics." As Lisle had predicted, the station lost money—over $100,000 a year, to be exact. "The only people who listened to it lived in Glenview," said Bob Morse, a former Bingham broadcasting executive, referring to the neighborhood where the Big House and Little House were located.

Barry Jr. was equally presumptuous and headstrong in his dealings with the staff. "The Bingham feeling about being a Bingham is something I can't understand," said one former staffer. "There is an arrogance there. I don't mean just haughty, but that belongs to them by birth. . . . You know, they [feel that they are] very, very special."

Barry Jr.'s ill-concealed contempt for print also won him few friends at *The Courier-Journal* and *Times*. He seemed confident that newspapers would eventually fade in importance, tipping the balance of power within the family in his favor. "I felt I was going to be the spokesman for broadcast and Worth was going to be the spokesman for the print side," he said. "I was personally convinced the future lay in broadcasting. If people perceived that Worth had the mantle of family leadership, I just don't know whether that's correct."

As if to demonstrate that he was, in fact, a leader, Barry Jr. threw himself into good works in Louisville, joining the board of the Cancer Society and the local Child Guidance Clinic. But his main interest was the arts. Soon after moving back home, he became one of three founders of Theatre Louisville and then its first president. Within a couple of years, the troupe merged with another acting group to become the celebrated Actors Theatre of Louisville.

Despite his many activities, Barry Jr. forged few personal ties. His only close friend was Ian Henderson, an attorney who lived just outside the Big House gates and shared his love of hunting. Several years after returning to Louisville, Barry Jr. went on an African safari with Ian. Once again he felt the intoxicating independence he had known during his years in New York and Washington. Whenever Barry Jr. was away from home, the mask of uncertainty and awkward arrogance fell away and he was funny and easygoing. "When things go wrong on trips, and they always do," said Ian, "he has this marvelous optimism. He doesn't brood, doesn't sulk."

———————

Soon after returning from Washington, Worth and Joan were forced to confront a political battle so personal and nasty that it might have taken place during Judge Bingham's reign. In 1946 and on two other occasions, *The Courier-Journal* and *Times* had endorsed Thruston Morton, a Republican and family friend, for Congress. But in the fall of 1962, when he ran for reelection to the U.S. Senate, the Bingham papers supported his challenger, Wilson Wyatt, a Democrat and even closer friend.

It was a vicious campaign. Morton attacked Wyatt for his leadership of Americans for Democratic Action in the 1940s, an organization he described as virtually communistic. Detractors scrawled hammer and sickles and pentagonal Stars of David on Democratic billboards. Morton went on WAVE radio, WHAS's chief competitor, and denounced *The Courier-Journal* as biased. "This is the only way I can get my word to the people of Kentucky undistorted," he thundered. Barry Sr. was both mortified and angry. He had been in Morton's wedding and, despite the *CJ & T*'s clear advocacy of Wilson Wyatt, he felt the papers had bent over backwards to be fair. The Binghams became social outcasts. "Many of our friends did not talk to us," said Joan. "Everyone [in Louisville] was for Thruston."

The deep freeze persisted even after Morton had won. On New Year's Eve, almost two months after the election, Worth and Joan sat on the floor of the Little House and spent the evening sipping champagne and polishing brass. No one had invited them out. Jonathan wandered over and joined them. He, too, was alone, a member of what at that moment seemed like a Bingham leper colony.

Worth did not seem to care. He was settling down, ripening, finding his equilibrium. And soon after the Morton debacle, he had a new center of gravity: Clara York Bingham, his first child, born in the last weeks of January 1963. Fatherhood transformed him. With Princess Clara, as he called her, he could shed his macho shell and display all the inner warmth and tenderness that, until then, only Joan had seen.

Worth took the little girl everywhere with him. She rode beside him in his golf cart and, on their annual summer trips to Nantucket, traveled around the island behind him in a special baby-size bicycle seat. In Louisville, Worth's at-home schedule revolved around his daughter. He got up about 5:00 A.M., read the paper, did his back exercises, wrote an editorial, and changed Clara's diapers. Then he piled back into bed with Joan and Clara and they played like toddlers.

Once he returned to Louisville for good, Worth threw himself wholeheartedly into *The Courier-Journal* and *Times*. He had the family's sense of entitlement and finesse, but he also possessed a street-fighter, one-of-the-guys virility that seemed most un-Bingham-like. "When he said 'Shit!' it sounded right," said John Richards. His common touch made him equally at home with social liberals—people he protectively referred to as "my Communists"—and ultraconservative businessmen.

When black journalist Carl Rowan came to Louisville, Worth announced to his parents that he was going to invite him to stay at the Little House and maybe even play a round of golf. Mary was apoplectic. "But what are we going to tell the servants?" she asked plaintively. "Just tell them we have a black man coming," said Worth with a shrug. When none of the usual country clubs would permit his guest on the course, Worth called some of his Jewish friends and arranged to play at the Jewish country club. "Mary was in a state of great anxiety and heaviness over this young man and what he was going to do," said Molly Clowes. "Worth just couldn't have been less concerned."

Worth's idea of being publisher was to do it all: news, advertising, and production. He wanted to call the shots on the editorial board and to shoulder the burdens of community service—the Rotary Club lunches, the fund-raising drives—that went along with the privilege of ownership. Bright rather than brilliant, he was a quick study and a quick decision maker. Most of all, he was inexhaustibly energetic. "He's going to be the ruin of you," Joan's mother wailed to her. "He's just going to wear you down to a little nub."

Neither Barry Sr. nor Barry Jr. felt comfortable with hands-on command. Worth had no such inhibitions and was not afraid to risk confrontations with the people who worked for him. Once, when he discovered that the sports editor, Earl Ruby, had decided to punish one of his reporters by refusing to let him cover a big boxing match, he strode angrily into the newsroom. "C'mere, Earl," he bellowed. Ruby trotted over. "What's this I hear about Larry not covering the fight?" Ruby gulped. "I'm taking him off boxing and putting Billy Reed on," he explained. Worth's eyes narrowed. "No, you're not." Ruby set his jaw. "I'm the sports editor," he said, his voice hardening. "Today," Worth said with exaggerated slowness. "At this point in time. Now, who's covering the fight?" "Larry," the editor said weakly. A *Courier-Journal* reporter who had witnessed the scene never forgot it. "There isn't another Bingham who would have done a thing like that," she said.

Worth was also at home with executive perks. He liked to buzz around the country in company planes and stay at fancy hotels on the papers' expense account. One of the first things he did when he arrived back in Louisville was to suggest that the company build an executive dining room. He also thought that top managers should get *CJ & T* stock as part of their compensation packages, something his father quickly shot down as inimical to family ownership.

Norman Isaacs agreed with Worth's you've-got-to-spend-more-to-get-more philosophy of journalism. In quick order, he and Worth tackled two costly projects: a design overhaul that made *The Courier-Journal* and *Times* the first successful six-column metropolitan daily in the United States, and a personnel policy that gave Norman license to recruit fresh talent from the best journalism schools in the country.

Worth's risk-taking personality also made him a high-stakes gambler. He could sit for hours at the gaming tables in Europe and Las Vegas, and loved to make bets over a game of poker or golf. He took losses hard, exploding at first, then stewing about his bad luck for days. Once, when Worth lost a tennis game at a local country club, he turned the air so blue that mothers had to whisk their transfixed youngsters out of hearing range. When several Louisville brahmins formed a syndicate to sponsor a talented young local boxer named Cassius Clay (who later became Muhammad Ali), Worth eagerly kicked in $2,000. The idea was to pay Clay's expenses, take half of his winnings and commercial earnings, then give the remainder to the boxer. It turned out to be a terrific investment, and Worth and Joan made a point of attending most of his matches.

A number of the fights were held in Las Vegas, where Worth was always in danger of losing his shirt. One night he won handsomely at The Sands's baccarat table, and he and Joan stayed up late talking about all the things they would buy with the money. The next evening they went to see Frank Sinatra's show and as they were walking out, they passed the baccarat table that had proven so lucky the night before. Worth's eyes lit up. He sent Joan off to bed and headed back to the casino. "I'll just play a little bit more," he assured her. "I won't be long."

At 4:00 A.M., Joan woke with a start, saw that Worth was not yet in, and began dressing to go look for him. Just as she was about to leave the room, she heard the sound of muffled sobs coming down the hall. Worth had lost all his previous winnings, plus the $10,000 he had borrowed from the house. Joan put her arms around him and made light of the disaster. "Just relax," she said. "All this money is gone. So what?" As he had done several times in the past, Worth asked friends and distant cousins to cover his losses, paying them back later and begging them not to tell his father.

––––––––––

Jonathan Bingham had been reluctant to go to Harvard. The summer before his junior year at Brooks School, he had worked as an intern at the Louisville papers, writing articles about park vandalism and civil defense exercises, and had concluded that journalism was not his calling. Nothing had gone wrong —Norman Isaacs remembered him as even more outgoing and popular than Worth. But as the third son, there seemed to be no obvious role for him to play.

The previous year, over Christmas vacation, he had had a long talk with his parents and told them he wanted to pursue science or medicine at Stanford or Caltech. The family's Harvard tradition was a burden, he insisted, one he was disinclined to bear. Although he did not say it, the thought of competing with his older siblings' college records terrified him. He was simply less ready to deal with the real world than most boys his age. "Jonathan was a charming child, and charming is the word for him," said Molly Clowes. "But he seemed very young, much younger than his sisters or brothers."

Barry Sr. was disappointed, but told Jonathan that the decision was, of course, his to make. At the same time, he could not resist trying to stage-manage events. He immediately arranged for a vocational test to analyze his son's aptitude for science. "My guess is that this [desire for schools other than Harvard] is a phase that will pass," Frank Ashburn, the headmaster at Brooks, advised Barry Sr. confidentially. "All it involves is an independent-minded cuss who may really be determined to go his own way."

Jonathan's friends never believed he would buck family tradition. They knew he was unconventional, but his sympathetic nature would not allow him to cause his parents any pain. When he dutifully entered Harvard in the fall of 1960, no one was surprised. Though he had once planned to plunge immediately into pre-med, he now elected to major in English. His parents had strongly urged him to get a broad liberal arts education before pursuing science, and he complied.

His freshman year, Jonathan shared a five-man suite in Thayer Hall with Peter Ardery and three classmates from Brooks—Joe Hammer, Charlie Hunt, and Ellery Sedgwick III. Charlie Bascom, his best friend from boarding school, did not have the grades to get into Harvard, but he was on the scene nonetheless, studying at Boston University. That first year, Charlie became an ex officio member of the suite, hauling a leather suitcase of contraband booze from Beacon Hill, where he lived, to Jonathan's room overlooking Harvard Yard almost every weekend.

Jonathan's freshman days were wild and raucous. For a while, life seemed like one of the all-night Louisville parties that had aroused such envy in his Brooks companions. After football games, Jonathan and his suite-mates would screw blue and red light bulbs into the ceiling sockets, play loud music, and drink their favorite cocktail: a nerve-numbing mixture of gin, bourbon, and fruit juice. One night, Jonathan showed up with a parking meter he had liberated from a nearby street. He planned to use it as a room decoration. "They were famous in the Yard," said Charlie Bascom. "They were showing off, like 'How outrageous can we be?' "

The quintet tried desperately to persuade women to go to bed with them, with occasional success. "It would be nothing for Jonathan and Peter to come back to the room with two women they'd picked up in Harvard Square at some mixer or something and they'd just stay all night," said Joe Hammer. "The three of us did some of that, too. But Jonathan and Peter were the ringleaders. Ellery just got dragged along. He was kind of the mascot, very shy. He loved to read in his bunk and eat raisin toast."

Of them all, Peter Ardery was the most outrageous. He talked provocatively of reading the Marquis de Sade, leering suggestively at the mention of the name. His feelings of social inferiority, already evident in Louisville, intensified at Harvard. To Peter, the Porcellian, Harvard's oldest and most exclusive final club, was "the ultimate club" and those who joined were "the ultimate people." Ellery Sedgwick III, whose family oozed brahmin sophistication, had "the ultimate name."

Eventually, Peter joined the Gas, Worth's old club. Jonathan went through punching season, agreeably attending the cocktail parties where he was looked over and judged, and, in the end, several clubs pursued him. But he had no interest and never joined, choosing instead to sing with the Gilbert and Sullivan Players and help out with Hasty Pudding theatricals. If Peter was obsessed with "ultimate" connections, Jonathan seemed embarrassed by them and blasé about his position as a member of Kentucky's First Family. Once, shortly before John F. Kennedy won the presidential election, he was invited to a party at the Kennedy compound in Hyannis Port. To his friends' astonishment, he announced that he was not going to go.

In their sophomore year, Jonathan and Peter roomed together in Adams House, known for its self-conscious bohemianism. Gradually, they drifted away from the old Louisville and Brooks crowd, which now seemed a bit unsophisticated for their avant-garde tastes. On the surface, however, Peter remained as frenetic and sodden as ever. When Sallie and Whitney invited him over for dinner at their Beacon Hill town house, he drank five martinis, passed out cold, and had to be revived in the shower. He began to experiment with marijuana and would stare for hours at a record turntable as it went around and around. "He was rolling his own dice," said Charlie Bascom.

Jonathan, on the other hand, began to retreat into his studies. He spent hours in the stacks of Widener Library and turned down invitations to parties in favor of trips to 52nd Street jazz clubs in New York. His friends noticed that he seemed more serious. "I have been thinking about how awful an atomic war would be," he told one. "Probably [none] of us would get out of it." His medical career was never far from his mind. He signed up for a Harvard-sponsored trip to the Yucatan to collect zoological specimens and wrote Catherine Luckett, a girlfriend from Louisville then attending Finch College in Manhattan, that he had started brushing his teeth with his left hand "because if you're a surgeon, you need to be ambidextrous."

In another letter to Catherine from Cambridge, written in the early morning, he described looking out a window at Harvard Yard.

Dawn is breaking over the Yard and the sky is blue with a light pink fringe. The trees are still wild, hairy, twisted arms which shake their fist at Heaven, and out in the streets the trucks growl by. Some people are just coming in from a binge. They must think it strange to see a light still on. . . . I pity the drunks, as they stumble about along the criss-cross paths that cover the Yard. I pity them for all their mirth, for the day is here and it is cold out there. . . . The birds flit by, low and high, gathering insects around the sky, like millions of chirping sweepers vacuum cleaning Nature's airy carpet.

Then, abruptly, in a typical Jonathan reversal that broke the serious mood, the tone changed and he ended on a comic note. "The time has come, my conscience says, to think of many things: of chemistry and H_2O, of poetry and wings. Of why the Yard is filled with light, and yet my eyes are closed, and why those little specks of dirt collect between my toes. In short, 'tis time for me to go, and so, with all my love, I close."

Women adored Jonathan for just such moments of boyish sweetness. At a Louisville debutante party his freshman year, he slipped up behind Ina Brown, the cousin of a childhood friend, put his hands over her eyes, leaned forward and whispered in her ear. "Tomorrow," he said, "tomorrow, you and I are going to drift down the Mississippi on a raft." Even secretaries at *The Courier-Journal* were smitten. "Oh, boy, they would just rave in their reports on Jonathan, what a wonderful guy he was," recalled Norman Isaacs. Barry Sr. thought his youngest son aroused a maternal feeling in the hearts of women, but he seemed to stir a protectiveness in many of his male friends as well.

Jonathan's childlike sensibilities contributed greatly to his decision to drop out of Harvard in 1963, at the end of his junior year. He had never wanted to go there in the first place and the fierce competition, so exhilarating in the early years, now seemed oppressive. When he looked ahead, he saw nothing but the frightening responsibilities of adulthood—an adulthood as a Bingham, which was even more daunting. "I think he felt quite threatened about growing up and living up to grand expectations," said Tani Cutchins Vartan, a Louisville girlfriend. "Like Peter Pan. Who wants to grow up? It all stops, you know. Senior year in college, it all stops." If Jonathan could remain a child a little longer, he was determined to do so.

He also felt increasingly suffocated by Peter Ardery, who still exercised a magnetic hold over him. No longer did Jonathan experience rebellious glee when he occasionally slipped and joined Peter in a boozy tear. Now he felt guilt and self-loathing. He longed to extricate himself from Peter's thrall. He avoided any mention of his roommate to his parents, though. Instead, he told them that he wanted time off to find himself. He was tired of Harvard and had lost his enthusiasm for it, he said. In particular, he wanted to think through whether medicine was the right career for him. He said he wanted to come back to Glenview, live in the Big House, and take chemistry courses at the University of Louisville.

Jonathan's Harvard friends were shocked. Later, as if grasping for answers, Charlie Bascom would conclude that Jonathan had felt "he was on the verge of running out of time, as far as deciding what he was going to do." Ellery Sedgwick III suggested that he suffered from "general ennui with coursework." But his Brooks friends would never really know for sure. They had barely seen Jonathan for over a year. He had been too consumed with Peter Ardery and his studies to spend much time with them.

His need to retreat to the security of childhood was apparent in his desire to bury himself in the familiar, unpressured life of Louisville. "It was a good place to feel comfortable in, to get some rest," said Tani Cutchins Vartan, who later dropped out of college and returned to Louisville herself. "It was very cushy, very soothing. We traveled between the outside world and Louisville. It was a very secure kind of life."

Mary heartily disapproved of Jonathan's decision. Barry Sr., whose own schooling had been erratic, was somewhat more understanding. Sallie and Whitney, on the other hand, cheered Jonathan on—until they found out that he intended to go home instead of hike through Nepal or register black voters in Mississippi. "The whole idea of leaving college was to go do something on your own and not be cooped up with your parents," said Mary. "But he was quite happy at home. He had his back quarters where he had a little sitting room and he could have his friends there."

Both Mary and Barry Sr. worried that Jonathan would never return to Harvard, but they comforted themselves with the thought that at least he wanted to use his time productively. In the fall of 1963, he signed up for two courses at the University of Louisville and studied mental illness firsthand at Central State Hospital. His main research interests were cancer and schizophrenia. Sometimes when he spoke of his ambitions, though, he seemed slightly out of touch with reality. He told his sister Eleanor that he wanted to grow plants in outer space.

During those months at home, Jonathan often sought Mary out for conversation and advice, acts of intimacy that rekindled the special love she had felt for him as an infant during the lonely years of World War II. Jonathan's wit and charm reminded her so much of her adored Barry Sr., but there was an emotional accessibility about Jonathan that went beyond that of anyone else in the family. His sensitivity shocked her sometimes.

As time passed, Jonathan also seemed to grow closer to Worth, whom he looked up to and even came to resemble in superficial ways. Worth loved fast cars while Jonathan spent hours admiring his friends' souped-up Harley-Davidson motorcycles. "They both had this mania for speed, I'm afraid," said Barry Sr.

In February 1964, Jonathan got his grades from the University of Louisville and was overjoyed to learn that he had earned an A and a B. He had never before gotten an A, and the satisfaction of it surprised him. Without the distraction of Harvard mixers and Peter's drunken sprees, he had turned into a model student. Still, he missed his friends. "I feel pretty isolated down here," he wrote one. "I have not met any new people, and there are damned few of the ones that I know from here anyway that are here now." He chose the moment of his first semester grades to tell his parents that he had reached a decision: Medicine was his calling, he felt sure. He would return to Harvard in the fall of 1964 and then go on to Harvard Medical School, if it would have him. Barry Sr. and Mary were thrilled and relieved.

On Thursday, March 5, Barry Sr. was out of town and Mary invited Jonathan to accompany her to the symphony. "We had such a nice evening," she said. "I don't remember what was playing, but it was something that was quite easy for him to enjoy like Beethoven's Fifth Symphony. We had a wonderful cozy evening and I've always remembered it."

That Saturday, Jonathan and several boyhood friends—Carl "Mac" McLaughlin, Spencer De Pree, and Corwin "Corky" Short, among others—set about preparing the Binghams' barn for a reunion of their Cub Scout troop. The party was to be held that night and the barn had no electricity. Jonathan had already done most of the basic work himself—running cords and hanging light bulbs—but he still had to wait for the local electric company to make the final hookup. For days there had been a torrential downpour and terrific wind, creating a backlog of repair requests. Jonathan had gone through the proper channels to get a crew to connect the power, but it had not yet arrived. Time was growing short; the rest of the troop would start gathering at the barn by nightfall.

In the early afternoon, Mary and Barry Sr. prepared to go beagling with several other couples, as they did on many Saturdays in the fall and the spring. The sport, which resembles fox-hunting but on foot, sends men and women chasing after a pack of howling beagles as they pursue a rabbit. No one seems to care whether the animal is actually caught; getting exercise and socializing with friends is the real purpose. The Binghams' hunt club, Fincastle Beagles, was famous for its tailgate parties after the chase, as well as a hunt ball in April to close the season.

As his parents walked out of the Big House, bundled up against the elements, Jonathan said that if the electric company did not come soon, he wanted to connect the lights to the barn himself. Mary paid little attention and casually murmured her consent. She knew that Jonathan liked to tinker with electrical gadgets and fancied himself an expert at such things. After all, hadn't he once set up his own telephone system in the Big House basement and, with Charlie Bascom, wired his room at Brooks to avoid the lights-out rule?

Jonathan waited impatiently for a couple of hours. But by about 4:30 P.M. he decided that the power company was not coming and he would have to do the job himself. He slid heavy electricians' gloves on his hands and gazed up at the twenty-foot-high utility pole outside the barn. He climbed up first, followed closely by Mac McLaughlin, who carried a set of pliers. When Jonathan got to the top, he reached down to get the pliers, slipped, and touched a wire charged with 7,200 volts of electricity. "Are you all right?" Mac shouted. "No," said Jonathan, his body paralyzed by the current and fear rising in his voice. "I need help." "What can I do?" Mac asked. "Pull me loose."

They were his last words. Mac yanked hard at Jonathan's trouser leg, trying desperately to avoid coming into contact with his body, which was by then as charged with electricity as the deadly humming wire. Finally, after several strong tugs, Mac managed to free Jonathan from the grip of the wire and he fell to the rain-soaked ground with a dull thud. Mac raced down the pole and administered mouth-to-mouth resuscitation while Spencer De Pree massaged his chest. Jonathan, his body blue-white, lay motionless on the ground like a fallen Icarus.

Mary and Barry Sr. had returned from their outing just moments before the accident occurred. They began walking over to the barn, which was at some distance from the Big House, to see how preparations were going. Just as they got within sight of the pole, they saw something fall. They rushed over and to their horror found that the tumbling object had been Jonathan. Mac, Spencer, and the others broke their huddle around Jonathan to let Barry Sr. and Mary through. "He wasn't responding to their efforts," Mary said. "I couldn't feel any pulse."

They ran to a neighbor's house to telephone for help, bumping into Jacques and Sophie Albert, who were visiting Louisville at the time, as they flew through the door. The county police arrived within fifteen minutes, the ambulance moments later. Medics administered oxygen and compressed Jonathan's chest, but like Mary, they could detect no flicker of life. His friends broke into sobs. Mac McLaughlin was particularly distraught; he was sure that his pulling and yanking had thrown Jonathan to the ground with such force that it was he who had killed him, not the electricity. "It was so horrible, so pathetic," said Jacques. "Mary and Barry just stood there looking at that boy while they were trying to revive him. I've never been so moved by anything."

Throughout the weeping and the activity, Jonathan's eyes remained open in a kind of deathly stare, as though he, too, were a witness to the grim event. Finally, when it was clear that he was gone, Barry Sr. bent down and gently closed his son's eyes.

In the end, it seemed that the very qualities that had endeared Jonathan to so many—his innocence, vivid imagination, and childlike impetuousness —had killed him. Later, Barry Jr. wrote a long letter to Fessenden Wilder, his Brooks tutor, and tried to explain why Jonathan had taken such an obvious risk—handling thousands of volts of electricity on a wet, dark day. "His accident was one of those freaks which could have happened to anyone who never found in inexperience a source of fear," Barry Jr. wrote.

———————

By sheer coincidence, Eleanor happened to be in Louisville the day Jonathan died. She had been temporarily suspended from Concord Academy, the girls' school in Massachusetts she was attending, for turning a hamster loose in chapel. That afternoon she was driving on the expressway when she heard the news on the radio. "She came home white as a sheet," Mary said. "I think she was more distressed than any of the children."

Word of the tragedy traveled quickly. Someone called Peter Ardery at Harvard and he called the rest of Jonathan's friends. Charlie Bascom and Joe Hammer were together in Winthrop House that Saturday when Ellery Sedgwick III came in and made the announcement. He and Peter and Joe left for Louisville immediately.

On Sunday, through a driving rain, a steady line of cars inched up the long driveway to the Big House as friends and employees of the Bingham companies came to pay their respects. President Johnson and Lady Bird sent a note of sympathy. Jonathan lay in a casket in the ornate music room, his bier flanked by two tall candelabra.

To the grieving visitors, the Binghams seemed remarkably contained. Some were even reminded of Jackie Kennedy's aristocratic fortitude four months earlier at the funeral of her slain husband. "They made us feel at home, as if you were the one who was suffering and they weren't," said Joe Hammer. Mary's show of strength, however, was for outsiders only. "I've never seen anything so awful in my life as Mary's reaction to Jonathan's death," said Joan Bingham. "She never stopped crying. . . . It rained and rained and rained, and she cried and cried and cried."

The funeral was held on Monday under the soaring roof of St. Francis in the Fields. After the Big House servants were shown to their seats, the congregation rose to sing "A Mighty Fortress Is Our God." For years afterward Mary broke into sobs whenever she heard that hymn. And she thought it cruelly ironic that the minister chose to read the passage from the tenth chapter of Matthew about God knowing when even the smallest sparrow falls. "Are not two sparrows sold for a farthing?" went the verse. "And one of them shall not fall on the ground without your Father."

After the service, scores of people returned to the Big House, where the servants offered drinks on silver trays and guided guests to tables heaped with food. The Binghams, true to their breeding, were "ambassadorial, no weeping openly, no public grief," said Charlie Bascom. At one point, with exquisite sensitivity, Barry Sr. gathered Jonathan's contemporaries together and told them that the autopsy had shown that his son had died of electrocution, not from the fall. Nothing could have been done, he said. The gesture was meant to absolve Mac McLaughlin of any guilt for the death.

As soon as she returned from the funeral, Mary rushed upstairs to Jonathan's room and began pulling his clothes out of the closet. "Here, can you use this?" she said to a niece who had several children. That night, to everyone's dismay, she insisted on reading aloud from Jonathan's diary. She was beside herself with anguish, in part because she felt that by giving him permission to make the hookup himself, she was partly responsible for what had happened.

Barry Sr. suggested that she go to church, where he had found some peace, but religion offered Mary no comfort. One day the Binghams' minister dropped by the Big House and together he and Mary knelt down and prayed. She felt nothing. "She tried to get the best of it through exertion of character [and] willpower, of which she has a tremendous store," Barry Sr. said. Sallie thought her mother might be helped by psychiatric care, but Mary would hear none of it. "What's the use of my going to a psychiatrist?" she said. "I know perfectly well what's wrong with me. I'm suffering from intolerable grief!"

Mary's sister Rose made a special pilgrimage to Louisville and together the two women wept for hours in an upstairs bedroom. Rose's daughter had committed suicide and she knew what it was like to lose a child. Together, they read a favorite passage in the third act of Shakespeare's *King John*. "Grief fills the room up of my absent child, lies in his bed, walks up and down with me . . . stuffs out his vacant garments with his form," it began. Then came its wailing conclusion: "O Lord! my boy, my Arthur, my fair son! My life, my joy, my food, my all the world!" Shakespeare's sad eloquence was one of the few things that consoled Mary.

Temporarily, the Bingham family seemed to draw closer. Mary appreciated their sweet, supportive gestures, but she was too lost in despair to take much nourishment from them. "I don't think she ever really found a comfort completely, or ever has," said Barry Sr. Instead, as she had so many times before, she clung ever more tightly to her husband. When a friend asked how she was doing, Mary replied, "Well, I'm doing the best I can. I can take it, you see, because I have Barry."

Soon after the funeral, Barry Sr. took Mary away to the Pink Sands resort, an emotionally neutral place of sea and sunshine in the Bahamas. There they spent long soothing days on the beach, walking for miles, and reading English poetry. But when they returned, Mary seemed no better. Often during those first grief-stricken days, she would get in her car, roll up the windows, and "really howl, just howl as loud as I could." She feared she was losing her mind.

In April, about six weeks after Jonathan's death, she traveled to Washington for a meeting of the Council for Basic Education. She had hoped that the work would divert her, but one afternoon she found herself pacing up and down in her room at the Shoreham Hotel "crying so that I really couldn't stop." She took a long walk in Rock Creek Park and suddenly the thought came to her: "I'm going to go talk to Kay Graham."

Katharine Graham, then president of *The Washington Post*, had recently lost her husband to suicide, and Mary thought she might have some words of counsel. So, without as much as a phone call of warning, Mary took a taxi to the *Post*, asked to see her old friend, strode into Kay's office, and sat down. "I want to ask you how you got through the terrible tragedy you suffered," she said. "[It is so] much worse than what I'm going through. I just don't know how to deal with it." Kay stared back at her with a stricken look. "I think she was pretty horrified," Mary said. She tried to be helpful, but Mary sensed her embarrassment and quickly withdrew. "I must have been quite mad," she later said of the impulsive visit.

Finally, after several months, a sort of numbness set in, a condition Mary considered a blessed provision of nature. As a memorial to their son, she and Barry Sr. endowed research at Central State Hospital, the mental institution where Jonathan had worked after he left Cambridge. Years later, at a college reunion, Joe Hammer and a dozen other friends established a financial aid fund in Jonathan's name to help bring Kentucky students to Harvard. Barry Sr. added some money of his own, gently insisting that the memorial also include Peter Ardery. By then, he, too, had been dead for several years. The daredevil personality that had so mesmerized Jonathan had led Peter to a drug overdose in India.

———

Jonathan's death matured Worth even more than his marriage and his daughter's birth had. He seemed suddenly aware of the brevity of life and tried to cram into each day as much activity as possible. Less than five months after the tragedy, he wrote his will and threw himself more energetically than ever into good works, joining the boards of a dozen local causes. He became active in newspaper organizations like the Southern Newspaper Publishers Association, swapping political tales over drinks with the cigar-chomping "bidnessmen" his father and Barry Jr. disdained.

He also became more aggressive about taking on his father when he did not agree with him. Vietnam became a particularly bitter and divisive issue. Worth, Lisle Baker, and most of the papers' editorial writers were adamantly antiwar. Barry Sr., characteristically, was more equivocal, in part because he thought the United States had a duty to keep South Vietnam out of Communist hands and in part because he hoped to make a second career in government once he turned the papers over to Worth. He did not want to alienate President Johnson, who was wholeheartedly committed to the effort. When Worth would insist that the papers speak out, Barry Sr. would say that opposition to the war could destroy his personal influence with the president, influence that could help bring the conflict to an honorable conclusion.

In the 1964 election, Barry Sr. saw to it that *The Courier-Journal* and *Times* supported Johnson and the full Democratic slate. Worth was also pro-Johnson, but he begged his father not to back the Democratic candidates in Louisville because, he said, they were incompetent and sleazy. Barry Sr. refused, insisting on a blanket endorsement. Worth was furious, but the move had the desired effect on the White House. L.B.J. sent Barry Sr. a personal note thanking him for his "vigorous" backing of the entire Democratic ticket.

To make sure the president was aware of his efforts on his behalf, Barry Sr. periodically mailed off notes and CJ & T clippings to the White House. Once he even arranged to have them pasted into a handsome scrapbook for easier reading. "I am deeply grateful for your support," Johnson wrote back after receiving a particularly glowing *Louisville Times* editorial about his policies. "I hope to rely on your counsel in the days ahead."

Worth considered his father's gentlemanly attempts to forge a friendship with the president self-serving and somewhat quaint. Neither he nor anyone on the editorial page staff thought Barry Sr. or the Louisville newspapers could possibly influence Johnson's position on Vietnam. "Barry has a considerable opinion of his own persuasive capacities," said Molly Clowes. "I never felt that he could have any effect on Johnson, who was an extremely hard-boiled man and knew what he wanted."

Molly was unaware, of course, that Barry Sr. was actively campaigning for a position in the administration. About a week after Johnson's inauguration in 1965, Carl Rowan, by then the head of the U.S. Information Agency, listed Barry Sr. as a possible pick for the USIA's oversight committee. That spring the State Department spoke with Barry Sr. about the assignment and reported back that he was "intensely interested in government service."

But the moment was not right. Worth was still too green for Barry Sr. to spend much time away from Louisville. After a more exhaustive talk at the White House with John Macy, chairman of the Civil Service Commission, Barry Sr. reluctantly took himself out of the running. A year from now, Macy advised the president in a memo, Barry Sr. "would be interested in a government spot and I believe he would be well-qualified for a major embassy."

By 1965, Vietnam was a growing quagmire, but Barry Sr. refused to let the papers take a firm stand against it. At the same time he knew he had to keep Worth, Lisle, and the many doves on the editorial board from outright mutiny. The result was a compromise that made the Bingham papers appear to be fence-sitters on the war. "The great majority of the American people are still willing to support President Johnson in his Vietnamese policy," said a typical CJ editorial at the time, "but their spirits are troubled."

Predictably, the neither-here-nor-there policy satisfied no one at Sixth and Broadway. The antiwar types wanted the CJ & T to come out squarely for disengagement while the papers' few hawks wanted editorials suggesting more forceful intervention. The mounting tension between the two camps exploded in the spring of 1966 when Weldon James, Barry Sr.'s wartime roommate in London and the editorial board's lone voice for military escalation, angrily resigned in a signed column headlined: "It's Past Time To Say To Hell With Ho!"

Weldon said he was unhappy with the papers' wishy-washy stance on the war and ostentatiously pointed out that he was backing up his personal beliefs by reenlisting in the Marine Corps. But Worth knew that Weldon's reasons for leaving had at least as much to do with wounded pride as political principles.

For the past several months, in an effort to put his own stamp on the newspapers, Worth had been searching for a new editor for the editorial page, even going so far as to interview nationally known figures such as Arthur Schlesinger Jr. When his first choice, Ben Bagdikian, then a contributing editor at *The Saturday Evening Post*, turned him down, he had offered the job not to Weldon, a twenty-year veteran of the CJ & T, but to Molly Clowes, the senior woman on the page. The move made Molly the first female editorial page editor of a major daily in the United States.

But that was not why Worth had selected her. He had chosen Molly because she was a dazzling compromise candidate. Everyone on the editorial page respected her, and Worth knew that her views on Vietnam, while dovish, were not as fixed or inflexible as those of her colleagues—something that made both him and his father happy. Best of all, Molly was sixty—exactly Barry Sr.'s age—and when she retired five years hence, so would Barry Sr., giving Worth a clear field to name an editorial page editor of his own generation.

Molly was thus a temporary member of what was slowly becoming, with his father's guidance, Worth's team at the newspapers. Barry Sr. wanted Worth to have the same kind of high-level triumvirate he had had while he was running the papers. Norman Isaacs had already demonstrated that he could play Mark Ethridge's role on the news side. But who would play Lisle Baker's role as the numbers man?

About two years before his sixty-fifth birthday, Lisle found his own successor—Cyrus MacKinnon, forty-eight, a printing executive from Chicago—and, with Barry Sr. and Worth's consent, he persuaded him to come to Louisville as his understudy. Cy, an urbane Dartmouth graduate and lawyer, hit it off instantly with Worth. He swore easily and had an off-the-wall sense of humor that the Bingham heir appreciated. On hot summer days, he could often be seen peeling off his shirt in the *CJ & T* parking lot, jumping into his red Fiat convertible, and roaring home bare-chested, an act of macho self-assurance that Worth respected. Intellectually, though, Cy was more compatible with Barry Sr. The two men shared a love of books, tennis, liberal causes, and well-informed conversation—just the sort of lively banter Barry Sr. considered "satisfactory" in a newspaper colleague.

Most *CJ & T* staffers, however, were unimpressed with Worth's general-manager-in-training. They considered Cy a transparent social climber, especially after he and his wife, "Wig," bought a house close to the Senior Binghams, built a tennis court and swimming pool, and started hobnobbing with the monied set at the Louisville Country Club. Cy considered such actions part of his job. His careful cultivation of movers and shakers helped soften the anger the city's conservative business establishment had long felt toward Barry Sr. and the papers. With Cy genially smoothing the way, Barry Sr. began to experience something he had never known in his hometown: popularity.

The same characteristics that made Cy a boon companion for Worth and Barry Sr. made him a less than meticulous manager. The half-dozen Bingham executives with whom Cy worked most closely found him confusing and hard to read. One staffer likened his mind to a police-radio scanner that skipped rapidly from channel to channel. Like Barry Sr., he avoided confrontation. Rather than make a decision, he appointed endless committees to study a problem, even such routine but sensitive matters as pay raises. Many thought he was secretly afraid of the Binghams and too concerned with their approval to contradict their often misinformed judgments about business. Cy, however, simply felt that newspapers like *The Courier-Journal* and *Times* did not need much managing. "It's a monopoly," he said. "It's like running a power company except you have no public works commission."

―――――――――

Five days after Christmas, 1965, Barry Sr.'s older brother, Robert, died of emphysema at the age of sixty-eight. For years he had battered his body— first with alcohol, then with cup after cup of coffee, and finally with nonstop smoking. At the end, he had to be physically restrained from lighting cigarettes in his oxygen tent.

Barry Sr. knew his older brother had died resenting, even hating, him for his vast wealth and the position he had held in their father's esteem. Robert and his second wife, Felice, had left their apartment in New York City in the early 1950s and moved into a house near Denver before finally settling in Genoa, Nevada, a little town outside Lake Tahoe. Once, Jacques and Sophie Albert came to the Colorado residence for a visit and were amazed at Felice's miserly behavior. "She had a notepad and would write down 'three cans of string beans' and then check off one because they'd eaten it," said Jacques. He ascribed the food inventory to Felice's compulsiveness rather than to financial need, but there was no denying that the house and location were barren and bleak.

Robert's main source of income was the annual $15,000 in *Louisville Times* dividends that Judge Bingham's will provided, plus returns from some investments. Barry Sr. thought his brother lived comfortably. It did not occur to him to supplement his finances in any regular way, and Robert did not ask. He loathed the idea of going hat-in-hand to his kid brother. Instead, he brooded on the injustice of it all, seething at how Barry Sr. had played up to the Judge and succeeded in winning his favor. Near the end, Barry Sr. asked Felice what she thought of his coming to Nevada to see his brother before he passed away. "No, I think you'd better not do that," she said. "So much bitterness has built up."

Robert was cremated soon after his death, but Felice did not bring the ashes back east for several months. On March 8, 1966, Robert Worth (né Norwood) Bingham Jr. (as Cave Hill Cemetery recorded it) was buried beside his father and mother. The interment took place the day before the second anniversary of Jonathan's funeral. It was just the sort of fateful symmetry that fascinated Barry Sr. and convinced him that the lives of the Binghams had somehow been choreographed by cosmic forces.

Less than a week later, on March 14, another Robert Worth Bingham Jr. was born: Joan and Worth's second child and first son. Though Worth was technically Robert Worth Bingham III, he decided to make his son a Junior

to simplify things. When Barry Sr. went to examine "Robbie," as he came
to be called, his pride in male sexual equipment, well known within the
family, was clearly in evidence. After seeing the baby in the bath, Barry Sr.
reported back to the rest of the family that the newest Bingham boy was
delightfully well endowed—an inherited trait, he was sure.

After the flurry of death and new life, the Binghams settled back into
their familiar routines. That spring, Worth added three boards to his long
list of outside activities and decided to attend a two-week current affairs
seminar in May at the American Press Institute at Columbia University. The
mental workout would do him good, he thought. Besides, it would help
him decide what issues the Louisville newspapers should stand for during
his reign as publisher. He was on the brink of assuming the job for which
he had been groomed all his life—head of *The Courier-Journal* and *Times* and
head of the Bingham family—and he felt increasingly up to the challenge.
"Worth was appointed to hold his family together," said Wayne Sargent, a
golfing and drinking buddy who was then a top executive at United Press
International. "It would splinter unless a strong leader takes over."

It was a habit of the Binghams to leave for the cool air of New England
sometime after Independence Day. Louisville was usually hot and muggy in
June, but it was July and August that were really unbearable. That summer
—the summer of 1966—Joan took Clara and the new baby to Nantucket
the day after the Fourth of July. Worth planned to follow at the end of the
week.

On Thursday, July 7, he stayed late at the office so that he could have
dinner with the copy desk staff. He was good at these informal gatherings,
mixing self-deprecating humor with serious newspaper talk. On Friday, he
left on a chartered plane for Washington, where he was scheduled to interview a prospective employee. He would travel to Nantucket on a commercial flight from there.

Harvey Sloane, a physician and liberal activist, accompanied Worth on
the Louisville-to-Washington leg. By coincidence, Harvey had been a
roommate of Whitney Ellsworth, Sallie's husband, at boarding school. His
father had died when he was quite young, making him naturally drawn to
male mentors and patrons. Soon after meeting Barry Sr. in 1964, Harvey
and the older man had become extremely close—so close in fact that Worth
once made a stinging comment about Harvey's secret desire to have been
born a Bingham. The crack made Harvey uneasy. He felt that Worth was
jealous because of the rapport he had with Barry Sr., the kind of natural
kinship Worth had yet to establish with his father.

Harvey and Worth were friends nonetheless, and Harvey's efforts to set up a community health center in Louisville had made them political allies as well. On the plane, they played gin rummy. Harvey won the first few games. Then Worth suggested that they raise the stakes. "By the time we hit National [Airport]," said Harvey, "I had paid for the whole flight."

Late Friday evening, Worth's plane touched down on Nantucket. It was a homecoming of sorts. His parents had stayed on the island briefly during their honeymoon, and he and Joan had vacationed there before. This year they had rented a house on Baxter Road in Siasconset, a village of small, gray-shingle cottages. On Monday, Worth spoke briefly by phone with Norman Isaacs. "The weather here is gorgeous," he said happily before ringing off.

Just after noon on Tuesday, July 12, Worth, Joan, and Clara climbed into a rented hardtop convertible and set out for a beach on the other side of the island. Worth wanted to go surfing, one of his favorite sports, and the waves near Siasconset were just too tame. In order to transport his eight-foot surfboard in the car, Worth had to roll all the windows down and rest the board on the back ledges so that the ends jutted out like wings. Like most convertibles, the car had no posts separating the front and rear windows.

Worth slid behind the steering wheel. Clara sat next to him and Joan next to her. Robbie, too young to come along on such an outing, stayed behind with a nurse. As they set out along Baxter Road, the street went up a hill, making it impossible to see whether a car was approaching from the other direction. Because the street was narrow and he could not see over the top of the rise, Worth prudently steered the convertible to the right side of the road. Up ahead, also on the right, was Eugene Cashman's station wagon, parked in its usual spot in front of his cottage.

As Worth veered, he miscalculated—or perhaps just forgot what he was carrying in the backseat. The right end of the surfboard smacked into the station wagon. The board pivoted sharply, shooting the left side forward with a violent snap. The edge hit Worth with a sudden, karatelike blow to the neck. His body slumped instantly like a dropped marionette. Joan frantically climbed over Clara and seized the steering wheel. The car continued on for about a hundred feet before she finally managed to stop it by putting it in park. They had been gone from their cottage for less than a minute.

Thinking that Worth was just unconscious, Joan tried to revive him by slapping his face and calling his name. Moments later, Richard Magee, a doctor vacationing from Altoona, Pennsylvania, drove by, saw that there had been an accident, and stopped. After quickly examining Worth, he looked up at Joan and said, "Your husband is dead." The swinging surfboard had fractured his cervical spine; Worth had died of a broken neck. Eugene Cashman's wife ran to call the police.

———

It was 12:30 P.M. in Louisville when Joan's call came for Barry Sr., who was in his office with Norman Isaacs and Lisle Baker. "Yes?" Barry Sr. said pleasantly as he picked up the receiver. There were a few moments of silence. All the blood seemed to drain from his face. "Oh, my God!" he exclaimed.

Norman and Lisle sat riveted in their chairs while Barry Sr. peppered Joan with questions. It was obvious that something terrible had happened. "There was nothing we could do but just keep our eyes on him," said Norman. "Finally he hung up the phone. His first words were, 'How am I going to tell Mary?' Then he looked at us and said, 'Worth is dead.' He had aged years in a couple of minutes."

A secretary summoned Barry Jr. from his office at WHAS. He phoned Edie and in a dull monotone told her that he and his father were setting out immediately for the Big House. They wanted to inform Mary before she heard the news from someone else. The day was sweltering and Mary had spent the morning playing tennis. She had just emerged from the shower when Barry Sr. and Barry Jr. appeared in the upstairs bedroom. It was highly irregular for them to come home in the middle of the day. She looked into their faces and instantly saw the grief and fear. "What has happened?" she demanded. "Worth has been killed," Barry Sr. told her. "Not again!" she cried. "Not again!"

Lisle arranged for Barry Sr., Mary, and Barry Jr. to fly up to Nantucket that afternoon in a private DC-3 owned by Brown-Forman, the Louisville-based distillery. In an effort to distract themselves, the family took Mary's sister, Helena, along, too. Helena's reactionary political views and her penchant for nonstop chatter made hysteria and tears less likely, something the Binghams certainly preferred. But Helena was no comfort to Joan, who had despised her ever since she had treated Jack Kennedy's assassination as a cause for celebration.

At the Baxter Road cottage, Barry Jr. was the first to venture into the bedroom to console his dead brother's widow. True to form, Helena never stopped talking. "I thought I was going to scream," said Joan. To escape, Joan announced that she was going to the funeral home to be with Worth's body. After a sleepless night, the entourage flew back to Louisville with the casket.

Sallie was at the airport in Louisville to meet the plane along with Stephen Davenport, the Binghams' rector. Eleanor, who had been spending the summer in France, was on her way home. Years later, she could not remember whether she had arrived in time for the funeral of "Saint Worth," as she and Sallie disparagingly called him. The last time she had seen her brother, they had quarreled bitterly on the Big House terrace, and he had slapped her so hard she thought her jaw was broken.

Once again, a coffin lay in the music room of the Big House and a somber procession of cars slowly made its way up the twisting driveway. As each group of guests arrived, a butler opened the door and invited them to sign a book of condolence. Other servants led them to the parlor where Worth's casket lay and then guided them quickly to refreshments. Throughout the steamy afternoon, Barry Jr. bravely played host, shaking hands, remembering people's names, and asking after staff members' families.

The funeral took place on a blistering Thursday, July 14, at St. Francis in the Fields, the same church where twenty-eight months earlier Jonathan had been eulogized. "There were trumpets and the most glorious, beautiful music you ever heard, tremendous, soaring, gorgeous, lovely music," said Mary Clowes Taylor, Sallie's childhood friend. "[It was] like somebody had gone to the trouble to make sure this was a joyous, triumphal kind of experience."

According to Sallie, Barry Jr. wept openly at the church service. "The way he sobbed and cried at Worth's funeral was absolutely heartbreaking," she said. Barry Jr. admitted that he was shattered. "I lost the closest person to me in my life, other than my wife. There was no one closer to me than my brother Worth," he said. But he stiffly maintained that he never cried in public. Sallie's version of events was just another example of her tendency to confuse imagined experiences with literal truth, he said. No one at the service can recall Barry Jr.—or anyone in the Bingham family—breaking down.

The Binghams maintained their composure even as Worth's body was lowered into the ground a few feet to the left of Jonathan and at the foot of his grandfather's grave. After the funeral, Melinda Page Hamilton, a cousin living in Manhattan, was agonizing about what to say to Worth's widow when Joan, desperate for escape, spied her and took her by the arm. "Come over here and talk to me," she said. "I've got to find out what's happening in the theater in New York."

The trauma of Jonathan's death two years earlier had anesthetized Mary. Emotionally spent, she found it almost impossible to mourn for Worth. "Sometimes I feel guilty because by the time Worth was killed, I'd had it," she said.

Barry Sr., on the other hand, had been stoic after Jonathan's death. But the premature loss of yet another son seemed to intensify the first, and the cumulative effect sent him spiraling into a black depression. While Mary had let out her grief for Jonathan in huge, heaving sobs, Barry Sr., typically, tried to distract himself. Two weeks after Worth's funeral, while he and Mary recuperated on Cape Cod, he sent an eleven-page handwritten letter to Molly Clowes defending his policy of not criticizing Lyndon Johnson on Vietnam. Inevitably, though, his mind drifted back to the tragedy, and he would try hard to come to an accommodation that would let him bury it.

Ever since his mother's death over fifty years earlier, Barry Sr. had dealt with personal pain by finding something positive in the thing that had wounded him, then comforting himself with the thought that it could have been worse. Now, in a characteristic mental contortion, he counted all the blessings in the deaths of his two sons.

They had died quickly and "went out completely themselves," he said, instead of lingering on in some horrible wounded state or dying of a debilitating illness. No one else had been hurt. Worth might easily have been driving too fast, or even driving drunk, and killed not only himself, but Joan and Clara and other innocent people. He and Mary had three more children; they could have lost them all in some cataclysm. Besides, he said, it was churlish to complain too bitterly. Most people had horrible things happen to them. For years, the Binghams had been bathed in abundance; perhaps this was just a case of the universe righting the balance.

Two years earlier, when he was trying to find the hidden comfort in Jonathan's death, Barry Sr. had told Mary that they had been lucky because he had died "right before our eyes." Had Jonathan been away at college, "we might never have known exactly what it was," he said. After Worth's death, Barry Sr. stood that argument on its head. It was a good thing they had not been with Worth on Nantucket, he said; at least they would not have to carry the ghastly memory around with them.

But try as he might, Barry Sr. seemed unable to talk himself out of despair. He seemed agonized by the fact that he remained alive while his children had been taken. "I had to fight very hard against a terrible feeling of guilt," he said. "Here I was, an old man facing the deaths of two fine sons with all that they had in front of them." It was not in the natural scheme of things, he argued.

Barry Sr. kept recalling a brief exchange he had had with a stranger at the Nantucket airport when he had gone to fetch Worth's body. In an attempt to be consoling, the man had put his hand on Barry Sr.'s shoulder and said, "This was an accident that just could not have happened." The phrase seemed pregnant with meaning and Barry Sr. had been momentarily overcome with an odd sense of helplessness. On that perfect July afternoon, he stood on the barren tarmac and sensed that a malignant fate was being visited upon his family. The feeling would not go away.

The funeral over, his second son buried, Barry Sr. once again focused his thoughts on the perpetuation of the newspapers. He tried to feel buoyed by the thought that at least Barry Jr. was left. But he found it hard to summon the optimism that had seen him through so many earlier hardships. "To have these golden people so cruelly treated," said Melinda Page Hamilton. "It just made you feel that no one was safe."

MR. CLEAN'S
NEWSPAPERS

A few days after Worth's death, Barry Sr. summoned his three top advisers—Norman Isaacs, Wilson Wyatt, and Lisle Baker—to his big corner office and told them that Barry Jr. wanted to take Worth's place at the newspapers. Norman's reaction was shock and dismay and he did nothing to hide it. While Worth's image had been powerfully masculine, the more delicate-looking Barry Jr. was known in the newsroom as "Baby Bear." He was, said one former Bingham executive, "that little boy, that little blond-headed guy over at WHAS."

With characteristic candor, Norman blurted out his doubts. Barry Jr. is not equipped to do the job, he told Barry Sr. He has nothing but disdain for print journalism. He's never wanted anything to do with newspapers. He'll be a fish out of water. Why don't you just keep the titles of editor and publisher for a while until we can think this thing through?

Barry Sr. listened to his executive editor with a look of sadness and concern. When Norman had finished, the room lapsed into an uneasy silence. Then Wilson broke the quiet. "Barry," he said softly, "what alternative do you have?" Leaning back in his swivel chair, the Bingham patriarch stared up at his old friend without saying a word. Finally, he sighed. "I suppose I don't have any," he said.

Father and son would later sharply disagree about who had pressured whom to take over Worth's responsibilities. Barry Jr. insisted that the day after the funeral his father asked him to come to the papers, adding Worth's duties to those he already had at WHAS and Standard Gravure. "I was flattered," he said. "I looked on it as a challenge . . . and an opportunity."

He acknowledged that he did not have to take on the burden. But he knew that refusing the torch might prompt his father to sell *The Courier-Journal* and *Times*—and that was unthinkable, if for no other reason than it would have diminished the memory of his beloved older brother. To Barry Jr., his duty was clear. And it was also apparent, if not explicit, that his father expected him to do his duty.

Barry Sr., however, hid behind the technical truth that he had never really insisted that Barry Jr. head the newspapers. As he recalled it, he had simply asked him what he wanted to do now that Worth was dead, and Barry Jr. had suggested taking his brother's place. "This was completely his decision, in which I was happy to concur," he said. "I didn't feel that it was by any means an open and shut thing that he would take over for Worth." But what if he had refused? "I really don't know," said Barry Sr.

The rest of the Bingham clan was not at all surprised that Barry Jr. had decided to step into the breach. As Wilson Wyatt had so clearly pointed out, who else was there? Bestowing the position on one of the Bingham daughters was unthinkable. Sallie and Eleanor had been away from Louisville for years and neither had shown any interest in journalism. Besides, the Binghams had a tradition of primogeniture that was as inviolate as if their name had been Plantagenet or Tudor. "There was never any question," said Melinda Page Hamilton, Mary's niece. "They would never consider a daughter ahead of a son."

━━━━━━━━

On July 21, 1966, a week after Worth's funeral, Barry Jr., thirty-two, became assistant to the publisher at *The Courier-Journal* and *Times*, a position calculated to give him a crash course in newspaper management. His father retained the titles of editor and publisher, with the understanding that, as soon as it was feasible, they would be transferred to Barry Jr. At the same time, it was announced that Lisle Baker, the papers' executive vice-president and general manager, would delay his planned retirement to help smooth the transition in the aftermath of the family tragedy.

Barry Jr. observed these changes with fear and fascination from a new office located next door to his father—an office that had recently belonged to Worth and, before that, Mark Ethridge. He was shaken by his brother's sudden absence and the overwhelming gravity of his new responsibilities.

But he could not help feeling a rush of excitement, even pleasure, as well. Not long after Worth's funeral, a *Courier-Journal* secretary heard someone whistling up the stairs. "It was him," she said. "It really shook me up."

Barry Sr. assumed that, as a newspaper executive, Barry Jr. would be like him—aloof from day-to-day headaches and consumed with politics and "socially useful" outside interests. He had no inkling that his artistic second son would make it his goal to be the hands-on manager Worth had seemed destined to become. Not long after Barry Jr. decided to take on Worth's job, Barry Sr. sat in his office with executive editor Norman Isaacs and looked into the future. "Well, Norman," he joked, "Barry Jr. is coming down here and you're going to get me all over again!"

But Barry Jr. was absolutely determined to fill Worth's shoes. He planned to be a working publisher, not a proprietor, even though the job he had inherited was bigger and more complex than what Worth had faced. Had he lived, Worth would have had Barry Jr. as his trusted partner and ally, looking out for Standard Gravure and the broadcast properties. Barry Jr. had no such lieutenant. When his father retired, he and he alone would be responsible for all the Bingham companies.

The Courier-Journal and *Louisville Times* were in the midst of tectonic shifts when Barry Jr. stepped into Worth's place. Worth had been back in Louisville for only four years, but in that time he had infused the staff with a sense of confidence and purpose. "It was an electricity," said Mary Phyllis Riedley. "You didn't even have to be on the same floor [with him]. If you knew he was in his office, you thought all was right with the world. This newspaper was going full speed ahead."

Worth had been ambitious. He had not minded spending money on innovative technical changes and top-flight people. He wanted to run nationally recognized newspapers and to be a member of "the club," as the small group of wealthy white men who published the nation's top newspapers were known. His father had always found newspaper publishers dull, parochial, and overly obsessed with profits, but Worth knew that they had the real power. He made a point of attending publishers' conventions, charming the old men on the golf course at Boca Raton, even as he outraged them by endorsing integration and opposing Vietnam. By the time of his death, he had already been elected to the board of the Southern Newspaper Publishers Association, a regional organization Lisle Baker had headed several years earlier.

The top aides Barry Jr. inherited—Norman Isaacs on the news side and Cy MacKinnon on the business side—were stylistically compatible with Worth, who had a confident vision of his role at the papers. But for Barry Jr., who had no knowledge of print journalism and little self-assurance, they were all wrong.

Colonel Bingham, left, reminiscing about the Lost Cause with a fellow Confederate veteran at the Bingham Military School in Asheville, North Carolina, circa 1923.

Robert Worth Bingham at thirty, just as he was diving into the murky waters of Louisville politics.

3

Barry with his mother, Eleanor, about four months before the tragic accident in which she died sheltering him in her arms.

4

When Barry was six, Bob Bingham played King Menelaus in an outdoor production of *The Trojan Women*. "I saw my father appear in armor on the stage in a helmet with a flowing mane coming out of it," Barry said. "I thought it was the most magnificent thing I had ever seen."

Mary Lily Kenan Flagler, the wealthiest woman in the United States, about 1916, the year of her ill-fated marriage to Bob Bingham.

5

6

Lubricated by Prohibition-era gin and plenty of money, Barry tried hard to look the part of the sophisticated jazz baby during his Harvard days. He and his sister, Henrietta, right, by then a darling of London's exotic Bloomsbury group, posed for this postcard, which they found hilariously tacky

From left, Henrietta, Bob Bingham, and his third wife, Aleen, in May 1933 aboard the ocean liner *Washington* en route to Britain and his new job as U.S. ambassador. Bob was one of the wealthy men, including Joseph P. Kennedy, who underwrote Franklin D. Roosevelt in his first presidential bid.

In the summer of 1936, Bob, far right, came back from Britain to campaign for the president, third from left.

Barry's dissolute older brother, Robert Jr., here with his first wife, Phyllis, lived in Britain on an allowance from his father; the couple reluctantly became regulars on the embassy social circuit.

11 Barry and Mary struck friends as unusually close—"not just wedded, but welded," as one put it. In the summer of 1934, they gazed adoringly at each other for London photographer Dorothy Wilding, who was later asked to do the official portraits of the British royal family.

12

Barry Sr., Sallie, Mary, and Worth arrive at
Louisville's Calvary Church on Easter Sunday,
1941, a month before Barry Sr. enlisted in
the navy.

Her brothers dubbed Sallie "Miss Priss"; she
looked upon them as barbarians.

In 1949, when Barry Sr. was appointed head of
the Marshall Plan in France, the family lived in
Paris. Worth, far left, was almost expelled
from his Swiss boarding school; Barry Jr.,
second from left, and Sallie studied together
every night but filial affection never took root.

13

14

15

This picture of Mary, dressed in a chic evening gown, had a prominent place on Barry Sr.'s office desk.

When Adlai Stevenson, right, made his first run for the presidency, Barry Sr. was a close adviser and later made a "fact-finding" trip around the world with him.

16

17

Barry Sr.'s top aides—Lisle Baker, left, and Mark Ethridge—helped propel *The Courier-Journal* and *Times* to greatness during the 1950s. "It was nirvana when those three men ran the place," said a former aide. Norman Isaacs, an adjunct member of the troika, was the curmudgeonly executive editor of both papers.

18

19

During a six-month African
safari in 1958, Barry Jr.
and Worth shot wild game,
watched pygmy dances, and
climbed to the top of an
active volcano.

After Joan and Worth, left,
returned to Louisville from
their European honeymoon,
the Senior Binghams threw a
party at the Big House with
Joan's mother, center.

20

21

As the Vietnam war became
a growing quagmire, Barry Sr.
refused to let the Louisville
papers take a firm stand
against it, in part because he
didn't want to alienate
President Lyndon B.
Johnson.

22

Christmas 1959: The Binghams at the height of their elegance, achievement, and togetherness. From left, Joan, Worth (standing), Whitney Ellsworth, Sallie, Jonathan, Barry Sr., Barry Jr., Eleanor, and Mary.

Joan, left, shows Edie around the Big House grounds shortly before Edie's marriage to Barry Jr. in November 1963.

In the spring of his freshman year at Harvard, Jonathan, far right, set out for his first Brooks School alumni day with boarding school pals, from left, Ellery Sedgwick III, Charlie Bascom, Joe Hammer, Bob Turner, and Charlie Hunt.

23

24

25

27

The surfboard that killed Worth Bingham in a bizarre summer auto accident on Nantucket in 1966.

26

Barry Jr. assumed Worth's mantle as heir and succeeded his father as editor and publisher in June 1971. Six months later he struggled with cancer, emerging gaunt, determined, and more rigid than ever.

Despite the diabolical cast of the eyes, Barry Sr. told friends this was one of his favorite pictures of himself.

28

A moment of apparent, if misleading, togetherness: Molly, Barry Jr., Sallie, and Eleanor (back row), with Edie and Emily soon after the Bingham sisters returned to Louisville.

Rowland, Eleanor's husband, here with son, Rowlie, felt besieged by the newspapers' critics at Louisville parties and accused Barry Jr. of "hating" him.

The "hired hands": George Gill, top left, was known as "The Barracuda"; his arch rival, Paul Janensch, top right, was nicknamed "Darth Vader." Bernie Block, bottom left, made a last-ditch effort to save the empire; Leon Tallichet held the Binghams' hands in financial matters large and small.

35

A grim Barry Sr. poses for *The New York Times* in January 1986, after announcing that the family's newspapers would be sold.

36

"I looked at it as an active rejection of my leadership," said Barry Jr., shown here at a picnic he threw for Bingham employees soon after *The Courier-Journal* and *Times* were transferred to Gannett.

Mary and Barry Sr. at a local benefit shortly before he was diagnosed with brain cancer.

Most of the reporters on the *CJ & T* had a love-hate relationship with Norman. They respected him as a newsman and editor but found him totally lacking in bedside manner. When riled, he would fly into foul-mouthed, table-pounding rages, an approach staffers considered abusive and unnecessary. He was proud of the fact that he had once called a reporter in from his day off so that he could fire him. "He could be brutal in the way he handled people," said George Gill, then managing editor of *The Courier-Journal*, who, despite his position as Norman's principal protégé, suffered like everyone else under his pit-bull style of leadership. "He would just rant and rave."

Cy MacKinnon was far less threatening to Barry Jr. but no better suited to serve as his guide and teacher. Barry Jr. was like an inexperienced, willful child-king. Cy was his prime minister, who maintained control by never challenging Barry Jr.'s views and limiting his access to other members of the management team. As a result, Barry Jr. had only Cy's version of what was going on—and that was a view other Bingham executives usually found misguided.

By alternately fawning over Barry Jr. and isolating him from the rough-and-tumble, Cy often appeared to be patronizing his boss. "Deep down, I don't think he [liked him very much]," said one executive, "although he worked very hard not to give that impression. I think he thought Barry Jr. was dumb."

It was true that Cy regarded the last remaining Bingham son as inconsequential and a bit odd. While Worth was still alive, Cy had invited Barry Jr. to attend meetings concerning the newspapers, but Barry Jr. had staunchly refused, saying he did not want to invade his brother's turf. Like his parents and siblings, he was ignorant of even the most rudimentary concepts of finance. "If you can teach my children what depreciation is, I'd be so grateful," Barry Sr. once told Cy. "I've never figured out what it is myself and I don't even want to know."

To make matters worse, Norman and Cy, while pleasant enough tennis partners, had little tolerance for each other's idiosyncrasies at the office. Cy thought Norman was "never in doubt and not always right." Norman, on the other hand, disdained Cy's preoccupation with budgets and his fondness for deliberation. He was particularly critical of one of Cy's innovations—a mass meeting of the top executives of all the Bingham companies every Monday morning. The only space large enough to accommodate such a crowd was the cavernous auditorium at WHAS. Norman railed that it was a complete waste of time.

Because Norman scared him and he had no direct access to other models, Barry Jr. emulated Cy, taking refuge in the predictability of procedures. Cy's dilatory management, his love of bureaucracy, and his quarantine

of Barry Jr. created an atmosphere of ill-will in the executive wing of the
CJ & T building that Barry Jr. only dimly sensed. At one point, the indecision and unhappiness became so pronounced that John Richards tried to
organize a revolt. He urged several other top executives to march into Barry
Jr.'s office en masse and blow the whistle on Cy. But they knew that Barry
Jr. was a man who played by the rules; he was unlikely to look favorably on
a palace coup. And then there was Cy's vengeance to consider. "Look, that
guy'll get you," warned one of the Bingham retainers. In the end, the revolt
fizzled.

———————

Barry Jr. was such a newspaper neophyte when he started at the CJ & T that
the company sent him to an American Press Institute seminar at Columbia
University just to learn the basics. "My knowledge of journalism is so limited
that I don't know a lobster shift from a bull-dog edition," he wrote a friend
at the time.* He was a blank slate, and had no particular goals in mind
except upholding the papers as paragons of liberal conviction.

Norman Isaacs ordered CJ managing editor George Gill to take Barry Jr.
in hand and "drown him in newspaper." George, a scrappy Indiana native
who had been at the Louisville papers since 1960, was pleased to have the
chance to get close to the man who would one day run the Bingham empire.
Perhaps he could even help mold him as a journalist in the process, he told
himself.

George intuitively liked Barry Jr., who was roughly the same age, although he found him strangely contradictory. Barry Jr. seemed to have
genuine sympathy for his employees and their problems, but sometimes he
blurted out inner thoughts that left George in a state of shocked disbelief.
On these occasions, George could not decide whether Barry Jr. was blindly
insensitive, naively honest, or simply mean.

Once, when they were driving back from a Kentucky Press Association
meeting, Barry Jr. started to complain about Norman Isaacs's gruff bluster.
Suddenly, he stopped. "Did you ever wonder why we've got Jews in key
positions around here?" he asked George. Then he answered his own question. "They work hard and you don't have to pay them very much." George,
whose wife was half-Jewish, was speechless.

As time went on, Barry Jr. turned out to be neither a charismatic leader
like his older brother nor a pragmatic statesman like his father. His strength
lay in being principled and high-minded. One of his first editorial efforts

* A lobster shift works in the middle of the night; the bull-dog edition is a very early edition of the
morning paper, usually published the previous evening.

was an impassioned defense of the clergy, who, he felt, had shown "moral leadership" by participating in demonstrations against the Vietnam War.

From earliest childhood, Judge Bingham's declaration that the newspapers were "a public trust" had been drummed into Barry Jr. Every morning when he arrived at the *CJ & T* building, he saw the phrase etched into the wall above the lobby elevators. Barry Jr. always assumed that, under his father and brother, the papers had adhered to the highest ethical standards. But as his induction into newspaper journalism progressed, he was chagrined to discover conflicts of interest that, he said later, "would have made a harlot blush."

The farm editor was plugging his tractor distributorship in his column. Reporters were taking all manner of free gifts, from theater tickets to bottles of whiskey. The aerial photographer was snapping extra pictures for the local gas and electric company during his assignments for the papers. One editorial writer had even composed speeches for a gubernatorial candidate while writing editorials about him!

It was a seminal moment. Barry Jr. had found the overriding theme of his tenure: ethical purity. He vowed to set the pace for the rest of the newspaper industry, establishing higher standards of right and wrong than ever before. This was to be his greatest legacy and, in many ways, it was a more enduring contribution than anything his grandfather or his father had accomplished.

Under Barry Jr., the Louisville papers soon became so ethically antiseptic that *The Wall Street Journal* referred to Barry Jr. and his father as the "Messrs. Clean" of journalism. No one on his staff ever doubted that Barry Jr. had the courage of his convictions.

But like Judge Bingham, Barry Jr. tended to elevate his personal judgment to the status of moral imperative. He became increasingly uncompromising, stubbornly ignoring the counsel of his aides and taking his noble ideals to ridiculous extremes. Eventually, the atmosphere at *The Courier-Journal* and *Times* came to resemble Lewis Carroll's *Through the Looking Glass*. The refreshing openness he fostered led to some brave journalism even as it encouraged reporters to publish stories in the name of full disclosure that were uselessly or deliberately cruel. Nothing was sacred or private. Editorial freedom became near anarchy.

In the early days of his tenure at the papers, however, Barry Jr. was a refreshing change. He questioned the status quo, innocently ignorant of the way it had always been. No one suggested that Barry Sr.'s or Mark Ethridge's leadership had been corrupt, but times and standards were changing. The bourbon-slugging, blue-collar brand of newspaperman had given way to a generation of journalists who were idealistic and college-educated. In keeping with the new thinking, Norman Isaacs had begun requiring reporters to buy their own drinks and pay their own way to events they covered. But there was no written policy.

Norman, in fact, was the chief perpetrator of "sacred cows." The term referred to the special interests of the Bingham family, which Norman insisted receive prominent coverage. Muffled choruses of "mooooo" would wash over the newsroom when Norman ordered up a big story on the English Speaking Union, one of Barry Sr.'s pet causes. Barry Jr. felt scalding shame. The news should be reported straight, he said, without regard to the publisher's Anglophilia or his wife's passion for bookmobiles and other educational causes.

As far as Norman was concerned, there was nothing unethical about paying attention to the concerns of a newspaper's owners. When Barry Sr. or Mary delicately asked his opinion of an organization or an event, he felt they were telegraphing interest. "And if something interested them," he said, "I was interested. I had no hang-ups about that."

In 1969, while he was still in the role of apprentice, Barry Jr. took up the problem with his father. The peculiar result was two memoranda from Barry Sr. tersely titled "Sacred Cows" and "More Sacred Cows." "It is our unvarying desire to see reporters play all stories straight down the middle, unaffected by their own prejudices or by what they believe are our prejudices," Barry Sr. declared in the first memo. In the second, he gave an exhaustive list of subjects in which he had a personal interest, from tennis to historic preservation. Given this broad involvement, he said, the only solution was "a clear understanding on the part of the entire news staff that the publisher's interests are not to be considered, either pro or con, in making normal news judgments."

The effort did not satisfy Barry Jr., who knew that Norman would continue to do precisely as he pleased. For all his talk about being Worth's "second Papa," Norman had treated the eldest Bingham son with considerable deference. In contrast, he could not seem to muster an ounce of respect for "Baby Bear." "Norman Isaacs didn't treat anyone the way he treated Barry Jr.," said Mary Phyllis Riedley. "He was always muttering about his ridiculous ideas."

Norman was playing a dangerous game. Initially, he had frightened the Binghams' sensitive second son with his tantrums and blunt manner. As Barry Jr. grew more confident, however, the fear became anger and then a consuming desire to replace his disrespectful lieutenant with a more congenial and like-minded aide. With no dearth of enemies in the newsroom, it was only a matter of time before the farewell parties commenced. Two years after Worth's death, Norman was forced off the fourth floor, where he had inhabited an office next to the newsroom. His new home was an isolated cubicle on the third floor—the executive floor—where Barry Jr., Cy MacKinnon, and other company managers could keep an eye on him.

Though Norman was still executive editor, his era at the Bingham papers was rapidly coming to a close. He started to look for a new berth, and soon found one as a journalism professor at Columbia University. He left Louisville in 1970, cushioned from financial hardship by a $25,000 consulting contract from the Bingham companies. Barry Sr. did not want him to go, but he yielded to his son, who insisted that Norman was an anachronism. When the day came for his old friend actually to walk out of the building for the last time, Barry Sr. became uncharacteristically emotional. At the moment of goodbye, he looked up from his desk, his eyes misty. "I'm going to be all alone," he said. Mark Ethridge had gone. Lisle Baker had retired two years earlier. Norman was the last of the Old Guard.

———

Barry Jr. was itching to have unbridled command of the papers. In late August 1970, he moved into Norman's old fourth-floor office and took on the title of "temporary executive editor," a position meant to give him a six-month taste of real, hands-on news management.

Newsroom regulars immediately began speculating about who Barry Jr. would choose as Norman's permanent successor. The appointment would be Barry Jr.'s first big personnel decision and it was expected to reveal not only the kind of papers he wanted to run, but something about himself. There were two candidates for the job: George Gill, managing editor of *The Courier-Journal*, and Bob Clark, managing editor of *The Louisville Times*. In the newsroom, the smart money was on George.

At *The Courier-Journal*, George's nickname was "The Barracuda." There was something menacing about the way he stood in the doorway of his office, languidly scratching his back against the frame as his eyes darted over the newsroom to see what his reporters were doing. Norman, his mentor, had considered George the best field-general he had ever known; he really knew how to marshal the troops for a big story.

He was also what Norman liked to call his very own "you're-full-of-shit" man—meaning that George, unlike practically everyone else in the newsroom, was not afraid to argue with him. In fact, Cy MacKinnon considered George inherently tougher than Norman. "Norman was mostly baloney," he said. "He would yell like hell across the newsroom and embarrass someone in front of other people, but he wouldn't do much about it. George would."

George had grown up as a poor boy on the east side of Indianapolis. He was street smart, with a withering sardonic wit and a clear talent for leadership. After being jilted by a woman, he had run off to the navy, then finished his degree in journalism at Indiana University and gone to work covering the space program and civil rights for *The Richmond News-Leader*. The experience had made him more liberal than his die-hard Republican upbringing.

One night in 1959 while he was still working in Richmond, he filed pictures and a story about a man accused of murdering a nun. The suspect had been chased through the night and into a pond, where he drowned. His editor would not even look at the pictures. "He said he was a nigger and that it wouldn't make any difference," George recalled.

Disgusted, he decided to quit and begged for a job at *The Courier-Journal*. He was hired as a copy editor and after a year went back to his old beat covering civil rights. He eventually returned to editing and was made managing editor of *The Courier-Journal* soon after Worth's death. Though his hard-drinking, chain-smoking ways were of the old school, George was very much in favor of ethical purity and cheered Barry Jr. on in his campaign for tougher standards. He was competent and cocky. Within the organization, he was considered the obvious choice to be executive editor.

George's rival for the job was Bob Clark, a man so mild that he was called "Mother Clark." The manner was deceiving: Bob was a decorated World War II combat veteran who carried a scar halfway around his waist from a Japanese bayonet. Still, there was something of the prudish old lady about him. His way of conveying dissatisfaction with articles, for instance, was to tear them out and write "ugh!" or "whew!" in the margin. Soft-spoken and gentlemanly, he was credited with boosting circulation at the *Times* by starting a feature-filled Saturday supplement called "Scene." Unlike George, he shied away from fights.

Although he had intelligence and plenty of opinions, Barry Jr. had little experience in management and even less real confidence. Did he want as his top lieutenant a tart-tongued veteran like George who would probably make him feel stupid and even defy him, or a less-capable man like Bob who would defer to rank and take orders without an argument? To Barry Jr., the answer was obvious. He named Bob Clark executive editor. "Bob was like a pillow," said John Richards. "Barry Jr. knew [Bob] was not going to push him around." Though he was disappointed and angry, George Gill stayed on as *CJ* managing editor and effectively ignored Bob, who agreeably seemed not to mind.

The Clark appointment came in January 1971. Six months later, on June 1, Barry Sr. formally retired as editor and publisher of the Bingham companies. Both titles went to Barry Jr., and Barry Sr. became chairman of the board, a title that had no operational meaning but reflected the fact that he remained the owner of most of the company stock.

Barry Jr. wasted little time throwing the money changers out of the temple. A month before taking over, he published the papers' first written conflict of interest policy. It went far beyond what most newspapers required. No gifts. No free tickets. No outside writing or photography for any profit or nonprofit organization, including outfits like the Salvation Army and the Community Chest. No work for a politician or political organization, either voluntary or paid.

The new rules infuriated some employees. "The policy really did deprive us of our civil rights," complained John Ed Pearce. "I imagine that Barry thinks grubby newspapermen are always out to get their hands on power. I don't think he trusts anybody." In general, though, the regulations were regarded as adding stature to *The Courier-Journal* and *Times*.

The news columns under Barry Jr. also suggested that sacred cows had been put out to pasture. The Binghams themselves were prominently featured in a long *Louisville Times* story about the city's power structure headlined, "Who Decides Where Louisville Is Going?" Although the article told readers nothing new about the clout of the community's First Family, it did boost the papers' credibility. Reading a frank analysis of newspaper owners in the owners' own newspaper was unprecedented in Louisville, and probably anywhere else in the country.

For the newsroom, the story was a breathtaking development that seemed to herald a new era of candid, no-holds-barred reporting. Barry Jr. was sending a message: No sacred cows! Not even the Binghams themselves!

In anticipation of his father's retirement and his ascension to the titles of editor and publisher, Barry Jr. had a physical in mid-1971 and was pronounced so fit that he could rejoin the Marine Corps. A few months later, the company wanted to take out a $1 million "key man" life insurance policy on him, and he had to undergo another battery of tests. "I bitched and moaned," he said. But the second physical proved alarming: New X-rays showed a mass the size of a grapefruit in his chest.

In November 1971, six months after taking over the companies, Barry Jr. flew up to Boston and entered Massachusetts General Hospital for diagnostic surgery. After the operation, a doctor came into his room and gave him the verdict: He had Hodgkin's disease, the same type of cancer that had killed his grandfather. Barry Jr. was sure he was going to die. "I said to myself, 'You kiss your wife goodbye, rewrite your will, call the funeral home, and order a box.' " Almost everyone else shared his fatalism. The word in Louisville was that the Binghams' sole surviving son was "a goner."

For Barry Sr., it was as though a malevolent force had singled him out for torture. "I thought, 'Here it comes again,' " he said. Soon after his son began cancer treatments, Barry Sr. reluctantly reclaimed the titles of editor and publisher. At *The Courier-Journal* and *Times*, letters-to-the-editor began to arrive saying that God was punishing the Binghams.

Barry Jr.'s doctors tried to be reassuring. Medical science had made great advances since the Judge had died, they said; there was a good chance Barry Jr. could lick the disease. Barry Sr., ever the optimist, was heartened by the news. But Barry Jr. was suspicious, convinced that the doctors were just trying to buck him up. He kept pressing the medical team to put a figure on his chances for survival. Were they 50 percent? Less? When the doctors hedged, saying that each case was different, he gave them a disdainful look and slumped back into despondency. He felt like a marked man; death seemed inevitable. "There were many times when I said, 'Maybe I'd be better off dead and maybe everybody else would be better off if I were dead,' " Barry Jr. recalled.

In late November 1971, a Louisville medical team removed Barry Jr.'s spleen and some lymph nodes. He found a local physician whom he trusted and for the first time was persuaded that he did, in fact, have a reasonable chance of surviving. Armed with this hope, he applied his remarkable will to conquering cancer. "He came within an eyelash of dying," said his friend Ian Henderson. "But if ever anyone was determined to beat it, he was and he did."

During December, he took radiation treatments in his chest several times a week. After a month's rest, the treatments resumed. It was a grueling, ghastly experience. The radiation scarred his lungs and blocked the functioning of his thyroid gland, producing hot flashes and preventing him from salivating. He went from being a trim man who continuously struggled against pudginess to a gaunt figure who looked almost anorexic.

Though the treatments made him weak and lethargic, he insisted on coming into the office as much as possible. He wrote upbeat memos about his progress and once even circulated a photo of himself taken during a radiation session: He had almost no hair and was wearing a lead girdle around his waist, but on his face was a broad, brave grin. The ebullience was deceiving. It took every bit of resolve he had to drive himself to work, sit at his desk, get up, drive himself to the hospital for treatments, then drive himself back to the office, where he worked until 6:00 P.M. each day. "After seeing that, his secretary said she didn't care what he did; she would always have tremendous respect for him," recalled Keith Runyon, then an obituary writer at *The Courier-Journal*.

As luck would have it, Barry Jr.'s family had moved out of the home on

River Hill Road and into the Big House the very weekend his cancer was diagnosed. The switch was symbolic as well as practical. Barry Jr. was the new editor and publisher of the Bingham newspapers; it was only fitting that he live in the Big House while Barry Sr. and Mary relocate to the Little House, where they had lived as newlyweds. Edie had packed all the boxes ahead of time and marked them for moving. But she wanted to accompany her husband to Mass General and could not stay in Louisville to oversee the details. "I just gave the keys and the money to my oldest son and left him with the movers," she said. "Those were very traumatic times, terrible times."

The result was that Edie not only had to cope with her husband's recovery, but with living next door to her in-laws. Worse still, Barry Sr. and Mary had bequeathed Barry Jr. and Edie the Big House servants—a Chinese couple who spoke almost no English and did not know how to cook anything but chicken or shrimp with stir-fried vegetables. "It was a zoo," said Edie, "and I was trying to keep things running smoothly so Barry could get well."

The situation was made more difficult by Edie's boys, Philip and Charles. Before Worth's death, Barry Jr. had had plenty of time to take them hunting and biking on weekends. The arrival of two daughters—Emily Simms in 1965 and Mary Caperton, known as Molly, in 1968—had enlarged the household just as the boys were entering adolescence. With the burden of being the Bingham heir rapidly settling onto his shoulders, Barry Jr. had had fewer and fewer hours to spend with his children, and the strain had begun to show. By the time of Barry Jr.'s cancer, Philip, a rebellious sixteen, and his younger brother, Charles, were locked in a sullen battle of wills with their stepfather. Both resented having to go to school and were so certain Barry Jr. would eventually force them into the family business that they demanded written assurances saying they would never be asked to work at the Bingham companies.

Philip was especially unsympathetic to Barry Jr.'s need for rest and quiet. All he cared about was the rock-and-roll band he had started. Once, when Barry Jr. was feeling violently nauseous from a radiation treatment, Mary came over for a visit and found the Big House shaking from amplified guitars and pounding drums. "Edie, really, what is going on?" she asked indignantly. "I promised Philip that he could have his group here to practice," Edie replied helplessly. "They've got an engagement and they've got to practice." With the total confidence of a queen, Mary said, "Edie, they cannot practice here." The aspiring musicians were soon sent packing.

Eventually, Barry Jr. banished Philip and Charles from the house altogether. They began smoking pot and he worried that they were having a malignant influence on Emily and Molly. "I felt awfully sorry for [Edie] because they were her children after all," said Mary. "It was one of the worst conflicts of interest I could imagine. In the end she had to go along with him when he told them they had to leave."

The radiation treatments ended in late February 1972, and Barry Jr. gradually increased his workload. In June, he resumed the titles of editor and publisher and his father went back into retirement. As she watched her ailing husband trudge wearily to work each day, Edie became increasingly concerned about his health and decided to ask Barry Sr. and Mary for help. Barry Jr.'s job is too much for one person to handle, she told them, especially someone who has just conquered cancer. He has no time for himself anymore, or for me and the children. Isn't there someone who could split the job with Barry Jr.?

To Barry Sr., installing such a person would be tantamount to handing over control of the Bingham companies to a non-Bingham. It was unthinkable. He shook his head sadly. "No, there isn't anyone," he said. Edie was shocked. "I can't believe that!" she cried, astonished at being turned down flat. Later, Edie would recall the incident with great bitterness. It was the first time she had seen evidence that the Binghams lacked sympathy for their son. Mary considered her daughter-in-law's pleas wildly exaggerated and Barry Jr.'s fatigue a product of his own compulsive habits. "Edie was great at fixing Barry Jr. as a martyr . . . that he works so hard, he's worked harder than anybody she's ever known," she said.

As the initial fright of his illness faded, colleagues began to notice subtle personality changes in Barry Jr. He had always been driven. Now he seemed obsessed with making every hour count. There was something sterner, more unyielding about him, as though he was determined to show a capricious God that he was in control of his own destiny. Billy Keller, a Louisville psychiatrist and old family friend, warned Barry Sr. and Mary that people who conquer fatal illnesses are often convinced that they are invincible and can do no wrong. At the same time, they feel terribly uncomfortable with risk. "Well," said George Gill of Keller's analysis, "that's Barry Jr."

The news of Barry Jr.'s illness attracted packs of prospective buyers. Throughout late 1971 and 1972, the newsroom was flooded with rumors that the papers were about to be sold to *The Washington Post*. Though he never actually negotiated with anyone, Barry Sr. for the first time began to talk with Cy MacKinnon about an eventual sale. What if the cancer recurs and Barry Jr. dies in the next few years, he wondered. The grandchildren are too young to take over; without a Bingham running the papers, maybe it would be better to sell.

Barry Jr. was disgusted by the ghoulish inquiries of the newspaper brokers and reacted to them with an extreme gesture that demonstrated just how stressful his illness had been. He suggested that the *CJ & T* take out a full-page ad in *Editor & Publisher*, the industry trade magazine, and print a picture of him lying in a coffin. Above the photo would be the headline: "Don't make a bid until you see me here." He was not joking, and had to be dissuaded.

The same sort of anger and willfulness was apparent in the way Barry Jr. handled the news side of the papers. In the summer of 1972, he insisted on running an editorial arguing that it was a mistake to let George Wallace's American party hold its presidential nominating convention in Louisville. Wallace, a staunch segregationist, was no admirer of the Binghams or their "Curious Journal," as he had once dubbed the morning paper. Barry Jr. was certain that Nazis and hippies would clash in the streets. Besides, Louisville should not play host to such virulent racists. "If income from the conventioneers is expected to offset these risks and problems," his editorial said, "they will have to be the biggest spenders this town has ever seen." The editorial board begged Barry Jr. not to publish the piece on the grounds that it was antidemocratic and contrary to the free speech principle for which the paper stood, but Barry Jr. remained firm.

The *CJ & T*'s opinion did not discourage American party organizers, who went ahead and held their convention in Louisville. During the proceedings, Barry Jr. ventured into the hall with one of his editors, who received a finger-wagging lecture for wearing a "provocative" red vest.* When, to his surprise, the gathering proved peaceful, Barry Jr. reacted with a "we wuz wrong" editorial. "Our dire prediction of tumult in the streets if Louisville hosted this convention have come back to us in the form of a heaping plate of crow (as we chew we are consoled only by the well-said maxim that if one must eat crow, the time to do it is while it's still warm)." The mea culpa was admirable, but there was an edge to both editorials that was unsettling.

A few months later, Barry Jr. used the editorial page of *The Courier-Journal* to suggest that demonstrators gather at Richard Nixon's inauguration to protest the secret bombing of North Vietnam. The statement, which Barry Jr. wrote himself, was widely viewed as a call for violent and illegal civil disobedience. Reaction in Louisville was so pronounced that it made the news pages of *The New York Times*. Barry Jr. stood by his editorial.

The personal routine Barry Jr. created for himself was equally rigorous and uncompromising. Winter and summer, snow or rain, he began his days

---

* Barry Jr. was annoyed when local conservatives referred to the intersection in front of the *CJ & T* building as "Red Square," but he was capable of seeing the humor in being called a Communist. "After all," he once said, "being a Communist means sharing your wealth and I have no intention of sharing mine!"

shortly after 5:00 A.M. with a jog around the looping driveway in front of the Big House, exercise meant to strengthen his radiation-scarred lungs. He fixed his own breakfast and ate in the kitchen as he unrolled *The Courier-Journal* and began to read. Then he headed to town. Almost always, other newspaper executives found him in his corner office by the time they arrived.

At the end of the day, he was often the last to leave, climbing into his battered Datsun and chugging out of the executive parking lot. If he and Edie had no social obligations, he would haul home a packed briefcase. Even at dinner parties, he kept the pressure on. He had no taste or time for social chitchat. "He'd come here to a meal and say, 'Goddamn it, let's eat,' " recalled Cy MacKinnon's wife, Wig. "If he was coming at seven P.M., he'd expect you to eat at seven-thirty and get home by eight-thirty or something. No relaxing."

He needed at least seven hours' sleep, which meant he had to be in bed by 10:00 P.M. There seemed to be no time for daydreaming, reviewing the day's events, or talking things over with Edie. "I'm one of those people who thinks bed is for sleeping in," he said. "The minute I slide between the sheets, I'm gone." By 1973, the breakneck schedule had taken its toll: He was diagnosed with a duodenal ulcer. The men and women who worked with Barry Jr. marveled at his self-discipline, even as they whispered that he was irrational and masochistic.

Compounding the strain was Barry Jr.'s refusal to acknowledge that he had a reading disability. He could easily have minimized the importance of reading in his job. Instead, he made reading the essence of it. Edie estimated that he spent 75 percent of his working day doing what he probably liked least in the world: reading. His colleagues watched his daily struggle with a mixture of awe and perplexity, as one might view a man with a terrible stutter who insisted on communicating only through speech.

Barry Jr. spent hours wading through pages and pages of memos and minutiae. Each day, his secretary read correspondence and magazine articles into a tape recorder so that he could listen to the information as he traveled to and from work. But the biggest chunk of Barry Jr.'s time was spent going through his own newspapers, which he spread out on a drafting table in his office. "He would sit at that easel and read the paper, starting at six A.M. or seven A.M., and he'd still be at it at noon," George Gill said.

Barry Jr. flared at the suggestion that he suffered from dyslexia, an all-inclusive term for reading disabilities caused by anything from eye malfunctions to psychological disorders. He insisted, as his mother did, that he had just been a victim of poor reading instruction. Regardless of the cause, the fact was that Barry Jr. had to read slowly and with intense concentration in order to retain information. As a young man, he had tried speed-reading courses and even hypnosis to improve his performance. "There is not a charlatan in the Western world I have not seen," he said. But the results had been marginal. "If there is anything which could have changed my life," he said, "it would have been to double or triple my reading speed."

As a result, unlike his father, who always felt a tingle of pleasure when he picked up his morning *Courier-Journal*, Barry Jr. came to look upon the daily mound of newspapers as an obligation and a burden. He saw newspapers primarily as data-delivery systems anyway, and not very efficient ones at that. Compared with broadcast journalism and computer-based "tele-text," they were slow and dull. He was convinced that an electronic newspaper, viewed on a home computer screen, would one day replace ink-and-paper publishing. No longer would readers have to endure what Barry Jr. characterized as the wasteful and frustrating task of going through page after page of useless information; with a single keystroke, they could just punch up the stories they wanted to read.

From Barry Jr.'s perspective, digesting every apostrophe and comma in *The Courier-Journal* and *Louisville Times* was his duty, but he was also motivated by the fear of being caught flat-footed by his staff. Virtually every Sunday he sat down with *The Courier-Journal*—which sometimes totaled three hundred pages—and slowly went through each story. "I didn't want to go into an editorial conference the next morning and have somebody say, 'Well, Mr. Publisher, what position are we going to take on the governor's budget?' And I'd have to say, 'Well, gee, I don't know. I haven't read it,'" he explained.

The "somebody" he had in mind was Bob Barnard, the *CJ*'s editorial page editor, who delighted in needling Barry Jr. about what he did not know. While Barry Jr. had chosen Bob Clark, a passive, noncombative man, as his executive editor, he had inexplicably saddled himself with Bob Barnard, who showed little respect for his boss and heavily edited his editorials.

Barry Jr. presided over the editorial page conferences, which were held twice a week at 10:00 A.M. Unlike his father, who had always arrived with a laundry list of topics he wanted assigned, Barry Jr. made one or two suggestions, then solicited ideas from the dozen or so writers present. Later in the day, after the editorials were filed, he made a point of proofreading both pages—one for *The Courier-Journal* and one for *The Louisville Times*. But he rarely changed anything substantive, limiting his corrections to grammatical mistakes or an occasional spelling error.

Barry Jr. took the same hands-off approach to the news department. Each afternoon, he would attend the news conference, where the papers' current and future coverage was planned. Although he was editor of both papers, he seldom expressed an opinion and almost never issued directives. "Everyone believed that Barry came in and said just exactly where to put every word on the page and how to write it," said Irene Nolan, then on the features staff. "Well, the fact was I never heard Barry say anything about what he thought or felt about a story. I used to wish he would have more to say."

Few people in Louisville realized that Barry Jr. was as remote as the Wizard of Oz at his own newspaper. Indeed, many were convinced that he slanted articles and schemed over the placement of stories to suit his own personal and political agenda. "Everybody outside the paper thought that Barry Jr. overmanaged the news," said Maury Buchart, a former Bingham executive. "We on the inside knew that he didn't manage the news at all."

Barry Jr. had his own reasons for not touching copy or expressing an opinion, but typically, they were somewhat peculiar. As a First Amendment purist, he felt uncomfortable interfering with anyone's freedom of speech, especially that of his reporters. He was also devoted to a military-style chain of command and disliked overruling editors, because he felt it undermined them in the eyes of their subordinates.

His dual roles of publisher and editor further limited his power. He was convinced that the business and news sides of the paper should be separate, like church and state. Because he was publisher—the top business position —he did not want to pollute the process by making decisions about news, even though he was also the editor-in-chief. Finally, he was terrified of being perceived as being like his father, someone with a herd of sacred cows and the inclination to impose them on the news staff.

The cumulative effect of these inhibitions was that Barry Jr. had only the most tenuous connection to the day-to-day operation of the newspapers. He almost never read sensitive articles before they were published and seemed to regard it as unethical to inject himself into the editing process. He was a journalistic anomaly: an editor who did not edit. He bragged, in fact, that he only learned what was in *The Courier-Journal* when it arrived in his delivery tube each morning, just like any other reader.

The approach salved his conscience and suited his temperament. He was no more comfortable with the boisterous culture of the newsroom than his father had been. Besides, blue-penciling stories was frightening. It would have exposed him to the critical judgment of his staff. And with his reading and writing difficulties, the potential for embarrassment was tremendous. "I think he thought as long as he read the paper and ran the editorial page and occasionally wrote an editorial, he was fulfilling the role," said George Gill.

Armchair psychiatrists at the *CJ & T* thought that Barry Jr.'s quirky personality was mostly a survival technique. He seemed to derive great satisfaction from self-discipline, they said. Discipline, after all, had rescued him from the misery of being overweight. It had gotten him through Harvard, despite his reading handicap, and had helped him excel at crew. It had led him to seek a commission in the Marine Corps rather than the less-rigorous navy, and it had given him the strength to battle cancer. Whatever genuine success Barry Jr. had had in life was due almost entirely to his unswerving pursuit of self-denial.

Others, however, saw Barry Jr.'s iron will as a sign of weakness. "It's perfectly possible for a person thrown into a situation that he knows he is not equipped to handle [to] instinctively react with authoritarian conduct," said Norman Isaacs. According to this analysis, Barry Jr. had little confidence in his own abilities. To compensate, he built a battlement of inviolate policies and principles to accommodate his personal tastes and fears. Because he disliked politicians, for instance, he made sure the papers' ethical guidelines forbade socializing with candidates and officeholders.

At bottom, Barry Jr. was a romantic about the family newspapers and in awe of reporters and editors. His driving ambition was to maintain the papers' reputation for quality and integrity, but his way of achieving that goal was to distance himself from the nuts and bolts of *The Courier-Journal* and *Times*. He established the ethical do's and don'ts of the papers and kept the news department well lubricated with funds, then stepped back and let reporters and editors do their jobs, with no interference or guidance from him.

Most news staffers considered the unbridled freedom intoxicating. But other Bingham employees—and many readers, as well—felt that *The Courier-Journal* and *Times* too often took on the air of an asylum run by the inmates. "Anything [the news side] did was OK," said Bernie Block, a Bingham executive. "They could walk into his office anytime, at any level. They were a separate camp from the rest of the company."

Nothing seemed to be off-limits, not even Barry Jr. A *Louisville Times* columnist wrote sneeringly about his bad breath. Bob Schulman, the *Times's* media critic, penned pieces so critical of the Bingham papers and broadcast outlets that Mary dryly suggested his column be called "Fouling the Nest." But Barry Jr. refused to exert control. He felt that would be tantamount to censorship. "Barry's whole approach is laissez-faire," said George Gill. "I don't know how many times I've heard him say, 'I'm not going to tell those people what to do.' If the reporter wrote it, it's got to be published."

The chaos extended to newsroom humor, which was often sophomoric and cruel. In December 1972, the *Times's* advice columnist received a letter from a woman asking how she should explain to her little girl that their puppy, "Willie," had died. "What do you tell a little girl whose best friend is dead?" asked the distraught mother. "That the angels took him, her sad-faced Willie? The angels took her Grandpa and her new baby brother last year, too. . . . Can you console her?" The columnist tacked the letter on the newsroom bulletin board, with a typed note inviting responses. One suggested reply:

> We have sad news for your little girl. Neither sad-faced Willie nor Grandpa could be located in Heaven by our newsperson there. Alas and alack, the *Times* has no man or woman in Hades, but we have asked our sister newspaper, *The Courier-Journal*, for help. The CJ, it can be reliably reported, has several staffers either in Hell or on their way, and they should be able to find your missing loved ones. Seasons Greetings, The editors.

"If we put notes on the bulletin board like they did—'we' being the business side—we'd get fired," said Bernie Block. "They were able to do it."

Barry Jr. was as likely to be the butt of bulletin board barbs as anyone. In the summer of 1973, during a safari in Kenya, he succeeded in bagging two one-thousand-pound man-eating crocodiles that had been terrorizing a local Samburu village. When he got back, the Sunday sports section printed an account of the grisly adventure, complete with a photo of Barry Jr. standing proudly beside one of the slain reptiles. The picture went up immediately on the fourth-floor bulletin board, along with several mock press releases.

One needled Barry Jr. for treating anything he or his family did as newsworthy. "Croc-O-Dial!" said one "announcement" pinned under the photo. "As a public service, and at no cost to you, *The Courier-Journal* and *Louisville Times* Public Relations Department will read over the telephone [Sunday's] account of the publisher's African exploits. . . . As a bonus, also free, they will recite an explanation of how the editorial integrity of these newspapers is not compromised by these and other seemingly contradictory acts."

The lambasting did not stop there. A month later, the staff held a raucous "Safari Soiree" at the home of one of the editors. As requested, Barry Jr. and Edie showed up in pith helmets and khaki shorts. The evening quickly devolved into a loud, drunken debauch. George Gill got so plastered that he locked himself in a bedroom with a secretary dressed in a loin cloth and refused to come out despite his wife's pounding and high-pitched threats.

The main entertainment was a slide show lampooning the Kenyan safari. At one point, a woman playing the character of Edie flashed on the screen. Her hair was disheveled, her shirttail was out, her pants were unzipped, and she was sporting the hat that had been seen earlier on the man playing the professional safari guide. In the script, the dim-witted Barry Jr. character explained. "I just came back from a hunt and called Edie out of her tent for a picture-taking session," he said, "and the poor dear didn't have time to get herself together."

The real Barry Jr. and Edie chuckled politely and left early. No one on the staff worried that the publisher would react with anger or vengeance. Indeed, many thought he did not realize he was being made fun of. "He never recovered from that croc stuff," said Jean Howerton Coady. "People thought he wasn't too smart."

They also had something new to snigger about. While on safari, Barry Jr. had let his beard grow. When he got back to Louisville, he shaved off everything except an unruly mustache, which he kept in line with thick applications of mustache wax. Eventually, he coaxed the blond and red hairs into a heavily waxed handlebar, which gave him the appearance of a British officer in colonial India.

In this free-wheeling, irreverent atmosphere, some impressive journalism also took place. In 1974, when *Time* magazine published its second-ever list of the nation's top ten newspapers, *The Courier-Journal* was there, as it had been a decade earlier. That same year, *Time* selected Barry Jr. as one of the nation's "200 Young Leaders of the Future." Five of the eight Pulitzer Prizes won by the Bingham papers were awarded while Barry Jr. was at the helm. Remarkably, one was for excellence in international reporting—a direct result of Barry Jr.'s faithfulness to his family's open-purse policy.

The Louisville papers' finest hour came in 1975 when the federal district court ordered busing to integrate the schools, which had become effectively re-segregated because of white flight to the suburbs. Riots and demonstrations erupted. While local politicians blasted busing and tepidly urged compliance with the law, Barry Jr. embraced the change as necessary and right. In late August, in an effort to prepare citizens for the change, *The Louisville Times* printed the names of newspaper executives and the schools their children attended. Barry Jr. dutifully reported that, despite his papers' support of busing, his two daughters went to private academies.

When busing actually started on September 4, 1975, opponents, powerless to hold back the inevitable, turned their rage on the newspapers. Ten thousand people gathered in front of the CJ & T building at Sixth and Broadway, shaking their fists and screaming abuse. Bricks were thrown through the windows; editions of *The Courier-Journal* and *Times* were ripped from their racks and burned. Some 3,500 subscribers canceled their papers. One man was so sputteringly furious that he sent Barry Jr. a note saying he was canceling his subscription "because of your Communistic position on busing"—even though he was not a subscriber. "In case I ever were to decide to subscribe," he explained, "this is my cancellation in advance."

The protest soon turned frighteningly personal. Barry Jr. was hanged in effigy. Death threats prompted him to hire bodyguards for his daughters and put bulletproof glass in his office windows. At one march, a demonstrator accosted a *Louisville Times* reporter and said: "You work for Barry Bingham

Jr., the thirty-third most powerful Communist in the United States? I'd like to get ahold of Barry Bingham and wring his neck. You can tell him that." Eventually, the governor called in the Kentucky National Guard.

Both Bingham papers gave the upheaval front-page coverage, but they also followed strict guidelines to make sure that only facts, not rumors, made it into print. A month before school opened, Bob Clark sent out a memo advising staffers to avoid inflammatory phrases like "forced busing" or "massive busing." Headlines were treated with special care. "Some people read no further than headlines," the memo pointed out. "Thus, it is imperative that headlines be true to the sense of the story. If there is doubt, write [the headline] on the side of caution."

From July 1975 until the end of the year, almost 1,200 articles on busing appeared in the Bingham papers, along with 330 photographs, over 200 maps, and hundreds of letters-to-the-editor—most of them opposed to the policy. "I am very proud that the hate crusade for the Binghams is gathering such momentum," said one. "God hates fools and hypocrites so we have no qualms." The cool-headed performance won distinguished service awards for both newspapers and for WHAS. The photo coverage was singled-out for a Pulitzer.

———

Barry Jr. barely had time to savor this triumph before the papers suffered two terrible wounds: the fall of the Binghams' first female managing editor, and the scaling back of *The Courier-Journal's* economic fortunes and editorial scope—two events that marked the beginning of a long decline.

The most visible blow was the public humiliation of *Courier-Journal* managing editor Carol Sutton, who had succeeded George Gill in 1974 to become the first female managing editor of a major metropolitan daily in the country. Carol, then forty, looked like a winsome Shirley MacLaine. She had started as a secretary at the papers in the 1950s and rapidly distinguished herself as a graceful feature writer. In 1963, she became editor of the women's section. Nine years later, she changed the name from "Women's World" to "Today's Living" in order to expand coverage beyond debutante parties to issues such as abortion and cohabitation. "Today's Living" became the prototype of the modern feature section.

Almost single-handedly, Carol redefined "soft" news. On Thanksgiving Day, 1972, Louisville readers were shocked to find a full-page picture of an open refrigerator with nothing in it but a jar of lard—the only food possessed by an elderly woman featured in the accompanying series, "Hunger in Kentucky." The next year, Carol wrote an exposé of the giveaways lavished on reporters by the fashion industry in New York. The article won

"Today's Living" a J. C. Penney–University of Missouri award. When the $1,000 prize arrived, Carol told her reporters that they could divide it among themselves or donate it to the University of Kentucky for a minority scholarship. "Our share would have been as much as a week's pay, but nobody dared tell Carol that we didn't want to start a scholarship," said Irene Nolan.

Carol treated her staff with almost maternal concern. She rarely forgot a birthday or a special anniversary, and when she went off to Central America, Mexico, and Europe to tour ancient ruins—her passion—she always came back laden with gifts. Her reporters loved her, and cheered when she was selected as *Courier-Journal* managing editor. As a gag, they made up a mock front page that announced her new position as "Managing Editress." "She's got the moxie," Barry Jr. replied when a local magazine asked why he had chosen her.

But even her admirers had misgivings about whether Carol had sufficient toughness and administrative skill to be an effective managing editor. As head of "Today's Living," she had agonized over decisions, shied away from confrontation, and been notoriously disorganized. "Carol was a marvelous people person," said George Gill. "What she lacked was experience in leading the troops. She was *not* prepared to be managing editor."

For Barry Jr., though, Carol Sutton's appointment represented a dazzling double coup. It was yet another "first" for the Bingham papers as well as further proof that *The Courier-Journal* was a top-rank liberal institution. "My God, it's a great thing for us!" Barry Jr. repeatedly told executives at the paper.

For a while, it appeared to be a great thing for Carol as well. Overnight, she became one of the nation's most celebrated editors. In 1975, she appeared on the cover of *Time* as one of a dozen "Women of the Year," and she was besieged with invitations to speak. Encouraged by Barry Jr. and Bob Clark, she accepted request after request and became a kind of traveling advertisement for the Bingham newspapers.

As a managing editor, though, Carol was clearly floundering. She watched in helpless frustration as the recession that gripped the nation in the mid-1970s battered *The Courier-Journal*. During her stewardship, the daily *Courier-Journal* lost 7 percent in circulation, suffering more than the *Times* or the combined Sunday edition. By the end of 1975, combined net profits for both papers had plunged to the lowest point ever—just over 2 percent.

The incessant globe-trotting to make speeches and appear on panels also took its toll. Although Carol was on hand for the most important moments, like the busing crisis, she was not in town often enough to master the complex day-to-day operation of the paper. "The [media] attention [to our female M. E.] . . . it's a little bit tiresome," one *CJ* reporter complained in a *Louisville Times* article.

Carol seemed pathetically uncertain about how to handle her new responsibilities. Having never had a secretary, she continued to compose her own letters on a manual typewriter. She tried to counter her image as a soft-news person by speaking in an unsmiling monotone, which she thought made her appear more serious. Those who had known her as head of "Today's Living" were baffled and dismayed; she seemed so unlike the animated, amusing friend she still was in private with them.

Barry Jr. did little to improve the situation. He seemed awkward and uncomfortable around his new managing editor. "Carol said she had a hard time meeting with him on a one-to-one basis because she felt he wanted to flee, almost. That he couldn't handle a woman in a position of authority," said one staffer who knew her well. Barry Jr.'s distress was shared by others. Despite the papers' vaunted liberalism, many male reporters and editors at the *CJ & T* openly disparaged women. Former city editor and ombudsman John Herchenroeder, exasperated at a female writer, once stormed, "I'd trade two women reporters for a good wastebasket."

As Carol's troubles deepened, neither Barry Jr. nor Bob Clark nor George Gill—who had recommended her as his replacement—stepped in to advise or help her, as they would surely have done had the editor been a man. The blood was in the water, and Carol was convinced that *Louisville Times* managing editor Michael Davies, a brash young Englishman, smelled it. "Davies was lurking in the weeds, nailing her every time he could and politicking with Barry Jr.," said George. "He was oozing his way up the ladder."

In May 1976, when the ax fell, even Carol's friends had concluded that a change was necessary. Barely two years after he had appointed her, Barry Jr. announced on the newsroom bulletin board that he had asked Carol to become "assistant to the editor and publisher." She was to take on the "major new responsibility" of studying the future of special interest publications, he said. Michael Davies would be the new managing editor of *The Courier-Journal.*

That, unfortunately, did not end the sad saga of Carol Sutton. A week after her fall, the *Louisville Times* media critic, Bob Schulman, reported in his column that there was an "untouched" story behind Carol's new assignment. Without naming any sources, he declared that she had been fired for incompetence and that her superiors had felt *The Courier-Journal* "needed a stronger hand."

He then quoted Barry Jr., who obligingly confirmed that Carol's new job was just a face-saving device. "Nobody wanted to look like he was knifing Carol," said Barry Jr., who went on to compliment Schulman's reportorial aggressiveness. "If one of our reporters or news editors smelled a story behind the story in [the personnel shifts at a local corporation], he'd have been after it like a barracuda . . . some of the most gifted don't see that if you 'go after' other people to get the full story, you must also go after yourselves."

The comments and the column were stunningly insensitive—all the more so because Barry Jr. had promised Carol that he would never publicly discuss the reasons she had been kicked upstairs. But while Barry Jr. the publisher might have pledged silence, Barry Jr. the editor felt obliged on principle to tell all he knew. As he was inclined to do, Barry Jr. took a commendable idea—openness—and followed it right out the window.

A week later, Carol struck back. In a confidential, two-page typed memo to Barry Jr., she castigated him for "shabby journalism," noting bitterly that the "newspaper game is still played by boys' rules" and that her position as a female M.E. had forced her to live in a "spotlighted fishbowl" for two years:

> I waited a week to write this, until the blood stopped flowing from the large wound in my back, but I do think you should know that I consider Bob Schulman's column of last Monday the ultimate betrayal. To treat a 21-year career and reputation—built, in my view, with a helluva lot of blood and brains and devotion and personal sacrifice—as grist for a public gossip mill is reprehensible. I don't know who his informed sources were, but I gathered from his column that you were eager to corroborate them. . . . The fact that I was never asked to comment on a story in which informed sources were taking whacks at my reputation is, to me, appalling. . . . You have regularly treated any criticism of the media critic as defensiveness. However . . . [this story] was not in the public interest, and it is not, contrary to your comment, the practice of these newspapers to treat others in this manner.

Barry Jr.'s handling of Carol's ouster revealed more than just his skewed zeal for openness. It showed his remarkable inability to empathize with others, a trait that would later prove fatal as he fought his sisters for control of the Bingham empire.

Despite the angry tone of her letter, Carol continued to work at *The Courier-Journal*. She felt loyalty to the place, she said, and could not find it in her heart to leave. By the time she died of cancer in 1985, she was a broken woman. Her smoking and drinking had escalated to dangerous levels. She had gained weight and appeared older than her years. "Some people thought she looked like a bag lady," said a friend. "She was sort of the walking wounded of that era." Although Barry Jr. made a point of visiting cancer victims because of his own experience with life-threatening illness, he could not bring himself to go see Carol.

Carol's removal in 1976 marked the beginning of a decade-long identity crisis at the Bingham newspapers. In a sense, she was the first casualty in a long, bitter struggle for the soul of the papers, a battle that came to figure heavily in the parallel war the Binghams eventually waged against each other.

The Courier-Journal and *Times* reached the pinnacle of their combined circulation in 1972, a year after Barry Sr. retired and Barry Jr. assumed operational control. The *Courier* was read in every county in Kentucky and much of southern Indiana. *The Louisville Times*, with its self-consciously local focus, dominated Jefferson County, which included Louisville itself.

Then came the economic recession, the gas crisis, the controversy over busing. Circulation began to drop, especially at *The Courier-Journal*, which was feeling competition from *The Lexington Herald-Leader*, a Knight-Ridder—owned daily based in the state's other major city seventy-five miles east of Louisville.

Soon after the busing protest subsided, *The Courier-Journal* conducted a probing study of its "personality." The conclusion, Bob Schulman wrote in his column, was that "if papers were people, the daily *Courier-Journal* would be a serious, often-stuffy, upper-crust schoolmaster who wears his hair long and occasionally plucks a guitar to prove he's with-it."

Stories rambled on endlessly and pocketbook issues were all but neglected. "Name an industry or business in Kentucky, and we don't cover it," the report said. Arts stories were far too high-brow to appeal to a wide audience. When Elvis Presley came to Louisville, for instance, the *CJ* did not even assign a reporter to cover his concert. The critical self-appraisal prompted a radical redesign and shift of emphasis. The new *Courier-Journal* tried to take the world less seriously, to be less "*The New York Times* of Mid-America" and more a selective digest for the average working man or woman.

Barry Jr. regarded the changes as repugnant and regrettable. He felt much as he had in 1975 when, after a decade of losses totaling almost $1 million, he had finally been forced to admit defeat and switch WHAS-FM from a classical music station to an all-news station. The awful truth was that *CJ & T* profits had sunk below even the family's modest expectations. After taxes, the papers barely broke even; most newspapers of comparable size earned well over 10 percent after taxes, and some made much more. To boost profits to an acceptable level, Barry Jr. would have to find new readers, attract more advertising, raise ad rates, and trim costs.

The in-house study recommended several ways to save money, including shrinking the space devoted to news, cutting the reporting staff by 5 percent, and reducing the number of pages in the edition of *The Courier-Journal* that was distributed in the distant, rural counties of Kentucky. Writing must be bright and polished. The paper should include more soft news and features to pull in the many readers who found the paper ponderous and stiff.

As unavoidable as the changes were, they violated Barry Jr.'s rarified interpretation of the Bingham newspaper tradition. His grandfather had shamelessly serialized potboilers to attract and hold readers, but Barry Jr. felt embarrassed—a word he used frequently—to have to trade in his Cadillac of a newspaper for a peppy new compact. In a bitter editorial that his top advisers begged him not to publish, Barry Jr. seemed to blame Louisville's yahoo readers for *The Courier-Journal*'s troubles. "The hard reality is that newspapers must change to match the taste of the communities they serve," he wrote, "or die a lingering and needless death."

The "new" *Courier-Journal* inspired a predictable protest from longtime subscribers and did not appreciably boost circulation. Reporters and editors, moreover, complained that *The Courier-Journal* and *Times* had stopped being like a family business and had become more like a corporation—interested only in the bottom line.

For Barry Jr., the next decade was an inexorable struggle. The price of paper and gasoline skyrocketed. The pressure for profits put an increasing squeeze on the news department, where most of the fat had settled during the spendthrift days of the 1960s and early 1970s. Instead of thinking about journalistic ethics and editorial positions, Barry Jr. spent his days consumed with business meetings and budgets as he tried to find ways to shore up the papers' eroding fortunes.

Although he had little to offer in the way of financial advice, Barry Sr. could easily have served as a sounding board for his son. He was someone Barry Jr. could trust, and he was also chairman of the Bingham companies and the controlling stockholder. But Barry Jr. made it an article of faith never to seek counsel from his father, and Barry Sr. never encouraged him to ask.

Except for gentle memos on incorrect word usage or run-on sentences, Barry Sr. had pointedly stayed out of his son's way since handing over the reins in 1971. "He was infinitely more stand-offish than we really thought was wise," said Wilson Wyatt, speaking for all the Bingham advisers. Few outsiders believed that someone in Barry Sr.'s position could relinquish control as totally as he insisted he had. But it was true. "He turned over the power and authority of the newspaper to me in a spectacular way," said Barry Jr. "No holds barred. He said, 'I'm not going to . . . tell you how to run these papers.' "

Barry Sr. had erected this wall in part because of his own personal history.

After all, as a young man he had had to battle the obsequious Mannie Levi for his father's confidence. Even after that fight was won and Mannie deposed, he had had to kowtow to the Judge's whims and directives—and would have had to continue to do so for years had his father not died in 1937. If anyone knew the value of having clear title to power, Barry Sr. did. The only control he retained for himself was the ultimate one: a majority of the voting stock.

The other reason Barry Sr. refused to step in and advise his son was because he usually did not agree with Barry Jr.'s decisions. By adhering to a principle of noninterference, he spared himself humiliation and embarrassment. When friends railed against the papers' policies or news coverage, as they frequently did, he could look sympathetic and say honestly that he had nothing to do with *The Courier-Journal* and *Times*. He could even add his own voice to the chorus of complaints. "Barry Jr. did things that made him really bite his lip," said John Richards. "God, it drove the old man up the wall!"

To reinforce the impression of distance, Barry Sr. refused to participate in the editorial page that he had once loved so much. When Bob Barnard invited him to write a regular, signed column, he declined. "He said the perception would be that he was still closely involved in [the papers]," Barry Jr. explained. "He thought that would be undesirable because it would appear to undermine my authority."

The truth was that many of the things Barry Jr. did baffled Barry Sr. A written conflict of interest policy, for instance, was something Barry Sr. had assiduously avoided when he was editor and publisher, because it would have diminished his flexibility. But to Barry Jr., having clear standards—knowing what was expected and then living up to it—was soothingly reassuring. By meeting a predetermined goal, he could prove to himself and perhaps the world that he was every bit the newspaperman his revered older brother might have been. "Worth became a kind of icon here after he died," Barry Sr. said. "That is a hard thing to compete with."

After a Louisville friend floated the idea and played intermediary, father and son had regular, once-a-week lunches, but they were usually perfunctory affairs, dominated by chat about the family and goings-on in the community. Though Barry Sr. maintained an office on the third floor, not far from Barry Jr., the younger Bingham rarely visited his father. He took pains to keep him informed about the business, but he never actively solicited his counsel. And Barry Sr. made it clear he had no interest in giving it. "I told my father the options we were considering," Barry Jr. said. "I assumed that if he thought one of them was absolutely off the wall he would have said [so]."

The result of this complex and formal relationship was that, as the pressure mounted for retrenchment at the papers, Barry Jr. found himself profoundly and rather poignantly alone. As time went on, he grew increasingly anxious and defiant and embattled. It was this frightened, besieged man that Sallie and Eleanor found at the helm of the family enterprises when they returned to Louisville in the late 1970s. Barry Jr. was already in a pressure cooker. His sisters would soon turn up the heat.

THE RETURN OF
THE SISTERS

Barry Sr. and Mary were overjoyed at the prospect of Sallie's and Eleanor's return to Louisville. After the deaths of two sons and Barry Jr.'s cancer scare, they looked upon their daughters' homecoming with a sense of relief and hope. It was a reunion of the family, and they felt satisfaction at the notion that, after many wanderings, disappointments, and heartaches, Sallie and Eleanor, like their brothers before them, had finally felt the primal pull of Kentucky and come home. They wanted to get to know Sallie's young sons, who had always lived so far away, and help Eleanor find a career and a mate. Most of all, as they entered their seventies, they longed for the comfort and intimacy of family ties.

Barry Sr., especially, hoped that Sallie and Eleanor would become more involved in the family business, invested in its health and perpetuation just as he, Mary, and Barry Jr. were. With his usual optimism, he had no inkling that his business goals and his family goals were on a collision course.

Keeping the newspapers in Bingham hands had been relatively simple as long as only one pair of hands was involved. Judge Bingham had chosen Barry Sr. over his siblings, giving Robert and Henrietta income from the companies but no stock and no power. Barry Sr. had subsequently selected Worth, then Barry Jr., to head the dynasty.

His daughters' return subtly altered his attitude toward how the empire should be governed. He had no intention of anointing them, but he found himself eager to include and please them and, despite his own relief at never having had to share power with his brother and sister, he felt certain that all three children would become closer if they functioned as co-owners. When another prominent family newspaper owner told him that he was courting trouble, Barry Sr. smiled and shook his head. "I know my kids," he said confidently.

Barry Sr. gravely underestimated the antagonisms, born in childhood, that still existed among his heirs, particularly between Barry Jr. and Sallie. Initially, Barry Jr. felt no threat to his power, but later he came to see the return of his patronizing sister as the beginning of his tumble from grace. "The best thing that could have happened to me was for Sallie to win a Pulitzer Prize for fiction every year," he said. "Then she would have stayed out of my hair. It was when she started to focus on her failures that the trouble began."

By her own admission, Sallie arrived back in Louisville in a state of complete demoralization. After the early years of promise, her writing had stalled, her agent had dropped her, and her second marriage had just broken up. She was worn out and artistically depleted from over a decade of living in New York City. She considered the manicured lawns of Kentucky a healthier environment for her growing boys and a safe refuge for her.

Sallie also came home to redress her conflicted feelings about her family, especially her father. In the years since the deaths of Jonathan and Worth, she had become increasingly distant from her parents, at times even blaming them for the freakish accidents that had snuffed out her brothers' lives. Barry Sr. and Mary had sheltered Jonathan and Worth too much, encouraging their recklessness by making them feel invulnerable, she told some family intimates; to others, she suggested that her brothers had committed suicide to avoid the weight of family expectations. She had had almost no contact with Joan or Eleanor, although all three had lived contemporaneously in New York. Her relations with Barry Jr. and Edie consisted of little more than an occasional Christmas visit. Yet the family continued to obsess her. For the sake of her children as well as herself, she wanted to rediscover what it meant to be a Bingham.

One of Sallie's major disappointments was her inability to succeed at marriage. Her storybook union with Whitney Ellsworth had ended in anger and humiliation. For the first several years, while she and Whitney lived in a little town house on Boston's Beacon Hill, Sallie seemed intent on reproducing her parents' life. Jeans, lovebeads, and brown rice were just coming into vogue in Cambridge coffeehouses, but Sallie, draped in tea gowns, resolutely served her guests the rich, buttery food of the Big House on thin china plates. Sallie would later say that beneath the pressed linen and finger bowls, she had been play-acting all the time, trying to live up to the paradigm of the ideal marriage her parents' union represented.

While Whitney worked at *The Atlantic Monthly*, Sallie wrote furiously. She was thrilled at the publication of her first novel, *After Such Knowledge*, in 1960, then crushed when the work was met with silence. She dedicated the book to Whitney, but its theme—"the dullness and sad triviality of most women's lives"—hinted at her underlying discontent. Perhaps to compensate for the failure of the book, she decided, against Whitney's wishes, to have a child. He was born in June 1961, the first Bingham grandchild, and she named him Barry Bingham Ellsworth, after her father.

The birth of the baby marked the beginning of the end of Sallie and Whitney's relationship. Sallie herself suggested the cause in a rueful short story she wrote at the time. In "The Ice Party," a new father leaves his wife with their baby boy in a Boston apartment while he goes to a skating party. As he guides an old girlfriend around the ice, he complains of being bored by his wife's obsession with the infant. "I suppose the whole thing has been hard on my vanity," he says, adding testily, "If I'd expected this in the beginning—but, you know, she was so gay, so lively, so interested in everything."

While the baby was still small, they moved to New York City, where Whitney quickly made a name for himself as the publisher and co-founder of *The New York Review of Books*. When *Time* wrote that the tabloid's arrival in September 1963 was "given the kind of hearty welcome usually reserved for long-awaited novels," the phrase fed Sallie's insecurities about the failure of her first book and her growing competitiveness with Whitney.

She felt out of her depth in the company of Norman Mailer, Susan Sontag, Gore Vidal, William Styron, and other established contributors. In the beginning, she volunteered to type envelopes for the *Review*, whose other founders included Jason and Barbara Epstein and a fellow Kentuckian, Elizabeth Hardwick, but their intellectual snobbery soon intimidated her. She retreated to the safety of her Upper East Side apartment, gave up writing novels, and concentrated on short stories, the literary form that had brought her such acclaim at Radcliffe. "It was easier for me to write short stories [than novels]," she said. "Then I wouldn't have so much invested in the reaction."

Sallie sold her work to the *Atlantic*, *Ladies' Home Journal*, and *Redbook*, but it did not satisfy the grand expectations she had for herself. She began to look upon the literary lions at the *Review* with contempt as well as fear. They did not take her writing seriously, she felt. She saw slights everywhere and began to pick fights with Whitney in public. A visitor to their apartment was shocked to discover that the young couple was sleeping in separate beds. Unaware of her daughter's troubles, Mary sank $10,000 into the

Review and offered to pay for a nanny for the baby. Saying they did not want their privacy invaded, Sallie and Whitney refused. "I've no doubt that domesticity without any help was quite a burden," said Mary. "That may have influenced her view of the unhappy state of marriage."

When the union finally ended amid great bitterness, Whitney wrote a "sensitive, considerate, really sweet" letter to the Binghams about the breakup. But Sallie never discussed the matter with her parents and did not consider coming home. "She just told us it was over," said Barry Sr.

Though Sallie was unwilling to talk to her parents about her deepest feelings, she was quite willing to write about them. Indeed, her parents began to look upon her short stories as letters home—they reflected her situation that closely. Though the details were different, she seemed always to write about herself, from the new mother of "The Ice Party" to a series of stories about women, generally divorced and victimized by men, who seemed ragged, desperate, and uncertain. Reviewers noted that the women in Sallie's works all had one quality in common: they "connect with nothing but themselves."

To allay her unhappiness, Sallie became even more obsessed with her infant son, refusing dinner invitations with friends so she could sit in the dark and watch him drift off to sleep. Years later she told her parents that the blond-haired little boy, an artistic, picture-book child, was the only person in her life she had ever really loved.

Soon after her separation from Whitney, Sallie became caught up in Freudian analysis. The sessions, which were billed to the Senior Binghams, lasted for almost ten years, giving her ample opportunity to explore the Oedipal roots of her distress, just as her aunt Henrietta had done decades earlier with Dr. Ernest Jones in London. Every time she was in her father's presence, Sallie told the psychiatrist, she got so emotionally overwrought that she could barely see straight.

More disturbing, from the Binghams' point of view, was the psychiatrist's encouragement of Sallie's already fertile imagination and her tendency to blame others for her misfortune. At his daughter's request, Barry Sr. agreed to come to New York for a session. The psychiatrist told him that one of Sallie's most vivid resentments from childhood was her persecution by her brothers, particularly the time Barry Jr. threw her cat in the fire. Astonished, Barry Sr. said that the family had never owned cats, indeed that he was allergic to them. "Oh, it doesn't matter whether those things happened or not," said the doctor, "because this is what is in her mind. That's the important thing."

Sallie took to the absolution of analysis as easily as she had once taken communion in the sweeping sanctuary of Calvary Church. In "Bare Bones," a short story published soon after she and Whitney broke up, Sallie wrote about a young divorced mother who is furious at finding herself lonely and miserable. "How could she have known what it would mean to be alone?" said Sallie's distraught heroine. "She had been taught to expect a great deal and it was not her fault if she were constantly disappointed. The world was simply not equal to her expectations."

Sallie's troubled state did not keep her entirely out of circulation. One night she turned up at a formal party in a black dress cut low in the back and caught the eye of a handsome young attorney named Michael Iovenko. The son of a Russian immigrant, Michael could not match Whitney's wealth or savoir faire, but he clearly adored Sallie. She was far more equivocal in her affections. "I don't think she was ever in love with him," said Mary. But she appreciated his kindness to her son and his solicitousness of her. In December 1965, less than a year after her divorce from Whitney, Sallie and Michael were married. They moved into a town house with a big bay window on East 95th Street, and within five years had two children of their own, Christopher and William.

Despite the disorder of a household with three small boys, Sallie continued to write, rising at 5:00 A.M. to work in her study and retiring to a small office in their country house in Rhinebeck, New York, on weekends. As the years passed and *The Touching Hand*, a collection of short stories, including a novella based on Nursie, and *The Way It Is Now*, another collection, were published to mixed reviews, her anger and desperation grew. Sallie seemed unable to extricate herself from the narrow, confining memories of the Big House. All of Sallie's characters, said *The New York Times*, were "poor little rich girls whose energy for life has presumably been sapped by having had to exercise a boring horse in adolescence or by mothers whose correctness was traumatic."

Increasingly, her writing seemed calculated to wound. In "The Way It Is Now," the title story of her third book, she painted a biting portrait of Michael Iovenko. In the story, a woman with a young son signs her divorce papers and then leaves for a rendezvous with the adoring man who now wants to marry her, a man she torments and manipulates, almost against her will. The woman invites pampering from men, even as she hates them for the stunted life their indulgence has caused. In a spasm of self-loathing and self-justification, the woman says to herself: "I have felt nothing, suffered nothing, and I will have my revenge for that."

Barry Sr. and Mary had seen Sallie frequently when she was married to Whitney. But after she married Michael, they glimpsed her only at Christmastime or on Labor Day weekend, when the whole family gathered in Chatham in the trim white house Barry Sr. had recently bought from J. Seward Johnson, heir to the Johnson & Johnson pharmaceutical fortune. Infrequent as these visits were, they cemented an unusual closeness between

Michael and Barry Jr., who had always felt dismissed by Whitney. The two men shared a love of classical music and a serious outlook on life. When Barry Jr. invited Michael to sit on the Bingham board of directors, the young lawyer gladly accepted.

At the time, Sallie was indifferent to the family business. She rarely read *The Courier-Journal* and seemed content to collect her dividends while her husband represented her interests. But she soon grew jealous of the affectionate regard in which Michael was held by her family and the company managers. Michael attended every board meeting, even the ones for WHAS and Standard Gravure, did his homework, asked good questions, and understood business procedures. "We all liked him because he was contributing, adding something," said John Richards. "That made Sallie real mad."

Michael also made life easier for the Senior Binghams. Despite Sallie's protestations that he was being imposed upon, he cheerfully agreed to look after the legal affairs of Henrietta, who lived alone in a second-floor apartment on East 75th Street. At Henrietta's request, Michael drafted several wills and codicils, but he never succeeded in getting her to sign any of them before she died, of a heart attack, in June 1968. By then Henrietta had grown fat and matronly, so dissipated by drink and drugs that a prominent vein trailed down one side of her cheek like a winding blue brook.

She had long ago traded Pineland Plantations, the Georgia hunting retreat left to her by the Judge, for cash, and sold off Harmony Landing, her Kentucky horse farm, to an automobile dealer. She had lived in New York since the early 1950s, chased out of Louisville, so legend had it, for making passes at a farmer's daughter. An ill-advised marriage to a younger man had lasted only a few months. But it had been long enough to deplete her investment in the country inn she had bought for him to run on Long Island Sound. She had been reduced to accepting an apartment and occasional gifts of money from Barry Sr.

The mercurial charm that had entranced John Houseman and Dora Carrington was still intact, though, and after her divorce Henrietta had several long-lived relationships. The most satisfying was with an older Englishwoman named Dorothie Poultney Bigelow, who had played the female lead in Cole Porter's first Broadway musical, *See America First*, in 1916 and lived in the apartment across the hall. But Henrietta continued to drink too much, once becoming so disoriented that she tried to clean up spilled bacon grease with a carpet sweeper. At a fund-raiser for Adlai Stevenson she got into an irrational, screaming fight with Tallulah Bankhead over a string of pearls.

On the morning of her death, she heard the maid come in, tried to get out of bed, and fell dead on the floor. Before Barry Sr. and Mary could fly up to New York, Michael Iovenko was in the apartment, opening silverware drawers, rummaging through closets, and throwing clothes left and right as

he searched to see if Henrietta had finally signed the will and other documents he had prepared. Sophie and Jacques Albert, who lived nearby and
had been summoned to locate something suitable for Henrietta to be buried
in, were appalled at Michael's behavior.

No signed will could be found. Henrietta died intestate. All she had of
value was her furniture and her jewelry, some of which went to Sallie. Years
later, in the flush of her newfound feminism, Sallie would describe her
relationship with Henrietta as unusually close. But at the time she told the
New York Surrogate's Court that she saw her aunt only once every two
months. In mid-June, just as the moist heat of Louisville was beginning to
blow in from the river, Henrietta was buried in Cave Hill Cemetery on the
right-hand side of the father who had both adored and ruined her. Every
year until she died herself, Dorothie Poultney Bigelow sent orange carnations to the grave.

Like Henrietta, Sallie loved turmoil. Hostilities, breakups, and reconciliations fed Sallie's writing and made her feel alive. Dinner parties at the East
95th Street house usually included a large helping of Sallie's lethal tongue
along with an elegant meal and witty conversation. "She would always offer
a cutting riposte about people who were not there," recalled a frequent
guest. No longer was Sallie the sensitive, precocious Radcliffe ingenue.
Early divorce and disappointment in the publishing world had hardened and
toughened her. Encouraged by therapy, she began to turn her anger outward.

Michael was ill-equipped to deal with a woman of Sallie's gathering fury.
By nature he was an understanding, peace-loving sort, a man who, like the
protagonist in Sallie's 1974 short story, "A Place in the Country," had "a
way with unhappy women." The quality might have endeared him to a less-
complicated mate, but it only made Sallie contemptuous. "Sallie could destroy him, destroy his whole life, and it wouldn't mean a thing to her," said
a Bingham in-law. "She's like one of these people that unless you kick her,
she doesn't respect you."

Bored with Michael, Sallie launched a flagrant affair with a psychiatrist in
Rhinebeck. She hoped, naively, that the man would marry her. When he
did not, Sallie filed for divorce from Michael even though he would have
forgiven the transgression instantly. She explained to her parents that Michael was simply not strong enough for her. "She said that he was like a
boudoir pillow—if you put your fist in it, it just collapses," Mary recalled.

Sallie's first child, Barry Bingham Ellsworth, appreciated Michael's gentle
ways. When he found out about the separation, he told Sallie that he
wanted to go live with him. Being rejected by the person she loved most in
all the world was more than Sallie could bear. She angrily refused, and
Michael told the young boy there was nothing he could do, since he was

not his biological father. Faced with the prospect of staying with his mother, Barry elected to go live with Whitney, who had remarried by then and had two small daughters. Sallie was shocked and hurt.

The air was thoroughly poisoned by the time Sallie and Michael went to court for the divorce. Michael fought hard to keep his children but the judge ordered joint custody, giving Michael the right to see Chris and Willy, as Sallie called her youngest son, only every other weekend.

The divorce from Whitney had left Sallie devastated, but the divorce from Michael left her enraged. He immediately went off the Bingham board of directors. She took his place and forbade her family to have any contact with him. For a while he continued to see Joan and her children at their summer place on Long Island and to visit the Senior Binghams in Chatham and Louisville. Finally, Barry Sr. and Mary sent him a letter saying that their relationship was causing a breach with Sallie and would only do damage to the children.

It was in this state of defeat, anger, and resentment that, soon after her fortieth birthday, Sallie packed up the two Iovenko boys and headed out for a new life in Louisville, the town she had once scorned. She came back not as a subversive but as a supplicant, a woman for whom the early expectations of success had never been realized. A change of scene, a return to the enfolding arms of the family, might reinvigorate her writing and heal her unsettled children, she reasoned.

Sallie had never been trained for adversity, something Mary and Barry Sr. had known so well and ultimately conquered in their own troubled childhoods. Now, she also had experienced misfortune and genuine disappointment, and it had been too much for her. She wanted to be surrounded by the thick, protective walls of the Big House again, to run away from the world as she had so many times in those long, languid after-school hours as a child. "I was floundering," she admitted. "It was seductive to think about going back where everybody knew me. I wanted to be safe for a while. I wanted to be in a safe, comfortable environment."

―――――――――

The Binghams tried hard to make Louisville a haven for Sallie. Barry Jr. sponsored his sister for membership in the River Valley Club. Barry Sr. and Mary threw a small party in her honor, helped her purchase a house close to Glenview and bought puppies for the boys. Barry Sr. felt a vague sense of guilt about Sallie, as though he was personally responsible for the Oedipal fixation and inflated hopes that were the cause of her troubles. He saw how desperate she was and yearned to heal her wounds.

As she had at almost every other juncture of her life, Sallie expected too much from her Louisville homecoming. Barry Sr. read to the boys and arranged private wrestling lessons for Chris, and Mary visited frequently. But Sallie wanted more. She had hoped that Barry Sr. and Mary would fully share the burdens of parenthood with her. When they made it clear they had no intention of playing such a role, she was bitterly disappointed.

Chris Iovenko, the older of the two, had outgrown an initial shyness and was a sanguine, even-tempered boy. But Willy had been a problem almost from birth. Even at the age of two, he stared out at the ocean from the balcony of his parents' room at the Chatham Bars Inn, silent and intense as a Buddhist monk. His quiet concentration made Sallie and Michael think he was a genius. Mary had a different interpretation. "I thought he was cooking up some ugly scheme."

Usually, boys and girls flocked to Barry Sr. like the Pied Piper, trailing after him, tugging at his sleeve, and building sandcastles with him on the beach. Willy never responded to his grandfather's overtures. While he was still quite young, he had stolen sleeping pills from his grandmother Iovenko and tried to sell them at school. As he got older and stronger, he became a bully. Soon after arriving in Louisville, he threw a little girl over a banister. Later, Willy and several other boys harassed a female classmate, jeering outside her bedroom window and throwing stones. When the girl's father, a WHAS executive, ordered the boys to leave, Willy identified himself as Sallie Bingham's son and threatened to have the man fired. A fistfight ensued, with Willy on the losing end.

The frustrations of motherhood aside, Sallie's confidence and sense of well-being grew as she spent more time in Louisville. In the fall of 1977, she began teaching introductory creative writing at the University of Louisville. She bought a little studio overlooking the Ohio River and started work on a novel.

At first her cultural horizons were narrowly defined by the standards of the Manhattan literary scene she knew so well. Like the rest of the Bingham family, she looked to New York and Europe, not Kentucky, for art, music, and literature. But as she became more comfortable in Louisville she began to appreciate a more homespun culture.

Bill Grant, an American literature professor at the University of Louisville, was a major influence in Sallie's changing focus. Bill and his colleagues had great respect for the music, crafts, and writing of the region. He took Sallie to folk fairs in his pickup truck, and she found herself curiously enchanted. At one point she even talked of developing a Kentucky crafts museum in Louisville.

Bill was an admirer of Sallie's early writing, and as their relationship deepened, she let him see a romantic novella she was working on. Slowly, Sallie began talking about her family. "She said more affectionate and positive things than negative," he recalled. "She was more critical of her brother than anyone else. Much harder on him."

In fact, just seeing Barry Jr. living in the Big House and running the family companies set Sallie's teeth on edge. In childhood, *she* had been the prodigy and he had been the cripple. Now the roles were reversed and she did not like it. Soon after her arrival, Barry Jr. had bluntly told *Fortune* magazine that he would "eventually have control [of the companies]. My mother and father feel it's important that one person have control." How maddening to think that Barry Jr., who could barely read a book, would eventually become the power in the family and have all the trappings that went with it! Worse still, Louisvillians still occasionally mistook Sallie for Eleanor, the family's chronic underachiever. "That almost killed me," Sallie said. "I hated that."

Though she had rarely read the Bingham newspapers when she lived in New York, Sallie had been proud to tell her Upper East Side friends that *The Courier-Journal* and *Times* were among the few liberal voices in the South. Many people were familiar with the papers and praised the Binghams' courage on civil rights. Now all she heard at dinners and cocktail parties were complaints.

To be sure, there were still rock-ribbed conservatives in Louisville who considered the papers near-Communist. But they mattered far less to Sallie than her new friends at the University of Louisville, who grumbled about what they considered to be *The Courier-Journal's* right-wing tone. The paper did not have enough blacks and women on staff, they said; it was not living up to its liberal reputation. Soon Sallie began to wonder herself.

Feeding her doubt was the case of Carl Braden, a militant leftist who had worked as a *Louisville Times* reporter and copy editor in the late 1940s and early 1950s. In 1954, Braden had provoked local fury by transferring a house he owned in a white neighborhood to a black man. To make matters worse, police found a pamphlet in his house entitled "How to Be a Good Communist," and he was promptly indicted as one.

The Binghams kept Braden on the payroll all during his trial, ending his employment only after he was convicted under an anachronistic state sedition law and sent to prison. He died shortly before Sallie's return, ending a lifetime of agitation for civil rights, labor unions, and other causes. Through his widow, Sallie became aware of the Binghams' role in the Braden affair. Because her father and the Louisville papers had not wholeheartedly embraced Braden's politics, Sallie considered her family hypocritical and began to view the entire Bingham mystique with suspicion. "She began to feel that I was not really the liberal I had professed to be," said Barry Sr. "And that Barry Jr. wasn't at all."

Eleanor, living with her boyfriend in Los Angeles, watched Sallie's return with interest. Unlike her older sister, who had pursued marriage, children, and a writing career with a ferocious determination, Eleanor had spent her early adulthood as a drifter. Her parents had never had any goals for her, she said, "other than the normal stuff of settling down, getting married, raising a family," and she had none for herself.

She joked that she was the family hippie and the description was apt. She had attended three undistinguished schools during her college years, sewn beads on flowered shirts during the Carnaby Street craze, lived in flop-houses, and experimented with drugs and group sex. Only in the early 1970s had she felt attracted to a profession—filmmaking—and even that was somewhat vague and unfocused. At the same time, she did not harbor any of Sallie's latent rebelliousness, perhaps because she had never felt that her parents cared very much what she did. "Sallie needs more recognition, emotional support, and attention from Mother and Daddy," she said. "It's a craving that I'm very familiar with in her." Though she did not admit it, Eleanor was just as starved for her parents' love and respect.

Jonathan's death had occurred while Eleanor was in her final year at Concord Academy, a girls' prep school in the same town as Barry Sr.'s dreaded Middlesex, and the tragedy had made her more sober. She spent the next summer working for the civil rights organization C.O.R.E. (Congress of Racial Equality) and teaching migrant workers how to read. She also interned at *The Courier-Journal*, where she achieved a certain notoriety for her lack of typing skills and her braless attire. "She wore miniskirts and had great bazooms," said George Gill. "Her appearance was quite an event in the newsroom." One day she asked her supervisor, Jackson Sellers, for the afternoon off. When he inquired why, she said, "I'm tired and my name is Bingham." Sellers told her those were very good reasons and let her go.

Eleanor graduated from Concord Academy in 1964 in what she called a watershed class. Although all of her classmates went on to college, as many as two-thirds of them dropped out or transferred by the end of their fresh-man year. The 1960s had begun in earnest and no group was more swept up in the do-your-own-thing philosophy of the era than the pampered children of the elite.

Eleanor's grades were too poor to get her into Radcliffe, but Mary politely went through the motions of writing to the admissions director and taking her to Cambridge for an interview. When the University of North Carolina at Greensboro accepted her, Eleanor decided to go there, mostly because, she said, her Concord guidance counselor had suggested a co-ed environment. But Eleanor had done virtually no research on the school and was shocked to arrive and find that all-female UNC-Greensboro was more than forty minutes by bus from its all-male counterpart in Chapel Hill.

Eleanor eventually stopped going to class altogether and never came back to UNC-Greensboro after her freshman year. Instead, she decided to pursue drawing and portrait painting at the Byam Shaw College of Art in London, a place she had heard about from "Daddy's English connections." The Bing-hams were dismayed at Eleanor's decision to drop out of college. When Jonathan had left Harvard two years earlier, Barry Sr. and Mary had comforted themselves with the thought that at least he had career goals. Eleanor's interest in art just seemed like another one of her sudden whims. True, she had an attractive, easy style of drawing, but she had given no evidence that she was as serious about art as Sallie was about writing. "One day I was interested in this, the next day I was interested in that," Eleanor said breezily. "I'm sure they were saying, you know, 'When is cooking school going to start?' "

To please her parents, Eleanor agreed to endure a round of debutante parties before she departed for England. Her horsey blond features had improved only slightly with maturity and she still struggled with a weight problem. But she had a reputation for being "fast" and the bachelors of Louisville were intrigued, if not exactly attracted, by the youngest daughter of the city's only newspaper owner.

That debutante season, one of Eleanor's prearranged dates was treated to a sight so absurd that it could have occurred during the Senior Binghams' jazz baby days at Harvard. When the young man arrived at the Big House, he was ushered into the library to wait while Eleanor finished dressing. As he was sitting there, drumming his fingers on his knee, he suddenly spied a strange figure coming toward him across the broad expanse of hallway. It was Barry Sr., dressed in full safari regalia, from khaki shorts to pith helmet, stepping smartly and playing the bugle. With Eleanor's astonished date watching his every move, Barry Sr. marched up to the door of the library, stopped, gave a loud blast on his horn as if in salute, turned on his heel, and progressed toward the kitchen. The young man decided it was Barry Sr.'s peculiar idea of a joke.

In London, Eleanor enjoyed a deliciously schizophrenic existence, sipping tea with her father's titled wartime friends, then pub crawling with the city's bell-bottomed hippies. One of her classmates lived in an ice-cream truck in front of the school. But after a year she was not invited to continue at Byam Shaw. "My draftsmanship just wasn't good enough," she explained. Several months after Worth's death, she enrolled at the University of Sussex in Brighton, an English seaside resort.

Barry Sr. and Mary disapproved of what they euphemistically described as Eleanor's "irregular living." During a trip on a Greek freighter, Eleanor seemed willing to sleep with almost anyone—the deckhands, the men in the boiler room. "She was hideously promiscuous," said a friend. "She's a little girl who grew up without much love and has a very loving nature."

When student rebellion swept through Europe, Sussex closed down and encouraged its students to aid their comrades across the English Channel. During the Six-Day War in 1967, Eleanor and her friends helped bring in the pear crop on an Israeli kibbutz in order to free farmers for the front. The breakdown in order drove Mary to lament that moderation was "about as fashionable as finger bowls and unbroken hymens" among college students of the era.

Barry Sr. and Mary threatened to cut off Eleanor's allowance if she did not finish school. The strategy worked and she finally received a degree in comparative literature from Sussex in 1969, but it failed to bring her home. For several years, she worked as a seamstress at Lord John, a Carnaby Street shop that sold gaudy shirts and tight satin pants to such rock-and-roll stars as Mick Jagger. "We had him come in for eight fittings," Eleanor said with a comic leer. She had a sexual fling with a married pop star and a chaste friendship with a gay fashion designer. In the early 1970s, the designer left London to manage a boutique on Ibiza, a small island resort in the Mediterranean off the coast of Spain, and she went with him.

Eleanor worked at the shop during the day and at night went home to a dilapidated seven-hundred-year-old sheepherder's cottage with no running water or electricity. The shower consisted of a tin bucket and a piece of rope. "It's worse than the pioneer women living on the plains," a distressed Mary told her daughter. "You're doing nothing but spending your whole time keeping body and soul together. You don't listen to music, you don't see pictures, you don't have any intellectual life. What are you getting out of this?" Eleanor's reply: "I'm eliminating the superficial and experiencing 'real life.'"

Even a modest life-style costs something, of course, and Eleanor continued to depend on her parents for money. As of her twenty-first birthday, she had legal access to income from a trust fund her father had set up in her name when she was small. But Barry Sr. and Mary were afraid that she would spend it on fair-weather friends or drugs and decided not to tell her that it existed. Instead, they ordered Leon Tallichet, then corporate secretary and treasurer, to pay her an adequate allowance and to use the trust fund dividends to buy more stock in the Bingham companies.

For years, Leon had held the Binghams' hands in financial matters large and small, graciously accepting Henrietta's shoeboxes of receipts at tax time and even helping family members pick out cars. "I think he literally slammed doors and kicked tires," said a colleague. Now he had to cable funds to Eleanor in places he could barely spell. The chore took on a crisislike air because Eleanor was careless with money, routinely underestimating how much she needed, and dispensing funds to friends with generous abandon.

Despite her unorthodox existence, Eleanor tried hard to keep the channels of communication open, writing long, amusing letters to her "aged P's," as she called her parents in an allusion to Dickens, and maintaining warm relations with the rest of the family. "Eleanor is a crazy kid," said Barry Jr.'s wife, Edie. "Lots of times we have wrung our hands and held our foreheads and tried not to be shocked by anything. But when she came home she was always loving and lavish in her affection."

While she was living on Ibiza, Barry Sr. and Mary flew to Portugal for a vacation and Eleanor met them there. With her, she brought an elaborate trunk of cosmetics. "Mother, you don't do enough for yourself," she explained as she sat Mary down and applied swirls of rouge. "I looked like a perfect clown," said Mary. "But she was that kind of child. I think she really cared about my appearance."

One day a film crew came to Ibiza to shoot a commercial for Fruit of the Loom underwear. Eleanor and her friends signed up as extras and obligingly pranced in front of the cameras in the company's briefs, bras, and panties. For the first time she came into contact with the new videotape cameras that were revolutionizing filmmaking, and she was intrigued by their ease, low cost, and portability. She did not actually use one until she came back to the States for good in 1971, tired of her ragtag life and ready for more adult challenges. "The sixties were over, you could really tell it," she said. "It was just time to move on."

Eleanor bypassed Louisville and flew directly to Aspen, Colorado, to take an unpaid job at an experimental public access cable channel called Grassroots Network. In this, as in so many other aspects of her life, family connections smoothed the way. This time it was Barry Jr. who helped out, prevailing on an old Harvard friend who ran the station to give Eleanor an apprenticeship. At Grassroots she did everything—producing, shooting film, and interviewing the offbeat celebrities who came through the resort, including the Guru Mahara-ji and the environmental artist Christo. One night gonzo journalist Hunter Thompson dropped by the studio to read the six o'clock news.

Back in Louisville, Mary took little notice of Eleanor's burgeoning interest in film. She considered photography of any kind to be "the last resort of people who don't know what else to do." Eleanor herself admitted she was still living for the moment. "I wasn't thinking seriously in terms of a lifelong career," she said. "I was just pursuing various interests and film was definitely one that I liked." During his recovery from cancer, Barry Jr. flew out to Aspen and, in a rare moment of intimacy, talked to his sister about what made him tick. "He said that duty was *the* motivating factor in his life," Eleanor recalled. "That had never occurred to me—to do your duty."

When Eleanor tired of the Aspen scene, she moved on to New York City, again on the advice of Barry Jr., who had suggested that she might want to follow in his footsteps and pursue documentary filmmaking. A job interview at the city's public television station went nowhere, though. Instead, Eleanor became involved with several videotape production groups on the fringe of the mainstream. One film captured a play performed on six levels of a tenement fire escape; another showed a group sex party in which Eleanor was clearly visible. "I was *riveted*," said Joan, Worth's widow, who viewed the tape at Eleanor's Soho loft. "She just thought it was funny."

Joan had remained in Louisville for several years after Worth's death, moving to New York in the late 1960s. There, she lived in an attic apartment at the Dakota, a dark Victorian building on Central Park West that was also home to Lauren Bacall and Leonard Bernstein. Although Robbie, her youngest, regularly got mugged for his lunch money on the way to school, Joan liked the hurly-burly of New York and made her apartment a lively gathering place for journalists and political junkies. Eleanor saw a great deal of Joan and the children in those years, often accompanying them to their Long Island house on summer weekends. She peddled her bicycle over to Sallie and Michael's house on East 95th Street, too, but the relationship was proper rather than close. Sallie was even cooler to Joan, and invited her out to the Iovenko house in Rhinebeck only once.

Eleanor's meanderings were not yet over. In 1975, she moved to Los Angeles to work for TVTV (Top Value Television), a production company that had a contract to do several one-hour specials for public broadcasting. In the process of working on documentaries such as "From the Underground: An Interview with Abbie Hoffman" and "Nixon in Exile," she met Leslie Shatz, a sound man about eight years her junior. Within months they had moved in together, formed their own production company, Image Audio Inc., and, with $40,000 of Bingham family money, launched a documentary on the Ku Klux Klan, the group to which her great-grandfather had belonged over a century earlier.

The Klan film was the high point of Eleanor's creative life. For a year, she went from Klan group to Klan group around the country, attending their rallies, bowling with their families, even dating some of the men. "They were horrified that I wasn't married and tried to make me go out with young Nazi types," she said. "We'd go listen to 'Deutschland über alles' in German beer halls. It was a riot." In every city, Barry Sr. called ahead and asked the local newspaper editor to watch out for his little girl. Later, he lent his sonorous voice to the film's narration.

In 1978, "The New Klan: Heritage of Hate" finally aired on the public broadcasting system. It won the John Grierson Award at the New York Film Festival and was the only American documentary invited to be shown at Cannes that year. Inadvertently, Eleanor had launched a career as a film-maker, but her personal and professional relationship with Leslie Shatz was falling apart and success seemed to mean little to her. After flying overseas for the Cannes screening, she returned to Louisville, not Los Angeles, to contemplate her next move. "I was not at all interested in staying in Louis-ville," she said. "It was just a good place to get Xeroxes of my résumé and try to find a new job."

Barry Sr. and Mary had sailed for Britain on the *Queen Elizabeth II* a few weeks earlier, so Eleanor had the Little House to herself. She enjoyed renewing childhood friendships and seeing Barry Jr. and Edie occasionally for dinner. Sallie had been back for almost a year when Eleanor arrived and she told her that, to her surprise, she was having a good time in Louisville. Barry Jr. did not encourage Eleanor to stay. But when she was turned down for a job with ABC-TV's documentary unit in New York, he felt duty-bound to tell her that WHAS, the family's television station, was always an option she could consider. "He mentioned it more out of a sense of being respon-sible, I think, than really wishing I would do it," said Eleanor.

Whatever the motive, the idea of working for the Bingham companies was attractive to Eleanor. She was now over thirty and most of her friends had long ago traded their feathers and granny glasses for steady jobs, wed-ding china, and children. The conservative currents that would culminate in Ronald Reagan's election two years hence were already beginning to flow through the country, and Eleanor, a conventional person at heart, was susceptible to trends. In the 1960s and early 1970s, it had been unfashion-able to live the opulent life-style that her family money could have made possible. Now the prospect of being a Bingham in Louisville, having a place and a name that commanded respect and, yes, money, seemed somehow all right.

In the fall of 1978, Eleanor arrived at the WHAS building, located in the same city block as *The Courier-Journal*, and was shown into a small, window-less office. Her job title, Director of Special Services, had little to do with her experience as a documentary filmmaker, but then, Barry Jr., fearful that WHAS managers would feel bound to air anything his sister produced, had forbidden her from operating a camera. Deep down he was afraid that she would embarrass him. "He acted like she didn't have a brain in her head," said a friend. "Eleanor felt that Barry's attitude was 'Don't be involved, don't get too close to me, and please, please, please don't *ever* tell me what to do.' "

Eleanor soon moved into a rented house in the country and met Rowland Miller, the young man she would eventually marry. After years of random living, everything seemed to be unfolding for the youngest Bingham child as if by benevolent design.

But the peace was soon shattered. Four months after she started work at WHAS, Barry Jr. asked Bob Morse, a young man who had served as the station's news director in the late 1960s and early 1970s, to come back from Philadelphia and take over the job of general manager. From the outset there was animosity and distrust between Morse and Eleanor, who was quickly given a new, catchall position that included promotion work and community relations and told to report directly to him. It was Morse's first job as a general manager, and he was nervous enough about it without having his boss's sister working under his command and looking over his shoulder. "I did not manage Eleanor well, I'd be the first to say that," he said. "And if anybody ever needed to be managed, she did."

Never having had a proper job, Eleanor was ignorant of office etiquette. She wore jeans and sweaters to work, took long vacations whenever she felt like it, wrote personal letters on WHAS stationery, and continued to parade through the corridors without a bra. Morse finally had to muster the courage to tell her that not wearing one was, well, unbusinesslike. "Oh, that was a big moment," said Eleanor. "I remember poor Bob telling me that. He said it was station policy."

The first indication that serious trouble was brewing, though, did not occur until Morse discovered that Eleanor had unilaterally redecorated her new office. The curtains were worn, she said, and she had simply gone out and ordered new ones—and a couch for good measure—at office expense. She did not bother to requisition the new furnishings, just as she had not asked permission months earlier to paint another office in broad, bright stripes.

The breach of procedure incensed Morse. He complained to Barry Jr., who felt acute embarrassment at his sister's actions. In Eleanor, the only Bingham who had failed to get into Harvard or conquer her weight problem, Barry Jr. saw a frightening sight: what he might have become without the stern whip of discipline. The similarity should have prompted compassion. Instead, it bred contempt.

Before Morse's arrival, Eleanor had helped launch a local public affairs program called "Louisville Tonight." The show was expensive to produce but it was topping the ratings, and her enthusiasm for production work was obvious. Partly to get her out of his hair, Morse pleaded with Barry Jr. to lift his ban on documentaries. "Give her $100,000," he said. "I'll handle it.

I'll make sure we don't put anything libelous on the air, I'll take the responsibility." Barry Jr. stood firm. Barry Sr. could have ordered his son to soften his position. But, Barry Sr. said, "Barry Jr. was in charge of things and I was trying very hard not to interfere."

By early 1980, relations between Morse and Eleanor had frayed to the snapping point. When Eleanor took notes at management meetings, Morse eyed her suspiciously. She was forever getting her facts jumbled, misstating information to Bingham friends like Cy MacKinnon during weekend social events that prompted frantic phone calls to Morse on Monday mornings. "I think she fried her brain on drugs," said a former WHAS employee. "She has a difficult time remembering things." After one top-level meeting at the station, she left a small pouch of marijuana in the ladies' room. A staff member discreetly mailed it back to her.

Finally, Morse had had enough. He went to Barry Jr. and told him that he was going to have a nervous breakdown if Eleanor continued in the organization. Though Morse had had one-on-one conferences with Eleanor every week since his arrival, he had never told her of his unhappiness, despite Barry Jr.'s explicit suggestion that he do so. "It wasn't until my parents blurted out that Bob was on the verge of some collapse that I knew anything was wrong," said Eleanor. "The only way to make it OK was for me to quit."

Just before Eleanor left WHAS, Barry Jr. asked Morse to write a critique of her performance. The "exit memo" was for his father, he explained. He wanted to use the information to help formulate a new policy on family members working for the companies. Morse was reluctant to put his views on paper. "Eleanor might own this place one day," he told Barry Jr. "I could be working for her." But Barry Jr. said "the shoe was on the table," an expression he used only when he wanted subordinates to know that they did not have a choice.

So Morse dutifully composed the evaluation, detailing Eleanor's many transgressions. Barry Jr. kept his word and gave the memo to his father. Unfortunately, he also gave a copy to Eleanor, who stormed into Morse's office and demanded an explanation. "She just came unglued," said Morse. "It took a long time before she and I could talk to each other again." When he angrily asked Barry Jr. why he had given his sister the memo, he got a lame answer. "He said he didn't mean to, it was a mistake and all that. Now I know he wanted to discredit Eleanor, but he wanted me to do it." The incident was not without cost. It hardened Eleanor's attitude toward Barry Jr. and created a permanent breach between Morse and the Senior Binghams, who felt that the WHAS general manager had maliciously undermined their daughter.

In many respects, though, Eleanor was content to leave WHAS. The previous fall she had married Rowland Dumesnil Miller, a Tulane-educated architect several years younger than she, and they had only recently decided to have children. Leaving work would free them both to travel before domestic concerns engulfed them.

Eleanor had turned down several proposals of marriage before meeting Rowland. Mary used to joke to friends that she did not care whom Eleanor chose as a mate as long as he was "not a Negro and was kind to her."

After the odd assortment of artists and hippies who had dated their daughter, Barry Sr. and Mary were thrilled at the prospect of Rowland, the oldest son of a Louisville family so well established that two streets, Rowland and Dumesnil, were named for ancestors. "One thing that made Rowland acceptable for Eleanor was certainly *him*," said a friend. "But his family, well, it may have been a step up for the Binghams in terms of Louisville as a whole."

The two had met at a private showing of the Klan film in the summer of 1978, but romance had to wait while Rowland disengaged himself from another relationship. It was not until the fall that he took up residence in Eleanor's country cottage, then a daring thing for a proper Louisvillian to do.

That Thanksgiving, Eleanor and Rowland invited both sets of parents to dinner. Mr. Miller sat grimly through the meal, furious at his son's illicit living arrangement and aghast at the Binghams' nonchalance about Eleanor's reputation. Barry Sr. and Mary, a full generation older than Rowland's parents, found the whole situation delightfully absurd.

Rowland's father had married the daughter of a monied old-line Louisville family, multiplying her riches through shrewd investments and real estate development. Rowland's early years were spent in the company of other Louisville Country Club Republicans, listening to them rail against *The Courier-Journal* and its endorsement of liberal causes and Democratic candidates. "He grew up in this atmosphere of hating the paper," said Joan. "The paper and the Binghams were anathema."

As a young man, Rowland briefly rejected his parents' conservative values. He worked at a New England racetrack, campaigned for Democratic presidential candidates Eugene McCarthy and George McGovern, wore his hair in a ponytail, and drove a yellow Mustang. But by the time he met Eleanor, he had completed his detour and was squarely back on the main road.

After the noisy disorder of her youth, Eleanor found Rowland's gentle wistfulness and whimsical humor appealing. He had a sensitive, almost mystical quality that reminded her of her dead brother Jonathan. When people were sick, he brought them poetry. When a childhood friend fractured her back, he helped her into her brace and took her out for walks. At the same time, Rowland had a wan and wounded air that appealed to the strong maternal streak in Eleanor. Instinctively, she felt an urge to protect him. It was Earth Mother meets the Lost Boy.

Rowland moved out of the house a week before the wedding—"so it would all be much fresher, I suppose," said Mary—and arrived at the altar in acceptably formal attire. The prospect of matrimony had stirred Eleanor's bedrock sense of convention and she insisted on an extravagant Emily Post wedding, complete with white dress and train, huge bursts of flowers, a reception for seven hundred on the Big House lawn, a "going away" suit and matching handbag, and a long European honeymoon.

Sallie, just back from a writing stint at the MacDowell Colony, was matron of honor. Barry Jr. and Edie hosted the wedding-day lunch. The *Courier-Journal* photography staff put in overtime to record the moment. "Well, my goodness, you'd think nobody had ever gotten married before," said Mary. "We were very much amused by it. It seemed so unlike the way she had been. It was, I think, Eleanor's notice that she was now a regular old-time girl."

Indeed, it was not until her marriage that Eleanor finally stopped running away from home. "I think the fact that Mother and Daddy were so crazy about Rowland helped make it happen," she said. "And working for WHAS was also something they could relate to. But I wouldn't say it happened much before then. I had as long an adolescence as anybody could possibly have."

Eleanor and Rowland bought a house two miles from the Senior Binghams and just a short walk from Lincliffe, where Mary Lily had died over sixty years earlier. Rowland spent his days working at a Louisville architecture firm and his nights studying for the licensing exam. On the weekends, the newlyweds scouted rundown real estate to renovate and develop.

When Joan came to town for visits, Rowland took her on long drives and questioned her about the family relationships. Edie enjoyed talking with her new brother-in-law about architecture and historic preservation, two long-standing interests. Rob and Clara, Joan's children, loved waterskiing with him and playing touch football on the beach. Rowland's position in the Bingham clan seemed secure.

By the Senior Binghams' fiftieth wedding anniversary in 1981, Eleanor and Rowland were well-integrated into the family. Early that June, fourteen Binghams converged on the Greenbriar Hotel in West Virginia to toast the Golden Anniversary couple. Barry Jr. executed his duties as master of ceremonies with a touch of wry humor. Edie compiled a scrapbook of keepsake photos chronicling Barry Sr. and Mary's life from childhood through their courting days and marriage, to the births of their five offspring, the Marshall Plan year, picnics at Chatham, European vacations, college graduations, and beyond.

The tranquility and familial fondness seemed touching, and certainly genuine. But it was more legendary Bingham breeding than deep affection on display that fine June day. "The unconscious aims of the family were to avoid friction, to keep things positive and sunny and friendly," said Sallie. "But that smoothness costs something, too."

ASSAULTED FROM ALL SIDES

Barry Sr. often spoke of what he called his "dual loyalties"—one to his family and one to the Bingham media empire. In his own life, he rarely felt those allegiances to be in conflict. With his cheery optimism, he saw no reason why his son and two daughters could not also balance their individual desires for fulfillment and security with the need of the companies to be financially successful and safely passed on to the next generation. Barry Jr. and Edie had long ago adopted Barry Sr.'s credo and frequently talked of the "shared dream." Sallie and Eleanor, on the other hand, had been distant from the family enterprise for decades. They received dividend checks but their emotional stake in the dynasty was based more on childhood memory and nostalgia than genuine involvement.

To remedy that, Barry Sr. suggested that Sallie and Eleanor take an active role in the oversight of the companies. Sallie had been on the Bingham board of directors since 1975, when her second marriage broke up, but she had rarely attended meetings. When Eleanor began working at WHAS in 1978, Barry Sr. asked her to join the board, too, and he invited both women to become more involved. Each had only a small amount of voting stock in the companies—about 4 percent, with another 7 percent to come when their parents died—and no business training or background. But that did not matter to Barry Sr. What counted was the comforting symbolism of bringing his daughters into the bosom of the Bingham empire. "I kept feeling that the family could be brought close together by a common association in the enterprises," he said. "I thought it was the most natural thing in the world." Mary already had years of experience on the board and Edie had been a member even before Sallie. Only Joan, Worth's widow, did not have a seat, although she often flew back to Louisville to attend the quarterly meetings as an observer.

Sallie and Eleanor were flattered by their father's graceful gesture; Barry Jr. seemed genuinely unconcerned about the change. "I really didn't think about it a whole lot," he said. "I was perfectly open to having family members on the board."

Still, the new arrangement preyed on Barry Jr.'s deepest insecurities. He was visibly uncomfortable around assertive women, as Carol Sutton, *The Courier-Journal*'s first female managing editor, had proved long ago. But at root, his fear was sex-blind. Though he often said he wanted people to level with him, he could not stand to have anyone, male or female, challenge his authority. As the months went by and his sisters became active in board discussions, Barry Jr. grew more remote and brooding. Cy MacKinnon, who had been promoted to company president in 1975, began telling colleagues that Barry Jr. was becoming "eccentric."

He was especially sullen around Sallie, the sister who had lacked respect for him since childhood. "There was no overt conflict of any kind," said Sallie. "I just noticed that he didn't have anything in particular to say to me. He was always completely silent at board meetings. . . . I think he was getting increasingly angry and paranoid. Something in my mere existence probably seemed like criticism."

Bingham board meetings in those days were so purely informational that company aides called them "show and tell" sessions. Virtually all decisions were made outside the boardroom by Barry Jr. and the half dozen or so lawyers and executives who actually managed the businesses. These men referred to themselves as the "hired hands," in gentle mockery of the gulf that separated the Binghams from those who did their bidding. The "hired hands" might have six-figure incomes, but they knew only too well that they worked on a plantation. Some even differentiated between "house slaves" and "field slaves." Outside lawyers, for instance, enjoyed a higher status than in-house senior vice-presidents. "We got invited to dinner at the Binghams more often than they did," explained one.

Sallie and Eleanor had inflated expectations of what it meant to have a seat on the board; as in most family businesses, it was essentially an honorary post. When board meetings turned out to be little more than a parade of eye-glazing presentations, the Bingham daughters felt cheated. They had begun to hear complaints from their friends about the news and editorial policies of the newspapers and were embarrassed to admit they could do little to influence them. "They felt that board membership gave them a sort of power in being, if not in fact," said Barry Sr. "I never felt that as members of the board that kind of power was within their jurisdiction. I must say that was an unrealistic expectation on their part." Typically, though, he said nothing to them about it.

Sallie and Eleanor's lack of business acumen was comically apparent. The director of circulation once made a report on the growing number of readers who called in to complain about late or missed papers. The lack of telephone operators, he said, meant that people are being put on "hold" for long periods of time. Then, for at least half an hour, the discussion came to a halt while Sallie and Eleanor debated whether the music following the "hold" message should be classical or Top 40.

Barry Jr. found Sallie's comments especially embarrassing. He cringed when she asked for over a thousand pages of material on cellular telephones —a business the Binghams had applied for a license to run—and then did not read them. When the newsroom was in the process of being computerized, she gratuitously remarked that no computer was ever going to run her life.

Time and again she harped on the responsibilities of monopoly ownership and stressed the importance of journalistic tradition, as though she alone among the Binghams cared about ethics and quality. She made it clear that, in her view, innovations like cable television were in conflict with the company's mission. Electronically delivered news was slick and without value, she said; moving a union printing plant to a right-to-work state in order to save money was immoral and illegal.

Pronouncements such as these from a person who knew nothing about business or journalism, who in fact had scorned both all her life, made Barry Jr. burn with anger and humiliation. As he had so many times during his tenure as head of the Bingham companies, he worried that the staff was laughing at him. "He felt, 'What are management people saying about my family, you know, having to provide this weird information,' " said Paul Janensch, then CJ & T executive editor. "He was embarrassed for the family."

Sallie and Eleanor were not the only burden weighing on Barry Jr. during the late 1970s and early 1980s. About a year after Sallie returned to Louisville, the board adopted a resolution establishing a goal of 12 percent operating profit for The Courier-Journal and Times, to be reached over three years.

In the Bingham-Baker-Ethridge era, profits had hovered around 10 percent. But Barry Jr. had had the misfortune to assume leadership of the companies during the 1970s, when double-digit inflation and high newsprint, postage, and energy costs eroded performance. The Louisville economy was hit hard by the national recession. To trim expenses, local

employers laid off thousands of people, and advertising revenue and circulation slumped. By 1977, when Sallie returned to Louisville, operating profit
for *The Courier-Journal* and *Times* stood at just under 4 percent. That same
year, *The Washington Post*, another highly respected family-controlled newspaper, posted an operating profit of 14 percent.

Wilson Wyatt and the hired hands had tried to convince Barry Jr. of the
importance of a healthier balance sheet, without much success. Every time
they brought up the subject at a board meeting, Barry Jr. and the two or
three top editors who attended as observers would protest in unison that
tightening belts would damage the Binghams' legendary news coverage. "We
couldn't get Barry Jr.'s attention," said George Gill, by then vice-president
and general manager. "He really didn't see the need for improved profits."
Finally, in frustration, the company managers, with Barry Sr.'s collusion, hit
upon the idea of a formally adopted goal. Barry Jr. responded to clear-cut
objectives like a good Marine, they figured, so why not give him one?

For months the hired hands worked to arrive at a reasonable figure, one
that would allow the Binghams to maintain quality, replace plant and equipment, and still produce sufficient dividends to keep Sallie, Eleanor, and
other family members happy. Once they had agreed on 12 percent, they
requested a private audience at the Big House with Barry Sr. and Barry Jr.
The idea was to isolate Barry Jr. from his Greek chorus of editors, spring
the 12 percent goal on him, and get him to agree to it before it was
presented at a board meeting the following week. "We didn't want any
arguments at the board meeting," said Gordon Davidson, an attorney who
in the early 1970s had taken on many of Wilson Wyatt's duties as the
family's chief counsel. "We wanted to show Junior that the phalanx had
formed."

Barry Sr. cooperated fully in the conspiracy. He barely knew an asset
from a liability, but he trusted company aides when they told him the papers
were courting financial ruin—and that was something he simply could not
allow, regardless of his promise not to interfere with Barry Jr.'s leadership.
So as the hired hands went through their spiel at the Big House, laying out
in detail the sorry state of CJ & T finances, Barry Sr. put on a convincing
performance. His eyes clouded and his lips pursed dramatically. His brow
furrowed with worry. "Oh, my God! You're right! You're right!" he cried, as
if hearing the predictions of doom for the first time. "This just can't go on
this way! We must do something!"

As hoped, Barry Jr. acceded to the 12 percent goal that weekend at the
Big House and the resolution passed unanimously at the board meeting.
Later, Barry Sr. would deny having gone behind his son's back to force
better performance. He was simply helping Barry Jr. see the light, he said.

"I felt convinced that this was the way the papers ought to go and that in the long run it would be something that Barry would appreciate," he said. George Gill remembered it differently: "We went around him, we sure did."

The new push for profits only heightened Barry Jr.'s innate pessimism. "You have to have a certain kind of personality to manage decline cheerfully," he said. "I find that wearing." The situation made him look at his father's stewardship of the properties with envy. In Barry Sr.'s day, Standard Gravure had been the cash cow of the Bingham empire, providing most of the money for family dividends and freeing *The Courier-Journal* and *Times* of financial pressures.

By the late 1970s, however, Standard's glory days were over. Newspapers were rapidly eliminating the Sunday supplements that had been the company's mainstay, and the magazines that remained, like *Parade*, wanted more modern printing techniques than Standard could provide. As a result, Standard dividends had to be cut in half in the early 1980s.

The development alarmed Sallie because, she said, it signaled trouble in the way the company was managed. But neither she nor Eleanor seemed worried that Standard's woes would affect their dividend income, which hovered around $100,000 a year when Barry Jr. took over in 1971 and rose steadily to about $300,000 by the mid-1980s. Because they lived almost entirely on dividends, Sallie and Eleanor regarded them as a worker might a salary—something independent of company performance. Annual increases, typically around 7 percent, were simply a given. To keep the funds close to the $300,000 level, the Courier-Journal and Times Company took up the slack for Standard, paying out more to Sallie and Eleanor than it had in previous years.

Despite these new financial pressures, the Binghams still expected *The Courier-Journal* and *Times*, their flagships, to maintain their historical preeminence in news. For a man more confident and realistic than Barry Jr., that should not have been difficult. The newspapers had long been a country club operation. In 1978, the papers had 178 more employees than *The Des Moines Register* and 138 more than *The St. Petersburg Times*, then both fine, family-controlled, morning- and evening-edition operations in towns comparable in size to Louisville. In payroll alone, the Binghams spent $5 million more than these papers did, with the CJ & T's outsized news staff consuming the lion's share of the cash.

At the Bingham papers, almost no one got fired. Reporters who were considered problems were moved to the Indiana bureaus, known in the newsroom as "the elephant burial ground," or just not given much to do. The fringe benefits, including a generous health-care package, maternity and paternity leave, and a subsidized cafeteria and day-care center, were unmatched in journalism. In the late 1970s, the papers maintained eleven bureaus, including eight in Kentucky, two in Indiana, and one in Washington, D.C.

The prospect of raising ad and circulation rates and scaling back personnel did not bother Barry Sr., who felt that the news side had gotten spoiled during the 1970s. Barry Jr. disliked retrenchment, but he felt he had no choice. Sallie, however, had heard U.S. presidents and foreign dignitaries exclaim about the quality of the *CJ & T* ever since she was a child. Even the modest economies that Barry Jr. imposed were troubling to her. She had little knowledge of what actually went into the production of a first-class newspaper, but she saw her brother's efforts to slash costs as a betrayal of family traditions. The fact that cutbacks were necessary at all was just another indication of his congenital incompetence, she felt.

The result was that Barry Jr. felt increasingly beleaguered by what he considered to be the family's incompatible demands for profits and quality. When his editors loudly complained that the cuts were causing difficulties on the news staff, Barry Jr. was genuinely sympathetic.

———————

Edie Bingham, Barry Jr.'s wife, saw herself as the truth-teller in the family and, in many ways, she was. The rest of the Binghams found it almost impossible to convey unfiltered emotion in person. As tension mounted on the board and at family meetings, a flurry of notes and letters began whirling through Louisville. The Binghams were determined to maintain appearances at all costs, regardless of the maelstrom that churned just below the surface, and the written word permitted a kind of merciful distance from confrontation. "That way, they can't see the agonized expression on your face," explained Sallie.

But Edie felt no such constraints. "I'm the one who can say [the truth] and that's why I'm a threat," she said. "I *will* go to the heart of something and I *will* bring up things that are a little hard to discuss." The trait should have endeared her to Mary, who alone among the Binghams had the capacity for what Barry Sr. delicately termed "moral outrage." But Mary's passionate honesty frequently had a brutal edge. When she disagreed with someone on an issue, her criticism took on a righteous, unforgiving air, and she tended to translate her dislike of the idea into a dislike of the person. With typical candor, she admitted that a less one-sided approach would probably be more effective. But, she said, "I find it most uncongenial."

Edie was more inclined to understand other viewpoints, even when she disagreed with them. That quality, coupled with her ability to remain unbowed in the face of Mary's sometimes determined power plays, made her a less-than-perfect companion for her mother-in-law. Only two years after

Edie and Barry Jr. were married, she and Mary had crossed swords over education. At the time, Edie was thinking of sending her sons to a new progressive school in Louisville run by the Episcopal Church. In the strongest possible terms, Mary tried to dissuade her on the grounds that permissive teaching methods had left Barry Jr. permanently handicapped as a reader. The discussion devolved into a stony silence. "There is nothing worse than an ill-educated person," Mary said finally. "I don't think we can have this conversation anymore. You don't know what you're talking about." Edie felt patronized and dismissed.

After Edie and Barry Jr. moved into the Big House in 1971, Mary took it upon herself to supervise much of the gardening. Edie would often find her magnolias trimmed without her permission. Mary felt that her son and daughter-in-law treated the mansion as though it were some kind of odious burden, shunning the festive soirees of the Senior Binghams' era in favor of stuffy staff functions, fund-raising dances for the Louisville Orchestra, and other dutiful entertainments.

Over the years, Barry Jr. and Edie began to sense that somehow they were not living up to the public image the heir to the Bingham empire and his wife were supposed to present. "Mary and Barry looked at us as fulfilling some kind of special role that we didn't know about," said Edie.

These undercurrents of unhappiness, long-lived but unacknowledged, burst into public view in the fall of 1979. Edie, the daughter of an architect, had been active for many years in the Preservation Alliance, a local group devoted to saving old buildings in Louisville, and in 1979 she was its chairman. At the time, the organization's most pressing concern was the rescue of the Will Sales building at Fourth and Liberty, a Victorian structure that had once been home to Walter Haldeman's *Courier-Journal* and *Times*. The decrepit building was in danger of being torn down because it occupied part of the space where many Louisvillians, in the hopes of revitalizing the downtown area, wanted to erect a three-story glass-enclosed shopping mall.

The project's developers, Oxford Associates, had already agreed to restore another old structure and incorporate it into the mall's design. But the Will Sales building, they felt, was too far gone to save without great expense. Despite heavy pressure from the business community, *The Courier-Journal* and *Times* and the Preservation Alliance stood firmly against the demolition of the Will Sales building under any circumstance, refusing to budge even after Oxford tried and failed to locate outside funds for its restoration. By the fall of 1979, the battle was at a standstill: Oxford would not move ahead with the mall unless it could tear down the Will Sales building—and that was something the Bingham newspapers and Edie, as the chairman of the Preservation Alliance, adamantly opposed.

Mary and Barry Sr. had more reason than anyone to want to preserve the Will Sales building. After all, it had been the birthplace of newspapers that had become synonymous with the name "Bingham." But they were not sentimental about such things. Mary, especially, felt that attracting retail business to Louisville's deserted downtown was far more important than preserving a crumbling structure that was not even on the National Register of Historic Places. She worried that Oxford would pull out altogether unless it could be demonstrated that powerful elements in the community still supported the project.

In October 1979, Mary decided that she would show Oxford and Louisville's business interests that the Bingham family was not united in its determination to save the Will Sales building at any cost. Without talking with Barry Jr. or Edie first, or even consulting Barry Sr., who was out of town, she composed a letter-to-the-editor and sent it to *The Courier-Journal.* "I wish to publicly disassociate myself from the position taken in the matter of the preservation of the Will Sales building by . . . Mrs. Barry Bingham Jr.," she wrote, adding that Edie and other preservationists were virtually ensuring "the desuetude and decay of Fourth Street."

Barry Jr. was shocked. That night, he took the letter home and handed it to Edie. "I wanted you to see what my mother has written about us," he told her. "We're going to publish it." Edie gulped and nodded weakly. She had certainly been aware of tension in her relationship with her mother-in-law, but a public repudiation was something else altogether. "That woman will eat you up!" she said.

A few days after the letter was published, Edie contained her anger and invited Mary over for lunch. Her effort at conciliation went nowhere. "She didn't budge and she didn't listen," said Edie. Barry Jr. never forgave his mother. Characteristically, Barry Sr. tried to remain aloof from the roiling dispute between his wife and his daughter-in-law. "Perhaps it would have been more tactful for Mary not to write the letter" was all he would say.

Meanwhile, other members of the family were sending clear signals that they, too, were restive and unhappy. Sallie, who at first had seemed so grateful to be accepted into the family fold, had begun to exhale some of the pent-up anger and resentment she had felt as a child. Once, during a talk with Worth's daughter, Clara, she had suddenly blurted out, "Your father was a dreadful person. I hated him," leaving the young girl startled and hurt.

Sallie's wrath spilled over into her literary work as well. In 1979, she wrote a play based on life in the Big House, and showed the script to her father. *Milk of Paradise* was a devastating portrait of the Senior Binghams, who took on the names of Robby and Alice in the play. At one point, Robby and Alice dance around in the background, completely absorbed in each other, while the Sallie character, a lonely little girl named Missy, stands forlornly in the foreground surrounded by servants.

The father figure was "very remote and somebody she couldn't count on," said Barry Sr. "She couldn't count on her parents for anything. They always ran out on her. They were always busy about their own affairs and they always were so absorbed in each other that they had no use for their children at all and no sympathy for them. This is the picture. I consider it a major distortion."

But the father character was more sympathetic than the mother, who was a careless and frivolous woman. Barry Sr. felt that the portrait of Alice was calculated to wound Mary and he begged Sallie to soften it. She refused, saying the play was a work of art and she had every right to do as she pleased. When the play was produced at the American Place Theatre in New York, Barry Sr. and Mary dutifully flew up for the premiere.

The experience was extremely uncomfortable. "It's not much fun to see yourself caricatured that way," Mary admitted. "But I thought it was just another of Sallie's exercises in building herself up as a neglected child." Secretly, Mary was pleased when a New York critic called *Milk of Paradise* a "self-indulgent biographical snippet" and described its young heroine as "a self-centered snit."

Overlaying Sallie's festering childhood wounds was her newfound commitment to feminism. The women's movement had passed her by when she lived in Boston and New York. In those days, she had felt rejected and overlooked, but she had not yet come to view herself as a victim of something larger. After she returned to Kentucky, she began to see sex discrimination everywhere, especially within her own family. Why else would her bumbling brother be running the empire when she had long ago demonstrated that she was the family's prodigy?

When a University of Kentucky journalism professor asked if she would agree to be interviewed for a story he wanted to write on the Bingham sisters, Sallie eagerly said yes. "It'll be a great article," she assured Eleanor. "It'll be our point of view for a change."

"The Bingham Black Sheep" came out in *Louisville Magazine* in June 1979 and was the talk of the town. Sallie and Eleanor described childhoods of rectitude, emotional restraint, and sibling rivalry fanned to a hot flame by their parents. They bluntly criticized what they called the "anti-women bias" in the upper levels of the family business, and said they felt unwelcome on the board of directors, where they had grave responsibilities but no authority. Even Eleanor, the more accommodating of the pair, complained that she could not speak out against company sexism without being labeled "a hysterical over-reactor." Both said they felt little more than "distant and restrained affection" for Barry Jr.

Mary was livid. "The whole tone of the article was just as wounding as it could be," she said, "and I told them so." Barry Sr. cringed at the public exposure, but eventually came to view the incident as just an unfortunate act of latent rebellion. Barry Jr., though, could not seem to slough off Sallie and Eleanor's allegations. He had tried hard to run the companies fairly and ethically. Now his own sisters had all but said that he was a sexist—and this after he had made Carol Sutton managing editor of the *CJ* and helped found the Jefferson Club, the first professional club in Louisville open to both women and men! He deeply resented what he considered to be a scathing attack on his character.

Eventually, the two women apologized to their parents ("Eleanor more than Sallie," noted Mary), and as the months went by, the fractured feelings of most members of the family seemed to heal. Only Barry Jr. continued to brood about the article. He felt angry and besieged. "He is a very thin-skinned person," said his father. "That's just his nature."

———

Later, no one could remember exactly how the idea got started, but by 1980 it seemed prudent for the Binghams to have an agreement to protect company stock from outside buyers. The era of the hostile takeover had begun and corporate raiders were sending shock waves through company boardrooms across the nation.

A common technique was to purchase small blocks of shares from dissi-dent shareholders and then use that stake as a wedge to create so much discord that the majority would find it easier to sell out rather than endure a carping interloper. Family businesses, insular by nature and unused to such hard-ball tactics, were especially vulnerable.

Takeover mania had not yet struck the newspaper industry, where many owners still regarded each other with a kind of clubby respect. As a matter of policy, Gannett, Knight-Ridder, and most of the other large chains refused to buy shares in any newspaper without an explicit invitation from the controlling owner. Even so, many family newspaper proprietors worried privately that the days of such gentility were numbered.

It was in this mood of caution and fear that Wilson Wyatt and Gordon Davidson set to work drafting a buy-back agreement for the Bingham family. The pact said that if a stockholder in the Bingham companies wanted to sell his or her shares to an outsider, the family had to be given sixty days to match the bid. The Binghams had never permitted anyone other than family members to own stock and Barry Sr. held the majority of the shares. With a signed buy-back agreement to discourage sharks, the Binghams could feel relatively confident of keeping the business in family hands for at least one more generation. "The buy-back made sense to me," said Leon Tallichet. "It was just another routine matter in the lives of those who have a company to pass on to children."

Barry Jr. was especially keen to execute a buy-back agreement. He was well aware that his sisters had little regard for his leadership and he feared what might happen after his parents' deaths. What if Sallie and Eleanor were approached by outside buyers and either used that as a threat to wring concessions out of him or, worse still, actually sold their stock?

Technically, there were circumstances under which a family member's stock could be acquired by an outsider, even with a buy-back. However, a buy-back would make that possibility far less likely. There were few customers for minority stock in private companies anyway, and virtually none who would be willing to negotiate a price if someone else had the option of reviewing the deal and then matching it. The agreement would eliminate one potential uncertainty from an already uncertain future.

In the spring of 1980, a few months after the premiere of *Milk of Paradise*, Leon Tallichet briefed Sallie and Eleanor on why the buy-back had been drawn up and how it might affect them. "I asked them, 'What do you think, how do you feel about this?' " he said. "And they were very nonchalant about it. They said 'Sure. No problem. That's what we'd do anyway, sell our stock back to the family.' "

But between then and June 13, when the family gathered on the west terrace of the Big House to sign the agreement, a dramatic change came over Sallie. After a few pleasantries, Wilson Wyatt passed out the buy-back documents, gave a brief presentation on the reason the agreement had been drawn up, and explained the mechanics of how it would work.

As the others leaned over to affix their signatures, Sallie announced in a hard and determined voice that she would not sign. Despite Leon's careful background briefing, she claimed she had never heard of the buy-back and was not going to be rushed into signing it before she had talked to a lawyer. "Look at all these lawyers here," said Mary in astonishment, sweeping her hand across the room.

Sallie said she felt that the assembled attorneys worked for her father and brother, not for her. She was being railroaded into rubber-stamping the buy-back, just as she had been railroaded into rubber-stamping policies on the board of directors. "I finally said that the buy-back agreement seemed to mean that there was some distrust in the family, and if there was distrust, signing this document was not going to erase it," she said. Taking her cue from Sallie, Eleanor said that she, too, was not yet ready to sign the documents.

The distrust that Sallie alluded to was in fact real, but in the best Bingham tradition it had never been addressed. "The Bingham Black Sheep" article had suggested that Sallie did not respect her brother. Now Barry Jr. saw

Sallie's refusal to sign the buy-back as an indication that she was openly hostile to him. He also concluded that she was irrational and using the issue to angle for attention.

Sallie, however, was correct to view the buy-back as something that would weaken her power. As long as she did not sign it, she had some slight leverage and Barry Jr. had to listen to her. Later, at a board meeting, Wilson Wyatt tried to minimize the importance of the agreement. He told Sallie that she would not be giving up anything if she signed the buy-back, and he told Barry Jr. he would not be losing anything if she did not sign it. "To me it was a non-issue," he said. "But they were rigidly in opposition to each other. It almost goes back to chemistry rather than logic."

In mid-July, about a month after the showdown on the Big House terrace, Sallie sent identical letters to Barry Jr. and Eleanor saying that she would not sign the buy-back and questioning what made family ownership of newspapers so special. She was unclear, she said, about the Binghams' goals for their papers. She assured them, however, that she had no intention of selling her stock to an outside buyer. She signed the letters, "with love."

The Binghams tried to address Sallie's concerns by writing down explicit goals for the family business, even though the companies already had such a document. George Gill had drawn it up in 1974, when he became general manager, and it had been subsequently published in *INTERCOM*, the companies' in-house newsletter. Barry Sr. and Barry Jr. thought that George's simple statements of purpose and philosophy were quite sufficient, but, at the insistence of Mary and Eleanor, they agreed to humor Sallie and go through a separate goal-setting exercise for the family.

The project, in which Sallie declined to participate, went on for several years. Some of the ideas, especially Eleanor's, were naive or too specific to have general applicability. But as windows on the gathering strife, the "goals memos" that circulated among family members were remarkably illuminating. In one, Eleanor complained about high newsroom costs and Barry Jr.'s refusal to acquire newspapers in other cities. She suggested that the company deny salary increases to managers who did not meet affirmative action goals. "Presently there is little written or verbal give and take between family members and Barry nor [*sic*] between family members and management," she wrote. "I do sense a lack of trust (as distinguished from disagreement) in the way management decisions are made. This makes me uncertain of our shared future."

Only two months after the buy-back debacle, Sallie and Eleanor were up in arms again. This time the issue was the dismissal of Will Morgan, the newspapers' architecture columnist, who had been let go as a result of company cutbacks. Morgan's removal saved the papers little money; as an outside contributor, he only received about $50 a column. But the Senior Binghams disliked the cynical tone of his writing and agreed with Barry Jr. that he was expendable.

Sallie and Eleanor admired Morgan, as did Edie. His columns satisfied Sallie's appetite for anti-Establishment writing and Eleanor's desire to please Rowland, her architect husband, who feared that his profession would otherwise go unremarked in *The Courier-Journal*. To voice their objections, the two women sent separate letters to Barry Jr. and David Hawpe, managing editor of *The Courier-Journal* and the man who first suggested that Morgan be axed.

Sallie hotly demanded that her brother give specific reasons for Morgan's dismissal. Eleanor's letter to Hawpe was more pointed. After reminding him that she was a shareholder as well as a reader, she launched into a full-bore blast. "This is the worst kind of short-sighted, pennywise, pound-foolish management," she said. "Your moves are gutting this newspaper of its heart and soul." She added that she looked forward to hearing his explanation at the next board meeting.

Sallie and Eleanor's attack appalled Barry Jr. He had not enjoyed listening to their barbs in the past, but at least they had confined their criticisms to the boardroom or family meetings. Now they had gone directly to one of his employees without consulting him and had even hinted at reprisals. They were interfering in his domain, he felt, and he bristled at their implicit suggestion that they should be included in day-to-day decision making at the papers. "Either you're going to let the family member who's running the companies make the decisions or not," he said. "[Otherwise] management becomes absolutely impossible."

The Will Morgan affair was less an attempt to challenge Barry Jr.'s power than an outgrowth of Sallie and Eleanor's frustration with their brother's inaccessibility. Another person might have sat down with them and talked out the problem. Instead, Barry Jr. scheduled a formal meeting in his office and invited his executive editor to sit in and write up a summary of the discussion. "If only he had met quite cozily with them for lunch once a month or something," said Mary. "If only he had said, 'This is what I'm thinking of doing. I'd like to know what your opinion is.' . . . But it would have taken an act of self-confidence on Barry's part to try something like that."

Barry Jr. did not seem to understand that he was head of a republic, not a dictatorship, and that much of his power derived from the confidence the rest of the family had in him. He clung to the rigid assumption that his authority should be almost total. He begrudged his sisters their seats on the board. He did not want them to have voting stock. And he certainly did not want them sticking their noses into the management of the papers. At one point, Eleanor tried to mediate with her brother. "There's no reason to go wild and start tearing your hair out," she told him. "You've got luggage in life and your sisters are part of it." Barry Jr. did not want to hear it. "He just blew me out of the water," said Eleanor.

Eleanor's husband, Rowland, was an added irritant. On the surface, he and Barry Jr. had ample reason to be friends. They were both fond of hunting and enjoyed talking about guns. But Barry Jr. had never liked this brother-in-law. "Barry's just got a thing about Rowland," said one Bingham executive. "And I can understand it. Rowland's not all that charming, let's face it."

Charm was the least of it. Rowland had little money of his own and Barry Jr. considered him a gold digger who was rapidly turning Eleanor, the family hippie, into the queen of consumption. When Edie was in the market for a new car, Rowland encouraged her to buy a Jaguar instead of the Japanese compact she preferred. "C'mon, why don't you live rich?" he taunted. "You can afford it."

Such comments annoyed Barry Jr., who had a kind of reverse snobbery about his own beat-up 1972 Datsun and cruelly disparaged any of his executives who drove big cars. Now Rowland's platinum tastes had infected Eleanor. Soon after their marriage, she and Rowland started buying property, including a building in downtown Louisville, a farm in adjacent Oldham County, and four hundred acres of timberland near the Tennessee border. Rowland drove a sleek green Porsche and Eleanor buzzed around town in a BMW. The purchases cost hundreds of thousands of dollars, and even with Eleanor's annual dividend income, the bills mounted up to more than they could handle. Faced with a cash squeeze, they borrowed money from the Senior Binghams and arranged for a loan from a Louisville bank.

Owing money was a concept beyond Barry Jr.'s comprehension. He seethed at the notion that Rowland was playing Monopoly with Bingham dollars and acting like a big shot. He also worried that his brother-in-law's profligacy would soon result in pressure on the companies for larger dividends.

In fact, Eleanor and Rowland seemed to need wealth and the sensation of power that comes with it just to feel good about themselves. Although they were in their thirties, neither could point to much in the way of accomplishment in their lives. Their status in Louisville derived almost entirely from the money and social position of their families, a situation that gave them both pleasure and anxiety. They wanted desperately to have pull in the community, and they felt that Eleanor's seat on the Bingham boards should, by rights, bestow it. Why *couldn't* they help friends who wanted to place stories in the newspapers? Why *couldn't* they contact the executive editor directly and tell him what they thought the papers should cover?

Edie gently tried to educate them about the traditional *cordon sanitaire* between family members and the news staff, but it did little good. Eleanor and Rowland smoldered in frustration when Barry Jr. blocked their attempts at influence. "They didn't like the fact that they had no power base, that they were shareholders and yet Barry was calling all the shots," said Edie.

Barry Jr., in turn, felt threatened by any glimmer of disrespect. While waiting for a plane at Louisville's Standiford Field, he was buttonholed by the president of a local bank, who told him in no uncertain terms that the Binghams' policy against electioneering in the *Courier-Journal* building was ridiculous. The banker wanted to lobby for a ballot issue authorizing the merger of city and county government, a position the papers had endorsed, and he could not understand why Barry Jr. would not allow him to talk to potential voters in the newsroom.

As the conversation became heated, Rowland, who was waiting for the same plane, sidled over. "Barry, you can run this company any way you want to," he said. "Can't you break that policy this one time?" Barry Jr. replied through clenched teeth that no, he could not and would not. He could not even bring himself to speak to Rowland about the incident for over a year.

By now, Rowland was included in every family meeting and his presence was a constant torment to Barry Jr. He wondered aloud why dividends were so low and asked to see comparative yields from other companies. He complained about "negativism" in news stories and "slanted" headlines. He prodded Barry Jr. to expand the business into new markets and different locations. "Rowland has never done anything in his life but he loves to give advice," said one of the family's chief advisers.

In fairness, Rowland did make an effort to learn something about the Binghams' business. He borrowed *The Kingdom and the Power*, *Death in the Afternoon*, and other books on newspapers from a friend at *The Courier-Journal*, and tried to assure Barry Jr. that his motives were not purely financial. "The Binghams are helping me. Why can't I help them?" he asked. "I know I could help Barry Jr. in something. . . . I would have sacrificed a lot of time just to be of some use to him."

That was precisely what Barry Jr. feared most. Soon after Eleanor's wedding, he and Edie had decided to build a small addition on the back of the Big House. When they consulted their regular architect about the job, Rowland was incensed. He had expected at least to be given a chance at the work. But Barry Jr. had no interest in being an employment agency for struggling relations, and he suspected that Rowland intended to use the family business to prop himself up professionally. "He wanted to be consulted about the redecoration of one of the companies and whatever building might be built," said Edie. "He got very upset when [he found out that] this was not the way the company worked."

Rowland maintained that he had no intention of mistreating the newspapers, Standard Gravure, or the broadcast properties. He just wanted not to be excluded from bidding on Bingham contracts because he was married to Eleanor. Otherwise, he said, he would be considered a liability by architecture firms and they would not hire him. In the fall of 1982, Barry Jr. issued a set of guidelines for family members doing business with the companies. The rules allowed Rowland to submit bids for jobs, but he never did. By then he had resigned his position with R. Jeffrey Points, a local architecture firm, and gone freelance. "He said he was just being asked to do the most dreary architectural jobs, and wasn't interested in being connected with a firm," Mary explained.

Mary watched the Barry Jr.-Rowland relationship with growing dismay. She felt fiercely protective of Eleanor's new husband, in part because he seemed so heartbroken over their protracted and painful attempts to have children. After several miscarriages, their first child, conceived in 1981, was diagnosed through amniocentesis as having Down syndrome and subsequently aborted.

It was not until the fall of 1982 that Eleanor and Rowland were able to have a healthy son, Rowland Antoine Miller. They treated "Rowlie" like a miracle child and imposed their sometimes offbeat notions of diet and discipline on him with an unswerving hand. At Rowlie's second birthday party, Eleanor and Rowland served a leg of lamb with candles stuck in it instead of cake because they were opposed to his ingesting sugar.

In such whimsical moments, Mary saw glimpses of Jonathan in her young son-in-law. There was something about Rowland's neediness that appealed to her, much as Jonathan's cries had appealed to her when she left for the office during World War II, and she rapidly became Rowland's fiercest champion. In 1983, just before Standard Gravure's new offset printing plant opened in Morristown, Tennessee, Barry Jr. chartered a plane to take the family and a few advisers to inspect it. After Mary had settled into her seat, she looked around and asked, "Is Rowland coming?" Barry Jr. said no, he was not. Eleanor, who was pregnant again, had been advised by her doctor not to fly, he said. The trip was just for directors and their spouses, and since Eleanor was not there, he saw no reason to include Rowland. Besides, he told his mother, all the seats were needed for Bingham company executives.

The incident troubled Mary. How could Barry Jr. ever expect to have a decent business or personal relationship with Eleanor when he treated her husband so uncharitably, she wondered. After several months of stewing, Mary finally confronted Barry Jr., who categorically denied arranging the trip so that Rowland could not go. Later, however, he confessed that he had deliberately made sure there would be no seat for his brother-in-law. He curtly apologized to his mother, but she would not let go of it. *"Why do you have this prejudice against Rowland?"* Mary demanded. *"Why* do you feel this way?" Barry Jr. shrugged and said that it was just "a matter of chemistry." Mary asked him if it was like the nursery rhyme:

"I do not like thee Dr. Fell.
The reason why I cannot tell.
But this I know and know full well,
I do not like thee Dr. Fell."

As she recited the verse, Barry Jr. got up and headed for the door. "Yes," he said as he looked back over his shoulder, his eyes glaring. "That's just it."

––––––––––

During the Christmas season, Barry Jr. and Edie traditionally held a square dance, clearing away furniture in the Big House hall, hiring a caller, and laying in extra stores of food and drink. Worth's friend Harvey Sloane and his wife, Kathy, also had a holiday tradition: a caroling party through the streets of Old Louisville. For years, both families had invited each other to these wholesome annual events. Barry Jr. and Edie's two daughters and the Sloanes' three young children had come to look upon them as essential ingredients of the holidays.

But Christmas, 1980, was different. Harvey Sloane, a doctor by training, had abandoned medicine for politics in the early 1970s, several years after accompanying Worth on his fateful journey to Nantucket. With the support of the Bingham newspapers, he had served one term as mayor of Louisville and in 1979 had made an unsuccessful bid for the governorship, losing out in the primary to Kentucky Fried Chicken magnate John Y. Brown. A year later he was back on his feet, announcing that he would run again for mayor in 1981.

On the first of December 1980, Edie wrote Kathy Sloane a polite but firm letter telling her that, because of Harvey's mayoral candidacy, she and Barry Jr. would not be coming to the Sloanes' annual caroling party. Edie added that the Sloanes should not expect an invitation to the Binghams' square dance either. "Barry has decided that the best policy for us is to refrain from entertaining or being entertained by political candidates or politicians in office. . . . Although at arm's length, we extend wishes to the family for a happy Christmas season."

The Sloanes were stunned. They were well aware of Barry Jr.'s distaste for politicians and his strict enforcement of the newspapers' conflict-of-interest rules, which prevented all officers and employees of the Bingham companies from contributing to political campaigns. But they could not understand how permitting their children to sing songs together and dance the Virginia Reel would damage the papers' integrity. "He was into blanket policies," said Harvey. "He took a very pure approach."

Deep down, Harvey suspected that Barry Jr. also felt threatened by the close, almost second-son relationship he enjoyed with Barry Sr., who had stoked Harvey's political career with advice, money, and valuable connections. He knew, too, that Barry Jr. resented his long-standing friendship with Cy MacKinnon. The joke at *The Courier-Journal* was that if a reporter wanted a quote from Harvey, he should call the MacKinnons' house, where he was sure to be found.

That comment hung over Barry Jr. like a rain cloud. He hated the idea that the Bingham papers might be perceived as being in the hip pocket of any politician, Democrat or Republican. But Harvey, who commanded so much affection and support from his family, annoyed him more than most.

In June 1981, several weeks after Harvey had won the Democratic primary, Barry Jr. ran a long, page-one story on Harvey's personal and political connections to the Bingham family to show that *The Courier-Journal* was still free of sacred cows. The article listed the amounts of money Mary, Sallie, and Eleanor had donated to Sloane for his 1979 gubernatorial bid, and went into detail about a $25,000 personal loan Barry Sr. had made to help retire Harvey's campaign debts. "Without question, a notion exists that Sloane flourished as a politician in part because of a cozy relationship at the newspapers," the *CJ* said.

When it came time to back a candidate for the general election, Barry Jr. was eager to show his independence. In mid-October 1981, *The Courier-Journal* endorsed Harvey's Republican opponent, George Clark, founder of the fast-food chain Druthers, for mayor. "We couldn't believe it," said Kathy Sloane. "It was as though somebody had dropped a bomb." All the other Binghams were outraged and embarrassed. How could Barry Jr. favor a political novice and Republican over an old family friend and Democrat?

The day before the endorsement appeared, Barry Jr. wired his parents in Amsterdam to inform them of his decision. Mary pleaded with Barry Sr. to put his foot down and insist that the papers support Sloane, but he refused. It had been ten years since he turned the papers over to his son, he said, and he would not start second-guessing him now.

Some people at *The Courier-Journal* thought the paper had legitimate reasons to back George Clark. When members of the editorial board had interviewed Harvey at the *CJ & T* building, as they did most political candidates, he had seemed listless and apathetic. He could not even promise that he would serve out his term if elected. "He was like a dead man, a zombie," said one staffer who was there. "It was as if he had been on drugs or something."

Few editorial writers actively favored Clark, but they thought endorsing him might at least wake Harvey up. They were right. Shocked by the papers' vote of no confidence, Harvey ran an energetic campaign and won in a landslide. Two days after the election, *The Courier-Journal* extended an olive branch to Sloane. "Now that the contests are over," said an editorial, "cooperation must begin."

For the Bingham family, at least, that would not be easy. The Clark endorsement had angered Sallie almost as much as it had Mary and Barry Sr. Instead of taking the issue up with Barry Jr. directly, however, Sallie shot off a letter to *The Courier-Journal* saying that the endorsement had "betrayed" the newspaper's "great liberal" reputation. *The Wall Street Journal* took note of the tiff in a small news story.

Barry Jr. seemed unruffled by the controversy. Barry Sr. never mentioned his feelings about the Clark endorsement during his once-a-week lunches with his son, although he and Mary complained bitterly to Marietta Tree and other close friends. And Sallie, who only five months earlier had refused to sign the buy-back, made no attempt to heal this latest break with her brother.

———

The flip side of Barry Jr.'s conscious isolation from politicians was his conviction that the Bingham operations should be open to public scrutiny. The idea was admirable, but as Barry Jr. was wont to do, he carried it to ridiculous extremes.

Public disclosure became not just desirable but an inviolate commandment in a kind of zealous fundamentalist religion. "We used to laugh about Barry's great desire to have a glass shithouse on River Road," said George Gill. "You know, so every morning he'd go out there and the whole world could see what he did." Barry Jr. guffawed as heartily as anyone when George made that joke. But in January 1980, Barry Jr.'s desire for total transparency was no laughing matter, least of all to George.

By then, company president Cy MacKinnon was a year away from early retirement and Barry Jr. had begun to focus on finding his replacement. Cy suggested that Barry Jr. get two candidates for the job, put them in positions of line responsibility for a year, see how they did, and then pick a winner at the end. Barry Jr. agreed. The hired hands quickly gave the neck-and-neck process a name. They called it "the horse race."

One of the candidates was Bernie Block, president of Dissly Research

Corp., a small Bingham subsidiary, who had carried papers for the *CJ & T* in high school, put in a stint at General Electric, and then been hired by Cy MacKinnon in 1970 as comptroller. The other was George Gill, who had started as a reporter, risen to managing editor of *The Courier-Journal*, been passed over by Barry Jr. for executive editor in favor of Bob Clark, then crossed over to the business side in 1974, where he had worked as vice-president and general manager. To the Senior Binghams and the hired hands, a contest between these two men was over before it started. Why would anyone pick a bean-counter like Bernie for company president over a seasoned manager like George, who had distinguished himself in both news and business?

Even Bernie was surprised to be in the running. Barry Jr. had invited him to be a presidential prospect over lunch in a downtown restaurant. For days before the appointment, Bernie speculated fretfully about why Barry Jr. wanted to see him. "I hadn't had lunch alone with Barry Jr. ever since I'd worked here," he said. "I didn't know whether he was going to fire me or what."

Still he was honored to be asked and pleased to discover that Cy Mac-Kinnon had suggested his name. But he also wanted to make certain that he was a serious candidate, not just a straw man tossed into the race to make it look like an open process. Barry Jr. assured him that the playing field was level. He was the only one who thought so. "To compare George to Bernie Block is like comparing me to Edward R. Murrow," said Bob Morse, then general manager of WHAS. "They're not in the same class."

For George, who felt that he had already earned Barry Jr.'s respect and trust, being pitted against Bernie was humiliating enough. Then Barry Jr. made the situation even more embarrassing. Early in January 1980, just before the horse race formally began, he summoned Bernie and George to his office and told them that he intended to announce the contest to the Louisville media, which virtually guaranteed a front-page story in *The Courier-Journal*.

For a week, George and Bernie desperately tried to talk him out of it. He could watch their performance, they said, but why let the entire world know they were competing? Why make a public spectacle out of it? Barry Jr. was unmoved. He not only announced that George and Bernie were vying for Cy MacKinnon's job, he announced precisely when he would decide the winner: at 9:00 A.M., January 16, 1981. "He always has to be open and honest about everything," said Bernie. "I think he would go to confession at the Super Bowl on a loudspeaker if he were a Catholic."

The horse race quickly became a standing joke in Louisville. People laughed about it at cocktail parties. Old-timers at the newspapers started a betting pool on who would win. Barry Sr., who had been informed of the contest only shortly before it was announced, felt acute discomfort. He did not mind Barry Jr. drumming up a rivalry between George and Bernie—that was his right, and maybe even good business practice—but he could not stand the idea that the Bingham companies were being held up to ridicule.

From January 1980 until January 1981, George and Bernie went about their duties with grim determination. For the purposes of the horse race, Cy MacKinnon's job was split in two, with each man taking half. During that period, Barry Jr. never gave either contender formal feedback. After about six months, each got a $10,000 bonus with a note that said, "You're doing a good job." But otherwise, Barry Jr. seemed to forget that he had set the competition in motion in the first place.

As the date for a decision neared, he started taking other company managers to lunch, asking them who they thought the winner should be, and scribbling down notes as they talked. When it was Bob Morse's turn, Barry Jr. showed up with Emily, his fifteen-year-old daughter. "Here I am evaluating two men in front of his kid!" said Morse in amazement. "I just told Barry, 'You don't have any choice—there's only one option.' "

In the minds of the hired hands, that option was without question George Gill, who despite his penchant for biting sarcasm, was a natural-born leader. During the horse-race year, he aggressively went outside the Bingham companies for new management ideas, even traveling to Japan to inspect the latest offset printing techniques, and he had a long history of business contacts in Louisville. Bernie, on the other hand, was like a chunky Mr. Peepers. His dependability, honesty, and accommodating manner made him a valued and trusted subordinate, but virtually everyone in the executive ranks felt that he was unsuited to be president of the Bingham companies.

Regardless of their own preferences, the top professionals felt protective of both George and Bernie. By conducting the horse race in public, Barry Jr. had already proven that he was capable of callousness. Now that the final decision loomed, they feared that one or both of their colleagues would again be subjected to unnecessary hurt and shame. So when Barry Jr. invited John Richards, then a senior vice-president, to give him advice on how to handle the announcement of the winner, he did not mince words.

In a long, forthright memo, John blasted Barry Jr. for conducting the horse race in front of an audience. "I think you have shown a frightening insensitivity to the feelings and concerns of the candidates and the rest of the executive group. . . . Frankly, we all look silly and most of us feel silly." He advised Barry Jr. to tell George and Bernie separately of his decision, in private, and not to require either of them to come into work that day. "You have no idea what level of intensity lurks in each of these guys," he wrote. ". . . Even the winner would be uneasy and embarrassed. The loser might want to take a three-hour walk, so let him."

He suggested that Barry Jr. inform his parents and sisters in advance and personally visit each of the Bingham subsidiaries to introduce the winner. "I have labeled you insensitive. You are not this way by design," he said in closing. "You have asked for help. I hope this qualifies." Barry Jr. wrote back: "Thanks for leveling."

January 16, 1981, dawned crisp and cold. Barry Jr. had a fire blazing in his study and coffee steaming in a silver urn when Bernie Block drove up to the Big House at 9:00 A.M. to find out whether or not he would be president of the Bingham companies, or even if he would have a job. Under the conditions of the horse race, it was up to the winner to retain or jettison the loser, a notion that had kept Bernie in a cold sweat for weeks. His wife was days away from delivering a baby. It was not a propitious moment to be out of work. Barry Jr. offered him a cup of coffee and a pastry. Bernie refused. "I just want to hear the answer," he said anxiously. Barry Jr. cleared his throat and said that he had decided to pick George Gill. "You lost by a field goal," he said sympathetically, touching Bernie on the shoulder.

George approached the Big House just as Bernie was leaving, and for a brief moment the two cars passed. Both men had speculated about the timing of their appointments—would Barry Jr. tell the winner at 9:00 A.M. and the loser at 9:45 A.M., or vice versa? Bernie gave George no hint as he continued down the Binghams' winding driveway and headed for home.

George's audience lasted only ten minutes. After getting the good news, he raced back to his house on Rebel Drive. "My wife was there waiting for me and we had a couple of moments," he said. "It was pretty emotional." That night, he invited Bernie over to talk about the future, and the two men drank whiskey for hours. "Block took it very hard," said George. "It was really God-awful. He just crashed and burned." George did manage to calm Bernie's fears of unemployment, though. He offered to keep him on as a senior vice-president, with responsibility for accounting and data processing, and Bernie agreed. "I still liked the Binghams and I liked George," Bernie said. "I knew if we could get over these wounds, it would be all right."

The Senior Binghams were pleased but somewhat surprised that Barry Jr. had chosen George. They were aware that he had executive ability and was well known in the community. But George was also strong-minded, short-tempered, and abrasive—qualities that made him ill-suited to be an adviser to their sensitive son. "George can be very sharp," said Barry Sr. "I think Barry was consciously not doing the thing that he would find most congenial. He was doing the thing that he thought was better for the papers."

In fact, the selection of George as company president was a brilliant stroke. Morale, especially in the top ranks, had suffered under Cy Mac-Kinnon, who in recent years had seemed more interested in building a retirement home in the Bahamas than running the business. On the dollars and cents side, George's energy, efficiency, and sense of direction was like a gust of spring air. For the first time in years, the Bingham executives had an organization chart with their titles and responsibilities clearly spelled out. Pay scales, raises, and evaluations had been a matter of whim under MacKinnon. Now, George convinced Barry Jr. to boost managers' salaries up to the level of comparable executives across the country. In some cases, the raises were huge. George's own salary soared well into six figures in less than three years.

As president, George tried hard to bring Barry Jr. out of the cocoon to which Cy MacKinnon had so long consigned him. He met with him informally every afternoon and included him in strategy sessions with the new corporate executive committee he had formed, a group made up of Bernie Block, John Richards, and Leon Tallichet.

George teased Barry Jr. about his enthusiasm for electronic journalism, but he also made an effort to translate his dreams into manageable realities, helping him launch a small chain of computer stores and a twenty-four-hour videotext service on cable TV. He even listened patiently when Barry Jr. suggested that the newspapers forgo the expense of moving to offset printing and instead wait to spend the money on electronic news delivery systems when the technology became available.

Barry Jr. hoped that George would be for him what Mark Ethridge had been for his father: a close friend and ally, someone who could discuss ad rates as easily as foreign policy and move gracefully between the business and the editorial sides of the papers, someone who would lift the weight of actually running the place from his shoulders and give him the freedom to do what he wanted. He repeatedly asked George to attend editorial board meetings, as Mark had done in Barry Sr.'s day. But even after Barry Jr. sent him a hand-lettered invitation with a blue ribbon around it, George refused. It was not appropriate for the financial side to participate in editorial policy, he felt.

Despite their differences in temperament, George Gill and Barry Jr. became close on a personal as well as professional basis. From 1981 until the middle of 1983, George enjoyed what he later came to look upon as a kind of golden honeymoon with Barry Jr. Both men owned chainsaws and loved to cut firewood and work outdoors. Occasionally on weekends they would tramp the forty acres around the Big House, flicking mosquitos away from their faces and talking.

One day Barry Jr. got misty-eyed as he spoke of the Big House and the land surrounding it. "You know, I just regret so much that I'm going to lose that place," he told George. "When my parents die it's going to be divided up into pieces. My sisters will get their part and I'll get mine. It'll just be gone." George stopped dead in his tracks. "Jesus Christ, Barry, that's not what your father thinks," he exclaimed. "He thinks you don't want to have anything to do with that place after he's gone."

Barry Sr. and Mary had always felt that the Big House was more of an encumbrance than a joy to Barry Jr. They had no idea that he wanted the property at their deaths. After George told Barry Sr. of his son's feelings, Barry Sr. invited Barry Jr. to sign a $250,000 promissory note for the house and ten acres of land, with the understanding that the debt would be forgiven in his and Mary's wills. Barry Jr. was elated at the gift—and very grateful to George for playing the role of intermediary. "They never thought of talking to each other," said George. "And that was just an *incredible* example."

George also took care of day-to-day details that plagued Barry Jr. When part of the driveway leading up to the Big House suddenly collapsed, he arranged for a contractor to get the road rebuilt. He replaced the rotting gutters at the Big House with copper ones and helped find a catering outfit to relieve Edie of the oppression of business entertainment. "They were so grateful," John Richards said. "George was in hog heaven with that relationship."

Slowly, Barry Jr. began to open up to George in a way he did with few people. When they were in Atlanta for a week-long seminar, Barry Jr. reminisced about his life in Paris during the Marshall Plan year and talked about the difficulties he was having with Edie's sons. Even Edie began to confide in George, complaining about Barry Jr.'s rigid work habits and his inability to relax. Did you realize, she said, that he reads the newspaper all day even when he's on vacation?

———

Despite her tangles with Barry Jr. over the buy-back, "The Bingham Black Sheep" article, and the newspapers' endorsement of George Clark, Sallie felt comfortable in Louisville. She had a busy existence, teaching at the University of Louisville, writing in her riverside study, and going out on dates. Several of the single women in town had taken note of Sallie's insistence on having a male escort with her at every social function—a strange position for a self-proclaimed feminist, they thought. "I took her to a party given by the Louisville Writers Club and she dragged along someone I'd never seen," said one. "It was as though she wasn't all right by herself."

In fact, Sallie's relations with men were as chaotic, dependent, and emotionally riven as they had ever been in New York. She was distraught when Bill Grant, the University of Louisville professor she had been seeing since her arrival back in town, became deeply involved with someone else, a woman he eventually married.

Soon thereafter she began dating Tim Peters, an ex-army officer six years her junior who had once been a student of Grant's. Tim, a building contractor, was less cerebral and articulate than the men Sallie normally went out with. But his imposing height, self-confidence, and down-to-earth personality made Sallie feel safe and protected. Because of her superior education and family name, she did not feel competitive with Tim as she had with Whitney Ellsworth, nor did she worry that he would collapse like "a boudoir pillow" like Michael Iovenko.

Barry Sr. and Mary told friends that Sallie had hooked up with "this character who wasn't interested in intellectual things." However, Wilson Wyatt, the family's wise old counselor, considered Tim a leveling influence on Sallie. "He is one of the least vicious people I know," said a friend. "Very supportive, honest, a real American Boy Scout type."

Even with Tim, though, Sallie could not restrain her native imperiousness. When they first started dating, Tim was drinking heavily. He had recently separated from his wife—another woman named Sally—and had gone to the bottle for comfort. One day, Sally Peters let herself back into the house to pick up their two young sons and noticed a note attached to the liquor cabinet. "Tim Peters is allowed one drink per day by order of the Queen," it said. She could not resist a retort. Underneath she scribbled, "Queen Sarah, I presume." That night, Tim phoned her in a rage to say that she had ruined his evening with Sallie Bingham, the woman Louisville wags had dubbed "Secondhand Sallie" out of deference to his wife.

As soon as Tim's divorce came through, Sallie moved into his rambling Victorian house in an old Louisville neighborhood and sent out printed announcements informing her parents and friends that their families had become amalgamated. "I have no talent for marriage," she added in a note to the Senior Binghams. "But I'm lonely so I'm going to live with Tim." The arrangement was still unusual in straitlaced Louisville. But, as they had with Eleanor and Rowland, Barry Sr. and Mary took the news in stride. Soon, Barry Sr. began showing up regularly to read to Tim's sons and the Iovenko boys.

Sallie's new location put her directly across the street from a good friend, *Courier-Journal* book editor Shirley Williams, who had once worked as Mary Bingham's secretary. Shirley became ill early in 1981 and was told she needed major surgery. When she worried aloud that the book page would suffer during her medical leave, Sallie's eyes lit up. "I'd love to take your place while you're recuperating," she told Shirley. "Would you mind mentioning my name to your editor?" Shirley said she would be delighted.

The news of Sallie's desire to be the paper's book editor raced up the chain of command. The editors were furious that Shirley had bequeathed her job, even temporarily, without asking their permission, but there was little they could do. A Bingham wanted a position at the paper: It was not up to employees to refuse. "When I heard about it, I just about had a fit," said Irene Nolan, then assistant managing editor of the features department. "Who wanted Sallie Bingham working for you, right?"

The matter was settled even before executive editor Paul Janensch ran into Barry Jr.'s office to tell him what had happened. "She does have good credentials," Paul said encouragingly. "We can live with this." Barry Jr. rolled his eyes, but he did not object. After all, it was only for a couple of months.

Being at *The Courier-Journal* was an epiphany of sorts for Sallie. For the first time in her life, she felt as if she belonged. After years of working alone in cluttered houses and apartments, she found the casual sociability of the fifth-floor features department immensely satisfying. She enjoyed going out to lunch with colleagues and sharing office gossip.

Initially, the work terrified her—she had to learn how to use the same computer terminals she had once maligned—but she soon discovered that the job was not at all strenuous and yielded easily to her disciplined work habits. "To her credit, she seemed to get the job done in fewer hours than Shirley required," said Paul Janensch. "Shirley complained that she couldn't do it in forty hours and needed help. Sallie seemed to get it done in twenty-five hours and took long lunches and days off."

Editors grumbled that Sallie confused her facts, misspelled words, and skewed the page too much toward obscure Kentucky authors and feminist writers. When a reporter suggested that she review a newly published book on Winston Churchill, she sent back a note saying, "I'm so tired of Winston Churchill." "Sallie had odd ideas," said Molly Clowes. "She didn't want to review any books that were best-sellers. . . . They had to be regional books. So we had people, bewildered people probably, who were suddenly big stars on the book page because they had written a vanity-published novel or some such thing."

Molly once drew Sallie's ire by writing a critical letter-to-the-editor about the book page. "Who is this old biddy?" Sallie asked John Ed Pearce, then a member of the Sunday magazine staff. John Ed was offended and a bit amused that a self-avowed feminist like Sallie was not aware of arguably the most successful woman ever to work at the Bingham papers. "Old biddy?" he said indignantly. "That woman graced this newspaper for twenty-five years with some of the most literary writing it has ever seen." Sallie shrugged. "Well, I never heard of her."

To Sallie, complaints like Molly's seemed inconsequential compared with the pleasure she found in the work. "It was really fun," said Sallie. "Instead of being an outsider as I always have been, there was also a little bit of the insider for me here."

But the book page belonged to Shirley Williams, and when she came back to the paper in the summer of 1981, Sallie reluctantly vacated the position. About a month later, though, the managing editor of *The Courier-Journal* called Shirley into his office and told her that she was being reassigned as a reporter in the features section. "Sallie has made wonderful suggestions for the book page and we're going to ask her to come back and edit it," he said. Shirley was stupefied, as were others at the paper. "I just about fell over when I heard the news," said Irene Nolan. "I couldn't believe it. It was just so ironic that Shirley had organized herself right out of a job."

In fact, Sallie's permanent installation as *Courier-Journal* book editor had less to do with the excellence of her past performance than with Barry Sr.'s desire to involve his daughter in the family business. Only a year earlier, Sallie had refused to sign the buy-back, saying she saw no value in family-owned newspapers. During the months that she had filled in for Shirley, however, Barry Sr. had seen Sallie become invested in *The Courier-Journal* and *Times* in a way he had never thought possible.

Perhaps if she were in the newsroom on a regular basis, working at the job her mother once held, he reasoned, she would come to understand the intense desire the rest of the family felt to perpetuate the Bingham empire. Sallie was thrilled and flattered at the prospect of returning to the book page. Barry Jr., however, boiled with anger and resentment. When he had bungled the horse race and endorsed Republican George Clark for mayor, his father had not interfered. He had gone along with the buy-back and had refused as a matter of principle to inject himself into the day-to-day running of the companies.

Now, for the first time in Barry Jr.'s memory, Barry Sr. had put his foot down: Shirley Williams was going to be shunted aside, Sallie was going to be book editor in her stead and that was that. Barry Jr. was told, not consulted, about the decision and there was little he could do about it.

Sallie did not need much persuading to participate in Shirley Williams's ouster. "Sallie pushed for [the position]," said Mary. "She wanted it very much." If she felt any feminist guilt about taking another woman's job, and a friend's at that, she did not indicate it. Once she was reinstalled in her small cubicle, she and Shirley passed each other primly in the hall but rarely spoke.

Barry Jr. was ashamed of his parents' insistent nepotism and mortified that one of his own employees had been dispossessed by a family member. He was also afraid of Sallie. It was one thing when she criticized his leadership at cocktail parties or board meetings. But to have her inside the building every day, watching his every move, gossiping in the ladies' room, cracking jokes about his ineptitude to the staff—that was too much. "I believe he felt that she would be an inimical force within the organization and would make comments that would be unfortunate," said Barry Sr. "I have no evidence that she did, of course."

In fact, Sallie took great delight in depicting Barry Jr. as an incompetent boob to her co-workers. "I knew that Sallie didn't approve of the way her brother was running the company because she told me so," said Irene Nolan, Sallie's boss. "When she'd start talking, it just used to amaze me some of the things she would say." Sallie also bruised Barry Jr.'s delicate ethical sensibilities by dispensing unreviewed books to the staff instead of paying publishers for them, as the conflict-of-interest policy then decreed. She incensed him further by saying that she tried to make sure her friends' books got friendly reviews so that when her work was published the favor would be returned. "Things like that really bothered me," said Barry Jr. "I thought we'd gotten the ethical question pretty well under control and suddenly here's someone who just made you want to blow your brains out."

Barry Jr. was especially distraught when, in the spring of 1982, Sallie joined a committee to lobby for a proposed tax to support Louisville's public schools. Soon after their arrival in Louisville, Sallie's sons, Chris and Willy Iovenko, had transferred from private school to the city's decaying public system. The schools cried out for improvement and Sallie felt strongly that a new levy was needed.

But as an employee, her involvement in a political committee was a direct violation of Barry Jr.'s conflict-of-interest guidelines. The news staff was forbidden from participating in any civic group other than a cultural or artistic organization. Barry Jr. ordered Paul Janensch to tell Sallie that she had to resign from the tax panel. "But I don't cover education," Sallie protested. "Can't you make an exception in my case?" Paul swallowed hard. "Well, I hate to put it this way, but you are going to have to make a choice," he said, implying that she was risking her position if she remained. "Let me know your decision by tomorrow."

Faced with such clear resolve, Sallie angrily left the committee and a day later dispatched a furious letter-to-the-editor, which Barry Jr. published. "At what point is the individual, who needs his job, willing to give up his rights as a citizen in order to keep it?" the letter asked. The Senior Binghams, horrified at what they considered to be Barry Jr.'s hidebound rigidity, requested that the conflict-of-interest rules be reviewed. "I did say to Barry [that] I felt [it] was a great mistake to carry [the policy] to that extent," said Barry Sr. "But he said he felt it was a matter of principle and that he must observe it." When the reexamination came back three months later, it revealed that the news staff was overwhelmingly in support of the ban against involvement in public controversies.

The tax panel imbroglio only intensified Barry Jr.'s suspicions of Sallie. She had long been an embarrassment on the Bingham board of directors.

Now she was an embarrassment, and a public one, on the newspapers as well.

His sense of being under siege was aggravated further by the continuing weakness of the Louisville economy, which had yet to rebound from the recession. Unemployment was 11 percent, one of the highest rates in the nation for a community its size; fifty thousand people were out of work.

To cope with declining advertising and circulation, the Binghams hired legions of outside consultants, a highly expensive and inefficient practice that often yielded conflicting advice. The board of directors, comprised of family members and the hired hands, was not up to the task of steering the business through such treacherous waters, Barry Jr. felt. He was especially concerned that board members did not have the expertise to bring about his dream: the electronic newspaper. "We were moving from the old ink on paper to a new form of communication, and I thought we needed people on the board who could help us make the transition," he said.

Barry Jr. did not keep his frustrations to himself. He began to vent his feelings to the hired hands, musing wistfully about how wonderful it would be to have a professional group of directors to guide him through this troubled period. One day in the fall of 1982, John Richards walked into Barry Jr.'s office and told him that he had found some people who might be able to help: Léon and Katy Danco. "They are a husband-and-wife team from Cleveland who counsel family businesses," he told him. "Léon has even written a book about boards of directors."

Barry Jr. stroked his handlebar mustache and listened attentively while George Gill stood sentry nearby. "I thought the idea had some hope," said George. "Particularly since Katy Danco was sort of an equal partner in this venture and the feminist part of Sallie was well known and Eleanor was kind of getting that way, too." But, he said, shaking his head, "I was dead wrong."

ONCE AT ODDS, NOW AT WAR

Léon Danco gingerly dipped a silver spoon into his soup, well aware that Mary Bingham was scrutinizing his table manners and finding them wanting. Barry Jr. had brought Léon and his wife, Katy, to Louisville in the spring of 1983 as high-priced family-business consultants, and the older Binghams had reluctantly invited them to lunch. "You'd have thought I was marrying into the family," Léon said, recalling his icy reception at the Little House.

From the moment John Richards told Barry Jr. about the Dancos, they had caused bickering within the Bingham clan. Barry Jr. had flown to Cleveland to spend a day with the couple in late 1982, and came away convinced that he had found the right team to help dig him out of his dilemma. He was especially delighted when Léon and Katy told him that they believed strongly in professional boards of directors. Unqualified family members, they said, had no place on the boards of family businesses. Had the hired hands known in advance that this was what the Dancos would advise, "we would've scrubbed the whole thing," said George Gill.

It is unclear whether the Dancos helped form Barry Jr.'s opinion or merely cemented a view he already held. Either way, he saw the couple as a godsend. Now he had a plausible rationale, seconded by experts, for dumping his sisters from the boards of the Bingham companies. The argument was simple: He needed professional directors to help guide him through the choppy waters ahead. His sisters contributed nothing. They had no useful professional or technical expertise, and their increasing demands on the family retainers were distracting and exasperating. Barry Jr. and the Dancos were of one mind. Sallie, Eleanor, and all the other "noncontributing" family members must go.

Barry Jr. immediately began lobbying Barry Sr. for a reconfigured board and pressed his parents to invite the Dancos to Louisville for a visit. He gave the family copies of the couple's books, including Katy Danco's *From the Other Side of the Bed*, aimed specifically at the wives of family-business owners. One of the chapters was entitled "We Make Lousy Directors." Barry Sr. and Mary reacted dubiously. Eleanor was offended. Sallie was outraged.

Edie suspected there were other reasons why Sallie, Eleanor, and the Senior Binghams balked at the prospect of a counseling session with the Dancos. "It was the first time that there was any delving into the dynamics of this family," she said. She hoped the Dancos would put the unacknowledged causes of the family tension on the table for discussion, including the Seniors' subterranean power plays and Sallie and Eleanor's delusions of self-importance.

Finally, in April 1983, Barry Sr. agreed to meet with the Dancos. But he had considerable misgivings. He had conceded only when Barry Jr. made the visit a test of personal loyalty, beseeching his parents to order Eleanor and Sallie to sit down with the consultants. Eleanor had warily said yes; Sallie had announced that she would not grant an audience to people whose role in life "was to talk women into getting off boards."

To be sure, when the Dancos arrived in Louisville, that was uppermost on their agenda. "I was down there to convince people of the need for an outside board," said Léon, "to tell them as gently as possible that they had no talent." Even if Léon and Baby (his pet name for Katy) had been Philadelphia WASPs, they would have had difficulty overcoming the Seniors' distaste for outside advice on family matters. As it happened, the Dancos were Roman Catholic arrivistes, and so short and squat that the hired hands privately referred to them as "the dinky Dancos."

Katy proved to be gracious and sensible. Léon, however, impressed the Senior Binghams as a chatty egomaniac. He insisted on being addressed as "LAY-on," in the fashion of his Belgian parentage, and frequently tacked "Ph.D." after his name, lest anyone forget his degree in economics from Case Western. Even Barry Jr., his most enthusiastic booster, was dismayed to find that Léon seemed more interested in talking than listening.

Despite his penchant for one-way conversation, Léon managed to leave Louisville with definite views on the five disputants—the Seniors, the Ju-

niors, Eleanor and Rowland, Sallie, and the hired hands, whose stake in
what happened was as great as that of any family member. George Gill and
the other top executives, he said, were "better managers than most families
are able to attract," and he gave Barry Jr. high marks for finding and retaining them.

He had a very different impression of Eleanor and Rowland. In a meeting
with the Dancos, Eleanor complained that Barry Jr. had rejected her goal-
setting exercise and other efforts to be helpful. She and Rowland feared that
boards made up of outsiders might not realize that the $300,000 they
received each year in dividends was a necessity, not a luxury. To Léon, such
concerns were tediously familiar, the "standard uninvolved daughter things"
of "greed" and "wanting involvement." "Eleanor wasn't brought up to contribute," he said. "She had nothing to contribute. She was an overindulged
child with no discipline who had married a self-seeker."

The Dancos' lunch at the Little House was even less successful. Léon had
barely launched into his speech on the merits of stripping family members
from the boards when Barry Sr. interrupted. Newspapers are not like other
businesses, he informed Léon stiffly. From the Judge's era on, family considerations had often overruled business considerations, frequently creating
moments of greatness at the papers. The quasi-public nature of *The Courier-
Journal* and *Times* set them apart from soap factories or clothing manufactur-
ers.

Léon listened politely, but as soon as Barry Sr. finished, he took up where
he had left off, firmly insisting that newspapers were no different from any
other family enterprise. With that, an uncomfortable silence settled over
the oval marble table. The Senior Binghams' disdain for the Dancos was
almost palpable. Their attitude went far beyond conflicting ideas; it was
rooted, Léon was sure, in his religion and his ancestry. "I come from what I
consider to be a fine European family," he said. "But I wasn't a member of
the white Anglo-Saxon Protestant gentry. I didn't pass the confidence test."
Mary was especially class-conscious, watching his every move in the hope
of catching him in an error of etiquette. "The only person I've ever met like
that is my mother," said Léon with a shudder.

Over coffee and dessert, Léon told Barry Sr. and Mary that Sallie was
blackmailing them with her refusal to sign the buy-back. If they really
wanted to perpetuate the family business, he said, they were going to have
to be ruthless with her. The Seniors rejected the message—and the messen-
gers along with it. "I felt the Dancos had a lot of rather slick gobbledygook
which didn't seem to apply terribly strongly to our situation," Barry Sr. said.
"Awfully common," said Mary with an imperious sniff.

Though she was haughtily dismissive of the Dancos, Mary was furious at
Sallie's refusal to see them. Sallie declined even to discuss her reasons, a

position Mary considered petulant and childish, both cardinal failings. At Barry Jr.'s urging, the Senior Binghams summoned the family to the Little House to try to break the impasse before the Dancos left town.

Barry Jr. began by arguing that Sallie was being unreasonable. "Well, if you feel that way," Sallie said curtly, "I don't intend to discuss the subject any further." At that, Mary unleashed her legendary tongue. Out tumbled accusations so fierce and ferocious that Barry Jr. was embarrassed to have her on his side. "You are acting like a child," Mary told her daughter in a hard and condescending voice. "Your behavior is irrational." Sallie blanched. "I won't take this!" she screamed as she turned on her heel and stalked out of the house.

Barry Jr., who had been on the receiving end of his mother's wrath many times, knew that Mary had not helped his cause. "She is a sledgehammer," he said. "Sallie needs help and every time Mother gets a crack at her, she absolutely smashes her flat." As it happened, Mary's words had struck Sallie in the one place she was most vulnerable: her mental stability. Accusing her of being irrational was, to Sallie's mind, tantamount to suggesting that she was psychologically unbalanced.

Sallie did not talk to her mother after the blow-up. "She wrote me a note that said, 'If you're going to attack me, we just won't see each other anymore,' " Mary recalled. Mary's reply gave no quarter, but simply restated her long-held belief that parenthood implied distasteful responsibilities. "If you think it's an attack, I'm sorry," she told Sallie. "But it's my maternal duty to tell you when I think you're behaving in an unreasonable way."

There the matter stood. With no hope of seeing Sallie, the Dancos flew back to Cleveland. "If I had known that Sallie wasn't going to play, I would never have gone to Louisville in the first place," Léon said later. After the brutal exchange at the Little House, Barry Sr. wanted the board issue to disappear. Grudgingly, Barry Jr. let it subside, at least for the time being.

But the tranquility was misleading. The Danco visit had moved the family from being at odds to being at war.

In the aftermath of the Danco imbroglio, Eleanor and Sallie sought out Wilson Wyatt, the one person trusted by all parties. For years, Wilson had labored on strategies to minimize estate taxes so that the Binghams could keep their empire intact and in the family after the deaths of Barry Sr. and Mary. If the Binghams were not successful in passing the newspapers, broadcasting stations, and printing company to another generation, Wilson's life's work would be for naught. He was therefore eager to play mediator.

When Sallie and Eleanor asked how they could remain directors and still satisfy Barry Jr.'s desire for outside professionals, Wilson thought he had a solution. Instead of family members leaving the boards, he said, why don't all but the most senior executives leave? Earlier, Barry Jr. had rejected the idea of simply adding three or four professionals to the mix because it would make the Bingham boards, which had swelled over the years to almost twenty people, too large and unwieldy. Editors and other managers of the various family businesses made up about half the membership and that seemed unnecessary. These aides could still report to the boards, said Wilson, and even sit in on meetings from time to time. But they did not have to be full members.

Barry Sr. hailed Wilson's plan as a "great agreement" and the hired hands indicated that they would be happy to give up their seats. Barry Jr., however, was not satisfied. Wilson's compromise begged the central issue, he said. His sisters did not contribute. They added nothing. To see how far his father would push the concept of "family," Barry Jr. pointed out that Eleanor wanted Rowland on the boards, too. "Well, that's just one more," Barry Sr. said genially. The prospect of his brother-in-law sitting across the table from him discussing corporate strategy and profit levels made Barry Jr. cringe, and only reinforced his conviction that all "noncontributing" family members must be purged.

A few weeks later, Barry Jr. gathered his management team at the River Valley Club for their customary Tuesday lunch. When the meal was completed, Barry Jr. quietly informed the group that he had made up his mind. His sisters would have to leave the company boards. He intended to insist on it.

He then said he would go around the table and give each executive a chance to express his view. As was his custom, he wrote down everything that was said. All of Barry Jr.'s advisers begged him not to throw his sisters off the boards. "Don't do this, it could be the worst thing you've ever done," Bob Morse told him. George Gill refuted Barry Jr.'s contention that his sisters were a burden on the staff. "We don't mind doing chores for Sallie and Eleanor," he said. "It's part of the job." Even soft-spoken Bernie Block made an impassioned plea. "You're threatening to break up this whole ownership because you won't tolerate your sisters," he said, shocking everyone with his accusatory tone. "Have you thought about us and our families?"

Barry Jr.'s only reaction was to scratch down their objections and anxieties on his notepad. After the last man had had his say, he looked up. "I've already made my decision, but I will convey what you've said to my father."

Only one person on the management team had been equivocal in his views: Paul Janensch. "I didn't say, 'That's great,' and I didn't say, 'Don't do it,'" Paul recalled. "I really felt that this was something for George Gill and Leon Tallichet to talk to him about." Paul understood Barry Jr. very well. Indeed, he had made a point of getting close to him since succeeding Bob Clark as executive editor in 1979. He knew that Sallie and Eleanor's feelings and other psychological considerations did not matter to Barry Jr. when he had persuaded himself that something was a matter of principle.

Barry Jr. was equally indifferent to business advice. For years the hired hands had argued that the family should buy newspapers in other communities. Such properties could serve as training grounds for reporters, editors, and even for the Bingham grandchildren, they said, allowing them to try their wings before graduating to *The Courier-Journal* and *Times*. But Barry Jr. had refused, saying that an owner should live where his newspaper is published. End of debate.

In much the same way, Barry Jr. dismissed his advisers' warnings about his sisters. Recognizing that the board issue was another example of Barry Jr.'s fierce intransigence, Paul kept his mouth shut. "To Barry, it was a matter of, 'Well, this is the right thing to do and we are just going to do it,'" he said.

———

Paul had another reason for not joining George Gill and the others as they alternately reasoned and pleaded with their resolute boss. Early that summer, Barry Jr. had tapped Paul to serve as acting editor and publisher of the papers during a nine-month sabbatical he intended to take starting in September 1984—a full year away.

Though Barry Jr. had already informed the Senior Binghams and his top lieutenants of his plans, he waited until August 1983 to tell Sallie and Eleanor. He and Edie would spend the 1984–85 academic year at Smith College, he said. She would finish her degree, and he would explore the practicality of electronic publishing.

Sallie and Eleanor greeted the news with unbridled enthusiasm. "They said, 'Whoopee! Wonderful! Wonderful! Do go away. Do leave soon. Don't hurry back,'" Barry Jr. recalled with considerable resentment. He felt his parents also seemed a bit too eager to see him off. All this fed his worst fear: that Barry Sr. and Mary were tilting away from him and toward his sisters, perhaps even conspiring with them to dilute his power.

The Senior Binghams and Sallie and Eleanor had indeed found common ground on one thing: their horror at the idea that Paul Janensch would be in charge of the newspapers during Barry Jr.'s absence. The depth and breadth of antipathy that Paul had managed to arouse in both the family and the staff was truly remarkable. Barry Sr. and Mary "despised" him, according to one of their close friends. Eleanor and Rowland "hated" him. Bob Morse could not understand why Barry Jr. was "so blind to the fact that Paul was totally inept." Maury Buchart found him "intellectually arrogant." Leon Tallichet thought Paul had damn little business sense. In fact, he said, "I'd question his news ability."

What had Paul done to warrant such feelings? As far as his critics were concerned, he was an abrasive tyrant who edited newspapers that were not nearly as good as he had convinced Barry Jr. they were. His Sunday column was hokey; the papers had become cynical and dull. Paul's physical appearance only exaggerated his natural hauteur. "He's a little cross-eyed, he's got some vision problems," said John Richards. "It often looks like a sneer is there when I don't think a sneer is meant." He was also a relentless social climber, hungry for prestige and power. And he had calculatingly ingratiated himself with the boss. "Paul was a great sycophant," said Mary, using the same tone she applied to descriptions of the loathed Mannie Levi.

Barry Jr. considered Paul the victim of an unjustified vendetta. "Paul is a resurrection," he said. "I mean, when Paul first went to work for us, he was such a son of a bitch [that] people used to cross the street just to avoid talking with him. He was a one-upsman of the first order."

Since then, Barry Jr. said, Paul had changed. He still considered him tough enough to deserve his newsroom nickname—"Darth Vader"—but he felt that Paul had learned to control his temper and muzzle his put-downs. This new Paul could "accomplish some things," Barry Jr. noted with approval. And these "things" were projects Barry Jr. cared about deeply, like boosting the number of women and blacks on the news staff.

Born in Winnetka, Illinois, a wealthy Chicago suburb, Paul had studied philosophy at Georgetown University before deciding on a newspaper career. Norman Isaacs had hired him straight out of the Graduate School of Journalism at Columbia University in 1964, and put him to work covering civil rights in Alabama and Mississippi. George Gill, then the CJ's managing editor, made him city editor in 1968. But after four years in the job, Paul hit a snag.

He thought he had earned a reputation as a can-do guy, but the truth was somewhat less flattering. "He was abusive," said Bernie Block. The consensus in the newsroom was that Paul was trying to imitate Norman Isaacs. Paul once asked a political reporter to do a story and he refused. "I can't," the reporter explained. "It would mean burning my sources." Paul's face grew red. He bent down, picked up a pile of old newspapers, and heaved them at the man like a sulky child. "You do it because I told you to do it!" he yelled. George Gill backed up the reporter and Paul later apologized.

Another time, a reporter inadvertently left a company tape recorder at a news scene. Someone returned it to Paul, who called the man into his office. "Where's your tape recorder?" he demanded. The reporter said he did not know, but he would go back to his desk and try to find it. At that, Paul pulled the tape recorder out of his drawer. "Don't you ever lie to me again," he said. Such exchanges did not win friends.

So, in 1972, when Cy MacKinnon was looking for someone to take over a Bingham subsidiary called *Pollution Abstracts*, Paul's name was at the top of everyone's list. Cy had been pushing to diversify, but Barry Jr., typically, had been unwilling to buy another news organization. *Pollution Abstracts*, a San Diego–based journal on oceans and pollution control, seemed like an agreeable compromise, and Cy snapped it up without auditing the books, only to find that it was a financial mess. He needed a good publisher and he needed one fast.

He asked each department head to recommend able people who needed broadening. "Every department sent me the guys they wanted to get rid of," said Cy. "George Gill sent me Janensch, and we took him because he was the only one who had any sense out of the whole damn lot." Paul was told to make the company profitable and bring it back to Louisville—or dump it. "He did a good job," George conceded.

Paul assumed that success in San Diego would pave the way to a top editor's job in Louisville, but he had made more enemies in the newsroom than he realized. In 1974, when reporters heard that Paul was lobbying hard from California to succeed George Gill as the *CJ*'s managing editor, they mounted a formal protest with Barry Jr. Soon thereafter, Barry Jr. appointed Carol Sutton to take George's place.

Paul made no secret of his disappointment, but returned to Louisville anyway, where he got a chilly reception. "The water just closed up behind him," said George. "There wasn't anything for him." Even Cy MacKinnon was helpless. "I thought we could squeeze him back in, but we couldn't," he said. "The newspeople wouldn't hear of his going back."

In 1975, after spending six months in a nothing job in the personnel department, Paul jumped at the chance to be managing editor of *The Philadelphia Daily News*, a tabloid owned by the Knight-Ridder chain. Barry Jr. felt terrible about losing him. He had been impressed with the way Paul had turned *Pollution Abstracts* into a going concern, and the very fact that a person left seemed to enhance his value and make Barry Jr. want to win him back.

When Carol Sutton's star began to fade in 1976, Barry Jr. went courting in Philadelphia. Executive editor Bob Clark was considered too nice to run a tight ship, and Carol was thought too enamored of soft news to continue as managing editor of *The Courier-Journal*. Maybe there was virtue to a hard-bitten type like Paul after all, Barry Jr. told himself.

Cy MacKinnon persuaded Barry Jr. that Paul Janensch was just the man for a top editorial position at the Louisville papers. Paul was tempted, but uncertain whether he wanted to uproot his family again. Barry Sr. and Mary happened to be in Philadelphia in April 1976, and took Paul and his wife, Gail, a onetime *CJ* consumer reporter, out to dinner. A few days later, Barry Sr. sent Paul a courtly letter encouraging him to rejoin the Louisville papers. It made a big impression. "You know," Gail told her husband, "it sure is different working for a family than for a corporation."

When reporters got wind that Paul might be coming back, they immediately assumed he would be replacing Carol Sutton as M.E. of the *Courier*. Once again they stormed into Barry Jr.'s office. This time, two of them even threatened to resign. Anxiety about "the second coming," as reporters called the second Paul Janensch-as-M.E.-scare, was so pronounced that Barry Jr. felt compelled to distribute a memo saying that Paul had taken a course in human relations and was "a changed man."

Not long afterward, the Louisville papers announced that Michael Davies would move into Carol Sutton's slot at the *Courier* and Paul Janensch would take Davies's job as managing editor at *The Louisville Times*. The story included high praise from Barry Jr., who said that Paul had "broad management experience and is known as an innovative editor." To Paul's many adversaries, the news augured ill. With a touch of black humor, they noted that Paul's return was scheduled for Midsummer Night, the summer solstice, fabled as a time when men went mad and fell in love with jackasses.

Barry Jr. was a major reason Paul returned to Louisville. He did not know the Bingham heir well at the time, but he admired his independence and his appetite for hard work. "I was comfortable with him," said Paul. "I liked him. I thought he was a decent guy, and I don't mean soft-headed or wimpy. But a decent guy. I thought he had good instincts."

And Paul, in many respects, was just right for Barry Jr. He did not poke fun at Barry Jr.'s electronic newspaper fantasy, unlike George Gill, who pooh-poohed the idea as inimical to democracy. "Everybody always hated to hear the wired city speech," said George. "He would get going and we'd say, 'Barry, don't give it to us again.'" Paul did not kid Barry Jr. that way. Ever.

As managing editor of *The Louisville Times*, Paul tried to show that he was no longer a hectoring bully. To suggest collegiality, he knocked down the walls of his office and replaced them with glass, a fishbowl effect that Ben Bradlee, executive editor of *The Washington Post*, had recently introduced to his newsroom. But the old Paul was not so easily exorcised. "He'd run out into the newsroom shouting at the top of his lungs, 'What idiot wrote this?'"

said Mary Phyllis Riedley. "I don't think there was a person on that staff that didn't have this feeling that he was out to get them."

Paul's determination to get the job done managed to survive the frenzy of self-improvement. When he returned to Louisville in 1976, economies had begun to be imposed at the Bingham papers. It did not go unnoticed that Paul Janensch was the only editor who did not treat his budget casually. He was also credited with infusing more hard news into the afternoon paper, which Barry Jr. feared had become too fluffy and feature-oriented in its effort to attract readers. To combat a string of rival weeklies that was nipping at the CJ & T's heels, Paul started several "Neighborhoods" sections to cover selected parts of the county with localized news and advertising.

When Michael Davies left the Louisville papers in 1978, few were surprised to see Paul tapped as *The Courier-Journal's* new managing editor. Less than a year later, Bob Clark resigned as executive editor, unhappy over being asked to slash expenses to reach the 12 percent profit goal the Bingham board of directors had recently adopted. Paul not only accepted the 12 percent goal as realistic and prudent, he had the stomach for the dirty work of reducing editorial costs. With little fanfare, Paul was made executive editor and given operational control over both papers.

Paul's first move as top editor was to institute a daily, one-on-one briefing with Barry Jr. Every morning, Paul would appear at his boss's door and the two of them would huddle together for thirty minutes or so. When Paul was managing editor of the *Times* and then *The Courier-Journal*, he and Barry Jr. had been cordial but distant, reflecting Barry Jr.'s chain-of-command style of management. As executive editor, Paul felt free to discuss more philosophical subjects with the publisher, like journalistic ethics and the importance of preserving editorial quality.

To his joy, Barry Jr. discovered that he and Paul agreed on most issues and shared many of the same approaches. They were both true believers, literalists, pragmatists by necessity, although not by inclination. In time, their professional similarities led them to venture into other critical subjects, such as Sallie and Eleanor and the mounting problems in the family.

Despite his many galling qualities, Paul had superb political instincts. He understood the importance of keeping the Bingham sisters on the reservation and he tried hard to accommodate them, if only for defensive reasons. In 1980, soon after Eleanor had begun work at WHAS, she invited Paul to lunch. At the time, she seemed eager to forge an alliance, and suggested that perhaps she could serve as a "communicator" between Barry Jr. and the managers at WHAS.

Paul did not want to alienate Eleanor, but he realized that it would be professional suicide for him to appear to line up with her against Barry Jr. His solution was to write a memo to Barry Jr. outlining the conversation and underscoring his loyalty. "I said that I would oppose any move that I thought might undermine Barry's effectiveness—no matter who favored it," he wrote.

In the same document, he tried gently to warn Barry Jr. that it would be unwise to shut his sister out. "I wish there was a way for the companies to tap Eleanor's energy, brains and talent," he wrote. ". . . it might be dangerous to have her feel she was being excluded." He then suggested that Eleanor be allowed to head a "small high-powered unit to make documentaries and special segments." Barry Jr. rejected the idea, never mentioning it to his parents, and Paul let it drop. In many ways, Paul was Barry Jr.'s dream lieutenant: unswerving, uncritical, and unfailingly respectful.

Soon, company president George Gill, who had his own audience with Barry Jr. each morning after Paul's, began to notice a subtle change. When he stuck his head in the door, Barry Jr. and Paul would fall silent. "Give us another minute," Barry Jr. would say, and George would withdraw. After a few months, when George stuck his head in, Barry Jr. would look up and say, "Got anything for the two of us?" George then had little choice but to come in and brief them both.

By late 1982, George had had enough. He refused to talk to Barry Jr. if Paul was present. He was befuddled by Barry Jr.'s shifting loyalties. He had considered his professional relationship with the Bingham heir rock-solid and his personal bond genuine, especially after all he had done to help him. Now he seemed to have been dropped with all the speed of a soured love affair. "There's something funny," George would tell the other hired hands. "I can't put my finger on it. There's just a chill in the air." George's wife thought she had it figured out. "Barry doesn't want anybody close to him," she told him, "and you were getting too close."

To be sure, George aggravated the situation by making astringent comments about Paul's management. He would often interrupt his reading of *The Courier-Journal* and *Times* to cry in a lamenting tone, "Where *are* the editors!" Stories were too long, he said. The front page was colorless and unfocused. George felt he had a right to make such judgments; after all, he had once been managing editor of *The Courier-Journal*. But Barry Jr. seemed to have forgotten that George had ever been a newsman. Increasingly, he saw his company president as a member of the conservative Louisville business establishment that he and Paul so distrusted. Finally, Barry Jr. told George to shut up about how the papers were edited. It was not his concern.

In late 1982 and early 1983, Barry Jr. confused the hired hands further by becoming obsessed with what he called "the regency." One by one, he called the top executives into his office and asked them who they thought should take over as editor and publisher if he were no longer around.

Presumably, a Bingham grandchild would eventually fill the top position, but no one in the fourth generation was old enough to assume leadership if Barry Jr. got hit by a truck or died in a plane crash. The hired hands suspected he had had a relapse of cancer and was just not telling them. But he insisted he was fine.

It soon became clear that Barry Jr. was wavering between George and Paul as designated regent, should the need arise. The hired hands were aghast. "To a man, everyone said, 'For God's sake, it can't be Janensch,' " said John Richards. They shared George's distaste for Paul, who they thought had gotten increasingly pompous and self-important as he had grown closer to Barry Jr.

In March 1983, Barry Jr. produced a six-page document setting out his hopes and requirements for the family member who succeeded him, in the event of his "death, incapacitation or other absence." It was a manifesto for future Bingham generations to follow. His successor, the letter said, should not use the papers "for his own aggrandizement, benefit or partisan support of individuals or causes. . . . [A] position of such responsibility should not be interpreted as an entree to privilege, but rather an opportunity for responsibility and service to the community and its citizens. I can in no way over-emphasize my devotion to this concept."

Although the document explicitly ruled out gender as a consideration, it took a swipe at Sallie by restricting potential successors to those who had signed the stock buy-back agreement. As for the "interim executive" who might be required to fill in until a suitable family member was ready, he said that the person would be designated in a "side letter" that he would sign and put in the company safe, to be opened only if circumstances required. Barry Jr. did not say whose name he would put in the "side letter," or even if he had written it.

A couple of months later, the mystery of Barry Jr.'s "regency" obsession was solved when, at one of their regular management lunches, he told the hired hands of his sabbatical plans. Since he did not indicate that anything would be different, except that he would be gone, they did not consider the news particularly alarming. George already ran things anyway; little would change while Barry was away.

After the lunch, Barry Jr. asked George to come into his office. As soon as he had settled into a chair, Barry Jr. looked his president and chief executive officer in the eye and told him that Paul Janensch would become acting editor and publisher from the fall of 1984 to the summer of 1985— the sabbatical year. What is more, he expected George to report to Paul just as he now reported to Barry Jr.

George reacted as if he had been clubbed. "This is un . . . un . . . unacceptable," he stammered to Barry Jr. With that, he got up, strode out of the office, down the corridor to the elevators, and out into the parking lot. "I didn't come to work the next day," he said. "That's the first time I'd ever done that." He sat on his patio with a yellow legal pad and thought about what to do.

He decided that he would not resign, nor would he accept what the Bingham heir had decreed. Instead, he told Barry Jr. that he would not under any circumstances report to Paul Janensch during the sabbatical year; neither would he demand that Paul report to him. Both would report directly to Barry Jr., using a modem and an uplink to pass messages between Louisville and Northampton. George would remain in charge of WHAS and Standard Gravure. Paul, as acting editor and publisher, would control all aspects of the newspapers, including the business operations and editorial pages.

Furthermore, George said, I want a management contract. The request was shocking: No Bingham executive had ever asked for a contract. At first, Barry Jr. balked, refusing to believe that companies even permitted such agreements. After finding out that they were common at other large Louisville firms, he reluctantly allowed one to be drawn up for George, and later for other top executives, including Paul Janensch. "This contract tells me you don't trust me," Barry Jr. protested. "I don't," said George.

The other hired hands were stunned at Barry Jr.'s apparent vote of no confidence in George and requested a meeting to air their concerns. "This is a Harvard case study of how not to run a company!" one wailed in hand-wringing despair. Barry Jr. did not dispute the assessment. "I know," he said. "But this is what I have to do. I have to test the bench. I have to find out if Paul is capable of being publisher of this company if something happens to me." All at once it became clear. Barry Jr. was seriously considering naming Paul as his "regent"; the sabbatical year was a tryout.

Though Barry Jr. told no one at the time, the most compelling reason he did not make George acting publisher was that it would have given him control of the editorial pages. To Barry Jr., that would have been comparable to Judge Bingham turning *The Courier-Journal* and *Times* over to Mannie Levi when he left for the Court of St. James's. Barry Jr. believed in rigid distinctions between church and state. And he considered George state, despite his credentials as a newsman. Only a fellow clergyman and true believer like Paul could be entrusted with the ultimate church, the editorial pages. Besides, George, who complained about high taxes and other business concerns, was beginning to sound too conservative to suit Barry Jr.

Shortly before Labor Day, 1983, in the pages of *The Louisville Times*, Barry Jr. went public with his sabbatical plans and his decisions about interim management of the papers. George squirmed in embarrassment. The incident was a stinging reminder of the horse race Barry Jr. had forced him to endure in 1980. Only this time, George was the one who lost. The humiliation of it all made George and Paul sworn enemies, and George's relationship with Barry Jr. never recovered. "It dropped right off the cliff, and never got back out," said Leon Tallichet.

——————

While Barry Jr. was hammering out the regency and his sabbatical plans, Sallie and Eleanor were embroiled in schemes of their own. Sallie's was straightforward, Eleanor's more subterranean.

Sallie had been bruised by her brother's accusation that she contributed nothing as a director. After all, she had attended meetings of the newspaper board fairly conscientiously and had never cast a nay vote. "I raised a ruckus but it was a genteel ruckus," she said. She had been terrified at first and had written down everything that was said, as though she were back in college taking lecture notes. She persuaded herself that maybe all she needed to do was to demonstrate to Barry Jr. that she was making a good faith effort to learn the ropes.

That summer, Sallie traveled to Cambridge to meet with Rosabeth Kanter, whose consulting firm, Goodmeasure, Inc., advised women on corporate boards. The result was a step-by-step blueprint for being a better board member. Sallie showed the recommendations to features editor Irene Nolan. "It was absolutely amazing," Irene recalled. "Perfectly detailed. Exactly what Sallie should do."

Part of the plan was for Sallie to meet independently with the family's top executives to learn more about the business, something they were eager to do. The sessions usually produced more heat than light, however. During one of Sallie's better-board-member interviews, George Gill suggested that she start thinking about how to prepare her sons and the other Bingham grandchildren to enter the family business. "You know," he said offhandedly, "there are seven little bastards in that generation and they're not getting any younger." To his astonishment, Sallie took offense at his language and later dissolved in tears. George had to pay her a visit and formally apologize before things were patched up. "I was dead wrong," he told her. "I didn't realize you'd be that sensitive."

Try as she might, Sallie could not seem to grasp the big picture at the newspapers. After each audience, she would return to Irene Nolan and talk in excited tones about some minor point that had captured her attention. "She just had no street smarts," said Irene. "The thing she always grabbed ahold of was women and minorities, and she would go off telling people,

'Oh, the *Courier* is just terrible on women and minorities.' I kept saying, 'Sallie, don't say that. The news department has one of the best records on women and minorities of any newspaper in the country.' And I would show her the figures and she would turn right around and do it again."

But facts did not interest Sallie. What preoccupied her was what she called "the politics of helplessness." She had just finished writing two plays, *Paducah* and *The Wall Between*. Both dealt with this issue. In *Paducah*, a woman who has left her husband comes home to take stock of her life, only to find her father unable to provide the emotional sustenance she craves. In *The Wall Between*, a play based on the Carl Braden case, a wealthy white woman and her black female servant develop a kinship after discovering they are both victims of society.

If Sallie felt drawn to helplessness, Eleanor longed to bask in the parental warmth she had been denied as a child, and she found that Sallie's fury and Barry Jr.'s rigidity had created an opening for her to do just that. While Barry Jr. and Sallie battled for their parents' favor, Eleanor crawled softly into their laps like a purring tabby.

Mary shared Eleanor's growing concern about what she considered the papers' "general aura of dour pessimism." The two women felt that, with Barry Jr.'s complicity, Paul Janensch had changed the tone of *The Courier-Journal* and *Times* from skepticism to hard-bitten cynicism. All politicians were scoundrels; headlines such as "Lame Duck Session . . . May Be Turkey" implied arrogance and scorn. To make matters worse, people in Louisville seemed to hold every member of the Bingham family responsible. Eleanor and Rowland, especially, felt besieged by the newspapers' critics as they made their way on the city's cocktail and dinner party circuit.

In her disgruntled daughter, Mary saw an ally to help her launch a corrective mission at the papers. Darts and arrows at dinner parties did not bother her when she felt the papers were in the right, but now she was taking heat for positions she frequently disagreed with. Worse still, people had begun to laugh at some of the things *The Courier-Journal* and *Times* did. She cared passionately about the reputation of the two newspapers she had read every day for fifty years. To think they were being held up to ridicule made her shudder.

Thus a sub rosa alliance was launched, fueled by dismay at the way Barry Jr. and Paul were running the papers. For months, letters flew between Eleanor and Mary as they compared notes on the latest outrage. Eleanor was flattered that her mother considered her a worthy confidante. It implied that Mary thought her intelligent and mature, qualities that Eleanor had never been sure she possessed. At one point, Mary drew up a laundry list of complaints about the papers and sent it to Eleanor and Rowland for their comments. Eleanor was effusively complimentary. "Thank you so much for letting us see your letter," she gushed. "We are really honored."

Later, in the spring of 1983, Eleanor wrote a confidential six-page memorandum to her father. It was a highly unflattering appraisal of Paul Janensch, Bob Morse, George Gill, and her brother, whom she charged with "abdication of responsibility." Although the memo was meant for Barry Sr.'s eyes only, he brought the document along to the March board meeting and left it on the table. Later, a secretary found it and gave the memo to Barry Jr., who returned it to Eleanor, along with a cover letter making it plain that he had distributed copies to Paul, Leon, and George. He signed the letter, "love, Barry."

To Barry Jr., the memo, which came to be known as the "Pumpkin Papers," was further evidence that Eleanor was a loose cannon and hostile to his management team.* But he was glad it had come to his attention. Maybe now the hired hands would realize that his sisters should be pushed off the board after all.

George Gill did not react that way. When Barry Jr. showed George the memo, George begged him to return it quietly to Eleanor and not make copies for the others. "It will just rub salt in the wound," he said. "Please don't." But Barry Jr. was determined to teach his kid sister a lesson. It did not bother him that Eleanor might find the disclosure embarrassing. "That's just the consequence of what she said," he said.

Eleanor regarded her brother's distribution of her memo as a treacherous assault intended to discredit her with the company's top managers. She was equally furious at her father, who, she strongly suspected, had left the memo behind on purpose so that her doubts about Barry Jr.'s leadership, which he shared, would be out in the open without his telltale fingerprints. "That was certainly not what happened," said Barry Sr., who insisted that the incident was inadvertent and "just the most unfortunate event."

The Pumpkin Papers had a very different effect from what Barry Jr. intended. Instead of discrediting Eleanor with the staff, it discredited Barry Jr. with Mary, who considered the whole affair mean-spirited and further proof that her son suffered from a martyr complex. His treatment of Eleanor demonstrated that he was rigid and unkind, she felt, just as Sallie was irrational and wrong-headed. In contrast, Eleanor seemed a model of reasonableness—a position not without power.

Indeed, even as Barry Jr. was telling the hired hands that he was deter-

---

* Pumpkin Papers refers to the microfilm *Time* editor Whittaker Chambers retrieved in 1948 from a hollowed-out pumpkin on his Maryland farm at the behest of Richard M. Nixon, then a young congressman on the House Un-American Activities Committee. The material helped convict alleged Communist Alger Hiss of perjury and launched Nixon's national political career.

mined to remove his sisters from the board, Eleanor and Rowland were using their leverage with the Senior Binghams to make their first real power play. They wanted more voting stock.

———

About the time Barry Jr. took command of the businesses in 1971, a plan was devised to pass voting control of the companies to him at the death of his parents while paying a minimum of estate taxes. Barry Sr. and Mary owned a majority of the voting and nonvoting stock. Over the years, they had given Barry Jr. mostly "voting preferred" stock, which paid a minimal dividend. At the same time, they had given Sallie and Eleanor mostly "nonvoting common stock," which paid hefty dividends. Barry Jr. thus had greater voting power and less cash, while Sallie and Eleanor had more dividend income and less clout. The idea was to create a power/money trade-off that would make each child feel that he or she had been treated equitably by Barry Sr. and Mary.

At a family meeting in the summer of 1983, shortly after the Dancos had left town, Eleanor made it clear that she thought the distribution of voting stock was unfair. Her grievance was soon lost in a chorus of other complaints ranging from her dissatisfaction with the division of the Glenview property to a demand that Bingham board members have special access to company officers.

As at most Bingham gatherings, there was no resolution, and Barry Jr. did not think twice about the voting-stock question, which he knew had been settled in 1971. But Eleanor did not drop the idea. Her father, in fact, came to think there might be something in it. If Sallie and Eleanor had a larger stake in the companies, he thought, perhaps they would play a more constructive role in their operations. And maybe Barry Jr. would start treating them with more tact.

Barry Jr. did not realize that his father had had a change of heart until Gordon Davidson, the family attorney, advised him that his total share of the voting stock, made up of the blocks he already owned and the additional voting stock he stood to inherit upon his parents' deaths, was going to shrink from 67 percent to 54 percent. Gordon said that Barry Sr. had informed him that, based on a conversation he had had with his son, Barry Jr. had "accepted the concept" of his sisters each owning 20 percent of the voting stock. After all, Barry Jr. only needed 50.1 percent to have control.

It was a classic Barry Sr. no-blood-on-his-hands maneuver. Barry Sr. and Mary were in Chatham at the time, and Barry Jr. recalled no such talk; he certainly had not "accepted the concept." He believed, as Judge Bingham had, that voting stock should be concentrated in one person. From time to time, he had even reminded his father with ill-concealed envy that Henrietta and Robert had been given no stock whatsoever.

Only by owning a large majority of voting stock, Barry Jr. argued, could he pass control on to the next generation of Binghams without having to pay huge inheritance taxes. What is more, a 20 percent block of voting stock would be far more attractive to an outside buyer than roughly 11 percent, the total Sallie and Eleanor would each own after their parents' deaths under the current arrangement. And his sisters were perfectly within their rights to sell. Neither had signed the buy-back pledge. Barry Jr. knew that Gordon was aware of these considerations, and he sensed that his father had put the lawyer in an uncomfortable position: as Gordon made his pitch, he could not even look Barry Jr. in the eye.

Barry Jr. suspected that the whole conspiracy had been cooked up by his sisters in partnership with his parents. That part hurt. "I'll wait until I hear some more reasoning behind this," he told Gordon coldly. And that seemed to end the matter. Barry Sr., fearful as usual of a confrontation, never pressed it, and Barry Jr. heard no more about it. "It just died," he said.

The voting stock incident occurred in late August 1983, shortly before Barry Jr. made his sabbatical plans public. That, combined with the Pumpkin Papers, Eleanor and Rowland's complaints about negativism at the papers, and his sisters' unabashed joy at the prospect of his leaving, if only for nine months, made Barry Jr. extremely uneasy. He did not want them making trouble on the boards of directors while he was exploring electronic journalism in Northampton. In the fall of 1983, he decided to force his parents to make a choice: Either banish Sallie and Eleanor from the boards by the time I leave one year hence, or I will be gone from the company.

Barry Jr. was tense when he met with his father in late September 1983. His distress was apparent as he told Barry Sr. that a solution had to be found to the family problems. "I can't continue doing this job for fifteen more years," he said, alluding to the gap between his present age and retirement at sixty-five. "We are in a declining business, which is demoralizing, and Sallie and Eleanor don't trust me."

The most difficult thing to deal with, he said, was "the feeling that the family was losing faith. That somehow we didn't have a shared dream anymore. . . . That, as I was trying to keep an ethical, high-quality operation [going], the family seemed to be becoming more critical and less supportive. . . . That's the most debilitating experience I've had, and I would put it way beyond Hodgkin's disease and way beyond the death of either of my brothers."

Then Barry Jr. dropped the bomb he had come to deliver: Maybe we should find someone else to run these companies, he said, someone you and Mother and Sallie and Eleanor *do* trust. Someone else. The ultimatum produced the desired effect. "I took it very seriously," Barry Sr. said. "I considered it a cry for help." But he felt that the idea of Barry Jr. stepping down was totally unacceptable. It would be nearly impossible to find a suitable outsider, he said. Of those available on staff, Paul Janensch would probably be his son's first choice—and that was highly unpalatable to Barry Sr. and Mary. Worse still, if Barry Jr. vacated his post, it would be an astonishing admission of weakness. Family pride was at stake.

A week after saying he could not go on, Barry Jr. gave his father a bleak "options" memo outlining three scenarios: (1) sell all three companies; (2) remove the "irrational element"—meaning his sisters—from the boards; or (3) get a new publisher.

Barry Sr. was in agony as he tried to find some way out of this dilemma that would keep the family and the business intact. "I kept on hoping in a Micawber-like way that some solution would develop," he said. But, in fact, a subtle sea change had occurred. Barry Jr. had put "Option X"—Bingham shorthand for selling the family business—on the table as a serious possibility for the first time.

Though he shrank from the thought of selling, Barry Sr. asked the hired hands to come up with an analysis of what each family member would get if the companies were put on the auction block. Unsure of how to read this latest change in strategy, Barry Jr. became alarmed. Although he had proposed selling as an option himself, he certainly did not want his father to choose it. Early in November, he confronted Barry Sr. again. "If we sell the companies," he told him, "I will have to say something about the options we passed up." Specifically, he said he would feel compelled to disclose the roots of family discord, including Sallie's intransigence over the buy-back and the Dancos.

This new threat sent Barry Sr. reeling. He told his son that he would look ridiculous. How else to describe a man who gives up a company just because his sister is an impossible person to do business with? Besides, Barry Sr. argued, such an attack could be very dangerous to Sallie's fragile psyche. He feared she would lash out with tremendous bitterness at her brother, and probably at him, too. She might even commit suicide. "Anybody with her history faced with that kind of violent, destructive criticism would be at risk," said Mary.

Barry Jr. coolly observed that it hardly seemed logical for his father to portray Sallie one moment as a very troubled woman and the next to say she should remain on the boards.

Despite the tempest swirling around them, the autumn of 1983 was particularly happy for Sallie and Eleanor. Eleanor was pregnant again.* Sallie had gotten married to Tim Peters earlier that summer and had managed to recapture a surface cordiality with her mother, although relations in the wake of the Danco affair were still strained.

The Seniors had helped heal the breach by hosting a wedding reception for Sallie and her new husband aboard the *Belle of Louisville*, an old river steamboat. Eleanor and Rowland felt closer than ever to Barry Sr. and Mary, and were delighted that they seemed to take such joy in Rowlie, their firstborn. With peace and serenity all around them, Sallie and Eleanor assumed that the "board issue" had drifted mercifully away. They were unaware of Barry Jr.'s threats and behind-the-scenes lobbying efforts that September; the Seniors had not told them.

But news like that was too explosive to be kept quiet for long. In late October, Gordon Davidson took Eleanor aside and, in a conspiratorial whisper, told her that "something terrible" was going to happen before Thanksgiving. He would not say what. Neither would her parents.

Shortly before the holiday, the Seniors invited Sallie and Eleanor to the Little House for dinner. Barry Sr. said he had something to tell them. After the meal, as they settled into the study for demitasse and cookies, Barry Sr. cleared his throat. For a moment, a look of panic swept over his face.

He told Sallie and Eleanor that he had reluctantly decided to remove all family members, including himself, from the Bingham boards of directors. By stepping down along with his wife, daughters, and daughter-in-law, Barry Sr. hoped not only to soften the blow to Sallie and Eleanor, but also to make plausible Barry Jr.'s contention that it was the "family," not just "women," he wanted off the board. Why had the Senior Binghams yielded to their son's demands? "It was Barry Jr.'s desperation, his obsession," explained Mary. "And the fact that he wouldn't listen to a reasonable compromise. We just felt that he wouldn't be able to go on."

Beyond that, though, Barry Sr. and Mary offered no explanation for their decision. "My father's attitude was, 'I don't understand this myself, but you must do it,' " Sallie said. "He probably thought everyone would do it. That was his experience with women, that they'd do it."

If so, Barry Sr. was in for a big surprise. Sallie defiantly said that she had no intention of resigning. It was nonsense. Barry Jr. had no right to strip her of membership on the boards. It was sexist. He was incompetent. Mary listened to the tirade until she could take no more. "You are trying to destroy your brother!" she said in a deadly tone. "You are being vengeful. Don't you care what we think of you?" Sallie stared back at her mother

---

* The baby was stillborn several months later.

through a blur of tears. She was in her mid-forties. The moment was symbolic. Was she going to remain a child forever? "No," she said firmly. "I really don't [care]."

Eleanor was more compliant. She seemed willing to go along, if that was necessary to keep her parents happy and the empire intact. All the same, the rejection stung and she could not bring herself to face her brother just yet. The next day she called Barry Jr. and Edie and canceled Thanksgiving dinner.

Agonized by Sallie's furious reaction and Eleanor's clear distress, Barry Sr. began to lose his resolve. By mid-December, the compact he had made with Barry Jr. started to unravel. "This is tearing me in two," he told his son in a halting voice. "I just cannot bring myself to pressure Sallie and Eleanor into leaving the boards. Why can't you compromise? Why can't you just ignore Sallie?"

His father's change of heart sent Barry Jr. into despair. At a gathering of the family shortly before Christmas, he seemed to be coming unglued. Again he offered to resign in favor of an outside publisher. Sallie and Eleanor looked at each other in amazement. They had no idea that that option was even on the table. Realizing how appealing the notion would be, especially to Sallie, the Senior Binghams had kept them in the dark. "It was painful," said Sallie. "Barry looked like someone who was pleading to be honorably relieved. . . . He just looked at me in the most piercing way and said, 'Maybe you can think of somebody who could run these companies.'"

Sallie seized on the offer. After the holidays she appeared in Barry Jr.'s office, and in her most silky and solicitous voice told her brother that she wanted to help him hire an outside publisher. Barry Jr. stiffened and informed her that she was being a bit premature. The family had not yet chosen that route and he had made it clear he wanted it only as a last resort. That may be so, said Sallie, but you did say "It's up to the family, it's the family's choice."

Undaunted, Sallie mounted a campaign to remove her brother from office that was as energetic and single-minded as was his effort to get her off the boards. In early January 1984, she requested a family meeting to talk about replacing Barry Jr. and began lobbying Eleanor for support, with surprisingly little success. "Sallie got the idea that anybody could do Barry's job," Eleanor said. "I never shared that feeling."

What was needed, Sallie said, was a wise, new publisher who could reinvigorate the family's liberal tradition, someone with vision, someone like, say, herself. "Isn't it perfectly plain that I could do just as good a job as Barry running these companies?" Sallie asked Eleanor, who gaped in horror at the thought. Mary was even more alarmed. "I would go mad if Sallie had the paper," she said. "She would have no compunction about using [it] for her particular causes and hobbies and interests. Sallie is curiously amoral. She doesn't tell the truth and she's just not liable."

The accusation was a painful rejection of Sallie, one that, to her, was even more insulting than being told she must leave the boards. A seat on the board was something she was entitled to by birth; no one expected her to "qualify" for it. Likewise, being tossed off the board was less a comment on her talents than an effort to shore up her teetering brother.

But the latest episode was something else again. She had tentatively suggested that she replace Barry Jr. as publisher and it had been dismissed out of hand by her parents and even by Eleanor. It had not even been worth serious discussion! It was a scalding humiliation.

Sallie had always looked down on journalism. She, after all, was a "real" writer. Reporters, with their potbellies, frayed clothing, and slavish devotion to facts, struck her as plebeian and a bit comical. Certainly her parents had never encouraged her to enter the family business, which was understood by all to be the province of males—specifically, the oldest male in the family, and then the younger ones in turn if the others faltered or proved unworthy. Once, in the late 1970s, after his only remaining son had recovered from cancer, Barry Sr. had confided to Eleanor that he would have sold the Bingham empire if Barry Jr. had died. As far as he was concerned, there were no other family members to take his place.

Despite their blindered belief in primogeniture, the Binghams encouraged their daughters in whatever field they chose to pursue. Woven into the fabric of the family was Barry Sr.'s almost total inability to refuse anything to his children. It was his way of showing love, of demonstrating closeness. Had Sallie taken an interest in the papers, Barry Sr. would probably have done whatever he could to ease her way and find a place for her.

Indeed, it is even plausible that he could have named her editor and publisher had circumstances and her own ambitions and talents been different—not likely, but possible even in the male-oriented Bingham family. On the other hand, had Barry Sr. actively pushed Sallie, demanding that she work at *The Minneapolis Tribune* like Worth or get a degree from Harvard Business School to prepare herself for leadership of the companies, "she would have flown right out the window," Barry Jr. said. "That was absolutely not in her line of interest."

Pointing out that she had no experience in journalism or business did little to salve Sallie's smarting ego. As far as she was concerned, she had been judged inferior next to a brother whom she had regarded since childhood as slow and pathetic. Within the family, if nowhere else, she had always assumed she had the mandate of heaven. Perhaps Worth and Barry Jr. had been favored in some ways, but Sallie had always been able to comfort herself with the sure knowledge that her parents considered her mind the quickest, her wit the sharpest. Now, measured against Barry Jr., she had been thought unworthy and a bit ridiculous. From her perspective, it was a great betrayal. Perhaps her parents had decided she was not really so exceptional after all.

DISASTROUS DECISIONS

When the Binghams finally met, at Sallie's insistence, to discuss finding a replacement publisher, Barry Sr. briskly declared that the proposal was "out," and Wilson Wyatt took up the program from there. But Sallie did not drop her quest so easily. She was like a boardroom Lorelei, calling down the table whenever there was a lull that an outside publisher would free Barry Jr. up to pursue activities he enjoyed more. "She didn't say, 'Wouldn't you be happier,' " Barry Jr. recalled. "It was, 'You *will* be happier. Let me tell you how much happier you will be when I relieve you of this burden.' "

Barry Jr.'s renewed talk of resigning had once again forced the Seniors to go along with his demand that the women leave the boards. Still, when the meeting adjourned, the only matter that had been firmly resolved was that Barry Sr. would, at the urging of his family, remain on the board. Mary thought Barry Jr. had been lukewarm when he asked his father to stay on for the sake of continuity; he would have been just as happy, she felt, to have the chairmanship vacated. But there was little chance of that. Mary was determined that Barry Sr. remain, and her bidding had been done.

Barry Jr.'s reluctance to retain his father only reinforced Mary's increasingly unsympathetic view of her son. At first, as she sensed his distress, she had felt worry and pity. But over the past few months, as his relentless demands mounted, she had grown suspicious. Barry Jr. and Edie seemed unwilling to settle for anything short of unconditional surrender as far as Sallie and Eleanor were concerned.

Barry Jr. fed these fears by continuing to pressure his parents on the subject of the buy-back agreement. Since Sallie refuses to sign it, he said, you should put your foot down and force her. At one point, he even suggested that the Senior Binghams disinherit Sallie if she did not sign. Edie backed him fully, and both she and Barry Jr. were dismayed when Barry Sr. told them he could never "cut Sallie out of my will because she disagreed with me on a matter of business."

Barry Jr. felt he had good reason to be obsessed with the buy-back. How else could he ensure that outside buyers would not make successful bids for chunks of the Bingham empire? No, he would not feel safe, he said, until his sisters had signed an ironclad agreement that gave the family the right-of-first-refusal on their stock. Without the buy-back, he was vulnerable, exposed. He stewed with frustration when his father dismissed the document as just "a matter of business," and felt more isolated and embattled than ever. Was he the only person who still believed that the present generation of Binghams had a duty to pass the papers safely on to the next, whatever the cost in wounded feelings? Did no one else see what was at risk?

Barry Sr., Wilson Wyatt, and the hired hands argued that Sallie's 15 percent portion of common stock was so minuscule that no shark would ever be interested. Even if she did sell to an outsider, they said, the companies would still be overwhelmingly family owned and controlled. Barry Jr. brushed these points aside. The issue, he said, was not whether he could live without the buy-back, but whether Sallie had an obligation to sign it as a sort of thank-you note for all those fat dividend checks. His father and the others were genuinely perplexed. Why was Barry Jr. so fixated on Sallie?

As this emotional tug-of-war dragged on, Edie called on the Senior Binghams to discuss the situation. Before a crackling fire in the back sitting room of the Little House, she said with clear distress that her husband simply had to have his parents' full support. They must remove Sallie and Eleanor from the boards, she said. They had to strike their daughters from their wills if they balked at the buy-back. The constant tension and worry were killing Barry Jr., she said. Cancer had left him frail; now his health was in real jeopardy.

Barry Sr. and Mary were touched by Edie's sincerity but bewildered by her failure to grasp the Solomon-like anguish of their situation. "To be asked to make decisions between our children is the most painful thing that can happen to us," Barry Sr. said pleadingly. Mary turned to Edie. "What if Molly and Emily were at odds about the paper?" she said. "Don't you see how difficult it is for us to take sides?" To their astonishment, Edie said, "No, I do not! I wouldn't have the faintest compunction about doing away with the one who was dissident." If it was right, she said, that would be all there was to it.

The March 27, 1984, election of board members was rapidly approaching, and still nothing had been firmly resolved. Barry Sr. continued to waffle. When Barry Jr. tried to build up his father's courage to remove his sisters, Eleanor begged her father to at least let her keep a seat on the WHAS board. Sallie was alternately furious and pleading, and had a haggard, drawn look. She told her parents that she was certain Barry Jr. would cut her dividends after their deaths.

To put Sallie's mind at ease, Barry Sr. asked his son to meet privately with her and he agreed. Instead of reassuring her, though, Barry Jr. used the occasion to plant an idea that he hoped would get her out of his hair once and for all. "If you think I'm so dishonest," he told Sallie sweetly, "you might want to sell your stock to the family. I'll do my best to accommodate you." A few days later, he repeated the proposal in writing and sent a copy of the letter to Eleanor. Neither sister took him up on the offer.

Shortly before the board meeting, Sallie humbled herself and sent her brother a conciliatory message through her attorney, Rebecca Westerfield. My client just wants to stay on the board, Rebecca told Leon Tallichet in a phone call; she does not want to be a troublemaker. Leon delivered the last-minute entreaty to Barry Jr. But "he wasn't interested," Leon said. "Absolutely a stonewall."

The Senior Binghams knew they had to come down on one side or the other. But which side? Edie's insistence that her husband was being crushed led them to think that Barry Jr. might be on the verge of quitting. He seemed gripped by a terrible, chronic anxiety. "It was very hard to determine whether he was holding our feet to the fire with a threat he never meant to carry out," said Mary, "or whether he was in such a hysterical frame of mind that he really meant all these things." In the end, the Senior Binghams decided he meant what he said: He would resign unless he got his way. To prevent that from happening, they would vote to remove Sallie and Eleanor from the boards.

Under pressure from Barry Sr. and Mary, Eleanor agreed to go along. She would not fight reconfiguration of the boards. Barry Jr. seemed on the brink of a breakdown. If this was the only way to keep him from cracking up and taking the companies and the dream down with him, so be it.

Promptly at 2:00 P.M. on Tuesday, March 27, 1984, the family gathered in the CJ & T conference room and quickly set about the main business of the afternoon: electing directors to sit on the Bingham boards. All the principal stockholders of the different companies—Barry Sr., Mary, Barry

Jr., Sallie, and Eleanor—were there. Barry Sr. acted as chairman. Barry Jr. made a motion to approve the minutes of the last stockholders' meeting. Sallie piped up with a brisk second. Then, his voice calm and deliberate, Barry Sr. called for the nomination and election of directors. Mary made a motion that the board be reduced to thirteen. After Eleanor's second, the motion passed.

Then Barry Sr. nominated everyone who had been on the board previously except Mary, Edie, Sallie, and Eleanor. He called for other nominations. Sallie nominated herself and asked that the record show that she would cast all of her votes for herself. Nominations thus closed, the Binghams cast votes by paper ballot. The only nonfamily member present was board secretary John Weeks, who tabulated the result. When he reported the winners back to Barry Sr., Sallie's name was not among them.

Fighting to keep her anger under control, Sallie made a motion to require that stockholders' meetings be held quarterly instead of once a year. Such gatherings were now the only means she had to stay informed about the family business, and she wanted them held more often. Barry Jr. enthusiastically seconded his sister's motion. He had no objection to show-and-tell sessions for shareholders, especially now that directors' meetings promised to be serious strategy-planning councils. Throwing the Bingham women off the boards had only taken ten minutes.

———————

Sallie's relations with her mother, icy before the vote, were now nonexistent. A few days after the stockholders' meeting, Mary phoned Sallie and, in a gesture of conciliation, asked her to go to a movie. Sallie curtly declined. She sent her parents a letter saying that she wanted no more "social commerce" with them. After all, she said, we cannot go on as though nothing has happened. Mary reluctantly agreed. "It is a bitter irony that our efforts to mediate the issues between you and Barry have resulted in a chilled and strained relationship with him and a break with you," she wrote back, "and for the same reason: you both feel that we have not given you the support you deserve in the hate-filled confrontations between you."

Indeed, Barry Jr. seemed no happier than Sallie. The Seniors had hoped —even expected—that since they had accommodated Barry Jr. on the board question, he would now be more accommodating on the buy-back. Instead, it soon became clear that giving in to one of his obsessions merely allowed him to concentrate more passionately on the other. Although the board issue had been resolved as he had demanded, Barry Jr. did not lift his threat to resign. He now said he "couldn't go on" if Sallie did not sign the buy-back. The Senior Binghams viewed such a stand as near madness.

Having already given in once to his son against his better judgment, Barry

Sr. was unwilling to budge. He would urge Sallie to sign the buy-back, he said, but he would not force her to do so with threats of disinheritance, as Barry Jr. wanted.

As the weeks passed and the board vote receded, Barry Jr. seemed more and more distraught. In April, he wrote an impassioned defense of his behavior, reminding his parents that it was Wilson Wyatt who had presented the buy-back, and it was the Dancos who had favored altering the boards. "I sometimes get the feeling that you think that I try to dream up issues . . . so as to create friction with Sallie," he told Barry Sr. and Mary. "That isn't the case."

After saying he had not written an editorial in months, Barry Jr. drew yet another line in the sand. "I don't intend to come crying to my parents about the hardships of my job . . . which I love . . . but I'm being forced to neglect my work by this unending debate about Sallie. . . . Either the issues must be settled or they will have to be dealt with by someone other than me."

To avoid this, he suggested what he considered to be a level-headed compromise. If his parents would not threaten to disinherit Sallie, would they at least put restrictions on the stock she stood to get after their deaths? With great reluctance, the Senior Binghams agreed. At a tearful meeting with Leon Tallichet and Gordon Davidson, they drafted language saying that family members had forty-five days after their deaths to sign a buy-back agreement. Anyone who refused would get nothing. When the new wills were typed up and ready for their signatures, though, the Seniors could not bring themselves to sign. Barry Jr. lapsed back into frustration and unhappiness.

Eleanor, too, was disgruntled. She had expected her brother to reward her for voting with him on the board issue by, at the very least, demonstrating a more generous attitude toward Rowland. But Barry Jr. had almost no political skills. As far as he was concerned, Eleanor's support showed that she was capable of clear-headed thinking—no more. He did not view the act as a favor that might require a payback. He continued to treat Rowland with frosty civility.

⸺

Shortly before Easter, 1984, relations took a turn for the worse. Rowland confided to Edie that he felt Barry Jr. "hated" him. "How truly preposterous," she said. In her usual frank manner, Edie explained that just because Barry Jr. might not consider him a chum or a buddy did not mean that he hated him. To Rowland's ears, that sounded like a distinction without a difference.

Word soon got back to Mary, who notified Barry Jr. that he was not to come to the family's traditional Easter lunch at the River Valley Club unless he could contain the "usual hostility and contempt" he displayed around his brother-in-law. Barry Jr. wrote back in a huff. "I've done my best to treat him in the same way I would like to be treated," he said. Besides, conditional invitations were not "a civilized way to treat anyone."

Despite these assurances, Mary remained suspicious. Early Easter Sunday, Mary phoned Edie and told her that under no circumstances were she and Barry Jr. to sit at the same table with the rest of the family at the River Valley Club. Poor Rowland was so hurt by Barry Jr.'s attitude that he could not stand to be near him.

Mary assumed that her son and daughter-in-law would take the hint and celebrate the Resurrection somewhere else. After all, Rowland's parents were going to be part of the River Valley Club ensemble, as well as Mary's unpredictable sisters, Harriette and Helena. No one wanted a scene, and Rowland had threatened not to come at all if Barry Jr. were present. "Well," Edie told Mary, "I have paid for our part of the reservations and we intend to go to the club for lunch. But we don't need to sit with you." With that, she ended the conversation and set out in her Easter best for church services.

A few hours later, Barry Jr. and Edie drove to the River Valley Club. They were the first to arrive and walked into the dining room to find the long Bingham table festooned with spring flowers and set for a banquet with place cards for everyone—including Barry Jr. and Edie. "My God, they've changed their minds again," Barry Jr. muttered as he and Edie sat down.

When the Senior Binghams and Rowland and Eleanor walked into the club and saw the dreaded Juniors sitting pertly at the table, they looked stricken. Mary hauled Rowland into a corner and began an animated discussion out of earshot. Suddenly, Barry Jr. realized that the staff had simply neglected to remove their place cards and he and Edie were unwelcome after all. He marched off in disgust to ask the maître d' to find them a table on the porch.

By then the room was filling up with Louisville's best families. How on earth would it look to have Barry Jr. and Edie publicly abandon the Bingham table and stalk out to a place of exile on the porch? Mary decided that would not do. She imperiously told her son that he and Edie must stay. She then began scurrying around the table snatching up place cards while Barry Jr. wearily informed the maître d' that he would not need a spot on the porch.

After a careful reshuffling of seat assignments, the Binghams enjoyed their spring lamb in tranquil good fellowship, with the combatants—Barry Jr. and Rowland—at opposite ends of the table. To Barry Jr., it was only one more piece of evidence that he was right about everything. "Some Easter!" he said with a snort. "It makes you understand why I couldn't do this for fifteen more years."

Three months later, Barry Jr. received news that suggested he might not have to endure fifteen more years of bickering after all, at least not from Sallie. In mid-July 1984, Sallie asked for a meeting with George Gill, Gordon Davidson, and the other hired hands. She brought her lawyer, Rebecca Westerfield, and said she wanted to sell her stock in the family companies. She wanted out.

In the months since she had been dumped from the boards, Sallie had been distant from the family, even from Eleanor, whom she now regarded as an undependable ally. She had brooded and seethed at first. The board vote had been a betrayal and a humiliating rejection. Being laughed at as a prospective publisher had been no less insulting. But the trauma had somehow helped sever the emotional umbilical cord that had both fed her and bound her to the family. She now felt free.

Four months after her wounding defeat, she was no longer angry, at least on the surface. Her main reason for wanting to sell her stock was a practical concern about her financial security. "My option was simply to sit here and collect my dividends," she said, "but I felt doing that without having any idea of how the company was being run would be just intolerable. After all, that's all I have to live on." Besides, she said, membership on the company boards had given her some prestige in Louisville. If she could not have that, she at least wanted the money it represented.

In a calm and even voice, Sallie told George, Gordon, and the others that she was quite prepared to sell to the family, but she would not accept the $6 million value that Management Planning, Inc., had placed on her stock. The Binghams had hired M.P.I., a professional appraisal company, to establish the lowest possible value for the family's shares that the I.R.S. would accept for estate tax purposes. Earlier that spring, George had told Sallie that M.P.I. had calculated the "whispered value" of her shares to be about $15 million, meaning that the stock might realistically be worth that much on the open market. The "whispered value" was never written down, lest the I.R.S. discover it and hike inheritance taxes accordingly. But even M.P.I.'s "whispered value" was too low for Sallie.

Though she owned only about 15 percent of the stock, she said she wanted one-quarter of the value of the companies. She was one of four Bingham inheritors, including Worth's line, she reasoned, so 25 percent seemed fair. Moreover, she declared, she would not accept a "minority discount" for her shares.

To Barry Jr., the news that Sallie wanted to sell was cause for jubilation, but he considered it unthinkable to pay what she expected. First of all, he said, she should be paid for the stock she actually owned, not a quarter of the companies. And what she owned certainly should be discounted as a minority stake; that was simply standard accounting practice.

Just as the I.R.S. places a premium on a controlling interest, it considers a minority interest to be less valuable. That meant that Sallie's 15 percent was actually worth less in dollars and cents than 15 percent of the companies' market value. In fact, minority stakes are normally considered to be worth about half of what they would bring if everything were sold and the full value realized.

On the open market, no one would dream of paying Sallie full value for her 15 percent share, because they could never get their money back unless all the companies were sold. And in a family business, that is usually unlikely. If anyone bought Sallie's stock at all, it would only be at a deep discount. By Barry Jr.'s reckoning, Sallie was lucky that the companies were willing to buy her stock at all, which they were not obliged to do. Certainly, he did not intend to buy it at anything but the "minority discount" price.

When Joan Bingham heard of Sallie's demands, she said flatly that Sallie was trying to force the Seniors to sell the companies. And that was something Joan, now living in Washington, D.C., was determined to prevent. Though the Binghams had never put Joan on any of the corporate boards, her interest in the family business was intense. Death had cheated her out of the role of publisher's wife; she had no intention of losing her chance to be the publisher's mother. If for no other reason, she wanted to keep the companies in family hands so that they could be passed on to Clara and Rob, the oldest Bingham grandchildren interested in the business.

The Senior Binghams agreed with Joan's assessment. "I think [Sallie] was very eager to bring down the temple around her," Barry Sr. said later with some bitterness. "I don't think getting the money was ever an important motive." Sallie enjoys money, he said, but she had "never shown any great greed" or been particularly acquisitive. No, it had to be something else. Barry Sr. and Mary concluded that, even then, Sallie had every intention of being the "engine of destruction."

But while Sallie may have wanted to force Option X to hurt her brother, she did not think she had a realistic hope of doing so. Her parents had just removed her from the boards to prevent such a thing, and it hardly seemed likely that they would now sell all the companies simply because she wanted out. "I thought there was a pretty good chance the family would just buy me out and that would be the end of it," she said. "That's what I hoped would happen."

The sticking point was price. Barry Sr. could have firmly told Sallie that the company would only pay M.P.I.'s "whispered value" of $15 million.

Take it or leave it. Instead, consumed by guilt over the board vote and a yearning to heal the rift with his daughter, Barry Sr. instructed the hired hands to retain investment bankers to do another valuation. Sallie should be involved in choosing whoever does the new analysis, he said, adding that George, Gordon, and the others must treat her with scrupulous fairness. Barry Jr. did not disagree with his father's actions or issue fresh threats to resign. He considered Sallie entitled to whatever was equitable. He wanted her out—not cheated.

Indeed, from Barry Jr.'s perspective, everything was working out exactly as he had hoped when he began issuing his nonnegotiable demands two years earlier. Sallie and Eleanor were off the boards and the hired hands were scurrying around the country looking for professional women and blacks to replace them. The buy-back was not signed, but Sallie had followed the spirit of the agreement anyway. She had offered her stock to the family, and by Christmas, with any luck, she would no longer be an owner. His parents seemed firmly committed to keeping the papers in the family. Option X was off the table.

Shortly before Barry Jr. left Louisville for his sabbatical, *The Courier-Journal* published an interview with him in which he talked about what he wanted to achieve during his nine months at Smith. He used the opportunity to restate his view that newspapers were arcane nineteenth-century vehicles for distributing information. Computers, he said, would allow readers to get news on demand without having to wade through hundreds of boring articles. To many readers, it was an old, familiar song. In 1983, in a speech before the annual meeting of the Associated Press managing editors, Barry Jr. had called ink-and-paper journalism the "last dinosaur in the swamp."

This time, as if to put a fine point on his argument, Barry Jr. said it would be a "catastrophe" for the price of gasoline to fall to thirty-five cents a gallon. Why? Without the whip of economic necessity, newspapers would continue to be delivered in the same way they had for decades—by gas-fueled trucks —putting off the day when electronic newspapers would be the norm. The *CJ & T* staff considered Barry Jr.'s comments insulting. The rest of Louisville merely wondered how out of touch with ordinary people one had to be to consider a thirty-five-cent gallon of gasoline a "catastrophe."

In the article, Barry Jr. also made a remark in passing that seemed of little importance to most but heightened anxiety among the hired hands and members of his family. He said that he was leaving open the possibility of restructuring his job at the papers when he returned, something that would be easier to do after an absence. He mentioned nothing specific, just some "fine tuning" of his responsibilities, he said, maybe a role with more visibility.

Barry Sr. and Mary read this suggestion of change at the top with keen apprehension. Eleanor and Rowland were acutely alarmed. George Gill and the other Bingham executives were fearful. None of them knew what Barry Jr. was talking about, but they all worried that it had something to do with Paul Janensch.

———————

It was a rainy Monday in September 1984 when the convoy of vehicles pulled away from the Big House bound for Massachusetts. Molly went first in the family station wagon. Barry Jr., Edie, and the family dog, Horatio, followed in a U-Haul truck stuffed with furniture, skis, bikes, a computer and two printers, a full silver coffee service, and two chainsaws for cutting firewood. Barry Jr. was bursting with the unencumbered joy his mother so aptly called a "holiday heart."

The whole sabbatical was like that. "I think it was the best year of our lives," said Barry Jr. They rented a semifurnished apartment near the campus, and Barry Jr. plunged into the academic feast of Northampton like a man long starved. While Edie studied for her degree in art history, he audited courses in Beethoven and opera, Shakespeare and fascism. For the first time since Harvard, he began rowing every day. The rowing coach, who had few other disciples, was thrilled to see this mustachioed zealot return day after day, whatever the weather, to take a shell out on Paradise Pond.

In the bracing air of New England, Edie discovered a new Barry Jr. Her husband actually wanted to play! For once, she was the one who was working hard and he was the one who was saying, "Come on, leave the books. You can go for a walk on a Sunday afternoon!" It was a total role reversal.

This Barry Jr. was not a grim loner. He was eager for intimacy and new friends. He savored the frequent dinners and lively conversation he and Edie had with the Smith faculty. He loved sitting across the table from his wife three meals a day and found discussions of *Othello* and other Shakespearean classics to be "surprisingly good family therapy."

As Barry Jr.'s U-Haul truck rumbled north, Paul Janensch moved his packing boxes and filing cabinets into the editor and publisher's large corner office. George Gill, still enraged by Paul's appointment, occupied the adjoining office, which was connected by an inner door. During the sabbatical, "that door never opened either way," said George.

Paul was keenly aware of George's resentment and tried his best to tread softly. As president, George still spoke for all three companies and ran the weekly management committee meetings. Paul's twin titles gave him control of the papers, but both men preferred to keep the division of authority somewhat blurred. "I just didn't want to draw a line in the sand," said Paul.

"I was a good sport about it. I thought it was a great opportunity and I didn't want to make everybody mad at me."

Soon, however, Paul had made a great many people mad at him. One reason was the widespread perception that he was using his temporary status as editor and publisher to claw his way up the social ladder. Eyes rolled as Paul regaled the editorial board with what Kentucky governor Martha Layne Collins had said over dinner at his house.

Paul and his wife, Gail, wanted desperately to be accepted by the Louisville establishment, and were miffed that the Senior Binghams did not embrace them as part of their social circle. The gossip about Gail Janensch's unshaven legs and armpits did not help. "She was of that school, sort of a flower-child type," said Mary Phyllis Riedley. "She always did look like a scrubbing would do her good."

Paul's romancing of the monied and the well connected skittered close to compromising Barry Jr.'s policy of rigorous independence, something the news staff prized highly. In the fall of 1984, Louisville played host to a presidential debate between Ronald Reagan and Walter Mondale. Paul arranged to sit directly behind First Lady Nancy Reagan. As he leaned forward to speak to her, a *Courier-Journal* reporter in the balcony stage-whispered to her companion, "I bet he's asking her over for dinner."

The Senior Binghams watched such antics with distaste. They considered Paul a commoner masquerading as lord of the manor in his master's absence. "We were a little distressed, I must say, by Janensch and his wife kind of throwing their weight around," said Barry Sr., who observed that Paul had a "rather grandiose" notion of the role of acting editor and publisher.

Paul damaged himself further with his tactless treatment of Sallie and Eleanor, whom he regarded as spoiled Southern belles. Sallie was furious when she heard that Paul had referred to her as "that bitch" in front of the editorial board, and Eleanor was equally unhappy when he sat next to her at a dinner party and called her "Sallie" all evening. Rowland complained that Paul pretended not to see him on the street. "He was so grand and haughty," he said, "he'd just walk right by me."

But it was Paul's stewardship of the papers that rankled the Senior Binghams the most. At Barry Jr.'s instruction, Paul headed a task force to study the possibility of merging the two papers, which would mean the death of the afternoon *Louisville Times*. The Senior Binghams realized that Louisville was virtually the only city of its size where a single owner published separate morning and afternoon newspapers. But they had emotional reasons for wanting to hang on to the *Times*, even if it made little financial sense. Paul favored jettisoning the paper and using the freed resources to restore *The Courier-Journal* to its former glory.

The fact that the *CJ* needed restoring at all was largely Paul's fault, as far as Barry Sr. and Mary were concerned. In January 1984, *The Courier-Journal* had not made *Time* magazine's ten-best list for the first time in two decades. "*The Courier-Journal* was cautious and static. It had a caretaker feel about it," said *Time* senior writer William A. Henry III, who compiled the list and wrote the accompanying article. "There were other papers that were doing a lot more." At the time, Barry Sr. and Mary appeared to take the demotion in stride. But there was a clear sense that the papers had lost stature on Paul's watch as executive editor.

The Senior Binghams also blamed Paul for the negative tone they detected in news columns and editorials. During the sabbatical year, Mary wrote several letters of complaint, pointedly addressing them to "Paul Jan-ensch, Office of the Publisher" as a subtle reminder that he only physically occupied the office and would not be publisher for long. Typically, Barry Sr. expressed no outright unhappiness, and only nodded in helpless agreement when friends groaned that Paul simply would not do as head of the papers.

The Binghams were especially outraged at the *CJ & T*'s coverage of their close friends, the Sloanes. Ever since 1981, when Barry Jr. had insisted on endorsing Republican George Clark instead of Harvey Sloane, a Democrat and Barry Sr.'s protégé, the Seniors had been on the look-out for slights and unfair treatment in the pages of the newspapers. While Barry Jr. was away, they found one.

Harvey was well into his second term as mayor when *The Courier-Journal* came out with an article insinuating that his wife, Kathy, was using her position as First Lady of Louisville to boost her real estate business. Kathy was aware that the article was in the works. Every other day, it seemed, her clients got calls from reporters asking whether she had used undue influence to persuade them to buy property.

After several such inquiries, Kathy stormed into Paul's office with a lawyer and angrily asserted that people were afraid to do business with her. In the end, the paper's investigation uncovered no wrongdoing, making Mary even more convinced that Paul, like Barry Jr., had it in for the Sloanes. Paul felt just as strongly that Kathy Sloane used Mary to muzzle the papers, and he made no attempt to hide his displeasure.

Such tensions paled, however, in comparison with a nasty confrontation over the papers' coverage of Humana, Inc., that occurred while Barry Jr. was happily rowing and reading Shakespeare in Northampton. Humana, one of the nation's fastest growing private health-care companies, was in many ways Louisville's brightest beacon of success. Begun in 1962, the business had made its scrappy, entrepreneurial founders, Wendell Cherry and David Jones, fantastically rich. Once, Wendell dropped by the New

York branch of Louis, Boston, a fine men's clothier, and walked out with $28,000 worth of apparel—a store record; the Cherrys' pied-à-terre in Manhattan had been featured in *Architectural Digest.*

As part of the city's new money, Cherry and Jones were generous patrons of the arts. The Cherrys had become friendly with the Senior Binghams and were frequent guests at the Little House. Dottie Cherry, Wendell's wife, was one of Mary's greatest admirers and confidantes.

But for all their polish, Wendell and David were gritty, driven hustlers. "They are as tough as two ten-penny nails," said Barry Jr. "If you cross them, watch out." Barry Jr. was suspicious of the way Humana courted doctors to put their patients in its profit-making hospitals. Wendell and David, in turn, were convinced that Barry Jr. resented brash, bold businessmen such as themselves, who were rising in power, challenging established Louisville families like the Binghams for preeminence.

About two months after Barry Jr. left for Northampton, an article appeared in the Louisville papers suggesting that an emergency room Humana managed for a public hospital was dispensing inferior care to indigent patients. Instead of venting their fury on Paul, Wendell and David phoned Barry Sr. directly and asked if they could come over right away to talk about it. He reluctantly agreed, then had his secretary buzz Paul and ask him to be present at the meeting.

When Paul arrived in Barry Sr.'s office, Wendell and David were already there. They were clearly unhappy to see him; they had hoped to talk to Barry Sr. alone. "I'm chairman of my company," David said, looking at Barry Sr., "and you are chairman of yours. That is why I felt that we should meet at our level." In polite but distressed tones, Barry Sr. explained that Paul was the one who had operational command of the newspapers. "If I'd wanted to deal with a flunky, then I'd have sent a flunky over," said David.

The Humana executives then angrily accused Paul of conducting a vendetta against them. They raised one objection after another about the papers' coverage, brusquely interrupting Paul's efforts to respond. "It was like being interrogated by two detectives, except they were both the bad guys," said Paul, who had a temper of his own and quickly lost it. "Don't call my staff liars!" he bellowed at one point, his face growing purple.

Barry Sr. watched the pyrotechnics in silence and extreme discomfort. When Paul at last managed to herd Wendell and David to the elevators, they were still so hot that they refused to shake hands. In a few days, the papers ran a quasi-correction that said that the original story had not been precise enough. Two weeks after the incident, Barry Sr. called Paul and said that he and Mary were planning to go to the Breeders' Cup, a horse race, with the Cherrys in a few weeks. "Do you think that will be a problem?" he asked tentatively. Paul told him he had no objection. It did not occur to him that Barry Sr. was not asking his permission; he was seeking his assurance that no embarrassing articles on Humana would appear while he was enjoying the Cherrys' company.

———————

Sallie was nearly two hours late for a presentation by Lehman Brothers, Kuhn, Loeb, the fourth of five New York investment banking firms that trooped to Louisville during the fall of 1984 to explain why it and it alone was equipped to give the fairest valuation of the Bingham companies. Thirty minutes after the meeting began, she was sighted shopping at Stewarts, a local department store, George Gill confided to Barry Jr. in the weekly memo he sent to Northampton.

George, who was orchestrating the new valuation and, it was hoped, quick purchase of Sallie's stock, knew that Barry Jr. delighted in anything that cast his sister in a bad light. Shortly after leaving for Smith, Barry Jr. had sent George a memo in which he copied a note from Sallie saying that she would not attend a dinner for the new directors of the Bingham boards. "It would be an awkard [sic] occasion for me," Barry Jr. had typed, painstakingly reproducing the whole letter so he could display her spelling error.

Though she missed most of Lehman's show, Sallie decided that she liked the firm and wanted it to evaluate her shares. Because of her feminist convictions, George had been sure she would pick another candidate, PaineWebber, which had sent a team headed by a woman. But Sallie had not cottoned to the female banker at all. "She said, 'I don't want that bitch doing this for me,' " recalled one of the hired hands. The Binghams' management team favored yet a third banker, Goldman, Sachs, but not passionately, and Barry Sr. had decreed that the choice was Sallie's, anyway. By mid-October Lehman Brothers was hard at work figuring out the market value of the companies and, more importantly, calculating how much Sallie's piece was worth.

Except for the flurry of excitement her decision to sell had caused, Sallie had all but dropped out of the family. She defiantly remained in her job as book editor and thus saw her father occasionally in the halls; otherwise, she stuck by her proclaimed desire to have no "social commerce" with her parents. Mary was regretful about the estrangement, but resigned. Barry Sr. took it much harder.

Since the board election, Sallie had worn her feelings of childhood neglect as proudly as a soldier might wear a Purple Heart. It was as though the board issue had cracked a dam holding back a lifetime of fear, rejection, and hurt feelings. "Did you know that my parents have never, ever told me they loved me?" she would say to friends, as if offering proof.

One of those who listened earnestly to Sallie's lament was her cousin,

Melinda Page Hamilton. Though Melinda felt a special loyalty to Sallie, she was also devoted to her uncle Barry and aunt Mary. She came to Louisville in the fall of 1984 filled with distress at Sallie's alienation. "You know," Melinda said to Barry Sr., "I think if you just went to Sallie and said in the simplest way, 'I really love you,' it would make a great difference to her." The Senior Binghams were skeptical. "We're not used to going around saying, 'I love you, I love you, I love you' the way people do now," Mary explained. "I've never thought it was necessary. Everything we've ever done, it seems to me, indicates our fondness for the children."

Barry Sr. thought so, too. He was as intensely uncomfortable with proclamations of love as Mary was, but he was willing to try anything to end his daughter's estrangement. "All right, Melinda," he sighed. "You know Sallie well, and if you think this will help, certainly I will tell her." Tim Peters, Sallie's husband, had suggested the very same thing only days earlier. Just say it, he had advised; just let her hear the words.

Barry Sr. was at a turning point. Throughout his life, he had resisted psychoanalyzing people. He considered it presumptuous to think that one could really understand what someone else felt deep down, perhaps because he knew his own motivations were endlessly tangled. He was quick to brush off the notion that he had been influenced by childhood trauma, for instance, and would argue that his mother's sudden death, his father's remoteness, and the humiliation of the Mary Lily affair had left no psychic scars. He did not try to explain why he had such an uncanny ability to sense pain in others. He just did. And though he could concoct an explanation for the suffering he recognized, he was disinclined to make a judgment, lest he be judged.

So Barry Sr. was doubtful when he was told that Sallie's alienation was rooted in her conviction that he did not love her. He was certain it was far more complicated than that. Even so, with considerable trepidation, he invited his daughter to lunch in the fall of 1984. And over a starched tablecloth, for the first time ever, he said, "I love you."

He felt intensely uneasy and clumsy. It was pathetic to have to convince one's grown child that she was loved. He thought it inconceivable that she would start to tremble, then weepingly embrace him as though finally, at long last, some invisible barrier had dissolved. It was much more likely, he thought, that she would at first be dumbfounded, and then mockingly chuckle, as though he had uttered a non sequitur and might even be senile. He felt absurd. He knew he had risked being ridiculed, and to what end? In the slim hope of reconciliation and because he had been told the words would mean a great deal to his daughter. In many ways, it was the most gallant, vulnerable moment of his life.

Just as he had feared, Sallie stared back at him, looking at first bewildered, then amused. Clearly she had not been moved either by the words themselves or by her father's out-of-character gesture. When she got home that night, she told her husband that her father had unaccountably blurted out a strange declaration of affection. Tim confessed that Barry Sr. had been prompted. Sallie lost no time turning the incident into a comical anecdote for her friends at the newspapers and the University of Louisville. To her, it was a humorous and poignantly revealing example of the family's inability to express love.

Then, as Sallie mulled over her father's awkward effort to win her back, it began to seem that the words had made a difference after all, but not as he had intended. Instead of the remote, longed-for father who never said "I love you," Barry Sr. had become very mortal indeed. He was now the supplicant, she the withholder.

This less godlike Barry Sr. made her angry in a new way. A wounded, fragile old man hardly seemed worthy of a lifelong obsession. By delicately tipping himself off his pedestal, Barry Sr. had betrayed Sallie in a way that was even worse than the board vote. He was beginning to look like that most scorned of objects: a boudoir pillow.

———

George Gill and Barry Sr. were becoming closer with each passing day. One reason was that George, together with Leon Tallichet, now did more work for Barry Sr. than for Barry Jr. As chief negotiators for the sale of Sallie's stock, they had a fiduciary responsibility to keep the other share-holders—Barry Jr. and Eleanor—at arm's length until a deal could be struck. George had even gone so far as to have the understanding written down and signed by Barry Sr. That way, he and the other hired hands would have some protection in the event of lawsuits—a prospect that appeared increasingly likely as family trust deteriorated.

Early on, Sallie had said that she was worried Eleanor would muck around in the negotiations and miscommunicate what was happening to her parents. Eleanor and Rowland, on the other hand, wanted to be kept closely informed, mainly out of concern that Sallie would be paid too much. On the theory that limited knowledge might reduce the potential for mischief, Barry Sr. had ruled that all shareholders should be treated equally. Once you inform one, you have to inform them all, he decreed.

As a consequence, George began to go to Barry Sr. for decisions on what shareholders could and could not know. It did not help relations with Barry Jr. when George coolly informed him that there were now certain things he could not tell him because of Barry Sr.'s guidelines.

During the sabbatical, George seemed determined to make Barry Jr. aware that he had burned his bridges when he had appointed Paul as acting editor and publisher. "The empire has survived another week without its leader," he wrote at the end of each weekly report to Northampton, a phrase dripping with sarcasm.

In December 1984, in a memo approving a hefty compensation package for George, Barry Jr. gingerly tried to repair the damage. "I would hope that, when I get back from our sabbatical, you and I could rediscover the close and trusting relationship which I feel we enjoyed until last summer," he wrote George. "I long for the kind of relationship my father had with Mark and Lisle and I hope that, after all the disruption of my absence and the buy-out are over, we can find it." George did not reply.

He was too angry over a new rumor that, if true, was even more wounding than the horse race or the elevation of Paul. Among the hired hands, a perception existed that, before going to Smith, Barry Jr. had executed the so-called side letter, naming Paul Janensch as his regent in the event of his death or incapacitation. No one had actually seen the document but almost everyone in the executive wing of *The Courier-Journal* and *Times* was willing to believe it had been written and signed.

George was especially vulnerable to such gossip. It infuriated him to think that, down the road, he might end up playing second fiddle to Paul Janensch. He nursed his hurt by ignoring Paul and trying never to mention him in his weekly memos.

———————

Shortly before Christmas, 1984, Lehman Brothers returned to Louisville to present a preliminary valuation. No one was worried. Earlier in December, *Business First*, a frisky local journal, had broken the story under a front-page headline: "Sallie Bingham Considers Selling Stock." In a follow-up article in *The Courier-Journal*, Sallie had explained that she was selling because she had been kicked off the Bingham boards. "No taxation without representation," she had quipped good-naturedly. She said she intended to remain as book editor and could not conceive of any reason why she would sell her stock outside the family.

Barry Jr. was so sanguine about the process that he did not come home from Smith for Christmas. Instead, he left with his family for a month-long trekking holiday in Nepal a few days after the article appeared. He felt sure Gordon Davidson, Wilson Wyatt, and the hired hands could work out an acceptable deal.

There was great speculation about what Sallie's portion of the pie was worth. *Business First* had guessed $30 million. The *Courier-Journal* reporter had estimated $20 million. Soon after the Binghams had hired Lehman Brothers, Eleanor and Rowland had gone to Barry Sr. and George Gill and urged them to "play hard ball" with Sallie. They said they feared the Seniors might offer her such a high price that one or more of the companies would have to be sold to pay the bill. "They . . . are very much in favor of trying anything to retain family ownership," George told Barry Jr. in his weekly memo. At the same time, he noted wryly, they seem to want to make sure there is enough money in the till to pay *them* off if they decide to yell "me, too."

On December 19, 1984, Lehman Brothers distributed its confidential report to the family and the hired hands. The firm estimated that the total value of the companies was between $210 million and $240 million. That would mean Sallie's 15 percent ownership, discounted 25 percent because it was a minority stake, was worth between $22 million and $28 million.

Sallie was furious. "That's not enough!" she cried. She was particularly suspicious of the rationale Lehman Brothers used for discounting, which was that no one was interested in buying a minority shareholder's stock. She did not believe that for an instant! Even though she had helped pick the firm, Sallie became convinced that Lehman Brothers was in the thrall of her parents and brother. The family was paying them, after all. And just as it was in her interest to have a high value placed on her shares, it was in the family's interest to keep the values low.

With Barry Jr. overseas, the Christmas holidays were quiet. In a surprising gesture of conciliation toward her mother, Sallie wrote a fond, nostalgic account of Christmas in the Big House during the war years, when she had gloried in playing a gap-toothed Columbia, the female symbol of the United States, for Mary's birthday play while Barry Jr. and Worth waved American flags in their Cub Scout uniforms. The article was supposed to run in *The Courier-Journal* on December 24, Mary's birthday. Because of the tension between Barry Jr. and Sallie, Paul Janensch vetoed the piece and it never appeared.

The remembrance would probably not have made any difference in family relations. Sallie was well aware that what she was about to do would catapult Mary to a new plane of dismay and alienation.

On January 13, 1985, Sallie told the world that she was willing to sell her shares in the Bingham companies to the highest bidder. With a media savvy that startled even her close friends, she contacted *The New York Times* and timed her announcement to make the Sunday *Courier-Journal*, which had a bigger circulation than the daily papers.

Her decision was automatically big news in Louisville. But *The New York Times* was less interested until Sallie agreed to hand over confidential financial data from the Lehman report, data which, the reporter knew, would provide an unusual window on the operations of a famous family business. Despite her years on the Bingham boards and many hours closeted with the hired hands, Sallie's understanding of finance was still rudimentary. She was convinced that Lehman Brothers had put too low a value on her shares, but she found the report itself an impenetrable muddle of perplexing terms and meaningless numbers. In order to extract revenue and profit figures, the *New York Times* reporter had to ask her to recite the whole report, category by category. Sallie did not seem to have the foggiest notion of what she was reading.

———————

The specter of an outsider coming into possession of Sallie's shares horrified the Binghams, who reacted as though the Visigoths and Vandals were at the very gates. "This is your children's patrimony," said Mary when she called Joan in Washington. "We're going to do everything we can to fight off Sallie." The Seniors, the Juniors, Eleanor and Rowland, Joan, the hired hands, and all the grandchildren (except for Sallie's sons, who were granted noncombatant status) made up the united front. "We were all in accord at that point," remembered Joan wistfully.

The family came up with a two-part strategy to stop Sallie. First, they decided to create a voting trust with Barry Sr. as trustee. He already controlled a majority of the voting stock, but if Barry Jr. and Eleanor gave him the power to vote their shares, he would control a daunting 95 percent of the votes. That would make it clear that the family was united against Sallie, a muscular gesture that would discourage even the most determined outside buyer.

Second, they agreed to offer Sallie a reasonable price for her shares, within the range that Lehman Brothers had recommended. Barry Jr. and George knew that it was almost unthinkable that any outsider would propose a sum close to the $22 million to $28 million that Lehman had suggested. A shark would not be interested in a fair price; he would want a bargain.

Since the family had not yet made her an offer, the plan was to let Sallie shop the shares around and get a sense of what an outsider would bid, a process they felt sure she would find discouraging. Then the family would propose a price, undoubtedly the best price she was going to get. She would accept it and the deal would be done. Simple.

From Northampton, Barry Jr. instructed George and Gordon Davidson to go to work putting together a voting trust document. There was no time to waste. A meeting was scheduled for February 5 to explain it to everyone and get signatures.

Barry Sr. had not seen Sallie except in passing since that ill-fated lunch when he had told her he loved her. He was still very much the supplicant, mourning the loss of his daughter. At the same time, he could not help admiring her spunk, a quality that reminded him of Mary. As Sallie's forty-eighth birthday approached, he began thinking of how he might use the occasion to send her a peace-feeler.

Sallie's birthday was on January 22, just nine days after she had invited outside buyers to make bids for her stock. She was sequestered as usual in her tiny fifth-floor office at *The Courier-Journal* and *Times* when, to her astonishment, her father appeared with an armful of roses. "She seemed so surprised to see me," he recalled. Sallie stood up and awkwardly took the flowers, but she was coolly diffident. Barry Sr. smiled and made birthday small talk. "Thank you, Father," she said in her most well-bred voice. The audience over, he scuttled back to the executive wing on the third floor.

Sallie had other things on her mind besides relations with her father. She had decided to use part of the millions she anticipated from the sale to establish the Kentucky Foundation for Women. With much fanfare, she announced that the Foundation would publish a literary and political quarterly, set up an archive for the papers of women in the region, and help finance women's education and career pursuits, especially in the theatrical arts. "We are committed to erasing the barriers between all classes and conditions of women who suffer from a common oppressor," she declared grandly.

The common oppressor was, without question, men. According to Sallie, women had only two choices open to them: "marriage-dependency-poverty or . . . being an accessory to a powerful man, through being his secretary, his wife, his mistress, or by collaborating with him." She was especially concerned that there were so few women at the top of corporations.

Sallie was also absorbed with how she could persuade Eleanor to add her 15 percent share of stock to the block that she had put up for sale. This bigger package would be more enticing to an outsider, because it would not only represent a far more significant stake in the companies, it would also indicate division in the family, one of the key predictors that a closely held business will eventually be sold.

At the moment, Eleanor did not seem to be solidly in anyone's camp. Out of obedience to her parents and a desire to avoid Option X—total sale —she had helped vote Sallie off the boards. Despite her complaints about negativism, and her clear preference for WHAS, she could not imagine the papers being sold. The idea of their being in non-Bingham hands was alien and frightening to her. The papers were like another sibling, an invisible but living presence at the dinner table. To have that seat empty would be terrifying. Besides, as a result of her acquiescence, she had drawn closer to her parents and wanted to maintain their approval.

But another thought had also begun to take root. Money! Imagine how life might change if she, like Sallie, got tens of millions of dollars in exchange for her stock. The arithmetic was intoxicating. If the family offered her $22 million, the lowest Lehman value, and the I.R.S. skimmed off a third of that in capital gains taxes, there would still be $14.5 million left. If she invested that money in tax-free bonds at 7 percent, she and Rowland would have an annual, after-tax income of over $1 million! Think of that compared to the $300,000 in dividends she got now, half of which went for income taxes!

What is more, Eleanor told herself, because of Barry Jr.'s rigid attitudes, she got almost no emotional reward from being part owner of the Bingham companies. Her "psychic income"—the pride, prestige, and status she derived—had been almost nil since she had lost her seat on the Bingham boards.

Barry Jr. seemed to think that passive ownership of an honorable, ethical organization was enough for any sensible person. He gave Eleanor the impression that listening to her views was a waste of time, and did not even seem grateful for her support on the board issue. In fact, he seemed to take her for granted. All he wanted, Eleanor fumed, was for her to keep her mouth shut and sign on the dotted line. What is more, Barry Jr. did not appreciate the fact that she had less of a stake in continuing the family business than he or Joan did. Her son, Rowlie, was far too young to be a candidate for editor and publisher in the fourth generation. Eleanor's line was probably always going to be shut out of the real power.

———

Barry Jr. and the hired hands were unaware of just how torn and ambivalent Eleanor had become. She needed to be courted if she was to remain loyal to Barry Jr. Sensing an opening, Sallie wasted no time in urging Eleanor to cross over to the dissident side. Not only was it in Eleanor's interest, she argued, but it would be a sisterly, feminist thing to do. Join forces with me! We can become financially independent and the papers can still remain in the family! It was a tempting notion.

The first sign that the Binghams' united front was cracking came on a Friday in late January 1985, when Rowland phoned George Gill. "Eleanor feels like a pawn in all this," he said. The problem was the voting trust. Eleanor was not sure she wanted to sign it. Her seat on the boards had already been taken away. Now Barry Jr. wanted to strip her of her power to vote her shares and turn it over to Barry Sr. George told Rowland to wait until the February 5 meeting where everything would be aired and explained. "Relax," he said, "and don't be so suspicious." In his weekly memo, George told Barry Jr. that Eleanor was getting restless. Unfortunately, Barry Jr. decided to reassure her himself.

Around 6:00 P.M. the day he got George's memo, Barry Jr. placed a call to Eleanor. He told her that he probably would not be coming home from Northampton for the February 5 meeting, since the matter to be discussed was fairly straightforward. Then he explained to her how important it was that she enter the voting trust, the key "shark repellent," as he liked to call it. Exactly what was said is not known. But Barry Jr. thought he had answered Eleanor's questions satisfactorily.

After the conversation, however, Eleanor was in great distress. She told her parents that Barry Jr. had said she would have "no voice" in fashioning shark repellents like the voting trust. Edie, who had been studying in the room with Barry Jr. when he made the call, chalked up the miscommunication to Eleanor's tendency to get hysterical in pressured situations. "She does not always understand what she hears," she said.

But Eleanor was convinced that her brother was trying to steamroller her. When the Senior Binghams told Barry Jr. of Eleanor's reaction, he was dumbstruck. From then on, he vowed, he would only communicate with the family in writing. "Eleanor's impression seemed to be that somehow a voting trust would be formed by the directors of the company without the stockholders approving it," he said, his voice suffused with exasperation. "Well, that's impossible. The directors can't form a voting trust. Only the stockholders can form a voting trust."

To clear up the matter once and for all, Barry Jr. sent Eleanor a letter meant to reassure her about having "no voice." But the tone was more condescending than comforting. "At no time in our telephone conversation did I say such a thing," he told her. "Moreover, I have never said—or even thought—that you and other family members have 'no voice' in matters regarding the companies." Like a law professor citing cases, he suggested that his sister review "my letter to you of Nov. 10" and "a memo of October 10," which clearly states "in paragraph (4) that . . . you and other family members are to be kept informed and their 'approval' will be sought. I did and do agree with this document and it certainly does not contemplate a 'no voice' position for any of us."

He ended with a patronizing slap. "I hope you won't mind my sharing a copy of this with Mother and Father in an attempt to clear up any confusion in their minds on this matter. . . . Honestly, it pains me that you and I should suffer such misunderstanding. Now is certainly the time for the family to pull together as best it can and not create more dissension than already exists."

This time Eleanor understood. But her anxiety over the voting trust and Barry Jr. had been sharply heightened nonetheless.

The February 5 meeting proved to be a showcase for Mary's talents as a back-street maneuverer. She considered the voting trust vital and had become alarmed when Eleanor began to hint that she might bolt. Then a solution occurred to her, and she put her shrewd mind to work forcing it through.

At the meeting, Gordon Davidson proposed, at Mary's prompting, a voting trust with co-trustees rather than a single trustee as had been originally envisioned. Mary immediately expressed great enthusiasm for the plan and nominated Barry Sr., Barry Jr., and Eleanor as the co-trustees.

Since Barry Jr. was still in Northampton, no final action could be taken. But to make sure that her son got the message that this was what she and Barry Sr. wanted, Mary arranged to have the meeting recorded and the tape sent to him. "I think it _most_ important for you to get the total impact of the discussions, whatever ambience, innuendo there might be that would not be clear in written notes," she wrote, adding how "pleased" she and Barry Sr. were by the proposal. "Joan agreed with our thinking and was most helpful throughout." She signed off: "Much, much love and thanks, Mother." Such an effusive leave-taking was highly unusual.

A week later, Barry Jr. wrote to his parents, who were by then taking their annual mid-winter spa vacation at the Pritikin Center in California. He had listened to the tape, he said. "I thought Gordon did a good job of describing the merits of the voting trust. I'm sorry that Eleanor still opposes the concept. Her suspicion that I'm determined to cut her out persists." The real importance of the voting trust, he said, was that it would allow his successor to control the companies with only "a tiny minority of voting shares." But, he added, "in the end, a voting trust must be based on the trust of family members in the person of the publisher. I only wish that I enjoyed more of that trust." Significantly, he made no mention of Mary's plan for three co-trustees.

FEELING A WAVE OF INEVITABILITY

By mid-February 1985, the family alliance seemed about to crack, but Sallie inadvertently came to its rescue by issuing an ultimatum. She had hired John Morton, a well-known Washington-based newspaper analyst, to do a quick evaluation of her holdings, this time from the seller's perspective rather than the buyer's. Based mostly on the Lehman documents Sallie had provided him, Morton estimated that a fair discounted value for her stock would be about $42 million.

Armed with this information, she laid out her terms to George Gill, Leon Tallichet, and Gordon Davidson. If the family wanted to buy her stock, she said, it would have to pay $42 million. Then she took a chapter out of Barry Jr.'s book and announced that the price was nonnegotiable. She would entertain no counteroffer below that figure. If the family failed to buy at this price, she said, she would aggressively peddle the stock to the highest outside bidder, no matter how odious. George, Leon, and Gordon promised to get back to her with an answer after the March 7 meeting of stockholders and directors.

The other Binghams were shocked by Sallie's price and outraged at her high-handed manner. Nevertheless, they hired a new investment banking firm—Goldman, Sachs—this time to calculate not what the stock was worth but how much the companies could afford to pay.

Soon after learning of Sallie's $42 million demand, Mary wrote Barry Jr. in Northampton to ask about his curious silence regarding the co-trustee proposal for the voting trust. "I cannot understand why you have neglected to respond to this suggestion or your statement that 'Eleanor still opposes the concept.' Eleanor does not 'oppose the concept' if the provision should include the appointment of the three trustees as I suggest."

Barry Jr. replied that he was worried about a three-way trusteeship. What would happen when Barry Sr. died? Would he appoint a successor trustee, and if so, who might that be? Would the three trustees have equal power? What about a 60 percent vote for Barry Sr. and 20 percent each for him and Eleanor?

With the voting trust effectively at an impasse, Eleanor moved steadily away from an alliance with either Sallie or Barry Jr., and toward a third position that was hers and hers alone. She considered Sallie unreasonable, but she viewed Barry Jr. as untrustworthy.

A week after Sallie issued her ultimatum for $42 million, Eleanor sent Barry Jr. a demand of her own that set him back on his heels. Eleanor said she was not interested in "staying in a relationship" in which her brother would be running the companies and she would be a passive stockholder receiving dividends. She was no longer willing to entrust the management of her birthright, and the dividend income she lived on, to Barry Jr. She wanted more say in protecting her interests and those of her family. Her letter did not suggest how such an arrangement might be effected. But the clear implication was that if she was not given a more active role, she would sell out, too.

Eleanor made a second demand that Barry Jr. found even more insulting. Over the past several weeks, she had become obsessed with the fear that her brother was out to cheat her. After the Senior Binghams died, she was sure Barry Jr. would sell his majority stake in the company for a premium price, leaving his sisters to barter with a new owner "who could basically offer [us] whatever price he wanted." To prevent this from happening, she wanted Barry Jr. to agree, in writing, that he would try to secure the same price for her stock as for his if he decided to sell.

Barry Jr. said he did not have a problem with such a "fair-pricing" pact, but "the implication of asking for it is a massive vote of no confidence in me." He seemed genuinely hurt and perplexed. Despite the Pumpkin Papers debacle, the board vote, and the erosion of her control that the voting trust implied, he could not understand why his sister seemed so distrustful of him. "There's just no track record for my performing in that way," he said in a bewildered tone.

Eleanor saw his track record quite differently. By his own admission, the economic future of the companies was bleak, and Eleanor felt certain it would degenerate further under his inept management. When Sallie had urged Eleanor to pool their shares and sell them as a block, one of her most persuasive arguments had been that now was the best time to sell; the companies would probably be worth far less in five years. Surely Barry Jr. knew that, too.

Another issue was the cumulative hostility Eleanor felt toward her brother. "The voting trust was not in itself particularly negative," she said. "But things were just leading up to a lessening of power. The idea was that Sallie and I as minority stockholders gave up a little bit more [each time] so that more power could be vested in Barry."

But even that did not seem to be the nub of the matter. What bothered Eleanor most was hearing her brother and the hired hands refer to "the sister problem," lumping Eleanor with Sallie as though both were equally annoying. Barry Jr. did not seem to give her credit for being helpful. "There were a lot of documents I had signed that Sallie had not," she pointed out.

In the end, no single incident prompted Eleanor's "fair-pricing" letter. "It had something to do with being on the sidelines and watching Barry maneuver Sallie out of the way," she said. "Since Sallie and I own exactly the same amount of stock and the situation is exactly identical in every way, it seemed to me very important that I not get moved down the tunnel with her. [A strong] statement . . . would obviously make everybody sit up, take notice, and pay attention." She did not want to be bought out. She wanted to be on the team, and treated accordingly.

Barry Jr. certainly took notice, although he "didn't want Eleanor around to muddle in his playpen," as George Gill acidly observed. But he decided not to do anything until he and Edie came back to Louisville for the March 7 stockholders' meeting.

The Senior Binghams, however, reacted to this new breach between Barry Jr. and Eleanor with weary despair. They had returned to Kentucky from the sunny regimen of the Pritikin Center only to find that relations among their offspring had become frostier than ever. Barry Jr., Sallie, and Eleanor could not seem to establish common ground. "Our optimism was crumbling," said Mary.

One afternoon in late February 1985, as the crucial stockholders' meeting loomed, Mary and Barry Sr. settled into the back sitting room of the Little House, stared into the fire, and began to talk, tentatively at first, then more boldly, about the possibility of a total sale. "This is something that we mustn't put out of our minds," they agreed. "This is something that is probably going to have to be faced."

The family was scheduled to gather on Thursday, March 7, for the stockholders' meeting and a showdown on the voting trust. Eleanor was determined not to be railroaded again. The Monday before the meeting, she hired one of Kentucky's toughest, savviest lawyers: Rucker Todd. A few years earlier, he had negotiated the sale of Louisville's family-owned WAVE to Orion Broadcasting, Inc., for a stunning amount. The deal had earned him a reputation as an expert in communications companies.

Like Gordon Davidson, Rucker made his living working for Louisville blue bloods. Both men were considered the sharpest attorneys in their respective law firms; as a result, a potent rivalry had sprung up between them. So Rucker's voice had a hint of smug satisfaction in it when he telephoned Gordon to tell him that he had been hired to represent Eleanor.

George Gill was delighted that Rucker Todd was joining the fray. Now, at least, he would be able to deal with a competent attorney instead of Eleanor herself, whom he considered to be vacillating and flaky. What is more, Rucker might reassure Eleanor, calm her down and help smooth relations between her and her brother.

Rucker did not share George's optimism. He had served on the board of the Louisville Orchestra with Barry Jr. and succeeded him as president. He considered the Bingham heir an autocrat whose style was to order, not persuade. "He's petulant," Rucker said. "If he wants to have his way, it's 'I'm going to take my baseball and go home.' "

Sallie had long ago urged Eleanor to hire her own attorney, as had her friends, who had grown concerned as they watched Eleanor become increasingly desperate and distrustful. The immediate reason she had called in Rucker, though, was to get his advice on the inch-thick voting trust document. During their first encounter, she had brought him up to speed on the family fracas, unloading all her fears and frustrations. What I really want to know, she had mused aloud, is how I fit into the family business.

On March 5, the day after Rucker was hired, he and Gordon Davidson met for lunch. They discreetly discussed the personalities of each of the players and considered all the logical possibilities that might help eliminate the lack of trust between Eleanor and Barry Jr. "Why can't we separate the holdings so that both Barry Jr. and Eleanor would have something of their own?" Rucker asked Gordon. Gordon stroked his chin. "I don't think Barry Jr. will go for that," he said. Rucker nodded understandingly. "I don't know if Eleanor will either." The two lawyers agreed to explore the idea anyway. Back in his office in the Citizens Plaza building, Gordon phoned George Gill and told him of Rucker's proposal to divide the empire up, with one part going to Barry Jr. and the other to Eleanor. George was intrigued.

The following day, Barry Jr. and Edie flew into Louisville from Northampton. Barry Jr. wanted to arrive a day before the critical Thursday stockholders' meeting so he could confer with George and Leon and catch up on doings at the newspapers. As they settled into their chairs, George handed Barry Jr. a document with Barry Sr.'s signature on it. "Your father calls these the Thirteen Commandments," George said with a grin.

Barry Jr. quickly scanned the sheet. The first twelve "commandments" dealt with how the family should respond to Sallie's $42 million demand and restated Mary's insistence that the voting trust include Eleanor as a co-trustee. All that looked fine. It was the final commandment that seemed ominous to Barry Jr. "Barry Bingham Jr. and Eleanor must establish a workable relationship in the future," it said. "If they cannot work together, then we must seriously consider the sale now of all of the properties. That is not a threat. It is a fact."

As Barry Jr. tried to absorb the implications of this latest thunderbolt, George went on to the business of Barry Jr.'s relations with Eleanor. "All she really wants is to own and operate something herself," he explained, echoing his recent conversation with Gordon Davidson. "She and Rowland want clout and cash, and they could get both by having something of their own." One way to do this, George suggested, would be for Barry Jr. and Joan to give their WHAS stock to Eleanor in exchange for her stock in the newspapers.

The proposal was news to Barry Jr., but, to George's utter astonishment, he told him to go ahead and put together a plan for "us each to do our own thing." He could understand Eleanor's feelings perfectly, Barry Jr. said. If Worth had lived, he might have wanted to own WHAS independently himself. The stock swap, as the plan came to be called, had surmounted its first hurdle, and the hired hands were ecstatic at the thought that perhaps this was the once-and-for-all solution to the family squabble.

The next day, at the March 7 stockholders' meeting, those hopes proved to be grossly inflated. As soon as the Binghams and their respective lawyers arrayed themselves around the conference room at Wyatt, Tarrant & Combs, Gordon's law firm, Rucker Todd asked that action on the voting trust be delayed until he could go over the documents more thoroughly.

Barry Jr. then laid the stock-swap proposal on the table. With a dramatic flourish, he suggested that he become 100 percent trustee of the voting stock of the papers, and that Eleanor become 100 percent trustee of the stock in WHAS. This would not literally require a stock swap, he hastened to add. Instead, he would put his WHAS voting stock under Eleanor's control, and she would put her voting stock in the papers under his control.

The family members present—Barry Sr., Mary, Eleanor, and Rowland— were stunned. Suddenly, Mary broke the stillness. "Why, this is just a sop to Eleanor to quiet her complaints!" she exclaimed. Barry Jr. responded in stony tones that his offer to step down was still an option. "Blackmail again!" Mary cried. Barry Sr. was dubious about the stock-swap idea, but said he would reserve judgment. His lack of enthusiasm, however, suggested that he had grave doubts Eleanor could run something as complicated as WHAS.

The meeting broke up bitterly. Edie took Mary's outburst as an indication that there was "some change in feeling about us" since they had been at Smith, and she was right: Barry Jr. and his mother could barely say goodbye to each other. The "sop" comment had stung. "She was talking about the company I [would] have operated if Worth had lived," Barry Jr. fumed. "If you really want to get the pie in the face, this is it."

It was true that Mary had nothing but contempt for broadcasting. It seemed not to matter that WHAS had won many prestigious journalism awards. Television and radio were "vulgar"; the people at WHAS were "just a bunch of promoters." "Her opinion was that to be involved with broadcast was to be dirtying your hands," said Cy MacKinnon. To Mary, an offer to saddle her daughter with the management of a local radio and television station was tantamount to no offer at all.

Eleanor, however, liked broadcasting. Shooting film and producing documentaries was all she had ever really done professionally. Still, she felt confused. The stock swap was generous and exciting, but it was also frightening. It seemed like an enormous overreaction to what she wanted, which was just to be treated with respect as an equal figure in the family business. Now she was being asked to take one entity while Barry Jr. took the other. "I mean, it was pretty extreme," she said. All the same, Eleanor gave a cautious go-ahead to pursue the deal.

Meanwhile, the conflagration over the stock swap and the voting trust had slowed down the Binghams' plans to respond to Sallie's $42 million demand. Sallie was no longer invited to family meetings where matters such as shark repellents were discussed, and she was almost totally out of touch with everyone but Eleanor. She had expected the family to tell her on Friday, March 8, that they would pay the $42 million, and had already announced her intention to resign as book editor. As scheduled, that evening she left her office on the fifth floor for the last time and Shirley Williams, the woman she had pushed aside four years earlier, took back her old job.

That same day, a glum Barry Jr. and Edie flew back to Northampton. Edie could feel the Seniors' support slipping away, and two days later wrote her mother-in-law a despairing letter. "Dear, dear Mary," she began. "Our leave-taking on Thursday afternoon was so abrupt and uncharacteristic . . . that I am deeply disturbed and alarmed. The bitterness and hostility which I sensed were all the more cutting because I simply do not understand their provenance." She defended her husband and, by implication, the stock-swap idea. Unless Barry Jr. and Eleanor have separate spheres, she said, they are apt to grate against each other like "two pieces of sandpaper."

Edie tried hard to contain her resentment of Mary, and softened her language for Barry Jr.'s sake. In the original longhand draft of the letter, she wrote, "I have repeatedly overlooked snubs and unkindness," then scratched it out in favor of, "I have repeatedly extended my love despite a discouraging reception at times." She signed it, "your devoted and far-away daughter-in-law."

Barry Sr. and Mary responded separately to Edie's letter. Barry Sr.'s seemed at first to be a frothy confection, but it turned dark at the edges. He pointedly avoided direct references to the turbulent March 7 meeting, nattering on instead about an upcoming festival at Actors Theatre and the recent death of his old friend, Weldon James. But then he casually mentioned that Sydney Gruson, vice-chairman of The New York Times Co., was soon to be a houseguest. Within the family, it was widely known that Sydney hoped to persuade Barry Sr. to sell the *CJ & T* to *The New York Times*. His presence at the Little House seemed to be a veiled warning to Barry Jr. to work something out with Eleanor or else. It was typical Barry Sr.: a harsh message delivered ambiguously, leaving no clear tracks.

In contrast, Mary's letter was all business. It started with conciliation. "I appreciate your efforts over the years to mediate differences between the members of this contentious and quarrelsome family," she wrote Edie. "As for the crisis that erupted on Thursday . . . I am obliged to say to you and Barry that I regret my intemperate and unkind remarks. They were the result of my failure to grasp the full import of Barry's generous offer of 100% trusteeship of WHAS to Eleanor."

The tone of the letter grew hotter as she went on to explain that her reaction sprang from Barry Jr.'s "habitual rejection of the idea of any sharing of power." It was clear, she said, that he was no closer to "recognizing Eleanor as a legitimate part of family ownership with a voice, even though a minority one, in certain decision-making instances." That Barry Jr. would prefer to resign as publisher rather than establish a working relationship with his sister left her "aghast and indignant." Her protective feelings toward Eleanor were based in part on her son's "inexplicable prejudice" toward Rowland, including "some very mean-spirited little plots." How Barry Jr. could think that "a friendly, brotherly relationship" could be built with Eleanor in the face of his "contemptuous rejection of Rowland . . . is preposterous." So much for conciliation.

In closing, she said that she had "to accept the hard fact that the suspicion and distrust that exist between Barry and Eleanor will always prevent them from being able to work together, or even to have normal family feelings for each other." For this reason alone, "I have now had to come to realize that a complete separation of responsibility and power is . . . the only practical expedient, and I hope that Eleanor will accept [Barry Jr.'s suggestion of a split trusteeship]."

But Eleanor, with Rucker Todd at her elbow, was aiming for a separation that would give her far more power than merely controlling WHAS through a voting trust. On the Monday following the rancorous March 7 meeting, Rucker sent Gordon Davidson a document entitled "Eleanor Bingham Miller Memorandum re: Present Preferences." The document was calculated to hold Barry Jr.'s feet to the fire.

The memo asserted that Eleanor did not want to enter the voting trust because that would "seriously disrupt her relationship with Sallie." Besides, signing it would further erode her already limited power. Eleanor "hopes that her mother and father will not regard this preference as a nonsupportive position," the memo said. "She does not want to see the companies sold, but she does not want to surrender the small measure of control that she now has."

However, Rucker artfully went on, Eleanor would be willing to join the voting trust if she could withdraw at any time. In effect, she would sign in order to give prospective sharks the impression that the Binghams were united, but if she changed her mind and decided to sell, she could do as she pleased. What is more, if the voting trust did come about, her stock had to be put in escrow so that she could retrieve it instantly if she decided to sell.

The memo amounted to an impressive power play, and Barry Sr., Mary, and Barry Jr. were over a barrel. They were about to turn down Sallie's $42 million demand, which meant the sharks would soon be gliding by to see if there was blood in the water. Some sort of voting trust was essential. They agreed to Eleanor's terms, and the sham voting trust was created.

Eleanor, however, was still not satisfied. Over the weekend, she had thought a lot about Barry Jr.'s proposal that she control WHAS as trustee of its voting stock. Rowland had pointed out that this would still leave most of her assets, in the form of stock in the papers and Standard Gravure, under Barry Jr.'s management. He would still have her security, and a big chunk of her dividends, in his hands.

The day after Rucker Todd's "preferences" memo went out, Eleanor called George Gill and told him she wanted nothing to do with anything her brother managed. She wanted none of her property or assets under his jurisdiction. Merely running WHAS through control of the voting stock was not satisfactory. There had to be a complete, total separation, Eleanor said. A literal stock swap.

When George called Northampton with the news, Barry Jr. reacted temperately. Actually swapping stock would be infinitely more complicated, but he was willing. Barry Jr. immediately phoned Joan, who would become his partner in the newspapers if the stock swap went through. Joan had thought the trusteeship plan was workable. She considered Eleanor's insistence on an actual exchange of stock bizarre. "I was horrified," she said, adding that she was sure Eleanor would never have put herself so far out on a limb without pressure from Rowland and Rucker.

But Joan wanted to keep a claim on the papers at all costs. If a stock swap was what was required, so be it. She sensed that Eleanor's ego was working overtime, conjuring up fantasies of a glorious reign at WHAS. Eventually, when the lovely vision had faded a bit, she was sure Eleanor's underlying insecurity would take over and she would begin to tremble at the thought of all that responsibility. Joan's deep concern was that, if Eleanor got scared and backed out of the stock swap, the Senior Binghams might sell all the companies. How strange, she mused. It seemed that her hopes for Clara and Rob at the newspapers might hinge on Eleanor's fragile self-esteem.

A week after Eleanor laid down her terms for signing the voting trust, *The Courier-Journal* announced that the Bingham family had formally rejected Sallie's demand for $42 million. In keeping with Sallie's instruction, no counterproposal was made.

The paper also portentously announced that Barry Sr., Mary, Barry Jr., and Eleanor had banded together in a ten-year voting trust representing 95 percent of the companies' voting stock. Barry Sr. was to be sole trustee, succeeded at death by Mary, and she by Barry Jr. There was no mention of Eleanor as a trustee.

The Courier-Journal was not told that a separate instrument had been signed allowing Eleanor to withdraw from the trust at any time. Unbeknownst to all but a handful of people, the much-ballyhooed voting trust was a paper tiger, a bluff that the family hoped would scare off potential sharks.

This sham trust vested Eleanor with new and genuine power, even though it was unwarranted by her stock holdings. Barry Sr. controlled a majority of the voting stock outright, and there was no real need for a voting trust to keep the companies from being sold. Adding Barry Jr.'s voting power made the family's strength even more unassailable. Still, Eleanor's threat to pull out had made the Binghams feel vulnerable. It was as though they had a secret that was not particularly important but were deathly afraid would be revealed.

The Binghams gathered again the next weekend, but the dynamics had changed considerably since the ugly March 7 meeting. Barry Jr., Edie, and Joan sensed that the Seniors were moving closer to a sale, and that, as expected, Eleanor was beginning to get cold feet about running WHAS. When a document was passed around the room showing how much money each Bingham would get if all the companies were sold, Barry Jr. felt the momentum jerk smartly toward total sale. He was also aware that his mother had trained a careful eye on him during lunch at a downtown restaurant to see how he and Rowland interacted. Barry Jr. took pains to treat his brother-in-law with magnanimous grace.

Later that afternoon, when Joan and Edie went to Eleanor's house to see little Rowlie, they tried to bolster her confidence about owning WHAS. Just as they had feared, she was having second thoughts. Eleanor was pregnant again and worried about how she could be a mother of two children and run WHAS at the same time. Don't worry! said Joan and Edie. The professional staff can do the day-to-day management. But, Eleanor ventured, wouldn't I still have to spend a lot of time in the building? "No!" said Joan. "You don't have to go down there every day." Eleanor wondered how people in Louisville would perceive her if she took a large salary from WHAS but was rarely there. That will be no problem, her sisters-in-law pleaded.

A few days after this unsatisfying exchange, Barry Jr. poured his heart out to his father. He would soon return to Northampton for the last weeks of his cherished sabbatical. He seemed softened, or chastened, or perhaps it was just one of those moments when he and his father were able to recapture the old intimacy, the old trust, the old shared dream. As they rode into town that morning, the Ohio River on their right was swollen with spring rain. Kentucky was in full flower and at its most beautiful.

Barry Sr. began to speak. "Your mother gets out of bed at 3:00 A.M. and writes letters I wish she would not send," he said. He apologized for her most recent missive, lacerating Barry Jr. for his "mean-spirited little plots" against Rowland. With that opening, Barry Jr. exposed his hurt. He said he had promised his mother that past incidents such as keeping Rowland off the plane to the Morristown plant would not happen again. He had admitted his mistake. Why couldn't she believe him? Why was she always "picking off scabs"?

Then Barry Jr. thanked his father for backing him during the very difficult last two years. This was a different kind of gratitude than before. This time, there was no air of entitlement or self-righteousness or resentment that the support had not been instantaneous and unquestioning. He thanked Barry Sr. like a man who realized he had asked a lot, and was sincerely appreciative that his father had come through for him. Barry Sr. was touched.

He and his son had not had such a moment of unalloyed affection in a long time. For both of them, the conversation seemed to herald a new start, and Barry Jr. flew back to Northampton with an optimism he had not expected to feel. No matter what his sisters did, he now felt more confident than ever that his father was on his side. When the chips were down, his father would support him. Not his sisters. Him. The son who had devoted his life to the family business.

Barry Jr. sealed the pact by writing his father as soon as he got back to Massachusetts.

> I . . . don't want to let this opportunity go by without thanking you for standing by me during the past difficult months. It has been a period during which I have seen my constituency dwindle among members of the family. I had expected that it would be just the reverse . . . being out of town should have reduced the opportunities for friction rather than increased them. But that isn't the way it has worked and it dismays me that my relationship with Mother and Eleanor suffers whether I'm near at hand or far away. I think you know me well enough to understand that I am not trying to cheat anyone out of anything. I am trying to run these companies in the tradition which you established in this era of considerable uncertainty and change in the world of journalism and communications. I'm sure I'll make mistakes (FM classical radio being one of the more expensive ones in the past) but I hope that you will continue to understand that they are not made out of malice or ill will towards anyone. I wish I could say this to Mother with some expectation that she would believe me. Every communication with her, however, seems to enhance rather than reduce her suspicions about me. I wish I could convince her that I'm just not the kind of conniving person she seems convinced I am.

He closed this poignant, gentle letter with a clear expression of unhappiness that his period of escape was about to end. "The year seems to be vanishing faster than the snow drops along the bank of the pond," he wrote.

Barry Jr.'s letter prompted Mary to make an effort to mend the breach with her son. As always, she tempered mercy with justice. "I do not, Barry, think you are a conniving or cheating person," she wrote. "I do think you have been insensitive and arrogant in your treatment of Rowland . . . [but] I shall not belabor this point."

Barry Jr. responded to Mary's overture with unusual tact, which suggested that, probably at Edie's instruction, he had learned that turning away wrath sometimes meant biting one's tongue. "I heartily share your desire to clear away misinterpretations and assumptions which have caused a rift between us," he wrote on one of the last days of his sabbatical. "This might be done better in conversation rather than in writing. . . . If it is satisfactory with you, we might get together sometime shortly after I return." Mary wrote back warmly: "I very much agree."

Sallie was genuinely shocked when the family turned down her $42 million offer. She had assumed they would buy her out, even at that price, if for no other reason than to prevent her from going elsewhere. She began to tell people that the family had made "a gross error in judgment." She set about finding an outsider to prove just how misguided their judgment had been.

She had no idea how one went about peddling something as unwieldy as a minority interest in a family communications business. What was needed was a New York lawyer to walk her through the tangled thicket of invest-ment bankers and media brokers. She promptly hired William J. Grant, a corporate attorney with Willkie, Farr & Gallagher, a large Republican firm that had once claimed Wendell Willkie, Franklin Roosevelt's 1940 presiden-tial opponent, as a partner.

With Grant at her side, Sallie sat through countless meetings with invest-ment bankers and listened to their estimates of how much she might get if she retained them to sell her stock. What she heard was discouraging. "Everybody was very pessimistic about my chances," she said. "All the New York investment people were saying it was hopeless."

Again and again she was told that the only certain value of her stock was the $300,000 a year in dividends it produced. One could invest $4 million in a money market fund and get that much in interest, so, in one sense, her stock was worth about $4 million. It was only worth more if all the compa-nies were sold, and that looked very unlikely. A patient investor might take a chance and pay $8 million for the stock. Even $10 million. But that was about it. What is more, the big investment banks were reluctant to sign Sallie as a client, fearing a backlash from other family newspaper publishers, who were apt to view the move as a hostile act and take their business elsewhere when it came time for them to sell.

There was one exception, however. Christopher Shaw, head of the U.S. branch of Henry Ansbacher & Company, a British banking outfit famous for its aggressive media deals, came to see Sallie at Grant's office. With his rosy plumpness and puckish demeanor, Christopher seemed like a character out of Dickens. But the impression was deceiving. He was as tenacious and ferocious as the wiliest Wall Street raider. "He is one of the strangest and most fascinating people I have ever met," said Sallie. "A first-class hustler." Christopher lived baronially, attended by a butler in a handsome Manhattan town house decorated in a manner befitting an English earl. "A little too new," Sallie said with a sniff, for she knew him to be from a background that was considerably less grand.

Christopher had made a fortune persuading owners of family newspapers to sell out. In the process, he had grown merrily cynical about the preten-sions of many of the nation's newspaper families. When it came time to sell, he found that most of them cared mainly about getting top dollar, amounts only the most ruthless chains were willing to pay. He thought the Binghams made an appealing target.

What he told Sallie was like a siren's song. If all the Bingham companies were put on the auction block and sold, her stock was worth from $82 million to $92 million, he said. Selling her 15 percent block alone would mean a considerable discount that would whittle the price down to about $32 million. However, if Sallie were willing to make an all-out public assault on her family, there was a pretty good chance the Binghams could be stampeded into selling the whole thing. Was she willing? Yes, Sallie said. She was very willing.

Christopher picked up the phone and called Jackie Markham, a public relations specialist who knew how to create what he called a "wave of inevitability." "It's like you're standing on the beach and the tide is coming in," he explained. "You can't stop it. All you can do is get out of the way." Christopher was always amused when such smoke-and-mirror tactics worked. "I'm surprised Barry Sr. didn't just say, 'Piss off!' because he held all the cards," he said much later. His plan, however, was to make Barry Sr. believe just the opposite.

Jackie Markham was a master at getting news organizations to run stories about her clients, and she found she had an instant rapport with Sallie. "She was a very interesting and engaging woman," Jackie recalled. "I considered her a godsend because so few people in that position want publicity. Most want it done quietly. Sallie was actually eager to have interviews."

Christopher had tried to interest Sallie in filing a lawsuit against her parents, but Sallie had not wanted to risk the negative press. Besides, she was unsure where it might lead. Instead, Jackie went to work calling contacts at various trade publications, offering interviews with Sallie and a spicy tale of sexism and family spite. Christopher hurriedly assembled a package of financial data to circulate among prospective buyers.

The "wave of inevitability" began to form in late April 1985. The Louisville tabloid *Business First* announced that Sallie had hired Ansbacher and expected to sell her shares for a price significantly higher than $42 million. Sallie claimed that fifteen "legitimate buyers" had already contacted her, most of them "large communications companies" and some private investors. WHAS-TV even put her on the air where, as Mary dryly observed, she looked "very jaunty" as she confidently said she believed her family would come back with an offer as soon as she decided to sell to someone else.

Sallie's assault began in earnest in early May when *Advertising Age*, a trade publication for the advertising industry, ran a long article about her campaign to sell her stock. The men in the Bingham family have a profound sexist bias, she was quoted as saying, and view female relations as "the girls" who are only interested in money. She portrayed Barry Jr. as a miserable man who hated newspapers and wanted to quit his job, but who had been thwarted by Barry Sr.'s determination to keep the papers in the family for the sake of the next generation. There was a similar article in *Editor & Publisher*, the trade weekly of the newspaper industry.

Sallie's selection of Ansbacher rattled the Binghams. "Of all the brokers she could have contacted, he was probably the worst," said Barry Jr. Christopher lost no time examining the voting trust. One of Eleanor's several demands had been that the only power the trust could have was to elect board members. Christopher trumpeted this fact in various articles, claiming the trust would not affect the "ability or duty of shareholders to consider an offer of sale."

Even more damaging was the fact that Eleanor had blabbed to Sallie about the side agreement permitting her to withdraw from the voting trust unilaterally. It is a possibility, Sallie told *Advertising Age*, that her sister would also sell because Eleanor "made it perfectly clear that she would not sign [the voting trust] if she couldn't sell." Barry Jr. was livid at what he considered to be Eleanor's double-cross, and Barry Sr. felt a little more sand washing out from under his feet.

The opening of Sallie's play, *Paducah*, in New York City presented an opportunity for the staff of the Bingham newspapers to take vengeance on Sallie, who, they now concluded, was their mortal enemy. When Mel Gussow reviewed the play for *The New York Times*, he described Sallie's characters as "tiresome . . . cold and self-centered." *The Courier-Journal* ran Gussow's review in its entirety, along with a slim paragraph from a more positive review by the Associated Press.

The impact of the Sallie-Ansbacher offensive hit Barry Sr. hard. He gloomily began to speculate out loud that perhaps selling was inevitable. Eleanor took her father's words as his customary way of saying something unpleasant without saying it directly. She was already having serious doubts about running WHAS, and Ansbacher's talk of $92 million for a block of stock identical to her own took her breath away.

In early May, on the same day Sallie's broadside appeared in *Advertising Age*, Rucker Todd told George Gill that Eleanor had changed her mind about the stock swap. Now she wanted to sell everything. He explained that Eleanor was worried that Sallie would be offered too high a price for her stock to enable the family to pass the companies along to the next generation. Selling now would give Barry Jr. years to do something else with his life.

As was often the case, Barry Sr. was of two minds. Despite his musings about a sale being inevitable, he now pleaded with Eleanor to view the stock swap as at least a possibility. Just consider it, he said. Eleanor agreed to do what her father wanted. Barry Sr. got word to his son that, as promised, he was supporting him. Eleanor was still on the reservation.

———————

In May 1985, a few weeks before Barry Jr. moved back to Louisville from Northampton, Wendell Cherry, David Jones, and their attorney came to see Paul Janensch about articles on Humana they knew were about to appear in *The Courier-Journal*. "Several people in town have called to tell me they're offended by the questions reporters are asking," Wendell began. Then, according to him, both sides agreed that the session would be off the record so that they could all feel free to say what was on their minds. At one point, David told Paul *The Courier-Journal* needed a "lesson in humility." Paul's attitude was equally unfriendly. "He acted like, 'This is our newspaper; we'll run it the way we want to,'" Wendell recalled.

But Paul also wanted to avoid angering the Senior Binghams or printing another embarrassing correction like the one the previous fall. So in a break with precedent, he asked to see the articles before they were published. Much of what he found appalled him. A lot of the reporting was sloppy and relied heavily on anonymous sources. The series absolutely has to be fixed, Paul said, or I will step in and stop it. "Of course, the staff was convinced that he was giving Humana special treatment because he wanted to be invited to Wendell Cherry's house," said Irene Nolan, one of the subeditors on the project. "But I knew that wasn't true."

In fact, the incident may have been Paul's finest hour. He showed leadership. He actually touched copy. When the series, "Humana: A Portrait of Power," appeared three days later, it was generally positive, prompting quiet grumbles from the principal reporter that the articles had been watered down. Humana's objections were more muted than usual.

But Paul could not resist taking a parting shot at Wendell and David while at the same time answering his critics in the newsroom. A week after the series ended, he wrote a column describing the meeting he had had with Humana's top executives earlier in the month. In the piece, he chided the two men for acting like "crybabies" and "playground bullies."

Wendell and David were apoplectic that Paul had made public what they had thought was an off-the-record conversation. The Senior Binghams were upset as well. Once again, it seemed, Paul had made it uncomfortable for them on the Louisville social circuit. As a corporate politician, "Paul was a disaster," said one top editor who observed him closely. But, the man added, "Janensch gets a bum rap because he was a good newspaperman. It was his style that got in the way."

That style was on full display at Paul's Kentucky Derby party, an event he considered to be the crowning social triumph of his nine-month tenure. By custom, Barry Jr. hosted a brunch at the Big House on the morning of the Derby, and Paul urged Barry Sr. to let him continue the tradition. Although he was uneasy, Barry Sr. smiled agreeably and Paul felt he had the Bingham patriarch's full support. "He thought it was a great idea," said Paul.

In years past, Barry Jr. had invited only top management from the companies and a select group from Louisville, including the director of the orchestra, the president of the University of Louisville, special political friends, and various representatives of the city's oldest and richest families. Paul added big advertisers, community leaders, and more staff members to the list, thus changing the party's tone from quasi-social to quasi-corporate. "I had to be a little more cold-blooded," he said.

The guest list swelled to such an extent that the company had to rent a local historic estate and throw up a tent. Cheese grits, scrambled eggs, bacon, beaten biscuits, and mint juleps were ladled out, to the Binghams' mind, at least, in a manner reminiscent of a soup kitchen. Paul was in ecstasy. "It was just one of those Kentucky mornings that I'll always remember," he exulted. "It was just like in the storybooks." But veterans of past brunches, especially the Binghams' closest friends, ridiculed the event as a tacky cattle call and sniggered at the Janensches' pretensions. The Senior Binghams were mortified.

By coincidence, the Class of '55—Edie's original class—was holding its thirtieth reunion the same weekend she graduated from Smith. Charles Kuralt came to do a segment for his Sunday television show and viewers saw Edie, beaming in a cap and gown, accept her undergraduate diploma in art history. Now that the time had come to leave Northampton, Edie felt "stronger, feistier, and at the same time more mellow and balanced, even more independent, if that is possible."

For Barry Jr., going back to the family wars was like a death sentence after these nine happy months. Even though he had never been farther from the combat than a phone call, a letter, or a plane ride, he had felt a glorious sense of distance between him and "it." In the tranquility of Smith, he and Edie had talked and talked about what might happen. Intellectually, he had persuaded himself that, if the papers were sold, he could use the rest of his life for any number of rewarding purposes. This was mostly self-administered psychology: imagining the worst. "He had to go back and either fight or cope," said Diana Fetter de Villafranca, Edie's former classmate and close friend who lived in Northampton, "and he was prepared to do both." Even such paper-thin equanimity about the situation was a vast change from the presabbatical Barry Jr., who had had the half-crazed, hypertense look of a man suffering battle fatigue.

There were reasons for optimism. The recent thaw with his mother seemed promising. Despite his intermittent comments about selling, Barry Sr. seemed genuinely committed to saving the papers for his grandchildren, and that was crucial. Eleanor skittered back and forth about the stock swap, but at least it was still on the table. And, ultimately, Barry Jr. thought it unlikely she would challenge the Senior Binghams, which made her caprice more a nuisance than a threat. True, Barry Sr. had issued the Thirteenth Commandment, saying he and Eleanor had to find a way to work together, but that, too, seemed manageable, one way or another.

That left the big problem: Sallie. The day after Edie graduated, Barry Jr. read an Associated Press interview with her that seemed intended to terrorize the family. "My aim is quite simple," she said. "To find the buyer who can offer me the most money. I don't feel much involvement with who it is." Barry Jr. knew that Sallie's real options were much narrower than her bombast made them sound. If he could only keep his parents from panicking, she would eventually have to come to the only plausible buyer: the family.

Still, something nagged at Barry Jr. as he morosely packed the silver coffee service and demitasse cups that had provided the finishing touch for those companionable college dinners he had so enjoyed. He had sensed something odd when he was in Louisville earlier in the spring. Something he could not quite put his finger on. It was an undercurrent he could feel, like a faint vibration. Something unspoken and veiled that was subtly poisoning the whole situation. But what?

LOADING THE GUN

The shift that Barry Jr. detected went far beyond anything he imagined possible. Even Paul was aware that a bizarre switch had occurred. Now the family and even some of the hired hands seemed more hostile to Barry Jr. than to Sallie, who had effectively dropped from sight. "It went from Sallie being on the outside to Barry Jr. being on the outside," Paul said later, still as mystified by the change as Barry Jr. Neither of them fully grasped how Paul's tenure as acting editor and publisher had alienated the Senior Binghams and undermined Barry Jr.'s position as he dealt with the family strife.

Despite these concerns, Barry Jr. seemed like a new man when he returned to Louisville in mid-May 1985. The tension was gone from his neck and he had lost the wary, hunted look around his eyes. What made his apparent ease even more remarkable was that he knew he needed to restore himself to the family's inner circle and seemed genuinely eager to mend fences.

To dispel what Edie called "the surge of ill-feeling" that had developed in their absence, Barry Jr. scheduled a private clearing-the-air session with his mother a week after his return. On the appointed day, he walked alone across the thick spring grass to the Little House. His father had delicately suggested that he not bring Edie.

Mary put in her usual bluntly sincere performance. She began by telling her son she did not believe he was a cheat and swindler, despite what Eleanor might think. But Eleanor and Rowland were very much on Mary's mind. Why don't you listen to Eleanor's complaints? Why don't you confide in her? Why do you so resent Rowland?

Barry Jr. wearily said he would listen to anything Eleanor had to say. As for confiding, he considered Eleanor "a walking security risk" because she was so casual with confidential information. He said he had forged a "satisfactory relationship" with Rowland. These were old grievances and he tried to be conciliatory, although he made it clear he had not changed his mind on the essentials.

Then Mary said something that made the hair on his neck quiver. Eleanor and Rowland feel that low dividends should entitle family members to more of a voice in oversight of the companies, she said. Barry Jr.'s face clouded and his response was icy. "That would be unmanageable," he said. Nevertheless, as the encounter drew to a close, both parties considered it a success, if only because Barry Jr. had managed to persuade his mother that he was no longer overtly hostile to his younger sister and her husband.

To reinforce this impression, Barry Jr. invited Eleanor and Rowland to the Big House that very afternoon. The mood was cordial and relaxed, although it was apparent that Rucker Todd had been fanning their unease about the stock swap with talk about how Trust #9, under which Judge Bingham had willed his grandchildren equal shares of stock in each of the Bingham companies, would have to be restructured in order to complete the deal. "I don't see how the stock swap could work," said Eleanor, hastening to add that, of course, she personally found the idea appealing. Then Rowland, again echoing Rucker, solemnly stated that Eleanor and Sallie's best interests would be served by selling everything now.

Instead of mounting a retaliatory strike, Barry Jr. listened thoughtfully and said he would ask the Senior Binghams about developing other options that might satisfy everyone's interests. Eleanor and Rowland were delighted at his temperate response. This, indeed, was a new Barry Jr.

The next day, to complete his diplomatic mission, Barry Jr. had a long talk with his father about the future. Each man came away from the discussion elated at how well it had gone, but with totally different understandings of what had been said. The depth of their miscommunication would have been comic had the conversation not proved so pivotal and, ultimately, so damaging.

Their talk began on a somber note with Barry Jr. asking his father what had gone wrong during his time away. Barry Sr. told him that Eleanor was whining and leaning on Mary a lot. "Sallie and Eleanor going off the board has been much more traumatic for them than I had ever realized," he said. He would like to step aside as chairman, he told his son; he would feel more comfortable.

At that point, Barry Sr. blurted out an idea that he hoped would satisfy everyone and put an end to the family squabbles. Why not sell WHAS and Standard Gravure? he asked Barry Jr. That would net several million dollars for each of the Bingham stockholders, and you and Joan could then use your share to buy Eleanor and Sallie's stock in the newspapers. Barry Sr. said he had already discussed the notion with Gordon Davidson. George Gill and Leon Tallichet were now busy analyzing whether it was financially feasible.

Barry Jr. found the idea intriguing and thought it might be a promising alternative if the stock swap did not work out. But he was left breathless and a little angry to find that his top executives had been working on such a major project without telling him.

Sensing his son's annoyance, Barry Sr. made a declaration that was intended to dispel Barry Jr.'s fear that he was being subverted. "He said he would support whatever I wanted to do, whichever option I wanted to pursue," recalled Barry Jr. "If I was absolutely convinced of the stock swap, he would support me in trying to get that. If I felt [this new proposal] was the best solution, he would support me in that. And if I ever decided everything should be sold, he would support me in that." Barry Sr. did not explicitly say he would impose whatever solution Barry Jr. favored. Neither did he mention conditions under which his support might be withdrawn.

To Barry Sr., "support" was a commitment comparable to a political endorsement, something revocable should the candidate prove unworthy or if events conspired to make the situation untenable. He had given his son an expression of intent, true. But, as always, he left himself plenty of room to maneuver.

As far as Barry Jr. was concerned, however, Barry Sr. had strongly reaffirmed the promise he made in 1971, when he had stepped back and turned the businesses over to him. During dark moments in the months ahead, he and Edie would draw comfort from Barry Sr.'s words, words that, Edie said, "remained an active on-the-table kind of commitment" to support Barry Jr. when the chips were down. Whatever evidence there might be to the contrary, they told themselves that, ultimately, Barry Sr. would side with Barry Jr.

Indeed, Barry Sr.'s promise of support made Barry Jr. feel so secure that he showed no alarm when the conversation drifted into what might happen if everything were sold. It would not be the end of the world, he told his father. "I have other interests. I don't have to be publisher of *The Courier-Journal.*"

His comments were almost word-for-word what he had told himself during those reflective evenings at Smith, when, it seemed, the whole world was open to him. He had no desire to see the companies sold, but Barry Sr. seized on his son's words as evidence that Barry Jr. had undergone a change of heart. No longer would he oppose a sale at all costs. As Barry Sr. remembered it, his son had not said that he would welcome a sale, "but that he would be willing to accept . . . whatever was the best solution from my standpoint. . . . There was not going to be this feeling that it was a battle to the death."

As the conversation wound down, neither father nor son sought to put too fine a point on what had passed between them. They went their separate ways that afternoon thrilled by the positive developments their talk had produced.

Barry Sr. was so happy with his son's new attitude that the next day he wrote him a note saying how delighted he was with his easy, relaxed outlook on things, and walked over to the Big House to deliver it personally. "After thinking about it constantly for the past 24 hours," he wrote, "I feel I must tell you that I am more at ease in my mind than I have been for a long while, as a result of our talk on Thursday. I am filled with admiration for the clear-headed, rational way you are approaching the situation so fraught with emotional problems. We are not through the woods yet, and there will be strains and challenges still to meet. For the first time, however, I see clear daylight ahead along the course you have charted."

Daylight to Barry Sr. meant that his son's new attitude had opened the door to accommodation with his sisters and perhaps even Option X. Barry Jr. read the ambiguous words and smiled because he saw them in a very different light—the comforting glow that came from his father's guarantee of support, which effectively blocked total sale or any other solution Barry Jr. did not agree with.

The following Monday, Barry Jr. resumed his duties as editor and publisher. His unprecedented ease and relaxation stunned those in the executive wing. He was clearly pleased at the way things had gone during the sabbatical, and had no idea that Paul Janensch's performance had helped push his parents into the enemy camp. Though Paul resumed his old title of executive editor, Barry Jr. asked him to continue sitting in on the daily editorial board meeting. George Gill, however, was still furious at Barry Jr. and jealous of Paul, and felt no hesitation about putting down the boss to his face. "He was brutal to Barry," said Bob Morse. "Really brutal."

Resolving the stock swap with Eleanor and the sale of Sallie's stock now dwarfed all other business problems. A few days after Barry Jr.'s return to work, George presented Barry Sr. and Mary with four options, and asked them to rank them according to preference.

After mulling it over for a few days, the Senior Binghams said that their top choice was selling WHAS and Standard Gravure. That way, they reasoned, Sallie and Eleanor could get the money they wanted and Barry Jr. and Joan could—at some unspecified date in the future—buy the sisters' share of the *CJ & T* and own the newspapers outright.

Their second choice was the original version of the stock swap, under which Barry Jr. would be 100 percent trustee of the papers and Eleanor would be 100 percent trustee of WHAS. This would give each heir control of the entity he or she wanted, but not actual ownership. That would not occur until after the Seniors' deaths, when Barry Jr. and Eleanor would literally swap WHAS stock for newspaper stock and vice versa. The beauty of this plan was that it avoided the legal complication of restructuring Judge Bingham's Trust #9.

The Senior Binghams rejected the other two choices, which were more complicated versions of the stock swap. "We are quite open to persuasion and/or discussion of other options," Barry Sr. wrote George in his letter outlining their preferences. "Please explain the plans in detail to Barry Jr. and let him know of our feelings." George went one better than that, putting on a thorough presentation of the four options for all except Sallie's branch of the family. The gathering broke up with clear momentum behind some variant of the stock swap.

The harmony was short-lived. Rucker Todd, Eleanor's lawyer, had been in China during the Bingham conference and did not get a chance to look at the "four options" memo until he returned. In late June, when the family reconvened to hammer out how a stock swap might actually work, Eleanor was present but Rucker did all the talking.

First, Rucker astonished everyone by delivering a lecture on fairness. After their scrupulous efforts to treat their children equally, the Senior Binghams were infuriated by Rucker's insolence. "Goddamn, it was awful," Gordon Davidson remembered with a grimace. "At one point I thought Mrs. Bingham was coming across the table."

The family planned to offer Sallie a price for her shares based on "minority" value instead of "fair" (meaning "full") value, Rucker said. That was fine; as the bad daughter, that was all that Sallie deserved. Eleanor, on the other hand, had not invited outsiders to make bids on her stock. Indeed, she had gone along with what her parents wanted and was willing to swap her stock to keep the papers in the family. Then, with a pause for effect, Rucker said that as compensation for being so cooperative, Eleanor wanted to be paid "fair" value for her stock, not a discounted value for minority ownership. The extra dollop for Eleanor came to be known as "the good-girl premium."

For Eleanor, the issue was how much cash she and Rowland would end up with after a stock swap. By swapping, Eleanor was going to be trading something very valuable—her newspaper stock—for something less valuable—Barry Jr.'s WHAS stock. Barry Jr. would then have to make up the difference in cash. The higher the stock values, the larger would be the difference between the two blocks—and the more Barry Jr. would have to pay her to equalize the trade. Instead of a cash equalizer of around $6 million at the minority rate, she might end up with around $20 million or more if the stocks were priced at "fair" value, with the good-girl premium.

Leon Tallichet was dumbfounded by Rucker's proposal. "That would sink the ship," he stammered. "The ship" was the future of the newspapers and all the years of effort that had gone into making sure they could be passed to the next generation. Putting a higher price on Eleanor's stock meant that the I.R.S. would put a higher value on the newspapers for inheritance tax purposes when the Seniors died. The values would be so great and the taxes so high that the papers would probably have to be sold.

Rucker's cheeky display enraged Barry Sr., who reacted with unusual decisiveness. He flatly told the attorney that all the stock was to be valued the same. There would be no good-girl premium. "So that was the end of that," said Eleanor. She dropped "fair" value as a condition of the stock swap.

But Barry Jr. knew that was not the end. If Eleanor's stock was to be valued at the same level as Sallie's for purposes of a swap, the two sisters now had a vested interest in Sallie receiving the highest possible price. Before, Eleanor had demanded that Sallie's stock be valued low. Now, the size of her "big cash pile," as Edie derisively called it, depended on how high a price Sallie could get.

———

The Senior Binghams soon left for their summer home in Chatham, more convinced than ever that Barry Jr. and Eleanor were nowhere near resolving the difficulties of a stock swap. Before driving north to Cape Cod, they dropped by to see Eleanor and their small grandson, and told her to make up her mind about what she wanted to do.

Barry Sr. said he was pessimistic that she and Barry Jr. could ever make the stock swap work. Eager to end the fighting and resume the pleasant existence he had known before the family trauma, he talked almost wistfully of selling everything. Think what new vistas it would open for each of us, he said.

Eleanor was all too familiar with her father's oblique way of communicating. She realized that he was delivering a message. Before, Barry Sr. had almost always spoken out strongly against a sale. Now, she decided, he was telling her that Option X was a solution he could accept, even embrace.

Barry Sr. and Mary had ample reasons to favor total sale. It might end the feuding and it would provide millions of dollars for them to give away, thus creating a grand string of monuments to their memory. Barry Sr. and Mary had always been generous with their wealth. Since 1952, Barry Sr. had had a policy of earmarking 5 percent of the companies' pretax profits for charity. But the amount had never been enough to make truly significant gifts. Doling out tens of millions in their final years would be a glorious way to go out. And what thrilling fun it would be to retake center stage after fifteen years in retirement.

Though they did not explicitly say so, the Seniors left Eleanor with the hazy impression that they favored total sale but also wanted to keep their hands clean. They wanted her to do the dirty work of putting Option X on the table. Eleanor did not have the appetite for such a move just yet. She told her parents she would let them know her preference very soon; with that, Barry Sr. and Mary drove off for Chatham.

The Seniors talked of nothing but the family morass as they settled into their summer routine, which included long walks on the beach and surreptitious skinny-dips in the ocean. Though she was now eighty, Mary had not lost her determination to look her best. Every morning she did a shoulder stand while furiously peddling in the air to a count of three hundred. She had a pamphlet called *How to Flatten Your Stomach for Women Over 35*, which she found so effective that she made copies for friends.

Barry Sr. had started jogging at the age of sixty and carefully monitored his intake of desserts and starches. He was so trim that his London tailor had never had to alter his measurements. His preoccupation with his own physique made him particularly observant of what others looked like. A female acquaintance about his age once dropped by for a chat on the beach. She was wearing a bathing suit cut high up the thigh, and it was apparent she had taken great pains to exercise and eat sparingly. As she rose to go, Barry Sr. said in unabashed admiration, "I can't let you leave without complimenting you on your marvelous figure. It's just a marvelous figure."

Though they were happy to be back at their old frame house on Water Street, with its miniature turret, green hedge, and small back garden, there was little peace on Cape Cod. The day they arrived, Eleanor called to say that she had concluded she could not trust Barry Jr.; therefore, the stock swap would never work. The deal depended on trading stock after her parents' deaths, and she felt she could not count on Barry Jr. to treat her fairly when the Senior Binghams were not around.

Barry Sr. and Mary hung up the phone and looked at each other with both despair and relief. They had had reservations about the stock swap from the start and Eleanor's positive declaration at least ruled out one option. In Chatham, the Seniors began debating about whether it would be better to sell WHAS and Standard and keep the papers, or to sell everything. Simply leaving things as they were did not seem like a realistic alternative because they assumed Eleanor would immediately pool her shares with Sallie's and put them up for sale.

Back in Louisville, Barry Jr. was blissfully unaware that Eleanor had told her father the stock swap was unworkable. Two days after she made the call to Chatham, he invited Eleanor and Rowland to the Big House to talk further about the swap. Joan and her two children, Clara and Rob, are in town and will be there, too, he said. Eleanor and Rowland accepted with some trepidation.

What started out as an informal social event turned into an intense effort to persuade Eleanor to accept the stock swap. The pressure was enormous. Joan had brought her children to Louisville from Washington, D.C., expressly for the purpose of making an appeal to Eleanor. Joan feared that, without a stock swap, the Seniors would sell all the companies. "I want a chance to run this paper," nineteen-year-old Rob said to Eleanor. "You had your opportunity, and now I want it, too. You owe it to me."

Eleanor and Rowland were not sure. Again and again, they came back to the fact that "this option gives no one a big pile of cash and Sallie gets screwed." Why screwed? Because Eleanor would end up owning WHAS, Barry Jr. and Joan would eventually own the papers, and Sallie would own nothing. Sallie would get $25 million or so in cash for her stock, but the assets the others would end up with would be worth at least twice that.

Sallie, however, did not seem to care about that—at least not publicly. As it happened, *The Courier-Journal* had recently announced that a stock swap was being considered and Sallie had been quoted saying she thought the deal would be great for Eleanor. Sallie's first and only priority seemed to be to get out, even if it meant her brother and sister died richer than she did.

The conversation went on and on. Eleanor had a close relationship with all her nieces and nephews. She cared what they thought, and was moved by Rob's and Clara's pleas. Joan wanted her to own and operate WHAS. Barry Jr. and Edie wanted it. The momentum was nearly irresistible. And Eleanor, much like her father, yearned to be loved and tried always to find a path that made that possible.

Finally, reluctantly, Eleanor agreed. She would go along with the stock swap. With whoops and tears, Edie and Joan opened bottles of champagne while Barry Jr. placed a call to Chatham to inform his parents that the consensus they had hoped for had at last been reached. The decision: stock swap! Only Rowland sounded a sullen note. "Eleanor is just doing this to keep the family together, not because she needs it," he said to no one in particular.

Barry Jr. ebulliently told his father the good news while Joan watched. Almost immediately, she saw his smile fade and his face take on the hard, tight quality that had been his trademark before the year in Northampton. He wearily handed her the phone. In a rapid torrent of words intended to overwhelm all resistance, Joan gushed to her father-in-law that Eleanor and Barry Jr. were getting along splendidly, that the agreement was genuine, the champagne toasts heartfelt. "We thought he was going to be so pleased because he'd been saying all along, 'You children work it out,' " said Joan.

Barry Sr. listened in silence. When the flood of words had stopped, he said, "It's never going to work." Only two days earlier, Eleanor had called him to say that the swap was off because she could not trust her brother. To Barry Sr., the news from Louisville seemed more like a temporary truce inspired by champagne and emotion rather than a real treaty.

Barry Sr. said that he and Mary would interrupt their vacation and fly back to Louisville to try and decide once and for all what course to follow. The family summit was set for July 8, 1985, Molly's seventeenth birthday. As Joan hung up the phone, Barry Jr. snorted in disgust: "Peace broke out and they don't like it!" Despite what they might say about wanting their children to "work it out," the Senior Binghams seemed to be the ones who wanted to control the outcome of the family strife.

———

In an odd twist, Barry Sr.'s doubts about the stock swap now made Eleanor and Barry Jr. allies. She, like her brother, had assumed that her parents would cheer any turn for the better in family relations, despite what she might have said two days earlier in her phone call to Chatham.

Why would Barry Sr. react this way? Eleanor thought she had the answer, based on how her father had spoken to her before he and Mary left for Cape Cod. "They're resigned to the papers being sold," she told the others, "and now they are deciding how they are going to spend all the money." To Barry Jr. and Joan, Eleanor's theory seemed terrifyingly plausible.

Barry Sr. had not really gone back on his commitment to follow whatever option his son chose, but Barry Jr. had sensed in his father's voice over the phone that he was returning to Louisville to push the idea of total sale. Option X was no longer just a desperate last resort. Now it was a definite possibility. This was an emergency!

Or maybe it was one of Barry Sr.'s elegant manipulations. Perhaps he was using reverse psychology to push his children together. As long as Eleanor and Barry Jr. thought he was leaning toward Option X, they would feel pressure to reach a genuine accord. Barry Sr. was such an enigma to his own children that no one knew for sure.

Three days later, Eleanor and Rowland went to see their lawyer, Rucker Todd. The champagne-graced agreement to pursue the stock swap had been only a declaration of intent, with the details of how it would actually work left unresolved. The nasty problems remained.

Eleanor told Rucker that Barry Jr.'s first choice was to leave everything as it was, and merely install Eleanor at WHAS. Rucker pointed out that this would do nothing to remove her assets from Barry Jr.'s management, which was what she had hired him to achieve.

The next day, Rucker ran into Gordon Davidson in the locker room of the Louisville Country Club and asked him what he thought would come out of the July 8 conclave with the Seniors. Gordon was taken aback. He knew nothing about such a meeting. He had only been told that Eleanor and Barry Jr. had agreed to the swap option and that the Seniors were "not all that enthusiastic." But a family summit? He had been kept in the dark, and concluded that Barry Sr. wanted it to be a strictly private affair.

Barry Sr. and Mary flew into Louisville on a sweltering Sunday night, July 7. They had closed up the Little House for the summer and did not want to go to the trouble of opening it for so short a stay, so they slipped quietly into the Seelbach Hotel, where the family was scheduled to gather the following day.

Business First was on prominent display in the Seelbach's lobby newsstand. In it was Christopher Shaw's latest attempt to make the Binghams feel that a "wave of inevitability" was rapidly approaching. The tabloid quoted one of Shaw's senior vice-presidents as saying that forty prospective buyers for Sallie's stock had been sent detailed information about the companies. Eight had said they had no interest, including David Jones of Humana. Twenty or so had said they "will get back to us." Two had made offers for "at least some of Sallie's shares," the article claimed.

On July 8, Barry Sr. met first with four of his eight grandchildren. Molly, Barry Jr.'s youngest, was home for the summer from boarding school. Her older sister, Emily, arrived from North Carolina, where she was interning at the Raleigh *News & Observer*, and Clara and Rob flew back from Washington. None of Sallie's line was present. Barry Ellsworth lived in New York and was more interested in art and film than the newspapers. Chris Iovenko, who wanted to stay on good terms with his mother, had removed himself from the struggle. Willy Iovenko, Sallie's youngest, had repeatedly run afoul of the law and was in a private youth rehabilitation center in Texas.

In one of the Seelbach's stiff, formal meeting rooms, Barry Sr. told his grandchildren that they must prepare for the worst. "I warned them that things were getting very difficult and that we couldn't go on forever like this," he said. "I just wanted them to feel that they had not been overlooked in our thinking."

One after another, the grandchildren asked Barry Sr. not to sell. Clara was forcefully direct. She wanted her chance to run the newspapers, she said, and Rob echoed her remarks. Emily's comments were a bit different. She did not want the papers sold, she said, but she did not want "Granny" and "Grandy" to worry about the future of the grandchildren. "We can all take care of ourselves," she said.

Barry Sr. was touched. "Why, that's the most liberating statement I've ever heard," he said, his voice tinged with the same whisper of relief that had greeted Barry Jr.'s statement that he did not have to be publisher of *The Courier-Journal*. Characteristically, Barry Sr. had been selective in what he heard. Emily, he felt, had absolved him on behalf of the grandchildren. Now he could do as he liked without feeling guilt about the next generation. After promising the grandchildren that he would consult with them again before making any decision to sell, they adjourned.

Eleanor and Rowland, Joan, Barry Jr. and Edie then filed into the room for the formal family summit. "People have said that so many of the problems of the family are derived from our not communicating with each other," Barry Sr. said later. "There may be something in that, but there was a very open communication on this occasion."

Mary began the gathering by distributing a memorandum she had composed on her battered manual typewriter at Chatham. The message, addressed to "shareholders from the Binghams Sr.," was brutally frank. It came to be known as "Mother's memo of distrust."

The document began by describing the stock swap as the option "preferable to all the others" but questioned whether it could ever work "in view of the lack of confidence that exists on both sides." This repeated Eleanor's statement that she could not trust Barry Jr. to treat her fairly when it came time to trade stock after the Seniors' deaths. Because of such "long-standing distrust and suspicion . . . we suggest that Option X ought to be seriously considered."

The pros of Option X were many, Mary went on. With her share of the sale price, Eleanor could "invest in and direct an independent, documentary-producing business for national distribution." A local station like WHAS, in contrast, would probably never give her "the opportunity to use her imagination, or to develop creative ideas about programming." Option X would also "resolve the . . . hostile distrust that now exists. Nothing would be held in common, therefore there would be no cause for disagreement."

Furthermore, a total sale would relieve family members of "the difficulties brought on by news and policy decisions at the papers with which we disagree, but for which we are held responsible by the public." Selling now would also bring top prices and spare Barry Jr. the burden of having to endure odious and inevitable developments, such as eliminating *The Louisville Times* and reducing *The Courier-Journal's* statewide circulation.

Compared with this long list of pros, the cons were skimpy indeed. Selling would end family ownership and the successor owner would be unlikely to keep up the companies' level of charitable giving to the community. Barry Jr. might have to leave Louisville to find new work. Loyal employees might be hurt. And selling would "end the opportunity for the next generation to have management careers in the three companies." Strangely, the possibility that the papers would decline in quality under new ownership was not mentioned. The Seniors seemed to feel that the papers were no longer exemplary news products that needed to be preserved.

With unusual candor, Barry Sr. told the group that one of the reasons he and Mary had returned to Louisville was that Eleanor had bluntly told them that she could not trust her brother to deal fairly with her. He turned to Eleanor and asked her why she now seemed so eager to go ahead with the same stock swap she had so recently rejected. Barry Sr. quoted her phone call to Chatham back to her word for word.

Visibly embarrassed, Eleanor stammered that she did not mean she could not trust Barry Jr. "in the long run"; she just felt now that the stock swap was "doable." A formula for valuing the stock could be made part of the agreement so that her interests would be protected after her parents died, she said.

Joan chimed in that the stock-swap plan was a wonderful solution. "The thing that will keep the family together is the family business," she asserted. "There'll be no more reason for everybody to come back here [otherwise]. Money isn't going to make anybody happy. Work is better than money!"

Barry Sr. arched his eyebrows. "Well, Joan," he said, "wouldn't you like a lot of money for *The Washington Weekly?*" He was referring to an upscale tabloid Joan had invested in that had recently folded. "Don't mind-fuck me!" she snapped back. "I took so much money, I gambled with it and lost. I'm not asking for anything."

Barry Sr. brought out a memo George had prepared, calculating how much Sallie should be offered for her shares if the stock swap were implemented. George suggested $25 million as "a prudent and fair minority value." WHAS would have to borrow funds to pay for its portion of the purchase and this would leave the company in debt for several years, with limited cash for such things as a new television tower. Was Eleanor prepared to go ahead with the stock swap knowing that WHAS would have such problems, at least for a while?

Eleanor waffled and wavered. The grandchildren turned to her with expectant faces. "You really haven't made a good faith effort," one of them said accusingly. Eleanor looked at Barry Jr. and Joan. "Could you be supportive of me as manager of the TV and radio stations?" she asked. They eagerly said yes, they could and would—gladly. Barry Jr. promised he would do all in his power to keep her *Courier-Journal* dividends, which she would continue to get until the stock was actually swapped, as high as possible.

Eleanor told her parents that she had met with her old boss Bob Morse. Despite their past differences, he had seemed amenable to her coming back to the station as president. He had even suggested that she do on-air editorials. Her experience with "Louisville Tonight" had given her confidence that she could produce programs and feed them to the CBS network through WHAS. There was also the possibility of expanding to other markets, acquiring more stations, building an empire.

"Yes," she said firmly. "I want to do it."

The matter was decided. Barry Jr. and Eleanor would execute the stock swap, coupled with an offer to Sallie of $25 million. The Binghams adjourned to reconvene at the Big House that night for Molly's birthday party.

Within hours, the deal would begin to unravel.

———

After the meeting broke up, Eleanor headed home. She was six months pregnant and wilting in the heat. Barry Sr. and Barry Jr. left quickly, too, but not for the Bingham compound at Glenview. Instead, they sped off to the newspaper building to compose a press release announcing the agreement.

That night, when Eleanor and Rowland arrived at the Big House for Molly's birthday, Barry Jr. handed Eleanor a copy of the press release. She hit the ceiling. "If you're going to write a press release, we'd like to be part of it," she stormed. "This must never happen again. If I am going to be running one of these companies, I certainly have to be the one there!"

Barry Jr. was exasperated. "It's a draft!" he said, rolling his eyes. "Edit it if you want!" Eleanor said she would rather not have the agreement announced in the next day's paper because she and Rowland were going to be in New York. But word had already begun to leak out that a deal had been made. Even without a formal announcement, she was bound to get questions.

Barry Sr. asked what they intended to say if reporters contacted them. "I don't know," snapped Eleanor. Mary was incredulous. "We had an agreement this afternoon. What has changed?" Eleanor and Rowland were silent. Reluctantly, they gave their consent to go ahead with the press release.

Barry Jr. watched Eleanor and Rowland angling to delay the announcement and gloomily concluded that the stock swap was not so firm after all. The next morning as he rode into work with his father, he said that he thought Eleanor and Rowland really wanted Option X and had only agreed to the stock swap because they did not want to be perceived as the ones forcing a sale. "They just don't want blood on their hands," he said.

Nevertheless, the historic agreement was announced that day as planned. Eleanor and Barry Jr. would enter a voting trust that would give them control of WHAS and The Courier-Journal and Louisville Times Company, respectively, the CJ said. An actual swap of ownership would not take place until after the deaths of the Senior Binghams. There was no announcement that Sallie had simultaneously been offered $25 million for her stock. The CJ only mentioned Sallie in passing, quoting her as saying how "delighted" she was that her sister was going to run WHAS.

Buried deep in the story, below the pleasantries and expressions of optimism, was a particularly telling paragraph. "The newspapers are worth more than three times the broadcast holdings," The Courier-Journal noted. "How that will be adjusted in the stock swap is one of the details to be worked out, Bingham Jr. said."

It had been six weeks since Barry Jr. had returned to Louisville, and in that time he had rapidly reverted to the beleaguered and suspicious workaholic he had been before his sabbatical. "I think he became even more intense," said John Richards. Colleagues noticed that he ate only lettuce for lunch, with a little salt and lemon juice. At social events, he shunned vodka or highballs—his standard drinks—and gulped club soda with a dash of bitters instead. The old Barry Jr. was back, more ascetic and self-denying than ever.

Fueling his anxiety was his conviction that Eleanor was masterminding a conspiracy to sell the companies out from under him. In March, Barry Sr. had issued the Thirteenth Commandment, requiring Barry Jr. and Eleanor to "establish a workable relationship" or resign themselves to Option X. Since then, Eleanor, with her on-again, off-again embrace of the stock swap, had seemed hell-bent on making a "workable relationship" impossible. Eventually, the Seniors might lose patience and carry out their threat, which, he was convinced, was what Eleanor and Rowland really wanted.

Adding to his sense of embattled isolation was a feeling that his parents no longer cared whether the papers remained in the family. Barry Sr. and Mary behaved as though the papers had lost that mysterious spark that, always before, had made them worth fighting for and sacrificing for. True, Barry Sr. had honored his pledge to go along with Barry Jr.'s wishes. But he felt he could almost smell their eagerness to sell.

He could not even trust George Gill and the hired hands. A few weeks after returning from Northampton, he had gone to his father and complained that they now kept things from him, on Barry Sr.'s orders. He even feared that they were working against him on behalf of Eleanor and Sallie. "The management team has become a cancer!" he told his startled father.

Barry Sr. said that he needed George, Leon, and Bernie Block to help him calculate the financial effects of various options and that he did not want to share the information with Barry Jr.—a minority shareholder just like Sallie and Eleanor—before the analysis was done. Barry Jr. enjoyed being lumped in with Eleanor and Sallie about as much as Eleanor enjoyed being considered part of "the sister problem."

With an air of brooding despondency, he concluded that he and Eleanor should not wait until the Seniors died. They should swap the stock now. With the help of the lawyers, who were paid to imagine every contingency, he had envisioned all sorts of doomsday scenarios. What if they agreed to swap now on the basis of WHAS stock being worth $100 a share, but Eleanor's inept management pushed its price down to $25 a share by the time the Seniors died?

In July, soon after the fractious gathering at the Seelbach, Barry Jr. called Eleanor, Rucker Todd, and Gordon Davidson together and proposed that the stock be swapped immediately. Eleanor, however, was more inclined to stick with the original agreement. Eager to end the constant wrangling, she now seemed more trusting of her brother than he did of her. She suggested that they set minimum performance standards, so "he wouldn't need to worry that I was over at WHAS running the place into the ground."

But Barry Jr. was adamant; there were too many uncertainties if they waited. What he failed to say, of course, was that he was reluctant to allow the fate of the papers to depend on negotiations with Eleanor without the Senior Binghams on the scene to referee. He had no faith in his own bargaining skills and his struggle with cancer had made him strongly averse to risk. He was almost incapable of leaving anything to chance.

Eventually, Barry Jr. won. The meeting broke up with Gordon Davidson under orders to proceed with the swap on the basis of an immediate exchange of stock. Because this would mean reconfiguring Trust #9, Eleanor thought it was more trouble than it was worth, but she agreed. Do it now.

Despite these difficulties, Eleanor had somehow managed to recapture the thrill and excitement about running WHAS that she had felt the previous spring when the idea was first proposed. When she and Rowland had dinner with CJ editorial page writer Keith Runyon and his wife, Meme, in late July 1985, they could talk of little else. "They were excited," recalled Meme. "It looked like it was going to work out and Eleanor was ready to go."

But Edie and Joan sensed that, below the surface, Eleanor was still riddled with anxiety and self-doubt. "I'm so worried that I won't be able to do a good job at WHAS," she moaned one day to Joan as they rode down Main Street. "And what will Barry Jr. think?" "Fuck him!" Joan shrieked. "Why do you care what he thinks?" Still, the moment was poignant. "She wanted his approval, just like Rowland wanted his approval," Joan said. "She wanted him to love her. She wants everyone to love her."

Edie's analysis was more pungent. "I think they wanted all the glory and money, but the prospect of working hard to make it happen was a little scary." When she tried to encourage Eleanor by reminding her of a woman who had successfully run another Louisville television station by coming in one day a week, Eleanor shrugged. She would have to go to work. Her time would not be her own. Maybe owning WHAS would not be so wonderful after all.

———

The Seniors returned to their New England summer house immediately after the July 8 meeting at the Seelbach, and by the end of the month, everyone else in the family had dispersed for vacations, including Gordon Davidson. As a result, the thick draft document outlining how a stock swap might be arranged was not ready until late August. Just before Labor Day, having taken a few days to look it over, Rucker Todd paid a call on Gordon to discuss the glaring inequity he saw.

By now, Rucker had become somewhat exasperated with Eleanor, who had switched from total sale to one variant of the stock swap and then another. "I remember one Saturday he phoned me," George Gill recalled. "And he said, 'I'm just lost. Can you shed any light on this? My client keeps changing on me.'"

But Rucker also saw that he could use Eleanor's wavering to his advantage, and hers. Eleanor was malleable, Rucker knew, and wanted above all to please people, especially her parents, who at the moment seemed to favor a total sale. Rowland, too, had made it clear that he would like a "big cash pile" and the power that went with it. At the same time, Barry Jr., Edie, Joan, and the grandchildren were urging Eleanor to take over WHAS and save the family business. "There was this pressure [on Eleanor] that she could have expressed to Rucker," Leon Tallichet theorized later. "And Rucker is a sly fox. Conspiracy is a tough word, but I think he explored all the avenues [to push a sale]."

Rucker's main tactic was to keep the pot bubbling at all times. Eleanor should receive "fair" value for her stock, he told Gordon, once again using his code word for the much higher market price rather than a discount for minority ownership. He proposed not swapping now, but waiting until the Seniors died and then trading on the basis of "fair" value. Either Barry Jr. or Eleanor could refuse to proceed at that time if "fair" value was too onerous, he said, but if they did, WHAS and the papers would be sold. As might have been expected from Eleanor's lawyer, such an arrangement was in Eleanor's best financial interest—if not the interests of anyone else.

Barry Jr. was incensed. Eleanor was demanding market value for her stock, but had insisted that Sallie be offered nothing more than minority value, which the family's $25 million offer represented. It was the good-girl premium in a different guise!

The move brought Barry Jr. back to the negotiating table, but not as Rucker had hoped. Through Gordon, Barry Jr. said he was willing to delay the actual swap until the parents' deaths, provided a precise formula was agreed upon now so that he did not have to negotiate with Eleanor later on. And the formula had to be based on minority value rather than what Rucker annoyingly continued to call "fair" value. Barry Jr.'s terms were absolutely firm, Gordon told Rucker. He would rather see Option X than have to negotiate with Eleanor after the death of their parents. Rucker was furious. "That was his response," he said, imitating Barry Jr. " 'I am unyielding! You'll do it my way, and if you won't, I'd just as soon have everything sold!' "

Faced with a new obstacle, Eleanor called a halt to all negotiations for the next month or so, until after her baby was born. She was becoming unglued emotionally. In part, the problem was due to anxiety over the imminent birth. The year before, she had delivered a stillborn son and was so traumatized by the experience that she could not bear to deal with the same maternity nurses and had switched hospitals.

That exacerbated her already deep ambivalence about the stock swap. Barry Jr.'s insistence on minority value and resolving all the questions now instead of after the deaths of their parents shocked and hurt her. After all, as Rowland pointed out whenever the opportunity availed, by agreeing to swap at all instead of pressing for Option X, she was making a sacrifice for the family.

Though she had toasted the swap in July, by September she was "not far away from hysteria," according to a friend who bumped into her in a local drugstore that month. "It's just awful what's happened," Eleanor had said, trembling. "The whole thing is falling apart." She had explained that Barry Jr. was building roadblocks. "He's just requiring so much of us," she lamented.

Eleanor's request for a hiatus seemed a blessing in disguise. Now everyone had a chance to cool down and reconsider.

Louisville's summer heat usually breaks in September, but that year the leaden atmosphere lingered on and on. The thickness of the air made any outdoor activity a trial. The only respite came at twilight, when the river stirred a languid breeze and a few mourning doves wailed from the darkening trees. With the family temporarily at truce, everything seemed slowed and blessedly peaceful.

Sallie soon disturbed the relative calm. Christopher Shaw's campaign to make the Binghams feel a "wave of inevitability" continued unabated. *Working Woman* magazine published Sallie's perspective in an article entitled "Family Feud: The War Between the Binghams." The author, a former *Courier-Journal* reporter, asked Sallie if her decision to sell was an act of revenge against the brother who appeared to hold her under his thumb. "Nobody's under his thumb," Sallie was quoted as saying, "because he's impotent."

The long article was the frankest look yet at the family. It even included a brief sketch of the Mary Lily scandal. Judge Bingham "had once been suspected of poisoning his new bride, a rich widow," the magazine casually observed in a photo caption.

When he read the piece, Barry Sr. blanched. This sort of story was his worst nightmare. If the "family feud" was going to attract journalistic interest, then there was all the more reason to end the squabble, one way or another. While Sallie's bragging about outside offers was dispiriting, the prospect of more articles dredging up the past he had wanted buried forever was infinitely more worrying.

In early October, Sallie responded to the family's $25 million offer with a statement saying she would take $32 million. She also wanted a ten-year "look-back," she said, an arrangement which meant that, in the event the companies were sold anytime in the next ten years, she would get a proportional share of the higher price.

Sallie had promised earlier that she would release a list of the written offers she had received. When a reporter asked to see the document, however, she said that her attorney had advised against it. Had it been released, it would have been very short and unimpressive. No outsider was willing to pay Sallie more than a pittance. As Christopher Shaw had known from the start, the family was the best prospect. The challenge was to scare them into paying the highest price possible.

Christopher Shaw was not alone in his assumptions. Barry Jr. and the management team were also operating on the belief that they would eventually buy Sallie's stock. The issue now was: How much could they afford to pay?

And how would buying Sallie out affect such things as inheritance taxes and the swap with Eleanor?

By mid-October 1985, Goldman, Sachs had prepared a detailed projection of what the companies could expect in the way of income, expenses, and profit over the next ten years, based almost entirely on figures supplied by George Gill and Leon Tallichet. Barry Jr., however, rejected the analysis out of hand, saying that Goldman was far too optimistic about the papers' financial future. George knew that the CJ & T could be run much more efficiently and had encouraged Goldman to project an annual increase of $2 million in profits—a figure Barry Jr. considered wildly unrealistic.

George seethed at Barry Jr.'s wholesale repudiation of the numbers. He saw it as yet another vote of no confidence in him, but he struggled to maintain a professional demeanor. He assured Barry Jr. that by merging the morning and afternoon papers, cutting editorial costs and boosting ad rates, profits could easily be hiked by $2 million a year. Then, in an effort to be comforting, George said that Barry Sr. had told him that no price would be offered to Sallie that Barry Jr. did not support. "Thank God!" Barry Jr. murmured to himself, reassured that he was still firmly in the driver's seat.

Despite George's cool-headed attempts to justify Goldman's projections, Barry Jr. was not persuaded. His fear of risk, so apparent since his battle with cancer, surfaced with a vengeance. "I just can't trust the numbers," he insisted. He made it sound as though George and Leon were actively trying to deceive him.

Well, George said curtly, since it is clear that you have no faith in me or Leon, perhaps you should find somebody else to come up with this kind of analysis, somebody you do feel comfortable with. Instead of reassuring two of his most senior aides that they did, in fact, have his confidence, Barry Jr. agreed. "Yes!" he said. "Maybe I *should* find somebody trustworthy to go over the numbers." That person, they all knew, was Bernie Block, the plodding, dependable executive who had lost the horse race "by a field goal" almost five years earlier.

Barry Jr. called Bernie and gave him his orders. "We've got to sit down and go through every line of this and make sure the taxes are right and the depreciation is right and the dividend level is right so I can go to Joan and Edie and Rob and Clara and say, 'This is a deal we can survive.' " Bernie threw himself into the assignment with the energy of a dervish. He worked day and night on a meticulous reanalysis, constructing spread-sheet projections based on doomsday assumptions about the economy and the newspaper industry, as Barry Jr. had demanded.

By then, Barry Jr. had concluded that Bernie and Paul were the only aides he could really depend on. Bernie had had little to do with the family negotiations, and therefore had avoided being painted with the same turncoat colors as the other hired hands. Paul, in the meantime, had become Barry Jr.'s daily confessor and confidant, remaining unfailingly sympathetic as he urged his harried boss to hang tough. Barry Jr.'s gradual loss of faith in his management team had pushed him steadily deeper into Paul's embrace. To the dismay of George and Barry Sr., Barry Jr. now seemed closer to Paul than to anyone but Edie.

The relationship had, in fact, taken a turn that neither George nor Barry Sr. was aware of. In late September 1985, Paul had written Barry Jr. a memo evaluating his accomplishments during the sabbatical year and outlining his goals for the future. "You need no longer be apologetic about having an all-white, all-male editorial staff," Paul wrote, citing the success of his efforts to boost minority hiring. He noted in passing that he was now "on the ladder" to become president of the Associated Press Managing Editors Association, a prestigious professional organization. This is "a compliment to the newspapers and their reputation, as much as to me."

As for goals, Paul suggested that the opinion page editors report to him instead of to Barry Jr. "This is not a power grab, but it would free you from administrative burdens." He closed on a note that Mary would no doubt have derided as sycophantic. "I will try to build more bridges between the newspapers and constituent groups. I have a good model to emulate—an editor and publisher who keeps his serenity in the face of the most hostile criticism. And finally, when the ducks are nibbling at my ankles, I remind myself that there is no place I would rather work and no person I would rather report to."

Barry Jr. responded warmly. First, he raised Paul's salary by $15,000 and thanked him for keeping up the pressure for more minority representation in the newsroom, which over the past five years had grown from less than 3 percent to over 10 percent, almost double the national average for newspapers. Barry Jr. had received an award from the National Association of Black Journalists because of Paul's energetic efforts.

Sale of the newspapers, he told Paul, was "a remote possibility." Then he delivered a paragraph that would have shocked his father. If George had seen it, "he would have been gone," said Gordon Davidson.

I have never worked with an executive at these companies who has been more helpful to me than you are. . . . I am happy to say that, if I do not have a troika Bingham-Ethridge-Baker management team, at least I have two legs of the stool: Bingham-Janensch.

The memo strongly suggested that Barry Jr. had made a decision about the future leadership of the newspapers, as the hired hands had feared. He had settled on Paul Janensch. The information was of extraordinary importance, but Barry Jr. did not share it with his father. He knew that Barry Sr. would not be pleased, and he did not want to antagonize him at such a critical moment.

Benjamin Worth Bingham Miller was born October 5. His first name honored one of Rowland's ancestors, but he would be known as "Worth." Despite her hippie past, Eleanor valued her heritage and took pride in being a Bingham. Her stationery identified the couple as "Rowland and Eleanor Bingham Miller."

The break from stock-swap negotiations had refreshed her, and she emerged primed to fight hard for what she wanted. And that, plainly said, was more than whatever Sallie got. Still, she seemed to have regained a bit of her former enthusiasm for running WHAS, albeit in her own peculiar fashion. About two weeks after little Worth was born, Bob Morse came to Eleanor's house to brief her on what was happening at the station. To Bob's astonishment—and acute discomfort—Eleanor chattered excitedly about WHAS affairs while breast-feeding her baby. In the background, Rowland cleaned his new shotgun, raising it to his shoulder and snapping the trigger on the empty chambers. The tale of this unorthodox meeting with WHAS's proprietor-to-be made the rounds among the hired hands under the code name "Tits and Shotguns."

Barry Jr. winced at the story. It reminded him of those humiliating board discussions about classical music versus Top 40 tunes and Eleanor's pouch of marijuana in the WHAS bathroom. Despite his sister's clear excitement about the stock swap, he was convinced that she was stringing him along and had no real desire to take over WHAS. "The only tangible thing Eleanor and Rowland ever did was to have a car telephone put in their cars at the expense of WHAS," Barry Jr. said. "They did absolutely zero to prepare themselves to own and operate the station. Zero."

But Barry Jr., the most uptight member of the Bingham clan, did not understand his laid-back sister. "She and Rowland would never prepare for a job the way you and I would," explained Bob Morse. "They live in a very unstructured world. . . . Their whole modus operandi is a very inconsistent, loose kind of life-style. Sometimes she shows up, sometimes she doesn't. That's Eleanor."

Bob Morse had been making such visits for several months—ever since the stock swap had been a viable option. He always went to her. She never came to the station. He thought Eleanor had some "off-the-wall ideas," but working for her was certainly preferable to taking his chances with a new corporate owner.

Bob thought Eleanor was genuinely interested in WHAS; she just wanted to run the station on her own terms. And she had made those terms crystal clear. "Number One, she wanted [my] office and she wanted me to move across the hall," he said. "She wanted to sit in on meetings when she felt like it. . . . She would be chairman of the board and approve budgets. If she wanted to spend $1 million a year on a little documentary unit, wonderful. I don't care. . . . It would have been perfect. And perfect for her."

The only real problem, as Bob saw it, was Rowland. At some point during Bob's visits, Rowland would inevitably say, "Eleanor is going to be chairman. But what am I going to do?" Rowland was always attentive and asked questions. But Bob hadn't the foggiest notion what role he might take. He wanted to ask why Rowland should have any role, but he didn't—"in the interest of tact."

———————

November 12, the date Barry Sr. had set to discuss ways in which the family might respond to Sallie's $32 million demand, was rapidly approaching. As the day neared, Barry Jr. closeted himself with Goldman, Sachs and his management team to battle it out over assumptions. Barry Jr. insisted on profit projections that George argued were unrealistically low. The wrangling went on and on, with everyone's eye on the calendar.

The stakes were enormous. George and the other managers felt that the Seniors were growing weary of the family feud; they could easily throw up their hands, they thought, and sell the companies. The only thing that could save the situation was to fashion a deal that Sallie, Eleanor, and Barry Jr. could all embrace. Sallie had demanded $32 million, and the closer they could come to that price, the more likely she was to accept it.

That would solve one problem, then would come the stock swap. The Senior Binghams had ruled that Eleanor must accept the same values for her stock as Sallie. So the more money Sallie was offered, the likelier it was that Eleanor would go through with the swap. And justifying an offer in the vicinity of $32 million required that Barry Jr. feel relatively optimistic about the future of the family business. George, in his push to get Barry Jr. to accept projections of ever-rising profits, was essentially trying to save both the empire and his job.

Barry Jr., on the other hand, had a different set of priorities. He felt confident that no one would give Sallie more than the $25 million the family had already offered. The more Sallie was paid, the more financial pressure he would be under at the papers after the swap with Eleanor. The more pessimistic the projections, the less the family could prudently offer Sallie. And though he hotly denied it, everyone around him knew that the price paid Sallie had become a bitter, personal contest.

On Tuesday, November 12, all the Binghams except Sallie, and their many retainers, lawyers, and top management advisers gathered in a corner room of the Seelbach Hotel to listen to Goldman, Sachs make its presentation.

The analysts elegantly outlined the choices, describing what the future of the Bingham companies would look like at four prices for Sallie's shares— $25 million, $26.3 million, $28 million, and $32 million. Goldman's verdict: The companies could pay Sallie anything up to $32 million. At that level there would be some years of debt and perhaps *The Courier-Journal* could not issue dividends for a while. But it was manageable. "Done every day in New York," said one analyst brightly.

Barry Jr. smoldered. In firm tones he said that the family should offer Sallie $25 million—"which is more than she has been offered on the street" —or, at most, the next highest option, $26.3 million. This was the "high Lehman value," he argued, meaning that it was in the upper range of what Lehman Brothers had said Sallie's stock was worth almost a year earlier.

Since the Binghams could not agree which of the four prices to offer Sallie, they decided to adjourn and reconvene in a week. But Barry Jr. would not let the matter rest. At a family-only lunch after the meeting, he continued to press his case. "There is no need to make any concessions to Sallie," he insisted. He brushed aside the argument that Sallie had dropped her demand from $42 million to $32 million, creating an obligation for the family to make a similar compromise. His view was, "Hold tight at $25 million."

Mary did not see how that would help get Sallie out of the way so that the stock swap could proceed. The family had to make some concession, she said, if only to save Sallie's face. Barry Jr. grimaced. He saw absolutely no need to make Sallie feel better. "It was at this point," Eleanor recalled, "that Mother and Daddy said, 'Squabble! Squabble! Squabble! Here you go again. That's all we ever hear from you guys.' "

Barry Sr. sighed. "I see no resolution here," he said. "We can't take this anymore. We're going to have to think about selling." He said that the Goldman, Sachs analysts had told him that a sale would not have to be an open auction; it could be limited to "people we'd all want to live with" such as *The New York Times* or *The Washington Post*.

Joan immediately sensed that Barry Sr. wanted to arrange a nice quiet little transaction. Over her dead body! If her children were going to lose their chance to run the papers, their birthright would not be sold cheap. Nor would Barry Sr. be spared the unpleasantness of dealing with a public auction. "If you sell, I will sue to see that it is a wide open list!" Joan said, her voice quavering. She had never been so ruthlessly defiant of her in-laws, and they were jolted. That seemed to silence the discussion of selling for the moment.

The debate turned back to what should be offered to Sallie. Barry Jr. saw only one genuine reason to go higher than $25 million. The stock swap could not be completed without re-forming Trust #9, and that would be difficult if Sallie objected, which she surely would do if there was no agreement on the purchase of her shares.

Grudgingly, Barry Jr. agreed to increase the offer to $26.3 million. But he said he would go no further despite pleas and remonstrances that Sallie was much more likely to accept $28 million. "No!" he said. This far, and no further.

Barry Jr., Edie, and Joan left the Seelbach believing that the family had agreed to pay Sallie $26.3 million and to proceed with the stock swap on that basis. Two days later, Barry Sr. told his son over lunch that Eleanor and Rowland thought no decision had been made about the stock swap. When Barry Jr. urged his father to set them straight, Barry Sr. said sheepishly that he was not sure a deal had been made either.

To Barry Jr., nailing down an agreement had become like grasping a greased eel. "It hurts me to say it," he thundered at his father, "but you have to decide what you want to reward. If it's dedication and hard work, you should help me keep control of *The Courier-Journal*. If it's Eleanor and Rowland and Sallie, sell!" Barry Sr. looked miserable and murmured something about just wanting to find a solution.

What was going on here? Barry Jr. wondered to himself. One minute an agreement was firm, the next it wasn't. Still, he comforted himself with one thought. He had a commitment from his father that any offer to Sallie and Eleanor had to have his approval. That he could take to the bank. Maybe the terms were undecided, but he still had veto power over whatever was offered.

After the Seelbach lunch, Eleanor and Rowland had turned, as usual, to Rucker Todd. He knew that the family was going to reconvene in about a week and that momentum was mounting for what Barry Jr. wanted: offering Sallie $26.3 million and swapping with Eleanor at minority value. From his perspective, that would be a financial mistake for Eleanor and a defeat for him. "You should tell your parents unequivocally that you favor an immediate sale of all the companies and should urge them to follow that course at once," Rucker wrote Eleanor. He was quite confident that such advice would not fall on deaf ears.

Rucker gave his letter to Eleanor on Friday, November 15, and she and

Rowland discussed it over the weekend. On Monday, they asked to have dinner with Barry Sr. and Mary. They absolutely had to come to some understanding of what the Seniors would and would not support before the next family meeting on Wednesday, they said.

Barry Sr. and Mary poured out their misgivings about offering Sallie $26.3 million. They were sure she would spurn it. And the stock swap looked more and more like an impossible tangle. The only solution seemed to be a sale. But they also felt an obligation to Barry Jr.; they did not want to be the ones pushing for Option X. Their son, they knew, was close to the snapping point. He would feel betrayed if they moved to sell out. Perhaps, Barry Sr. mused to Eleanor and Rowland, perhaps there was a way. "If someone other than us put Option X on the table, the whole family could discuss it," he coyly suggested to Eleanor. "The time has come for us all to debate it."

Eleanor and Rowland got the message. They left the dinner convinced that Barry Sr. and Mary wanted to sell, but just needed an agent provocateur. Early the next morning, Tuesday, November 19, Eleanor called Barry Jr. and told him that she needed to see him before the Wednesday meeting. "I have something I need to present," she said.

Later that day, the family gathered in Barry Sr.'s office and she delivered what came to be called her "I want out" memo to her brother. "I firmly believe that the sale of all the companies would best satisfy the needs of all the members of the family," she wrote. Swapping would be "a mistake for me." She said a sale would give everyone "ample money" for their various interests. "The family could begin to function again as a family," she argued.

Barry Jr. listened calmly before responding. "I will resist selling all the companies," he announced, "and anyone who thinks that selling will bring peace in the family is crazy." He accused Eleanor of only being interested in the swap in the first place so that she could turn around the minute she owned WHAS and sell it. The remark hit close to the truth; after all, how else would Eleanor and Rowland have the "big cash pile" they so obviously wanted? But the swipe prompted a sharp rebuke from Mary, who accused Barry Jr. of always assuming the worst about Eleanor. Barry Sr. said decisively, "We'll discuss it tomorrow." Eleanor went home in tears. At least tomorrow would be the day it all ended, she thought.

PULLING THE TRIGGER

The next morning, a Wednesday, the family reconvened in the boardroom at *The Courier-Journal*. Rucker Todd was there, as were the other lawyers, hired hands, and advisers. Barry Jr. started off by saying that he wanted the family feud resolved. He stated Eleanor's position and then said that he and Joan were unalterably opposed to selling. "My father has developed an alternative solution," he said. At the mention of Barry Sr.'s name, Eleanor's and Rowland's faces clouded with confusion. Had Barry Sr. not told them only two days earlier that he favored a sale? How could he now be in league with Barry Jr. on yet another plan?

In disbelief, they listened to Barry Jr.'s proposal. WHAS would be sold and Barry Jr. would buy out his sisters' interest in *The Courier-Journal*. Both Sallie and Eleanor would get $37 million in cash, and Barry Jr. and Joan would carry on with the papers. The scheme was nearly identical to the proposal Barry Sr. had casually mentioned to his son the previous May, just days after Barry Jr. returned from his sabbatical. Now, six months later, the notion was out in the open for the family to consider. Because it was presented on Wednesday, November 20, the proposal was promptly dubbed the "Wednesday Plan."

Rowland grasped Eleanor's arm and they swung back their chairs from the boardroom table. "It was like God had struck them from above," said Joan.

They thought the subject that day was going to be total sale. Instead, Barry Sr. had double-crossed them. Rowland recovered his senses sufficiently to look across the table at Mary and choke out his intuitive first reaction. "If that happened," he said, "we would be so humiliated that we would have to leave town." He did not need to add, "and take Rowlie and Worth with us."

Joan fumed. "It was emotional blackmail," she said. "Mary is so interwoven in their lives. She's losing all her children and Eleanor's the only one she has left." Mary was genuinely puzzled. She considered the Wednesday Plan an admirable compromise and dazedly asked Rowland why he and Eleanor would have to leave town. Much later, Rowland would assert that it was because, after all the concessions Eleanor had made, "it seemed unfair to be liquidated just to fulfill Barry's and Joan's desires." But at the time, he said nothing. "There was just a lot of shrugging," Edie recalled.

To be sure, there were financial reasons for Eleanor to be distressed. Selling everything would yield considerably more than the $37 million she stood to get under the Wednesday Plan. Even the stock swap was a better deal from Eleanor's perspective. At least that offered her a good-girl premium, for even if Sallie got what she had asked for, it would be no more than $32 million. The stock swap would give Eleanor ownership of a business worth $55 million or more, which she could operate or eventually sell. But the Wednesday Plan treated both sisters exactly the same. In effect, Sallie got more than she expected, and Eleanor got less.

Just as important to Eleanor was the unpleasant prospect of the smirking looks she would have to endure if WHAS were sold, as the Wednesday Plan envisioned. Everyone in town knew that she had agreed to take over the stations. It had been announced in the paper. Now it would look as if the family had concluded she was incompetent. "I could just not imagine walking down the street every day and having people say, 'How did this happen?' " she said. If everything were sold, the failure would be spread evenly among all members of the family. If only WHAS were sold, Eleanor would be the goat. "I remember it being a really weird feeling that all these people were around the table and everybody was looking at Eleanor and saying, 'Okay, you take the fall,' " Rowland recalled.

Eleanor stuck up for herself as best she could, but her arguments sounded hollow. After all, the Wednesday Plan seemed to solve everyone's problems. This way, the papers could stay in the family, Eleanor and Rowland would have the millions they had always wanted, and she had said herself that the stock swap was a mistake. There was little to say beyond Rowland's threat to leave Louisville. The couple went home immediately after the meeting.

Barry Sr.'s embrace of the Wednesday Plan made Joan and Edie and Barry Jr. ecstatic. At last, a deal! Joan hugged Barry Sr. with tears in her eyes and said, "Thank you so much." Later, in the ladies' room, Mary asked Joan, "Why isn't this enough money for Eleanor and Rowland?" Joan thought Mary seemed disgusted at their apparent greed, and "rather happy that a solution had been found to save the papers."

Eleanor wasted no time letting her mother know just how betrayed she and Rowland felt, and Mary was appropriately remorseful. That evening she wrote her daughter a letter. "We are distressed," she began. On Monday evening, she and Barry Sr. had indeed agreed that "sale would be to the best financial interest of all of us." But, she said, both she and Barry Sr. had "grave and deeply felt reservations."

They worried what effect a sale would have on Barry Jr., who seemed on the verge of a breakdown. The strain and tension in his face was frightening. And Joan's threat to sue had closed off the possibility of a quiet transaction with a first-class newspaper company. "You must understand that we cannot be indifferent to the quality of the ongoing management of *The Courier-Journal*," she wrote.

Mary went on to say that on Tuesday, after Eleanor had delivered her disavowal of the stock swap and Barry Jr. had reacted with such fury, she and Barry Sr. had called Gordon Davidson in desperation to figure out what selling WHAS might bring. She ended her communication on a despairing note: "It seems to us now that we cannot favor any option without alienating one or the other of our children."

Eleanor argued back that there were lots of reasons beyond financial ones to favor selling, such as the constant frustration of being held responsible for CJ policies over which stockholders had no control and were in violent disagreement. "Irksome as this situation often is," Mary countered, "it cannot be weighed against the anguish we would be subject to should Barry be destroyed (as we greatly fear would happen) by the sale of the CJ and the consequent cutting off from what has been his whole life."

Her arguments spent, Eleanor resigned herself to the fact that the agreement with her parents that had seemed so definite five days earlier had been a mirage.

Soon after Barry Sr. put forward the Wednesday Plan, Eleanor sent a frosty letter to her brother. "Since the option of a total sale at this time has been rejected by Mother and Father, I would like to reconsider the swap option, as I find it more attractive than the sale of WHAS." The reversal effectively swept the Wednesday Plan from the table.

Joan had left for the South Seas for a Thanksgiving holiday and Barry Jr. tried to call her in Fiji and Vanawatu to tell her that the deal had once again come unglued. When he finally reached her, she was incredulous. "Why isn't your father making it stick?" she demanded.

Selling everything was still her first preference, Eleanor said, but she knew her parents would not accept that. So instead, she proposed proceeding with the swap—but "at not less than $28 million" instead of $26.3 million. Sallie had to be satisfied before she would go ahead, she said.

To the Seniors, this looked manageable. Barry Sr. believed that Sallie would be likely to accept an offer in the range of $28 million, and that would allow everything else to move forward. Perhaps Thanksgiving, three days away, would finally merit its name this year. All Barry Jr. had to do was agree to increase the offer to Sallie.

<hr>

As Thanksgiving approached, Barry Jr. and Bernie Block spent hours and hours huddled over spread-sheets, substituting numbers, and analyzing every aspect of what would happen if Sallie were offered $28 million. Barry Jr. had tried to persuade his father to tell Eleanor she had to choose between the Wednesday Plan and the swap at $26.3 million, but Barry Sr., fearful as ever of a confrontation, squirmed at the thought.

Instead, Barry Sr. inquired hopefully about offering Sallie $28 million. Barry Jr. said that it did not look good, but he and Bernie were going over the spread-sheets and would get back to him on Thanksgiving eve. Before the holiday, he would know.

As Barry Jr. was leaving the office, Barry Sr. tried in his oblique way to warn his son that he might soon lose the thing he cared about most. "You have paid too high a price for the women leaving the boards," he said quietly, referring to the trouble and pain that had resulted from that single act. But Barry Jr. was a literalist and missed his father's point entirely. He snapped back that it was strange indeed for Barry Sr. to be urging him to pay Sallie more if $26.3 million was too much.

George Gill, on the other hand, was well aware of the patriarch's growing desperation. He had noticed that Barry Sr. no longer walked into the building with his usual bouncy step and sighed a lot for no apparent reason. He had the weary, glassy-eyed look of a man who had been up late too many nights, George thought. He felt certain that Barry Sr., tired of the constant squabbling, was leaning toward a sale. But he also knew how cagey Barry Sr. could be; the elder Bingham would not have revealed such deep distress to an employee like George unless he wanted him to act as a go-between with his son. George felt sure Barry Sr. wanted him to convince Barry Jr. of just how high the stakes were.

As Thanksgiving drew near, George sensed that the situation had reached the moment of crisis. If Barry Jr. did not agree to up his offer to $28 million, George thought Barry Sr. would sell everything. The other hired hands, who had watched Barry Jr.'s increasing inflexibility and his father's advancing despair, also believed that something had to give. The strain was just too great.

All that week, the occupants of the executive wing kept mind-numbing hours going over the documents. Barry Jr. spurned George's counsel. Only Bernie Block would tell the truth. Only Bernie Block could be counted on not to cook the books.

Barry Jr. had insisted that Bernie's calculations include not only a conservative profit projection, but $73 million for new color presses. In their daily closed-door sessions together, Paul Janensch had argued strongly that color photos and ads were essential to attract readers now that *The Louisville Times* was being phased out.

George, on the other hand, had pleaded with Barry Jr. to drop the presses from the calculations. Under the circumstances, he said, they were a luxury, not a necessity. He offered figures that indicated that the introduction of color would not boost advertising enough to justify the investment. Barry Jr. cited Paul's editorial quality argument and insisted that buying the presses be included.

On the Tuesday before Thanksgiving, Bernie Block presented his detailed analysis of five different options—all including new presses and based on 1 percent to 2.5 percent annual growth in profits until the year 2006 instead of the higher profits George had thought plausible. Using these ultraconservative assumptions, Bernie concluded that $26.3 million was viable, and $28 million was not. There was a note at the bottom of the page, however, saying that the Goldman, Sachs team thought $28 million was easily doable. Barry Jr. ignored it. He was content that Bernie, the last honest man, had blessed his judgment that $26.3 million was as far as he should go. He asked Bernie to make the same presentation to Barry Sr. on Thanksgiving eve.

But Bernie was not as convinced as he seemed to be that $26.3 million was the highest figure that could safely be offered. And he was in a state of near terror that the empire was about to crumble—mainly because of Barry Jr. "He was about to crack up," Bernie said. He, too, had tried to talk Barry Jr. out of insisting that new presses be included in the analysis. "I cried, I begged, I pleaded," he said. Like the other hired hands, Bernie felt Barry

Jr.'s position had less to do with business than with his obsessive need to vanquish Sallie.

Bernie also blamed much of Barry Jr.'s intransigence on the influence that Paul exerted in those daily closed-door meetings they had. He had been especially suspicious after hearing Paul describe Wilson Wyatt as "a senile old man" some months earlier. The comment was prompted by Wilson's unrelenting push for profitability, which had created pressure for cuts in the outsized news budget. To Bernie, a staunch loyalist to the Bingham tradition, saying such a thing about Barry Sr.'s close friend was like spitting on an altar.

For weeks Bernie had been working on the numbers at Barry Jr.'s behest. "I was crazy, staying up nights and weekends trying to save the empire," he said. And after all that time, he found that it came down to one Wednesday night, Thanksgiving eve. Using the firearms imagery Barry Jr. favored, Bernie said, "It was my day in the barrel."

About 4:00 P.M., Barry Jr. and Bernie walked into Barry Sr.'s office to put the new analysis on display. Despite Bernie's pleas, the new presses were still in the projections. Bernie showed Barry Sr. what he had done, and why he had labeled $26.3 million viable and $28 million not viable. Barry Sr. looked at the columns of numbers in tight-lipped silence.

Steeling himself, Bernie decided that it was now or never. With a brief glance at Barry Jr., he began to fly solo. He told Barry Sr. that the analysis was, in his opinion, terribly flawed because of the assumptions it made. Out of the corner of his eye, Bernie could see Barry Jr.'s face turning a bright scarlet. "I was standing up, showing the numbers to Barry Sr., who caught on very quickly. And I said, 'Now in my opinion we can afford more than $26.3 million and here's why. Boom. Boom. Boom.' And I looked at Barry Jr. and he just was very upset because he didn't want to hear that."

Barry Jr. did not make a sound. "Thank you very much," Barry Sr. said, and Bernie left father and son alone together. Even as he walked down the hall, Barry Sr. was saying to his son, "Now even Bernie, the man you said you could trust, has told you that you can do it."

Bernie went back to his office and waited nervously. About an hour later, Barry Jr. stuck his head in and said coldly, "Twenty-six three is it," followed by a curt "good night." The bitter tone of voice made it evident that Barry Jr. had concluded that even honest Bernie Block had been pulled into George's nest of vipers.

Bernie went home, poured himself several stiff drinks, and brooded about what had happened. Finally, he roused himself. "There's only one way to stop Barry Jr.," he told his wife. "I'm going to call Paul Janensch and see if he can turn this thing around."

His wife was appalled. "If George finds out, he'll fire you," she cautioned. In effect, Bernie had decided to go hat in hand to Paul and say, "George can't save the empire, can you?" Bernie assured her that George would want him to do it, and to prove it he would call George and tell him what he was about to do. He let George's phone ring, then hung up before anyone could answer. He decided his wife might be right.

He did not tell George. Instead, he called Paul at home and, clearly distraught, asked him to meet him at the office the next morning, Thanksgiving, at 7:00 A.M. "It's the most important thing I've ever asked you to do," Bernie pleaded. Reluctantly, Paul agreed.

The next day Bernie laid out the options for Paul just as he had for Barry Jr. and Barry Sr., and then told him what had happened the night before. Bernie said he was convinced that, unless Barry Jr. agreed to go to $28 million, the Seniors would sell. "You're the only guy now who has any influence," he told Paul. "Not any other employees, not his father, not his sisters, nobody but you. You're our last hope."

Paul protested that he planned to leave on vacation early Friday morning. There isn't enough time, Bernie said. It has to be now. "Fuck your vacation! Get in here tomorrow!" Paul sighed and said he would think about it.

Paul was not persuaded by Bernie's histrionics. "I just couldn't conceive of the family selling," he said. But he respected Bernie and had never seen him in such a state. On Friday, Paul called Barry Jr. and asked him to come to the office, saying he wanted to go over the spread-sheets again. Barry Jr. had already shown Paul everything once, and Paul had thought his boss's position justified.

Perhaps Paul's greatest strength was his ability to make things easier for Barry Jr. When Sallie had been imposed on the news staff as book editor, Paul had shown the excellent judgment to go to Barry Jr. and say, "Don't worry about it. We can make it work." And he had done so. By not forcing a showdown with George over their division of responsibilities, he had also made the sabbatical work. Such flexibility had gone a long way toward earning Barry Jr.'s confidence.

Now he tried the same tack. "We can make $28 million work," Paul told the Bingham heir. "We can do it. You don't have to stick to this rigid standard." As he had so many times before, Paul emphasized the positive and, knowing how much Barry Jr. hated to have his authority challenged, avoided telling him he was making a mistake.

Barry Jr. listened, and then told Paul, "I've got to be very careful. I've got to be responsible. I can't gamble with the company and the family." That was the end of the audience. Paul called Bernie to say that he had gotten nowhere, and left on his vacation.

It had been six months since the sabbatical ended, and Edie had watched her husband's thin emotional armor crumple. His nerves were raw and he was clearly desperate. She was afraid he was going to die.

The day after Thanksgiving, Edie and Barry Sr. played doubles with Molly and a friend at the Mockingbird Valley Tennis Club. The grass was brown and the trees bare, but there was still enough autumn sun to make it a lovely day for tennis.

She was not there for exercise, however, but to talk to Barry Sr. alone in the car on the ride home. "I feel it is unreasonable and unfair of you to pressure Barry to raise the price to Sallie to $28 million," Edie began. She berated her father-in-law for putting her husband in such a terrible bind and for not laying down the law to Eleanor and Sallie. Barry Jr. was the one who had to keep on running the companies. "This is crushing Barry, this pull, this conflict," she said. Barry Sr. became quiet and stared straight ahead. He looked as if he was going to cry. He shook his head ever so slightly, the tension apparent in his neck. "Barry is crushing me," he said slowly, in a voice barely above a whisper. That was the end of the conversation.

Barry Sr. was all the more rattled because of something his son had said a few days earlier while going over some stock-swap documents with Gordon Davidson. One of the papers included the term "willful default," and Barry Jr. had asked Gordon if his death would amount to willful default of the agreement. When Gordon said no, Barry Jr. had inquired, "What if I commit suicide?" Then he laughed. Gordon had laughed, too, but he had promptly reported the incident back to Barry Sr. and Mary.

As soon as Barry Sr. got to the Little House, he told Mary about the scene with Edie. Mary was incensed. "Your conversation with Barry this morning amounted to no less than blackmail, which I deeply, deeply resent," she wrote Edie in a letter that Barry Sr. persuaded her not to send. She accused her daughter-in-law of trying to manipulate them by insinuating that they were responsible for Barry Jr.'s diminished physical and emotional health. "The threat is made horrendously effective," she wrote, because of what Barry Jr. had said to Gordon, raising the specter of suicide. "So, we are faced with the intolerable dilemma: unless Barry gets his way and defeats his sisters, he will commit suicide. I cannot tell you in acceptable language how this cowardly maneuver affects me. My disgust at the willingness you and Barry show to descend to the use of such a stratagem and to put Barry Sr. in this hideous dilemma is more than I can possibly express."

Though the letter was never sent, the rumor that Barry Jr. had threatened to kill himself streaked through the family. Eleanor called Sallie with the news. When Barry Jr. heard it, he strenuously denied it was true. It was ridiculous to think that his inquiry about suicide meant he was considering ending his life, he said. Mary was not mollified. Maybe Barry Jr. does not intend to commit suicide, she thought to herself, but he and Edie are fighting dirty.

———————

Edie's denunciation did not stop the family and Bingham employees from pressuring Barry Jr. to agree to $28 million, although the tactics changed. Barry Sr. offered to cover the difference between $26.3 million and $28 million himself. "If you can't do it yourself, I will fill in the gap," he told his son. Barry Jr. responded that he just did not see how that could work.

Eleanor and Rowland tried their hand at persuasion. Rowland infuriated his brother-in-law by suggesting the difference could be made up by cutting back employee benefits. "You all want to offer her so much, why don't you give her the money?" Barry Jr. replied. Eleanor took him seriously and, after talking it over with Bob Morse—another terrified hired hand—she came back to her brother with a proposal. Since WHAS owed no money, perhaps it could make up the $1.7 million. Barry Jr. declined. "He wouldn't consider it," said Eleanor. "No matter where it came from, he didn't seem to want to do it. He said it would saddle WHAS with too much debt."

Despite the fact that Barry Jr. stood virtually alone in his view that $28 million was an impossible hurdle, he continued to insist that his obduracy did not spring from a personal vendetta against his sisters. "I'm not a game player," he said. "If people think that this was a big poker game for me and I was trying to put Sallie down or put Eleanor down or put me up by sticking with a price which they didn't agree with, that's not the motive. It really isn't. I take this place too damn seriously to play with it like poker chips. . . . My total concern was the financial welfare of the company."

Almost everyone else, however, felt that Barry Jr.'s arguments rested on a fragile foundation. Bernie's analysis, based on Barry Jr.'s bleak assumptions, showed that, at $26.3 million, the company could anticipate one year with a "BB" credit rating from Standard & Poor's. At $28 million the company could anticipate three years as a "BB" company. A very high rating—"AA" —means that a company's indebtedness is minuscule compared to the money it makes each year and it can easily borrow additional funds. A "BB" rating indicates that a company's resources are stretched thin to cover existing debt, and that borrowing money will be more difficult.

Goldman, Sachs told Barry Jr. repeatedly that being categorized as a "BB" company was probably avoidable if new presses were taken out of the projections. And even if the companies were "BB" for a time, they said, that did not mean they could not borrow more money if they needed it.

But Barry Jr., like his father, had had little experience with debt. The Binghams had virtually never owed anything, and always kept a large cash reserve at the papers. He was obsessed by the fear that, during the period when the company was "BB," there would be some unexpected need to borrow money and no bank would lend it. He envisioned potential bankruptcy, a distress sale, or—the worst possible scenario—having the papers placed under the control of a financial institution.

His professional advisers told him he was behaving like a man who insisted on wearing both a belt and suspenders. He did not care. "I am no financial wizard and don't pretend to be," he said defending his concern about the Standard & Poor's rating. "Perhaps if I were an M.B.A. or a Ph.D. in finance, I'd [look at it differently]. Maybe I'm overly impressed with those things, but since I'm the person who's going to have to face the music, I think it's understandable that I'm inclined to be conservative. How much of a crapshoot do you want to take when it is you who is going to operate it and it is your future and the futures of your children? I want a margin, a comfort factor."

There was also the matter of dividends. The various projections indicated that money for dividends would be scarce for a while, and he felt he was asking his own wife and daughters as well as Joan and her children to face the potential of several years without dividend income. "So all the eggs are being put in one basket," he said.

But underlying this complex rationale were two fundamental convictions that formed the real heart of his refusal to budge. First was his certainty that Sallie had nowhere else to go, and that $26.3 million was the highest offer she would get. Eventually, she would have to accept it.

And second, he was sure that, when the chips were down, his parents would go along with him. Despite the warnings of the hired hands and his own sense that his parents' preference was for Option X, he simply could not believe that they would turn their back on a life's work and sell out their grandchildren's birthright. "Basically he just didn't believe his father would do it," said Joan, who considered Barry Jr.'s attitude a huge bluff. "He thought, 'Because I am so good and so right, the right will out.'"

On the Monday after Thanksgiving, it looked as though Barry Jr. had won. Eleanor backed down.

After meeting with Rucker, she agreed to go along with $26.3 million for Sallie and a stock swap based on that number. She had retreated first from "fair" market value to $28 million and then to the $26.3 million that Barry Jr. insisted upon. But she imposed one major condition: Sallie had to agree to that price before Eleanor would proceed with the swap.

On Wednesday, December 4, Sallie and her lawyer, Rebecca Wester-field, met to hear the family's counterproposal to her demand for $32 million. They listened quietly as Sallie was offered $26.3 million. Sallie had asked for $8 million down and 15 percent interest on the balance; Barry Jr. offered her 12 percent.

Sallie had also wanted a ten-year look-back, which Barry Jr. agreed to offer on the newspapers. Eleanor was not so generous with her sister. She offered Sallie only a five-year look-back on the broadcasting properties, with a cap of $65 million, meaning that if WHAS was sold in five years and one day, Sallie would get nothing; if it was sold before that, she would not share in any amount over $65 million. Barry Jr. had surmised that the five-year look-back was Rucker's idea, calculated to poison the deal with Sallie, which would be another push toward Option X. When Rebecca Westerfield heard the conditions on WHAS, she was outraged, and astounded to be told that they were Eleanor's doing, not Barry Jr.'s.

A week later, Sallie rejected the whole package and withdrew her offer to sell for $32 million. If anyone was bluffing at this point, it was Sallie. "I was trying to hold out for $30 million, but I might have gone to $28 million," she said later. "I was ready to accept just about anything they were willing to give me at that point because I'd exhausted all my other options." Still, she spurned the offer out of pride. "I was insulted that they came back with $26.3 million," she said.

Ironically, both Sallie and Barry Jr. had arrived at the same conclusion: Eleanor was trying to scuttle the stock swap without bloodying her hands. When Sallie learned that Eleanor had made buying her out a condition of the swap, she tried to talk Eleanor out of it. "I asked her not to, because it didn't make any sense to me," Sallie said. Eleanor wanted "to have somebody to blame, I think. I think she was scared to death [of running WHAS]. She'd have so many people gunning for her. So I think it was this queer thing of wanting something, but ensuring that it wouldn't happen."

Eleanor insisted to friends that she was bending over backward to protect Sallie. "How could I screw her?" she would say. But the day after rejecting the $26.3 million offer, Sallie was quoted in *The Courier-Journal* voicing particular objection to the five-year look-back and $65 million cap. "It will probably be worth a lot more in five years," Sallie said. "I might be a substantial loser." Barry Jr. was quoted as placing the responsibility for that condition squarely in the lap of "Mrs. Miller." Eleanor was not available for comment. Much later, she said she would have been willing to alter the look-back, but never got around to it.

At the Bingham companies, employees were becoming increasingly nervous. As article after article appeared citing Sallie's multimillion dollar demands, she had been adjudged the cause of all the family's problems and a threat to *The Courier-Journal's* future. At one bar, reporters erected "The Sallie Bingham Dartboard." A cartoon of Sallie—with crow's feet around her eyes, huge teeth, and a jutting jaw—was dead center. At the top: "$42 million points for a bull's-eye." At bottom: "$26 million—It's not enough; hold out for more."

On the third floor, George Gill and the other hired hands had become fatigued and pessimistic—especially George. Still, they felt duty-bound to find a solution. Now that Sallie had rejected $26.3 million, what was next? Barry Sr. hoped that Barry Jr. would be willing to up his offer to $28 million. Barry Jr. wanted to go ahead with the swap or the Wednesday Plan.

George was past caring. He was burned out and embittered. "I was just exasperated by Junior's inflexibility," he said. "We were all very tired and working very hard in his best interests and in the best interests of everybody, and we were getting nowhere." Barry Jr. had made it plain that he did not trust George, and George had made it equally clear that he considered Barry Jr. a stubborn fool. Although nothing had been said, Paul was the obvious choice to be Barry Jr.'s right-hand man in whatever configuration the company took after the dust settled, assuming, of course, that Barry Sr. did not sell it all. The thought of having to report to Paul made George's guts curdle.

Barry Jr.'s refusal to budge on $26.3 million nettled all the hired hands. Their frustration became anger and then disgust. Barry Jr. did not believe anything they said. He had no confidence in them. Well, they had no confidence in him, George, Leon, and John muttered to themselves as they brooded about their options. Barry Jr. was probably going to get the whole damn thing sold. Even if he didn't, what did they have to look forward to? Paul and Barry Jr., the unholy alliance. As they bitterly drank their Scotches, they confessed that they had no reason to stay. They did not want to work for Barry Jr. and Paul. They agreed that it really didn't matter what happened. Either way, they were gone.

———

Wreaths and red Christmas bows decorated almost every door in Glenview, but there was little cheer in the Bingham compound. The family seemed to be at an impossible impasse. Barry Jr. wanted his father to tell Eleanor that she had to choose between going ahead with the stock swap or the Wednesday Plan. Eleanor threatened to leave town if the Wednesday Plan went through, and would only proceed with the stock swap if Sallie was satisfied. Sallie had rejected $26.3 million, and Barry Jr. refused to go higher.

Even then, Barry Sr. was unwilling to pull the plug. The hired hands had thought that he would throw up his hands when Sallie turned down $26.3 million, but he had not. Instead, he went back to the grueling task of trying one more time to devise a new proposal for Sallie that Barry Jr. would embrace.

A few days before Christmas, George and Leon gathered once again in Barry Sr.'s office to go over yet one more set of documents and projections, trying to figure out a way to save the papers for Barry Jr. They hunched over Barry Sr.'s desk and went to work.

Barry Sr. was bone tired. The years of stressful quarreling had taken their toll and, for once, the Bingham patriarch looked like the seventy-nine-year-old man he was. He was used to being in control, but the situation had somehow gotten out of hand and he felt increasingly manipulated by his rigid, single-minded son. As Barry Jr. had issued ultimatum after ultimatum, he had reluctantly tried to accommodate him. Throw the women off the board. Make Sallie sign the buy-back. Now his son had refused, against expert counsel, to go above $26.3 million. As a result, he and the hired hands were back at square one and Barry Sr. resented it. At this stage in his life, he wanted love and tranquility, not internecine warfare.

As much as he hated to admit it, Barry Sr. was also increasingly unsure that the newspapers he had loved for over six decades were worth preserving. He was weary of hearing complaints about the papers' cynical tone and sloppy editing, and tired of feeling dismissed by Barry Jr. and Paul Janensch. He had even begun to feel that he had made a terrible mistake by stepping back so completely from the management of the business in 1971 and giving in to Barry Jr. every time he threatened to resign. "The papers are not fun anymore," he now told close friends. "Boy, I'd like to cash in and spend the rest of my life giving money away."

But when Judge Bingham had willed Barry Sr. the papers, he had made it clear that he expected him to pass them on, in time, to yet another generation of Binghams. Throughout the family feud, Barry Sr. had felt an obligation to the memory of his father as much as to the future of his grandchildren. Indeed, one thing that had kept him from selling out had been the thought of what the Judge would have said. Allowing the papers to pass from Bingham hands would abort his father's dream and call into question what Barry Sr. had always maintained was the raison d'être of his own life. Though he wanted to sell, and thought it wisest to sell, the ghost of the Judge simply would not let him do it. Like Eleanor, Barry Sr. did not want blood on his hands. He would dearly love to find a way out of his misery. But how? Reluctantly, he turned back to the business at hand.

George was just as depleted as Barry Sr., and had even more cause to be furious with Barry Jr.—the man who had put him through the humiliation of the horse race, who had spurned him in favor of Paul Janensch during the sabbatical year, and who had openly distrusted him during the negotiations over what price to offer Sallie. As George gazed at Barry Sr. he was torn about whether he should reveal what he knew would be a blockbuster piece of information. Should he or shouldn't he? In a sense, it was his duty. And it was so, so tempting. It would let Barry Sr. know just what a numb-skull his son was and it would be repayment for all of Barry Jr.'s slights. It would serve Barry Jr. right. And anyway, Barry Sr. should know. It was George's fiduciary duty as a top executive to tell him.

George cleared his throat. "Barry Jr. sure is going to have a tough time getting a team to work for him," he said nonchalantly. Barry Sr. looked up from the spread-sheets, puzzled. "What do you mean?" he asked. As George well knew, Barry Sr. had an unspoken assumption that the hired hands, and especially George and Leon, would be there to help his boy through the rough times ahead. And if Eleanor proceeded with the swap, he certainly expected them to be at her elbow over at WHAS, guiding her, watching out for her. These men were important—no, essential.

"Well, John Richards is going to take early retirement," George said, "and Leon here is probably going to do the same." Leon looked at his colleague in amazement. He had never expressly told George that he was planning to retire early, but they had discussed the possibility, and Leon did not contradict him now. "And I'm leaving as soon as my contract is up," George said matter-of-factly.

George went on to say that he and many of the other hired hands had agreed among themselves that they would not work for Barry Jr., even if the stock swap or the Wednesday Plan went through. The message was clear: We are fed up with running into brick walls, fed up with having our counsel ignored, fed up with being distrusted, and fed up with working for a man who is clearly irrational. We are fed up with Barry Jr.

Barry Sr. seemed confused. George went on, in a humorously mocking tone. "Yup, Barry won't have old George to kick around anymore and he won't have Leon either." Then he landed the real killer. "No, Barry and Paul Janensch are going to have to run this thing by themselves."

There was silence. Barry Sr. stared into space. He seemed to be looking at some terrible vision. Finally, he quietly said, "That's right. I never thought of that." Leon watched Barry Sr.'s face as Paul's name was mentioned. "I could see the shock of recognition," he said. "It was something he hadn't contemplated before."

Leon and George walked out of the room, leaving Barry Sr. sitting at his desk in a kind of daze. Leon was trembling. "I think you just did it, George," he said in a frightened voice as they made their way down the hall. "You just tipped him in favor of selling."

THE END OF AN ERA

For several moments after George and Leon left the room, Barry Sr. sat motionless behind his desk. George's words had changed everything. Suddenly, after months of indecision, he saw with stark clarity the radically different futures he had the power to bring about.

The stock swap now seemed unthinkable. Barry Sr. had never been confident that Eleanor could run WHAS. Without George and Leon there to help, he feared for Eleanor's welfare and the future of the broadcast properties.

The Wednesday Plan was equally repugnant. Like the stock swap, it left the family's crown jewels—the newspapers—in the hands of Barry Jr. and Paul Janensch. Barry Sr. had been able to stomach that possibility as long as he knew that George and the hired hands would continue actually to run the business, tempering Barry Jr.'s stubborn willfulness and acting as a counterweight to Paul's unsavory influence and ambition.

With the professional staff gone, however, Barry Jr. would be left to face debt and economic uncertainty with a lieutenant who had almost no business experience. Without George and the others to keep the ship financially afloat, it seemed all but certain that the papers would eventually become organs he would not want associated with the name "Bingham." Ironically, Barry Jr.'s pessimistic spread-sheets had convinced Barry Sr. that tough times lay ahead. But by repeatedly ignoring the counsel of his aides, Barry Jr. had also demonstrated that he did not have the common sense to run a complex enterprise during a precarious period. The assumption that Paul would serve as his top adviser made the future even less appealing.

Without the hired hands, Barry Sr. could foresee *The Courier-Journal* slipping in prestige and value while Barry Jr. ruined his life struggling to save it. "I thought this would have left Barry in a dreadful position," he said. "Think of staff morale if so many of the principal people had moved out. He would have had an impossible job to undertake."

Suddenly, as he sat ruminating in his office, Barry Sr. realized that George's declaration was a wonderful gift. It eased his conscience. For Judge Bingham's sake, Barry Sr. had felt duty-bound to go as far as he could to keep the newspapers in family hands. Now his indecision could at last be honorably resolved and he could do what he had been long inclined to do: sell. "Mr. Bingham was somewhat Machiavellian," observed an aide who had known him for years. "I can see him taking [what George said] and using it to justify his own position."

Despite the months of ambivalence, Barry Sr. now felt no anxiety about the idea of total sale. Mark Ethridge and Norman Isaacs had always marveled at Barry Sr.'s ability to leave a problem behind the minute he chose a course of action to deal with it. No second thoughts. No lingering doubts. It was a talent they admired and suspected was rooted in his mother's death, the psychic hurt Barry Sr. had managed to bury by not dwelling on the past.

Before he could finally cut the Gordian knot, however, he had two things yet to do. He had to convince Mary that the companies must be sold and then decide with her on a public justification that would do the least damage to their son and still approximate the truth.

The first was harder than one might expect. When Mary Bingham made a commitment, it went deep. Her strongest commitment, of course, was to Barry Sr. But second to that was her devotion to the newspapers. Despite her sometimes menacing talk of sale in the past, she was bound to the papers in an emotional way her husband was constitutionally incapable of sharing. Yes, he had loved and enjoyed them, but always at a distance, the way he loved and enjoyed so many things. Now that he no longer took pleasure in them, his ardor had dissipated. The newspapers still had a powerful claim on Mary's heart, though, a claim more intense in many ways than the pull of her own children. "You would think she would be less distressed than I was," said Barry Sr. "If anything, she was even more distressed and more determined to see what could be done to try to preserve the papers."

Now, with the news that George and Leon were going to leave, Barry Sr. had information so devastating that it overwhelmed even Mary's bulldog resistance. She viewed Paul Janensch even less favorably than did her husband, and the thought of him as commander-in-chief of the family papers sickened her. Shortly before Christmas, 1985, Mary reluctantly brought herself to agree with Barry Sr.: The Bingham properties, including the beloved newspapers, must be put on the auction block.

Barry Sr. and Mary still had to devise a rationale for the sale that would save face for Barry Jr. and perhaps even make the two of them look wise and benevolent. As the holiday neared, the Senior Binghams' private conversations came to resemble a sort of catechism as they crafted reasoned statements to answer the questions they quite rightly anticipated would come from the family and the public about why they had decided to sell.

They could not say that the hired hands were prepared to bolt; that would be too embarrassing for Barry Jr. Indeed, Barry Sr. could not even bring himself to tell his son in private what George had said. That would shatter him, he felt, and provoke the kind of painful confrontation Barry Sr. had spent his life trying to avoid. There was also no way to predict Barry Jr.'s reaction. With his penchant for total disclosure, he might publish the news on page one. Or maybe he would try to appease his senior managers and put the team back together. Perhaps George's decision to leave was revocable. Perhaps Leon's early retirement was not cast in stone. Perhaps some compromise could be reached. If Barry Jr. were made aware of this new catastrophe, he might come up with an alternative. He would certainly try. And Barry Sr. was so spent, he just wanted the family strife to end.

At a party shortly before Christmas, however, Barry Sr. did confide to Eleanor and Rowland that George and the others were bailing out. With considerable theatricality, he shook his head in dismay, his blue eyes wide, unfocused, and terribly sad. It was a pose Barry Sr. used whenever he wanted to convey the idea that something fateful had happened and there was nothing to be done. For a moment, it crossed Eleanor's mind that her father hoped she would deliver the information to Barry Jr., but she and Rowland decided not to be the bearers of such tidings and told no one.

Of course, Barry Jr. also had a secret of vital importance. He had never shown his father the letter describing Paul as his new Mark Ethridge. And though he had realized months ago that there would be no need for many of the hired hands under the changed ownership contemplated by the stock swap and the Wednesday Plan, he had never raised the subject with Barry Sr. He knew such a discussion would automatically focus attention on who would get the top job of running the papers. His parents undoubtedly preferred George, and Barry Jr. knew that declaring publicly for Paul would only alienate them further. In such a pressure-cooker atmosphere, he decided to spare himself yet another fight and hope that the issue would never come up. Unfortunately for him—and unbeknownst to him—it had.

As the Christmas holidays neared, Barry Sr. and Mary talked endlessly about how to frame their decision for their children and the press. Barry Sr. wanted the deed done as kindly and gently as possible, sparing Barry Jr. and the family the humiliation of public failure. This was his only remaining son, his favorite. He did not want to add hurt to a situation that was sure to devastate him anyway.

Besides, the exodus of the hired hands was just the final straw. There were plenty of other reasons for choosing Option X, reasons that not only sounded plausible, but were true. Barry Jr., Sallie, and Eleanor clearly could not work together. Both the stock swap and the Wednesday Plan would leave the papers in a vulnerable economic position and, eventually, estate taxes would add to the burden. Standard Gravure had long since ceased to make money and without the ability to call on WHAS for revenue, it was almost inevitable that *The Courier-Journal* and *Times* would plummet in quality. Besides, Barry Jr. had never liked newspapers; selling would free him from a miserable life of unending toil.

Prices were at a historic high and the papers and WHAS might be worth far less later. Selling would also provide ample money for each child and grandchild to craft a satisfying life and would free up $100 million or so for the Senior Binghams' personal philanthropy. And it held the promise of resolving the family fracas once and for all by removing the reason for fighting. In time, with some luck, peace might finally come to the Bingham family.

All of the reasons were true. They were just not the whole truth.

The other causes of the sale remained unspoken: the Seniors' lack of confidence in Barry Jr., their dislike of Paul Janensch, even their own emotional divestment in the newspapers. Barry Sr. had become convinced that every scenario except selling would mean endless bickering among his children and that eventually they would devour each other fighting over the spoils. Acting now meant that he and Mary could face the furor together. It would also ensure that the outcome he preferred would actually happen. As a man accustomed since childhood to getting his own way, he was determined to have the last word in the resolution of this ghastly situation.

———————

Unaware that his father had made up his mind to sell, Barry Jr. continued to badger him to impose the Wednesday Plan. Eleanor has had her shot, he told Barry Sr. over their weekly lunch. Now is the time for you to tell her that you have decided on the Wednesday Plan and she has no choice but to go along with it. Barry Sr. said he was unwilling to do that.

By Christmas week, Barry Sr. was visibly tense, anticipating the announcement he knew he would soon have to make. The holiday itself was a gloomy affair. Instead of paying Sallie a yuletide visit, Barry Sr. left a pile of presents heaped on her front porch, and she, too, managed to drop off gifts for her parents without actually seeing them.

Barry Jr. and Edie dutifully invited Barry Sr. and Mary over to the Big House for Christmas Eve dinner. It was Mary's eighty-first birthday, but family plays honoring the occasion had long ago been abandoned. As a substitute, Barry Jr. had started showing home movies taken over the previous year. After dinner he put on his production as usual, but no one could muster much enthusiasm. Eleanor and Rowland were conspicuously absent, committed to spending the holiday with Rowland's family. Early the next morning, the Seniors left for The Homestead, a resort in Hot Springs, Virginia, where they planned a relaxing visit with Eddie Warburg, a friend of Barry Sr.'s from Middlesex and Harvard, and his wife.

The Warburgs found the Senior Binghams in a state of despair and nervous exhaustion. Over dinner Christmas night, Mary solemnly asked Eddie to help her plan a double funeral. She could not live without Barry Sr., she explained, and she intended to commit suicide if he died, which she feared was quite likely because of the enormous pressure he was under. Horrified, Eddie said he would not be a party to any such scheme, and the matter was quickly dropped.

Barry Jr. and Edie left Louisville as well, flying to Elbow Key in the Abacos the day after Christmas for a week's vacation. Even with the azure sky and gentle sea to soothe him, Barry Jr. could find no peace. Emily, their oldest daughter, later told Mary that she had never had such a wretched time. "I knew we were coming down to the line," said Barry Jr. "I didn't know what the line was going to be, but I knew this wasn't going to go on for another six months. A decision was going to be made."

Even then, he felt certain that his father would back him as he had so many times over the past fifteen years, from the moment he had decided to start up an unprofitable classical music station to the day he had demanded that the Bingham women leave the board. And he tried to comfort himself with the commitment of "support" his father had given him the previous May. "We kept thinking that Barry Sr. would have our interests at heart," said Edie.

Barry Jr. returned to Louisville on January 3 and immediately sensed that something was up. First, his father called a meeting with Barry Jr. and Eleanor for January 8 without explaining its purpose. Then, on January 7,

Gordon Davidson phoned Barry Jr. in a near panic and urged him to buy the papers outright from the family. Such a move would mean assuming a huge debt, and Barry Jr. knew Gordon would never have suggested the idea unless he was sure it was the only way to avoid disaster.

As usual, the unseen hand of Barry Sr. was at work, delivering a message indirectly. Hours earlier, he had called Gordon and told him of his decision to sell. It was now up to Gordon to force Barry Jr. to do something that might prevent that from happening.

Barry Jr. rightly smelled a rat and demanded to know whether Gordon's frantic buy-out plea meant that his father had chosen Option X. Barry Sr. had sworn Gordon to secrecy about his plans, but had also made it clear that he wanted the lawyer to warn Barry Jr. in the strongest possible terms that he was on the verge of total sale. Barry Jr. turned the buy-out down flat as too risky. Gordon reported back to Barry Sr. that he had delivered the message to no avail.

———————

At 10:00 A.M. on Wednesday, January 8, Barry Jr. and Eleanor gathered in the book-lined study of the Little House. Neither knew that what they were about to hear would put an end to almost seventy years of Bingham tradition and change their lives forever. Barry Jr. perched stiffly on a rose-colored couch facing his parents while they sat nervously in front of the sepia and white tiles that bordered the blazing fireplace. Eleanor fidgeted in a chair to one side. Mary poured coffee but no one took a sip.

After a few moments of strained silence, Barry Sr. stood up, cleared his throat, and said that this was the hardest decision he had ever had to make but he had concluded that all the companies must be sold. He looked at Eleanor and said he knew how disappointed she was that she was not going to own and operate WHAS. Then he turned to Barry Jr. and said he knew he could find other things to do with his life, echoing almost word for word what Barry Jr. had told him soon after arriving back from his sabbatical the previous May.

Barry Sr.'s draft statement, which he read aloud, spoke of the rising costs of materials and equipment, and of the increasing difficulties families faced when they tried to pass control of their businesses from one generation to the next. There was no mention of the Bingham family feud, and certainly no hint that Barry Sr. lacked confidence in his son. Indeed, he praised Barry Jr. for his high ethical standards and his wisdom in recruiting outside directors for the boards.

While his father read his statement, Barry Jr. sat motionless on the couch. Despite the strong signals he had gotten that Option X was coming, he seemed totally unprepared for his father's decision. For years, he had kept his emotions tightly under wraps. When he had been teased about his weight or his slow reading as a child, he had shrugged it off. When cancer had threatened his life, he had become stoic and subdued. But the news that the papers were being sold made him crackle with rage. "To this day I find it amazing that he didn't realize that this could happen," said Barry Sr.

Eleanor, who had inherited her father's distaste for conflict, gently suggested that the press release include a phrase saying that the companies had been well run. "Who cares!" Barry Jr. said hotly. "They've been so wonderfully run that now we've decided to sell them. Spare me!"

To mollify his son, Barry Sr. tried to explain why he could not embrace the Wednesday Plan, as Barry Jr. had wanted. "It will leave you with such a heavy financial burden," he told him. "The newspapers will be in jeopardy." Barry Jr.'s eyes flashed. "No, that's wrong!" he said. "It will put the newspapers in exactly the same financial position as if we had offered Sallie $26.3 million. If that's the problem—your misunderstanding of the Wednesday Plan—let me come back tomorrow and present it again."

Barry Sr. nodded weakly. He had no intention of changing his mind but he could not bring himself to tell Barry Jr. the real reasons for the sale. "It's too bad Daddy presented it that way," said Eleanor later. "It wasn't a financial decision." When the meeting broke up, Barry Jr. vowed to return the next day with a new workup of the Wednesday Plan along with a "very angry" statement of his own.

Thinking that the issue would be resolved once and for all that day, Barry Sr. had asked George, Gordon, and a few other top executives to meet him at the CJ & T building, and he wearily drove into Louisville to keep the appointment. Most of those assembled were not sure why they had been so hastily summoned, but they suspected the worst. When Barry Sr. walked in, he was ashen. "Gentlemen," he sighed as he lowered himself into his chair. "You're looking at a man who has lived too long." The family is considering selling everything, he told them, but Barry Jr. is assembling further documentation on the Wednesday Plan and there will be another private family meeting tomorrow. Please stand by.

That evening, Barry Sr. began phoning the grandchildren and reading them his statement about the sale. Emily, reached at Harvard, told him that he was leaving out the key factor in the decision: family disharmony. "You've got to admit there's a problem," she insisted. Reluctantly, Barry Sr. agreed and penciled in a vague allusion to "divergent interests" in his children's generation.

He reached Clara and Rob in Hong Kong, where they were spending the holidays with their mother. It was 5:00 A.M. Hong Kong time and still dark in the Peninsula Hotel when the phone rang. Barry Sr. spoke briefly with Clara, who was shocked but sleepily sympathetic. She and Rob shed a few tears.

Joan, however, was furious. Barry Sr. had gone back on his promise, made at the Seelbach Hotel the previous July, to consult with the grandchildren one more time before reaching a final decision. Now they had been told that their birthright was to be sold off like so much used furniture and they would have no say about it whatsoever. "When he phoned it was a fait accompli," she said. "To this day I will never forgive myself for having gone [to Hong Kong] for Christmas."

At 10:00 A.M. the next morning, January 9, Barry Jr. and Eleanor arrived once again at the Little House. Barry Jr. came armed with facts and figures about the Wednesday Plan. But Barry Sr. said he had no interest in hearing new arguments. His mind was made up: He was going to sell.

Barry Jr. then thrust a copy of the two-page statement he had drafted the previous night at his father. "What you are doing is a concession to stunning greed," he said, glaring at Eleanor. Barry Sr.'s eyes welled as he read his son's press release.

The statement began by denouncing the sale as "irrational" and "ill-advised." "While my father has kind words for my stewardship," it said, "his decision to sell all the companies I have managed clearly indicates that he holds other family member's [sic] personal interests and priorities at a higher value than my service to the companies. It is difficult not to view this action as a betrayal of the traditions and principles which I have sought to perpetuate. It fails to meet any standard of fairness that I can comprehend. Had I thought, in the early nineteen-sixties, that my career would be abbreviated by my parents in this summary way, I would have dedicated my life's work to other enterprises." Attached was a formal letter of resignation, signed in Barry Jr.'s flamboyant hand.

All of the old half-buried slights and unspoken grudges of Barry Jr.'s life had surfaced, it seemed, in one grand fireworks display—the wounding comparisons with Worth, his mother's biting criticisms, his father's empty assurance of "support." "It was just an explosion that was impossible to contain, you know, the feelings that Barry had," said Edie.

Barry Sr. was deeply offended by his son's characterization of him as irrational. "You're calling me senile!" he said in astonishment when he came to the word. "No, I'm not," responded Barry Jr. "I'm saying that the reasons you have given do not make sense." Barry Jr., of course, was on to something. He knew how equivocal his father could be about the truth, especially unpleasant truth. Although he had no knowledge that the hired hands were set to leave, he sensed correctly that Barry Sr. had not come clean about his motives for the sale. "I looked at it as an active rejection of my leadership," said Barry Jr. "What [my parents] were saying is, 'We're sick of the way this guy is running the newspaper.' "

Barry Sr. pleaded with his son to take out the words "irrational" and "betrayal." "It's going to hurt you with the public," he warned him. "I wish you would think better of it." But Barry Jr. was not persuaded. Mary, who had been listening to the exchange in silence, could no longer contain herself. "We gave you the best job in Louisville and you and Edie acted like martyrs!" she said in a hard voice. "You've treated your father and the rest of the family in a most ungentlemanly way."

After that remark, the Binghams had little to say to each other. The decision had been made. Now they had to tell the newspaper staff, the heads of the other Bingham companies, and the world. Barry Jr. turned on his heel, headed out to his car, and sped off for the CJ & T building.

At about twenty minutes of eleven the phone rang in George Gill's office. It was Barry Sr. In numb tones he asked George to round up Gordon Davidson, Leon Tallichet, and Bernie Block and meet him in his office at 11:00 A.M.

Even as they spoke, Barry Jr. was walking into the building, flashing his I.D. to the guard, and ascending to his spacious third-floor office. Minutes later, Paul Janensch, working at his desk a floor above, got a call from Barry Jr.'s secretary. "Barry Jr. would like to see you," she said. "Can you come down right away?" Paul's heart beat fast. "I'll always remember that morning," he said later. "I just knew."

Barry Jr. was taut as a piano wire. "Well, old friend, the family is going to sell," he said. "My father is going to call a meeting of top management in about an hour. He doesn't know I'm telling you this so please don't tell anyone else. I know it's a big story but you're just going to have to sit on it until 11:30 A.M." Paul nodded and stumbled back upstairs.

Meanwhile, down the hall in Barry Sr.'s office, Gordon, Leon, Bernie, and George had assembled just as the Bingham patriarch had requested. They talked in nervous tones until Barry Sr. arrived, stylishly dressed as always but chalk-white and haggard after the draining session at the Little House.

Moments later, Barry Jr. walked into the room, still bristling with anger, his embarrassment wrenchingly obvious. Averting his eyes from his son, Barry Sr. told the family advisers that he had definitely decided to put the Bingham companies up for sale. "I've called a meeting of all the managers at 11:30 A.M. in the third-floor conference room," he said. "Shouldn't we be getting down there now?"

The other executives were already arrayed around the table when Barry Sr. and Barry Jr. arrived and settled into seats at opposite ends of the room. Few of the men had any idea what the Binghams' announcement was going to be. "I would not have bet money," said John Richards. "It could have been either a solution or a dissolution."

After a curt "good morning," Barry Sr. passed out copies of his statement and read it aloud while the white stack traveled from hand to hand around the room. Then Barry Jr. distributed his, along with his letter of resignation. "The bitterness in that memo shocked everybody," said Leon. "I was bowled over by it." As a dozen pairs of eyes scanned the stapled sheets, no one said a word, choosing instead to stare at the pieces of paper rather than glimpse the pain on the faces of Barry Sr. and Barry Jr.

Finally, Paul Janensch broke the silence. He asked how *The Courier-Journal* and *Times* should handle the story now that Barry Jr. was technically no longer in charge. The sale was the hottest story of the day, if not the year; it should get into the afternoon cycle for that day's *Louisville Times* if possible, he said. Barry Sr., displaying his well-known prejudice for the morning paper, said no, he wanted the news kept confidential so that *The Courier-Journal* could break it the following day. With that, he cut off the exchange and walked back to his office.

As soon as Barry Sr. was out of earshot, Paul turned to George. "It's not going to work!" he said. "This story will be all over town in hours. And the employees are going to be wondering what's happening and they won't know until they read it in the paper tomorrow—people who work here!" George knew Paul was right, but he was not about to go out on a limb for his old enemy. "Screw it, I'm not going to make that decision," he said. "Let's go see the chairman."

Paul and George trooped down to Barry Sr.'s office, where Paul made an impassioned plea for a page-one story in that afternoon's *Times*. "The worst thing you can do is let rumor take over," he told Barry Sr. "If we don't do this now, by eight o'clock tomorrow night you won't be able to recognize the truth." Frazzled to the point of indifference, Barry Sr. had no energy left for argument. He waved his hand weakly. "Do anything you like," he said.

There was no time for a formal press release, so Paul quickly put several secretaries to work duplicating the statements of Barry Sr. and Barry Jr. and tacking them up on every bulletin board in the building. He assigned a reporter to the story and stopped the presses, which were set to spew out the *Times*'s early edition. By 1:00 P.M., the shocking news that the Binghams had decided to sell *The Courier-Journal* and *Times* and subsidiary companies was racing through the building. Soon, a revised edition of *The Louisville Times* rolled off the presses and into the papers' delivery trucks. "Bingham Sr. to Sell Communications Firms," said the headline. "Bingham Jr. Calls Father's Act 'Irrational.' "

Sallie, enjoying a hamburger in a Louisville restaurant with friends, was unaware of the discussions at the Little House over the past two days. Shortly after 1:00 P.M., she was called to the telephone. It was a *Courier-Journal* reporter. "Your father has just posted an announcement that the newspapers are going to be sold," she said. "Do you have any comment?"

Sallie was terror-struck. Despite the media campaign orchestrated by Christopher Shaw, Sallie had never seriously believed that putting her 15 percent share in the companies up for sale could be the catalyst for the collapse of the entire empire. As angry as she still was at her brother, this was not what she had intended. All she had ever wanted was to make her point, grab some attention, get her money, and get out. "I was scared to death," she said. "It was like a massive castle falling down. I knew everyone would blame me."

Later that afternoon Sallie called her father, who had tried to reach her at the Kentucky Foundation for Women hours earlier. The conversation was stiff and perfunctory. Sallie and Barry Sr. had not spoken for months and the strain showed. When she told him that she had already heard about the sale, he did not respond. "I'm sure this is a terribly hard time for you and Mother," she ventured cautiously. "Yes, it is," her father agreed. Then he hung up. By early evening, Sallie had recovered sufficiently to tell a *Courier-Journal* reporter that the decision was good news for her. It will make my stock worth more, she said confidently, and it could improve the newspapers.

The next morning, January 10, readers awoke to a *Courier-Journal* stuffed with analysis of the sale, elegiac reminiscences from the staff, and words of sadness and praise from state leaders and publishers. Even Congressman Mitch McConnell, a Kentucky Republican who over the years had received both applause and damnation at the hands of *The Courier-Journal*, found ample reason for regret. "It is tragic to see this family breaking up," he said. "Especially in public."

That day and for weeks afterward, the Binghams were besieged with requests for interviews. The dissolution of the Bingham media dynasty and the family fight behind it seemed to strike a profoundly human chord. From the Mary Lily affair to the Judge's ambassadorship, to the deaths of two sons, Barry Jr.'s cancer, and Sallie's vocal estrangement, the Binghams had conducted their lives in the glare of public scrutiny. Now was no exception. Had they wanted to, they could have cut off the persistent publicity. Instead they embraced it, partly because they viewed it as a journalistic duty and partly because it gave each one of them a chance to justify the position he or she had staked out in the family feud.

With the exception of Eleanor, who shunned the spotlight, the Binghams agreeably went on television and radio and granted audiences to reporters from *Time*, *Newsweek*, *The New York Times*, *The Washington Post*, and *The Los*

Angeles Times. Privately, Barry Sr. felt flattered to think that national publications such as these considered his family's saga worthy of notice. It reassured him that the newspapers still had the weight and prestige he feared had been lost under Barry Jr.'s leadership.

At 3:00 P.M. on the day after the announcement, several hundred newspaper employees jammed into the *CJ & T* cafeteria for what Paul called an "address to the troops." With awkward grace, Barry Jr. rose to speak, reassuring his co-workers that it was a "failure of family," not of management, that had caused the downfall of the Bingham dynasty. But try as he might, his words betrayed the desperate guilt and insecurity that had haunted him all his life. "In my proprietorship here, I've tried to operate these companies so that none of you would be ashamed of the man you work for," he said. "You do not need the burden of a publisher who's an embarrassment to you."

The clapping started quietly at first, then grew. In moments, the employees were on their feet in a tearful standing ovation that honored the beaten man before them and paid tribute to the passing of the Bingham tradition. When Paul took the podium, he said that he could understand why staffers might seek jobs elsewhere but he hoped most people would remain. "As for me," he said hoarsely, "I'll be at my post to the end."

Many reporters, even those who had had little good to say about Paul in the past, found his expression of loyalty touching. The selfless image was tarnished somewhat two weeks later when the rank and file discovered that Barry Jr., at George's urging, had given Paul, George, and twenty-seven other top Bingham executives "golden parachutes"—guarantees of three years salary if they were fired by a new owner. "Why, they're really no different from Wall Streeters," said one staffer in disgust.

In the weeks following the sale announcement, Barry Sr. was lionized in the press while Barry Jr. seemed rarely to merit a word of praise—or even a word at all. As Barry Sr. had predicted, his son's intemperate accusations of betrayal and irrationality won him more resentment than sympathy.

Letters of advice and consolation poured in from around the country. Ann Landers, a family friend, wrote that she was "heartsick" at the news of the sale. A publisher from the ravaged coal-mining area of eastern Kentucky praised the newspapers' efforts on behalf of strip-mining legislation. For poor mountain folk, he said, "the Binghams have been a court of last resort." A reader from Pineville, Kentucky, said he hardly knew how to face the sunrise without *The Courier-Journal.*

Not everyone was sad to see what former governor A. B. "Happy" Chandler once called "the wind tunnel at Sixth and Broadway" change hands. In late January, Democrat Carroll Hubbard Jr. stood on the floor of the U.S.

House of Representatives and told his colleagues that he and "tens of thousands of Kentuckians" were "overjoyed" to see the demise of Bingham ownership.

As Sallie had feared, most people in Louisville cast her as the villain in the family drama. Eleanor was too immature to have been a factor, they reasoned—unaware, of course, that she had refused to go along with the Wednesday Plan and threatened to leave town. Barry Jr., in fact, considered Eleanor far more responsible for the sale than Sallie. But his was a minority opinion. "Everybody felt that Eleanor really didn't have much say in it, that she played the child role and other people did the negotiations," said Catherine Luckett, Jonathan's childhood friend.

Eleanor was perfectly happy to encourage the impression that she had been the good daughter willing to go along with "whatever Mother and Daddy wanted." The day the sale was announced, she dropped a letter off at Sallie's house imploring her not to talk to the press. "That made me so angry," said Sallie. "There's just something that she does not want to disclose. Her interest is to let it be me who caused everything to break down. Which is all right. I don't care. I don't mind taking my share, but I don't want the whole load."

Within days, however, Sallie seemed to relish her role as the woman who had tumbled an empire. With consummate skill, she took what had begun as a devastating vilification and turned it into a personal triumph. She was charming, witty, controlled, and thoroughly believable as she told questioner after questioner that the sale of the newspapers was "liberating for the family" and good for Louisville, that it demonstrated to the leaders of other family businesses that they could assume acquiescence on the part of women only at their peril. On "The Phil Donahue Show," she won a round of applause when a woman in the audience asked her whether, when she was a child, she had ever wished she were like everyone else. "No, I didn't," said Sallie bluntly. "I loved [being rich and being a Bingham]."

At last, Sallie was getting the kind of attention and recognition she craved, attention she hoped would eventually transfer to her writing. "The most gratifying part of all this is that, because of this interest [in me], I can get people to read what I wrote," she told one magazine writer. "That is important, to make the link." Important indeed: Sallie had four finished novels sitting in a drawer that she had been unable to get published.

Barry Sr. did not know quite what to make of the media star he had inadvertently launched. In interviews, he tried hard to portray the family debacle as devoid of heroes or villains. As he had when other tragedies had struck, Barry Sr. found comfort in the rather ennobling conclusion that God Himself had touched the Binghams, and there was little any individual could have done to alter the outcome. "I can't pin [the sale] on any one person or any one act or any one episode," he said. "It's been a gradual development with the subtle inevitability of a Greek tragedy. . . . There is that feeling that some sort of fate has been decreed for us and that we seem powerless to break away from it."

Barry Sr. spoke of a healing process, of "peace in our time." But it was not to be. The Binghams, it seemed, had followed in the footsteps of the Haldeman family, whose bickering had made the Judge's purchase of the newspapers possible in 1918.

The grandchildren were gently supportive of "Granny" and "Grandy," even as they tried to offer aid and comfort to their battered parents. "Something feels pierced," wrote Molly, Barry Jr. and Edie's youngest. "Perhaps it is my heart." Back at Brown University, Rob composed a letter to Barry Sr. full of grief and anger. "Like it or not, you have let your son down," he wrote. "This is something that you will have to live with." But Rob was also concerned that Barry Sr. would auction the papers off in "a firesale" to friends like Katharine Graham of *The Washington Post* or the Sulzberger family of *The New York Times*, who might not pay the proper price. "Why not be deceptive and make them believe there is a possibility that we might sell it to a Ganet [*sic*] or even worse!" he said. "All's fair in love and war."

Barry Sr. used the occasion of Rob's letter to justify his decision to the rest of the Bingham clan. In late January, he sent copies of his three-paged, single-spaced response to everyone in the family. He said that to his "lasting regret" he had not had time to reconvene all the grandchildren before deciding to sell, as he had promised he would. He described how difficult it had been for him and Mary to live with "this aching problem" for the past two years, and said he had assumed, quite wrongly, that whatever he finally decided would be "accepted, reluctantly . . . but without public rancor" because he was head of the family. At his age, he said, he did not expect to live long enough to "see the quarrels and divisions of recent years resolved." His only hope was that the "disease of suspicion and lack of faith" that had touched his children's generation would not infect theirs.

Barry Sr. closed by saying he wanted no response to the letter, as if he were afraid of not having the final word. But Joan Bingham had not communicated with her father-in-law since the sale announcement and was determined to vent her feelings about the decision. In measured tones, she wrote back that she worried what effect the sale would have on Clara and Rob. "Having a lot of money . . . does not build character," she said. "I still don't think my children know the satisfaction that comes from hard work . . . and the money doesn't help this."

Barry Sr. was acutely aware that the sale of the papers meant a permanent end to the dreams Joan had had—for her son, especially—so he tried, as usual, to find a silver lining. But his clumsy attempts at rationalization only caused more hurt and dissension. In a long letter to Joan, he speculated that, had the Binghams kept the papers, the "heavy burden of family expectations might have forced [Rob] into a delayed sense of rebellion." Rob's understandable desire to live up to the memory of his father "could have had a crippling effect," he said. "I have always detested the idea of men so determined to shape family tradition that they placed a dead hand on their heirs. I have tried to do the opposite."

Joan was devastated by the letter's subtle suggestion that Rob did not have the ability to be publisher. She made the mistake of showing it to Barry Jr., the Bingham most haunted by Worth's long shadow, and he hit the ceiling. "I'm embarrassed for you to have written a letter like that about any of your grandchildren," he told his father over lunch. "If it had come from Sallie, I wouldn't have been surprised."

Barry Sr. found the comparison to his errant daughter deeply offensive, almost as offensive as being called "irrational." Edie had a darker interpretation of Barry Sr.'s letter. "It was indicative of his anxiety, of his realizing how little control he would have had down the line," she said. "I think he always would have wanted to dictate [who would be publisher]."

Nonetheless, that same month, Edie wrote the Senior Binghams a cautious note of conciliation, saying she hoped they could all "break the silence of woundedness" and "effect a restoration of relationships." Barry Sr. and Mary's answer was as strange as it was curt: Let's wait until we see how things go on "60 Minutes."

The Binghams' friends were flabbergasted that they had agreed to go on the popular CBS television news magazine show. Hadn't the family suffered enough without that? Even Don Hewitt, the show's executive producer, was surprised. "You won't believe it," he told a *New York Times* reporter incredulously once the filming dates had been set. "They're all going to play!"

Mary said later that the "60 Minutes" segment, aired in April 1986, "made a pageant of our bleeding hearts," and indeed it did. Sallie triumphantly declared herself the winner of the family feud and said that her mother had accused her of trying "to destroy" Barry Jr.; Barry Jr., in turn, all but called Sallie crazy on camera. Barry Sr. decried the lack of communication in the family, and Eleanor compared her parents and siblings to the warring Ewing clan on the television program "Dallas."

But the comment that caused the most lasting damage came from Mary, who described Sallie as living in a fantasy world, with her portrayal of herself as a neglected, unloved daughter and the victim of a sexist Southern family. Mary's words suggested to Sallie that her mother thought she was insane, and sent her into fresh waves of fury. "I didn't want to say, 'Sallie is a liar,' " Mary explained later, "and yet I did want to point out that the things she says are not true."

Sallie did not like being portrayed as a member of a rich family squabbling over petty things. It made her complaints seem trivial. But she felt that the "60 Minutes" segment at least gave each of the Binghams a chance to hear what the others thought and felt. "Thank God for '60 Minutes,' " she told a reporter in Lexington, Kentucky. "We got to see each other on TV. . . . Down the road, I think good things will happen."

Communication within the family, however, did not improve. Shortly after the show aired, the Senior Binghams invited Barry Jr. and Edie to a concert. Now that the nightmare of "60 Minutes" was over, Edie hoped to see some signs of rapprochement. None was forthcoming. At the bar during intermission, Barry Sr. turned to Edie and said, "Well, what did you think of '60 Minutes'?" She said she thought it had been relatively even and fair. Barry Sr. nodded and said nothing.

By early spring 1986, the process of selling *The Courier-Journal* and *Times*, WHAS, Standard Gravure, and smaller Bingham subsidiaries such as Data Courier, an electronic data-base firm, had begun in earnest. For Barry Jr., the period was particularly awkward. He had been persuaded by his father to tear up his letter of resignation and stay on as editor and publisher until the last Bingham company was sold. Barry Jr. said he would do it to protect the interests of the employees. To the Seniors, the arrangement, which Barry Jr. insisted on being codified in a legally enforceable contract, was as much to keep Paul Janensch away from the top position at the newspapers as it was to bring Barry Jr. back in.

Barry Sr. had realized within hours of the sale announcement that he would have to put someone in charge of the companies if his son stepped down. George Gill had suggested that Barry Sr. simply take back the title of editor and publisher during the sale period and that he and Paul Janensch fall back into their sabbatical roles, with George running the business side and Paul running the news operation. Barry Sr. reacted to the idea with uncharacteristic vehemence. "No way are we going to do that!" he said. "Paul will have nothing to do with news and editorial if I have anything to say about it."

One condition of Barry Jr.'s continued employment at the family companies was that he was to have no more information about the sale process than his sisters. The action was precautionary—to avoid an ugly legal challenge from Sallie. So, like a wounded animal, Barry Jr. slipped quietly back into his old office routine, reading the newspaper for hours and going to news and editorial conferences. But he now spent more time than ever talking with Paul. His relations with George, who was head of the oversight committee charged with selling the companies, were pro forma and his visits with his father infrequent and strained.

Barry Sr. chose Goldman, Sachs to represent the family at the sale and charged them with finding a benevolent buyer for the companies. He assured Bingham employees that the family would do its best to convince the new owners, whoever they might be, to maintain the day-care center, subsidized parking, and other benefits that had been hallmarks of his family's stewardship and to continue the Binghams' practice of giving 5 percent of pretax earnings to local charities.

Such cheery promises did little to lift the mood of anxiety and anger that hung over the newsroom. Several employees tried to organize a chapter of the Newspaper Guild, something that had not been attempted at the Bingham newspapers since 1961. Columnist Bob Hill erected a miniature "golden parachute" above his desk and did a brisk business in green and white buttons poking fun at the "key" employees who got them. The buttons sported an old-fashioned door key with a slash across it and the words "Official Non-Key Employee."

In March, Goldman, Sachs sent prospectuses on all the Bingham companies to potential bidders. Throughout the spring of 1986, executives from The New York Times Co., The Washington Post Co., Gannett Company Inc., Hearst, and the Tribune Co. of Chicago strolled through the *Courier-Journal* and *Times* newsroom, studied the accounts, and, over the din of the newspapers' printing presses, asked pointed questions about ad lineage and penetration of market.

Eleanor was interested in acquiring WHAS, or at least said she was. "But she doesn't understand the complexity of any given situation," said Bob Morse. "When we told her it would take [at least $70 million] she couldn't fathom spending that amount. . . . We could not even get her to consider going on, nor her lawyer, Rucker Todd." The deal died, although four WHAS executives, including Morse, still managed to scrape together enough money from other sources to enter a respectable bid for the TV station.

Barry Jr., too, considered buying back a piece of the family business. He was interested in Data Courier, the small electronic publishing subsidiary he had acquired in 1973, but in the end decided not to be a contender. It would be unethical for him to bid on the company, he said, since he knew so much more about its operation than his competitors. Mary found his high-minded argument unconvincing. "I think the truth is that Barry Jr. could not tolerate the idea of living in Louisville as the head of Data Courier while somebody else ran the papers," she said.

Sallie, meanwhile, was as distant from the deliberations as she had been during the eighteen months leading up to the decision to sell. She continued to have her lawyer represent her at stockholders' meetings while she basked in her newfound celebrity and waited patiently to receive her millions. Two months after the sale announcement, she signed a contract with Alfred A. Knopf, reportedly for six figures, to produce a memoir of her life. "It's the largest income I've ever made so far from any of my writing," she said excitedly.

Her most cherished dreams seemed to be materializing even as her status as the wicked witch of the Bingham drama became more pronounced. Reporters and editors who had befriended her during her days at *The Courier-Journal* now snubbed her. When she and Tim went to a farewell party for the newspaper's food editor, no one spoke to them. "These people believed that everything that had happened to them had been Sallie's fault," said Irene Nolan.

While doing a live call-in show on a Louisville radio station, Sallie found herself fielding hostile questions. "How does it feel to be hated by 2,200 people?" asked one listener, alluding to the total number of employees at the three Bingham companies. If Sallie ever experienced any guilt over her role in the family empire's downfall, she did not show it. "I don't feel responsible for that," she said. "I feel as though that's part of the problem of being a woman in this society."

Détente between Sallie and the rest of the family was impossible largely because, for months, she had been helping David Chandler, a *People* magazine reporter, and his wife, Mary Voelz Chandler, delve into the Mary Lily incident. David Chandler had come across the allegations of wrongdoing while researching a book on Henry Flagler, Mary Lily's first husband. The book on Flagler was completed by the time the Bingham feud burst into the nation's headlines and would be available in stores early that summer. In the sudden notoriety of Kentucky's First Family, Chandler saw a news peg for his next publishing project, one focused mainly on the Judge and what he provocatively called "the murder conspiracy."

In mid-January 1986, Barry Sr. had agreed to see the Chandlers, who said they were working on a story about the family quarrel for *People*. After asking several questions about the demise of Mary Lily, Chandler told Barry Sr. that he was not just there to write a magazine piece; he was also working on a book about Judge Bingham. Barry Sr. was horrified.

His fears were not allayed when, three weeks later, David Chandler sent him a five-page list of follow-up questions about the Judge and the murder rumors. Was it true that Robert Worth Bingham sought out Mary Lily because he was heavily in debt? he asked. Was there animosity between Mary Lily and the Bingham children? Barry Sr. had spent his whole life trying to forget the public disgrace that had rocked his youth, but he knew sooner or later he would have to reply. He turned the letter over to the family law firm and wrote Chandler a stiff note saying that he would be back in touch when he had answers to his queries.

Sallie, however, was only too happy to talk to the Chandlers, as she had to every other reporter. She agreeably supplied quotes that supported "the murder conspiracy" even though she had no firsthand knowledge of the Judge and had done no independent research herself. She found the suggestion that her grandfather had committed murder oddly appealing. It added color to her family history, she felt, and bolstered her conviction that all women, even rich women, were victims of powerful men.

Mary could not understand why Sallie insisted on being so cruel to the father she still professed to love. "She seems to get great satisfaction out of fouling her own nest," Mary said. Under such circumstances, relations between Sallie and her parents inevitably grew more tense. After all, if she had been willing to tell the Chandlers that her grandfather killed Mary Lily, what was she apt to say in her own book?

By late April, the strain on Mary began to show. When WHAS-TV ran a promotional contest called Bingham Bucks Sweepstakes, Mary called Barry Jr. and demanded that he take it off the air. When they had previewed it, Barry Jr. and Bob Morse had seen no problem with the offending ads, which opened with the theme music from "Dallas" and described the Binghams as "Louisville's megabucks family." "In other days the Seniors would have thought it was a riot," said Bob Morse. "They had a sense of humor and they would have gone for that kind of thing. . . . It never occurred to us that they would care." But care they did. Mary denounced the "obscene vulgarity" of the spots in *The Louisville Times* and phoned Morse personally to bawl him out. "She really told me what she thought of me," he said. "That was the only time she ever called in ten years."

Barry Sr. assumed that *The New York Times* or *The Washington Post* would jump at the chance to own *The Courier-Journal* and *Times*. "Punch" Sulzberger, the publisher of the *Times*, and Kay Graham, chairman of the *Post*, were old friends and had served with him on several editorial boards and journalism committees. But the *Times* did not put in a bid, and the *Post's* offer was too low to be competitive. Even a last-minute plea from Barry Sr. failed to improve it. Louisville was economically depressed, said executives from both companies, and the papers were fat and overstaffed. No offense intended, but it just did not make good business sense to buy *The Courier-Journal* and *Times*.

In the end, Gannett, the nation's largest chain of newspapers, made the best offer: $305 million, more than twenty times the cash flow of *The Courier-Journal* and *Times*. Jack Kent Cooke, the owner of the Washington Redskins and *The Los Angeles Daily News*, came in a distant second with a bid of about $265 million. The decision was clear. Gannett would get the papers and there was little left to do but draw up a formal agreement and collect the money.

At 10:00 A.M. on Friday, May 16, the family gathered in a conference room at the Seelbach Hotel to formally select buyers for the newspapers, Standard Gravure, and Data Courier. The meeting—which was also attended by the hired hands; the lawyers for Barry Jr., Sallie, Eleanor, and Joan; and the bankers from Goldman, Sachs—lasted almost three hours but was generally civilized and subdued.

Barry Sr. looked relieved, even jaunty, as he strode out of the Seelbach, gently declining to reveal the identity of the newspapers' new owner to the throng of reporters who had staked out the location. "We will make the announcement at a press conference Monday morning," he said. "You'll just have to wait till then." But soon after he spoke, an enterprising reporter spotted Gannett's corporate jet parked out at Standiford Field and the secret was out.

Two days later, on Sunday, May 18, Al Neuharth, Gannett's brassy chairman and chief executive officer, swept into Louisville to participate in the announcement of the sale agreement. At sixty-two, Neuharth was a short, dark Horatio Alger of a man, a former sports reporter from South Dakota who, in 1970, became president of a little-known chain of thirty-five daily newspapers. Within a decade, he had turned the company into a household name. The acquisition of *The Courier-Journal* and *Times* would bring Gannett's inventory of newspapers to ninety, including the trend-setting national daily, *USA Today*.

The empire had come a long way since Frank Gannett, a pious teetotaler and Democrat-turned-Republican, bought his first paper, the Elmira, New York, *Gazette*, in 1906. Neuharth shared with his company's founder a relentless urge to succeed. His early associates had only half-jokingly dubbed him "The Black Prince."

Neuharth favored flashy gold jewelry and the garish trappings associated with the worst of the nouveau riche. His office in the Washington, D.C., suburb of Rosslyn featured snakeskin wallpaper, copper air-conditioning vents, electronically controlled maps, and gold flatware for luncheon guests. He felt no qualms about commissioning two huge busts of himself for Gannett's corporate headquarters. Neuharth's philosophy of journalism was equally lacking in subtlety. He believed in positive stories, lots of color, and rigorous cost control. Gannett papers generally had profit margins three times that of *The Courier-Journal*. Neuharth liked to boast of the company's ever-increasing earnings, and within the industry, Gannett was viewed as putting the bottom line ahead of journalistic distinction. With the acquisition of *The Courier-Journal* and *Times*, Neuharth hoped to bring a touch of class to the Gannett chain.

When Neuharth alighted from his limousine at the Brown Hotel, George Gill rushed up, took his arm, and escorted him through the crowd of shouting reporters. George had made special arrangements to get Neuharth's room key and, within minutes, he whisked the startled chief executive up to his suite. The room, per George's instructions, was well stocked with Neuharth's standard accoutrements: an exercise bicycle, a bowl of fruit, chilled Pouilly-Fuissé, and an antique Royal manual typewriter, which *CJ* staffers had had to scour the city to find.

Intrigued by the meticulous advance work, Neuharth asked George to stay and talk for a bit. During the negotiations for the Bingham papers, Barry Sr. had told Neuharth that he would be pleased if Gannett chose George as publisher. In checking around, Neuharth had found that George had a reputation for leadership and was highly respected as a manager. On the plane ride to Louisville, he had thought seriously about offering him the job of publisher in the hope that continuity would ease the transition. "Would it be appropriate when we sign this contract tomorrow and hold the press conference for me to publicly announce that you're going to stick around and run this place for us?" he asked.

George was pleased, flattered—and taken aback. No, he said; it would not be appropriate. There is too much bad blood in the family at the moment. You have to realize that Barry Jr. favors Paul, he told Neuharth, and it would just rub salt in the wound if you came out and said you wanted me. It might be better to ask the family whether they have any candidates, to bring them into the process. Neuharth nodded knowingly and thanked him for his frankness.

That evening, the Binghams, the hired hands, Neuharth, and several Gannett aides mingled awkwardly over drinks and dinner in the English Grill at the Brown Hotel. Moments earlier, Mary and Sallie had encountered each other in the hotel parking garage. For the first time in months, Sallie walked up to her mother, embraced her, and kissed her. Mary remained stiff and impassive. "She had just made one of those awful statements about her father being a sexist beast and Barry and the papers never having been fair to women," said Mary. "I really cannot pretend to Sallie that this does not make a difference to me. So I did not respond. . . . I must say I was quite chilly."

As was his habit, Al Neuharth was up at 6:00 A.M. the next morning,
Monday, May 19, jogging around Louisville. When he was through, he
loped unexpectedly into *The Courier-Journal* and *Times* newsroom, still damp
from his run and decked out in shorts and a T-shirt. Although it was very
early, there were dozens of staffers milling about the room, talking in
hushed tones. Some were waiting to walk down the street to the Brown
Hotel for the press conference that would announce the new owner. Others
were on their way to what one reporter called "a power breakfast for the
powerless" before the proceedings began. Neuharth looked around. "I'd love
a cup of coffee," he announced brightly. "Can anybody loan me a quarter?"
An editor rushed to comply.

After showering and changing into his signature black suit, Neuharth
kept his appointment at Wyatt, Tarrant & Combs, the Bingham family law
firm, where the agreement of sale was to be signed. As soon as the deed was
done, he motioned for George to step into Wilson Wyatt's office and closed
the door. Again he asked George if he would take the position of *Courier-
Journal* and *Times* publisher under Gannett. Confident now that Neuharth
had no intention of making the news public, George said yes. "OK," said
the Gannett chairman. "Just sit tight and we'll try to play this thing out
between now and the closing date in the least offensive way possible."
George said he would keep quiet.

By 8:30 A.M. hundreds of reporters were packed into the Crystal Ballroom
of the Brown Hotel. All of the Binghams showed up. Neuharth mounted
the platform. "It feels like winning the Triple Crown," he said, referring to
Gannett's acquisition in the past year of *The Des Moines Register*, *The Detroit
News*, and now Louisville's "sparkling jewel."

Barry Sr. and Barry Jr. then made statements that were so much in keeping
with their philosophies of life that observers later wondered if the phrases
had somehow bubbled up from the depths of their unconscious. Barry Sr.,
the cheerful fatalist, said he was heartened by the new owner's promise
to try and continue the generous benefits and local philanthropy that
had characterized his family's stewardship. His quote from the Old Testament—"there is a time to sow, a time to reap"—made it sound as
though the passing of the papers from the Bingham family, Kentucky's
chosen people, was as inevitable and divinely ordained as the fall of Israel
to the Babylonians.

Barry Jr.'s thoughts were darker and more troubled. "I hope Mr. Neuharth
and the Gannett executives will pardon my candor when I say this is a day I
had hoped never to live to see," he said. He recited a list of accomplishments, including the papers' crusade against strip-mining and the ethics

policies that "have made Louisville a beacon to other journalists." He concluded with a quote describing the printing press as "God's last and greatest gift."

The quote was from Martin Luther, who as a young man was struck by lightning and, in his agony, cried out to St. Anne for help, promising to become a monk if spared. He went on to lead the Protestant Reformation. Like Luther, Barry Jr. had faced death and been saved, pursuing his work ever after with an ascetic zeal. By invoking Luther, Barry Jr. seemed to be saying: "I have kept up my end of a holy pact, denying myself leisure and earthly pleasures to perpetuate the family business. Why hasn't my father kept up *his* end? Why hasn't God?"

As soon as the press conference was over, Al Neuharth, Barry Sr., and Barry Jr. returned to *The Courier-Journal* and *Times* to speak to the employees. On the way, the Binghams could not help but notice that the ever-efficient Gannettoids, as the company's minions were called, had already installed a blue and white *USA Today* vendor box in front of the building. In the newsroom, a funeral wreath of black carnations arrived from the staff of *The Cincinnati Enquirer*, which had been bought by Gannett in 1979.

In the ensuing months, the remaining Bingham businesses were sold off in rapid succession. Data Courier went to Bell & Howell for $12 million. Standard Gravure, the printing firm that Judge Bingham had bought in 1921 to give his oldest son something to do, went to Michael Shea, an Atlanta businessman, for more than $22 million. WHAS-TV brought a handsome price—$85.7 million—from the Providence Journal Co. of Rhode Island, proving that it was hardly the "sop" Mary had considered it when the stock swap was first proposed. Clear Channel Communications Inc. of San Antonio scooped up the AM and FM radio stations for a little over $20 million. After all the sales were settled, the Binghams were out of the media business in Louisville for the first time since 1918 and were richer by some $448 million, including interest and miscellaneous items.*

Sallie watched with satisfaction as the properties changed hands. *Ms.* magazine, which only six years earlier had saluted Barry Sr. for his support of the Equal Rights Amendment, put her picture on the cover of its June 1986 issue and featured a long article by Sallie called "The Truth About Growing Up Rich." That same month, the *Radcliffe Quarterly* included a first-

---

* Excluding the $93,948,554 allocated to Trust #9, Barry Sr. and Mary received $115,083,842; Barry Jr. and his children received $51,242,481; Sallie and her children received $64,761,083, including $11,441,804 earmarked for the Kentucky Foundation for Women; Eleanor and her children received $63,695,061; and Joan and her children received $50,690,776. The remainder went for fees associated with the sale, including $4,715,512 to Goldman, Sachs.

person piece by Sallie entitled "Biting the Hand." In both articles, Sallie attacked her family, her stifling childhood, and the sexist policies of the newspapers. Her view of herself was archetypal—she was "woman as Other," a heroine, a rebel, a surrogate for all women who are victimized by a male-dominated society. "Saint Sallie," said one acquaintance wryly.

She was in great demand as a speaker and seemed to relish the role, but her weakness for fabrication sometimes got her into trouble. During a talk before a national conference of women coal miners, Sallie recalled with some pain that she had been left in the car at the age of fourteen while her father and brothers toured a mine in eastern Kentucky. "They told me I had to stay behind because the mine roof would fall down if I went inside because women in the mines bring bad luck, just like women in the news business bring bad luck," she said.

It made a wonderful story. Unfortunately, said Mary, "there was not one iota of truth in it." Barry Jr. could not recall ever being in a mine. Neither could his father.

Now that she felt she had won the family feud, Sallie was more conflicted than ever about her father. Before, she had been willing to use her fiction to attack her mother, leaving her father generally unmolested out of a combination of awe and love. The decision to sell ended what awe remained, and the love seemed to vanish with it. In deciding to sell, Barry Sr. seemed to have given Sallie what she wanted most: her freedom from him.

Sallie was only half-informed about the reasons for the sale, but she was convinced that the ultimate cause was a collapse of her father's will. It diminished her father in her eyes to think that he could be so weak and it redoubled her rage. How could she have allowed herself to be emotionally tortured by such a man for so many years? It made a mockery of her Oedipal adoration and she fought back ferociously, attacking him in his most vulnerable spot: the death of Mary Lily. By embracing the worst gossip about Judge Bingham, she was wounding her father in the way she knew would hurt him most.

Mary begged her daughter to avoid the scandal in her memoir. "Sallie, if you go ahead and publish this book it will break your father's heart," she said. "There's no way you could have known your grandfather; you don't know anything about him." But Sallie would not let go of what she knew was her most potent weapon. "Mother," she said, drawing herself up with haughty grace, "the truth lies in many places."

―――――――

The Binghams agreed to sell *The Courier-Journal* and *Times* to Gannett in mid-May, but many matters still had to be settled before the money could actually change hands and the transition be made complete. A key issue was who would be named publisher under the new ownership—at least, the Binghams assumed that was a key issue. They did not know, of course, that Al Neuharth had already decided on George Gill.

For the next two months, Gannett officials went through the motions of holding formal talks with Barry Sr., Barry Jr., and Paul Janensch, but it was all an elaborate charade. Barry Jr. even sat down and wrote two unsolicited letters to Gannett. In one he tepidly recommended George for publisher; in the other, he vigorously endorsed Paul Janensch. "[Gannett] was trying desperately to weave its way through this family thing and get out of it with as little damage as possible," said one executive close to the process.

Paul did not officially apply to be publisher until mid-June. "I hadn't intended to put in for [it]," he said. "But one day I was sitting out on my back deck, on my second martini, and I turned to Gail and said, 'You know, I'm what they need. I know the community and I come out of the news side and I've got a vision for the place. I think I should put in for the job.'"

Several days later, Paul made his pitch to John Curley, the new Gannett CEO. In a letter, he compared himself with England's wartime prime minister, Winston Churchill, saying he felt born to lead the Louisville papers. In early July, Gannett flew him up to its Washington headquarters in the corporate jet, met him with a limousine, and ushered him in to talk with Curley. "It was very businesslike, very crisp," said Paul. "I knew I had no better than a fifty-fifty chance and probably a lot less."

In fact, Paul was wasting his breath. On Monday, July 7, the day before Paul's visit, George had huddled for hours with Curley and several other of the newspaper chain's executives ironing out the final details of his continued employment. That night, Gannett officially offered George the job of publisher and president, formally sealing the verbal contract that Neuharth had made in Wilson Wyatt's office. The company said it would announce his selection, and that of the papers' new editor, when the sale was finalized in Louisville on July 14, exactly one week hence.

Gannett officials had made it clear from the beginning that they wanted their own man to run the news side of the Louisville papers, which George had told them was in need of a thorough housecleaning. Their choice was Michael Gartner, former editor and president of *The Des Moines Register*, one of the three "crown jewels" of which Neuharth had spoken so glowingly in mid-May. At forty-seven, Gartner was energetic, ambitious, and respected for his ability to be tough and genial at the same time—just the sort of manager Gannett felt it needed to oversee the painful cuts, belt-tightening, and editorial changes it had in mind for the Bingham newspapers.

Barry Jr. had no knowledge that the Gill and Gartner appointments had been made when the Louisville chapter of Sigma Delta Chi gave him its coveted First Amendment award in early July. But it was very much on his mind that his days at the family's newspapers were drawing to a close and with them, he feared, the ethical purity that had been his one shining achievement. In his speech that night, he exhorted Bingham writers and broadcasters to try to keep their hands clean "under new skippers who may take their sightings from different stars."

Rigorous editorial integrity was the one thing that was truly, wholly his, that had separated him from his older brother and given his time at the papers purpose and meaning. He was not charming and politically astute like his father, nor was he an outstanding intellect like Mary, or a natural leader like Worth. He was not artistically brilliant, as Sallie felt she was, or endearing like Jonathan, or outgoing and needy like Eleanor. But he could create and follow rules, he could strive for grace and, like Martin Luther, don the robes of a monk after wrestling with a thunderbolt. "[Your] philosophy," wrote Paul Janensch in his final Sunday column, "can be summed up in these three words: 'Do what's right.' Barry, we will."

<hr />

In mid-July, Barry Sr. and Mary came back from Chatham to sign the final papers of sale and collect their share of the cash. The price for *The Courier-Journal* and *Times* had already been ballyhooed as one of the highest ever paid for any newspaper. But many media analysts were not aware that, as of the day of sale, the debt-averse Binghams had $31 million in cash on the books that went to Gannett, as well as $45 million in an overfunded pension that was immediately transferred to the Gannett Company pension fund.

Paul Janensch did not find out that he would not succeed Barry Jr. as publisher of *The Courier-Journal* and *Times* until the day the papers actually changed hands—Monday, July 14, 1986. At 8:00 A.M. that morning, he had breakfast in the Brown Hotel with Gannett CEO John Curley and John Quinn, editor of *USA Today*. Curley did not waste time. As soon as the three men had ordered their eggs, he told Paul that George Gill was going to be the new publisher and president. "It's a business job and he's got strong business credentials," he said simply. "As for you, we would like to move you to headquarters for a couple of months, then ship you out to another Gannett paper somewhere. We prepared two press releases coming in on the jet last night. One says you're exploring opportunities with Gannett. The other says you're quitting. Which one should we put out at ten-fifteen?"

Whatever other faults they may have had, the Binghams had always treated their employees with velvet politeness. Power plays, when they occurred, were orchestrated with a kind of Southern courtesy that made them both harder to fight and easier to take. Gannett's raw bluntness was like a splash of cold water and for a moment Paul was left speechless. "I made one of these nano-second calculations and figured, well, I'm not going to just quit and have no job," he said. "So I told them I'd stay."

Later at the press conference, Paul saw Michael Gartner standing in the crowd and he knew instantly that Curley was about to introduce him as the new editor. During the question and answer period, a reporter asked why both George and Paul would not remain together at the Louisville newspapers. "Chemistry," Curley said, using the same word that Barry Jr. had employed long ago to explain his dislike of Rowland. "We thought George Gill would like to have an editor he felt comfortable with."

For George, the moment was deliciously sweet. He still recalled the sting of hurt and embarrassment he had felt when Barry Jr. had chosen Paul instead of him to run the papers during the sabbatical year. Now the tables were turned. Paul had not only lost the race to be publisher, he had essentially been banished from Louisville. Barry Jr. had had his life's work sold out from under him by his father. And now George, the poor kid from Indianapolis who had started on the *Courier-Journal* copy desk, was to take on Barry Jr.'s title and move into his office. It was like a dream come true.

Afterward, in the newsroom, Al Neuharth, George Gill, and Michael Gartner made short, predictable speeches about their hopes for the papers while Barry Sr. sat quietly in the back, watching the formal changing of the guard as though it were one of his beloved Shakespearean plays. At last, Barry Jr. got up to make his final address. "I speak to you for the last time as editor and publisher of *The Courier-Journal* and *Times*," he said. "Wherever you go in the tradition of these newspapers, I will be with you. Preserve this shrine of quality and integrity which I have tried to help you build during the past fifteen years. May you prosper and do great things under the leadership of George Gill. May God's peace be with you always. Farewell."

That afternoon, the front page of *The Louisville Times* sported a new legend: "A Gannett Newspaper." While the paper was still rolling off the presses, Barry Jr. walked into his office, took off his coat, and began packing up his belongings. A sixty-eight-year era of journalism in Kentucky had come to a close. In the company newsletter, Don Towles, a thirty-year veteran of *The Courier-Journal* and *Times*, wrote a tribute to the papers and to the family that was alternately fond, proud, angry, and sad:

Every major progressive step taken by Kentucky in the 1900s to drag itself into the 20th century, screaming and protesting much of the time, was suggested, encouraged and supported by the Louisville papers. . . . The poor were helped, the needy were served, the helpless and the infirm were tended because the newspapers did their jobs. . . . That's quite a legacy left to us by the Binghams. All of us who earned our keep at the hands of the

Binghams had a part in it, regardless of our job with the companies. There is a heritage here, don't you see? A heritage fashioned by a family with enormous wealth but with more enormous commitment. . . . Oh, those cynics and ignoramuses . . . will say this piece has turned into a glorification essay about the Binghams and the past. . . . To [them], I say, "You can go to Hell—in a two-horse wagon."

With an eerie kind of symmetry, *The Courier-Journal* and *Times* had been transferred to Gannett exactly twenty years to the day that Worth Bingham, the anointed heir to the family empire, had been lowered into his grave in Cave Hill Cemetery. Back on that steamy day, July 14, 1966, the men and women standing solemnly around the freshly turned earth had only the vaguest notion that Worth's death might launch the downward spiral of the Bingham papers and even the family itself. "We didn't know it at the moment, but as the time has gone on we look back and say, 'Yes, I see it,'" said Norman Isaacs. "The tragedy of the Bingham family began then. It was the end of all our dreams."

Even Sallie agreed that her hated and feared older brother would never have kicked her and the other women off the board of directors. Had she decided to sell her shares, he would have paid whatever it took to get rid of her. "He was a great pragmatist," she said.

Barry Jr., though, felt that the sale was the result of a loss of nerve within the family to keep the companies together. "If either of my parents had said, 'The number-one goal is preserving family ownership, that is the North Star and that is what we steer by,' I think we could have pulled this off," he said. "They never were willing to say that. The only thing they could say is: 'We all have to agree.'"

Leon Tallichet knew better than most that agreement was unlikely ever to happen. He had felt certain for some time that the companies would eventually run afoul of the siblings' determined selfishness. "There's no give at all [in this family]," he said. "It's always their own interests. I don't think it would ever have survived after the Seniors' deaths. They were the glue."

Now, the best that could be hoped for was healing, something that Barry Sr., with his usual optimism, felt was not only possible but inevitable. Even after suffering through his mother's early death, his father's subsequent rejection, the premature demise of two sons, and more than two years of an emotionally corrosive family battle, Barry Sr. continued to feel stubbornly convinced that the future contained promise. "Nothing can be so painful as these family divisions and I've really dreaded them all my life," he said. "Now I'm confronted with them, but I cannot help but feel that these things can be repaired."

Others were not so sure. "It'll never happen," said Bernie Block. "They can't sit down, have a beer, and talk." The family that seemed to have everything, that had begun its life in America in a rude North Carolina schoolhouse, survived the devastation of the Civil War, remade itself in the urban image of the Industrial Revolution, served alongside Franklin Roosevelt and Averell Harriman, created newspapers that had brought light and goodness to a dark land, could not, in the end, assuage its own internal, lonely torment. "Probably no family was the subject of more gossip or misrepresentation than the Binghams because they were remote in a way," said Keith Runyon, a *CJ* editorial writer who had grown up admiring the Binghams. "They had an aura about them that inspired speculation and jealousy. It's funny, isn't it? Because all those people who might have been jealous for so many years are probably not too jealous now."

EPILOGUE

Early in the summer of 1986, Barry Sr. stopped off at the Hawley-Cooke bookstore on Shelbyville Road to look over the new arrivals. He was particularly eager to locate David Chandler's recently released biography of Henry Flagler, hoping that it would provide clues to how the author intended to treat the subject of his next book—Robert Worth Bingham. When Barry Sr. finally located the volume, his eyes gravitated to the inside flap of the dust jacket. Mary Lily Kenan Flagler, it said, was "very probably murdered" by her new husband, Robert Worth Bingham, "as she changed her will in his favor on her deathbed."

Trembling, Barry Sr. purchased the book, climbed into his dark green Volvo, and raced home. "His outrage was the closest to furious that I've ever seen him when he showed me that," Mary said. "Barry not only loved his father, he really revered him. To have his character assassinated this way is just about the worst thing that can happen to him."

Barry Sr. had thought that the decision to sell would put an end to the family agony, at least for him. But now events were spinning out of control again. Just as he had feared, David Chandler and his wife were preparing a book that would say that Judge Bingham had murdered Mary Lily. And Sallie was helping them! The greatest shame of his childhood had reappeared like a vengeful ghost to haunt his old age. The thought made him cold-sweat desperate, something that he had not been even at the height of the family troubles.

Sallie, busy writing her own memoir about the family in her River Road studio, professed not to understand what all the fuss was about, and played down her role in the Chandlers' work. Because she knew so little about the Mary Lily affair, she told her father, she had been unable to help the two reporters much. Sallie treated his alarm as an old man's irrational panic about a trifle and Barry Sr. felt patronized. "She said, 'Oh, Daddy, I'm sorry you're so disturbed about this,' as though it was surprising to her that I was upset," he recalled indignantly.

Gordon Davidson had already told Barry Sr. that it was legally impossible to libel the dead, but the Bingham patriarch was determined to find other ways to stop David Chandler and his publisher, Macmillan Company, from making their "sordid set of charges" public. When he obtained a set of galleys of *The Binghams of Louisville: The Dark History Behind One of America's Great Fortunes* early in 1987, and learned that Chandler was going to say not only that his father had killed Mary Lily, but had given her syphilis, he went from being a man concerned to a man obsessed.

Using the attorneys of Wyatt, Tarrant & Combs and his own personal historian, Barry Sr. mounted a mammoth campaign to disprove Chandler's thesis. A young law firm associate, Mark Wilson, was dispatched to Asheville, the Johns Hopkins Hospital in Baltimore, and Wilmington, North Carolina, where Mary Lily was buried. Letters and phone calls went out across the country. Through an intermediary, Barry Sr. contacted Thomas Kenan III and even talked to him briefly by phone. But he could not bring himself to go personally to Chapel Hill, North Carolina, and meet with the custodian of the controversial autopsy report. "To go crawling down there asking for mercy was really more than he could do," said Mary.

In the spring of 1987, shortly before the Kentucky Derby, Barry Sr. flew to New York and paid a call on Thomas Mellon Evans, the principal owner of Macmillan and a casual social acquaintance. When the two men were seated, Barry Sr. presented Evans with a five-volume set of memoranda weighing fourteen pounds that challenged the accuracy of the Chandler book. An accompanying memo, prepared by the Bingham lawyers, charged that the Chandler text contained over 160 "misstatements of fact" and managed to make a "devoted public servant" and "loving husband and father" look like an "unprincipled, greedy individual" who caused Mary Lily's death to get her money.

Barry Sr. had also gone to the trouble of copyrighting seventeen of his father's letters, as well as a letter and a memo he had written himself, as soon as he had the Chandler galleys in hand. Because Chandler had not obtained written permission to use this material, Barry Sr. now charged, he may be in violation of copyright laws. Although the book was in production and due to be released in June—finished copies were already sitting in a New Jersey warehouse—Evans suspended publication so that Macmillan could look into the accusations.

Barry Sr. had defended the First Amendment all his life. Now he seemed not to see that his crusade against the Chandler book made a mockery of all that. The fourteen-pound rebuttal should not be interpreted as a threat to sue Macmillan or to muzzle free speech, he said. As a leading publisher, "Macmillan should be as concerned as I am about preserving editorial integrity and protecting society from the propagation of unjustified attacks and factual errors."

For a while, it seemed that Barry Sr. had once again managed to control events and shield his father, whose reputation had always appeared to mean more to him than his own. In July 1987, Macmillan announced that it had canceled *The Binghams of Louisville* due to "substantive disagreements" with the author. But any sense that Barry Sr. had put the genie back in the bottle was quickly dispelled.

Sallie publicly denounced her father in a fashion calculated to give credence to Chandler's wildest theory about a murder conspiracy. Only a year earlier she had tried to calm Barry Sr.'s fears by telling him she knew so little about the Mary Lily incident; now she expressed the view that Chandler was right about the Judge. "Through suppression of a book," Sallie wrote in an angry boilerplate letter she sent to book editors around the country, "powerful people are able to deprive a professional writer of his livelihood."

David Chandler and his wife did not have to look far for a new publisher; three other companies immediately expressed interest in their book. In December, Crown brought out *The Binghams of Louisville* with only minor corrections. At first Barry Sr. was determined to battle this version of the Chandler book as well, and began drawing up lists of reviewers to whom he could send the five-volume refutation. But that fall, during a lunch with Mary and Gordon Davidson at the Jefferson Club, he abruptly decided against it. "I'm tired of the publicity," he told them. "I'm tired of this regurgitation in the newspapers. I'm just not going to do it." Taken aback, Mary and Gordon urged him to reconsider, but he would not budge. By then, Gordon said, "the fight was out of him." Both he and Mary were baffled as to why.

———————

Not everything in the lives of the Senior Binghams was unpleasant. With their share of the sale proceeds—$115 million—they established the Mary and Barry Bingham Sr. Fund, moved into a suite of offices in downtown

Louisville with a commanding view of the river, and began giving away money. Leon Tallichet found a second career as the fund's financial manager while John Richards acted as executive director. In short order, the fund made grants of $43 million, including $4 million to the University of Louisville for a faculty and staff club, $4.7 million to health organizations such as Planned Parenthood and the American Cancer Society, and over $2 million to the Kentucky Center for the Arts.

Barry Sr. was especially excited about a $2.6 million donation to the city of Louisville to build the world's tallest floating fountain, a structure that, when completed and anchored in the Ohio River, would spray water four hundred feet in the air in the shape of a fleur-de-lis. He had seen a similar geyser in Lake Geneva while on a trip to Switzerland some twenty years earlier, and hoped that the Louisville Falls Fountain would come to symbolize his hometown much as the Gateway Arch did St. Louis.

The sheer number and size of the gifts gave Barry Sr. and Mary a power and a platform they had not known since Barry Jr. was named publisher in 1971. After so many years on the sidelines, they were thrilled to be back at center stage, beloved and admired by all. "We will give as much [money away] as we can during our lifetime rather than leaving things in our will," Barry Sr. explained to *The Courier-Journal* in an article about their philanthropy. "This way we'll have the pleasure of seeing some of those things come to pass."

Eleanor and Rowland, too, seemed delirious finally to have the clout and cash they had always craved. When Mary gave $3.5 million to Open Court Publishing Co., a producer of progressive children's books, Eleanor kicked in $250,000. But she and Rowland spent a sizable portion of their new fortune on themselves. In the summer of 1987, they took a grand tour of Europe with Barry Sr. and Mary, sailing over and back in first-class staterooms aboard the *Queen Elizabeth II*. The family hippie who had once lived in a dilapidated sheepherder's cottage now checked into the Connaught in London, the Bristol in Paris, and the Cipriani in Venice, trailing her two small children, a nanny, and a van full of expensive luggage. Rowland stopped by Anderson & Sheppard, Barry Sr.'s Savile Row tailor. In Paris, he and Eleanor went shopping for museum-quality art deco furniture. "It defies description," said Joan in disgust. "The conspicuous consumption is so vulgar that even my children get it."

So did many Louisvillians, who considered Eleanor and Rowland's live-rich behavior unseemly and ostentatious. "People feel that they are throwing their weight around, putting on airs, wanting to have influence in the city," said Catherine Luckett, Jonathan's childhood friend. Eleanor did not care. She had gotten what she wanted in the family feud—money, power, and the parental warmth and attention that had eluded her as a child. People smiled knowingly when Eleanor decided to conduct her business affairs from an office next door to her father's.

Sallie, on the other hand, was the family outcast. The other Binghams rarely saw her and Barry Sr. no longer even kept a picture of her on his office wall. For public consumption, she pretended not to mind, but the rejection stung. "She desperately wants to be reconciled," confided Mary Clowes Taylor, a Collegiate classmate. Still, Sallie consoled herself with the knowledge that she, too, had gotten what she wanted from the fractious family battle—national attention and a large book contract. Like Eleanor, she went on a spending spree, acquiring a $1.1 million farm outside Louisville, a vacation home in Key West, and an apartment in Manhattan. But the bulk of her new riches was devoted to gaining an audience for her writing: Soon after she gave a $1 million gift to the Women's Project, a subsidiary of the American Place Theatre, it staged a rehearsed reading of two of her plays-in-progress.

Sallie dropped by the offices of her Kentucky Foundation for Women only once a week or so, yet managed to run the place with an iron hand nonetheless. Grants were small—mostly under $20,000—and successful applicants invariably shared Sallie's political agenda. Artists who had talent but no particular commitment to "dealing with female stereotypes in Western culture" usually found their projects rejected. "We don't just support women who make beautiful things," Sallie explained. "After all, they will have an easier time surviving than women who are attacking the issues— the issues I'm interested in." But Sallie's own commitment to feminism was not always clear. In the fall of 1986, she fired several women on the staff but retained Frederick Smock, the lone man and editor of the foundation's literary magazine. "We just had too many people," she shrugged.

Of all the Binghams, Barry Jr. was the most fretful, angry, and unhappy. He and Edie traveled furiously at first—to Europe for the opera, to Canada to hunt moose, to Oregon to visit friends, to California to see Edie's son, even back to Africa to shoot big game. But the whirlwind schedule provided only momentary relief. At fifty-three, Barry Jr. had had his life's work abruptly ripped out from under him and, try as he might, he could not get over his feelings of loss and bewilderment. Edie set up an office for him on the second floor of the Big House and he began looking for magazines, newsletters, and data bases to buy. But his heart was not in it. He missed the prestige of his former position and even his daily routine at the papers. "At home, there's nobody to drop in on," he complained.

Several employment consultants told him that before deciding on his next step, he should schedule a formal "exit interview" with his father. "When an executive is fired," Barry Jr. said, "he's got the right to go in and say to the chairman, 'Just so I don't screw up again in the next job, tell me what went wrong.' " So in the summer of 1987, Barry Jr. invited Barry Sr. to lunch. At last, he thought as he drove into town for the meeting, at last I will have an honest conversation with my father. But it was not to be. Barry Sr. still could not bring himself to tell his son the real reasons for the sale. When Barry Jr. asked his father point blank whether it was his management that had caused him to put the papers on the block, Barry Sr. shook his head. "No, no," he said emphatically. "You didn't do anything wrong. Everything was just wonderful."

The obvious pretense only redoubled Barry Jr.'s sense of indignation. In some ways, his father had been uncommonly good to him since the breakup of the empire. When he discovered that Barry Jr. had received less money than his sisters from the sale, for instance, he had quietly given him $5 million toward the difference.* At the same time, Barry Sr. had not abandoned his habit of indirect communication, instructing Gordon Davidson to ask Barry Jr. about his future housing and employment plans rather than inquiring himself. Your father is worried, Gordon informed Barry Jr., that if you decide to leave Louisville, you will sell the Big House to outsiders. The question infuriated Barry Jr. "My parents think Edie and I are the kind of people who would sell the house without offering it to them first!" he said, his voice suffused with pain. "They are obviously more concerned about real estate than they are about us."

Barry Jr. could also not help but notice that his father eagerly submitted articles to the op-ed page of *The Courier-Journal* now that the paper was owned by Gannett, something he had refused to do under Barry Jr.'s management. His parents seemed unperturbed by the fact that Gannett had shut down *The Louisville Times* early in 1987, devoted less space to news, accepted ads for wrinkle-eraser cream and other dubious products, serialized popular books, and established a 25 percent after-tax profit goal that had resulted in early retirements for scores of loyal employees.

He did not expect them to mourn Paul Janensch's departure—first to Gannett headquarters in northern Virginia and then to the company's Westchester-Rockland papers outside New York City. But he was shocked that Barry Sr. and Mary were not more critical of George Gill's cozy relationship with Louisville's business community. George had even turned over executive office space at *The Courier-Journal* to one of his pet causes—a group raising $10 million for local economic development.

Worse still, George had shown a vindictive streak. Soon after assuming the job of president and publisher, he had taken Barry Jr.'s huge, kidney-shaped desk, whittled it down to a coffee table, and gleefully installed it in

---

* The reason for the difference was because much of Barry Jr.'s stock was voting preferred, which was redeemed at its face value, while his sisters had more nonvoting common stock, whose value was determined by the sale price of the companies.

his office. George also told the editorial board that he had kept a detailed diary during the Bingham feud and was now trying to peddle it to one of several authors writing books about the family. His asking price: $100,000. None of this seemed to ruffle Barry Sr. and Mary. They had long ago distanced themselves from the papers that had once been the center of their lives. "I've completely adjusted to it," Mary said of the change in ownership. "I can look at *The Courier-Journal* now as a Gannett publication and I don't have any rise in my gorge at all."

Under such circumstances, the prospects for détente in the Bingham family seemed bleak indeed. Mary was wounded when Barry Jr. regularly walked by her without saying hello while she was working in the Little House garden. Barry Sr. felt hurt and slightly silly when he made a lunch date with Sallie and she did not show up. At parties, Barry Jr. and Edie huddled in one corner while Eleanor and Rowland eyed them warily from another. "It's almost like a divorce," said Frank Q. Cayce, a retired Louisville rector who witnessed several such encounters. "Which one do you talk to?" Barry Sr. still clung to the hope that, eventually, the sale would bring healing. But his son had felt all along that, in a family as unschooled in communication as the Binghams, that was naive and unrealistic. "The concept that healing is automatic, like a cut on your hand, is a concept that doesn't work in relationships," Barry Jr. said. "You've got to work at it. Somebody's got to get the ball rolling. And that's just not happening."

———————

Barry Sr. was playing tennis shortly before Thanksgiving, 1987, when he became aware that his vision was blurry and his balance was off. "I think I'm going to have to give up tennis," he told Mary when he got home. "I'm afraid I may fall down." A CAT scan the following week confirmed the worst: Barry Sr. had a half-inch lesion at the base of the brain. It was highly likely that the mass was cancerous. His Louisville doctor, Bill Blodgett, administered steroids to shrink the tumor and urged him to go to Massachusetts General Hospital for more sophisticated tests. The Senior Binghams promptly began packing for Boston.

Except for his sickly childhood, Barry Sr. had been blessed with exceptional health. He and Mary enjoyed a sex life well into their seventies, and he was vigilant about his eating and drinking habits. Now, even though the prospect of a debilitating, possibly fatal, illness loomed, his native buoyancy did not waver. "He was extremely calm and collected about it," Mary said, "the way he met all crises." He seemed almost serene as he bid farewell to his office staff, assuring them that he had lived a fine life and was not afraid to die.

Before leaving for Boston, Barry Sr. called Eleanor and Barry Jr. to tell them about his condition. He wrote a letter to Sallie, but stipulated that it not be delivered until after his plane had left Louisville. He was simply not up to dealing with her at such a moment. None of the Bingham children accompanied their parents to Mass General. Eleanor and Rowland kept in touch by phone, while Barry Jr. and Edie took off on a long-planned vacation to Europe.

Barry Jr. had volunteered to cancel his trip, but, typically, Barry Sr. and Mary had given him conflicting signals. "Don't be ridiculous. This isn't that important. This isn't that serious," they said, all the time hoping that Barry Jr. would ignore their protests and come with them to Boston. To Barry Jr., who had faced cancer himself at Mass General fifteen years before, the comments sounded like yet another painful rebuff. In mid-December, he and Edie left for Europe. "They really didn't want us around, whether he was sick or well," he said bitterly.

The doctors at Mass General were mystified by Barry Sr.'s illness. The steroids had reduced the lesion in his brain to an almost imperceptible dot, making accurate diagnosis impossible without a biopsy. But such a measure was considered dangerous at Barry Sr.'s advanced age of eighty-one. What is more, there was no evidence of malignancy anywhere else in his body— highly unusual for brain cancer victims. "Mary and I are in a Catch-22 situation," Barry Sr. wrote one of his many well-wishers. "The little visitor who has decided to make his abode in my cerebellum cannot be clearly identified except by surgery [but] surgery is deemed unwise. Therapy, radiation or otherwise, not now advised as they don't know what they are treating. . . . So I dose on cortizone [sic], start to bulge [and] take more tests. . . . It's a frustrating experience!" In a letter to the CJ editorial board, he said he thought of the tumor as "E.T.," the extraterrestrial in the movie by the same name. "I just wish he would phone home," he wrote wistfully.

After about a week, the Mass General doctors sent Barry Sr. back to Louisville, advising him to continue taking steroids for now and to come back for more tests after Christmas. The cortisone had weakened Barry Sr.'s muscles, making it difficult for him to walk without a cane. Still, during the holidays he read The Night Before Christmas to Eleanor's little boys and seemed genuinely to enjoy the presents, carols, and festive decorations.

On Wednesday evening, December 30, Barry Sr. had difficulty getting out of the tub. Mary tried desperately to assist him but she was not strong enough. Finally, after a half hour of tugging, she phoned Rowland, who immediately drove over to the Little House, scooped up his father-in-law, carried him to bed, and went back home. Neither of the Senior Binghams slept much that night. Toward dawn, Mary realized that her husband was burning with fever; his temperature was 103.

The sky was still dark when she called Dr. Blodgett, who rushed right over and did a quick diagnosis: pneumonia. "Barry really shouldn't be moved," he said, "but I want him to go to Boston immediately." So, on New Year's Day, 1988, Mary helped load Barry Sr. into a special ambulance plane and they flew back to Mass General, where he was put under the care of Dr. Fred Hochberg, a brain lymphoma specialist. Mary checked into the Ritz-Carlton Hotel.

When Barry Jr. and Edie arrived at O'Hare Airport three days later on the final leg of their return trip from Europe, there was an emergency message waiting from Mary. "The signals had clearly switched from, 'Don't be concerned, he's got plenty of time,' " said Barry Jr. "Suddenly, the S.O.S. went out." Barry Jr. and Edie continued on to Louisville, dumped their bags, and by noon the following day were at Barry Sr.'s bedside in Boston.

They were unprepared for the sight. The steroids had undermined Barry Sr.'s immune system and the doctors' constant demands for blood tests had made him anemic. "It was a goddamn nightmare," said Barry Jr. "They literally bled the man to anemia." Barry Sr.'s spirits were equally depleted. All his life he had been in control—of himself, his family, his newspapers. Now he lay helpless in a hospital bed, wheeled from the brain scan machine to the X-ray machine from morning till night and awakened before dawn for more poking and probing.

The memory of his own battle with cancer made Barry Jr. intuitively sympathetic, and despite the rage he still felt about the sale of the papers, he magnanimously tried to comfort his father. "Sometimes I don't understand you," he told Barry Sr. soon after he arrived. "But I do love you and I want to help." Barry Sr. nodded, but neither man used the rare moment of intimacy to open up a discussion of the past. "I just didn't think I ought to say, 'Now let's talk about why you sold the companies,' " Barry Jr. said. "I don't think he needed that."

After a battery of tests, Dr. Hochberg announced that he wanted to try chemotherapy. "We're going to use methyltrexate to attack this tumor," he told Mary and Barry Jr. "If he can tolerate three rounds, he has a good chance of surviving the disease." Barry Sr. barely lived through the initial injection. A blood clot sprouted in his leg, blackening one toe with gangrene. He developed a fissure in his lungs and was rushed to intensive care. "He went from being a man who was ill to being a man at death's door," Barry Jr. said. "It was clear they were never going to try chemotherapy again."

Early Sunday morning, January 17, Barry Jr. arrived at the intensive care unit to find a minister in the hallway comforting Rob Bingham, who had come up from Brown University to visit his grandfather. The boy was practically in tears. "Grandy just asked me to shoot him," Rob told Barry

Jr., his voice quavering. "He says there's no way for him to escape and he doesn't want to live any longer."

Barry Jr. strode into his father's room, sat down next to the bed, and asked him whether he had asked Rob to kill him. Barry Sr. said that yes, he had, and he repeated the request to Barry Jr. "Please shoot me," he pleaded. Barry Jr. shifted uncomfortably in his chair, his face impassive. For decades, his father had had almost limitless power over Barry Jr.'s life. When he had asked Barry Jr. to leave Washington and the job he loved and move back to Louisville, he had dutifully done so. When Barry Sr. had made it clear that the papers might go out of the family unless Barry Jr. stepped into the void created by Worth's death, he had again done what his father wanted. And when Barry Sr. had abruptly terminated his son's career by selling the companies, Barry Jr. had had no choice but to accept it. Now, almost exactly two years after Barry Sr.'s decision to sell, the roles were dramatically reversed. On that cold January morning in Boston, it was Barry Jr. who had power—the ultimate power—over Barry Sr.'s life. Despite the anguish of the moment, he felt a surge of satisfaction at the thought. After a long pause, Barry Jr. looked directly at his father. "I love you," he said, "but I am not going to go to the penitentiary for you. I am not going to blow your brains out in a hospital bed. That's just not going to happen."

Mary was aghast when she heard what her husband had said, and later that day, accompanied by Barry Jr., she made her own plea for him to press on. "Don't you want to walk on the beach in Chatham again, darling?" she asked Barry Sr. "Don't you want to see the good works of our foundation come to fruition?" Barry Sr. shook his head. "No," he said firmly. "I just want to die."

Mary's eyes welled with tears and she took a different tack, appealing to Barry Sr.'s optimism and fighter instinct. "Go on with the therapy," she urged. "It's worth a try, even if the chances of survival are not great." That, too, had no effect. Finally, Mary played her last card, one she was certain would change his mind. "I want you to live for me," she said, looking Barry Sr. straight in the eye. Barry Sr. did not hesitate. "I want to die," he repeated adamantly, with a hint of impatience. "I won't live for you."

At that, Mary dissolved in tears while Barry Jr. stood stunned beside her. Like everyone else in Louisville, he had considered his parents unusually close—not just wedded, but welded, as one friend had put it. Indeed, he knew that he and his siblings had probably suffered psychologically from being locked out of such an impenetrable union. No one—not the Bingham children, not the family's closest friends—had ever seen Barry Sr. deny Mary anything that was within his power to give. Now even that myth, the myth of the perfect marriage, the perfect relationship, had shattered right before his eyes. For a moment, Barry Jr. felt as devastated and betrayed as his sobbing mother.

Dr. Hochberg tried to comfort Mary by telling her that her husband had "intensive care psychosis," a sort of temporary madness common among severely ill patients, and she clung willingly to the explanation. But Barry Jr. had no doubts about his father's sanity. For years, he had watched Barry Sr. say one thing while thinking another; he was all too familiar with his talent for high-gloss obfuscation. On the subject of his own death, however, Barry Sr. had been uncharacteristically clear. In 1970, he had sent a "letter of understanding" to his Louisville physician, explicitly stating that, when the time came, he wanted no medical heroics if "there is no reasonable prospect of any improvement and no hope for the slightest enjoyment of life." Later, he and Mary had executed living wills. Now that Barry Sr. was seriously ill and had said that he wanted to die—not just once but many times—Barry Jr. had no reason to disbelieve him.

But Mary wanted more proof, and flew two of his most trusted friends— Wilson Wyatt and Dr. Bill Blodgett—up from Louisville to talk to Barry Sr. The results were inconclusive. On the one hand, Barry Sr. told Wilson, "I want to turn my face to the wall and go to heaven." On the other, he did not ask Wilson or Bill to kill him. Dr. Blodgett, in particular, felt that Barry Sr. was just suffering from intensive care psychosis and should not be taken seriously. The upshot was that, against Barry Sr.'s wishes, Mary decided to proceed with more treatment.

Since chemotherapy and surgery were clearly out of the question, the doctors tried radiation and, by the end of January, Barry Sr.'s tumor had again shrunk to the point of invisibility. Despite the marked improvement, he seemed increasingly alienated from everyone except the grandchildren. His wife, his son and youngest daughter—they were all obstructors, people who refused to give him what he wanted. "He was a man who all his life had expected to get his way, and usually had," Barry Jr. said. "It came as an appalling revelation to him that in a hospital you can suddenly become a prisoner." Barry Sr. was especially sullen around Mary and would not speak to her. "He turned quite hostile toward me," she said. "Really the last vocal and completely intellectual communication I had with him was when he told me he didn't want to live anymore."

Despite her own hurt and despair, Mary kept up a grueling routine. Each morning, she arose at the Ritz, did her exercises, ate breakfast, walked to the hospital, and by 10:00 A.M. was at Barry Sr.'s bedside. When Emily, Barry Jr.'s oldest, learned of her grandfather's illness, she cut short her foreign study program in Italy and checked into a room next door to Mary. Eleanor came as often as she could, accompanied by her children and a nurse. Molly, who was at Harvard, and Clara, who was working for Michael

Dukakis's presidential campaign, were also frequent visitors. But on many weekends, Mary had only Barry Jr. and Edie for dinner partners. She greatly appreciated her son's frequent trips to Boston, but, like Barry Sr., she did not use the occasion to discuss the sale of the newspapers. "That was a nonsubject," she said. "We never have talked about it, and probably never will."

One night, soon after Barry Sr. began radiation, Mary got a call at the hotel. "It's your husband," said the physician on the other end of the line. "He's not going to live through the night unless you put him on a respirator." Mary rushed over to Mass General and found Barry Sr. unconscious. In desperation, she called Barry Jr. and Eleanor in Louisville and asked them what she should do. They both told her it was her decision. "We're not there, so we really can't advise you," said Eleanor. After a long consultation with the doctor, Mary agreed to put Barry Sr. on the respirator. She was not yet ready to give him up. "Looking back on it, it would have been better to let him die then," she said later. "From then on it was just one crisis after another."

Barry Sr. was somewhat improved by February 10, 1988, his eighty-second birthday, but he was having a hard time sleeping. His room was located across the hall from where the bedpans were cleaned and he was continually awakened by the wheezing sound of the sterilizer. To ensure that he was well rested for his birthday, Mary had asked the doctors to give him a sedative the night before. But the orders got garbled and the nurses administered the injection at 1:00 A.M. instead of 6:00 P.M. So by the time Barry Jr., Edie, Eleanor, Rowland, and the grandchildren arrived with a cake, get-well banners, and balloons, Barry Sr. was sound asleep. By the time he finally woke up, everyone but Mary had left.

Sallie sent an affectionate birthday card, which Barry Sr. refused to answer. "He was so deeply hurt by her statements about the family and his father," Mary said. "He really felt completely estranged." Not one to be so readily dismissed, Sallie decided to take matters into her own hands.

About a week after Barry Sr.'s birthday, Mary was conferring with one of the doctors about whether to install feeding and breathing tubes when Sallie suddenly appeared with her husband, Tim. Mary looked up, startled. "I'm having an important conversation," she said coldly. "Go in and see your father and I'll be finished in a few moments." Sallie and Tim cautiously peeked in Barry Sr.'s room, but he was barely conscious and gave no indication that he knew they were there.

Mary told the doctor to go ahead with the tracheotomy. Then she turned to Sallie. "They're going to move him to another room, and I plan to stay to see where he is put," she said. "So don't you wait. Go back to the hotel and I'll join you later." Sallie looked stricken. "Don't you want me to sit with you?" she asked her mother. That was the last thing Mary wanted, but her Montague breeding remained firmly in place. "No, don't do that, because I don't know how long it will be," she said. "Go back and I'll join you as soon as I can." When Mary appeared at the Ritz hours later, she found that Sallie and Tim had checked out. "I'm sure this was a conciliatory effort on Sallie's part," she said, "but I was not in a condition to meet her halfway."

After the tracheotomy, Barry Sr. could speak only with great difficulty. From then on, none of the Binghams were able to coax more than a few words out of him. "Is it really so painful or does he just not want to speak to me?" Barry Jr. often wondered as he moved about his father's room, plumping up pillows and chatting about the latest doings in Louisville.

By the end of February, the Mass General doctors felt there was no more they could do for Barry Sr. Radiation had temporarily shrunk the tumor, but after a while it began to grow back. Since chemotherapy and surgery were impossible, they decided to send him home on the theory that he would at least be happier in familiar surroundings. On March 4, Barry Sr. again boarded an air ambulance, flew back to Louisville, and entered Norton Hospital, where his sense of despair remained unchanged. He refused all visitors, even old, old friends, and seemed ashamed of his appearance. The radiation had caused most of his hair to fall out and what was left was snow white. He had lost weight in Boston and had a gaunt, weathered look— "like a refugee from Auschwitz," Barry Jr. told friends. One day, Mary ran into Wilson Wyatt, who was visiting another patient at Norton, and she suggested he open Barry Sr.'s door and wave to him. Wilson was appalled at what he saw. "I will regret that to my dying day," he later confided to a CJ reporter.

After several weeks, Barry Sr. was considered stable enough to move into the Little House, which Mary had had air-conditioned for his comfort. Each morning around 6:00 A.M., Harry Chenoweth, one of three private nurses, would arrive to shave and bathe Barry Sr. and hoist him into a wheelchair. Then Mary would roll him out into the garden, where she would read aloud from The Courier-Journal, Jane Austen novels, or Shakespeare. A speech therapist dropped by regularly to help him talk, but Barry Sr. seemed completely uninterested in communication.

Still, it was clear that inside his failing body, Barry Sr.'s mind was amazingly alert. His eyes followed people around the room, and on Derby Day in early May, he managed to tell a nurse which horse he wanted to bet on. His pick came within inches of winning. The incident left Mary bereft. Her husband's condition was nightmarish enough without the added burden of feeling he was mentally capable of understanding it. "That tormented me," she said. "I had really hoped by that time that he didn't know how bad it was." The only solid indication of what Barry Sr. was feeling came from

Harry, the male nurse, who told Barry Jr. that his father cried a lot at night. "I think he was extremely lonely," Barry Jr. said of Barry Sr. "I expect he lay in that bed hour after hour saying, 'Whatever sins I've committed in my life, they weren't bad enough to deserve this.' "

The summer of 1988 was one of blazing skies and terrible heat. As the days wore on, Mary wrote sorrowful letters to the Asia Foundation, the Gannett Foundation, the National Portrait Gallery, and a host of other organizations, telling them that Barry Sr. was too sick to continue on their boards and would have to resign. To make her husband's life a little less empty, she bought a VCR and rented several of their favorite films. One selection was *Oklahoma*, the musical they had seen on Broadway in 1944 the night before Barry Sr. had had to return to the navy. They sat in silence as the show flickered on the screen. After a few minutes, Barry Sr. looked so displeased that Mary got up and ejected the cassette. "He did not seem to want to revisit even things which had given him pleasure," said Barry Jr., who tried without success to interest his father in an old home movie of Judge Bingham and Henrietta.

Eleanor had pinned all her hopes on getting Barry Sr. back to Louisville. Now even she had to admit that he would probably be better off dead. One day, as she watched the nurses suction out her father's lungs, something snapped and she demanded that Bill Blodgett, Barry Sr.'s Louisville physician, stop all life supports. Dr. Blodgett gently reminded Eleanor that her father was not on life supports. "Well, cut off his feeding tube then," she said defiantly. Mary refused to let her husband die of starvation and dehydration, although she did agree to reduce Barry Sr.'s food supply.

When the end seemed imminent, Eleanor phoned Sallie and invited her to come see her father one last time. Sallie spent several minutes staring into Barry Sr.'s glazed, water-blue eyes and kissed him lightly on the forehead. He did not respond. "Everything seemed controlled, beautiful, even serene," she later wrote of the experience. "I felt I was witnessing Mother's masterpiece." Mary purposely made herself scarce.

Around 3:00 A.M. on August 15, 1988, the night nurse roused Mary and told her to come quickly to the sickroom. Eleanor and Rowland were summoned, as were Barry Jr., Edie, and Emily. No one called Sallie. By 5:15 A.M., Barry Sr. was dead, surrounded by everyone in his immediate family except the daughter he had once characterized as an "engine of destruction."

Although Barry Sr.'s death had been expected for months, newspaper and political leaders from around the country overflowed with grief and adulation. "He ran a paper that was a model for the industry," said *Washington Post* chairman Katharine Graham, who stayed with Mary at the Little House the night before the funeral. Kentucky's Republican governor, Wallace Wilkinson, lamented that "a great voice had been stilled." Even Sallie was quoted as saying she admired her father's "great relish for life." The entire op-ed page of the *CJ* was given over to excerpts of Barry Sr.'s editorials, speeches, and essays.

The day after his death, Barry Sr.'s plain oak coffin sat in the Little House living room covered with a pall of white brocade as dignitaries and ordinary citizens alike streamed in from the hundred-degree heat to console the Binghams. Mary, looking remarkably composed in a crisp white linen dress, headed up the informal receiving line, followed by Barry Jr., Edie, Emily, and Molly. Rowland sat in a corner with Eleanor, who had been injured in a recent riding accident and was incapable of standing. Servants hovered attentively, offering trays of white wine, ice water, summer punch, and small tea sandwiches.

Suddenly, Sallie and Tim entered the room and the conversation went down several decibels in a sort of collective gasp. Sallie clearly felt awkward, but she bravely walked over to Eleanor and greeted her with a smile. Then she turned and shook hands with Barry Jr. Gradually, slowly, person by person, Sallie worked her way through the family and friends until finally there was nothing left to do but confront her mother. Mary looked up indifferently at her daughter and offered her cheek for a kiss. Sallie complied with the barest brush of the lips, and after a few words, Mary turned back to her duties at the door. Sallie was a guest at her own father's wake. Her mother, brother, and sister were receiving; she was being received.

About seven hundred mourners attended the funeral the following morning at Calvary Church. Barry Jr. escorted his mother to the front pew, followed by Eleanor and Rowland. Sallie and Tim came last and made a point of crowding into the front pew with the others. "Sallie, rather oddly, cares about being a member of the family in public, in spite of all the things she does," Mary said later.

Barry Sr. had planned his funeral service years before and, in accordance with his wishes and the rites of the Episcopal Church, there were no eulogies or references to him by name. Even so, the readings and psalms revealed Barry Sr.'s firm belief in a sort of celestial barter system in which good works are exchanged for a place in heaven. All his life, he and his family had been blessed by angels and stalked by devils. But nothing—not the rumors of Mary Lily's murder, the freakish deaths of two sons, or the sale of the papers—had weakened his conviction that the Binghams were God's chosen people. "If God be for us, who can be against us?" went one reading from the eighth chapter of Romans. "Who shall lay anything to the charge of God's elect?"

More than two hundred people clustered around Barry Sr.'s grave in Cave Hill Cemetery in the shimmering Louisville heat. The trees rustled softly as the minister issued the final "dust to dust" benediction and, for a moment, a wave of reconciliation seemed to wash over members of the Bingham family. Standing stiffly by their limousines, they seemed briefly united in contemplation and grief, starkly aware that all of them had been shaped, molded, blessed, and cursed by the charming, lonely, and elusive man who was now about to be lowered into the ground. For Mary, the moment was fraught with terror. "You see, I don't think there's anything after this life," she explained, her voice cracking. "So I just have to face the fact that he is no more."

Many friends feared that Barry Sr.'s death would send Mary into a spiraling depression or perhaps turn her into a recluse, but the imminent publication of Sallie's memoir proved a bracing tonic. Overnight, Mary became as protective of Barry Sr.'s reputation as Barry Sr. had been of his father's. Fueling her ire was her absolute belief that the stress Sallie had inflicted on Barry Sr. during the family feud and the battle over the Chandlers' book had brought on the mysterious form of brain cancer and greatly hastened his death. "Sallie is a murderess," she told family intimates.

By December 1988, Mary had managed to obtain galleys of Sallie's book, *Passion and Prejudice: A Family Memoir*. She was appalled at what she read. Without offering a shred of evidence, Sallie hypothesized that Eleanor Miller had not died accidentally in 1913, saving Barry Sr., but instead had committed suicide by hurling herself in front of the interurban, and that Judge Bingham had very probably killed Mary Lily.

The "maliciously skewed" assertions so angered Mary that she decided to mount an aggressive campaign against her daughter, and sought out John Scanlon, one of New York's savviest p.r. men, for guidance. In mid-January 1989, an inch-thick "response document," signed by Mary, Barry Jr., Edie, Eleanor, Joan, and Clara, was mailed out to book reviewers around the country. In a cover letter, the Binghams took care to say that they had not contacted Sallie's publisher, Alfred A. Knopf, nor had they tried to restrain publication. Their sole aim, they said, was to prove that Sallie's claims rested on "erroneous suppositions, leaps of logic and, in some cases, outright fabrications."

Sallie responded in kind. Only five months earlier, at the reading of her father's will, she had discovered that Barry Sr. had left $2 million trust funds to each of her three children. Barry Sr. had felt they ought to have at least some inheritance since Sallie had repeatedly said she planned to leave her sons nothing. My father bypassed me "because he did not approve of the way I give my money to women," she wrote at the time. Now, her family had attacked her credibility as a teller of the Bingham tale and had even implicitly questioned her sanity.

Sallie characterized the corrections as "hamburger" and tartly asked why her family didn't use their money instead to help the homeless. Her parents, she told a New York reporter, were "gifted manipulators . . . used to controlling . . . and defining reality." But in Louisville, at least, many people thought it was Sallie who had been unfaithful to reality. In late January, a week before *Passion and Prejudice* was to appear in the nation's bookstores, the *CJ* published an editorial cartoon of a seated Pinocchio, his nose long with leaves growing out of the end, holding a copy of Sallie's book. "Q: What characteristics does this puppet have in common with this book?" asked the line under the figure. "A: For openers, both were fabricated from pulp products."

The cartoon hit Sallie in her most vulnerable spot—her mental stability—and prompted her to write an angry letter-to-the-editor. "I think anyone who reads the book with care will conclude that its only connection to Pinocchio is that it shows a woman turning into a human being instead of remaining a wooden puppet," she stormed.

Sallie soon found herself under attack from other quarters. Shirley Williams, her predecessor on the *CJ* book page, sued her for damage to her professional reputation; she was furious at passages in the book suggesting that her work at *The Courier-Journal* had been unsatisfactory. A Louisville radio announcer began doing cruel imitations of the elder Bingham daughter on his afternoon drive show. In one, "Sallie" calls the station to say that she is deeply offended by the Louisville Falls Fountain, inaugurated just days after her father's death, because it reminded her of the male sex organ. "If I had done the fountain," said the radio announcer in a shrill, superior voice meant to suggest Sallie, "it would be in the shape of a *woman!*"

The Binghams managed to mute their disagreements during the wedding of Barry Ellsworth, Sallie's oldest son, in a Manhattan loft. But the tensions were still palpable. As a reggae band played in the background, Mary kept to one side of the room while Sallie staked out her turf in the other. "[My mother] snubbed me at my son's wedding," Sallie complained later. "It's just one rejection in a long series of rejections."

———

Despite the differences still roiling the older generations of Binghams, the grandchildren remained on good terms and, at Clara's instigation, gathered in the summer of 1989 to talk about pooling 5 percent of their pretax income each year for a new "Bingham cousins" foundation. In an attempt to mend the rift among their parents, they asked Barry Jr., Sallie, and Eleanor to contribute as well, with Mary matching the donations dollar-for-dollar. Barry Jr. and Eleanor agreed to kick in $1.5 million each, but Sallie declined to participate.

The wounds in the warring Bingham clan had gone too deep, it seemed, ever to heal. Contact with Sallie was almost nonexistent, and she, in turn, referred to her mother, brother, and sister as "my ex-family." Eleanor occasionally brought her boys over to the Big House to play, but her relations with Barry Jr. and Edie were merely civil. Mary remained close to her youngest daughter, but despite all Barry Jr. had done to ease the pain of Barry Sr.'s illness and death, she was still severe and reserved around her son. "Barry Jr. is thoroughly correct, you know, and does all the right things," she said. "But we have no real intimacy."

Barry Jr. no longer talked of buying a magazine or a data-base company and moving away from Louisville. His father had left him the Big House free and clear in his will and he now seemed content to remain in the place he had grown up, with all its familiar ghosts. "There are too many stayers in this family," said Sallie, who continued to live most of the year on her farm outside town. "You'd think he'd want to move on."

To occupy his time, Barry Jr. acquired office space in downtown Louisville and began producing *FineLine*, a monthly newsletter about journalism ethics. Although his millions could have easily subsidized the operation, Barry Jr. insisted that the publication be run on a strict business basis. At the same time, he refused to accept advertising because it might compromise *FineLine*'s integrity. As a result, the subscription rate—almost $300 a year—put *FineLine* out of reach of the journalists it sought to serve. "I think Barry Jr. feels a tremendous pressure to prove himself as a businessman, almost to prove it to his father," said Mary.

It was true that Barry Jr. was still haunted by the sale of the newspapers, all the more so because Barry Sr. had died without revealing the real reasons behind his decision. It was not until a year after the funeral that Barry Jr. learned for the first time of George Gill's bombshell conversation with Barry Sr. in December 1985, the one that had convinced him to put the papers on the auction block. Barry Jr. was silent and showed no visible sign of anger or hurt. "I've never heard that before," he said carefully. "But if my father saw the management team disappearing, with just me left, I can understand his apprehension [about the future]."

Barry Jr. sat pondering why his father had not come clean with him. After all, he was the one person who yearned most to make sense of the sale. He tried to reconstruct the events of those days with the missing piece of the puzzle in place. "Maybe he felt he was protecting me or something, I don't know," he ventured. Then, suddenly, he blinked and looked as if he finally understood it all for the first time. "The problem with him telling me things is that I always had a response, I always came back with something he didn't want to hear," he said. "I would have gone back and somehow gotten George and Leon to change their minds [about quitting]. Or at least tried to. And that was not what he was looking for. I think he had already made the decision [to sell]. He was just looking for a trip wire."

If there was any wisdom to be gleaned from what had happened to him and the rest of the Bingham clan, he said, it was that it is a mistake not to communicate clearly with people. "If you've got a real problem with somebody, you ought to sit down and talk about it. You may think you're protecting someone by not telling them the truth. But you'd better be certain before you act that way, because most people want to be participants in their own destiny. . . . If I were ever in business with [my daughters], I'd be much more candid with them than I feel my father was with me."

———

For Mary, the task now was simply to endure, which she did mainly by throwing herself into a host of philanthropic projects. The summer following Barry Sr.'s death, she decided to return alone to the sunny, weathered, and beloved white summer house in Chatham on Cape Cod.

She and Barry Sr. had first vacationed in Chatham in 1939, the year Mary had lost a baby that had almost come to term. Barry Sr. had hoped that the sea air and bright, spare houses would somehow take his wife's mind off her grief and loss. Now, fifty years later, Mary was back again to grieve and to try to find some comfort. In the parlor of the Water Street house, she looked out at the blue hydrangeas lining the terrace. "This house is really haunted," she said. "I guess I ought to be glad to be haunted. But it's horrible. He was so much a part of this life in Chatham, you know."

While Barry Sr. was alive, he and Mary had had a set routine. They took picnic lunches to North Beach, swam, played tennis, then showered before sitting down to a satisfying dinner, a nice bottle of wine, and a few hours of reading or a game of Scrabble. "That established kind of life, it's just knocked to pieces," said Mary. "Now I have dinner alone, read a book or the paper, and try to face the evening."

Mary told visitors she was worried about Rowland, who was deeply depressed about being perceived as a kept man. "Eleanor likes to have him on hand, you know, to go to the Caribbean in the winter and to New York for art auctions," Mary said, "but I'm afraid it comes in for a good deal of comment." He and Eleanor are both seeing marriage counselors, she confided.

She said she was also concerned about Barry Jr., aware that he desperately needed to make a success of his newsletter, and about Edie, whose sons continued to cause problems. "They ought to be sent to Africa with a small allowance, never to be seen again," Mary said of the two Franchini boys, shaking her head. She said she was even able to muster a small scrap of sympathy for Sallie, who had recently thrown her youngest son, Willy, a high school dropout, out of the house.

Aware of how grim it all sounded, Mary hastened to add that her own life was not gloom every minute. "I go to the movies with friends and I get great satisfaction out of dispensing money to good causes," she said.

Then there was a long, long silence while she struggled for control. She cast her eyes around the room as if searching for a distraction. But she found none. Sighing, she uttered a phrase that could have been said by any of the Binghams, so much had their lives and destinies revolved around Barry Sr.

"I never stop missing him."

NOTES

T he main source for most of the material in this book is hundreds of hours of interviews with members of the Bingham family, particularly Barry Bingham Sr. and his wife, Mary. Because the interviews with them, and with other members of the immediate family—Barry Jr., Edie, Joan, Sallie, Eleanor, and Rowland—are so numerous, the reader should assume unless otherwise noted that quotes attributed to these individuals come from tape-recorded sessions with the authors.

We also interviewed more than one hundred friends, acquaintances, family retainers, and present and former staff members of *The Courier-Journal* and *Times*, WHAS, Standard Gravure, and Data Courier.

Other primary sources include the voluminous correspondence between Barry Sr. and Mary on file at the Arthur and Elizabeth Schlesinger Library on the History of Women in America at Radcliffe College, as well as the papers of Robert Worth Bingham at the Library of Congress, the National Archives, and the Filson Club in Louisville. The presidential libraries of Franklin D. Roosevelt, John F. Kennedy, Lyndon Baines Johnson, and Jimmy Carter provided a window on the Binghams' involvement in Democratic politics over the years and in public causes ranging from literacy to mental health.

Much of the information about the family's early life in America comes from the Southern Historical Collection and the North Carolina Collection at the University of North Carolina at Chapel Hill. The papers of Mark and Willie Snow Ethridge, also at the Southern Historical Collection, were invaluable in fleshing out life at the Louisville newspapers in the 1930s, 1940s, 1950s, and 1960s, as were interviews with *CJ & T* principals conducted by the University of Louisville Oral History Project. The correspondence of Col. Edward House at Yale University, which includes many letters to and from Robert Worth Bingham, was equally useful in our research.

When conversation or dialogue occurs, the reader may assume that it is based on the recollection of at least one participant or observer and, in some cases, several such persons.

Abbreviations:

RWB   Robert Worth Bingham
BBS   Barry Bingham Sr.
MB   Mary Bingham
BBJ   Barry Bingham Jr.
SB   Sallie Bingham
EBM   Eleanor Bingham Miller
CJ   *The Courier-Journal*
LT   *The Louisville Times*
LOC   Library of Congress, Robert Worth Bingham Papers
SL   The Arthur and Elizabeth Schlesinger Library on the History of Women in America, Radcliffe College, Mary (Caperton) Bingham and Barry Bingham Papers

Epigraph

"Paradise," by BBS, *The Harvard Advocate* 113, no. 2 (Nov. 1926).

Chapter 1 BEGINNINGS

21   The man he had come to see: Many of the details about Robert Worth Bingham's physical condition and frame of mind during his final illness are taken from BBS's unpublished account of his father's last years, BBS private papers. Also see *CJ* and *LT* accounts Nov. 26 through Dec. 19, 1937.

22   Three days earlier: RWB to Franklin D. Roosevelt, Dec. 8, 1937, LOC.

22   Krock had his own reasons: An account of Krock's motive for revealing the Kennedy appointment can be found in Michael Beschloss, *Kennedy and Roosevelt: The Uneasy Alliance* (New York: W. W. Norton, 1980), pp. 153–55.

23   In 1936, Kennedy had visited: Peter Collier and David Horowitz, *The Kennedys: An American Drama* (New York: Summit Books, 1984), pp. 82–83.

23   Unfortunately, there was no proof: Information about the Binghams' antecedents and the family's early life in America is taken from *Descendants of James*

Bingham of County Down, Northern Ireland, compiled by James Barry Bingham (Baltimore: Gateway Press, 1980); Rose E. McCalmont, *Memoirs of the Binghams* (London: Spotteswood & Co., 1915); and telephone interviews with James Barry Bingham.

25 The first moment came in mid-June: An account of the battle at the South Anna Bridge and Bingham's capture can be found in Robert Bingham, "A Reminiscence of 1863," in *The Bingham Military School Annual*, 1916, North Carolina Collection, University of North Carolina at Chapel Hill.

26 Instead, Bingham and his companions: Descriptions of Northern prisons are taken from William Best Hesseltine, *Civil War Prisons* (New York: Frederick Ungar Publishing Co., 1930).

26 He was particularly offended when: Robert Bingham Civil War diary, Bingham Papers, Southern Historical Collection, University of North Carolina at Chapel Hill.

26 On Palm Sunday, 1865: Bingham's physical appearance taken from RWB to Margaret Mitchell, Feb. 16, 1937, LOC. Bingham's account of Appomattox can be found in A. J. McKelway, "Appomattox—An Anniversary," *Harper's Weekly*, Apr. 15, 1916, p. 411, and in Gene Smith, *Lee and Grant: A Dual Biography* (New York: McGraw-Hill, 1984), pp. 281–82.

27 The sliver of prosperity: For the effects of the war on North Carolina, see Hugh Talmadge Lefler and Albert Ray Newsome, *North Carolina: The History of a Southern State* (Chapel Hill: University of North Carolina Press, 1963), pp. 433–36. Slang words for Confederate currency are taken from Bell Irvin Wiley, *Embattled Confederates: An Illustrated History of Southerners at War* (New York: Harper & Row, 1964), p. 121.

27 When Robert arrived home: Bingham describes what he found upon his return in *Bingham School v. P. L. Gray et al.*, Supreme Court of North Carolina, 1898.

28 The Bingham Military School that Rob knew: Descriptions of the school during Reconstruction are taken from Anna Barringer, *The Natural Bent: The Memoirs of Dr. Paul B. Barringer* (Chapel Hill: University of North Carolina Press, 1949), and William E. Ellis, "The Bingham Family: From the Old South to the New South and Beyond," *The Filson Club History Quarterly* 61, no. 1 (Jan. 1987).

28 "We who were born here": as quoted in Richard Nelson Current, *Those Terrible Carpetbaggers: A Reinterpretation* (New York: Oxford University Press, 1988), pp. 52–53.

28 While he was still a toddler: RWB recollects seeing his father in Klan regalia in RWB to Margaret Mitchell, Feb. 16, 1937, LOC. Accounts of Klan violence in Alamance County and the Binghams' involvement in it are taken from the proceedings of the impeachment trial of William W. Holden (Sentinel Printing Office, Raleigh, 1871), pp. 583–85, 600–602, 2276–77, 2537–38; Allen W. Trelease, *White Terror: The Ku Klux Klan Conspiracy and Southern Reconstruction* (New York: Harper & Row, 1971), pp. 205, 408–409; and Ellis, "The Bingham Family."

28   "Dr. Black" or "Dr. Brown": *Raleigh News & Observer*, May 20, 1927.

29   He clearly favored: Description of Robert Bingham riding with Rob taken from M. C. S. Noble to RWB, Feb. 24, 1933, Noble Papers, Southern Historical Collection, University of North Carolina at Chapel Hill.

29   "Melanie to the last emotion": RWB to Margaret Mitchell, Feb. 16, 1937, LOC.

29   "nervous prostration": Colonel Bingham's depression after Dell's death is detailed in *Bingham School* v. *P. L. Gray et al.*, Supreme Court of North Carolina, 1898.

30   "promotive of various evils": Archibald Henderson, *The Campus of the First State University* (Chapel Hill: University of North Carolina Press, 1949), p. 249.

30   When Bob ran for chief ball manager: An account of the election and Bob's dance with Irene Langhorne is contained in W. W. Davies to Shepard Bryan, May 31, 1933, Bryan Papers, Southern Historical Collection, University of North Carolina at Chapel Hill.

30   "a social success always": William J. Andrews quoted in caption beneath photo of RWB's college class, University of North Carolina general alumni association files.

30   His academic performance: Student Records and Faculty Reports, Vol. 5, University Archives, University of North Carolina at Chapel Hill.

31   he contracted malaria: Grover M. Hutchins, M.D., to Mark Wilson, Mar. 31, 1987, in Memorandum to Macmillan Publishing Co. from BBS, Apr. 27, 1987.

31   These quarrels with his father: Hugh Young describes RWB's experience in Charlottesville in *Hugh Young: A Surgeon's Autobiography* (New York: Harcourt, Brace and Co., 1940), p. 504.

31   "quick, decisive manner": Obituary of Hugh Young, *Baltimore Sun*, Aug. 24, 1945.

31   "crazy incendiary": Details of the fires and their causes can be found in *Bingham School* v. *P. L. Gray et al.*, Supreme Court of North Carolina, 1898.

32   Colonel Bingham had attended UNC: In his prison diary, Robert Bingham notes that two of his classmates from the University of North Carolina are with him: "Tillett & Keenan [sic]." Mary Lily's uncle, Thomas S. Kenan, was in the class of 1857.

32   "an affair": *The New York Herald*, Nov. 6, 1916.

32   He wore his gray officer's cape: According to William J. Miller, who was a small boy in Asheville in the early part of the century. William J. Miller to Susan E. Tifft, Oct. 27, 1987.

32   So ridiculous was the sight: Wolfe's use of Bingham as a prototype for Joyner is made clear in Floyd C. Watkins, *Thomas Wolfe's Characters: Portraits from Life* (Norman: University of Oklahoma Press, 1957), pp. 151–52.

32   Silk "sensed the right thing": Thomas Wolfe, *The Hills Beyond* (New York: Plume Books, 1935), p. 220.

33   It was summer: A description of the Battery Park Hotel can be found in *Health Resorts of the South*, 1891, pp. 277, 312.

33 "I am safely conscious": RWB to Henrietta L. Miller, undated, Bingham Papers, The Filson Club, Louisville, Kentucky. Hereinafter referred to as The Filson Club.

Chapter 2 BEAUTIFUL BOB BINGHAM

35 "No more to wade": As quoted in George H. Yater, *Two Hundred Years at the Falls of the Ohio: A History of Louisville and Jefferson County* (Louisville: The Heritage Corporation, 1979), p. 129.

36 A slender man with thinning hair: A more detailed profile of Samuel Miller can be found in J. Stoddard Johnston, ed., *Memorial History of Louisville from Its First Settlement to the Year 1896* (Chicago: American Biographical Publishing Co., 1896), pp. 498–500.

37 There were eight bridesmaids: CJ, May 17 and 21, 1896.

37 Louisville at the time: Descriptions of Louisville and Kentucky taken from *Old Louisville* (Louisville: University of Louisville, 1961); Isabel McLennan McMeekin, *Louisville: The Gateway City* (New York: Julian Messner, 1946); George R. Leighton, *Five Cities: The Story of their Youth and Old Age* (New York: Harper & Brothers, 1939); Neal R. Peirce, *The Border South States* (New York: W. W. Norton, 1975); and Yater, *Two Hundred Years.*

39 After several years with the firm: *The National Cyclopedia of American Biography,* Current Volume D (New York: James T. White and Company, 1934), pp. 32–33, and *Hubbell's Legal Directories 1906–1910.*

39 "doing the great club and society act": W. W. Davies to William H. Tayloe, Aug. 6, 1898, The Filson Club.

39 "nothing more. . .than an ordinary drunkard" and "a gentleman at all times": William H. Tayloe to W. W. Davies, Aug. 2, 1898, The Filson Club.

39 He took an expensive cure: For details of Bingham's health and his preoccupation with his ancestry, see Grover Hutchins, M.D., to Mark Wilson, Mar. 31, 1987, in Memorandum to Macmillan Publishing Co. from BBS, Apr. 27, 1987; RWB to Sadie Grinnan, June 13, 1905 and RWB to Col. Robert Bingham, Oct. 2, 1905, The Filson Club. The Juniper Hunt Club is described in *Hugh Young: A Surgeon's Autobiography,* p. 506.

40 It took him four years: Details of RWB's financial state are taken from James J. Holmberg, "The Use of Filson Club Manuscripts in *The Binghams of Louisville," The Filson Club History Quarterly* 63, no. 3 (July 1989): 372–73, and Internal Memorandum Re: Courier-Journal research, Wyatt, Tarrant & Combs, Mar. 25, 1986.

40 Although he had been professionally established: RWB returned $3,500 in Worth Manufacturing stock but not the $2,500 his grandfather had borrowed against it. In 1899, however, he did begin paying Dr. Worth interest on the note. See *In Re Last Will and Testament of J. M. Worth,* in the Supreme Court of North Carolina, August term, 1901, pp. 45, 249.

40 As it turned out: *In Re Last Will and Testament of J. M. Worth,* in the Supreme

Court of North Carolina, August term, 1901, and in the Superior Court of North Carolina, December term, 1901.

40   Vowing that he would "not stop": RWB to Thomas C. Worth, Apr. 16, 1900, The Filson Club.

40   "Bob seems to care": Berta W. Boyd to RWB, Apr. 26, 1900, The Filson Club.

40   "The most contemptible": RWB to R. T. Grinnan, Apr. 19, 1900, The Filson Club.

40   But after court costs: Memorandum to Macmillan Publishing Co. from BBS, Apr. 27, 1987.

41   The municipal election: Details of the 1905 election and Bingham's role in it are taken from William E. Ellis, "Robert Worth Bingham and Louisville Progressivism," *The Filson Club History Quarterly* 54 (Apr. 1980); Arthur Krock, *Myself When Young: Growing Up in the 1890s* (Boston: Little, Brown, 1973), p. 179; Yater, *Two Hundred Years*, pp. 146–49; LT, Oct. 14, 1910.

41   In April 1907: An account of the court's action, Bingham's selection as mayor, and his term in office can be found in Yater, *Two Hundred Years*, pp. 149–150, and Ellis, "Robert Worth Bingham and Louisville Progressivism."

42   One day, a Whallen strongman: *Hugh Young: A Surgeon's Autobiography*, pp. 504–505.

42   Fed up with the abuse: RWB to BBS, Sept. 26, 1935, LOC.

42   "If you crossed him": Interview, Norman Isaacs, Aug. 29, 1989.

43   But he could not resist: LT, Oct. 14, 1910.

44   She provided: Memorandum to Macmillan Publishing Co. from BBS, Apr. 27, 1987.

44   The furnishings were Bob's responsibility: RWB to Col. Robert Bingham, June 18, 1907, The Filson Club.

45   On summer afternoons: "Growing Up in America—Barry Bingham's Louisville, Kentucky," *CJ Bicentennial Monthly*, May 1976.

45   For his fifth birthday: MB to BBS, Jan. 23, 1944, SL.

45   "slight feminine air of mystery": BBS, "Town Mice Have Their Fun, Too," *CJ*, Feb. 6, 1957.

46   "a gentleman of the old school": Memorandum, BBS to family members, Aug. 30, 1985.

46   The evening was warm: BBS describes this special July 4 in *CJ Bicentennial Monthly*, May 1976, and *The New Voice*, July 1, 1987.

47   Several weeks later: The circumstances of the drive, the accident, and Eleanor's death are taken from *CJ* and *LT*, Apr. 28 and 29, 1913; *The Louisville Herald*, Apr. 28, 1913; *Louisville Evening Post*, Apr. 28, 1913; and Memorandum to Macmillan Publishing Co. from BBS, Apr. 27, 1987.

Chapter 3 THE MAD WOMAN IN THE ATTIC

51   A few months after her funeral: Interview, Sophie and Jacques Albert, Feb. 27, 1987.

51　His grades, in the 90s: Male High School academic records, 1913–14.

52　When she entered Louisville Collegiate: Henrietta's athletic successes are recorded in *The Transcript*, the school's student-run magazine, Dec. 1915 and Mar. 1916.

52　"He was in love with her": Interview, John Houseman, Feb. 4, 1987.

54　When he was well enough: BBS, "Is the Dining Car a Dinosaur in the Modern World?," *CJ*, June 23, 1957.

54　Another time, provoked by the taunts: MB to BBS, July 16, 1944, SL.

54　"My life at that age": BBS to MB, Apr. 2, 1944, SL.

55　He once promised to bring: Mrs. Nathan Bronstein to CJ, July 11, 1977.

55　"Isn't Barry the essence": *Courier-Journal Junior*, Dec. 9, 1917.

55　"Won't somebody take pity": *Courier-Journal Junior*, June 4, 1916.

55　"The rainbow is beautiful": *Poems by Barry Bingham* (privately printed, 1923), p. 3.

56　"healing breath of the pine": *Health Resorts of the South*, 1891, p. 234.

56　Mary Lily Kenan Flagler had been driven: *Asheville Citizen*, July 18, 1915.

57　To be sure, her own family: Details of the Kenan history and Mary Lily's early years are taken from A. C. Howell, *The Kenan Professorships* (Chapel Hill: University of North Carolina Press, 1956), pp. 4–10; William Rand Kenan Jr., *Incidents by the Way* (privately printed, 1946), pp. 9–21; Alvaretta Kenan Register, *The Kenan Family and Some Allied Families* (Statesboro, Ga., privately printed, 1967), pp. 47–54; and *The National Cyclopedia of American Biography* (New York: James T. White and Company, 1953), p. 427. Also see *Durham Morning Herald*, July 29, 1965, and *Raleigh News & Observer*, May 15, 1966.

57　She also had her share of beaus: Mrs. Eleanor Hope Cobb to *Time*, Feb. 25, 1936.

58　She met the creator of this improbable oasis: Details of Mary Lily's first meeting with Flagler can be found in Edward N. Akin, *Flagler: Rockefeller Partner & Florida Baron* (Kent, Ohio: The Kent State University Press, 1988), pp. 148–49; Noel Yancy, "The Kenan Legacy," *The Spectator* (Durham, N.C.), Mar. 20, 1986; and *Raleigh News & Observer*, June 9, 1963.

58　"quick to see an advantage": Ida M. Tarbell, *The History of The Standard Oil Company* (New York: Macmillan, 1925), pp. 50–51.

58　She held seances: Akin, *Flagler*, p. 148. Also see David Leon Chandler, *Henry Flagler: The Astonishing Life and Times of the Visionary Robber Baron Who Founded Florida* (New York: Macmillan, 1986), pp. 110–15.

58　He loved her singing: Interview, Thomas S. Kenan III, Nov. 10, 1986.

58　Soon, Mary Lily and her friend: Akin, *Flagler*, pp. 149–51; Chandler, *Henry Flagler*, pp. 117–18.

59　The couple grew closer and bolder: *The New York Times*, May 10, 1901.

59　"You've tainted her": Interview, Thomas S. Kenan III, Nov. 10, 1986.

59　By 1903, to no one's surprise: William Rand Kenan Jr., *Incidents by the Way*, pp. 51–53.

59　On August 24, 1901: Unable to jettison Alice in New York, which permitted divorce only on the grounds of adultery, Flagler established legal residence in Florida and was instrumental in the passage of a bill permitting divorce in that state on the grounds of insanity. He allegedly bribed some members of the legislature to pass the bill, which was signed into law on Aug. 13, 1901. See Akin, *Flagler*, pp. 149–51.

59 The groom arrived: *The New York Herald Tribune*, Nov. 15, 1959, and *The New York Times*, Nov. 7, 1976.

59 He even brought his own orchestra: Details of the wedding are taken from the Duplin *Times-Progress Sentinel*, Aug. 27, 1970, and *The Spectator* (Durham, N.C.), Mar. 13, 1986.

59 By the spring of 1902: Description of Whitehall and its distinguished guests taken from William Rand Kenan Jr., *Incidents by the Way*, pp. 14–15; *The New York Herald Tribune*, Nov. 15, 1959; *The New York Times*, Jan. 22, 1961, Nov. 7, 1976, and Feb. 7, 1980.

60 Mary Lily's cocktail: Interview, Thomas S. Kenan III, Nov. 10, 1986.

60 As a practical matter: Alcohol and opium use among Victorian women is detailed in John S. Haller Jr. and Robin M. Haller, *The Physician and Sexuality in Victorian America* (Urbana: University of Illinois Press, 1975), pp. 274–302.

60 No one heard him cry out: Flagler's accident, death, and funeral are described in Chandler, *Henry Flagler*, p. 262, and *The Atlanta Constitution*, May 21, 1913.

60 "born at the age of 15": *The Chapel Hill Weekly*, Oct. 28, 1962.

60 All the same, she wished: Interview, Thomas S. Kenan III, Nov. 10, 1986.

61 Dinners at Fernihearst: Mary Lily's social life during the summer and fall of 1915 is chronicled in *The Asheville Citizen*, July 8, 18, 27; Aug. 13, 17, 20, 21, 31; Sept. 8, 10, 12, 19, 26; and Oct. 2, 1915.

61 Reluctant to be accused of fortune hunting: A. C. Howell, *Kenan Professorships*, pp. 22–23.

61 Cupid's only conquest: *The Asheville Citizen*, Aug. 15, 1915.

61 Her new beau: Battle and Mary Lily are mentioned together in the social columns of *The Asheville Citizen* on July 27, Aug. 8, 13, 17; and Sept. 10, 1915.

   On Oct. 6, 1915, Col. Robert Bingham wrote to the president of the University of North Carolina, informing him that Mary Lily "is said to be about to marry Dr. Westry [sic] Battle," see A. C. Howell, *Kenan Professorships*, pp. 19–20.

   Description of Battle is taken from Samuel A. Ashe, ed., *Biographical History of North Carolina From Colonial Times to the Present*, vol. 6 (Greensboro: Charles L. Van Noppen, 1927), pp. 47–54, and William S. Powell, ed., *Dictionary of North Carolina Biography*, vol. 1 (Chapel Hill: University of North Carolina Press, 1979), p. 117.

62 In mid-August: Memorandum to Macmillan Publishing Co. from BBS, Apr. 27, 1987.

62 "young, radiant and full of life": Ethel Thacher to RWB, Aug. 5, 1917, The Filson Club.

62 Her dress, an afternoon gown: Details of the wedding are from *The New York Herald*, Nov. 16, 1916, and CJ, Nov. 16, 1916. Value of pearl necklace taken

from *Final Settlement in Re: Estate of Mary Lily Kenan Flagler Bingham*, Jefferson County Inventory and Settlement Book 152, Dec. 22, 1927.

63 The Ballards, the Whittys: Samuel W. Thomas, "Let the Documents Speak," *The Filson Club History Quarterly* 63, no. 3 (July 1989): 326. Watterson's lunch at the Pendennis Club is mentioned in the social column of the *CJ*, Nov. 26, 1916.

63 "wouldn't trade places with any woman in the world": Interview, Thomas S. Kenan III, Nov. 10, 1986.

63 Within three months of their marriage: Mary Lily's gifts to RWB are detailed in Transcript of Record, *Louisville Trust Co., etc.* v. *Robert W. Bingham and William R. Kenan and William A. Blount, Trustees*, Court of Appeals of Kentucky, Nov. 14, 1917, p. 78. Hereinafter called Transcript of Record.

By written agreement with Mary Lily, however, RWB got only the income from the securities; he did not own them. At her death, they reverted to her estate.

63 Even Sadie received: According to BBS, Sadie later decided to sell the necklace and was told that the pearls were "worthless paste" and that Mary Lily had been defrauded by a dishonest jeweler; see BBS memorandum to family members, Aug. 30, 1985. But the idea is improbable. An inventory of Mary Lily's estate reveals that she was a connoisseur of pearls and bought almost all her jewels at Tiffany & Co. Moreover, she had a history of extravagant gift-giving. It is more likely that it was Sadie, unschooled in fine jewelry, who was swindled by an opportunistic appraiser.

63 But he knew the honor: A. C. Howell, *Kenan Professorships*, p. 20.

64 The moment she saw the presents: Interview, Thomas S. Kenan III, Nov. 10, 1986.

64 The room where: *CJ*, Dec. 31, 1916.

64 "The Judge really ruined": Interview, John Houseman, Feb. 4, 1987.

64 She began to take long naps: According to Sophie Albert, a Louisville teenager at the time, BBS and his siblings saw "so very little of Mary Lily because she was always asleep." Interview, Sophie and Jacques Albert, Feb. 27, 1987.

65 On the advice of his physician friend: RWB to Herbert Hoover, May 28, 1917, BBS private papers. Mary Lily's alcoholism during her marriage to RWB is detailed in notes made by Hugh Young for his 1940 autobiography and contained in Memorandum to Macmillan Publishing Co. from BBS, Apr. 27, 1987.

65 Perhaps thinking that a return: *CJ*, July 28, 1917.

65 Soon after Mary Lily came back: Description of Lincliffe taken from Kentucky Historic Resources Inventory, Site No. JF-531.

65 For weeks, attendants unpacked: Mary Lily's possessions are detailed in *Appraisement of Household Goods in Re: Estate of Mary Lily Kenan Flagler Bingham*, Jefferson County Court, Feb. 1, 1919.

65 When the Binghams' four hundred guests: Accounts of the party can be found in *CJ*, June 10, 1917, and *Louisville Evening Post*, June 11, 1917.

66　Thrilled with the praise: In her book, *The Road to Dream Acre* (Louisville: The Standard Printing Company, 1928), Jennie C. Benedict writes that the Monday after the party, "Mrs. B_____" brought her "an exquisite platinum pin, set with forty-two beautiful diamonds" and told her that the charge for the dinner was so reasonable she had "added the price of an automobile to the check." See pp. 67–69.

66　The Judge, who suffered from eczema: Mary Lily may have also had skin disorders. Henry M. Flagler to Rev. J. N. MacGonigle, Aug. 24, 1903, and Sept. 16, 1903, the Henry M. Flagler Museum.

66　Bingham knew him to be an able physician: Ravitch was a long-standing member of the American Medical Association and, with two other "prominent Louisville medicos," spoke before its national convention in 1908. See RG 115, Jefferson County Medical Society Records.

　　By 1917, he was an assistant editor of the *Kentucky Medical Journal*, to which he contributed numerous articles, many of them co-authored with clinical pathologist Sol A. Steinberg.

66　His second wife's insanity: Allan M. Brandt, *No Magic Bullets: A Social History of Venereal Disease in the United States Since 1880* (New York: Oxford University Press, 1985), p. 9.

67　All four were negative: Grover Hutchins, M.D., to Mark Wilson, Mar. 31, 1987, in Memorandum to Macmillan Publishing Co. from BBS, Apr. 27, 1987.

67　Ironically, alcohol only exacerbated: Ravitch makes clear that victims of cardiovascular syphilis should not drink because, he says, the "aorta's resistance is lowered through use . . . of alcohol." See M. L. Ravitch and S. A. Steinberg, "Chronic Syphilitic Aortitis," *Kentucky Medical Journal* 15 (Apr. 1, 1917): 146–47.

67　According to one account: CJ, July 28, 1917, says "14 years ago Mrs. Bingham suffered an attack of heart trouble." According to her death certificate she had suffered from myocarditis, an inflammation of the heart muscle, since Sept. 1916.

67　"disastrous results have been encountered": M. L. Ravitch, "The So-Called Important Drugs Used in Dermatology," *The Journal of Cutaneous Diseases Including Syphilis* 35 (1913): 469.

　　Ravitch also urges caution with regard to Salvarsan, or arsphenamine, as it would be called today, in "Common Sense in Dermatology," *Kentucky Journal of Medicine* 13 (Oct. 1, 1915): 487, and with S. A. Steinberg, "Principles in the Modern Treatment of Syphilis," *Kentucky Journal of Medicine*, Dec. 1, 1915, pp. 588–91.

　　He was probably wise to be conservative. Early doses of Salvarsan were highly toxic. In 1914, 109 deaths were attributed to the drug. Although a less toxic compound was available in the U.S. by 1915, universal acceptance in the medical community did not come until the 1920s. See Brandt, *No Magic Bullets*, pp. 40–46.

67　Instead, he relied on mercury: Ravitch's articles in the *Kentucky Medical Jour-*

nal, 1913–17, make clear that he relied almost entirely on mercury to treat syphilis.

68   "a complete cure is a difficult thing": M. L. Ravitch and S. A. Steinberg, "Chronic Syphilitic Aortitis," *Kentucky Medical Journal* 15 (Apr. 1, 1917): 146–47.

68   After the housewarming party: Hannah Bolles is first mentioned as being at Lincliffe in *CJ*, May 27, 1917, and was at the residence during Mary Lily's final illness and death, according to *CJ*, July 28, 1917.

68   In two afternoon drives: Davies recounts his conversations with Mary Lily, the early drafts of the codicil, and the signing of the final document in Ravitch's office in Transcript of Record, Nov. 14, 1917, pp. 72–85.

68   In 1913, when her first husband: Akin, *Flagler*, p. 227.

69   "she was a woman" and "her brother William": Transcript of Record, Nov. 14, 1917, pp. 77, 82.

69   In early July, Judge Bingham purchased: RWB to W. W. Locke, secretary and treasurer, Cave Hill Cemetery Co., July 5, 1917, The Filson Club.

   Eleanor Miller Bingham was buried three times in three different locations in Cave Hill Cemetery: in the Miller family plot immediately after her death; in Lot 99, Section 13, purchased by RWB on Oct. 15, 1913; and finally in Lot 101, Section 13, purchased by RWB in 1917. RWB also bought Lots 84, 85, and 102 in the summer of 1917. See Cave Hill Cemetery records.

69   "severe attack": *CJ*, Sept. 24, 1917.

69   At some point, Walter Boggess: Boggess's medical background taken from *Polk's Medical Register and Directory of North America* (Baltimore: R. L. Polk & Co., 1917). See also Memorandum to Macmillan Publishing Co. from BBS, Apr. 27, 1987.

70   As for the baths: Mercury vapor baths were a common treatment for syphilitics. See Brandt, *No Magic Bullets*, p. 12.

70   "I love to think that you made her": Ethel Thacher to RWB, Aug. 5, 1917, The Filson Club.

70   The action shocked: Kentucky finally received $3,279,179 in taxes from Mary Lily's estate. See Summary of Response Document by Members of the Bingham Family to SB's *Passion and Prejudice*, Jan. 1989.

71   "Everybody thought Bingham": Interview, John Herchenroeder, Jan. 19, 1987.

71   Jacob had treated: RWB to Col. Robert Bingham, Dec. 5, 1904, The Filson Club.

71   As a result, relations with the Flexner family: Hugh Young recounts the feud in notes to his 1940 autobiography, contained in attachments to Summary of Response Documents by Members of the Bingham Family to SB's *Passion and Prejudice*, Jan. 1989.

   There are several inaccuracies in Young's account, however. He places the conflict around 1918, for instance, when it more likely happened in 1905, the year Flexner closed his school. He says that Flexner then left Louisville to join the Carnegie Foundation for the Advancement of Teaching, when in fact he left to study at Harvard and then Berlin and did not join Carnegie until 1908. And finally, Young says RWB brought court action against Flexner, although there is no record of litigation.

For more information on Flexner's school, see Abraham Flexner, *I Remember: The Autobiography of Abraham Flexner* (New York: Simon and Schuster, 1940). For RWB and Jacob Flexner's connection to Louisville Medical College, see catalogues 1904-1908, University of Louisville Medical School Library.

72   "Judging from the testimony": Transcript of Record, Nov. 14, 1917, p. 91.

72   Several days earlier: *The New York Tribune*, Sept. 21, 1917.

72   That left Davies: Davies testimony is included in full in Transcript of Record, Nov. 14, 1917, pp. 72–85.

73   "He could never rest": Interview, Thomas S. Kenan III, Nov. 10, 1986.

73   "the only detective of genius": *The Encyclopedia of American Crime.*

73   One of his agents' first acts: According to John Herchenroeder, a Louisville teenager in 1917 and, eventually, a city editor and ombudsman at the *CJ & T*, it was also rumored that political enemies of RWB had masterminded the break-in. Interview, John Herchenroeder, Jan. 19, 1987.

73   In late September, just as Bingham: *The New York Herald*, Sept. 21, 1917; *CJ*, Sept. 22 and 25, 1917; *The New York Tribune*, Sept. 22, 1917; *The Asheville Citizen*, Sept. 23, 1917.

73   "badly scared Negroes": Notes made on the case of Mrs. Mary Lilly (sic) Bingham by Hugh H. Young, Mar. 13, 1933, Alan Mason Chesney Medical Archives, The Johns Hopkins University Medical Institutions, contained in Memorandum to Macmillan Publishing Co. from BBS, Apr. 27, 1987.

73   "I'll never forget it": Interview, Sophie and Jacques Albert, Feb. 27, 1987.

73   Hugh Young later secured: Notes made on the case of Mrs. Mary Lilly (sic) Bingham by Hugh H. Young, Mar. 13, 1933.

The men involved in the autopsy were Dr. William G. MacCallum, author of *Textbook of Pathology* (1916) and then in-coming dean of Johns Hopkins Medical School; Dr. Charles Norris, director of laboratories at Bellevue and Allied Hospitals in New York and after 1918 chief medical examiner of New York City; and, from Chicago, Dr. Ludvig Hektoen of the Rush Medical College and director, McCormick Institute for Infectious Diseases. The chemistry work was performed by Alexander O. Gettler, Bellevue's chief chemist and later chief toxicologist.

74   The transaction cost: Southern Motors Co. to RWB, Aug. 23, 1917, The Filson Club. In May 1919, RWB bought a Packard Landaulette from Mary Lily's estate for $3,800. See *Final Settlement in Re: Estate of Mary Lily Kenan Flagler Bingham*, Jefferson County Inventory and Settlement Book 152, Dec. 22, 1927.

74   "Mary Lily's brother just said": Interview, Thomas S. Kenan III, Nov. 10, 1986.

74   Accordingly, on July 27, 1918: Mary Lily's estate paid the federal taxes but

RWB eventually paid $146,575 in Kentucky state inheritance tax. See S. W. Thomas, "Let the Documents Speak," p. 353.

74   Nor did the remaining millions: The fates of the various Kenans are taken from Akin, *Flagler*, pp. 230–35; Register, *The Kenan Family*, p. 47; *The New York Times*, Nov. 7, 1976; and Cholly Knickerbocker columns, Nov. 3, 1939, and Nov. 30, 1940.

As for the Russian-born Dr. Ravitch, he became infatuated with the Bolshevik Revolution in the months following Mary Lily's death, and later wrote a rhapsodic book about medicine in the era of Lenin and Stalin. Despite his alleged role in the "murder conspiracy," Ravitch's practice thrived. He remained in Louisville, treating patients and publishing articles, until 1923, eventually moving to Hollywood—no doubt a lucrative location for a dermatologist. See Michael Leo Ravitch, *The Romance of Russian Medicine* (New York: Leveright Publishing Corp., 1937), and American Medical Directories 1917–40.

75   According to Thomas Kenan III: The maid, Ida Remly, was, in fact, white, not Haitian. She continued in Judge Bingham's service after Mary Lily's death and in her old age was paid a pension by the family. See Emily Overman to BBS, Sept. 20, 1935, LOC.

Chapter 4 EDEN WAS A LONELY PLACE

76   In December, Henrietta: Stuart Hall records.

77   "I was obliged to goose-step": BBS, "Only Memories Remain of the Richmond School," *CJ*, Sept. 20, 1958.

77   "I marveled that with his wealth": Interview, Wilson Wyatt, Jan. 20, 1987.

77   He applied for the Officers Reserve Corps: RWB to Herbert Hoover, May 28, 1917, BBS private papers.

78   "Abstention in wartime": as quoted in Arthur Krock, *Memoirs: Sixty Years on the Firing Line* (New York: Funk & Wagnalls, 1968), pp. 45–48.

78   Perhaps he did not realize: Account of the Haldeman feud is taken from Denis Cusick, "Deja Vu," *Louisville Magazine*, Mar. 1986, and Joseph Frazier Wall, *Henry Watterson: Reconstructed Rebel* (New York: Oxford University Press, 1956), pp. 314–15.

78   "worthy of the paper's heritage": Krock, *Memoirs*, p. 43.

79   "no need to apologize": *CJ*, Aug. 7, 1918.

79   "justly and wisely": Louisville Fifty Years Ago: A Souvenir Issue, *CJ*, Mar. 9, 1923.

79   Ensconced at the Plaza: *Courier-Journal Junior*, Aug. 11, 1918.

80   "He was like Lord Chesterfield": Interview, Billy Keller, Jan. 24, 1987.

80   It seemed somehow fitting: Joe Ward, "The Binghams: Twilight of a Tradition," *CJ Magazine*, Apr. 20, 1986.

81   The library eventually contained: After RWB's death, BBS gave the collection of Joan of Arc books to the municipal library in the French city of Orleans. See *CJ*, May 8, 1952.

81 Up the broad, maroon-carpeted staircase: Judge Bingham's household effects and their locations are taken from Appraisement and Inventory, *Final Settlement of Executor in the Estate of Robert Worth Bingham*, Jefferson County Court, Apr. 22, 1938.

81 "He was so good": Interview, Sophie and Jacques Albert, Feb. 27, 1987.

81 He then enrolled: Tulane alumni records.

82 A social climber became: Interview, Sophie and Jacques Albert, Feb. 27, 1987.

83 "I am very eager": RWB to Frederick Winsor, Feb. 1, 1921, Middlesex records.

84 "Barry is a young boy": Preston Boyden to Frederick Winsor, Mar. 31, 1921, Middlesex records.

84 "sought out . . . minor transgressions": Philip Dunne '25, "In Memory of Sir, 1920–1925," Middlesex School *Bulletin*, Summer 1985.

84 The Middlesex regimen: Taken from John E. Knowlton '22, "Middlesex Remembered," Middlesex School *Bulletin*, Summer 1977.

85 By the end of Barry's first quarter: Report of George Barry Bingham, Class IV, Middlesex School, year ending June 9, 1921, Middlesex records.

85 "[Barry] is naturally appreciative": Ray Allison Spencer to RWB, 1921, Middlesex records.

85 "This is highly irregular": Frederick Winsor to RWB, Nov. 14, 1921, Middlesex records.

86 "His condition is not alarming": RWB to Frederick Winsor, Dec. 12, 1921, Middlesex records.

86 On the appointed night: BBS, "The Nimble Tread of the Feet . . . ," *CJ*, June 27, 1987.

86 But by the end of his junior year: Report of Barry Bingham, Class II, for term ending Mar. 22, 1923, Middlesex records.

87 During her long lifetime: Details of Mina Kirstein's life taken from Smith *Alumnae Quarterly*, Winter 1986; Smith alumnae records; and interview, John Houseman, Feb. 4, 1987.

88 "gentle, encompassing warmth": Interview, John Houseman, Feb. 4, 1987.

88 "the perfect oval of a Buddha": David Garnett, *The Golden Echo* (London: Chatto and Windus, 1962), pp. 9–10.

88 At a winter party: Ibid.

89 "the face of a Giotto Madonna": David Garnett, ed., *Carrington: Letters and Abstracts from Her Diaries* (London: Jonathan Cape, 1970), p. 254.

89 "I hardly ever speak": Ibid., p. 294.

90 "with a mixture of embarrassment": Interview, John Houseman, Feb. 4, 1987. See also John Houseman, *Run-Through: A Memoir* (New York: Simon and Schuster, 1972), pp. 55–56.

91 "The overwhelming experience of Harvard": BBS, "Harvard at 350," *CJ*, Sept. 8, 1986.

Chapter 5 BABY'S AWAKE NOW

93 Helena Caperton, a descendant: George William Montague, comp., *History and Genealogy of Peter Montague* (Amherst: Carpenter & Morehouse, 1894).

93 "one of the famous wits": *Richmond Times-Dispatch*, Oct. 16, 1932.

94 Receiving an invitation: Details about The German are taken from "Autumn Garner," a recollection by Sallie Montague Lefroy for her grandchildren, and Helena Lefroy Caperton, *A History and Record of the Richmond German* (Richmond: The Virginia Historical Society, 1939).

94 When Buffalo Bill: Helena Lefroy Caperton, "When the Wild West Came to Richmond," *The Richmond Quarterly* 7 (Summer 1984): 19–23.

95 The Richmond Mary Caperton knew: John A. Cutchins, *Memories of Old Richmond 1881–1944* (Verona, Va.: McClure Press, 1973), pp. 111–19.

97 "Looking back on my childhood:" MB to BBS, Dec. 10, 1944, SL.

98 "hold a baby on one knee": *Richmond Times-Dispatch*, Dec. 5, 1950.

99 "voluntarily and with good will": "Reflections of a 'Miss Jennie's Girl,' " St. Catherine's *Alumni Magazine*, Summer 1972.

99 "whose attainment, honor and influence": C. Dillon Barnett Jr., Director of Development, St. Catherine's, to Susan E. Tifft, Feb. 27, 1987.

99 "a more or less inattentive": Helena Lefroy Caperton, "How We Raised Our Six Daughters," *Women's Home Companion*, Dec. 1930.

100 Mary found that she was one of only two: The other Southerner in her class was also from Virginia. *Annual Report of the Dean*, 1928, Radcliffe College Archives.

100 " 'Harvard is a nursery' ": Undated speech by MB.

101 "I used a pen": Essay by MB written in 1968 for a volume of college reminiscences, Radcliffe College Archives.

103 "resound as the most stirring": BBS, "Harvard at 350," CJ, Sept. 8, 1986.

104 "a Prohibition concoction": BBS, "Too Good to Last," *Harvard Gazette* 82, no. 38 (June 5, 1987).

104 To buy it, Barry sometimes sold his lecture notes: A Symposium of the Harvard Class of 1928 on the Occasion of Their Fiftieth Reunion, June 6, 1978, p. 25.

104 "her love for John": BBS, "White Carnation," *The Harvard Advocate* 111, no. 9 (May 1925).

106 "a combination of blond beauty": BBS, "Too Good to Last," *Harvard Gazette* 82, no. 38 (June 5, 1987).

106 "I do wish I could always": BBS to MB, Mar. 24, 1931, SL.

108 They claimed they did not have the money: Sallie Bell, "Debutantes of Today," *The Black Swan: The Magazine of Virginia* 1, no. 10 (Dec. 1927).

108 "It looked as though the good times": Interview with BBS, June-July 1982, University of Louisville Oral History Project.

112 "who brushes her hair with a toothbrush": BBS to MB, Mar. 25, 1930, SL.

112 "we went out on the town": Ibid.

112 "I miss you so intensely": BBS to MB, Aug. 17, 1930, SL.

112 To dispel the notion: Interview, John Herchenroeder, Jan. 19, 1987.

113 "I don't know how long": MB to BBS, Oct. 29, 1930, SL.

113 "most numbing sense of loneliness": BBS to MB, Nov. 2, 1930, SL.

113 "I feel that you are naturally": MB to BBS, Nov. 18, 1930, SL.

114 "I realize that I've been a troublesome": BBS to MB, Dec. 2, 1930, SL.

114 "Despite all that has been written": BBS to MB, Mar. 24, 1931, SL.

114 Earlier that spring: Telephone interview, Helena Stevens, Oct. 16, 1987.

Chapter 6 THE FAMILY JEWELS

116 Of the seven dailies: "Mirror of a Century: *The Courier-Journal,* 1868 to 1968," *CJ,* Nov. 10, 1968.

117 "to satisfy and to subserve an ambition": as quoted in Oswald Garrison Villard, *The Disappearing Daily* (New York: Alfred A. Knopf, 1944), p. 270.

117 "It can lead one to believe": "Mirror of a Century," *CJ,* Nov. 10, 1968.

117 "feminine freaks" and "horsey girls": *CJ,* Mar. 12, 1919, and Mar. 7, 1918, respectively.

117 "their goddesses in the role": *CJ,* Aug. 27, 1918.

118 "Day after day we printed": RWB to BBS, Aug. 18, 1937, LOC.

118 "a fad" and a "petty conceit": "True Story of Watterson's Retirement," *CJ,* May 18, 1949.

118 "Watterson loved the Irish": as quoted in Villard, *The Disappearing Daily,* pp. 269–70.

118 Before the sale: Krock tells his version of the showdown with Bingham in *Memoirs,* pp. 49–50.

119 While Henry Ford's *Dearborn Independent:* Frederick Lewis Allen, *Only Yesterday: An Informal History of the 1920s* (New York: Harper & Row, 1931), pp. 53–54.

119 "un-American and un-patriotic": Michael Lesy, *Real Life: Louisville in the Twenties* (New York: Pantheon Books, 1976), pp. 95–96.

119 The winning reporter: "Dark Carnival," *American Heritage,* Oct. 1976; John Hohenberg, ed., *The Pulitzer Prize Story* (New York: Columbia University Press, 1959), pp. 264–68; Lesy, *Real Life,* p. 224.

120 To help put these new groups: Information about RWB and tobacco co-ops taken from RWB to Col. Edward M. House, Sept. 4, 1932, House Papers, Yale University Library; RWB to BBS, Aug. 18, 1937, LOC; Joseph C. Roberts, *The Story of Tobacco in America* (New York: Alfred A. Knopf, 1949), pp. 201–202; Bernard Baruch, *Bernard Baruch: The Public Years* (New York: Holt, Rinehart and Winston, 1960), p. 159; interview with BBS, Apr. 2, 1975, University of Louisville Oral History Project; and William E. Ellis, "Robert Worth Bingham and the Crisis of Cooperative Marketing in the Twenties," *Agricultural History* 56, no. 1 (Jan. 1982).

120 "Like all human beings": RWB to Col. Edward M. House, Dec. 4, 1936, House Papers, Yale University Library. Hereinafter called House Papers.

120 According to at least one account: Leighton, *Five Cities,* pp. 91–92.

121 "North Carolina mountain carpetbagger": *Congressional Record,* June 4, 1920, p. 8582.

121   "If the Democrats win here": RWB to Col. Edward M. House, Oct. 31, 1931, House Papers.

122   "a gentleman": Writing to Col. Edward M. House, July 5, 1932, RWB says: "In every great crisis I think any people does well to pin its faith to a gentleman. I believe the Revolutionary War would have resulted in failure if George Washington had not been a gentleman. I have no idea the Confederacy could have lasted as it did for those four years except for the fact that Gen. Lee was a gentleman, and I am very thankful that in this great crisis this country has an opportunity to rely on a gentleman." House Papers.

122   "to secure the Kentucky delegation": RWB to Col. Edward M. House, Nov. 5, 1931, House Papers.

122   "for pre-campaign expenses": RWB to Col. Edward M. House, Oct. 31, 1931, House Papers.

122   "That same year": Interview, John Herchenroeder, Jan. 19, 1987.

122   In late October 1932, Bingham checked into: Grover Hutchins, M.D., to Mark Wilson, March 31, 1987, in Memorandum to Macmillan Publishing Co. from BBS, April 27, 1987.

123   To his delight: RWB to Col. Edward M. House, Oct. 25, 1932, House Papers; interview, John Herchenroeder, Jan. 19, 1987.

123   "There are plenty of people": RWB to Shepard Bryan, Oct. 24, 1932, Bryan Papers, Southern Historical Collection, University of North Carolina at Chapel Hill.

123   The Judge had set his sights: Arthur M. Schlesinger, Jr., *The Crisis of the Old Order, 1919–1933* (Boston: Houghton Mifflin Company, 1956), p. 280; Raymond Moley with the assistance of Elliot A. Rosen, *The First New Deal* (New York: Harcourt, Brace & World, Inc., 1966), p. 86; Emanuel Levi to RWB, Jan. 17, 1933, LOC.

123   "alter ego": William E. Leuchtenberg, *The Perils of Prosperity, 1914–1932* (Chicago: The University of Chicago Press, 1958), p. 50.

123   "There is no doubt": RWB to Col. Edward M. House, Sept. 29, 1925, House Papers.

123   "I have never known you": RWB to Col. Edward M. House, Sept. 13, 1932, House Papers.

124   After peddling the story: Notes made on the case of Mrs. Mary Lilly (sic) Bingham by Hugh H. Young, Mar. 13, 1933.

124   "mysterious and suspicious circumstances": *Congressional Record*, Mar. 15, 1933, p. 491–94.

124   "longest time and the lowest rate": RWB to Col. Edward M. House, Feb. 6, 1923, House Papers.

124   "England has had about as much": Thomas Tollefson to President Roosevelt, Mar. 18, 1933, Robert W. Bingham Papers, File No. 123, The National Archives.

125   Furious, Hull cabled Bingham: State Department Document File Note, Oct. 27, 1934, Bingham Papers, The National Archives. Also CJ, Oct. 24, 1934.

125   From 1933 to 1936, he took: Edgar B. Nixon, ed., *Franklin D. Roosevelt and*

Foreign Affairs, Volume III: September 1935–January 1936 (Cambridge: The Belknap Press of Harvard University Press, 1969), p. 569.

126   By 1936, an ambassadorial allowance: Wilbur Carr, State Department, to RWB, July 1, 1936, Bingham Papers, The National Archives.

127   He and Phyllis danced at balls: RWB to Col. Edward M. House, June 19, 1934, House Papers.

127   When Judge Bingham offered to buy: Robert Bingham to RWB, June 3, 1936, LOC.

127   "It might come out publicly": RWB to BBS, Oct. 18, 1935, LOC.

128   "She knew that if she went": Interview, John Houseman. Feb. 4, 1987.

129   "You know I've no right": Garnett, *The Golden Echo*, p. 15.

129   Helen and Henrietta had met: Helen Hull Jacobs to Susan E. Tifft, Aug. 6, 1987. Also see *The New York Times*, Aug. 15, 1933.

129   "I don't believe I've ever seen": BBS to RWB, Oct. 3, 1935, LOC.

129   "Our friendship was a very placid": Helen Hull Jacobs to Susan E. Tifft, Aug. 24, 1987.

130   "more magnificent than anything": BBS to RWB, Oct. 22, 1935, LOC.

130   "on account of the health of his wife": *The Secret Diary of Harold L. Ickes: The First Thousand Days 1933–1936* (New York: Simon and Schuster, 1954), p. 567.

130   "to wind up the things": BBS to RWB, Nov. 18, 1936, LOC.

131   "I hate the thought": Ibid.

131   "It was a grand letter": RWB to BBS, Dec. 4, 1936, LOC.

Chapter 7 COMING OF AGE

135   "It was a particularly brilliant": BBS to MB, Sept. 23, 1943, SL.

136   "The Prince had an unerring instinct": BBS to Norman L. Johnson, Jan. 2, 1982, BBS private papers.

137   "The story in the newsroom": Interview, John Herchenroeder, Jan. 19, 1987.

138   "Flossie Flirt" dolls: "Mirror of a Century: *The Courier-Journal* 1868–1968," CJ, Nov. 10, 1968.

138   "stumped": BBS to RWB, Oct. 8, 1934, LOC.

138   "Unalterably opposed to entire plan": BBS to RWB, Oct. 7, 1934, LOC.

139   "Greatly relieved": Cable, BBS to RWB, Oct. 8, 1934, LOC.

139   "I am pleased and proud": BBS to RWB, Oct. 8, 1934, LOC.

139   "I am completely undecided": BBS to RWB, Nov. 4, 1934, LOC.

139   "You have built up two splendid papers": BBS to RWB, Oct. 8, 1934, LOC. BBS feared that the Judge's connection to *The Herald-Post* "would leak out just as it has done in the case of WAVE," referring to the acquisition of a competitor to the Bingham-owned station, WHAS, by Republican George Norton Jr., Aleen's nephew, in 1932, which sparked embarrassing allegations that Judge Bingham was assembling a family monopoly in Louisville. See *The Herald-Post*, Dec. 9, 1932.

140   "called off the *Herald-Post* matter": RWB to BBS, Oct. 15, 1934, LOC.

140   "tendency to prejudice": RWB to BBS, Nov. 5, 1934, LOC.

141   "much moved": RWB diary, LOC.

142   "has good qualities": RWB to MB, Mar. 16, 1935, MB private papers.

142   It was not until February 3, 1935: RWB diary, LOC.

143   "Nothing that embarrasses anybody": Kenneth Stuart and John Tebbel, *Makers of Modern Journalism* (New York: Prentice-Hall, 1952), p. 383.

143   "the worst feature [of work]": BBS to MB, Feb. 1, 1930, SL.

143   "disappointing that he should even": RWB diary, LOC.

144   "The more I talked to him": Ibid.

144   "You couldn't do better": Stuart and Tebbel, *Makers of Modern Journalism*, p. 380.

144   "I want to be a newspaper proprietor": RWB diary, LOC.

145   Lisle was a native Kentuckian: Interview with Lisle Baker, Apr. 28, 1981, University of Louisville Oral History Project.

146   "such a large lump in my throat": RWB diary, LOC.

146   There was "an audible cheer": BBS to RWB, Dec. 2, 1936, LOC.

146   The rain began on Christmas: George H. Yater, "A Flood of Memories," *Louisville Magazine*, Jan. 1987.

147   "I Dare You to Catch Me Not Smiling": Clyde F. Crews, "The '37 Flood: It May Have Been a Blessing in Disguise," *CJ*, Jan. 18, 1987.

147   Mark worked the newspapers like a general: Unpublished autobiography of Mark F. Ethridge, W. S. Ethridge Papers, Southern Historical Collection, University of North Carolina at Chapel Hill. Hereinafter called Ethridge autobiography.

148   "I do not thank you for *Gone With the Wind*": RWB to Margaret Mitchell, Feb. 16, 1937, LOC.

149   The following day, the Judge decided: RWB diary, LOC.

149   a "trustworthy" chauffeur: RWB to BBS, Sept. 14, 1936, LOC.

149   "like some damned jack-ass": *The Asheville Citizen*, Apr. 20, 1937.

149   "with full honor and dignity": RWB to Col. Edward M. House, June 4, 1937, House Papers.

151   "I've had a hard time": Transcript of transatlantic telephone conversation between RWB and Hull, Nov. 17, 1937, Bingham Papers, The National Archives.

151   "As I bent over him": *Hugh Young: A Surgeon's Autobiography*, p. 515.

151   President Roosevelt provided his special: Funeral details are taken from *CJ & T*, Dec. 19, 1937, and *CJ*, Dec. 20, 1937.

Chapter 8 A VERY SATISFACTORY LIFE

154   "[My father] has bequeathed me": BBS to President Roosevelt, Dec. 24, 1937, File 716, Franklin D. Roosevelt Library.

155   "My information," Brown said: Contained in W.D.H. to Stephen Early, March 31, 1939, File 1387, Franklin D. Roosevelt Library.

155   "[The Sunday magazine] not only": Interview with Lisle Baker, Apr. 28, 1981, University of Louisville Oral History Project.

155   "all for the betterment of Louisville": Ethridge autobiography, p. 108.

157   "One's children do not seem": MB to BBS, May 7, 1944, SL.

159   "Way down South": BBJ to BBS, Sept. 13, 1942, SL.

160   "I feel so deeply identified": BBS to MB, June 17, 1945, SL.

161   "The first key to strong national health": CJ, Apr. 13, 1941.

161   "deliberate assault": CJ, Apr. 23, 1941.

161   "Those objecting to the paper's conduct": Ibid.

162   "All of us were breathing fire": Jimmy Pope to BBS, Feb. 1, 1974, BBS private papers.

Chapter 9 WARTIME

166   "rich, personable Lieut. Barry Bingham": Time, Oct. 20, 1941.

166   Barry and Adlai had first come: John Bartlow Martin, Adlai Stevenson of Illinois (Garden City, N.Y.: Anchor Books, 1977), p. 180.

168   "You were looking so particularly lovely": BBS to MB, July 25, 1943, SL.

168   "When you'd get to doing business": Interview, Bill Walton, Aug. 23, 1986.

169   "nothing but a distant and decorous smile": BBS, "Even Bombs Are No Match for Show Business," CJ, Dec. 21, 1960.

169   "I think it very unlikely": Interview, Bill Walton, Aug. 23, 1986.

170   "The greatest joy in life": MB to BBS, Jan. 31, 1944, SL.

170   "It sounds so attractive": MB to BBS, Sept. 23, 1942, SL.

170   On her first day, she "marched off": MB to BBS, Sept. 16, 1942, SL.

170   "she may turn out to be a more efficient": MB to BBS, Jan. 3, 1943, SL.

171   Later, Sallie would say: Newsday, Aug. 7, 1986.

171   "He nearly jumps out of his skin": MB to BBS, Mar. 10, 1943, SL.

171   "I know that I have probably": MB to BBS, Nov. 29, 1944, SL.

171   "It all sounds offensively": MB to BBS, Sept. 27, 1942, SL.

171   "To Sallie!": MB to BBS, Jan. 24, 1943, SL.

172   "The only thing to do": MB to BBS, July 26, 1945, SL.

172   "I knew in my heart they were not worthy": SB, "Growing Up an Episcopalian," Mademoiselle, Mar. 1970.

172   "as though they had a good deal": BBS to MB, June 5, 1943, SL.

173   "I'm afraid he has . . . absolutely no idea": MB to BBS, Jan. 3, 1943, SL.

173   "But, Mother, isn't that a rather common name?": MB to BBS, Apr. 24, 1945, SL.

173   "Barry was in the midst": MB to BBS, June 16, 1945, SL.

173   "It has an eerie and rather frightening": MB to BBS, Apr. 22, 1943, SL.

174   "God will, God will not": Ibid.

174   "Do you think it is possible": BBS to MB, May 2, 1943, SL.

175   When Barry Jr. shot Curtis: MB to BBS, Mar. 10, 1943, SL.

176   "a creature of . . . forlornity": The tale of Worth's transgression is taken from MB to BBS, Apr. 12, 1944, SL.

176   "normally aggressive, normally egocentric": Speech by MB before a joint meeting of the Council of Jewish Women and the Y.W.C.A., Oct. 11, 1962.

177   "I wore Sallie Bingham's clothes": Interview, Melinda Page Hamilton, Oct. 13, 1986.

177   "If you were not the most generous": MB to BBS, Apr. 23, 1944, SL.

177   "I'm afraid I rouse": MB to BBS, July 13, 1943, SL.

178   "All of us who grew up": MB to BBS, Aug. 6, 1944, SL.

178   "In peacetime," he said: MB to BBS, Apr. 18, 1943, SL.

179   "She has a sharp, shrewd eye": MB to BBS, Dec. 10, 1944, SL.

180   "This effort of mine": MB to BBS, Sept. 20, 1942, SL.

180   "Mary, let's call up Barry": Ethridge autobiography, p. 151.

180   "He's a God-damned son-of-a-bitch": Ibid.

180   "I have always wanted the *Courier*": BBS to MB, Jan. 17, 1943, SL.

180   "[*The Louisville Times*'s editor] said the other day": Mark Ethridge to BBS, Jan. 11, 1943, SL.

181   One day he encountered: Interview, Mary Phyllis Riedley, Feb. 27, 1987.

181   a real "Toonerville number": MB to BBS, Sept. 23, 1942, SL.

181   "I'm afraid I am a very unnatural mama": MB to BBS, June 13, 1945, SL.

181   "I believe I can manage": MB to BBS, Sept. 20, 1943, SL.

182   "I cannot hide the fact": MB to BBS, Oct. 21, 1942, SL.

182   "The quite bald and simple truth": MB to BBS, Jan. 23, 1944, SL.

183   When she learned what her husband had done: A more daunting obstacle may have been the U.S. Army, which forbade women to cover the invasion. Gellhorn managed to stow away on the first hospital ship to arrive off the beach at Normandy and filed stories to *Collier's* anyway. See Julia Edwards, *Women of the World: The Great Foreign Correspondents* (New York: Ivy Books, 1988), p. 124.

184   "It had to be done this way": BBS to MB, June 11, 1944, SL.

184   "There was a feeling that Americans": Telephone interview, John Templeton-Cotill, Sept. 7, 1989.

185   "I was more heavily assailed": BBS to MB, Sept. 8, 1944, SL.

185   "It is the very most lovely": MB to BBS, Nov. 19, 1944, SL.

185   "a pretty sharp feeling of anguish" and "It does not shine": MB to BBS, Dec. 25, 1944, SL.

185   "I am bigoted enough": MB to BBS, Mar. 2, 1944, SL.

185   "The choice [of boarding school]": BBS to MB, Apr. 9, 1944, SL.

186   "horror-loving imagination": MB to BBS, Feb. 28, 1944, SL.

186   "All the masters are married": MB to BBS, May 19, 1944, SL.

186   "I am already beginning to think": MB to BBS, July 29, 1944, SL.

186   "low and . . . narrowly partisan": MB to BBS, July 16, 1944, SL.

187   "The President seems convicted": MB to BBS, July 22, 1944, SL.

187   But in a veiled admission: Ethridge autobiography, pp. 163–73.

187   "I think you have made": Ibid.

187   "I didn't get you up here": Ibid.

187   "I am a stern and disciplining parent": MB to BBS, Sept. 4, 1944, SL.
187   "The conduct and attitude": BBS to MB, Sept. 8, 1944, SL.
188   "There was a sudden swish": MB to BBS, Sept. 23, 1944, SL.
188   "He does love his home comforts": MB to BBS, Feb. 28, 1944, SL.
188   "I cannot say that there has been": MB to BBS, July 25, 1944, SL.
188   "I by some mastake [sic]": BBJ to Nursie, Oct. 1, 1944, SL.
188   Now, in his dreary cubicle: MB to BBS, July 29, 1944; and MB to BBS, Nov. 19, 1944, SL.
189   "waves of color": MB to BBS, Nov. 19, 1944, SL.
189   "model boarding school career": BBS to MB, Nov. 25, 1944, SL.
189   "I think Worth is": MB to BBS, Dec. 20, 1944, SL.
189   "I feel quite capable": BBS to MB, Dec. 4, 1944, SL.
189   Little girls, Mary felt: MB to BBS, Dec. 3, 1944, SL.
189   It was hardly surprising that: MB to BBS, Oct. 25, 1944, SL.
189   "I believe that blue-stockingness": MB to BBS, Aug. 15, 1944, SL.
190   "I had hardly realized": MB to BBS, Oct. 1, 1944, SL.
190   "I think that the thing that must be avoided": MB to BBS, Apr. 18, 1945, SL.
190   "pleased at her fine efforts": MB to BBS, Aug. 25, 1944, SL.
190   "with long, loving strokes": MB to BBS, July 25, 1945, SL.
190   "It would have been nonsense": BBS to MB, May 13, 1945, SL.
190   "banished, as poor Romeo": MB to BBS, Nov. 29, 1944, SL.
191   "However this decision came about": MB to BBS, Dec. 25, 1944, SL.
191   "I believe of all our goodbyes": MB to BBS, Mar. 13, 1945, SL.
191   "passionate regret" and "anguish and heartbreak": MB to BBS, Mar. 21, 1945, SL.
191   "I want the maximum amount": BBS to MB, Oct. 17, 1943, SL.
192   "It would mean a grind": RWB to BBS, Oct. 1, 1934, LOC.
192   "It made me quail": BBS to MB, July 1, 1945, SL.
193   "I can truthfully say": BBS to MB, July 15, 1945, SL.
193   "I am seriously contemplating": Ibid.
193   "I couldn't find anyone": BBS, "Victory Came to Piccadilly, But Not to the Pacific," CJ, May 9, 1965.
194   "It was such an anticlimax": Interview with BBS, June-July 1982, University of Louisville Oral History Project.
194   "Practically every one of us cried": Interview, Sophie and Jacques Albert, Feb. 27, 1987.
195   "Wherever we go, the thought": BBS to MB, Aug. 25, 1945, SL.

Chapter 10 RETURN TO NORMALCY

197   "Now there is no doubt": Internal Time memo, Feb. 21, 1946.
197   "It was nirvana": Interview, John Richards, June 21, 1987.
198   "Nobody, not even in the newspaper business": Internal Time memo, Feb. 21, 1946.

198 "the real boss": FBI memorandum, Oct. 24, 1942.

198 "Mark Ethridge made the paper": Interview, Molly Clowes, Feb. 23, 1987.

199 "He had a presence": Interview, Maury Buchart, Apr. 26, 1987.

200 For public consumption: *The New York Times*, Sept. 29, 1948, and *CJ*, June 12, 1986.

201 "For the younger child in a big family": Michael Kirkhorn, "The Bingham Black Sheep," *Louisville Magazine*, June 1979.

202 "It's one of those partnerships": Alanna Nash, "The Woman Who Overturned an Empire," *Ms.* magazine, June 1986.

202 "Do you remember how we used to notice": MB to BBS, June 13, 1945, SL.

203 "[Even now] we are hard-pressed": Interview, Mary Clowes Taylor, Feb. 26, 1987.

203 She picked up *The Pied Piper of Hamelin*: MB to BBS, Apr. 18, 1945, SL.

205 "Sallie's later attitude [of being unloved]": Interview, Molly Clowes, Jan. 19, 1987.

206 "I was so busy [in Paris]": Interview with BBS, June-July 1982, University of Louisville Oral History Project.

206 His best subject was Bible study: Phillips Exeter academic records.

207 "very untidy, unpunctual": Application to Lawrenceville School, Jan. 1, 1949, Lawrenceville School records.

207 "uncooperative, unfriendly and very inattentive": Bill Saltonstall to BBS, Dec. 18, 1948, Lawrenceville School files.

208 "He is a boy who may be reacting": Thurston Chase to Fred A. Eichelberger, Dec. 21, 1948, Lawrenceville School files.

209 "I am a little concerned at leaving him": MB to Allan Heely, Apr. 29, 1949, Lawrenceville School files.

210 "It was hard to swallow this revolutionary idea": Worth Bingham to Allan Heely, Sept. 27, 1949, Lawrenceville School files.

211 In the fall of 1949, he had written: BBS to Richard Gummere, Sept. 27, 1949, Lawrenceville School files.

211 "That was when the needle really went in": *Kentucky Opera News* 3, no. 3 (Jan. 1987).

213 "The Lord preserve me": SB, *Passion and Prejudice* (New York: Alfred A. Knopf, 1989), p. 263.

214 "Why leisurely Louisville should be blessed": "The Prudent Publishers," *Fortune*, Aug. 1950.

214 "He was a Machiavellian character": Interview, John Ed Pearce, Feb. 25, 1987.

215 "Mr. Bingham and the Ethridges seemed to have": Interview, Mary Phyllis Riedley, Feb. 27, 1987.

215 To thank the Ethridges for their hospitality: Ethridge autobiography, p. 287.

215 "I have only read a little": MB to BBS, Apr. 1, 1944, SL.

216 "I really can't imagine when I look at her": MB to BBS, Mar. 14, 1943, SL.

216 "Barry has one weakness": Interview, Norman Isaacs, June 22, 1986.

216   "I don't think he ever understood": Interview, John Ed Pearce, Feb. 25, 1987.
217   "I would call it enlightened despotism": Interview, Jean Howerton Coady, Mar. 2, 1987.
217   "Mark's conferences were better": Interview, Molly Clowes, Jan. 19, 1987.
217   "We'd ask him, 'What did you discuss' ": Ibid.
218   After Stevenson lost to Eisenhower: The others on the world tour were *Look* magazine writer Bill Attwood, University of Chicago professor Walter Johnson, and Stevenson's personal secretary Bill Blair.
218   As news of the decision was read: *New York Post*, Sept. 16, 1956.
218   Less than two hundred miles away: "A Quiet Social Revolution in a Gateway to the South," *The New York Times Book Review*, Aug. 23, 1957.
219   "It amazes me that any child": MB to BBS, July 14, 1945, SL.
221   "I told him that Jimmy Pope was a bigot": Interview, Mary Phyllis Riedley, Feb. 27, 1987.

Chapter 11 AN AMERICAN IDYLL

222   "It was an idyllic life": Interview, Marietta Tree, Jan. 17, 1987.
223   "Certainly no out-of-town guest": CJ, May 3, 1981.
223   Appalled by Kentucky's high illiteracy rate: Information about Mary's bookmobile project comes from *Time*, Aug. 17, 1953; *Library Journal*, Sept. 15, 1953; CJ, June 6, 1954, and Oct. 20, 1955; and LT, Sept. 17, 1954.
223   "I don't think there was a lack of love": Interview, Catherine Luckett, Jan. 23, 1987.
224   "He could make up rhyming operettas": Interview, Tani Cutchins Vartan, Jan. 27, 1987.
225   "That's Jonathan": Interview, David Morton, Jan. 31, 1987.
226   "She was a fat, dirty-faced kid": Ibid.
227   Like Barry Jr., Jonathan became manager: Brooks School yearbook, 1960.
227   He got C's and D's in English: Brooks School records.
228   "those horrible people from Long Island": Interview, Charles E. Bascom, June 3, 1987.
228   "Jonathan didn't toe the line": Interview, Joe Hammer, May 5, 1987.
228   "He was somewhat of a Gatsby figure": Ibid.
229   "every cherry in town": Alanna Nash, "The Woman Who Overturned an Empire," *Ms.* magazine, June 1986.
230   Once, at a Boston party, he unzipped: SB, *Passion and Prejudice*, p. 282.
230   When Boston Psychiatric Hospital: Interview, Charles J. Egan, July 5, 1990.
230   "I was his second Papa": Interview, Norman Isaacs, June 22, 1986.
231   Late one summer, Joe Creason: Joe Creason, "Kentucky's Forbidden Land," *CJ Sunday Magazine*, Aug. 19, 1951.
231   His SATs were poor: Brooks School records.
231   "I for one will never forget": BBJ to Fessenden Wilder, Mar. 16, 1964.
232   "I said to myself, 'If that little black box' ": Frances C. Locher, ed., *Contemporary Authors*, Vol. 106 (Detroit: Gale Research Company), p. 58.

232 "gorgeous and divine": Interview, Melinda Page Hamilton, Oct. 13, 1986.

232 "He was an absolutely charming, delightful boy": Interview, Marietta Tree, Jan. 17, 1987.

233 "not so unreasonable": Transcript of Young Churchmen's meeting prepared by Mrs. James Pitman Sams, Mar. 13, 1951.

233 One short story written in high school: "Sand Castles," *The Transcript*, Louisville Collegiate School, 1954.

234 "a bitch in heat": SB, *Passion and Prejudice*, p. 323.

234 "We led sheltered lives": Interview, Mary Clowes Taylor, Feb. 26, 1987.

234 When her freshman creative writing professor: Interview, Jane O'Reilly, Sept. 2, 1986.

235 "What a shame!": SB, "Notes on a Freshman's Diary," 1968, Radcliffe Archives.

235 "They all seemed more iron-willed": Ibid.

236 "wondered how much of her desire was passion": SB, "Winter Term," *Mademoiselle*, July 1958.

236 "all sex and wants to be": Jonathan Kozol, *The Fume of Poppies* (Boston: Houghton Mifflin Co., 1958), p. 7.

236 Arthur Kopit, a Harvard contemporary: CJ, Feb. 26, 1989.

236 "I like distances": SB, "The Flavor of Solitude," *Mademoiselle*, June 1959.

237 "I don't know who that is": SB's quote according to BBS.

237 Why, the Ellsworths lived at One Sutton Place: Information on the Ellsworths comes from obituary of Duncan Steuart Ellsworth in *The New York Times*, Dec. 4, 1967.

238 While in one of the antique shops: Appendices, Response by Members of the Bingham Family to *Passion and Prejudice*, p. 31.

238 Worth went along, so family legend has it: BBJ denies that he seriously entertained notions of staying in Africa.

238 A hotel manager in the Congo: Details of the trip taken from BBJ to Mr. and Mrs. Fessenden Wilder, Oct. 8, 1958.

238 Two flower girls and four bridesmaids: CJ, Sept. 28 and Oct. 5 and 12, 1958. Also *The New York Times*, Oct. 12, 1958.

Chapter 12 THE HEIR RETURNS

242 "This young man turned out to be the stereotype": As quoted in a *Time* file, 1960.

243 "For Pete's sake, listen to what I say": Norman Isaacs to Worth Bingham, Jan. 13, 1957.

243 "I feel that everyone else is more worried": Worth Bingham to Norman Isaacs, Jan. 26, 1957.

243 "Once Worth got that thing": Interview, Norman Isaacs, June 22, 1986.

247 Each morning, a beaker of fresh orange juice: The food served to Big House guests comes from William Pahlmann, "Kentucky Home," Publishers-Hall Syndicate, Jan. 2, 1972, BBS private papers.

248   The Stevens family imported their own pastor: Details of the wedding taken from *CJ*, Feb. 7, 1960; *The New York Times*, Feb. 14, 1960; and *San Francisco Chronicle*, Feb. 23, 1960.

250   That November, when Kennedy won: BBS is mentioned as a possible candidate for the Court of St. James's in *The New York Times*, Jan. 8, 1961.

250   "The President liked Barry a lot": Interview, Bill Walton, Aug. 23, 1986.

252   Every week, he and two other trainees: Frances C. Locher, ed., *Contemporary Authors*, Vol. 106, p. 59.

253   "He was a *vitellone*": Telephone interview, Diana Fetter de Villafranca, May 28, 1987.

255   "You'd think you had him in a weak spot": Interview, John Richards, June 21, 1987.

257   "Since Mr. Ethridge's efforts to secure an interest": Memorandum, SAC-Louisville to Director, FBI, Nov. 29, 1962.

257   "She beat my ear": Interview, John Richards, June 21, 1987.

257   She thought Mark had been treated shabbily: Regardless of her other complaints, it was unfair of Willie Snow to hold up *The Washington Post* as an example of generosity, since the main reason that paper's editors became millionaires was because they owned stock when the company went public —a fortunate accident of timing. Had Mark been given stock in the *CJ & T*, he would have become wealthy only if the papers went public or were sold. Both were unlikely events at the time.

258   "the world's greatest living, working newspaperman": *CJ & T*, Sept. 8, 1963.

258   "He made it possible for *The Courier-Journal* and *Times*": Ethridge autobiography, p. 101.

258   "I will always be proud of these papers": Ibid, pp. 438–40.

259   "I feel sort of like a fellow": Ibid.

Chapter 13 DEATH OF A DREAM

261   In 1964, two years after leaving NBC: BBJ to Fessenden Wilder, Mar. 16, 1964.

261   "nor did they deserve more than they got": BBJ to Alex S. Jones, Sept. 11, 1989.

262   "Some people may doubt that we made a good business decision": BBJ to Fessenden Wilder, Sept. 22, 1966.

263   "The only people who listened to it": Interview, Bob Morse, Apr. 24, 1987.

263   "When things go wrong on trips": Interview, Ian Henderson, Apr. 23, 1987.

264   Morton attacked Wyatt for his leadership: Wilson Wyatt Sr., *Whistlestops: Adventures in Public Life* (Lexington: The University Press of Kentucky, 1985), p. 172.

264   "When he said 'Shit!' ": Interview, John Richards, June 21, 1987.

265   "Mary was in a state of great anxiety": Interview, Molly Clowes, Feb. 23, 1987.

265 "There isn't another Bingham": Interview, Mary Phyllis Riedley, Feb. 27, 1987.

265 He also thought that top managers should get: But in 1957 and again in 1959, the CJ & T company did buy shares of common stock in Photon, Inc., as a means of giving options to several top executives. Photon made typesetting equipment—the precursor of computer typesetting.

266 When several Louisville brahmins formed: "The Eleven Men Behind Cassius Clay," *Sports Illustrated*, Mar. 11, 1963.

266 The previous year, over Christmas: Frank Ashburn to BBS, Jan. 9, 1959.

266 "Jonathan was a charming child": Interview, Molly Clowes, Feb. 23, 1987.

267 He immediately arranged for a vocational test: BBS to Frank Ashburn, Dec. 30, 1958.

267 "My guess is that this [desire]": Frank Ashburn to BBS, Jan. 9, 1959.

267 "They were famous in the Yard": Interview, Charles E. Bascom, June 3, 1987.

267 "It would be nothing for Jonathan": Interview, Joe Hammer, May 5, 1987.

268 When Sallie and Whitney invited him over: Interview, Charles E. Bascom and Ellery Sedgwick III to Susan E. Tifft, Sept. 22, 1989.

268 "because if you're a surgeon": Interview, Catherine Luckett, Jan. 23, 1987.

268 "Dawn is breaking over the Yard": Jonathan Bingham to Catherine Luckett, Oct. 12, 1960.

269 "Tomorrow," he said: According to interview with David Morton, Jan. 31, 1987.

269 "I think he felt quite threatened": Interview, Tani Cutchins Vartan, Jan. 27, 1987.

269 No longer did Jonathan experience rebellious glee: SB, *Passion and Prejudice*, p. 341.

270 "general ennui with coursework": Ellery Sedgwick III to Susan E. Tifft, Sept. 22, 1989.

270 "It was a good place to feel comfortable": Interview, Tani Cutchins Vartan, Jan. 27, 1987.

271 "I feel pretty isolated down here": Jonathan Bingham to Embry Rucker, Feb. 16, 1964.

272 "Are you all right?": This quote and other details about the accident come from CJ, Mar. 8, 1964, and Autopsy No. A 64-117, Louisville General Hospital, Department of Pathology, Mar. 7, 1964.

272 "It was so horrible, so pathetic": Interview, Sophie and Jacques Albert, Feb. 27, 1987.

273 "His accident was one of those freaks": BBJ to Fessenden Wilder, Mar. 16, 1964.

273 "They made us feel at home": Interview, Joe Hammer, May 5, 1987.

274 "Here, can you use this?": According to telephone interview with Helena Stevens, Oct. 16, 1987.

276 L.B.J. sent Barry Sr. a personal note: Lyndon B. Johnson to BBS, Sept. 14, 1964, Lyndon Baines Johnson Library.

276 "I am deeply grateful for your support": Lyndon B. Johnson to BBS, Oct. 8, 1964, Lyndon Baines Johnson Library.

276   "Barry has a considerable opinion": Interview, Molly Clowes, Jan. 19, 1987.

276   About a week after Johnson's inauguration: In January 1965, Rowan's first choice was Ralph McGill, the racially liberal editor of *The Atlanta Constitution;* BBS was listed as number two. By March, BBS had become his top pick, mainly because he had "traveled widely and demonstrated concern about foreign policy." See Memorandum, John W. Macy Jr. to Lyndon B. Johnson, Jan. 29, 1965, and Memorandum, Carl T. Rowan to the President, Mar. 26, 1965, Lyndon Baines Johnson Library.

277   "intensely interested in government service": Memo for the record, William Little, Department of State, Apr. 1, 1965, Lyndon Baines Johnson Library.

277   A year from now, Macy advised: Memo for the record, John W. Macy Jr., Apr. 15, 1965, Lyndon Baines Johnson Library.

277   "The great majority of the American people": CJ, Dec. 30, 1965.

277   Weldon said he was unhappy: On Apr. 2, 1966, about two weeks before his "To Hell with Ho!" column appeared, Weldon sent a confidential letter of resignation to BBS. In it, he bluntly told BBS that

you have spread yourself so thin . . . with your countless commitments to admirable causes everywhere . . . that you can not [sic] have had the time to . . . ponder the fact that in this building the qualities of fire and grace have been diminishing almost to the zero level. The lesser men to whom you have been delegating more and more of the responsibilities you and Mark once shared demonstrate the truth of James Conant's dictum that there is no substitute for the first-class man.

In my own case the fairly rapid erosion of my once considerable influence on our editorial councils dates from the time two of our executives went to a frightened lecture, read a frightened paper, and appeared overnight as frightened experts with a simple solution for Southeast Asia: U.S. withdrawal. The invidious suggestion then and later that my views owed more to my ties with the Marine Corps than to reason and logic could scarcely fail to influence Worth . . . and I am not at all sure it has not influenced you. At any rate, it was not long before Worth asked me to "soften" one editorial [that] I was aware . . . that our once forthright editorial expressions on foreign policy were gradually becoming more and more Hamlet-like.

I do not mean for that to sound like a vote of no-confidence in Worth. . . . I admire his combination of conscientiousness and tough-mindedness. He is already a first-class newspaperman. . . . You are already entitled to be proud of him. . . .

But the immediate situation is one in which I see no livable future for myself. Somewhere along the way you and I lost our old ease and frequency of communication. . . . I write this with a heavy heart.

As ever,
Weldon James
Associate Editor

278 On hot summer days: *LT*, Apr. 22, 1976.

279 "It's a monopoly": Interview, Cy MacKinnon, Apr. 26, 1987.

279 "She had a notepad": Interview, Sophie and Jacques Albert, Feb. 27, 1987.

280 "Worth was appointed to hold his family": Interview, Wayne Sargent, 1986.

281 "By the time we hit National": Interview, Harvey and Kathy Sloane, Feb. 22, 1987.

281 "The weather here is gorgeous": Norman Isaacs, "A Promising Career Cut Short," *CJ*, July 13, 1966.

281 The edge hit Worth with a sudden, karatelike blow: Many details of the accident are taken from *CJ*, July 13, 1966; *The New York Times*, July 13, 1966; *The Nantucket Athenaeum*, July 14, 1966; and Certificate of Death, Town of Nantucket, July 12, 1966.

282 "There was nothing we could do": Interview, Norman Isaacs, June 22, 1986.

283 The last time she had seen her brother: Interview, Irene Nolan, Feb. 26, 1987.

283 "There were trumpets": Interview, Mary Clowes Taylor, Feb. 26, 1987.

285 "To have these golden people": Interview, Melinda Page Hamilton, Oct. 13, 1986.

Chapter 14 MR. CLEAN'S NEWSPAPERS

286 "Barry," he said softly: According to interview with Norman Isaacs, June 22, 1986.

287 "There was never any question": Interview, Melinda Page Hamilton, Oct. 13, 1986.

288 "It was an electricity": Interview, Mary Phyllis Riedley, Feb. 27, 1987.

289 "He could be brutal": Interview, George Gill, June 22, 1987.

289 "Deep down, I don't think he [liked him]": Interview, John Richards, June 21, 1987.

289 "If you can teach my children what depreciation is": Interview, Cy MacKinnon, Apr. 26, 1987.

290 "My knowledge of journalism is so limited": BBJ to Fessenden Wilder, Sept. 22, 1966.

290 "Did you ever wonder why we've got Jews": Interview, George Gill, June 22, 1987.

290 One of his first editorial efforts: BBJ to Fessenden Wilder, May 19, 1967.

It was Barry Sr., however, who wrote most of the papers' Vietnam editorials during this period. "He did not feel that he could entrust anyone on the editorial staff [to] represent his exact feelings," Barry Jr. explained.

Those feelings changed rapidly after the Tet Offensive in late January 1968. Sometime that winter, BBS walked into an editorial board meeting and said he had written an editorial announcing a new policy for the papers: The *CJ & T* was now squarely against the war. The reason behind the switch probably had less to do with the carnage of Tet, however, than with the new editorial stance of *The New York Times*. In the years before Tet, the *Times* had moved from measured support for military intervention to advocacy of a negotiated settlement. After Tet, the paper became much more pessimistic and began to insist on settlement and withdrawal. On Feb. 8, 1968, the *Times* declared that "neither side is entitled any longer to illusions about military victory." The change in the *Times*'s stance gave Barry Sr. the comfort of good company and he duly mimicked the paper's position on the editorial pages of the *CJ & T*.

291 "Messrs. Clean" of journalism: *Wall Street Journal*, July 11, 1974.

292 The peculiar result was two memoranda: Memoranda, BBS to Robert Clark and George Gill, Aug. 29 and Sept. 5, 1969.

293 He left Louisville in 1970, cushioned: The $25,000 consulting contract was to last only until his sixty-fifth birthday. Memo to Norman Isaacs, Apr. 24, 1970, BBS private papers.

293 "I'm going to be all alone": BBS quote according to interview with Norman Isaacs, June 22, 1986.

293 "Norman was mostly baloney": Interview, Cy MacKinnon, Apr. 26, 1987.

294 "He said he was a nigger": Interview, George Gill, June 22, 1987.

294 "Bob was like a pillow": Interview, John Richards, June 21, 1987.

295 "The policy really did deprive us": Interview, John Ed Pearce, Feb. 25, 1987.

296 At *The Courier-Journal* and *Times*, letters-to-the-editor: Interview, Molly Clowes, Feb. 23, 1987.

296 "He came within an eyelash of dying": Interview, Ian Henderson, Apr. 23, 1987.

296 "After seeing that, his secretary said": Interview, Keith Runyon, Jan. 22, 1987.

299 "Don't make a bid until you see me": *Fortune*, June 19, 1978.

299 "If income from the conventioneers": *CJ*, June 11, 1972.

299 "Our dire prediction of tumult": *CJ*, Aug. 6, 1972.

299 Reaction in Louisville was so pronounced: *The New York Times*, Jan. 3, 1973; *LT*, Jan. 5 and 6, 1973.

300 "He'd come here to a meal": Interview, Wig MacKinnon, Apr. 26, 1987.

300 By 1973, the breakneck schedule had taken: BBS to W.E. Chilton III, Mar. 12, 1973, BBS private papers.

300 "He would sit at that easel": Interview, George Gill, June 22, 1987.

301 "Everyone believed that Barry came in": Interview, Irene Nolan, Feb. 26, 1987.

302 "Everybody outside the paper": Interview, Maury Buchart, Apr. 26, 1987.

303 "It's perfectly possible for a person": Interview, Norman Isaacs, June 22, 1986.

303 "Anything [the news side] did was OK": Interview, Bernie Block, Apr. 24, 1987.

303 A *Louisville Times* columnist wrote sneeringly: *LT*, Nov. 1, 1974.

303 "Barry's whole approach is laissez-faire": Interview, George Gill, June 22, 1987.

304 "If we put notes on the bulletin board": Interview, Bernie Block, Apr. 24, 1987.

304 In the summer of 1973, during a safari: CJ, Aug. 19, 1973.

305 "He never recovered": Interview, Jean Howerton Coady, Mar. 2, 1987.

305 Five of the eight Pulitzer Prizes: However, the most prestigious Pulitzer—the one for public service—was won in 1967 for the papers' crusade against strip-mining, a campaign led by Worth and BBS, not BBJ.

305 In late August, in an effort: LT, Aug. 29, 1975.

305 When busing actually started: Details of busing and the protests that ensued come from The New York Times, Sept. 5, 6, 11, 28, 1975; LT, Sept. 5, 13, 1975; CJ, Sept. 7, 1975; Time, Sept. 8, 15, 22, and 29, 1975; and Testimony by BBJ before U.S. Commission on Civil Rights, Louisville, June 14–16, 1976.

305 "because of your Communistic position": "The Bingham Tapes: A Candid Interview, Part One," Louisville Today, Nov. 1976.

305 "You work for Barry Bingham Jr.": LT, Sept. 5, 1975.

306 "Some people read no further": Guidelines on Coverage of Busing, Aug. 7, 1975.

306 From July 1975 until the end of the year: CJ, Apr. 1, 1976.

306 "I am very proud that the hate crusade": Eileen Meredith to BBS, May 3, 1976, BBS private papers.

307 "Our share would have been as much": Interview, Irene Nolan, Feb. 26, 1987.

307 "She's got the moxie": Louisville Magazine, Sept. 1974.

307 "My God, it's a great thing": Interview, Norman Isaacs, June 22, 1986.

307 By the end of 1975, combined net profits: LT, Dec. 11, 1975.

307 "The [media] attention [to our female M.E.]": LT, Aug. 27, 1974.

308 "I'd trade two women reporters": Interview, John Herchenroeder, Jan. 19, 1987.

308 "Davies was lurking in the weeds": Interview, George Gill, June 22, 1987.

308 She was to take on the "major new responsibility": Memorandum, BBJ to All Concerned, May 19, 1976.

308 "Nobody wanted to look like he was knifing": LT, May 24, 1976.

309 "I waited a week to write this": Carol Sutton to BBJ, June 1, 1976.

309 Although Barry Jr. made a point of visiting: In fairness, Carol died while BBJ was away from Louisville. He spent the 1984–85 academic year at Smith College and came back only for family meetings. But his reluctance to see Carol was real nonetheless, according to friends interviewed by the authors.

310 "if papers were people": LT, Dec. 11, 1975.

310 "Name an industry or business": Report to Carol Sutton by Ken Loomis, fall 1975.

310 He felt much as he had in 1975: It took the all-news station only two years to lose $1 million. In 1980, when BBJ finally surrendered and gave the Louisville market what it wanted—country music—the station was an overnight success.

311   "He was infinitely more stand-offish": Interview, Wilson Wyatt, Oct. 20, 1989.

312   When Bob Barnard invited him to write: BBS may have also refused because he had had bad experiences with Barnard, who once heavily edited an obituary BBS had written about an old friend.

Chapter 15 THE RETURN OF THE SISTERS

315   "I know my kids": The warning came from Nelson Poynter, owner of *The St. Petersburg Times*. In order to keep his paper independent, Poynter effectively disinherited his wife and children, leaving the *Times* to a nonprofit educational institution, with voting control invested in a nonfamily editor. Poynter argued that the paper was too important to be left to grandchildren he did not really know, and he tried to persuade BBS to follow his example.

316   "the dullness and sad triviality": *Library Journal*, Feb. 1960.

316   "I suppose the whole thing has been hard": SB, "The Ice Party," *Atlantic Monthly*, Dec. 1963.

316   "given the kind of hearty welcome": *Time*, Dec. 8, 1963.

317   "connect with nothing but themselves": *The New York Times Book Review*, Apr. 2, 1972.

318   "How could she have known": SB, "Bare Bones," *Redbook*, Mar. 1965.

318   "poor little rich girls": *The New York Times Book Review*, Apr. 2, 1972.

318   "I have felt nothing": Ibid.

319   The most satisfying was with: Charles Schwartz, *Cole Porter: A Biography* (New York: The Dial Press, 1977), pp. 40–43, 274. Also interview, Sophie and Jacques Albert, Feb. 27, 1987.

319   At a fund-raiser for Adlai: Interview, Sophie and Jacques Albert, Feb. 27, 1987.

320   But at the time she told the New York: Proceeding for Letters of Administration, Estate of Henrietta Bingham McKenzie a/k/a Henrietta Bingham, Deceased, Surrogate's Court: County of New York, File No. 6644.

320   "a way with unhappy women": SB, "A Place in the Country," *Redbook*, Mar. 1974.

321   He immediately went off the Bingham board: Sallie was formally elected to the board Dec. 1, 1975.

321   Barry Jr. sponsored his sister: BBJ to Vertner Smith, July 20, 1977, BBS private papers.

322   "She said more affectionate": Telephone interview with William E. Grant, July 13, 1987.

323   "eventually have control": *Fortune*, June 19, 1978.

323   In 1954, Braden had provoked: Details about the Braden case come from *LT*, Oct. 12, 1948, June 13, 1952, Sept. 21, 1954, Oct. 4, 5, 1954, Dec. 7, 14, 1954, Feb. 19, 1975; *CJ*, Aug. 28, 1954, Oct. 6, 1954, Dec. 2, 9, 1954, Jan. 21, 1955, Sept. 13, 1967, Apr. 2, 1972, and Jan. 9, 1977.

Also see Mark Ethridge to Edith Conrad Turpin, Feb. 24, 1955, M. F. Ethridge Papers, Southern Historical Collection.

324 "She wore miniskirts": Interview, George Gill, June 22, 1987.
324 "I'm tired and my name is Bingham": Joe Ward, "The Binghams: Twilight of a Tradition," *CJ Magazine*, Apr. 20, 1986.
326 "about as fashionable as finger bowls": Essay by MB, 1968, Radcliffe College Archives.
330 "I did not manage Eleanor well": Interview, Bob Morse, Apr. 24, 1987.
331 "Eleanor might own this place": Ibid.
333 Barry Jr. executed his duties: *The Voice* newspapers (Ky.), June 17, 1981.

Chapter 16 ASSAULTED FROM ALL SIDES

337 "He felt, 'What are management people saying' ": Interview, Paul Janensch, Mar. 9, 1987.
338 "We couldn't get Barry Jr.'s attention": Interview, George Gill, June 22, 1987.
338 "We didn't want any arguments": Interview, Gordon Davidson, Oct. 20, 1989.
338 "Oh, my God!": Ibid.
339 In 1978, the papers had 178 more: Minutes, quarterly meeting of *CJ & T* company, June 15, 1978.
343 "self-indulgent biographical snippet": *New York Post*, Mar. 6, 1980.
344 "The buy-back made sense": Interview, Leon Tallichet, Jan. 21, 1987.
345 "I asked them, 'What do you think' ": Ibid.
345 "I finally said that the buy-back": Alanna Nash, "The Woman Who Overturned an Empire," *Ms.* magazine, June 1986.
346 "To me it was a nonissue": Interview, Wilson Wyatt, Jan. 20, 1987.
346 "Presently there is little written": Goals memo, EBM, Dec. 1, 1983.
347 "This is the worst kind of short-sighted": Joe Ward, "The Binghams: Twilight of a Tradition," *CJ Sunday Magazine*, Apr. 20, 1986.
352 "He was into blanket": Interview, Harvey and Kathy Sloane, Feb. 22, 1987.
352 "Without question, a notion": *CJ*, June 21, 1981.
352 "We couldn't believe it": Interview, Harvey and Kathy Sloane, Feb. 22, 1987.
353 "Now that the contests are over": *CJ*, Nov. 5, 1981.
353 "We used to laugh": Interview, George Gill, June 22, 1987.
354 Dissly Research Corp., a small Bingham subsidiary: The name was later changed to Computer Emporium, Inc.
354 "I hadn't had lunch alone": Interview, Bernie Block, Apr. 24, 1987.
354 "To compare George to Bernie": Interview, Bob Morse, Apr. 24, 1987.
355 "I think you have shown": Memo, John Richards to BBJ, Jan. 2, 1981.
356 "Thanks for leveling": Memo, BBJ to John Richards, Jan. 2, 1981.
356 "My wife was there waiting": Interview, George Gill, June 22, 1987.
358 Barry Jr. was elated at the gift: In July 1988, the Senior Binghams sold the

remaining thirty acres and buildings, including the Little House, a garage, barn, and another small house on the property, to BBJ for $850,000 cash. The deed reserved a "life estate" for the joint lives of the sellers. As survivor, MB retains ownership privileges and responsibilities for her lifetime, and title will pass to BBJ at her death. Leon Tallichet to Alex S. Jones, Nov. 3, 1989.

360   "She does have good credentials": Interview, Paul Janensch, Mar. 9, 1987.

360   "Sallie had odd ideas": Interview, Molly Clowes, Feb. 23, 1987.

360   "That woman graced this newspaper": Interview, John Ed Pearce, Feb. 25, 1987.

362   "I knew that Sallie didn't approve": Interview, Irene Nolan, Feb. 26, 1987.

362   "Well, I hate to put it this way": Interview, Paul Janensch, Mar. 9, 1987.

363   Unemployment was 11 percent: *The New York Times*, May 21, 1982.

Chapter 17 ONCE AT ODDS, NOW AT WAR

364   "You'd have thought": Interview, Léon Danco, July 21, 1987.

365   "was to talk women into getting off boards": Joe Ward, "The Binghams: Twilight of a Tradition," *CJ Sunday Magazine*, Apr. 20, 1986.

365   "I was down there to convince": Interview, Léon Danco, July 21, 1987.

368   "Don't do this": Interview, Bob Morse, Apr. 24, 1987.

368   "We don't mind": Interview, George Gill, June 22, 1987.

368   "You're threatening to break up": Interview, Bernie Block, Apr. 24, 1987.

369   "I didn't say, 'That's great' ": Interview, Paul Janensch, Mar. 9, 1987.

371   "Every department sent me": Interview, Cy MacKinnon, Apr. 26, 1987.

372   "You know," Gail told her husband: Interview, Paul Janensch, Mar. 9, 1987.

372   "broad management experience and is known": *LT*, June 22, 1976.

372   "He'd run out into the newsroom": Interview, Mary Phyllis Riedley, Feb. 27, 1987.

374   "I said that I would oppose": Memorandum, Paul Janensch to BBJ, Apr. 15, 1980.

374   "Give us another minute": Interview, George Gill, June 22, 1987.

374   "Barry doesn't want anybody": Ibid.

375   "for his own aggrandizement": Letter of Instruction to My Trustees by BBJ, Mar. 2, 1983.

375   "This is un . . . un . . .": Interview, George Gill, June 22, 1987.

376   "This contract tells me you": Ibid. The contract was highly unusual in that it bound George as much as BBJ. Under the agreement, if George left the *CJ & T* before he turned fifty-five, he owed BBJ the equivalent of his salary for the entire term of the contract—potentially a huge sum. "I later showed that to a couple of guys I respect out in the real world and they were incredulous," George said. "They couldn't believe it."

377   "She just had no street smarts": Interview, Irene Nolan, Feb. 26, 1987. BBJ began a concerted campaign to hire blacks, Hispanics, and other minorities in 1979, when less than 2 percent of the *CJ & T*'s professional staff fell into these categories. Paul Janensch headed up the drive and by 1985, 10.3

percent of the papers' professional staff was minority, almost twice the industry figure nationwide.

During the years that Sallie complained about the lack of women in management positions at the family companies, the Binghams had a female vice-president of WHAS and a female president of Data Courier.

378 "general aura of dour pessimism": MB to BBJ, Feb. 2, 1983.

379 "Thank you so much for letting us": EBM to MB, Feb. 2, 1983.

379 Later, a secretary found it: BBJ to EBM, Mar. 9, 1983.

379 "It will just rub salt": Interview, George Gill, June 22, 1987.

380 The idea was to create a power/money trade-off: The plan called for Barry Jr. to amass 40 percent of the voting stock. When his parents died, he stood to inherit more voting stock from Trust #9, established by Judge Bingham's will. At the same time, his parents' voting stock was to be repurchased by the company and retired. With less voting stock in circulation, the pie would be smaller and Barry Jr.'s slice would automatically grow to an estimated 67 percent—well above the 50.1 percent he needed to "control" the company.

The beauty of the plan was that Barry Jr. would not inherit voting control from his parents' estate—he would get it from stock he already owned. The I.R.S. puts a premium on the power represented by "control" of a company. If an estate passes "control" to a beneficiary, the I.R.S. considers the estate to be worth far more, and the taxes balloon accordingly. Inheritance taxes on an estate that does not pass "control" are significantly lower.

383 "My father's attitude was": Judith Adler Hennessee, "Louisville Slugger," *Savvy* magazine, Aug. 1986.

Chapter 18 DISASTROUS DECISIONS

389 Promptly at 2:00 P.M.: Minutes, annual stockholders' meeting, CJ & T company, Mar. 27, 1984.

390 "It is a bitter irony": MB to SB, Apr. 10, 1984.

391 "I sometimes get the feeling": BBJ to BBS and MB, Apr. 3, 1984.

392 "I've done my best": BBJ to MB, Apr. 21, 1984.

395 This time, as if to put a fine point: CJ, Aug. 26, 1984. The "last dinosaur in the swamp" comment comes from LT, Nov. 3, 1983.

396 "surprisingly good family therapy": Edith Stenhouse Bingham, "Coming Back as an Ada," Smith *Alumnae Quarterly*, Summer 1985.

396 "I just didn't want to draw a line": Interview, Paul Janensch, Mar. 9, 1987.

397 "She was of that school": Interview, Mary Phyllis Riedley, Feb. 27, 1987.

398 *The Courier-Journal* was cautious": Interview, William A. Henry III, Apr. 8, 1988.

398 In the end, the paper's investigation: CJ, Feb. 3, 1985.

399 "I'm chairman of my company": Interview, Paul Janensch, Mar. 9, 1987.

399 "If I'd wanted to deal with a flunky": Ibid. Cherry, however, says that no "uncivil" language was used. Interview, Wendell Cherry, Apr. 23, 1987.

400   Thirty minutes after the meeting: Memorandum, George Gill to BBJ, Oct. 5, 1984.

400   "It would be an awkard [*sic*]": Memorandum, BBJ to George Gill, Sept. 13, 1984.

400   " 'I don't want that bitch' ": Interview, Gordon Davidson, Oct. 20, 1989.

402   George had even gone so far: Memorandum, George Gill to BBJ, Oct. 12, 1984.

403   "I would hope that": Memorandum, BBJ to George Gill, Dec. 2, 1984.

403   Among the hired hands: BBJ said that he never actually executed this instrument and Leon Tallichet said that he did not find such a letter in the company safe when he cleaned it out months later.

403   "No taxation without representation": CJ, Dec. 11, 1984.

403 $30 million: *Business First*, Dec. 10, 1984.

403 $20 million: CJ, Dec. 11, 1984.

403   "play hard ball": Memorandum, George Gill to BBJ, Nov. 2, 1984.

404   "That's not enough": Interview, Leon Tallichet, Jan. 21, 1987.

406   "marriage-dependency": Alanna Nash, "The Woman Who Overturned an Empire," *Ms.* magazine, June 1986.

408   "At no time": BBJ to EBM, Feb. 14, 1985.

409   "I think it <u>most</u>": MB to BBJ and Edie, Feb. 7, 1985.

409   "I thought Gordon": BBJ to BBS and MB, Feb. 14, 1985.

Chapter 19 FEELING A WAVE OF INEVITABILITY

411   "I cannot understand why": MB to BBJ, Feb. 19, 1985.

411   Barry Jr. replied: BBJ to BBS and MB, Feb. 25, 1985.

411   "staying in a relationship": EBM quote according to interview, BBJ, Jan. 13, 1986.

413   "He's petulant": Interview, Rucker Todd, Apr. 25, 1987.

413   "Why can't we separate": Ibid.

414   "Barry Bingham Jr. and Eleanor must establish": Confidential memorandum, Comments and Conclusions of Mr. and Mrs. Barry Bingham, Sr., following Discussion on Mar. 5, 1985, with Messrs. Leon Tallichet, George Gill, Wilson Wyatt, Sr., Tom Luber, and Robert Maddox.

415   "Her opinion was that to be involved": Interview, Cy MacKinnon, Apr. 26, 1987.

415   "Dear, dear Mary": Edie Bingham to MB, Mar. 10, 1985.

416   "I appreciate your efforts": MB to Edie Bingham, Mar. 14, 1985.

417   "seriously disrupt her relationship with Sallie": EBM Memorandum re Present Preferences, Mar. 11, 1985.

420   "I . . . don't want to let": BBJ to BBS, Mar. 28, 1985.

420   "I do not, Barry, think you are a conniving": MB to BBJ, Apr. 4, 1985.

420   "I heartily share your desire": BBJ to MB, Apr. 16, 1985.

420   "I very much agree": MB to BBJ, Apr. 25, 1985.

421   "a gross error in judgment": *Advertising Age*, May 6, 1985.

422   "It's like you're standing on the beach": Interview, Christopher Shaw, Apr. 11, 1988.

422   "She was a very interesting and engaging": Interview, Jackie Markham, Apr. 11, 1988.

422   Sallie claimed that fifteen "legitimate buyers": *Business First*, Apr. 22, 1985.

422   The men in the Bingham family have: *Advertising Age*, May 6, 1985.

423   There was a similar article: *Editor & Publisher*, May 4, 1985.

423   Christopher trumpeted this fact: *CJ*, Apr. 26, 1985.

423   "made it perfectly clear that she would not sign": *Advertising Age*, May 6, 1985.

423   "tiresome . . . cold and self-centered": *The New York Times*, Apr. 21, 1985.

424   "lesson in humility": *CJ*, May 19, 1985.

424   "Of course, the staff was convinced": Interview, Irene Nolan, Feb. 26, 1987.

424   "crybabies" and "playground bullies": *CJ*, May 19, 1985.

425   "He thought it was a great idea": Interview, Paul Janensch, Mar. 9, 1987.

425   "stronger, feistier": Edith Stenhouse Bingham, "Coming Back as an Ada," Smith *Alumnae Quarterly*, summer 1985.

425   "He had to go back": Interview, Diana Fetter de Villafranca, May 28, 1987.

426   "My aim is quite simple": Associated Press, May 20, 1985.

Chapter 20 LOADING THE GUN

427   "It went from Sallie being on the outside": Interview, Paul Janensch, Mar. 9, 1987.

428   "I don't see how the stock swap could work": Rucker was right to alert Eleanor to the need to restructure Trust #9. Income from the trust went to Barry Sr. and Mary, and, upon their deaths, the trust's corpus was to be divided in four equal shares: one quarter each to Barry Jr., Sallie, and Eleanor and the fourth quarter to Worth's children. As a result, each of the four beneficiaries would eventually receive exactly the same number of shares in all three Bingham companies.

    To complete a stock swap, Trust #9 would have to be legally altered to allow Eleanor to receive Barry Jr.'s and Worth's WHAS shares. In exchange, Barry Jr.'s and Worth's heirs would receive her *Courier-Journal* stock. Without the cooperation of Sallie, who had equal legal standing as a beneficiary, such an alteration would be extremely difficult.

429   "I have other interests": BBJ's remark according to interview, BBS and MB, Aug. 4, 1986.

430   "After thinking about it": BBS to BBJ, May 31, 1985.

431   George presented Barry Sr. and Mary with four options: Memo, George Gill, Leon Tallichet, and Gordon Davidson to BBS and MB, June 7, 1985.

431   "We are quite open": Memo, BBS and MB to George Gill, Leon Tallichet, and Gordon Davidson, June 12, 1985.

431   "Goddamn, it was awful": Interview, Gordon Davidson, Oct. 20, 1989.

432   Instead of a cash equalizer: Memo, Rucker Todd to EBM, Sept. 7, 1985.

432   "That would sink the ship": Interview, Leon Tallichet, Jan. 21, 1987.

433   But the amount had never been enough: The Bingham Enterprises Foundation, established in 1952, made a total of $14 million in gifts before closing its books in 1986. John Richards to Alex Jones, Sept. 25, 1989, and Oct. 24, 1989.

434   "I want a chance to run": Rob's comments according to interview, Joan Bingham, Jan. 25, 1987.

437   "We can all take care of ourselves": Emily's comments according to interview, BBS, Aug. 7, 1986.

438   "a prudent and fair minority value": Memo, George Gill, Gordon Davidson, and Leon Tallichet to BBJ, Re: Counteroffer to Sallie, July 8, 1985.

440   Nevertheless, the historic agreement was announced: CJ, July 10, 1985.

442   "There was this pressure [on Eleanor]": Interview, Leon Tallichet, Jan. 23, 1987.

443   "That was his response": Interview, Rucker Todd, Apr. 25, 1987.

444   "Nobody's under his thumb": "Family Feud," *Working Woman*, Sept. 1985.

444   When a reporter asked to see: LT, Oct. 3, 1985.

446   "You need no longer be apologetic": Memo, Paul Janensch to BBJ, Sept. 30, 1985.

446   "I have never worked": Memo, BBJ to Paul Janensch, Oct. 1, 1985.

447   To Bob's astonishment: Interview, Bob Morse, Apr. 24, 1987.

447   "She and Rowland would never prepare": Ibid.

451   "I firmly believe that the sale": Family Memorandum by EBM, Nov. 19, 1985.

Chapter 21 PULLING THE TRIGGER

454   "We are distressed": MB to EBM, Nov. 20, 1985.

454   "Since the option of a total sale": EBM to BBJ, Nov. 23, 1985.

456   "I cried, I begged": Interview, Bernie Block, Apr. 24, 1987.

458   "I just couldn't conceive of the family": Interview, Paul Janensch. Mar. 9, 1987.

459   "Your conversation with Barry this morning": MB to Edie Bingham, written but not sent, Nov. 29, 1985.

460   "If you can't do it yourself, I will fill in the gap": BBJ said he has no recollection of either his father's or his sister's offers to make up the $1.7 million difference between $26.3 million and $28 million.

461   But she imposed one major condition: Memoranda, EBM to BBJ, Nov. 27 and Dec. 1, 1985.

462   "It will probably be worth a lot more": CJ, Dec. 13, 1985.

464   "The papers are not fun anymore": BBS's remarks according to interview, Gordon Davidson and Wilson Wyatt, Oct. 20, 1989.

465   "Barry Jr. sure is going to have a tough time": Interview, George Gill, June 22, 1987.

465 "And I'm leaving as soon as my contract is up": George's contract was set to expire in the summer of 1989.

466 "I think you just did it": Interview, Leon Tallichet, Jan. 23, 1987.

Chapter 22 THE END OF AN ERA

471 Instead of paying Sallie a yuletide: SB, *Passion and Prejudice*, p. 511.

471 The Warburgs found the Senior Binghams in a state: Interview, Edward and Mary Warburg, May 24, 1990.

473 "Gentlemen," he sighed: Interview, Gordon Davidson, Oct. 20, 1989.

473 "You've got to admit there's a problem": Joe Ward, "The Binghams: Twilight of a Tradition," *CJ Sunday Magazine*, Apr. 20, 1986.

475 "Well, old friend, the family is going": Interview, Paul Janensch, Mar. 9, 1987.

476 "It's not going to work": Paul's comments according to interview, George Gill, June 22, 1987.

476 "Do anything you like": Interview, Paul Janensch, Mar. 9, 1987.

477 "I was scared to death": Judith Adler Hennessee, "Louisville Slugger," *Savvy* magazine, Aug. 1986.

477 It will make my stock worth more: CJ, Jan. 10, 1986.

477 "It is tragic to see this family": Ibid.

478 "In my proprietorship here": CJ, Jan. 11, 1986.

478 "As for me," he said hoarsely: Richard Harwood, "The Binghams of Louisville: A Media Dynasty Self-Destructs," *The Washington Post*, Jan. 19, 1986.

478 The selfless image was tarnished: CJ, Jan. 26, 1986.

478 "Why, they're really no different": *The Washington Post*, Jan. 19, 1986.

478 "court of last resort": Thomas E. Gish, ed. and pub. of *The Mountain Eagle*, Whitesburg, Ky., as quoted in CJ, Jan. 10, 1986.

478 In late January, Democrat Carroll Hubbard Jr.: *Congressional Record*, Jan. 23, 1986.

479 "Everybody felt that Eleanor really didn't": Interview, Catherine Luckett, Jan. 23, 1987.

479 "liberating for the family": Judith Adler Hennessee, "Louisville Slugger," *Savvy* magazine, Aug. 1986.

479 "No, I didn't": Transcript, "The Phil Donahue Show," Feb. 20, 1986.

479 "The most gratifying part of all this": Judith Adler Hennessee, "Louisville Slugger," *Savvy* magazine, Aug. 1986.

479 Important indeed: Sallie had four finished novels: *Baltimore Sun*, Mar. 6, 1986.

480 "Something feels pierced": Molly Bingham to BBS and MB, Apr. 27, 1986.

480 "Like it or not": Rob Bingham to BBS and MB, Jan. 16, 1986.

480 He said that to his "lasting regret": BBS to children and grandchildren, Jan. 24, 1986.

480 "Having a lot of money": Joan Bingham to BBS and MB, Feb. 10, 1986.

481 In a long letter to Joan: BBS to Joan Bingham, Feb. 17, 1986.

481   Nonetheless, that same month, Edie wrote: Edie Bingham to BBS and MB, Feb. 6, 1986.

481   Barry Sr. and Mary's answer was: BBS to Edie Bingham, Feb. 8, 1986.

481   "made a pageant of our bleeding hearts": MB to Diane Sawyer, July 8, 1986.

482   "Thank God for '60 Minutes' ": *Lexington Herald-Leader*, June 29, 1986.

482   "No way are we going to do that": BBS remarks according to interview, George Gill, June 22, 1987.

483   Bob Hill erected a miniature: Judy Rosenfield to Alex S. Jones, 1986.

484   "It's the largest income": *Baltimore Sun*, Mar. 6, 1986.

484   His fears were not allayed when: David Chandler to BBS, Feb. 4, 1986.

486   In the end, Gannett: Figures according to telephone interview, Leon Tallichet, May 24, 1990.

486   His office in the Washington, D.C., suburb: *The Washington Post*, Oct. 31, 1986.

487   "Would it be appropriate": Interview, George Gill, June 22, 1987.

488   "a power breakfast for the powerless": LT, May 19, 1986.

488   "I'd love a cup": Ibid.

488   "It feels like winning the Triple Crown": The purchase of *The Courier-Journal* and *Times* was Neuharth's last act as chief executive officer. The following day he startled Gannett shareholders and media reporters alike by relinquishing the title to John Curley, forty-seven, thus ending years of speculation over who his successor would be.

489   In the newsroom, a funeral wreath: *Washington Journalism Review*, July/Aug. 1987.

489   Data Courier went to Bell & Howell: Figures according to telephone interview, Leon Tallichet, May 24, 1990.

489   *Ms.* magazine, which only six years earlier: Gloria Steinem to BBS, May 13, 1980, BBS private papers.

490   "They told me I had to stay": *Lexington Herald-Leader*, June 29, 1986.

491   In a letter, he compared himself: Paul Janensch to John Curley, June 30, 1986.

491   That night, Gannett officially offered George: Interview, George Gill, June 22, 1987.

492   "[Your] philosophy," wrote Paul: CJ, July 13, 1986.

492   But many media analysts were not aware: Figures taken from telephone interview, Leon Tallichet, May 24, 1990.

492   "It's a business job": Curley's remarks according to interview, Paul Janensch, Mar. 9, 1987.

493   "Chemistry": CJ, July 14, 1986.

493   "I speak to you for the last time": Ibid.

493   "Every major progressive step": Don Towles, "The Torch is Passed . . . ," *INTERCOM* 12, no. 6 (June 1986).

494   "We didn't know it at the moment": Interview, Norman Isaacs, June 22, 1986.

495   "Probably no family was the subject": Interview, Keith Runyon, Jan. 22, 1987.

EPILOGUE

497 Because she knew so little: SB to BBS, June 12, 1986.

498 "Macmillan should be as concerned": Memorandum, BBS to Macmillan Publishing Co., Apr. 27, 1987.

498 "Through suppression of a book": *Newsday*, July 29, 1987.

498 "I'm tired of the publicity": Interview, Gordon Davidson, Oct. 20, 1989.

499 In short order, the fund made grants: John Richards to MB, June 9, 1989. Of the $115 million in the Senior Binghams' proceeds from the sale, $25 million went for taxes, $12 million went to Barry Jr. and Joan as gifts to "equalize" them with the rest of the family, $16 million went to the grandchildren as bequests, and $43 million was dispensed to various charities from the fund, leaving $19 million in The Mary and Barry Bingham, Sr. Fund as of Sept. 1989. John Richards to Alex S. Jones, Sept. 25, 1989.

499 "We will give as much": CJ, Oct. 7, 1987.

499 Rowland stopped by: BBS to Anderson & Sheppard, Ltd., Apr. 6, 1987, BBS private papers.

499 "People feel that they are throwing": Interview, Catherine Luckett, Jan. 23, 1987.

500 But the bulk of her new riches: Soon after giving $1 million to the Ms. Foundation, Sallie also appeared on the cover of *Ms.* magazine.

502 His asking price: $100,000: George Gill approached the authors of *The Patriarch*, but they refused to pay for his diary or for any other information used in this book.

502 "It's almost like a divorce": Interview, Frank Q. Cayce, Mar. 2, 1987.

503 "Mary and I are in a Catch-22": BBS to Alex S. Jones, Dec. 16, 1987.

504 "Barry really shouldn't be moved": Blodgett's comments according to interview with MB, July 22, 1989.

504 "We're going to use methyltrexate": Hochberg's comments according to interview with BBJ, Oct. 19, 1989.

504 "Grandy just asked me to shoot": Ibid.

505 "Please shoot me": Ibid.

506 "there is no reasonable prospect": BBS to Dr. William Blodgett, Apr. 22, 1970, BBS private papers.

506 Since chemotherapy and surgery were clearly out: CJ, Jan. 27, 1988.

507 "It's your husband": Physician's comments according to interview, MB, July 22, 1989.

507 "We're not there": Ibid.

507 "Don't you want me to sit with you?": Ibid.

509 "Well, cut off his feeding tube": Ibid.

509 "Everything seemed controlled": SB, *Passion and Prejudice*, p. 518.

509 "He ran a paper that was a model": CJ, Aug. 16, 1988.

509 "a great voice has been stilled": Ibid.

510 "great relish for life": Ibid.

511 "erroneous suppositions, leaps of logic": Response Documents by Members of the Bingham Family to SB's *Passion and Prejudice*, Jan. 1989.

511   My father bypassed me "because he did not approve": SB, *Passion and Prejudice*, p. 519.

512   "gifted manipulators . . . used to controlling": Daphne Merkin, "The Last Taboo," *Seven Days*, Mar. 8, 1989.

512   "Q: What characteristics": CJ, Feb. 1, 1989.

512   "I think anyone who reads the book": Ibid.

512   Shirley Williams, her predecessor: The suit was dismissed in the fall of 1990.

512   "If I had done the fountain": According to interview with EBM, June 16, 1989.

512   "[My mother] snubbed me": *The Boston Globe*, Feb. 8, 1989.

512   Sallie declined to participate: Information about Sallie's refusal to participate comes from other family members. When asked directly about her involvement in the cousins' foundation, she declined to comment, saying the matter was "personal." SB to Susan E. Tifft, May 23, 1990.

513   As a result, the subscription rate: In 1990, BBJ lowered the rate to $49 a year.

513   It was not until a year after the funeral: BBJ learned the real reasons why his father sold the papers during a final interview for this book.

514   She said she was even able to muster: Sallie's domestic life continued to be tempestuous. In June 1990, her third husband, Tim Peters, filed for divorce and sought maintenance.

Index

ABOUT THE AUTHORS

Susan E. Tifft is an associate editor at *Time*, where she has worked since 1982. She holds a master's in public administration from the John F. Kennedy School of Government at Harvard and a bachelor's degree from Duke, where she also served on the board of trustees. She did much of the early work on *The Patriarch* while a Fellow at the Gannett Center for Media Studies at Columbia University.

Alex S. Jones is the press reporter for *The New York Times*, which he joined in 1983. He holds a bachelor's degree from Washington & Lee University and also attended Harvard as a Nieman Fellow. In 1987, he won a Pulitzer Prize for his coverage of the Binghams. His family has been in the newspaper business in East Tennessee for four generations.

The authors are married to each other and live in New York City.